D1569904

CONSERVATION
OF COINAGE

Frontispiece. Denier of Vich 'whereon oxen are shown',
according to texts of 1083

CONSERVATION OF COINAGE

Monetary Exploitation
and its Restraint in
France, Catalonia, and Aragon
(*c.* A.D. 1000–*c.* 1225)

THOMAS N. BISSON

OXFORD
AT THE CLARENDON PRESS
1979

Oxford University Press, Walton Street, Oxford OX2 6DP

OXFORD LONDON GLASGOW
NEW YORK TORONTO MELBOURNE WELLINGTON
KUALA LUMPUR SINGAPORE JAKARTA HONG KONG TOKYO
DELHI BOMBAY CALCUTTA MADRAS KARACHI
NAIROBI DAR ES SALAAM CAPE TOWN

© *Oxford University Press 1979*

British Library Cataloguing in Publication Data

Bisson, Thomas N
    Conservation of coinage
    1. Coinage–France–History
    2. Coinage–France–Political aspects
    3. Coinage–Aragon (Kingdom)–History
    4. Coinage–Aragon (Kingdom)–Political aspects
    5. Coinage–Spain–Catalonia–History
    6. Coinage–Spain–Catalonia–Political aspects
    I. Title
    332.4'042'0944   HG976   77-30359
    ISBN 0-19-828275-3

*Printed in Great Britain
at the University Press, Oxford
by Eric Buckley
Printer to the University*

To Carroll

PREFACE

MEDIEVAL coinages have received ample (if not yet sufficient) attention from the numismatic point of view and not much less from the economic, but they have seldom been studied by historians interested in institutional or social processes. This book attempts to improve the balance without pretending to right it altogether. It deals with the ways in which communities of people in a considerable expanse of Western Europe began to assert their interests in the administration of coinages. I had hoped at first to pursue this theme from its apparent origins in the eleventh century down to its parliamentary manifestations and the theory of Oresme in the fourteenth. But the earlier phases of this history proved more absorbing than had been anticipated, pushing the later ones beyond the reasonable limits of a single volume; moreover, it became clear that the story down to about 1225 was sufficiently distinct from its sequel to justify postponing the latter.

The chronological and geographical limits of the present work have been determined chiefly by the survival of evidence for payments made or demanded to secure the stability of coinage (or 'money-taxes') and for confirmations of coinage in the societies which succeeded to the West Frankish realm. Within this territory two broad areas where the coinage assumed evident constitutional importance have been selected for emphasis: (1) northern France, in which the Île-de-France, Normandy, Picardy, and Burgundy are foremost in view; and (2) those regions included in, or bordering on, old Septimania, Novempopulania, and the Frankish March of Spain that were known (or would be known) as Gascony, Languedoc, Roussillon, Cerdanya, Catalonia, and Aragon.[1] Sharing a fundamental inheritance of Carolingian institutions,[2] both of these blocs of lands had one or two coinages widely circulating by the twelfth century, and in each could be found lesser rights of *moneta* in profusion. Both areas were economically diverse, neither was quite in the forefront of commercial revival. How the nascent social interests in the coinages of these regions were related to differences or divergences in provincial experience is a major problem to be examined.

No one who ventures into medieval institutional history can attribute his shortcomings to the obscurity of his materials. The sources for these studies—narrative, diplomatic, and numismatic—have, with a few

[1] I sometimes refer to the non-Catalan southern domains as 'Occitania', an artificial designation for regions more extended than the historical Languedoc.

[2] Or mostly so; Aragon and Gascony were clearly peripheral.

exceptions, long been known to historians. Of the fundamental texts, most have been reliably edited, some more than once. The money-taxes came early to the notice of great scholars: of Zurita, Du Cange, and Brussel, to name but three. If the dissertations of the two latter on the *focagium* and the *tallia panis et vini* can still scarcely be bettered for fullness of description, that is a measure of their erudition as well as of their regional specialization. Léopold Delisle and Émile Bridrey nearly exhausted the subject of the Norman *monetagium*, and their evidence and conclusions figure prominently in the reassessment offered here. For regions other than the Île-de-France and Normandy, new research has afforded an improved basis for comparative study of the money-taxes. The practice of confirming the coinage has not heretofore been investigated as a matter of constitutional interest, but if I am not mistaken it provides our best approach to understanding the deeper processes of related historical change.

While the types, weights, alloys, and values of coins are considered in so far as these seem to be matters of institutional or social consequence, it must be admitted that these studies draw on numismatics and economics far more than they contribute to them. The work could hardly have been done without reliance on the researches of (among others) Faustin Poey d'Avant, Adolphe Dieudonné, and Jean Lafaurie relating to France; of Joaquím Botet y Sisó, Pío Beltrán Vilagrasa, and Felipe Mateu y Llopis for Spain; and of Marc Bloch, Philip Grierson, Carlo Cipolla, Robert S. Lopez, and Georges Duby in general. My stress is necessarily on the documentary evidence and the problems it presents, and some particular attention to the formal and contextual aspects of this evidence has seemed warranted. In the analysis of economic and monetary conditions, I have not attempted to quantify the data for regional and chronological differentiation. Scribal allusions to coinage are, in degrees impossible to control, conventional and arbitrary; moreover, I have been obliged to rely on cartularies uncritically edited or in manuscript somewhat more than I should have liked. The time is not yet ripe for the systematic economic comparison of the regional societies here in question, work that must be based on the kind of exhaustive analysis of the documentation that is only beginning in our days. I shall be content if my evidence and conclusions help to improve the formulation of some larger problems of economic change.

Nomenclature presents considerable difficulty in a work so oblivious to modern political geography as this. Apart from the names of popes, kings, and certain other persons conventionally Latinized or Anglicized (e.g. Gelasius, Innocent, Peter of Blois), I have preferred the modern vernacular forms most nearly corresponding to those familiar, in the several regions, in the twelfth century: e.g. Pierre in the North, Pere in the South; Ramon in Catalonia, Raimond in Occitania. Names of places in Spanish Catalonia are given in Catalan, except for Lérida and Vich, of which the native forms might seem obtrusively unfamiliar to some readers. What this system loses in simplicity will be compensated, I hope, by its consistency with my stress on the historical reality of cultural diversity.

The study was undertaken in 1964–5 when I held a fellowship of the John Simon Guggenheim Memorial Foundation. Further research was supported by the Humanities Institute and the Institute of International Studies (both of the University of California at Berkeley), the American Council of Learned Societies, and the American Philosophical Society; and much of the writing was done during my membership in the Institute for Advanced Study, Princeton, in 1971–2.[1] Without the unfailing kindness of the Institut de Recherche et d'Histoire des Textes, my documentation would have been immeasurably poorer, while for the study of extant coins I have relied on the expert classification and photography of the American Numismatic Society and the Gabinete Numismático de Cataluña. Subsidies in aid of publication were generously provided by the University of California; the Stiftung der Münzen und Medaillen AG zur Förderung Numismatischer und Archäologischer Forschung, Basel; and the Jubilee Fund of the Numismatic Department of Bank Leu Ltd., Zürich.

As for the individuals who have helped me, whether in the institutions mentioned above or in the archives, libraries, and universities of Europe and the United States, it would be impossible to name them all. Those to whom I am most indebted—some for expediting my research, others for criticizing and improving my results—include John F. Benton, Giles Constable, Philip Grierson, Miquel S. Gros, Jean Guerout, Olivier Guillot, John Le Patourel, Manuel Mundó, Lucien Musset, Kenneth J. Pennington, and Joseph R. Strayer. My wife traversed the archive-towns of France and Pyrenean Spain with me, she has helped in countless ways, and—she has borne with this book to the end. To all these persons and organizations I express my cordial thanks.

T. N. B.

Berkeley, California
July 1976

---

[1] Since this book was completed (1973–4), important new work touching its subject at many points has appeared. Some references to this work have been incorporated, but it has been impossible to revise very thoroughly in this respect.

CONTENTS

LIST OF MAPS   xiii

LIST OF PLATES   xiii

SELECTED COINS   xv

ABBREVIATIONS   xxi

I. INTRODUCTION: THE PROPRIETARY COINAGE   I

II. THE MONEY-TAX OF NORMANDY   14

III. THE MONEY-TAXES OF CAPETIAN FRANCE   29

IV. CONFIRMATIONS OF COINAGE IN THE SOUTH   45
    A. Aquitaine in the Eleventh Century   45
    B. Catalonia: *Cunctis pateat* (1118) and its Background   50
    C. Melgueil in the Twelfth Century   64
    D. Aragon and Catalonia (1155–1213)   74
    E. Toulouse and Quercy (1205–1212)   104
    F. Toward a Parliamentary Custom of the Confirmed Coinage   112

V. CONFIRMATIONS OF COINAGE IN THE NORTH   120
    A. Burgundy (1101–1203)   120
    B. Blois and Champagne (1165–1224)   126
    C. Nevers: the Charter of Corbigny (1188)   135
    D. Picardy (c. 1080–1215)   144
    E. Toward a Redefinition of the Public Interest   156

VI. THE CORRELATIONS OF THOUGHT   166
    A. *Quanto personam tuam* (3 *Comp.* 2.15.4; *X* 2.24.18)   166
    B. Pecuniary Obligations   172
    C. Profit and Taxation   180
    D. Wealth: the Almighty Coin   183

Contents

VII. CONCLUSION   189

    APPENDIX: Select Documents   199

    BIBLIOGRAPHY   207

    INDEX OF CHARTERS, DECRETALS, AND REGULATIONS   231
        PERTAINING TO COINAGE

    GENERAL INDEX   233

MAPS

I. The South (Occitania, Catalonia, Aragon)   46–7

II. Northern France   122–3

PLATES

Frontispiece. Denier of Vich, later eleventh century. Museo Episcopal de Vich
(*Photograph courtesy of Gabinete Numismático de Cataluña*)

AT END

I. Selected coins, 1–9

II. Selected coins, 10–18

III. Selected coins, 19–27

IV. *Scriptum de foagio*. Biblioteca Apostolica Vaticana, MS. Ottoboni 2796, fo. 46rb
(*Photograph courtesy of Biblioteca Vaticana*)

V. Charter *Cunctis pateat*, 4 April 1118. ACA, Cancillería, Registro 4, fo. 42^{rab}
(*Photograph courtesy of Archivo de la Corona de Aragón*)

VI. Philip Augustus's charter for Orléans, Fontainebleau 1183. AM Orléans, AA. 1
(*Photograph courtesy of Archives départementales du Loiret*)

VII. Confirmation-charter for coinage of Vich, 13 December 1174. ACA, Canc., pergaminos Alfonso I, 160
(*Photograph courtesy of Archivo de la Corona de Aragón*)

VIII. Royal charter for Vich, March 1197 (N.S.). ACA, Canc., pergaminos Pedro I, 26
(*Photograph courtesy of Archivo de la Corona de Aragón*)

IX. View of Blois from an engraving in Jean Bernier, *Histoire de Blois* . . . (Paris, 1682), p. 1.

X. Portal inscription of Blois from the facsimile by Bernier, *Histoire de Blois* (1682), p. 301

XI. Papal letter *Quanto personam tuam*, Lateran 5 April 1199. ACA, Canc., Bulas, Inocencio III, legajo 3, no. 4

(Photograph courtesy of Archivo de la Corona de Aragón)

SELECTED COINS

The list of coins described here and illustrated in the Frontispiece and Plates I, II, and III has been facilitated by the collaboration of the American Numismatic Society (New York, abbreviated as ANS) and the Gabinete Numismático de Cataluña (Barcelona, GNC). I wish to thank Dr. Jeremiah D. Brady, Associate Curator of Mediaeval Coins at the ANS; Dr. Pedro Vegué Lligoña, Director of the GNC; and my colleague Professor John M. Smith, Jr. Titles abbreviated by authors' names are fully cited in the Bibliography.

Frontispiece. Vich (Ausona). Denier (enlarged). Late eleventh century. Æ. Diam. 15·5 mm. Wt. 1·01 g. *Obv.* + s. PETRVS* ꟾVꟾVꟾꟾ .ꟾ Field: heads of saints facing each other. *Rev.* AVSO NA (2 lines), cattle-herd driving pair of oxen with rod. Botet y Sisó, i. 177–8, nos. 149, 150. Museo Episcopal de Vich.

1. Normandy. Denier. Eleventh century. Æ. Diam. 21 mm. Wt. 0·851 g. Classification uncertain. Inscriptions illegible. *Obv.* field: cross with dots in quadrants. Cf. Poey d'Avant, i, nos. 131, 144 (Plate 4, 17; Plate 5, 9). ANS, photo 75.0118.

2. Laon. Denier. Early eleventh century. Æ. Diam. 19 mm. Wt. 1·061 g. Inscriptions illegible. *Obv.* facing head (of king?). *Rev.* facing head (hooded?). Cf. Poey d'Avant, iii, no. 6531 (Plate 152, 2). ANS, photo 75.0119.

3. Étampes. Denier. Louis VI (1108–37). Æ. Diam. 19 mm. Wt. 0·936 g. *Obv.* + LODOVICVS REX. Field: described by Lafaurie as E with ringlet, bezants, and cross. *Rev.* STANPI[.......], cross with ᴧ in 2 quadrants. Lafaurie, i, nos. 113, 114 (Plate 4). ANS, photo 75.0123.

4. Orléans. Denier. Louis VII (1137–80). Æ. Diam. 20 mm. Wt. 1·249 g. *Obv.* + LVDOVICVS REX. Field: town gate. *Rev.* + AV[REL]IANIS CIVITAS. Cross with v and o in 2 quadrants. Lafaurie, i, no. 154; cf. no. 130 (Plate 5). ANS, photo 75.0124.

5. Denier *parisis*. Louis VII (1137–80). Æ. Diam. 20 mm. Wt. 1·30 g. *Obv.* LVDOVICVS RE +. Field: FRA NCO (2 lines). *Rev.* + PARISII CIVIS. Cross. Lafaurie, i, no. 138 (Plate 5). ANS, photo 75.0126.

6. Denier *parisis*. Philip Augustus (1180–1223). Æ.   Diam. 19 mm. Wt. 1·044 g. *Obv.* PHILIPVS REX. Field: FRA NCO (2 lines, reversed). *Rev.* + PARISII CIVIS. Cross, with emblems in quadrants. Lafaurie, i, no. 181 (Plate 6).
ANS, photo 75.0127.

7. Denier *tournois*. Philip Augustus (1180–1223). Æ.   Diam. 18 mm. Wt. 0·770 g. *Obv.* PHILIPVS RE +. Cross. *Rev.* SCS [MART]INVS. Castle. Cf. Lafaurie, i, no. 193 (Plate 7).
ANS, photo 75.0128.

8. Limoges. Denier *barbarinus*. Late eleventh or twelfth century. Æ. Diam. 19 mm. Wt. 1·232 g. *Obv.* SCS MARCIAL. Bearded facing head. *Rev.* + LEMOVICENSIS. Pearled cross with 8 ringlets evenly distributed in quadrants. Poey d'Avant, i, no. 2291 (Plate 50, 16).
ANS, photo 75.0130.

9. Angoulême. Denier. Probably twelfth century. Æ.   Diam. 20 mm. Wt. 1·181 g. *Obv.* + LODOICVS. Cross. *Rev.* + EGOLISSIME. 4 ringlets centred on small cross. Poey d'Avant, ii, nos. 2655, 2662 (Plate 57, 5).
ANS, photo 75.0131.

10. Barcelona. Mancus. Eleventh century. N.   Diam. 20 mm. Wt. 1·912 g. Imitation of dinar of Yaḥyā al-Mu'talī (1021–35). *Obv.* RAIMVNDV(?S) COMES.

Field:

ولى العــهـد	Lord of the Age
الامام يحيى	the Imām Yaḥyā
المعتلى بالله	(caliphal regnal name)
امير المومنين	Commander of the Faithful
ادريـــس	Idrīs (proper name)

(5 lines)

Rev. الدينر بمدينة . . . بسم الله ضرب هذا In the name of God, this dinar was struck in the city of . . .

Field: القا

لا الــه الا	no god but God.	
الله وحـده	who has no	the Distributor
لا شريك له	associate	
مسم		

(5 lines)

Arabic transcribed from Lavoix, *Catalogue des monnaies musulmanes* . . . ,
ii. 523. See also Botet y Sisó, i. 72–3, no. 19; G. C. Miles, 'Bonom de
Barcelone', *Études d'orientalisme dédiées à la mémoire de Lévi-Provençal*,
2 vols. (Paris, 1962), ii. 692, and references there.

11. Barcelona. Denier. Ramon Berenguer IV (1131–62). Æ. Diam.
17 mm. Wt. 0·773 g. *Obv.* [?] CHINO. Fleur-de-lis (?) *Rev.* Cross with 4
ringlets in quadrants. Botet y Sisó, i. 73–4, no. 22; Gil Farrés, *Historia*,
no. 91.
GNC, no. 15155.

12. Béarn. Denier. Late eleventh or twelfth century. Æ.   Diam. 19 mm.
Wt. 1·258 g. *Obv.* CENTVLLO COM. Cross with bezants in upper 2 quad-
rants. *Rev.* + ONOR FORCAS. Field: PA +. Poey d'Avant, ii, no. 3233
(Plate 69, 8); Blanchet and Dieudonné, iv. 87, Fig. 41.
ANS, photo 75.0135.

13. Roussillon. Denier. Guerau II (1164–72). Æ.   Diam. 17·5/17 mm.
Wt. 0·862 g. *Obv.* [G]IRARDVS COM. Cross with unexplained emblem in
quadrant. *Rev.* + ROSILIONVS. Field: + PAS. Poey d'Avant, ii, no. 3539
(Plate 76, 15); Blanchet and Dieudonné, iv. 350, Fig. 213.
GNC, no. 34088.

14. Toulouse. Denier. Twelfth century. Æ.   Diam. 19 mm. Wt. 1·076 g.
Obv. RAMVNDO COME. Cross. *Rev.* TOLOSA CIVI. Field: PA +. Poey
d'Avant, ii, no. 3677 (Plate 80, 10); cf. Blanchet and Dieudonné, iv. 235.
ANS, photo 75.0136.

15. Melgueil. Denier. Twelfth century. Æ.   Diam. 19 mm. Wt. 1·084 g.
Obv. RAMVNDVS (?), with characteristically stylized cross. *Rev.* NAIDONA,
with 4 ringlets centred on small circle. Poey d'Avant, ii, no. 3842 (cf.
Plate 85, 17); cf. Blanchet and Dieudonné, iv. 240–1, and Fig. 137.
ANS, photo 75.0137.

16. Aragon. Denier *iaccensis*. Alphonse I (1104–34). Æ.   Diam. 18·5 mm.
Wt. 1·116 g. *Obv.* ANFVS REX. Head of king facing left. *Rev.* ARAGON, with
adorned cross. Heiss, ii, Plate 71 (Alfonso I, no. 1); Beltrán, p. 81.
ANS, photo 75.0139.

17. Aragon. Denier *iaccensis*. Alphonse II (1162–96). Æ. Diam. 19·2 mm.
Wt. 1·044 g. *Obv.* Head of king with diadem facing left. *Rev.* ARA GON
(2 lines), with adorned cross. Heiss, ii, Plate 71 (Alfonso II, no. 1);
Beltrán, p. 87.
GNC, no. 2124.

18. Aragon. Denier *iaccensis*. Peter II (1196–1213). Æ. Diam. 18·5/17·7 mm. Wt. 0·936 g. *Obv.* PETR RE +. Crowned head of king facing left. *Rev.* ARA GON (2 lines), with adorned cross. Heiss, ii, Plate 71; Beltrán, p. 90.
GNC, no. 2200.

19. Barcelona. Denier. Alphonse I (1162–96). Æ. Diam. 19/18 mm. Wt. 1·039 g. *Obv.* BARCINO between 2 circles of points. A full-length cross forms quadrants occupied by a cross, a ring, and crescents. *Rev.* CI VI RE X, with full-length cross. Botet y Sisó, ii. 29, no. 159, and Frontispiece, no. 1.
GNC, no. 34112.

20. Barcelona. Denier. Peter I (1196–1213). Æ. Diam. 21/18 mm. Wt. 1·035 g. *Obv.* PE TR RE X, full-length cross with 4 ringlets in quadrants. *Rev.* BAR[.]INONA, between 2 circles of points. Indented full-length cross, centred over cross within field. Botet y Sisó, ii. 35, no. 161.
ANS, photo 69.222 (P. K. Anderson bequest, no. 2069).

21. Cahors. Denier. Bishop Guillem IV (1208–34). Æ. Diam. 17 mm. Wt. 0·866 g. *Obv.* + EPISCO[PV]S, crozier with 2 crosses in field. *Rev.* + CATVRCENSIS, cross with 3 grouped ringlets in one quadrant. Poey d' Avant, ii, no. 3907 (Plate 87, 10).
ANS, photo 75.0144.

22. Dijon. Denier. Hugues III (1162–92). Æ. Diam. 17 mm. Wt. 0·667 g. *Obv.* + VGO DVX BVRGDIE, field design incompletely legible. *Rev.* + DIVIONENSIS, cross in field. Cf. Poey d'Avant, iii, no. 5658 (Plate 130, 16).
ANS, photo 75.0145.

23. Dijon. Denier. Eudes III (1193–1218). Æ. Diam. 18 mm. Wt. 1·028 g. *Obv.* + ODO DVX BVRG:DIE, *annille* in field with bezants above and below. *Rev.* + DIVIONENSIS, cross in field with 2 arrowheads in opposite quadrants. Poey d'Avant, iii, no. 5659 (Plate 130, 17).
ANS, photo 75.0146.

24. Blois. Denier. Late eleventh or early twelfth century. Æ. Diam. 21·5/20·5 mm. Wt. 1·289 g. *Obv.* warrior's head facing right. *Rev.* + BLESI[......], cross in field. Cf. Poey d'Avant, i, no. 1680 (Plate 32, 9).
ANS, photo 75.0147.

25. Meaux. Denier. Bishop Étienne de La Chapelle (1161–71). Æ. Diam.

19/18·5 mm. Wt. 0·945 g. *Obv.* ⊕ STEPHANVS EC, mitred head facing left. *Rev.* + MELI CIVITAS, cross with 2 crescents and 2 lilies in quadrants. Poey d'Avant, iii, no. 6027 (Plate 139, 23).
ANS, photo 75.0149.

26. Nevers. Denier. Hervé de Donzy (1199–1223). Æ. Diam. 19 mm. Wt. 0·959 g. *Obv.* + COMES ERVEUS, sickle and star in field. *Rev.* + NIVERNIS CIVIT, cross in field, with a point in one quadrant, star in another. Poey d'Avant, i, no. 2135 (Plate 46, 18).
ANS, photo 75.0151.

27. Vermandois. Denier. Aliénor (1183–1214). Æ. Diam. 19·5 mm. Wt. 1·052 g. *Obv.* X CO. VIROMEND[.]. Field: ALI ENO (2 lines). *Rev.* + S. [Q]VINTIN[..], cross in field, 2 stars in opposite quadrants. Poey d'Avant, iii, no. 6690 (Plate 156, 6).
ANS, photo 75.0154.

ABBREVIATIONS

Abh.	*Abhandlungen der Gesellschaft der Wissenschaften in Göttingen, Philologisch-historische Klasse*
AC	Arxiu (or Archivo) capitular (Spain)
ACA	Archivo de la Corona de Aragón (Barcelona)
AD	Archives départementales (France)
AEM	*Anuario de Estudios medievales*
AHDE	*Anuario de Historia del Derecho español*
AHN	Archivo Histórico Nacional (Madrid)
AHP	*Archives historiques du Poitou*
AM	Archives municipales (France), Archivo (or Arxiu) Municipal (Spain)
AN	Archives nationales (Paris)
BEC	*Bibliothèque de l'École des chartes*
BEHE	*Bibliothèque de l'École des hautes études*
BN	Bibliothèque nationale (Paris)
BRABLB	*Boletín de la Real Academia de Buenas Letras de Barcelona*
BRAH	*Boletín de la Real Academia de la Historia*
BSAN	*Bulletin de la Société des antiquaires de Normandie*
BSN	*Bulletin de la Société nivernaise des lettres, sciences et arts*
BSS	*Bulletin de la Société archéologique, historique et scientifique de Soissons*
CCDT	*Collection des principaux cartulaires du diocèse de Troyes*
CFMA	*Les Classiques français du Moyen Âge*
CSIC	Consejo Superior de Investigaciones Científicas
DI	*Colección de documentos inéditos del Archivo General de la Corona de Aragón*, ed. Próspero de Bofarull y Mascaró, 42 vols. Barcelona, 1847–1973
EcHR	*Economic History Review*
EEMCA	*Estudios de Edad Media de la Corona de Aragón*, 10 vols. Zaragoza: CSIC, 1945–75
HF	*Recueil des historiens des Gaules et de la France*, ed. Martin Bouquet et al., 24 vols. Paris, 1738–1904
HL	Claude Devic and J.-J. Vaissete, *Histoire générale de Languedoc avec des notes et les pièces justificatives*, new edn., 16 vols. Toulouse: Privat, 1872–1904
IEC	Institut d'Estudis Catalans
ISAD	*Inventaire-sommaire des Archives départementales* . . . (France)
JL	*Regesta pontificum Romanorum ab condita ecclesia ad annum post Christum natum MCXCVIII*, ed. Philip Jaffé, Samuel Loewenfeld, et al., 2nd edn., 2 vols. Leipzig, 1885–8

LB	Landesbibliothek (Germany)
LFM	*Liber Feudorum Maior. Cartulario real que se conserva en el Archivo de la Corona de Aragón*, ed. Francisco Miquel Rosell, 2 vols. Barcelona: CSIC, 1945–7
LTC	*Layettes du Trésor des Chartes*, ed. Alexandre Teulet *et al.*, 5 vols. Paris, 1863–1909
MGH	*Monumenta Germaniae Historica*
MRABLB	*Memorias de la Real Academia de Buenas Letras de Barcelona*
MSAA	*Mémoires de la Société académique d'agriculture, des sciences, arts et belles-lettres du département de l'Aube*
MSAF	*Mémoires de la Société des antiquaires de France*
MSAHO	*Mémoires de la Société archéologique et historique de l'Orléanais*
MSAM	*Mémoires de la Société archéologique de Montpellier*
MSAN	*Mémoires de la Société des antiquaires de Normandie*
MSAP	*Mémoires de la Société des antiquaires de Picardie*
MSHPIF	*Mémoires de la Société de l'Histoire de Paris et de l'Île-de-France*
MSO	*Mémoires de la Société académique d'archéologie, sciences et arts du département de l'Oise*
NC	*The Numismatic Chronicle and Journal of the Royal Numismatic Society*
Olim	*Les Olim, ou registres des arrêts rendus par la cour du roi*..., ed. Arthur Beugnot, 4 vols. Paris, 1839–48
PL	*Patrologiae cursus completus . . . Series latina*, ed. J.-P. Migne, 221 vols. Paris, 1844–64
Po.	*Regesta pontificum Romanorum inde ab anno post Christum natum MCXCVIII ad annum MCCCIV*, ed. August Potthast, 2 vols. Berlin, 1874–5
PSANA	*Publicaciones del Seminario de Arqueologia y Numismática aragonesa*
PU	*Papsturkunden in [Frankreich or Spanien]* (see Bibliography)
RHDFE	*Revue historique de droit français et étranger*
RN	*Revue numismatique*
SATF	*Société des anciens textes français*
SB	Staatsbibliothek (Austria, Germany)
SHF	Société de l'Histoire de France
Structures	*Les Structures sociales de l'Aquitaine, du Languedoc et de l'Espagne au premier âge féodal.* . . . Paris, 1969 (reprinted from *Annales du Midi*, lxxx, 1968)
VL	Jaime and Joaquín Lorenzo Villanueva, *Viage literario a las iglesias de España*, 22 vols. Madrid, 1806–1902
X	*Liber Extra (= Decretales Gregorii IX)*..., ed. Aemilius Friedberg in *Decretalium collectiones*, Leipzig, 1881; ed. with glosses, e.g. Lyon, 1553
ZRG Kan.	*Zeitschrift der Savigny-Stiftung für Rechtsgeschichte, kanonistische Abteilung*

art.	article
canon.	canonistische (Handschrift)
c.	*capitulum*
lat.	latin
n a (fr.)	nouvelles acquisitions (françaises)
p.j.	*pièces justificatives*

I

INTRODUCTION: THE PROPRIETARY COINAGE

'NOTHING pertaining to the king or to whatsoever lord is so much handled by men', observed Ptolemy of Lucca, 'as the coin.'[1] For all its immediacy in an age of expanding business, this was an old truth. In coinages peoples and rulers had durable instruments of contact, tangible and symbolic. What was the ruler's in name was the people's to use, a paradox which entailed a delicate balance of interests in the political relationship. Would the people be content to circulate their ruler's coins openly, forsaking all others, without hoarding or mutilating them? Would the ruler, who alone could guarantee currency and intrinsic value, resist the temptation of misrepresenting or altering the value of minted money? Historical experience has usually tended to impose a favourable resolution of such issues, to define a convergence of economic and fiscal interest through which the ancient conception of coinage as a matter of public utility is perpetuated. But, for reasons to be examined in this volume, the balance of interests in coinage was upset in the post-Carolingian centuries by rulers claiming virtual propriety in the money and seeking to exploit their mints for profit. When some of these men arbitrarily altered their coinages or otherwise took advantage of their monetary rights, the remonstrance of their subjects was aroused. Kings and lords were urged to maintain the currencies sound and stable—'to conserve the coinage', in the words of the decretal *Quanto personam tuam* and of other medieval texts. The history of this issue, with some rather curious manifestations and solutions, is a little-travelled by-way in medieval constitutionalism. It is a way worth taking, not only for the interest of the historical scenery through which it passes, but also because it surely leads into the great age of medieval parliamentarism, the origins of which, perhaps still imperfectly

---

[1] *De regimine principum*, ii, c. 13; ed. R. M. Spiazzi, *Divi Thomae Aquinatis doctoris angelici opuscula philosophica* (Rome, 1954), p. 291 (§899). On the nature and general history of coinage, see Ferdinand Friedensburg, *Die Münze in der Kulturgeschichte*, 2nd edn. (Berlin, 1926); Alfons Dopsch, *Naturalwirtschaft und Geldwirtschaft in der Weltgeschichte* (Vienna, 1930); Walter Taeuber, *Geld und Kredit im Mittelalter* (Berlin, 1933); A. P. Usher, *The Early History of Deposit Banking in Mediterranean Europe*, i (Cambridge, Mass., 1943), ch. 7; Marc Bloch, *Esquisse d'une histoire monétaire de l'Europe* (Paris, 1954); Carlo Cipolla, *Money, Prices, and Civilization in the Mediterranean World ...* (Princeton, N.J., 1956).

understood, it may help to explain. Few were the Estates, Cortes, and parliaments of the later Middle Ages that failed to claim a share in the administration of coinages; and these claims found support in a revolutionary political theory according to which the money belonged to the people.[1]

The right to mint coins (*jus monetae* or, more usually and simply, *moneta*) was a prerogative of composite character in the Middle Ages. In its legitimately authoritarian form, it was a 'sovereign' or 'regalian' right. It was an attribute of that supreme power enjoyed, in theory, only by emperors or kings. The right was justified in Roman law as a service in the public interest, the money being recognized to be a publicly guaranteed means of exchange. The money was political in the sense that it enabled the ruler to propagate his portrait and his principles (or pretences); it was jurisdictional in that it rendered him the corrector of counterfeiters and other violators of coinage; and it was fiscal in that proceeds of the mint and fines accrued to the state. 'The integrity of coinage'—so ran the emperor's commission to mint-men in the sixth century—'on which our visage is impressed and through which the general utility is procured, ought to be fully maintained, for what will be safe if our effigy is violated . . . moreover, all marketing is disrupted . . . when it is necessary to reject what seems corrupt in transactions . . . for if injury to one is held to be punishable by laws, what shall he deserve who has offended such a multitude of men?'[2]

The *moneta* long retained, indeed never entirely lost, some residue of its public and utilitarian character. In this it was sustained by Carolingian legislation, of which the Edict of Pîtres (A.D. 864) was the last great monument. Carolingian moneyers were obliged to swear to exercise their *ministerium* faithfully.[3] But the publicity of coinage survived as an administrative principle which made no allowance for popular restraints on wayward rulers. The Gothic and Frankish kings who enjoined from rejecting coin of good weight or counterfeiting do not seem to have allowed for the possibility that they themselves might administer the *moneta* fraudu-

[1] On concepts of property in coinage, see Émile Bridrey, *La Théorie de la monnaie au XIVe siècle. Niçole Oresme* . . . (Paris, 1906), and René Gonnard, *Histoire des doctrines monétaires dans ses rapports avec l'histoire des monnaies*, 2nd edn., 2 vols. (Paris, 1935–6), i. 103–38—both works to be used with caution. Bridrey's remarkable book had the importance, among other things, of drawing attention to parliamentary interests in coinages. The considerable dimensions of that subject in the South, which I attempted to bring out in *Assemblies and Representation in Languedoc in the Thirteenth Century* (Princeton, N.J., 1964), was the stimulus for looking further afield. There is a useful sketch by Peter Spufford, 'Assemblies of Estates, Taxation and Control of Coinage in Medieval Europe', *XIIe Congrès international des sciences historiques* (Louvain–Paris: *Études présentées à la Commission internationale pour l'histoire des assemblées d'états*, xxxi, 1966), 113–30.

[2] Cassiodorus, *Variae*, vii. 32; ed. Theodor Mommsen (Berlin: *MGH, Auctores Antiquissimi*, xii, 1894), p. 219. On Roman coinage, see generally Harold Mattingly, *Roman Coins from the Earliest Times to the Fall of the Western Empire*, 2nd edn. (London, 1967).

[3] See Maurice Prou, *Catalogue des monnaies françaises de la Bibliothèque nationale: les monnaies carolingiennes* (Paris, 1896), pp. xlvi–lxxi.

lently.[1] Moreover, the utilitarian function of coinage was obscured when, in turbulent tribal societies suffering from shortages of minted coin, the economic behaviour of money ceased to be well understood. Georges Duby has contended that the later Merovingian gold coinage, so incongruous in commercial terms, must have served a chiefly political, palatial purpose.[2] Philip Grierson, finding no good evidence that the introduction of Charlemagne's heavy silver denier had any economic justification, has plausibly connected that reform with a reorganization of weights and measures.[3] In fact, the Frankish capitularies, while reminiscent of the Roman law on monetary fraud, betray some weakness of the regalian sanction. Not merely the imprint but also the weight of the coin must now be lawful to ensure its currency;[4] springing ultimately, perhaps, from old tribal suspicions of coined money, the test of weight was for long to remain a critical determinant of monetary soundness.

In the tenth and eleventh centuries the monopoly of coinage slipped from the king's hands. By the late eleventh century some sixty to eighty mints were active in (greater) France alone, no more than about twenty of which were royal, with another eight to ten in the Spanish March. The economic localism implied by this development was not in itself new. Frankish rulers had recognized the function of regional, or, more exactly, of mercantile currencies, and they had minted in many places. From the ninth century onward, grants of *moneta*—meaning, usually, profits of the local mint—were often coupled with market rights (*mercatum*) and toll (*teloneum*).[5] The fragmentation of monetary rights was better indicative of political change. It corresponded to the multiplication of territorial powers. What

---

[1] *Leges Visigothorum*, ed. Karl Zeumer (Hanover–Leipzig: *MGH, Legum Sectio I*, i, 1902), pp. 309–11; and citations in n. 4 below.

[2] Georges Duby, *Guerriers et paysans* ... (Paris, 1973), pp. 74–83; tr. H. B. Clarke, *The Early Growth of the European Economy* ... (London, 1974), pp. 61–70. See also Joachim Werner, 'Fernhandel und Naturalwirtschaft im östlichen Merowingerreich nach archäologischen und numismatischen Zeugnissen', *Moneta e scambi nell'alto medioevo* (Spoleto, 1961), 571–94.

[3] Philip Grierson, 'Money and Coinage under Charlemagne', *Karl der Grosse: Lebenswerk und Nachleben*, ed. Wolfgang Braunfels, 4 vols. (Düsseldorf, 1965–7), i. 528–30.

[4] *Capitularia regum Francorum*, ed. Alfred Boretius and Victor Krause, 2 vols. (Hanover: *MGH, Legum Sectio II*, 1883–97), i, nos. 28 (art. 5), 44 (art. 18), 63 (art. 7), 139 (art. 18); ii, nos. 192 (art. 8), 201 (art. 9), 271, 273 (art. 8); ninth-century formula quoted by Levin Goldschmidt, *Handbuch des Handelsrechts*, 3rd edn. (Stuttgart, 1891), p. 312, n. 54; and there is a law of Reccesuinth to the same effect, Zeumer, *Leges Visigothorum*, p. 311 (vii. 6. 5). Whether such regulations represented a significant change is not perfectly clear to me, for the Roman law was less than categorical on the matter. But the pertinent texts cited by Theodor Mommsen, *Römisches Strafrecht* (Leipzig, 1899), p. 674, make no such allusions to weight as figure in the barbarian law; see Paulus, *Sententiae*, v. 5. 1; Arrian, iii. 3. 3; and cf. *Codex Theodosianus*, viiii. 22. 1. I owe thanks to Professor David Daube for help on this point.

[5] Prou, *Monnaies carolingiennes*, pp. xlix–l, liv–lxxxix. See generally the remarkable study by Françoise Dumas-Dubourg, *Le Trésor de Fécamp et le monnayage en France occidentale pendant la seconde moitié du Xe siècle* (Paris, 1971).

mattered was not so much the number of mints as the increasing number of independent coinages that issued from them. But even in this respect the extent of the breach with older practice should not be exaggerated. For the devolution of monetary rights did not keep pace with that of other jurisdictional powers, not even with that of banal justice. This fact can most easily be observed in Anjou, Burgundy, and the Île-de-France, where the *consuetudines* have been best studied, but wherever one looks it is apparent that castellans and viscounts could not, as a rule, pretend to mint money on their own authority. While shares in the revenues of mints were often ceded in alms or in fief to the depths of society, the *moneta* in the full sense—with exceptions, notably in Berry and in the Midi—remained a comital function at the comital level of power. It was typically as concessionaires of the *comitatus* that prelates and churches exercised the right of coinage.[1] To the extent that the regal element was thereby diminished, the kings themselves were affected: the early Capetians retained their comital mints with familiar local issues for many generations until at last Philip Augustus began to promote the distinctively royal moneys of Paris and Tours.[2] In Normandy and Brittany the dukes may have been in advance of the king in consolidating their issues. Certainly they monopolized the coinages of their domains together with most other comital rights, a fact that lent substance to the belief that they ruled 'kingdoms' (*regna*).[3] There is little to show that the magnates of France conceived of their rights to mint as fiefs held of the king. Less still could such have been the situation of Pyrenean Spain, where great lords having to rely on their own resources under duress were able to make good the regalian pretensions they shared with the French marcher dukes, becoming kings in the eleventh and twelfth centuries.

---

[1] Prou, pp. liii–lx; J.-Adrien Blanchet and Adolphe Dieudonné, *Manuel de numismatique française*, 4 vols. (Paris, 1912–36), iv. 5–10; Olivier Guillot, *Le Comte d'Anjou et son entourage au XIe siècle*, 2 vols. (Paris, 1972), i. 395, and chs. 4, 5; J.-F. Lemarignier, *Le Gouvernement royal aux premiers temps capétiens (987–1108)* (Paris, 1965), esp. chs. 1, 2; Georges Duby, *La Société aux XIe et XIIe siècles dans la région mâconnaise* (Paris, 1953), pp. 88–116, 155–71, 205–29; new edn. (Paris, 1971), pp. 89–108, 137–48, 173–90.

[2] Maurice Prou, 'Esquisse de la politique monétaire des rois de France du Xe au XIIIe siècle', *Entre Camarades* (Société des Anciens Élèves de la Faculté des lettres de l'Université de Paris, 1901), 76–82; Jean Lafaurie, *Les Monnaies des rois de France*, i. *Hugues Capet à Louis XII* (Paris, 1951), pp. 1–18.

[3] For Brittany, see Dieudonné, *Manuel de numismatique*, iv. 121–5; *Chronicon Briocense*, ed. Hyacinthe Morice, *Mémoires pour servir de preuves à l'histoire ecclésiastique et civile de Bretagne...*, 3 vols. (Paris, 1742–6), i. 35–6; Ferdinand Lot and Robert Fawtier, *Histoire des institutions françaises au moyen âge*, 3 vols. to date (Paris, 1957–62), i. 268–71; for Normandy, Adolphe Dieudonné, 'La numismatique normande. Les monnaies féodales', *BSAN*, xxxvi (1927), 301–6; C. H. Haskins, *Norman Institutions* (Cambridge, Mass., 1918), pp. 38, 280, 283; *Recueil des actes des ducs de Normandie de 911 à 1066*, ed. Marie Fauroux (Caen, 1961), nos. 3, 61, 62, 67, 74, 92, 95, 122, 158. See also K. F. Werner, 'Königtum und Fürstentum im französischen 12. Jahrhundert', *Probleme des 12. Jahrhunderts...* (Stuttgart, 1968), 177–225.

Thus the regalian attributes of coinage survived the collapse of Frankish government. Toward the middle of the eleventh century the comital *moneta* at Dinant could be defined in terms of office and jurisdiction virtually unchanged from the past, and the rights at Saintes were substantially the same.[1] In other respects, too, the proliferating coinages remained a conservative institution. The *moneta* enabled its possessor to 'renew' the coinage or to 'change' it. In either case profits resulted from returns of the mint or from leases at farm or, where the lord was strong enough and so inclined, from the obligatory exchange imposed on the people.[2] The moneyers continued to work the lord's dies on terms that were mutually profitable;[3] and the fixed revenues from mints—often called 'moneyage' (*monetagium* or *monetaticum*), and much later, *seigneuriage*—did not, so far as we are informed, vary significantly from the 4·5 per cent of the issues allowed to their moneyers by the early Carolingian rulers.[4] The silver continued to be struck in deniers (or their fractions) according to the Carolingian monetary system, wherein the sou of 12 d. and the pound of 20 s. were fictive units of account. So it was too in the design of the minted pieces, for many lords had clung to Carolingian types and devices, even when introducing their own inscriptions.[5]

Nevertheless, for all this traditionalism, most coinages ceased to be fully public institutions in the eleventh and twelfth centuries. The common interest, save where it coincided with the fiscal interest in prosecuting fraud, lost whatever protection had been afforded by Carolingian legislation. Revenues from the mint, together with the amends levied on violators, tended to be confused with patrimonial income; they were often divided

[1] 'Malleus et incus, moneta et monetarius, et percussura et inscriptio nummismatis ad comitem pertinent, et delicta eorum et falsitas ad suam pertinent justitiam. Quamdiu voluerit stabit; quamdiu voluerit mutabitur', *Actes des comtes de Namur de la première race, 946–1196*, ed. Félix Rousseau (Brussels, 1937), p. 89, art. 4; for the significance of the final clause, see p. 6 below. For Saintes, see *Cartulaire de l'abbaye royale de Notre-Dame de Saintes . . .*, ed. P.-Th. Grasilier (Niort, 1871), nos. 51, 77.

[2] *Cap. reg. Franc.*, i, nos. 90 (art. 9), 28 (art. 5), 150 (art. 20); ii, nos. 18 (art. 18), 273 (arts. 10, 11). In 864 the public exchange ordered by Charles the Bald had its term on Martinmas (11 November), and we find November indicated with curious frequency in the dated references to such exchanges in the twelfth century: see pp. 8, 10.

[3] On Carolingian moneyers, see Edict of Pîtres, *Cap. reg. Franc.*, ii, no. 273, esp. arts. 13, 14, 16–18; and R. S. Lopez, 'Continuità e addattamento nel medio evo: un millenio di storia delle associazioni di monetieri nell'Europa meridionale', *Studi in onore di Gino Luzzato*, 4 vols. (Milan, 1949–50), ii. 74–117. For negotiations with moneyers at Saintes in 1047 and before, see *Cart. Notre-Dame de Saintes*, nos. 1, 77; and see below, pp. ??, ??.

[4] *Cap. reg. Franc.*, i, no. 13 (art. 5); cf. Joaquim Botet y Sisó, *Les Monedes catalanes . . .*, 3 vols. (Barcelona, 1908–11), i, apèndix, no. 5; *Cartulaire de Maguelone*, ed. J.-B. Rouquette and Augustin Villemagne, 7 vols. (Montpellier, 1912–24), i, nos. 47, 161; Adolphe Dieudonné, 'Le melgorien. Exemple de variations de monnaie médiévale', *RN*, 4th ser., xxxv (1932), 34 (table). Cf., generally, Philip Grierson, 'Mint Output in the Tenth Century', *EcHR*, 2nd ser., ix (1957), 462–6.

[5] See generally Faustin Poey d'Avant, *Monnaies féodales de France*, 3 vols. (Paris, 1858–62); Dieudonné, *Manuel de numismatique*, iv, esp. ch. 3.

or alienated.[1] By a significant identity in terms, the *moneta* came to mean the place of the mint as well as the authority to mint; and in many towns the newly rising stone citadels of coin must have become objects of popular suspicion.[2] Who could trust the minters?—or, for that matter, the lord? In 1056 the count and countess of Barcelona turned over their silver coinage to Marcus and Bonfill Fredal for two years in return for monthly renders in grain. The contract was renewed when it expired in 1058, this time for five years; and still another contract, naming Bonfill with two new moneyers, is extant from 1066.[3] These were private contracts, not public charters; each is termed *convenientia*. They refer to the coinage in awkwardly proprietary terms—*ipsa moneta illorum argento*—without the slightest concession to economic and political realities. By comparison, references in Domesday Book show that moneyers in contemporary England worked on terms that were more profitable to the ruler than in Barcelona but also more commonly known;[4] and the controlled recoinages of the late Saxon period underscore the contrast. What people had now to fear in West Frankland was the arbitrariness of the monetary prerogative. In the ominous expression which concludes the list of the count's rights in the money at Dinant: 'Whenever he wishes, it [the coinage] will be stable; whenever he wishes, it will be changed.'[5] If few lords were that blunt, most seem to have acted accordingly; the increasing diversity of weights and alloys betrayed the weakening of exchange and the trend toward particularism. What is distinctive about these coinages—even about their peculiar numismatic behaviour so often noted by analysts of the 'feudal theory of money'—is not so much their relation to vassalage or fiefs[6] as their lordly,

[1] In fact, the term *moneta* in charters more commonly refers to revenue from coinage than to the mint right itself. See the great dissertation on *moneta* in Charles Dufresne Du Cange, *Glossarium ad scriptores mediae et infimae latinitatis*, 1st edn., 3 vols. (Paris, 1678); or in nineteenth-century editions.

[2] The *turris monetaria vetus* at Carcassonne is mentioned in 1126, *HL*, v. 921, iii. 923, viii. According to Camille Piton, 'Les premiers hôtels des monnaies à Paris', *RN*, 4th ser., xii (1908), the earliest reference to such a building at Paris is dated 1227; among existing 'houses of money' in France and Spain, none seems to be older than the late medieval period. In 1106 the houses (*case*) at Jaca 'ubi moneta solebat fieri' adjoined the cathedral church, *Colección diplomática de la catedral de Huesca*, ed. Antonio Durán Gudiol, 2 vols. (Zaragoza, 1965–9), i, no. 97.

[3] Botet y Sisó, *Monedes catalanes*, i, apèndix, nos. 4–6 (ACA, Cancillería, pergaminos Ramón Berenguer I, nos. 182, 228, 361).

[4] *Domesday Book*, 2 vols. (London: Record Commission, 1783), i. 56, 172, 179, 252, 262; see also S. Harvey, 'Royal Revenue and Domesday Terminology', *EcHR*, 2nd ser., xx (1967), 221–8.

[5] Text quoted above, p. 5 n. 1; cf. the custom of Jaca, quoted p. 11 n. 1, below.

[6] The feudalistic forms of engagements relating to the coinage of Melgueil (see below, pp. 65–71) appear exceptional to me; the grant of *dies* in fief, as apparently occurred at Ponthieu (below, p. 155), must not be confused with the tenure of the *moneta*. Cf. Ernest Babelon, 'La théorie féodale de la monnaie', *Mémoires de l'Académie des inscriptions et belles-lettres*, xxxviii: 1 (1909), esp. 287–311, with review by Dieudonné in *RN*, 4th ser., xiii (1909), 90–109; and Adolphe Dieudonné, 'Les lois générales de la numismatique

private, potentially exploitative character. The usual designation 'feudal' as applied to post-Carolingian coinages is unsatisfactory; if a label is needed, it should preferably be 'proprietary' or 'seigneurial'.

Such coinages did not have to be manipulated to return profits. As in the past, mints were active when the supply and price of silver allowed. At Melgueil the combined shares of lord and moneyer were fixed in 1174 at 8⅓ per cent of the strike,[1] an amount that would not have been thought extravagant at the time. What was ultimately critical for the ruler's advantage and reputation was the relation established between newly minted money and that already in circulation. In the eleventh and twelfth centuries, as in other times, monetized metal could be moderately over-valued in exchange without repercussion. Rulers could mint on accustomed standards without calling in the old coinage. This seems to have been common practice, especially in profitable or productive mints, such as at Melgueil or Morlaas, and since it required no publicity, it probably lent itself readily to successive petty debasements. An accumulation of these in time would help to explain the gradual depreciation of currencies in the West that went unnoticed as such by contemporaries, so far as we know.[2] Or else rulers could alter the coinage more abruptly and more drastically by changing types, weights, or alloys, or by making some combination of these changes; and they might impose these changes by prohibiting the use of old coins after a given date. Such mutations would soon become evident even if they were not announced.

The facts known directly and surely about abrupt mutations down to about 1200 are all too few. One of the best documented instances is also an early one: a reduction in weight of the gold mancus of Barcelona in 1056.[3] It was alleged of Bishop Gaudri II of Laon (1106–12) not only that he suffered his coinage to be badly debased, but that he changed types as well.[4] In the same years the coinage of Poitou was notoriously unsteady. 'There was great tribulation' in 1103, according to the *Chronicle of Saint-Maixent*, 'and silver coins were exchanged and minted for bronze.' In 1112, 'again the coins were altered and others made with grains' (meaning, perhaps, with deficient weights); and in 1120 'the coins were changed

féodale', *RN*, 4th ser., xxxvi (1933), 155–70. My view has independent support in Françoise Dumas, 'Le début de l'époque féodale en France d'après les monnaies', *Cercle d'Études numismatiques, Bulletin*, x (1973), 65.

[1] *Cart. Maguelone*, i, no. 161.
[2] Carlo Cipolla, 'Currency Depreciation in Medieval Europe', *EcHR*, 2nd ser., xv (1963), 414–22. For a different explanation, see Duby, *Guerriers et paysans*, pp. 278–9; *Early Growth*, pp. 250–1.
[3] Pierre Bonnassie, *La Catalogne du milieu du Xe à la fin du XIe siècle . . .*, 2 vols. (Toulouse, 1975–6), ii. 672. (See Plate II, no. 10.)
[4] See p. 9. At Verdun (in Lorraine) a comparably disastrous debasement occurred toward 1130 (below, p. 157).

in the month of November'.[1] King Ramiro II of Aragon changed his money of Jaca on 12 November 1135 and his successor, Alphonse II, did the same in November 1174.[2] The coinages of Melgueil and Toulouse, both of which lost intrinsic value progressively from the later eleventh century, both declined abruptly in the twelfth, the former passing from 5 d. to 4 d. fine silver in 1130 and the latter from 8 d. to 7 d. in the 1170s, when the weight of the melgorian also slipped.[3] Less satisfactory evidence of mutations may be found in altered types or legends on extant coins, as for example, on those of Normandy, Carcassonne, and the realms of the Spanish March. In some cases new legends suggest approximate dates for alterations according to the years when princes acceded to power.[4] But changed dies do not necessarily imply changed standards, and efforts to press the numismatic evidence to demonstrate such coincidences appear hopeless in the present state of our knowledge.[5] Such is the extent of the direct evidence. From references in texts to 'new money' or the like, we can identify a few other mutations (or probable mutations) within the regions of our concern and date them approximately: at Barcelona about 1071, and in Aragon at the accession of Peter I (1094–1104) and again about 1128; and in Catalonia as well as in Aragon there were several manipulations during the three decades commencing in 1181.[6] In France, where the episcopal coinage of Amiens fell toward 1100, the archiepiscopal coinage of Lyon was weakened shortly before 1139, reinforced toward

---

[1] *Chronicon sancti Maxentii Pictavensis*, ed. Paul Marchegay and Émile Mabille, *Chroniques des églises d'Anjou* (Paris, 1869), pp. 421, 425, 429 (readings verified in BN, MS. lat. 4892, fos. 205ra, 205va, 206rb); for the entry relating to 1103, see below, p. 9 n. 5.

[2] 'Documentos para el estudio de la numismática navarro-aragonesa medieval (1.a serie)', ed. Antonio Ubieto Arteta, *PSANA*, i (1951), 116, no. 4; 'Documentos . . . (2.a serie)', *PSANA*, ii (1953), 95, no. 33. (Plate II, nos. 16, 17.)

[3] *HL*, v. 932ii–933; *Cart. Maguelone*, i, nos. 47, 55; Paul Guilhiermoz, 'De la taille du denier dans le haut moyen âge', *BEC*, lxxxiv (1923), 272 n. 1; Dieudonné, *Manuel de numismatique*, iv. 236; Mireille Castaing-Sicard, *Monnaies féodales et circulation monétaire en Languedoc (X^e–XIIIe siècles)* (Toulouse, 1961), pp. 16, 31. On the Toulousan mutation, see below, p. 75. (Plate II, nos. 14, 15.)

[4] Poey d'Avant, *Monnaies féodales*, i. 24–32; ii. 271–7; Aloïss Heiss, *Descripción general de las monedas hispano-cristianas desde la invasión de los Árabes*, 3 vols. (Madrid, 1865–9), ii. 2–7, and lámina 71; Pío Beltrán Villagrasa, 'Los dineros jaqueses, su evolución y su desaparición', *PSANA*, i (1951), 73–83; Lafaurie, *Monnaies des rois*, pp. 6–18.

[5] Consider e.g. the case of Poitou, where we know that the coins were changed at least three times from 1103 to 1120. Dieudonné, *Manuel de numismatique*, iv. 334–8, shows two types prior to the accession of Richard I in 1169, of which one survives in exemplars weighing between 1·60 gr. and 1·30, the other—subsequent, according to Dieudonné—between 1·50 gr. and 0·90. This evidence is suggestive but hardly conclusive. For more likely possibilities, see *Manuel*, iv. 70–1 (Angoulême); 236 (Toulouse).

[6] Botet y Sisó, *Monedes catalanes*, i. 41; Beltrán, 'Los dineros jaqueses', 79; 'Documentos para el estudio de la reconquista y repoblación del Valle del Ebro . . .', ed. J. M. Lacarra, *EEMCA*, ii (1946), no. 56; 'Documentos', ed. Ubieto, no. 15; for the mutations in 1181 and after, see below, pp. 84–8. Stipulations of 'new money' or 'new deniers' cannot safely be interpreted in isolation, for the allusion may be simply to unworn coins. (Plate II, nos. 17, 18; Plate III, nos. 19, 20.)

1150, and debased again after 1184.[1] Having perhaps been altered under Raoul II (1102–52), the comital money of Vermandois was changed at the accession of Philippe d'Alsace (1164–7).[2] The ducal money of Dijon fell in value between 1179 and 1185, and the comital money of Nevers was lightened at about the same time.[3] There were changes in royal coinages of the Île-de-France during the twelfth century, although it seems impossible to determine their dates very precisely.[4]

How arbitrary were these abrupt mutations of coinage? Perhaps the most blatant instance is that of Laon, and it is worth pausing for a moment over Guibert de Nogent's relation of the troubles there, for despite its passion and, on some points, obscurity, it is the most informative record of its kind. The minters of Bishop Gaudri II, we are told, had issued bronze counterfeited to resemble silver,[5] a fraud which deceived sellers and rewarded the bishop, who tolerated it to the 'misery' of many people of the region (*provincia*). Gaudri then tried to put 'very corrupt' obols[6] of Amiens into circulation, and when this expedient failed, he issued a coinage depicting the pastoral staff in token of himself. The latter, says Guibert, was so scorned as to be valued less than the debased issues. Meantime, the bishop's proclamation at each minting that the coins were to be accepted without cavil occasioned frequent accusations and fines; more-over, a 'most vile' monk from Tournai abetted the debasements by bring-ing large amounts of silver to the mint at Laon and by purchasing the silence of powerful men. 'No hostility, no plunderings, no burnings have done worse damage to this province', Guibert concluded, 'since the Roman walls held the ancient and very satisfactory mint of this city.'[7]

Troubles of this description could hardly have resulted from honest mistakes. There was deception in the mint and in other exchanges, prob-ably collusion between the prelate and his moneyers to make fast profits; and if Gaudri's alternative policies are well represented, it looks as if he found himself an unwitting victim of economic forces beyond his compre-hension as well as beyond his control. What effectively exposed the fraud,

[1] See below, p. 146; and Étienne Fournial, *Les Villes et l'économie d'échange en Forez aux XIIIe et XIVe siècles* (Paris, 1967), p. 498.

[2] Below, pp. 148–9.

[3] Jean Richard, *Les Ducs de Bourgogne et la formation du duché du XIe au XIVe siècle* (Paris, 1954), p. 371; Dieudonné, *Manuel de numismatique*, iv. 301.

[4] Adolphe Dieudonné, 'Histoire monétaire du denier parisis jusqu'à Saint Louis', *MSAF*, lxxi (1911), 132–5, 142–4; Lafaurie, *Monnaies des rois*, pp. 11–18. And see below, pp. 31 ff.

[5] Were they influenced by the recent example of Poitou? Cf. *Chron. sancti Maxentii*, p. 421: 'MCIII.—Fuit magna tribulatio, et nummi argentei pro aereis mutati et facti sunt.'

[6] i.e. coins of less than a denier's worth.

[7] Guibert de Nogent, *De vita sua*, iii, c. 7; ed. Georges Bourgin as *Histoire de sa vie (1053–1124)* (Paris, 1907), pp. 158–60; the translation of C. C. Swinton Bland as edited by J. F. Benton, *Self and Society in Medieval France* . . . (New York, 1970), pp. 168–70, is convenient, but, in this very difficult passage, problematical.

and worsened its consequences, was the relatively developed economy of exchange, based on viticulture, by which Laon and its countryside were bound to Amiens and the Flemish towns, among other places, by 1100. When foreign merchants recognized the weakness of the excessively over-valued bronze, they contrived to buy it cheaply on the exchanges and to disburse it at nominal rates for purchases in or around Laon. Inflation presumably wiped out this advantage; but the flight of the good money would then have been followed by that of the bad, which may be why the bishop tried to establish local currency for the obols of Amiens. But since these pieces, too, had to be overvalued, the former problem was reproduced, to be resolved at last—too late for an exasperated populace—by the issuance of an improved denier which, meeting other objections itself, had to be imposed by decree.[1] If Guibert's account can be trusted on this point, it seems to afford a rare glimpse of the moment when a traditional type was replaced by a seigneurial one.[2] The mutation of types cannot have been popular in the best of circumstances; when done to celebrate a ruler like Gaudri, it can only have been an aggravation.

In Poitou as at Laon the manipulations involved debasements, at least in 1103 and 1112, and the first of these was likewise linked to popular discontent. Yet even in the condensed expression of the annalist there sounds a more open and orderly note. To say that 'coins were exchanged' as well as changed (1103) and that they 'were changed in the month of November' (1120) suggests the procedure of public exchange, or demoneti-zation, whereby a new coinage was imposed on the people by proclaiming that after a certain date the old money would no longer have legal currency. If this is what happened in 1103, we can be sure that the exchange was at rates unfavourable to the people. New coinages must often have been unpopular for this reason. The same procedure seems more certainly in evidence in the Aragonese mutations of 1135 and 1174. These are mentioned in royal charters as elements of the dating protocol, just as, to similar effect, expeditions, battles, and other incidents of common knowledge were sometimes noted.[3] Public events, these mutations were most likely in keeping with the *antich fuero* of Jaca, which says that 'the king can change

[1] See Renée Doehaerd, 'Un paradoxe géographique: Laon, capitale du vin au XIIᵉ siècle', *Annales: Économies — Sociétés — Civilisations*, v (1950), 145–65; esp. pp. 146–9. In the main, I follow this interpretation of Guibert's account.

[2] The numismatic evidence is consistent with this suggestion but by no means proves it. Extant deniers of Laon cannot be dated between the early eleventh and mid-twelfth centuries. The earlier coins bore modified Carolingian monograms, without the staff; no coins are known to correspond to Guibert's description. See Poey d'Avant, *Monnaies féodales*, iii. 350–4; Adolphe Dieudonné, . . . *Les Monnaies capétiennes ou royales françaises*, Iᵉʳᵉ *section* . . . (Paris, 1923), pp. 41–2; and the collections in the Cabinet des Médailles (BN) and in the museum at Laon. (Plate I, no. 2.)

[3] Cited above, p. 8 n. 2. See also Ricardo del Arco, 'Referencias a acaecimientos históricos en las datas de documentos aragoneses de los siglos XI y XII', *EEMCA*, iii (1947–8), 291–354.

his money when he pleases and can establish a table of exchange in each city of his realm to which the peoples must come . . . who wish to exchange the old money according to the constitution and the order of the king, and the king's table should last forty days and no more'.[1]

Recoinages of this sort were probably more usual in the eleventh and twelfth centuries than can be demonstrated from surviving evidence, for they had Frankish as well as Gothic precedents.[2] In later Saxon England they occurred regularly and periodically, the term being six years, later reduced to three.[3] Traces of periodic emissions or renewals can be found in Normandy, perhaps also in the Île-de-France,[4] as well as in Aragon.[5] They cannot have been all bad in intent, nor even in effect. They were sometimes called 'renewals of coinage' (*renovationes monetae*) on the Continent,[6] a term that suggests some recognition of their social utility. Yet even when it was only a matter of changing types or legends, they must have seemed a disagreeable price for a standard and sufficient coinage. And in giving occasion for mutations of intrinsic value and rates of exchange they surely fostered abuses. As a Limousin chronicler was to put it in the thirteenth century, the count of La Marche 'renewed his coinage for the worse'.[7] Surreptitious changes of standards had nothing to commend themselves to popular favour and the profits they brought must have been harder to control than those of renewals. Nevertheless, we have no basis for assuming that all mutations in France and Spain had the dignity of public proclamation.

So it may be said that, like other aspects of monetary practice, mutations

[1] *El Fuero de Jaca*, ed. Mauricio Molho (Zaragoza, 1964), p. 156 (Redacción A, art. 301): 'Antich fuero es e prouat que quan plazdra al Rey pot mudar so moneda Ζen cada ciutat de so regne pot establir taula de cambi a la qual los pobles deuen uenir per deute los qui uolen cambiar uiella moneda segunt la constitution e·l mandament del Rey. E la taula del Rey deu durar .XL. dias e no plus.' The article recurs in other redactions (pp. 207–8, 304, 305, 515), in a form that stresses the king's discretion in establishing the exchanges; it was evidently the basis for the revised text which appears in the *fueros* of Aragon (see below, p. 192).
[2] Edict of Pîtres (864), *Cap. reg. Franc.*, ii. 314–17, esp. art. 15.
[3] Michael Dolley, *Anglo-Saxon Pennies* (London, 1964), pp. 24–30; R. H. M. Dolley and D. M. Metcalf, 'The Reform of the English Coinage under Eadgar', *Anglo-Saxon Coins: Studies presented to F. M. Stenton . . .*, ed. R. H. M. Dolley (London, 1961), pp. 152–7; Philip Grierson, 'Numismatics and the Historian', *NC*, 7th ser., ii (1962), ix–xiv.
[4] In the form of triennial levies of the money-tax; see below, pp. 18–19, 29 ff.
[5] See below, p. 75. I pass over mint contracts and such evidence as makes no allusion to recalls of coinage.
[6] Grierson, 'Numismatics and the Historian', x, and works cited there, notably Stanisław Suchodolski, '*Renovatio monetae* in Poland in the 12th Century', *Polish Numismatic News* (1961), pp. 57–75.
[7] *Anonymum S. Martialis chronicon . . .*, ed. Henri Duplès-Agier, *Chroniques de Saint-Martial de Limoges* (Paris, 1874), p. 176 (cf. p. 177): 'Eodem anno [1280], comes Marchie monetam suam renovat in deteriorem.' The line is repeated almost verbatim *sub anno* 1282.

of coinage were exploited in the eleventh and twelfth centuries without losing all touch with a steadier past. But how self-serving was this exploitation in fiscal reality? What impact did mutations have on the economies in which they occurred? The interest of these questions is more than matched by their difficulty. Next to nothing is known about seigneurial incomes before the thirteenth century, still less of the place in them occupied by returns from mutations or recoinages. As we shall see, the proceeds of taxes to secure the stability of coinage constitute indirect evidence on the point; but of those proceeds themselves we know very little before the thirteenth century and not much more before the fourteenth. We can infer from this evidence, such as it is, and so with a considerable margin of error, that mutations were only modestly profitable in prior centuries.[1] Whatever their form, they cannot normally have been so lucrative as the regulated operations of mints. Short-lived and unpredictable in their returns, abrupt manipulations answered to immediate, perhaps often desperate, fiscal needs, but if repeated they threatened to destroy the source of the bounty. The coinage of Poitou, where Duke Guilhem IX had been fighting costly local wars, lost popularity after those successive mutations in the early twelfth century;[2] and it looks as if Count Bernard IV of Melgueil was in debt for similar reasons when he borrowed 13,000 s. on security of stabilizing his money in 1128, and then debased it in 1130.[3] The coinage of Laon seems to have been interrupted for more than a generation after Bishop Gaudri's time.[4]

How manipulations of coinage were related to the regional economies is a more promising if not much easier question to investigate. For there survives considerable information about money and exchange, even though historians have yet to put it to much use. It enables us to form rough estimates of the relative amounts of specie in circulation and to imagine how people tended to regard the stability of a given coinage. It suggests that the disappearance of the uniform Carolingian denier and the progress of commercial exchange combined to foster a heightened sensitivity to monetary value. At Laon the dawning of popular awareness may have been depicted on Guibert's agitated canvas; and while less explicit in the usual documentation, the tendency is perceptible in many regions. To be obliged to accept unfamiliar or lightened or debased coins in payment or exchange must have been regarded as a bother at best and a swindle at

[1] See below, pp. 25–6, cf. p. 97.
[2] Alfred Richard, *Histoire des comtes de Poitou, 778–1204*, 2 vols. (Paris, 1903), i. 461, 486–7; 'Cartulaire de l'abbaye de Saint-Cyprien de Poitiers', ed. Louis Rédet, *AHP*, iii (1874), nos. 66, 76, 111, 388, 394, 417, and *passim*; 'Chartes poitevines de l'abbaye de Saint-Florent près Saumur (de 833 à 1160 environ)', ed. Paul Marchegay, *AHP*, ii (1873), nos. 30, 95.
[3] *HL*, iii. 644–6, 658–60, 667–8; *Cart. Maguelone*, i, nos. 47, 55.
[4] Poey d'Avant, *Monnaies féodales*, iii. 350; Émile Caron, *Monnaies féodales françaises* (Paris, 1882), pp. 370–1.

worst; and unlike most other bothers and swindles the incidence of this one was, theoretically, universal.

Whether as periodic recoinages or as disruptive debasements—both of which were mutations to contemporaries—such impositions became thoroughly unpopular. But they can hardly have been more advantageous to rulers than to the people. Apart from the diminishing returns of irregular mutations, which answered poorly to the requirements of sound fiscal policy, obligatory exchanges were open to fraud and resistance. So the idea of commuting manipulations into regulated taxes cannot have failed to interest those who collected from them; and such agreements, once made, satisfied some rulers enough to retain them or renew them. This is not to say that the commutative tax was always imposed by fiat; on the contrary, its effect was plainly that of a quid pro quo and it must usually have been preceded by consensus if not always by discussion. But the fact remains that when the prince agreed not to change his coinage in return for grants of money, he was ostensibly expressing his prerogative quite as profitably as ever, merely less capriciously. The prerogative character of such taxes is suggested none too subtly by the very names which some of them bore: 'tallage' (*tallia*) in the Île-de-France, *monetagium* (*monnéage*) in Normandy, and *monetaticum* (*monedatge, monedaje*) in the Spanish March. The latter terms referred originally, and did not cease to refer, to the ruler's returns from the mint. The 'money-tax' was 'moneyage' (or *seigneuriage*) in another form.

It is through this institution—at once an expression of the monetary prerogative and a condition of its limitation—that the principle of conserving the coinage seems first to have become concrete. Once recognized, that principle enabled lords and communities alike to conceive of money-taxes in compensatory as well as commutative terms, or, indeed, of uncompensated confirmations of coinage. But what precisely did it mean to stabilize the coinage? Did it make sense—and if so, to whom?—to prohibit all mutations, including the *strengthening*, of coinage? Was the conservation of coinage a practical solution to the problem posed by grasping lords-proprietor? Who was competent to advise in such matters? The resolution of these issues was by no means uniform either in substance or in chronology in the lands examined in this volume. But if it was clear by the early thirteenth century that arbitrarily exploited coinages could not survive in the moral and economic circumstances then prevailing, it was also becoming clear that the social interests in coinage and the economic behaviour of money were too complicated to be easily or permanently adjusted.

II

THE MONEY-TAX OF NORMANDY

THE first of the money-taxes was probably that of Normandy.[1] There it can be traced back to the middle of the twelfth century and very likely to the later eleventh, but nothing is known certainly about how it was instituted. The probable circumstances of its beginnings can only be reconstructed from texts of the thirteenth and fourteenth centuries, as Émile Bridrey conclusively showed. Of these texts, two have outstanding importance:

(1) The chapter *De monetagio* in the *Summa de legibus Normannie*. This codification of Norman custom dates from the middle of the thirteenth century, but it incorporates observances that were old even then. The chapter in question begins as follows: '*Monetagium* is a certain pecuniary aid to be paid to the duke of Normandy every third year, so that he will not cause the form of coins circulating in Normandy to be changed for others.' The passage goes on to specify the incidence of the tax and exemptions from it in accordance with personal status, order, property, and place of residence; it concludes with the remark that 'all jurisdiction of coinage in Normandy is known to pertain to the duke', a regulation we know to have been in force at the time of the Conqueror.[2]

(2) The memorandum *De foagio Normannie*, written in all probability by an official familiar with ducal administration shortly after Philip Augustus conquered Normandy in 1204. This text responds to the question: how is the money-tax levied?—and the answer it gives explains its title. The tax is imposed, every third year, on hearths (*foci*) at the rate of 12 d.

---

[1] The money-tax of Norman custom, although well known to jurists of the *Ancien Régime* and to historians since Du Cange, could still rightly be called 'a forgotten page' when Émile Bridrey wrote his massive 'Une page oubliée des Coutumiers normands. Le chapitre *De monnéage*', BSAN, xlviii (1940–1), 76–519. For references to the older legal commentators and their sources, see this work, 76–99 and *passim*. Among historical discussions of the early period other than Bridrey's, one need only mention Du Cange, *Glossarium mediae et infimae latinitatis*, articles on *focagium* and *monetagium*; Nicolas Brussel, *Nouvel Examen de l'usage général des fiefs en France . . .*, 2 vols. (Paris, 1750); Léopold Delisle, 'Des revenus publics en Normandie au douzième siècle', *BEC*, xiii (1852), 103–6; and Dieudonné, 'La numismatique normande', BSAN, xxxvi, 306–7. Bridrey's account of the origins of the *monnéage* is at pp. 100–35, with addenda at 494–7, but the juridical method employed throughout this work results in important observations elsewhere on the original nature of the institution.

[2] *Summa de legibus Normannie in curia laicali*, ed. E.-J. Tardif (Rouen–Paris, 1896), c. 14 (pp. 40–3); *Consuetudines et iusticie*, ed. Haskins, *Norman Institutions*, p. 283, art. 13.

per hearth. The collectors are villagers, four or six (or more), appointed *ad hoc* and sworn to faithful service; they are responsible to the *baillis*, to whom the money is brought together with the names of those paying *fouage*. The *De foagio* also specifies exemptions which correspond closely to those recorded in *De monetagio*.[1]

Taken together, these neatly complementary documents provide a remarkably explicit account of the Norman money-tax as it was administered in the thirteenth century. They also suggest, especially in their joint stress on customary general exemptions, that the institution was already respectably aged.[2] This testimony is borne out by Angevin administrative records. The great rolls of the Norman Exchequer, extant only for the two decades preceding the Capetian conquest, refer regularly to *monetagium* or *focagium*, while among acts of Henry II granting immunities or, occasionally, proceeds, the usual term is *focagium*.[3] When we push back earlier than the mid-twelfth century, however, the trail of texts is lost. Lost, that is, unless—like a blaze on some distant towering tree—the famous chapter on *monetagium* in the English charter of liberties issued in 1100 marks the same Norman trail. 'The common *monetagium*', said Henry I, 'which was collected through [*per*] the cities and through the counties, which did not exist in King Edward's time, this I utterly abolish from now on.'[4]

This text, taken together with some allusions in Domesday Book,[5] proves that a money-tax of Norman contrivance was known in England after the Conquest. Does it also establish the existence of such an institution

---

[1] The best edition of this text, pending its publication in the *Recueil des actes de Philippe Auguste*, is Léopold Delisle, *Le Premier Registre de Philippe-Auguste: reproduction héliotypique du manuscrit du Vatican* (Paris, 1883), reproducing MS. Ottoboni 2796, fo. 46ʳ (reproduced Plate IV, and transcribed below, Appendix, p. 204). For other editions, all older, see Bridrey, 82, and nn. 12, 14. Although *de foagio* was included in some early manuscripts of Norman custom, it was not part of the original *Très Ancien Coutumier*, ed. E.-J. Tardif (Rouen, 1881), nor yet among the jumble of items that were gathered, probably toward the end of Philip Augustus's reign, to form the second part of this collection. Bridrey plausibly links *De foagio* 'au petit mouvement législatif auquel nous devons la composition du *T.A.C.*', p. 82; but Tardif was probably right in choosing to omit it from his edition: see his pp. xii–xxvi, xxxi–xxxviii, xli–lxxvii.

[2] See Bridrey, 'Le chapitre *De monnéage*', 215–69, and my discussion below, pp. 19–20.

[3] *Magni rotuli scaccarii Normanniae sub regibus Angliae*, ed. Thomas Stapleton, 2 vols. (London, 1840–4), i. 21–2, 32, 110, 199, 246, 249, 252, 276, 285; ii. 342, 450–1, 466, 523, 554, 558; other edited fragments of Exchequer rolls contain no more evidence; *Recueil des actes de Henri II, roi d'Angleterre et duc de Normandie, concernant les provinces françaises . . .*, ed. Léopold Delisle and Élie Berger, introduction and 3 vols. (Paris, 1909–27), i. 260, 350, 519; ii. 236, 249, 297, 316, 334, 345, 355, 383, 411 (the allusions to *focagium* at ii. 121 and 160 are not to the Norman money-tax).

[4] *Chartes des libertés anglaises (1100–1305)*, ed. Charles Bémont (Paris, 1892), p. 4, c. 5; or in William Stubbs, *Select Charters and Other Illustrations of English Constitutional History . . .*, 9th edn. (Oxford, 1913), p. 118.

[5] *Domesday Book*, i, fo. 336B; below, p. 18 n. 1; and cf. Charles Oman, *The Coinage of England* (Oxford, 1931), p. 85.

in Normandy before 1100? Many scholars have thought so.[1] Given the unambiguous Norman evidence of later date, it has seemed reasonable to suppose that King William I simply imported the tax from Normandy. Yet it is by no means clear that the exaction renounced in 1100 was identical with that described in subsequent Norman documents. For the administration of the mints in England continued to follow Saxon procedures that were probably unlike those customary in Normandy. The Norman kings minted their English coinage in many localities, renewed it periodically, but maintained it stable as to weight and alloy.[2] In Normandy they had only two mints at most, the issues from which had no reputation for regularity, stability, or workmanship.[3] If the types of English coins continued to be changed and their intrinsic value to be maintained, it seems difficult to interpret the *monetagium* of Domesday and the charter as a compensation for renouncing mutations. Amidst a variety of explanations, the suggestion has even been made that the levy was intended to protect the king against depreciation of the currency,[4] a purpose quite the opposite of that later manifest in Normandy. To argue for a money-tax in the duchy on the basis of the English evidence is no simple matter.

Yet it seems equally difficult to dismiss the English texts altogether. They do not, after all, tell against the simultaneous existence of a ducal money-tax that was certainly collected half a century later and whose origins are undated. It rather strains the imagination to conceive of Norman conquerors imposing on the English without precedent an unpopular exaction for which the word if not precisely the function was identical with that applied to the tax later collected in Normandy and nowhere else in the North. One could argue, to be sure, that Henry I instituted in the duchy only after 1100 what he had abandoned in the kingdom, and as we shall see, this possibility cannot be entirely ruled out. But let us assume for the moment, despite the difficulty there may now seem to be in doing so, what has always seemed most reasonable to assume: that the English *monetagium* was the same sort of tax as the one later attested in Normandy.

---

[1] See e.g. Gabriel Lecointre-Dupont, *Lettres sur l'histoire monétaire de la Normandie et du Perche* (Paris, 1846), p. 9; Anatole de Barthélemy, 'Essai sur la monnaie parisis', *MSHPIF*, ii (1876), 149; Bridrey, 'Le chapitre *De monnéage*', 120–1. While most of these writers adduced other considerations, none found independently authoritative evidence that the Norman institution antedated 1100. Cf. Du Cange, *Glossarium*, s.v. *monetagium*, and Grierson, 'Numismatics and the Historian', *NC*, 7th ser., ii. ix, who are more cautious.

[2] Oman, *Coinage of England*, pp. 80–98; R. H. M. Dolley, *The Norman Conquest and the English Coinage* (London, 1966), pp. 6–29. The Anglo-Saxons had, however, altered weights.

[3] *Consuetudines et iusticie*, ed. Haskins, *Norman Institutions*, p. 283; cf. p. 280; Dieu-donné, *Manuel*, iv. 302–5.

[4] Stapleton, *Magni rotuli*, i. xvi, argued so, followed by F. M. Powicke, *The Loss of Normandy, 1189–1204 . . .*, 2nd edn. (Manchester, 1961), p. 36 n. 2, and others. See also Oman, *Coinage of England*, pp. 85–6; Grierson, 'Numismatics and the Historian', ix; H. R. Loyn, *Anglo-Saxon England and the Norman Conquest* (London, 1962), p. 124.

What other considerations can be adduced to suggest that this tax could have originated in Normandy—or have been known there—before 1100?

Bridrey, who assumed without question what we are now supposing *ex hypothesi*, argued that the English *monetagium* implied an importation from Normandy, where it originated during the reign of William Rufus (1087–1100) and probably between 1097 and 1100, when Rufus was in control of Normandy. Three reasons were offered for this thesis. First, Bridrey found no evidence that ducal coinages were at all plentiful before the middle of the eleventh century or that they were unstable in the time of William I (1035–87). Second, he observed that Norman legislation down to 1091 made no reference to the money-tax. Finally, he found that William Rufus, unlike his father, was notorious for having made damaging mutations of coinage.[1]

So supported, however, the argument collapses. A review of the evidence shows that the first of Bridrey's reasons is unsound, the second an inconclusive argument from silence, and the third quite mistaken. The numismatic data are not only desperately few but also ambiguous; the studies Bridrey cited did not establish what he drew from them, while at least one work he overlooked pointed to erratic minting and manipulations in the eleventh century.[2] And to make a point of the fact that the money-tax was not mentioned in the statutes of Lillebonne (1080) and the *Consuetudines et iusticie* (1091) was to forget that it was likewise unnoticed in all other extant Norman legislation down to the thirteenth century.[3] Yet even to Bridrey, it seems, these reasons were of value chiefly as props for the third, which he thought 'decisive'. So it is curious to learn that among the many charges levelled against William Rufus by contemporaries, that of manipulating the currency, so far from being common, is conspicuously absent. Bridrey cited Orderic Vitals and Henry of Huntingdon, Freeman and Delisle, none of whom support his point. Apart from the silence of the chroniclers he adduced (and of others he did not), the evidence of English coins indicates that Rufus's standards were held stable, although the issues declined in workmanship.[4] Nothing is known of his coinage (if

---

[1] Bridrey, 'Le chapitre *De monnéage*', 122–8.

[2] Victor Luneau, 'Quelques deniers normands inédits du XIᵉ siècle: nouvelle trouvaille', *RN*, 4th ser., xv (1911), 86–96; cf. idem, 'Deniers normands inédits du XIᵉ siècle', *RN*, 4th ser., x (1906), 306–16; Poey d'Avant, *Monnaies féodales*, i. 17–32; and Dieudonné, 'La numismatique normande', 304–7. A new coinage shortly before the Conquest seems indicated by BN, Coll. Moreau, xxi. 22–4, cited by Lucien Musset, 'Sur les mutations de la monnaie ducale normande au XIᵉ siècle: deux documents inédits', *RN*, 6th ser., xi (1969), 292. The hoard of Fécamp suggests that deniers of Rouen were plentiful in the later tenth century; see Dumas, *Trésor de Fécamp*, pp. 6–19, 71 ff.

[3] Bridrey urged that so patently regalian a practice would surely have found a place in such texts, but as Haskins pointed out, *Norman Institutions*, p. 278, 'the inquest of 1091 expressly disclaims completeness'.

[4] Oman, *Coinage of England*, pp. 90–1; G. C. Brooke, *English Coins*, 3rd edn. (London, 1950), p. 82.

any) in Normandy, where he ruled but briefly. In general, a king so demanding of impositions and gelds as Rufus was reputed to be cannot have
been interested in debasing the money he wished to receive.

Yet perhaps, after all, Bridrey was right in seeking the origins of the
Norman money-tax in the later eleventh century. Continuing to assume
an identity between the English and Norman *monetagia*, we may imagine
that if he had not overlooked the references in Domesday Book, Bridrey
would presumably have felt less inclined to attribute the invention of
these taxes to William Rufus. Domesday alludes explicitly to *monedagium*
(*sic*) as a 'king's geld', so there can be little doubt that the Conqueror
himself first imposed it on England.[1] Several other facts may have some
bearing on the problem. First, the Norman kings were notably reluctant
to replace the native moneyers with Normans after winning England. Not
only did they retain Englishmen in the mints, but well into the reign of
Henry I they were still allowing Englishmen to succeed to these posts.[2]
Although the shortage of Norman monetary experts would help to explain
this policy, it looks as if the Conqueror and his sons saw no point in
favouring Norman minting practices at the expense of Anglo-Saxon ones.
Second, there is evidence—less explicit than we could wish, it is true—of
a monetary reform in Normandy in the Conqueror's time. The *Consuetudines et iusticie* not only specify the ducal mints and jurisdiction over
coinage, but also fix the weight and alloy of legitimate coins to be struck.[3]
It is hard to understand why William I would have been willing to articu-
late his standard if he had meant to reserve his freedom to alter the coinage;
and even harder to understand why Robert and William Rufus would have
committed themselves to that standard in 1091 had they not recognized it
to have good and lawful precedent.

Third, let us recall that the texts *De foagio* and *De monetagio* plainly
indicate a triennial term for collection of the Norman money-tax. There
is reason to think that this interval was customarily observed in the twelfth
century.[4] Now if the three-yearly term dates back to the origin of the money-

---

[1] *Domesday Book*, i, fo. 336B: Aluredus has three tofts at Lincoln 'in quibus habet
omnes consuetudines praeter geldum regis de monedagio'; cf. 203: at Huntingdon 'rex
Willelmus geldum monete posuit'. I am inclined to agree with Carl Stephenson, *Borough
and Town: A Study of Urban Origins in England* (Cambridge, Mass., 1933), pp. 100–1, that
there may be other disguised allusions to the money-tax in Domesday, although I do not
find his understanding of the nature of the tax satisfactory.

[2] Oman, *Coinage of England*, pp. 80–1.

[3] ed. Haskins, *Norman Institutions*, p. 283, art. 13.

[4] Since *Rec. des actes de Henri II*, ii. 121 and 160 are not Norman *fouages*, there is
nothing in its references to indicate that the Norman money-tax was an annual levy
(citations, p. 15 n. 3, above). Extant Exchequer rolls refer to collections of *focagium* in
1180, 1184 (perhaps levied in 1183), 1195, 1198 (above, p. 15 n. 3), but not in 1200–1
(*Magni rotuli*, ed. Stapleton, ii. 501–2, a mere fragment, however); *Miscellaneous Records
of the Norman Exchequer, 1199–1204*, ed. S. R. Packard (Northampton, Mass., 1927),
pp. 9–11, 34–9, possibly 45–50; other records in Packard's collection cannot be dated

tax, it must have been derived from the actual or conventional terms of
minting then in effect. We know that in England the coinage was minted
at triennial, or sometimes biennial, intervals in the eleventh and twelfth
centuries; whereas in Normandy there is no early evidence of fixed periods
of any length and the numismatic data, if anything, tell against any such
orderly practice.[1]

Finally, we have to notice a fact that is hardly less treacherous than tan-
talizing. According to *De foagio* and later texts, the populations of several
march districts were wholly exempt from the money-tax.[2] Now it seems
clear that these territorial immunities dated back to the early days, if not
to the very origins, of the institution. Nothing so sweeping could have
arisen piecemeal. *De monetagio* says firmly that the regions in question
'were never subject to the aid'.[3] So if we ask why these exemptions were
allowed, we may hope to find another clue to the age of the tax itself. By
the testimony of an undated *jurea* from the time of Henry II (*c.* 1150?–74),
ducal rights of jurisdiction, including the justice of coinage, had been
'general throughout Normandy, save only in the marches where the
[duke's?] money did not circulate'.[4] The ambiguities of this assertion need
not trouble our inference that people in the marches had been free from
fouage because they did not use the coinage it secured. This interpretation
of the texts has support in the fact that the marches enumerated in *De
foagio*—lands extending from the castellany of Saint-James, bordering on
Brittany, eastward through Mortain and Alençon, opposite Maine, as far
as Breteuil—were certainly regions where foreign moneys had prevailed
in the past. But the dukes do not seem to have insisted on exclusive

closely enough—and most, indeed, are too brief—to be helpful on this point). For those
disposed to carry the argument to its logical extreme, 1180 would have marked the thirty-
fourth triennial levy on a cycle of years carried back to 1078, a possible year of origin for
the money-tax: see below, p. 20.

[1] Oman, *Coinage of England*, pp. 82–4; Brooke, *English Coins*, 3rd edn., pp. 79–101;
Dolley, *Norman Conquest*, pp. 9–29; Dieudonné, 'La numismatique normande', 301–6.

[2] *Premier Registre*, ed. Delisle, fo. 46ʳ: 'Sciendum uero quod hec terre quite sunt de
foagio, videlicet totum feodum Britolii quicumque illud teneat, et Vallis Moritolii usque
ad Petras Albas et usque ad Doet Herberti, et tota terra de Passeis et Alenconii et Alenconesium usque ad Pissotum Heraudi, et Molins et Boens Molins et terra ad ea pertinens,
et castrum de Aumenesche in ballia de Argenton. In ciuitate Lexouiensi capietur foagium
per manum episcopi Lexouiensis et extra ciuitatem ut alibi capietur.'

[3] *Summa leg. Norm.*, c. 14 (p. 42): '6. Sciendum autem est quod sunt quedam loca in
Normannia que nunquam fuerunt huic auxilio subrogata, ut castellaria Sancti Jacobi et
vallis Moritolii, et si qua sunt hujusmodi que nunquam monetagium persoluerunt.'
This list of exempt localities is shorter than that of *De foagio*, but evidently not meant
to be complete; it begins with the same places at the head of the former list. See Bridrey's
resourceful discussion of the territorial exemptions, 'Le chapitre *De monnéage*', 218–31.

[4] *Très Ancien Coutumier*, c. 70 (pp. 64–5): 'Dixerunt eciam quod . . . similiter omnis
justicia de exercitu, vel de moneta, ad solum Ducem pertinent. Hec autem supradicta
fuerunt generalia per totam Normanniam, nisi solummodo in marchis ubi moneta non
currebat.'

currency for their money (as distinct from exclusive jurisdiction over it) anywhere in the duchy, and the invasion by *mançois*, *angevins*, and other coinages continued unchecked during the reign of Henry I.[1] Therefore it is a little easier to conceive of the territorial exemptions being granted in the later eleventh century than in the twelfth. And there are secondary reasons for preferring the earlier period. We find no mention, among the enumerated marches, of the stronghold of Bellême and its immediate environs. The omission can hardly be accidental, for no less than three castles just to the north are listed, as are also the lands around Alençon and Domfront, traditionally dependencies of Bellême, but garrisoned by the Conqueror.[2] Now in the decade of the 1070s the security of Normandy had been threatened by uprisings not only in Bellême itself but also in Maine and Brittany: that is, in just those lands marching with the exempt districts.[3] If military exigencies had anything to do with this fiscal favour —and we may note in passing that knights were exempt from the money-tax throughout the duchy[4]—it would be hard to find a better conjunction of the political and geographical facts than in these troubled later years of William I.

On the basis of these circumstances and criticisms, the following explanation may be proposed. The Conqueror arrived in England to discover there in effect a much better organization of coinage than that of his duchy, save in one respect: that he could not profit from manipulations of specie as he was used to doing in Normandy. So he attempted to make up the difference by imposing a 'common money-tax', which had, therefore, the same commutative purpose as the Norman *monetagium*. We may imagine that this imposition was not very successful in England. What the kings regarded as a rightful return on the mints, the English people deplored as an unwarranted novelty, a kind of revocation of their traditionally good currency. For a general tax, the English *monetagium* left surprisingly

---

[1] A charter listing benefactions to the collegiate church at Mortain in 1082 and after 1106 shows that the count of Mortain's tolls were accounted in money of Le Mans in his immediate march domains and in money of Rouen only in places more central to the duchy proper, ed. Jacques Boussard, 'Le comté de Mortain au XIe siècle', *Le Moyen Âge*, lviii (1952), 258–68; see also Delisle, 'Des revenus publics', *BEC*, x (1849), 183 n. 4, 190–2; and Jacques Boussard, *Le Gouvernement d'Henri II Plantagenêt* (Paris, 1956), pp. 302–3.

[2] Bridrey, 'Le chapitre *De monnéage*', 223; Jacques Boussard, 'La seigneurie de Bellême aux Xe et XIe siècles', *Mélanges d'histoire du moyen âge dédiés à la mémoire de Louis Halphen* (Paris, 1951), pp. 43–53. Orderic Vital, *Historia ecclesiastica*, ed. Auguste Le Prévost, 5 vols. (Paris, 1838–55), viii (iii. 262), implies that Bellême, too, was garrisoned, but the suzerainty of the seigneury was still in doubt, and Robert of Bellême was quite likely in control of his capital when he rose with neighbouring lords in 1078 (next note). See also J.-F. Lemarignier, *Recherches sur l'hommage en marche et les frontières féodales* (Lille, 1945), pp. 60–9.

[3] D. C. Douglas, *William the Conqueror* . . . (London–Berkeley, Calif., 1964), pp. 223–39. Boussard, in works cited in previous note, does not discuss the rising of 1077–8.

[4] *Premier Registre*, ed. Delisle, fo. 46; *Summa leg. Norm.*, c. 14, arts. 2, 4 (pp. 40–1).

few traces in the sources, and it may well have been abandoned before 1100. One reason for not insisting on it can perhaps be found in the heavy payments the king received from moneyers 'when the coinage was changed' —that is, when types were changed and when, possibly, demonetization took place.[1] In the end William I found that the English *moneta* was no less lucrative for being orderly. He therefore decided to bring the Norman coinage into better correspondence with the English, going at least as far as to stabilize its standards. Accordingly, the *monetagium* was introduced into Normandy, where it could more reasonably be defended and tolerated, as a quid pro quo, than in England. A triennial minting term may have been adopted as a part of the Norman reform and so have determined the interval of the money-tax from its inception; or else this interval may have been fixed at some later date—conceivably after the reunion of kingdom and duchy in 1106—when the tax assumed (or recovered) its definitive form. The possibility of an origin some time after 1100 remains, although it has nothing in its favour except the perfect silence of extant records, none of them fiscal, down to the time of Henry II. And lest that silence be unduly credited, we should observe that clergy as well as knights—the most usual recipients of charters—were probably immune from the beginning.[2]

The agreement or acquiescence that marked the foundation of this institution is also problematical. Bridrey thought that the money-tax was expressly contractual at the outset and that quite possibly the duke received it by the concession of a general assembly of Normans. He pointed to traditions of the fourteenth and later centuries that the *fouage* had been 'granted' to the duke, to the presumable analogy with other areas where money-taxes demonstrably originated in consent, and to known assemblies in Normandy whence issued decisions of comparable importance in the eleventh century.[3] These arguments may seem vulnerable prima facie, but if we bear in mind that the documentary record of early Norman history 'has in large measure disappeared',[4] we shall be cautious about dismissing the possibility of a formal concession. Especially since, among what is left, there survives no such evidence as in England that the Norman money-tax was ever regarded as an unjust exaction.

Nevertheless, in the absence of anything like a constitutive monument, Bridrey's case is open to question. His first two reasons we may pass over for the moment, for they are clearly indecisive by themselves. As for the

---

[1] G. C. Brooke, '"Quando moneta vertebatur": The Change of Coin-Types in the Eleventh Century . . .', *British Numismatic Journal* xx (1929–30), 105–16.

[2] *Premier Registre*, ed. Delisle, fo. 46; *Summa leg. Norm.*, c. 14, arts. 2, 4 (pp. 40–1). I have reserved for later discussion the mode of levy recorded in *De foagio*, because it seems to me without demonstrable bearing on the problem of origins.

[3] Bridrey, 'Le chapitre *De monnéage*', 100–16; esp. 115–16.

[4] Haskins, *Norman Institutions*, p. 241.

third, relating to the likelihood of a grant in some early assembly, what seems doubtful is not so much the possibility of such an event as Bridrey's conception of it. Quite true it is that the dukes convoked major assemblies; and to those of 1047, 1066, and 1080 cited by the French scholar, one could easily add others on the evidence of chronicles and charters. What is more, there are allusions to unspecified general *negotia* in some of these meetings, in those, for example, of 1074, 1075, and 1107.[1] But it is hard to conceive of an agreement or bargain such as Bridrey postulates emanating from one of these great courts. For since the tax bore on the mass of Normans, we should have to imagine either a thoroughly parliamentary or representative assembly, or else a great charter having a comprehensiveness of address perhaps without example before the *Charte aux Normands* of 1315. Such a conception is excessively juridical and anachronistic. If the money-tax was instituted in assembly, then that assembly was much more probably conciliar than parliamentary in nature, political rather than contractual. The men who were to pay the tax—villagers and townsmen— were just those who quite certainly did not attend ducal courts and councils, nor were then understood to be legally represented in them. The magnates, on the other hand, were exempt.

Must we necessarily suppose an assembly? The decision could perhaps equally well have been an administrative one, approved in inner counsels and put into effect by directives to the *vicomtes* and stewards of domain. Such records, like any writs, were far less likely to survive than narratives and charters alluding to assemblies and legislation.[2] Still another alternative to the theory of a consenting assembly is that the Norman money-tax might have originated in local agreements, conceivably with mercantile communities, and then have been generalized by administrative order and the acquiescence of magnates. If these possibilities have no better support than that urged by Bridrey, they may nevertheless be found more consistent with what we know about the political character of William the Conqueror and his sons and about their conceptions of the prerogative of coinage.

The economic evidence, while inconclusive in itself, is consistent with an early date for the money-tax, and it suggests that the dukes and lords had as much interest in a stable currency as villagers and townsfolk. Monetary exchange, stimulated by trade, conquest, and pious enterprise, was already important in the duchy's economy in the first half of the

---

[1] Robert de Torigni, *Chronique* . . . , ed. Léopold Delisle, 2 vols. (Rouen, 1872–3), i. 59, 60; Orderic Vital, *Hist. eccles.*, xi, c. 30 (iv. 269). See also iv, c. 2 (ii. 168), x, c. 7 (iv. 37), xi, c. 21 (iv. 233–4); Ferdinand Lot, *Études critiques sur l'abbaye de Saint-Wandrille* (Paris, 1913), recueil des chartes, no. 37; Haskins, *Norman Institutions*, pp. 54–5; and in general, Lucien Valin, *Le Duc de Normandie et sa cour (912–1204)* . . . (Paris, 1910), pp. 101–6, 171–6; Douglas, *William the Conqueror*, pp. 143–5, 284–7.

[2] Grierson, 'Numismatics and the Historian', viii–xiv.

eleventh century. It continued to progress thereafter, the social ascent of the moneyers being symptomatic.[1] Haskins and Musset agree that Normandy was in advance of other provinces in respect of wealth in money.[2] Not only big payments but also small and regular ones were made or stipulated in specie. Ducal revenues, larger and more numerous than those of other feudal states, were commonly in coin, notably tolls, which were especially bountiful in Normandy.[3] It appears, however, that the supply of coin did not always keep pace with economic needs. Extant deniers are relatively few, perhaps an indication of recoinages or of export to Italy where they would have been melted down and of a prevailing disinclination to value them enough to hoard them;[4] but what seems more significant is that large payments were sometimes transacted partly or wholly in kind, and that in such cases the monetary value of the horses or chalices or other goods was often indicated.[5] Nor were payments in weights of precious metal uncommon.[6] These may point not only to deficiencies of specie but also to an awakening of interest in the intrinsic worth and stability of available coins.

People did not usually specify what deniers they wanted in Norman transactions until the twelfth century.[7] One reason for this may be that the prevailing ducal coins, neither attractive nor dependable, were by no means preferred to those from neighbouring provinces; the dukes for

---

[1] Lucien Musset, 'A-t-il existé en Normandie au XIe siècle une aristocratie d'argent? ...', *Annales de Normandie*, ix (1959), 285–99.

[2] Haskins, *Norman Institutions*, pp. 44–5; Musset, 'Une aristocratie d'argent?', 286. Their evidence is supported by the newly recovered hoard of Fécamp, in which more than 35 l. of pieces were buried some short time before 975–6, Dumas, *Trésor de Fécamp*, pp. 12–19.

[3] Delisle, 'Des revenus publics', *BEC*, x. 178–82; Haskins, *Norman Institutions*, pp. 39–45, 299, no. 10, 300–2, no. 11; Lucien Musset, 'La vie économique de l'abbaye de Fécamp sous l'abbatiat de Jean de Ravenne, 1028–1078', *L'Abbaye bénédictine de Fécamp ... XIIIe centenaire*, 3 vols. (Fécamp, 1958), i. 70–5; *Rec. des actes des ducs de Normandie*, nos. 45, 80, 83, 86, 91, 98, 101, 112, 118, 120, 123, 130, 135–6, 139, 143–4, 153–4, 156, 163 *bis*, 165, 167, 171–2, 180, 186, 189–90, 193, 197, 202–3, 206, 218, 220, 222, 224–5, 232.

[4] Poey d'Avant, *Monnaies féodales*, i. 17–18; Dieudonné, 'La numismatique normande', 304–6. Philip Grierson informs me, however, that specimens of the 'blundered-temple' type are not rare.

[5] Musset, 'La vie économique ... de Fécamp', i. 70–2; Delisle, 'Des revenus publics', *BEC*, x. 179–80; idem, *Histoire du château et des sires de Saint-Sauveur-le-Vicomte ...* (Valognes, 1867), *p.j.*, no. 12; Haskins, *Norman Institutions*, p. 307, no. 22; Lot, *Saint-Wandrille*, chartes, no. 145; *Chartes de l'abbaye de Jumièges (v. 825 à 1204) ...*, ed. J.-J. Vernier, 2 vols. (Rouen–Paris, 1916), i, nos. 46, 56; *Rec. des actes des ducs de Normandie*, nos. 63, 89, 113, 135, 188.

[6] Delisle, 'Des revenus publics', *BEC*, x. 206–7; *Rec. des actes des ducs de Normandie*, nos. 89, 234; Musset, 'La vie économique ... de Fécamp', i. 70–2.

[7] For exceptions, see Musset, 'La vie économique ... de Fécamp', i. 70 (Senlis); Lot, *Saint-Wandrille*, chartes, no. 117 (Rouen); Delisle, 'Des revenus publics', *BEC*, x. 178–9; *Rec. des actes des ducs de Normandie*, nos. 63, 136 (Rouen), 232 (Le Mans); *Cartulaire des Îles Normandes ...* (Jersey, 1918–24), no. 150.

their part made no effort to exclude other currencies nor, so far as we know, to allow their mutations to be determined by public rates of exchange. The moneys of England, Maine, and the Île-de-France were of better alloy and reliability than the dukes', although Capetian coinages seem to have fallen into rough parity with the Norman at the start of the twelfth century.[1] Then too, or a little later, Angevin money was interchangeable with that of Rouen, which it eventually replaced.[2] But there are stronger reasons for thinking that the Normans early became sensitive to the value and steadiness of the deniers in their mixed bag. As far back as 1012, to judge from extant charters, large payments were made or specified in 'pounds of coins',[3] and this practice became so common as to be the rule during the middle third of the eleventh century.[4] When it was a matter of 30 or 60 l., to say nothing of 200 (!), it was safer as well as easier to measure by weight than by count. Allusions to payments by weight of coin become scarcer in the later eleventh century.[5] While these facts must certainly be handled with care,[6] they are consistent with the possibility that the Conqueror finally improved a Norman coinage that had been especially unreliable in his early years. If that is what happened, some were not at once convinced. An explicit reservation as to the stability of coinage may be found in a charter by which, toward 1100, the nuns of Sainte-Trinité of Caen farmed their revenues in Jersey. The price of the farm was 26 pounds of deniers for ten years, during which time the concessionaire was to receive payments of 100 s. on the festivals of Pentecost, Peter and Paul, and Christmas, the last of which was to be in 'strong money' in case 'the coinage shall have been changed'.[7] Such declarations are most uncommon in Norman texts of the twelfth century, perhaps because people gained

---

[1] Dieudonné, 'La numismatique normande', 304–7. Luneau, 'Quelques deniers normands', 87; Dolley, *Norman Conquest*; Dieudonné, *Manuel de numismatique*, iv. 289–91; idem, 'Les conditions du denier parisis et du denier tournois sous les premiers capétiens', *BEC*, lxxxi (1920), 45–60.

[2] Delisle, 'Des revenus publics', *BEC*, x. 182–7; Boussard, *Gouvernement d'Henri II*, pp. 302–3; *Chartes du prieuré de Longueville . . .*, ed. Paul Le Cacheux (Rouen–Paris, 1934), nos. 14, 26, 39, 49, 53, 91.

[3] *Rec. des actes des ducs de Normandie*, no. 14 *bis*: 'XXX^ta. libras nummorum'.

[4] Ibid., nos. 74, 83, 86, 112, 118, 121, 123, 130, 139, 143, 153, 163 *bis*, 167, 188, 190, 197, 200, 206, 220, 224; *Cart. Îles Normandes*, nos. 150, 300; *Cartulaire de la Sainte-Trinité-du-Mont, de Rouen . . .*, ed. Achille Deville (in *Cartulaire de l'abbaye de Saint-Bertin*) (Paris, 1841), nos. 28, 30, 78.

[5] *Rec. des actes des ducs de Normandie*, no. 234; Lot, *Saint-Wandrille*, chartes, nos. 117, 118.

[6] Some of the references to *libre denariorum* may be the result of scribal habit, and may not signify payments by weight. Cf. citations in next note.

[7] BN, MS. lat. 5650, fos. 32^v–33. Cited by Delisle, 'Des revenus publics', *BEC*, xiii. 106 n. 3, this text was drawn to my attention by Professor Musset, who has since then discussed it in 'Sur les mutations de la monnaie ducale', 292–3. Cf. *Rec. des actes des ducs de Normandie*, no. 83 (1030–5): 'datis denariorum probatę monetę sexaginta libris, emit'; and 'Actes inédits du XIᵉ siècle. I.—Les plus anciennes chartes du prieuré de Saint-Gabriel (Calvados)', ed. Lucien Musset, *BSAN*, lii (1952–3), 122.

confidence in the coinage.[1] Occasional references to 'new money' or 'new sous of Rouen' probably indicate recoinages rather than debasements,[2] although we might infer from *De monetagio* that mutations of any sort had been precluded. The Plantagenets closed the ducal mints, or at any rate suppressed the old coinage of Rouen in favour of that of Angers.[3] Whatever the reasons for this, the decision left them no less free to change the money as counts of Anjou than to collect the money-tax as dukes of Normandy.

The fiscal importance of the early Norman money-tax is difficult to estimate. What we should most like to know is how the imposition was related to profits of the mint; but since our ignorance of the latter is total, the inquiry would be frustrated even if we could be sure that 12 d. was the original rate per hearth.[4] There can have been no very successful effort, if any at all, to translate mutations (and/or *seigneuriage*) into determined proportions of value. From the table of exemptions, we deduce that 4 d. to 20 s. of annual income was the maximum ratio of admissible return claimed by the duke, but 1·67 per cent would have been an extremely poor rate of profit from mints by any standard.[5] So it seems more likely that the calculation was made more roughly in terms of desired proceeds. And, by chance of survival, we have a figure for the probable net proceeds from a *fouage* of 1183 or 1184. The *bailli* of Gisors, accounting for sums applied to the works of castles in the march, acknowledged receipt of 1700 l. sterling *de focagio* from the treasury at Rouen.[6] Since the levy

---

[1] For two examples see Delisle, 'Des revenus publics', *BEC*, x. 186, n. 5–187; *PU Frankreich. Neue Folge. 2. Normandie*, ed. Johannes Ramackers (Göttingen: *Abh.*, 3rd ser., xxi, 1937), no. 122.

[2] Delisle, 'Des revenus publics', *BEC*, x. 181 n. 2, 182 n. 2; xiii. 106 n. 3. At least one of these mutations occurred in the year (1135) when a new duke came to power. The earliest instance dates from 1030 to 1060, Musset, 'Actes inédits du XIᵉ siècle', 122.

[3] Boussard, *Gouvernement d'Henri II*, pp. 302–3; and references, p. 24, n. 2, above. Some scholars have thought, indeed, that the imposition of the money-tax corresponded to the closing of the mints, e.g. Lecointre-Dupont, *Lettres sur l'histoire monétaire*, pp. 9–10; and Poey d'Avant, *Monnaies féodales*, i. 18; and this mistaken opinion was adopted by Lot and Fawtier, *Hist. des institutions*, ii. 211. It is expressly contradicted, e.g. by Henry I's cession of revenues from the mint of Rouen to Fontevrault, Haskins, *Norman Institutions*, p. 106.

[4] There is no good reason to doubt that this was the original rate. See below, p. 27; and cf. Bridrey, 'Le chapitre *De monnéage*', 149, and n. 179, who speculates as to why the sum was not spoken of as an even sou.

[5] *De foagio*, ed. Delisle, *Premier Registre*, fo. 46: '. . . et si in eadem domo manserint quatuor homines uel plures siue pauciores de quibus unusquisque uiuat de suo proprio et habeat de catallo xx. solidos aut amplius, quislibet illorum reddit foagium.' Cf. above, p. 5.

[6] *Magni rotuli*, ed. Stapleton, i. 110. Stapleton himself noticed the significance of this passage, 'Observations on the Great Rolls of the Exchequer of Normandy', ibid., p. cxxxvi, as later did Bridrey, 'Le chapitre *De monnéage*', 210 n. 316. Both writers assumed, probably correctly, that the figure was a total of receipts. The fact that it was reckoned in sterling suggests that it had been collected and re-counted at Rouen for some such purpose as attested. Moreover, the item indicates a large number of paying hearths—possibly as high

itself can be assumed to have been collected in local deniers, most likely those of Anjou, Maine, or Tours, we can safely multiply this sum by a factor of 2 to 4 to arrive at values prevailing in France.[1] The maximum resultant figure would be 6,800 l. (*tur.* or *andeg.*); and the relative importance of such a sum, even if it were much less than total proceeds of *fouage* for the duchy—which is unlikely—was modest. Calculated on a yearly basis, it amounted to something under 2,300 l., at a time when the fixed farms of Normandy were producing about 20,000 l. *andeg.* per annum.[2] Still less favourable is the comparison with the special aids known from the end of the century. In 1198 the town of Caen alone was tallaged for 4,000 l.[3] On the other hand, the *fouage* continued to be more valuable than the old *graveria* and *bernagium*, Carolingian imposts incompletely revived in the eleventh century.[4] Assuming a fairly constant ratio between the farms and the *fouage*, the conclusion seems justified that the money-tax had been at first just about what average returns from mints tended to be: an important but unspectacular financial resource.

That the tax continued to be valued by the rulers of Normandy in the age of the Capetian conquest is proved not only by the drafting of *De foagio* but also by the evidence of rights to *fouage* in the early thirteenth century. The summons of four or six local men to report as well as to collect points to a concern for enforcement that may have been new in the Angevin period. There is some analogy with the administration of the Saladin Tithe (1188), as recorded by Hoveden, whereby four or six men of the parish were to assess the property of those suspected of underpaying.[5] The *fouage* on his tenants was a major issue in the archbishop of Rouen's settlement with Philip Augustus over the manor of Andeli.[6] And while the relative value of the *fouage*, even allowing for increasing population, surely declined in the Norman inflation of the thirteenth century, the

---

as 136,000, if all payments were in, or accountable in, deniers of Anjou or Tours— a figure which, properly corrected, is probably the earliest solid evidence of the population of medieval Normandy. It bears a plausible relation to the 79,748 hearths reported in Brittany in 1392, text cited by Bridrey, 211 n. 317.

[1] Cf. Dieudonné, *Manuel de numismatique*, iv. 42; *Recueil des actes de Philippe Auguste, roi de France*, ed. H.-F. Delaborde, Charles Petit-Dutaillis, Jacques Monicat, and Jacques Boussard, 3 vols. to date (Paris, 1916–66), ii, no. 844.

[2] Powicke, *Loss of Normandy*, 2nd edn., p. 234.

[3] *Magni rotuli*, ed. Stapleton, ii. 348; see generally Delisle, 'Des revenus publics', *BEC*, xiii. 130–1; Powicke, pp. 234–5.

[4] Delisle, 'Des revenus publics', *BEC*, xiii. 120–2; Lucien Musset, 'Recherches sur quelques survivances de la fiscalité ducale', *BSAN*, lv (1959–60), 9–18. The latter is cautious and convincing about the Carolingian ancestry.

[5] *De foagio*, transcribed below, p. 204; Stubbs, *Select Charters*, 9th edn., p. 189. In the light of recent Capetian practice (e.g. *Rec. des actes de Philippe Auguste*, i, no. 224 [art. 32], no. 345), it cannot be maintained that the four or six men are specifically English.

[6] *LTC*, i, no. 821; see generally Powicke, *Loss of Normandy*, 2nd edn., pp. 108, 113–16, 136, 190, 251–2, 255–6.

Capetian kings were reluctant to alienate the tax or its levy or to exempt from its payment.[1]

The fiscal facts together with the administrative ones recorded in the thirteenth century tell us something about the political and social significance of the original Norman money-tax. They tell of a duchy full of houses and of a duke capable of imposing himself directly upon every household. No lesser lord could abstract his tenants from this obligation; and few were the lords who had any rights in the collection of *fouage*.[2] The general exemptions of knights, clergy, and indigent persons reflect a combination of military and pious interests that were especially characteristic of the Conqueror, although at no time uncommon in the eleventh and twelfth centuries. From the summary in *De foagio*, it would appear that the two former of these exemptions were a kind of reward for service to the duke or duchy: they were extended to millers and oven-keepers in the employ of prelates, barons, and such knights as served their lords for any part of a knight's fee; while prelates and barons could designate seven sergeants quit of *fouage*.[3] Hearths, better than the ancient manses, were the measure of a population growing in bourgs and towns as well as in vills. In terms of revenue, the immunity of march lands cannot have been so important at the beginning as it became when the borders were secured and opened to new enterprise.[4] The fixed triennial sou was probably a modest assessment even in the eleventh century, perhaps roughly the wages of a day's field work per year; and if not perfectly geared to a growing economy, it had the advantages of being predictable in its returns and easy to collect. Granted the accomplishments of the great dukes, these

[1] *LTC*, i, no. 977; ii, no. 2833; *Rec. des actes de Philippe Auguste*, iii, nos. 966, 1000; *Chronicon Rotomagensis*, in *HF*, xxiii. 332. For an estimate that prices rose 50 per cent in Normandy from 1180 to 1260, see Édouard Perroy, *Le Moyen Age . . .*, 3rd edn. (Paris: *Histoire générale des civilisations*, iii, 1961), 363.

[2] The bishop of Lisieux was privileged to collect *fouage*, but only in his city proper, *De foagio*, as quoted above, p. 19 n. 2. The only concession I have found for the twelfth century is *Rec. des actes de Henri II*, i. 350 (1156–62), the king's sergeant Baudri is to have 'totum pasnagium hominum suorum et focagium'. For exemptions in consequence of sergeanty, see also ii. 345 and 249; cf. n. 3 below. In 1180 some lords were fined *pro monetagio retento*, doubtless on report of the sworn receivers, *Magni rotuli*, ed. Stapleton, i. 21–2. Raoul Taisson accounted for the *fouage* of his land in 1198 and 1203, Bridrey, 'Le chapitre *De monnéage*', 197; *Magni rotuli*, ii. 523; cf. 554, 558.

[3] *De foagio*, ed. Delisle, *Premier Registre*, fo. 46: 'Molendinarii etiam et furnarii episcoporum et abbatum et baronum et omnium militum qui deseruiunt dominis suis per membrum lorice exinde quiti sunt. Et preterea quilibet episcopus et abbas et baro habet .vii. seruientes quoscumque uoluerint quitos de foagio.' Cf. *De monetagio, Summa leg. Norm.*, c. 14, art. 4, p. 41.

[4] Jacques Boussard, 'Hypothèses sur la formation des bourgs et des communes de Normandie', *Annales de Normandie*, viii (1958), 423–40; Lucien Musset, 'Peuplement en bourgage et bourgs ruraux en Normandie du Xe au XIIIe siècle', *Cahiers de civilisation médiévale*, ix (1966), 177–208; Georges Duby, *L'Économie rurale et la vie des campagnes dans l'Occident médiéval*, 2 vols. (Paris, 1962), i. 159–61, 208–9; tr. Cynthia Postan, *Rural Economy and Country Life . . .* (London, 1968), pp. 80–1, 117.

were still appreciable advantages for the government of the late eleventh or early twelfth century.

In sum, the origins of the money-tax, like those of other Norman institutions, are shrouded in obscurity. The first imposition probably occurred in the later years of William the Conqueror, although possibly not until some time in the next generation. It post-dated the English *monetagium* in either case. The decision to institute the tax could have been made in great council or in small and the measure was quite likely related to a reform of the coinage. The precocious development of the Norman economy suggests that neither ducal nor public interests suffered from the arrangement, which may be another reason why so little is heard about it. Of moderate fiscal importance, the levy corresponded in form and incidence to conditions prevailing in Normandy under the Conqueror and his sons. By the later twelfth century, when it comes clearly into view, it was a flourishing institution apparently divorced from the administration of coinage. Yet it might then have seemed justified in its results as well as sanctioned by custom, for the coinages circulating in Normandy were effectively secured in public ratios of exchange at the time of the Capetian conquest.[1]

[1] See below, p. 164.

III

THE MONEY-TAXES OF
CAPETIAN FRANCE

NORMANDY lay on the threshold of 'France'. There, in the region later known as the Île-de-France, the Capetian kings began in the early twelfth century to collect money-taxes of their own.[1] And although the history of these taxes is scarcely less obscure than that of the Norman *fouage*, we are somewhat better informed about the origins of the Capetian imposition. Whereas for Normandy the best evidence dates from a century or more after the beginnings, in the case of France we are fortunate to have records which, if not quite foundation charters themselves, cannot have long post-dated the institution of the money-taxes.

Louis VII granted major charters to the men of Étampes and Orléans within months of his accession to the throne in August 1137. These towns were old resorts of Capetian authority and both had active mints. The charters they received dealt with various issues arising from local adminis-tration and commerce, but in each the initial and principal concession was the assurance that the coinage would be stabilized. The terms were similar though not identical. To Étampes the king promised to maintain the money without mutation or lightening in weight or alloy during his lifetime, while in return, 'for the redemption of the same coinage', the knights and burghers of Étampes were to pay 100 l. in money of Étampes on the All Saints' Day of every third year.[2] According to the charter for Orléans,

---

[1] Capetian money-taxes have never been thoroughly studied. The Parisian tax, finding no place in regional custom, was not a subject for applied legal commentary. The tax at Orléans was known to local jurists in the seventeenth century, when it had lately dis-appeared, but only as an adjunct of the consolidated tallage with which it had been asso-ciated since 1183 (below, p. 35); see Jacques de La Lande, *Coutume d'Orléans . . .* , 2nd edn., 2 vols. (Orléans, 1704; 1st edn., 1673), ii. 386–8. Du Cange, *Glossarium*, on words *relevatio monetae* and *tallia panis et vini*, cited some of the texts, and many subsequent historians have mentioned these institutions. But the fullest account remains that of Nicolas Brussel, *Nouvel Examen de l'usage général des fiefs*, i. 216, 524–31. Among other discussions, it suffices to cite Barthélemy, 'Essai sur la monnaie parisis', 170–1; Achille Luchaire, *Histoire des institutions monarchiques de la France sous les premiers capétiens* (*987–1180*), 2nd edn., 2 vols. (Paris, 1891), i. 99–101; Lot and Fawtier, *Hist. des institu-tions*, ii. 211. For Adolphe Dieudonné's curiously unsatisfactory contribution to the subject, see p. 37 n. 3, below. (Plate I, nos. 3–7.)

[2] Basile Fleureau, *Les Antiquitez de la ville et du duché d'Estampes . . .* (Paris, 1683), pp. 103–4 (reproduced in *Ordonnances des roys de France de la troisième race*, 22 vols. [Paris, 1723–1849], xi. 188; indicated by Achille Luchaire, *Études sur les actes de Louis VII*

which probably followed that for Étampes—perhaps by several months—
the coinage of Orléans that was circulating at the end of the lately past
reign was to be maintained without mutation or lessening of alloy during
the king's lifetime, in compensation for which the king was entitled to
collect a triennial 'redemption' of the money. The tax of Orléans, however,
was specified in its application: two deniers on each measure (*modius*) of
wine and winter wheat, one denier per measure of (spring) oats.[1]

In regulating the future, these charters betrayed an uneasy past. Louis
VII had been greeted by a communal uprising at Orléans as he passed
through to claim the throne in 1137, and in the latter part of his father's
reign there had been unrest at Étampes as well as at Orléans.[2] The concessions of 1137–8 both originated in complaints or appeals. In Étampes it
was the knights and burghers who took the initiative and 'their humble
petition' may have been brought to the king by one Luc de Male, knight of
Étampes, who at the request of the king swore surety for the king's observance of the monetary pact.[3] In Orléans the burghers alone are said to

(Paris, 1885), catalogue des actes, no. 7; in the transcription, I have suppressed Fleureau's
italics and one minor slip): 'In nomine ... Ego Ludovicus Francorum Rex, & Dux
Aquitanorum, notum fieri volumus cunctis fidelibus, tam praesentibus quam futuris, quod
universis Stamparum hominibus, tam militibus, quam Burgensibus, humili ipsorum
petitione; & fidelium nostrorum concilio, concessimus, quod praesentem Stamparum
monetam, quae ibi à Patris nostri decessu habebatur, nos omnibus diebus vitae nostrae
neque mutabimus, neque lege, neque pondere alleviabimus, neque alleviari ab aliquo
patiemur, quamdiù milites, & Burgenses Stampenses, unoquoque tertio anno, à festivitate
omnium Sanctorum, pro ejusdem monetae redemptione, libras centum, de eadem moneta
nobis dabunt. Et si ipsi eandem monetam falsificari, aut alio modo alleviari cognoverint, nos
ab ipsis moniti, eam probari, & tentari videbimus. Et si falsificata, aut alleviata fuerit, nos
de falsificatore, aut alleviatore, consilio militum, & Burgensium Stampensium, justitiam
faciemus. Luc de Malus autem, miles Stampensis, praecepto nostro, & pro nobis jura-
mento firmavit, quod nos hujusmodi pactionem eis praedicto modo tenebimus, & ob-
servabimus. . . .'

[1] BN MS. fr. 11,988, fos. 24–5 (ed. Eugène Bimbenet, 'Examen critique de la charte
octroyée par le roi Louis VII aux habitants d'Orléans, en l'année 1137', *Mémoires de la
Société d'agriculture, des sciences, et des belles-lettres et arts d'Orléans*, 2nd ser., xvi
[1874], 67): 'In nomine Domini amen. Ego Ludovicus, Dei gracia Francorum rex et dux
Aquitanorum. Notum facimus tam futuris quam instantibus quod nos burgensibus
Aurelianensibus pro gravamine civitatis aufferendo istas que secuntur consuetudines in-
dulsimus:
Monetam Aurelianensem que in morte patris nostri currebat in tota vita nostra non
mutandam eis concessimus et eam neque mutari neque alleviari paciemur. In tercio autem
anno pro redempcione eiusdem monete de singulis modiis vini et hyemalis annone binos
denarios et de singulis modiis avene singulos denarios, sicut in tempore patris nostri
fiebat, capiemus. . . .' A garbled version of this charter in the 'First Register' of Philip
Augustus (Vatican, MS. Ottoboni 2796, fo. 58ra), where it is dated 1187, in the fifth (*sic*)
year of an unnamed king, has misled scholars, including Delisle: see his *Catalogue des
actes de Philippe-Auguste* ... (Paris, 1856), no. 201; also Babelon, 'Théorie féodale de la
monnaie', 326; and many others.

[2] Suger, *Histoire du roi Louis VII*, ch. 1, ed. Auguste Molinier (Paris, 1887), p. 165;
Achille Luchaire, *Louis VI le Gros. Annales de sa vie et de son règne (1081–1137)* (Paris,
1890), nos. 437, 505, 531; Introduction, pp. cxc–cxci.

[3] Fleureau, *Antiquitez d'Estampes*, p. 103; quoted above, p. 30 (continued note).

have complained; but since people well outside the urban limits were soon paying the money-tax,[1] it seems that the agreements covered more than just the city. The participation of knights at Étampes points to a similar conclusion, while dramatizing the depth of an issue that had united the classes. There can be no doubt that the coinages had come under debate in communal assemblies in both places. Nevertheless, the form of the agreements suggests that the king's prerogative was maintained foremost. The decisions were recorded in charters of grace, not conventions, and were dated at Paris. The charter for Étampes alludes to counsel with the king's *fideles*, but the final protocols afford no hint that either document issued from an assembly; the *signa* are those of the court officers and are, in fact, identical in the two texts.

Here, then, we have solid information to work with. People of the royal domain are anxious about the coinages as a new king comes to power, they want the old, familiar deniers to continue in use without so much as a change of type, and they are willing to pay for assurances to such effect. So much seems clear. But it seems equally clear that these were neither the first nor the last such agreements in the Île-de-France, a circumstance which complicates the inquiry because we have no other such direct evidence to employ. It develops that, in reference to the money-tax, the charter for Orléans was not a novelty but a confirmation and that, by the later twelfth century if not before, the same sort of imposition was being collected in and around Paris.

'We shall take [it]', added the king in 1138, alluding to the redemption tax on wine and grain at Orléans, 'just as it was done in the time of our father.'[2] Perhaps it is safe to imagine that the levy was first established at Orléans by way of petition and charter, as it was at Étampes in 1137; but how far back in the reign of Louis VI must we go in search of its origin? Unfortunately, no general charter for Orléans survives among the memorials of that reign.[3] Nor does the numismatic evidence help much. Types, to be sure, were changed at Orléans, as they were elsewhere in the Île-de-France, but—save for the possibility of a new type under Louis VII (in

---

[1] See *Cartulaire de l'église cathédrale Sainte-Croix d'Orléans (814–1300)...*, ed. Joseph Thillier and Eugène Jarry (Paris, 1906), no. 54, or Luchaire, *Actes de Louis VII*, no. 113; *Rec. des actes de Philippe Auguste*, i, no. 5; 'Compte général des revenus ... du Roi pendant l'an 1202', ed. Brussel, *Nouvel Examen des fiefs*, ii. cl (reproduced by Ferdinand Lot and Robert Fawtier, *Le Premier Budget de la monarchie française: le Compte général de 1202–1203* [Paris, 1932]).

[2] Quoted p. 30 n. 1 above.

[3] Luchaire, *Louis VI*, pp. clxxxix–cxc; cf. Charles Petit-Dutaillis, *Les Communes françaises...* (Paris, 1947), pp. 42–3, where, despite two errors in copy or print, it is made clear that there are no charters for Orléans during the reigns of Philip I and Louis VI. According to La Lande, *Coutume d'Orléans*, 2nd edn., ii. 387, the *taille du pain et du vin* at Orléans is sanctioned in a charter of Henry I dated 1037; he was probably misled by a misdated reference to the charter of 1137 in his source.

spite of his engagement to the contrary)¹—these changes can no more be dated than the gradual debasement that is only perceptible over the century from Philip I to Philip Augustus.² Some writers have supposed that the *Chronicle of Saint-Maixent* referred to the royal coinage when it mentioned mutations in 1103, 1112, and 1120. This opinion, though it received the sanction of Lot and Fawtier, is extremely improbable.³ When we look for clues in contracts or charters of the Île-de-France, we find occasional reservations, or implied reservations, about the stability of coinage scattered between the years 1116 and 1164;⁴ but none of these has especial pertinence to Orléans, nor for that matter to Bourges, Étampes, or (until probably toward 1160) Paris, among near-by mints, and no argument can be based on them.

We are reduced in the end to a single hard fact, but a most important one. It is in the form of a record which, although not relative to Orléans, significantly illuminates the circumstances in which Capetian money-taxes originated; it also supplies us with a probable *terminus a quo*. In 1120 (or early in 1121) Louis VI reported that the men of Compiègne, another mint town, had opposed his project to make money there. Trouble had developed, the townspeople had petitioned the king, and in response Louis promised that neither he nor his successor would mint a new coinage at Compiègne and that only such money would henceforth be put in circulation there as had circulated in the past. This unaltered coinage, the king added, was to be *ad medietatem*.⁵

¹ See Lafaurie, *Monnaies des rois*, nos. 130, 154; cf. Blanchet and Dieudonné, *Manuel de numismatique*, ii. 211. The extant deniers inscribed LVDOVICVS cannot surely be assigned to Louis VI or Louis VII; and even if Louis VII did issue a changed coinage, he may not have done so at once.

² Dieudonné assigns to Louis VI a debasement of alloy from 7 d. fine to 6 d., 'Histoire du denier parisis', 133–5, 143; *Manuel de numismatique*, ii. 146. But the evidence is neither ample nor clear.

³ See above, pp. 7, 9 n. 5. E.g. Adolphe Vuitry, *Études sur le régime financier de la France avant 1789*, 3 vols. (Paris, 1873–83), i. 437; Babelon, 'Théorie féodale de la monnaie', 316; Maxime Legrand, 'Essai sur les monnaies d'Étampes', *RN*, 4th ser., xvi (1912), 407–8; Lot and Fawtier, *Hist. des institutions*, ii. 211; cf. Dieudonné, 'Histoire monétaire du denier parisis', 132, and *Manuel de numismatique*, ii. 146 n. 2, who supposes the references were to the *tournois* of Saint-Martin. But if the local chronicler failed to specify what coinage he meant, it was surely because he alluded to the familiar money of Poitou, as Richard, *Hist. des comtes de Poitou*, i. 461, 486–7, rightly assumed. Capetian coinages were not current in Poitou in the early twelfth century.

⁴ *Cartulaire de l'abbaye Saint-Corneille de Compiègne*, ed. Émile Morel, 2 vols. (Compiègne, 1904–9), i, no. 38; *Le Cartulaire du prieuré de Notre-Dame de Longpont de l'ordre de Cluny . . .*, ed. (anonymously) Jules Marion (Lyon, 1880), no. 7; *Cartulaire de l'église Notre-Dame de Paris*, ed. Benjamin Guérard, 4 vols. (Paris, 1850), i. 267, 71; 'Recueil de chartes et documents de Saint-Martin-des-Champs, monastère parisien', ed. Joseph Depoin, *Arch. France monastique*, xvi (1913), nos. 193, 205, 210, 263, 335, 380; Luchaire, *Louis VI*, nos. 435, 497; *Cartulaire de l'église d'Autun . . .*, ed. Anatole de Charmasse (Paris–Autun, 1865), part 2, no. 12.

⁵ Jean Mabillon, *De re diplomatica . . .* (Paris, 1681), p. 598; copy in *Cart. Saint-Corneille*, i. 87–9, under the rubric: 'De moneta non facienda apud Compendium'; in-

This charter has been diversely interpreted since it was first printed by Mabillon from an original now lost. The prevailing view, perhaps most authoritatively expressed by Luchaire, is that Louis had issued a debased money and then, upon complaint, promised not to do so again. Luchaire thought that by the words *ad medietatem*, the king meant to direct that the weakened money continue to circulate at one-half of its nominal value.[1] Most numismatists have interpreted this expression as a reference to the alloy of a coinage that was 6 d. (that is, six-twelfths) fine in 1120,[2] although Maurice Prou argued that *ad medietatem* must allude to the sharing of mint rights at Compiègne.[3] Of these opinions, only the interpretation of *ad medietatem* as pertaining to alloy is tenable. The charter, closely paraphrased above, says nothing about a debased coinage. It makes clear that the opposition was to any new coinage as such at Compiègne.[4] And, while this is less clear, it seems to be worded in such a way as to allow the king the option of continuing to mint on the accustomed type and standard.[5] The customary alloy was 6 d., which is about what we should expect of a royal money that had been at 8 d. and then 7 d. in the later eleventh century and was to slip to 5 d. a hundred years later.[6] In short, just as at Étampes and

dicated by Luchaire, *Louis VI*, no. 296. The date can only be fixed as between 3 August 1120 and the next 25 March or 10 April, Luchaire, pp. 297–8; Georges Tessier, *Diplomatique royale française* (Paris, 1962), pp. 225–6.

[1] Luchaire, *Louis VI*, no. 296, and p. cxci; also idem, *Institutions monarchiques*, 2nd edn., i. 100; W. M. Newman, *Le Domaine royal sous les premiers capétiens (987–1180)* (Paris, 1937), p. 27. See also François Le Blanc, *Traité historique des monnoyes de France* (Paris, 1690), p. 162; Vuitry, *Régime financier*, i. 437; Barthélemy, 'Essai sur la monnaie parisis', 149; Dieudonné, 'Conditions du denier parisis', 47, 53.

[2] Le Blanc, *Traité historique des monnoyes*, p. 162; cf. Barthélemy, 'Essai sur la monnaie parisis', 149; Dieudonné, 'Histoire du denier parisis', 133, 143; idem, 'Conditions du denier parisis', 47, 53.

[3] Maurice Prou, review of Engel and Serrure, *Traité de numismatique du moyen âge*, ii (Paris, 1894), in *RN*, 3rd ser., xii (1894), 524. Prou thought that the term had no textual parallel for reference to alloy, but the Norman *Consuetudines et iusticie* (1091) affords a close analogy, referring to coinage 'mediam argenti', Haskins, *Norman Institutions*, p. 283. Prou subsequently abandoned his argument.

[4] This was evident to an early copyist at Compiègne (see rubric, quoted above, p. 32 n. 5); and among modern writers, to Poey d'Avant, *Monnaies féodales*, iii. 349, and Georges Bourgin, *La Commune de Soissons et le groupe communal soissonais* (Paris, 1908), p. 242, the latter noting Luchaire's view in passing.

[5] If, that is, it implies that any coinage at all had recently been minted there. Knowledge of the activity of the mint at Compiègne (*Cart. Saint-Corneille*, i, nos. 7, 10) has little support other than a LVDOVICVS denier that cannot be dated better than 1108–80, Lafaurie, *Monnaies des rois*, no. 149, and a reference in 1127, *Cart. Saint-Corneille*, i, no. 48, to an annual revenue of 12 d. 'Compendiensis monete' payable at Compiègne. Even if the latter were but a money of account, it suggests that a royal mint had recently been active at Compiègne. In 1164 some were in doubt as to what was the 'public money' at Compiègne, *Veterum scriptorum . . . amplissima collectio*, ed. Edmond Martène and Ursin Durand, 9 vols. (Paris, 1724–33), i. 874. Cf. *Cart. Saint-Corneille*, i, nos. 46, 50, 59, 84, 97, 98, 116.

[6] Dieudonné, 'Conditions du denier parisis', 52–4; cf. Paul Guilhiermoz, 'De la taille du denier dans le haut moyen âge', 280.

Orléans in 1137, the men of Compiègne in 1120 contemplated *any* new coinage with alarm, perhaps even new mintings of old. The mutation of types was no more tolerable than that of standards, presumably because it led to confusion and suspicion.

How valuable was this concession by Louis VI? Since we have no Capetian deniers of Compiègne that could not have been minted before 1120, it is possible that the charter marked the end of the coinage at Compiègne. But whether the king so fully observed his promise or not, he was certainly limiting his prerogative in a way that was to fetch a good price when it was done elsewhere. So it is difficult to believe that the charter for Compiègne was gratuitous. Sixty to eighty years later a hearth tax (*fumagium*) figures among customary payments at Compiègne, and since *fumagium* was to be an alternate term for the Norman money-tax, one may be tempted to draw a connection between the imposition and the events of 1120 at Compiègne.[1] But in the absence of early evidence such as is found elsewhere, it is perhaps more plausible to suppose a single fee at the time of the concession. And if fee there was—whatever its form—we may reasonably identify it as the first of the Capetian money-taxes. For there is no reason to think that other mints of the royal domain had ceased to function during the early years of Louis VI, and the more important mints, including those at Étampes, Orléans, and Paris were quite certainly active after 1120.[2] That Compiègne's charter is unique of its kind and time can hardly be an accident of survival. The agreements of 1137–8 seem more sophisticated, were perhaps, indeed, improved models; and they were so soon followed by the first evidence of collections that we must doubt that they had then any long history. All things considered, the initial understanding to institute a money-tax at Orléans should probably be placed in the latter half of the reign of Louis VI, if not, indeed, near its close. The arrangement

[1] *Cart. Saint-Corneille*, i, no. 146; Brussel, *Nouvel Examen des fiefs*, ii, 'Compte général pendant l'an 1202' (Lot and Fawtier, *Premier Budget*), clxxviii; Bridrey, 'Le chapitre *De monnéage*', 117; *Cart. Îles Normandes*, no. 164. The *fumagium* of Compiègne was a round 100 s. in 1202–3, and was figured in hens in 1240, *Cart. Saint-Corneille*, ii, no. 468. On *fumagium* as a rural exaction, see also Du Cange, *Glossarium*; Delisle, 'Des revenus publics', *BEC*, xiii. 105, n. 1; and idem, *Études sur la condition de la classe agricole et l'état de l'agriculture en Normandie au moyen âge* (Paris, 1903), p. 63, and n. 53: 'Et a quaque domo (ex qua) exit fumus dabunt unam gallinam contra Natale et v ova contra Pascha.'

[2] See generally Émile Caron, 'Essai de classification des monnaies de Louis VI et Louis VII', *Annuaire de la Société française de numismatique*, xviii (1894), 249–75; Lafaurie, *Monnaies des rois*, pp. 6–18, esp. nos. 93–159. And specifically, *Recueil des chartes de l'abbaye de Saint-Germain-des-Prés . . .* , ed. René Poupardin, 2 vols. (Paris, 1909–32), i, nos. 89, 101, 118, 177; *Cartulaire de l'abbaye de Saint-Martin de Pontoise*, ed. Joseph Depoin (Pontoise, 1895–1901), nos. 39, 125, 165, 172, 177; *Cart. Notre-Dame de Paris*, i. 380; 'Chartes de Saint-Martin-des-Champs', *Arch. France monastique*, xiii, nos. 76, 94; xvi, nos. 217, 263, 268, 295; Luchaire, *Actes de Louis VII*, nos. 177, 284; *Cartulaire du chapitre de Saint-Avit d'Orléans (1112–1418)*, ed. Gaston Vignat (Orléans, 1886), nos. 39, 40; *Cart. Sainte-Croix d'Orléans*, nos. 5, 73.

was accepted at nearby Étampes upon the accession of Louis VII when its advantages had become apparent to all concerned.

The two communities were not to keep company very long thereafter. Nothing survives to show that people of Étampes ever paid the money-tax. The imposition had certainly been abandoned there by the end of the twelfth century and it had quite likely been suppressed when, years before, the king ceased to mint at Étampes.[1] At Orléans it was otherwise. Just when the people of Orléans began to pay the money-tax we cannot say, but Louis VII was granting exemptions from it as early as 1143–4.[2] That year corresponded to the term of a second triennial levy, counting from 1137–8, which may be accidental; but it is interesting that the only other twelfth-century charters of exemption from this tax date from December 1159 to March 1160,[3] just following a year on the same triennial cycle, and from 1180,[4] a year squarely on that cycle. Perhaps then it is not accidental that Philip Augustus chose the year 1183 to grant the men of Orléans a charter from which it is clear that the money-tax had been customarily paid on exactly the conditions that had been established half a century before. The imposition had apparently satisfied king and people alike and its redemptive effect was now extended. As his price for remitting the arbitrary tallage on Orléans, Philip Augustus made the triennial tax a fixed annual levy of 2 d. per measure of wine, winter wheat, and fodder, such that the proceeds of two years would compensate for the tallage, while those of the third would continue to secure the 'stability of coinage'. Men formerly exempt from the tallage at will were to continue to pay the money-tallage every third year at the old rate, which allowed a denier less per measure of fodder. Finally, it was laid down in 1183, probably to regulate what had been developing in customary practice, that the tax was to be collected each year by a sergeant from court, other royal sergeants at Orléans, and ten 'legitimate' burghers to be chosen by assembled townsmen themselves; these collectors were to swear to work fairly.[5] The money-tax thus became the cornerstone of a system of regular royal taxation at Orléans.[6]

---

[1] While these are admittedly arguments from silence, the documents for Étampes are very comparable to those for Orléans, which tell a different story. Moreover, the royal account of 1202–3 records money-taxes at Orléans and Paris but not at Étampes, Brussel, *Nouvel Examen des fiefs*, ii (Lot and Fawtier, *Premier Budget*), cl, clvi, clxxiv, clxxv, clxxxix; cf. cxliii–cxlviii, cli, clxxi. The large tallage there accounted for Étampes probably resulted from a recent commutation of the tallage at will restored by the king when he quashed the commune in 1199, *Rec. des actes de Philippe Auguste*, ii, no. 616; cf. Petit-Dutaillis, *Communes françaises*, pp. 130, 143–4. Cf. below, p. 36 n. 6.

[2] *Cart. Sainte-Croix d'Orléans*, no. 54 (Luchaire, *Actes de Louis VII*, no. 113). The text makes clear that a levy had been made.

[3] AN, K 24A, no. 3 (1).

[4] *Rec. des actes de Philippe Auguste*, i, no. 5.

[5] AM Orléans, AA 1 (original, reproduced in Plate VI; imperfectly edited by Delaborde, *Rec. des actes de Philippe Auguste*, i, no. 84): the most essential of the pertinent clauses read: 'Sed sciendum quod duorum annorum collectio sic facta de blado et uino, que

[*See overleaf for note 5 cont. and note 6*

The money-tax of Orléans was generally known as the 'tallage on bread and wine' (*tallia panis et vini*), for reasons that should now be clear. Said in 1183 to be the common usage, the term had not yet become so in 1143–4, when it appeared as *talliata* . . . , nor perhaps yet even in 1159–60, when in keeping with the charters of twenty years before Louis VII spoke of the 'relief of the coinage'.[1] By 1202–3 the popular expression had made its way into the administrative language. The *tallia panis et vini* figures not only in the first extant royal accounts, but in later ones too. And the accounts and charters, from 1202 on, disclose that the tax so called was being collected at Paris as well as at Orléans.[2]

That the Parisian tallage on grain and wine was also a money-tax was established by Du Cange, or by texts he gathered, and has been accepted by most scholars since.[3] But the demonstration is more difficult than they have realized. For by 1202, as we have found, the *tallia panis et vini* at Orléans, without ceasing to be a money-tax, had become the regulated form of the general tallage. One cannot argue from the analogy of terms

quidem collectio uulgo nuncupatur tallia panis et uini, erit pro quitatione tolte et tallie et pro supradictis consuetudinibus eis concessis; cuiuslibet uero anni tercio collectio erit pro stabilitate monete. Et illo quidem anno tercio alii homines quam illi quibus supradictas immunitates concedimus qui uidelicet talliam nobis non debebant nisi panis et uini talliam pro moneta, illam panis et uini talliam pro stabilitate monete nobis exsoluent eodem modo quo consueuerant, uidelicet de singulis modiis uini et hibernagii duos denarios, de singulis modiis marceschie unum denarium. Singulis autem annis unum e domesticis seruientibus nostris mittemus Aurelianis, qui et alii nostri seruientes uille et decem burgenses legitimi, quos burgenses uille communiter elegerint singulis annis, talliam illam panis et uini facient. . . .'

[6] Texts cited n. 2 below, plus an *enquête* of *c.* 1220–3, AN, JJ 26, fo. 277rb. On the progress toward enfranchisement at Orléans, see Marc Bloch, *Rois et serfs: un chapitre d'histoire capétienne* (Paris, 1920), pp. 51–2, 54–6. As Carl Stephenson showed, 'The Origin and Nature of the *Taille*', in *Mediaeval Institutions: Selected Essays*, ed. Bryce D. Lyon (Ithaca, N.Y., 1954), pp. 61–8, tallages often burdened tenants other than serfs, and the distinction is plain at Orléans when one compares the enfranchisement of 1180 (*Ordonnances*, xi. 214, discussed by Bloch) with the charter of 1183. Stephenson was unaware of the original nature of the *tallia panis et vini* (for the term, see next paragraph), but he was right in relating the commutation of 1183 to that of 1185 at Laon (*Institutions*, p. 84). When it is observed that the charter of 1183 has some echoes in the abbatial charter for townsmen of Saint-Denis in 1186 (Stephenson, pp. 41–2), the importance of Philip II's early years for regulating and commuting tallage becomes even clearer.

[1] *Rec. des actes de Philippe Auguste*, i, no. 84; *Cart. Sainte-Croix*, no. 54; AN, K 2[A], no. 3 (1).

[2] Brussel, *Nouvel Examen des fiefs*, ii (Lot and Fawtier, *Premier Budget*), cl, clvi, clxxiv, clxxv, clxxxix; *HF*, xxi. 270; xxii. 740, 742; *Rec. des actes de Philippe Auguste*, iii, nos. 1071, 1105, 1195; *LTC*, i, nos. 901, 1554.

[3] Du Cange, *Glossarium*, s.v. *tallia panis et vini*; an editor later made the connection explicit. Also Le Blanc, *Traité des monnoyes*, p. 167; Brussel, *Nouvel Examen des fiefs*, i. 524–31; Delisle, 'Des revenus publics en Normandie', *BEC*, xiii. 105; Achille Luchaire, *Manuel des institutions françaises: période des capétiens directs* (Paris, 1892), pp. 336, 341; Bridrey, 'Le chapitre *De monnéage*', 107. Lot and Fawtier, *Premier Budget*, p. 61, expressed reserved adherence to the traditional view. They were surely aware of Dieudonné's recent attack on it (cited below, p. 37 n. 3).

alone. Nevertheless, the evidence, although very slight, sustains the traditional view. An inquiry in 1222 revealed that the king customarily collected the *tallia panis et vini* each third year at Paris, that is, at the same interval as the money-tax of Orléans.[1] And in the later thirteenth century the *taille du pain et du vin* was invoked specifically, at Paris, as the security for a good royal coinage.[2] It cannot be doubted that this was its original significance.[3]

There is a singular pointer to this significance in the moral *Summa* of Peter the Chanter, dating from *c.* 1180–92. With reference to the problem of fixed payments in unsteady coin, and taking the Parisian money for example, the Chanter spoke of the 'price of the money' increasing 'in the third year'.[4] Now it might be argued that by 'third year', he simply meant some given interval without ulterior implication; but given the context— 'in [?the] third year when [not 'if'] the price of the money increases'—it seems more likely that he meant to refer to the local minting term with which, as a Parisian, he would have been familiar. If so, his point must have been that deniers fresh from the mint, even when their standard was unchanged, were more highly valued than the darkened pieces already many months in circulation. The natural inclination of moneyers or changers to take advantage of such a situation would help to explain why some people in the Île-de-France feared the simple replenishment of silver as well as debasement or demonetization. There was cost in any case, and it is conceivable that the cost to which the Chanter alluded was among those which were understood to be commuted by the fixed triennial levy.

Apart from this clue (if such it is), there is little to show when and how the Parisian money-tax originated. As regards the date, the year 1159 has sometimes been taken as a *terminus ad quem*.[5] The only evidence is a charter

[1] AN, JJ 26, fo. 274vb.
[2] 'Avis sur la question monétaire donnés aux rois Philippe le Hardi, Philippe le Bel, Louis X et Charles le Bel', ed. Paul Guilhiermoz, *RN*, 4th ser., xxv (1922), 79: 'Item . . . [speaking of *tournois* and *parisis*] li rois est tenus a tenir les en bon point, car il encherit la taille du pain et du vin de la terre. . . .' Guilhiermoz showed that this counsel was given about 1278; Du Cange, *Glossarium*, had cited it as dating from about 1320.
[3] In an uncharacteristic note contributed to the *Bulletin de la Société des antiquaires de France* (1927), 202–4, Adolphe Dieudonné undertook to deny that the *tallia panis et vini* was ever a money-tax, either at Paris or at Orléans. His argument was invalid. He suggested, first, that allusions to this tallage never make the connection with coinage; but this was to overlook the charter of 1183, where that connection is explicit. Second, he proposed that the *avis* alluding to *taille du pain et du vin*—which text he misdated, following Du Cange instead of Guilhiermoz, whose edition he was citing—meant that the king should keep a good coinage so that taxes *of that kind* could better be paid; but this was a blatantly forced reading of a reasonably clear passage (quoted in preceding note). Dieudonné repeated his argument without improving it in a review of Lot and Fawtier, *Premier Budget*, *RN*, 4th ser., xxvi (1933), 252; to my knowledge his opinion has been neither accepted nor refuted, Lot and Fawtier keeping silence on the point when they returned to it in *Hist. des institutions*, ii. 211.   [4] Text quoted below, p. 175 n.
[5] Le Blanc, *Traité des monnoyes*, pp. 167–8; Brussel, *Nouvel Examen des fiefs*, i. 216, 527;

for Saint-Magloire of Paris, in which Louis VII, listing the customs from which the abbey was exempt, mentioned the 'relief of the coinage which is collected by us in each third year'.[1] If this was a reference to the money-tax *at* Paris, it was the first and last of its kind—for the term *relevatio monete* is not otherwise found there—and it was the last of any kind before 1202. Moreover, among surviving charters that allude to the imposition at Paris, this seems to be the only one in which the king fails to reserve his right. Perhaps, therefore, it was the money-tax at Orléans that Louis VII had in mind in 1159. The term *relevatio monete* echoes the sense of *re-dempcio monete* found in the charters of 1137–8. And—what may be more significant—we find a house at Orléans among the possessions of Saint-Magloire that were confirmed in 1159. The matter remains doubtful, but the charter for Saint-Magloire can only be regarded as poor evidence for the date of the institution at Paris. Again we must fall back on the circumstances.

The Parisian coinage had a very different history from those of Étampes and Orléans in the twelfth century. While the latter were in decline under Louis VII, the *parisis* was extending its dominion.[2] It is true that Parisian types were stabilized, but this happened only after Louis VII had introduced a characteristically new legend.[3] Moreover, the alloy seems to have weakened to 5 d. fine around mid-century or a little later.[4] Neither of these mutations was consistent with the engagements made to Étampes and Orléans, which suggests that the Parisians still lacked such security in the early years of Louis VII. On the other hand, these alterations help us to understand why reservations as to the stability of the *parisis* were expressed

cf. Delisle, 'Des revenus publics', *BEC*, xiii. 105 n. 4. Le Blanc, followed by Bridrey, 'Le chapitre *De monnéage*', 106 n. 75, said that a Pepin (III?) had anticipated this 'relief' of the coinage, but I find no evidence, in Le Blanc or elsewhere, for this assertion.

[1] AN, K 24A, no. 3 (1), an original. A mediocre text from a copy may be read in *Gallia christiana ...*, 16 vols. (Paris, 1715–1865), vii, *inst.*, 70; the first critical edition of the piece may be expected from Mme Fossier and Mlle Terroine. W. M. Newman, *Catalogue des actes de Robert II, roi de France* (Paris, 1937), p. 158, dismisses this document as a forgery without explaining why; on palaeographical grounds, in any case, the piece may be dated to the reign of Louis VII: see Françoise Gasparri, 'Études sur l'écriture de la chancellerie royale française de Louis VI à Philippe Auguste ...', *BEC*, cxxvi (1968), 299 n. 1. For Saint-Magloire's holdings at Paris, see Charles Braibant, 'Études sur le temporel urbain du monastère de Saint-Magloire de Paris', *École nationale des chartes: Positions des thèses ... de 1914*, pp. 23–31.

The pertinent language, from K 24A, no. 3 (1), is: '... precipimus [Louis VII] ut ... predia, possessiones, beneficia libera sint et quieta ab omni exactione, redibitione, consuetudine et releuatione monete, quę tercio anno a nobis exigitur ... in ciuitate Aurelianensi claustro uidelicet sancti Evvreii domus una cum uineis in suburbio ciuitatis positis ab omni redditu et consuetudine et exactione liberis et quietis. ...'

[2] Barthélemy, 'Essai sur la monnaie parisis', 150–2; Dieudonné, *Manuel de numismatique*, ii. 113–14, 206–21; idem, 'Histoire du denier parisis', 132–45; Lafaurie, *Monnaies des rois*, pp. 11–22.

[3] i.e., FRA/NCO: see Plate I, no. 5; Lafaurie, *Monnaies des rois*, nos. 138–44.

[4] Dieudonné, 'Conditions du denier parisis', 53.

in charters dated 1164 and 1185,[1] and they underscore the importance of Philip Augustus's decision, probably early in his reign, to hold the coinage steady and to encourage others to do the same.[2] The *parisis*, although it bore the new king's name, was little changed from that of Louis VII. Philip continued to promote it at the expense of local Capetian currencies. By the early thirteenth century it had become the standard money of the old royal domain and enjoyed a good reputation.[3]

These considerations, together with the certainty that the *tallia panis et vini* was paid by Parisians in 1202 or 1203, suggest that this money-tax originated in the last two or three decades of the twelfth century. Other evidence helps us to limit this period a little more. Observing that the tax was represented as a fixed revenue in round figures in the accounts of 1202–3, we may infer that it had ceased to be a novelty by that time. The inference is perhaps strengthened when we find that the Parisian tallage on bread and wine figures not among the *bailli*'s receipts, as it does in the case of Orléans, but among those of the *prévôt*.[4] These facts seem to take us back to a time, probably before 1190, when the *prévôts* were still doing most of the local accounting themselves.[5] And if we seek to relate the institution of the Parisian money-tax to other measures of fiscal commutation or consolidation as well as to the decision to stabilize the coinage, we are unlikely to be far wrong in assigning it to the last years of Louis VII or the first ones of Philip Augustus.[6] The form and substance of the

---

[1] *Cart. Notre-Dame de Paris*, i. 71; *Rec. des actes de Philippe Auguste*, i, no. 145. A loan by the monks of Longpont to a knight of neighbouring Montlhéry in 1146 was accounted in l. of Provins with stipulation of repayment in pure silver 'si moneta mutata fuerit', *Cart. Longpont*, no. 7.

[2] See below, pp. 42, 44, 149 ff., 162, 164.

[3] See Dieudonné, *Manuel de numismatique*, ii. 113–15, 146–7, 219–22; Lafaurie, *Monnaies des rois*, pp. 18–22.

[4] Brussel, *Nouvel Examen des fiefs*, ii (Lot and Fawtier, *Premier Budget*), cl, clxxiv, clxxv, clxxxix. It is true that the *prévôté* of Paris developed so as to exclude the *bailli* there; but there was a *bailli* for Paris in 1202 (of whom it was said expressly at All Saints that he had not accounted for the *tallia panis et vini*, clvi), and his accounts are clearly distinguished from those of the *prévôt*: see L. L. Borrelli de Serres, *Recherches sur divers services publics du XIIIe au XVIIe siècle*, 3 vols. (Paris, 1895–1909), i. 542–56; *Premier Budget*, cxlvi, clv–clvi, clxxiv, clxxxii, clxxxix, cci–ccii.

[5] Henri Gravier, *Essai sur les prévôts royaux du XIe au XIVe siècle* (Paris, 1904), pp. 20–36; Lot and Fawtier, *Premier Budget*, pp. 7–11, 20–2; idem, *Hist. des institutions*, ii. 143–7.

[6] For the coinage, see just above. For Louis VII's finance, see Marcel Pacaut, *Louis VII et son royaume* (Paris, 1964), pp. 139 ff., esp. 147–60. (Pacaut does not discuss the money-taxes.) Philip Augustus seems to have been especially interested in fixing and consolidating revenues in money. See above, p. 36 n. 6; the king who instituted the Saladin Tithe in 1188 (*Rec. des actes de Philippe Auguste*, i, no. 229) was already experienced in finance. Apart from the extension of the money-tax at Orléans, Philip had converted confiscations of Jews' houses into collective leases to the furriers and drapers of Paris for annual rents amounting to 173 l. *paris.* in 1183 or 1184 (*Actes*, i, nos. 94, 95). He was busy selling communal charters, e.g. *Actes*, i, no. 129; and see generally Achille Luchaire, *Les Communes françaises à l'époque des capétiens directs*, new edn. (Paris, 1911), p. 282.

agreement are scarcely less in doubt. The landlord-kings were notoriously stingy with charters for Paris and there need not have been one in this case. Philip seems to have imposed the responsibility for the wall of 1190 on the men of Paris[1] and this may have happened with other matters. We do know that the tallage on bread and wine was not consolidated with the general tallage at Paris as it was at Orléans. At Paris as well as at Orléans the money-tax must have been a sort of assessment on provisions, and collections were probably administered similarly in the two cities. We may imagine the sergeants and deputy burghers setting to work after the harvests, trudging, door to door, up and down the streets, and taking care not to overlook the traffic at the gates. But the round figures of 1202–3 point to the farming of the revenue, a practice which may in turn have encouraged some simplification or commutation of the levy. This would explain why the king was said in 1222 to be entitled to a customary payment of 60 sous every third year for the tallage on bread and wine in the old Bourg Saint-Germain.[2]

That Capetian money-taxes were originally assessed on grain and wine was symptomatic. Even around the year 1150 the economy of the Île-de-France was probably more retarded than Normandy's had been in the latter half of the eleventh century: less wealthy in specie and movables, less commercial, less diversified in productive enterprise, more bound to the simpler products of the soil. If kings and monks remained preoccupied by bread and wine, it cannot have been different with the poorer folk. The money-tax was not the only revenue to be measured or paid in these foodstuffs.[3] Markets of the domain towns, awkwardly located between the

Similar impulses are manifest in the great Parisian abbeys: Saint-Germain-des-Prés, *c.* 1174–5 (*Chartes de Saint-Germain*, i, no. 159); Saint-Denis, 1186 (*Gallia christiana*, vii, *inst.*, 75). A study of commutation in relation to fiscal policy in the Île-de-France would be rewarding.

[1] Louis Halphen, *Paris sous les premiers capétiens (987–1223)* . . . (Paris, 1909), p. 19.

[2] *LTC*, i, no. 1554: '. . . Habet siquidem dominus rex in veteri burgo Sancti Germani sexaginta solidos pro tallia panis et vini, de tercio anno in tercium annum, sicut hucusque habuit.—' For the determining *enquête*, see AN, JJ 26, fos. 274ᵛ–276ʳ.

[3] Ecclesiastical tithes were, of course, commonly in grain, sometimes in wine too, as elsewhere. See e.g. *Cart. Notre-Dame de Paris*, i. 35, 83–5, 357, 365; *Rec. des actes de Philippe Auguste*, i, no. 56; cf. no. 27; *Cartularium abbatiae Morigniacensis* . . . , ed. Ernest Menault, . . . *Morigny: son abbaye, sa chronique et son cartulaire* . . . (Paris, 1867), *p.j.*, p. 155; *Cart. Longpont*, nos. 93, 111; Vuitry, *Régime financier*, i. 274–5; Delisle, *Condition de la classe agricole en Normandie*, pp. 96–7; and generally, Marc Bloch, *Les Caractères originaux de l'histoire rurale française*, new edn., 2 vols. (Paris, 1955–6), i. 84–5; Duby, *Économie rurale*, i. 175; ii. 436–7, 472–3 n. (*Rural Economy*, pp. 92, 213, 239 n.). For the king's *decima* (not to be confused with the *tallia*) *panis et vini*, often remitted to monastic foundations of the Île-de-France, see *Recueil des actes de Philippe Iᵉʳ, roi de France (1059–1108)*, ed. Maurice Prou (Paris, 1908), no. 31; Luchaire, *Actes de Louis VII*, nos. 108, 138, 378, 448, 512, 530, 614, 652, 718; *Rec. des actes de Philippe Auguste*, i, nos. 79, 98, 111, 119, 120, 150, and *passim*. The *tensamentum* was sometimes in grain and wine, e.g. at Bagneux in 1118, *Cart. Notre-Dame de Paris*, i. 257; and for royal receipts in grain, 'Compte général pendant l'an 1202', ed. Brussel, *Nouvel Examen des fiefs*, ii (Lot and Fawtier, *Premier Budget*), clix, clxi, clxxvii. And see below, p. 42 n. 2.

trading centres of Champagne and the lower Seine, were mostly limited to regional produce; and even at Paris, where the Water Merchants gained an important share of the river trade, economic expansion rested largely upon agrarian settlement.[1] Those Parisian scholars who debated whether a pig was led to market by a man or a rope[2] were not entirely academic.

The use of money in this economy—by no means a *Naturwirtschaft*— was characteristically modest but steady. While transactions in coin were never rare, they do not seem to have been commonly in such large amounts as in Normandy.[3] We hear less about payments by weight of deniers in the Île-de-France and less, too, about shortages of coin.[4] Only exceptionally before 1100 did Frenchmen indicate what sort of deniers they wanted in payments, nor did they specify with regularity before the later twelfth century.[5] Quite possibly deniers were more current in local market transactions than in customary renders until a late date; there is little evidence that the kings had important revenues in coin before the second half of the twelfth century.[6] It would appear from these circumstances not only that

---

[1] The economy of the Île-de-France in the eleventh and twelfth centuries has yet to be studied thoroughly. See provisionally Guy Fourquin, *Les Campagnes de la région parisienne à la fin du moyen âge* ... (Paris, 1964), chs. 1, 2. Also Frédéric Lecaron, 'Les origines de la municipalité parisienne', *MSHPIF*, vii (1880), 93–107. Marcel Poëte, *Une Vie de cité: Paris de sa naissance à nos jours*, 3 vols. (Paris, 1924–31), i, has a wealth of information without documentation; see esp. chs. 8, 12, 13, 17–19. The summer fair of Lendit, just north of Paris, had a certain importance. See also Robert Bautier, 'Les foires de Champagne. Recherches sur une évolution historique', in *La Foire* (*Recueils de la Société Jean Bodin*, v, Brussels, 1953), 107.

[2] John of Salisbury, *Metalogicon*, ed. C. C. J. Webb (Oxford, 1929), i. 3, p. 10.

[3] This impression can hardly be demonstrated statistically; but see evidence cited for the eleventh century, above, pp. 22–3, footnotes, and cf. *Cart. Notre-Dame de Paris*, i. 292, 297, 363, 365, 366, 380, 387, 389, 391, 397; *Cart. Saint-Martin de Pontoise*, nos. 24, 30, 125, 133, 177, 189; and *Cart. Longpont*, nos. 7, 288, with *Antiquus cartularius ecclesiae Baiocensis* (*Livre Noir*), ed. V. Bourrienne, 2 vols. (Rouen–Paris, 1902–3), i, nos. 7, 11, 13, 15, 42, 59, 61, 112, 119. François de Fontette, *Recherches sur la pratique de la vente immobilière dans la région parisienne au moyen âge* ... (Paris, 1957), finds that real sales were often still disguised as donations in the twelfth century.

[4] Clarius, *Chronicon sancti Petri Vivi*, in *Spicilegium, sive collectio veterum aliquot scriptorum* ... , ed. Luc d'Achery, 2nd edn. Étienne Baluze and Edmond Martène, 3 vols. (Paris, 1723), ii. 482A; Luchaire, *Louis VI*, nos. 157, 353, 435; idem, *Actes de Louis VII*, no. 359; *Cart. Notre-Dame de Paris*, i. 236, 267, 292; *Cart. Longpont*, nos. 22, 225.

[5] *Chartes de Saint-Germain-des-Prés*, i, nos. 62, 70, 72, 74, 75, 82, 89, 93, 100–3, 110, 118, 133, 139, 140, 150, 173, 177, 179, 198, 216; ii, nos. 235–8, 244, 251, 254, 257, and *passim*; *Cart. Saint-Martin de Pontoise*, nos. 7, 8, 17, 21, 30, 39, 52, 54, 56, 125, 132, 133, 141, 165–214 *passim*; *Cart. Sainte-Croix d'Orléans*, nos. 3, 5, 8, 11, 12, 15, 17, 50, 51, 53, 58, 60, 73, 75, 78, 83, 84, 86, 88, 101, 104, 107, 110, 116, 119, 120.

[6] Luchaire, *Actes de Louis VII*, nos. 7, 15, 53, 90, 98, 112, 183–4, 186, 203, 205, 209, 216, 218, 221, 226, 246, 279, 284, 337, 353, 361, 522, 555, 591, 645, 687, 744; *Rec. des actes de Philippe Auguste*, i, nos. 2, 28, 31, 34, 54, 74, 82, 84, 94, 95, 143, 175, 270, 360; ii, nos. 537, 573, 620, 664, 669, 908–12; iii, nos. 1,034, 1,210, 1,245; 'Compte général pendant l'an 1202', ed. Brussel, *Nouvel Examen des fiefs*, ii (Lot and Fawtier, *Premier Budget*), cxxxix ff. For the 'penny's worth' (*denariata*) of bread or of wine, see *Rec. des actes de Philippe Auguste*, i, no. 40 (55, art. 11); *Cart. Notre-Dame de Paris*, i. 377.

the values in exchange tended to be small but also that the numerous active mints within and surrounding the Île-de-France sufficed for regional needs. Perhaps we may also infer that no one of the prevailing currencies had any distinctive value or repute.[1] And we can understand why, in such an economy, the first impulses to stabilize the coinage were popular, and were conservative to the point of misconceiving the economic function of minting. Directed as much to the custody of coins in circulation as to preventing profiteering on new coinages, these impulses surely contributed to the improvement of monetary administration under Louis VII. On the other hand, the increasing liquidity of royal revenues made the mainten-ance of a steady coinage a better and better bargain for the Crown. The money-tax itself was paid in coin and, in being calculated on measures of produce, it was better suited to a growing economy than the hearth tax of Normandy.

Nevertheless, the Capetian impositions cannot for long have satisfied the kings as well as it did their subjects.[2] The triennial levy of 100 l. instituted at Étampes was not much better than the 'old tallage' of 10 l. and very much poorer than the (new) 'tallage' of 500 l., the latter sum probably less than total, both of which were accounted in 1202–3;[3] the Crown can hardly have regretted the abandoned money-tax of Étampes. Since the mode of levy adopted at Orléans was not only confirmed at a later date but also, apparently, extended to Paris, we may suppose that it had been more productive than that at Étampes from the outset. In 1202–3 Orléans ac-counted for 450 l., probably *pro toto*, and Paris twice for 500 l., probably *pro tertiis*; and when allowance is made for the triennial periods, we obtain the figure of 650 l. for a year's total receipts in money-taxes prior to the conquest of Normandy.[4] This amount may be set against the general tallage on Paris alone, amounting to 2,955 l. for the year,[5] or against 29,117 l., the minimum uncorrected sum from farms of the *prévôtés*.[6] The second of these comparisons yields a proportion of barely more than 2·2 per cent, as contrasted with a corresponding 11·5 per cent for Normandy; and the money-tax was much less than 1 per cent of total ordinary receipts

---

[1] See citations in preceding note. As early as 1099, 2 d. of Beauvais money were recog-nized to be worth 3 d. of Paris, *Cart. Saint-Martin de Pontoise*, no. 39. But there is little other data of this kind before the late twelfth century, probably because most of the local currencies were thought to be in rough parity with one another.

[2] It is tempting to see especial pertinence in Louis VII's famous lament over the superiority of Plantagenet wealth: 'We in France have nothing except bread and wine and contentment', Walter Map, *De nugis curialium*, ed. M. R. James (Oxford, 1914), p. 225. Cf. p. 40 n. 3 above.

[3] Luchaire, *Actes de Louis VII*, no. 7; Brussel, *Nouvel Examen des fiefs*, ii (Lot and Fawtier, *Premier Budget*), cli, clxxxi, cxcvii; and cf. Lot and Fawtier, *Hist. des institutions*, p. 60.

[4] Brussel, ii (Lot and Fawtier, *Premier Budget*), cl, clvi, clxxiv, clxxv, clxxxix.

[5] Ibid. ccii.   [6] Lot and Fawtier, *Premier Budget*, p. 11.

in France (perhaps 100,000 l. at most) for 1202–3,[1] a calculation we cannot make in the case of Normandy. Even if we estimate Louis VII's domain revenues at 60,000 l.,[2] while assuming the same return from money-taxes as in 1203, the fraction is barely over 1 per cent. These ratios are echoed when we reckon in another way. Taking the prices for wheat, wine, and oats that prevailed in the Île-de-France in 1202, we can determine the approximate rates of taxation at Orléans on the basis established in 1138 and still in effect at the century's end. Two d. per *muid* of wine would have been barely above 1 per cent *ad valorem*; 2 d. per *muid* of bread-grain very much less than 1 per cent; and 1 d. per *muid* of spring oats scarcely more than the rate for winter grain and still under 1 per cent.[3] Even allowing for some increase in prices since 1138, these ratios remain unimpressive, corresponding closely to the proportion of money-taxes to over-all receipts. No ordinary proceeds from mints, to say nothing of abusive ones, can have determined the scale of Capetian money-taxes. Adding a penny to the tax on oats in 1183—and then only for men newly subjected to the tax at Orléans!—was a pathetic gesture by a king who was perhaps already looking to more promising fiscal resources. This is another reason for supposing that, at least in some places, the original form of assessment was simplified—it was not worth the trouble. If other districts composed for a customary quota as did the old Bourg Saint-Germain, it is hardly surprising that the global triennial proceeds of the Parisian *tallia panis et vini* increased by only 100 l. (7·5 per cent) in the half-century after 1203.[4] That these impositions were so inadequate resulted not only from economic but also from political circumstances; and it is in their political aspect that they are revealed as most significantly unlike the Norman money-tax.

The royal institution was, ironically, at once less regalian and more seigneurial than that of Normandy. Years after the dukes had effected their monopoly of coinage, the kings were still minting different deniers in half a dozen places and allowing towns and abbeys to share or enjoy the jurisdiction over false moneyers.[5] From the single ducal coinage—itself a *consuetudo Normanniae*—sprang a tax on men almost everywhere in the

---

[1] Ibid., pp. 7–26, 42, 48. When exceptional receipts for the war year are subtracted, there remains a figure somewhere between 95,000 and just over 100,000 l. See J. F. Benton, 'The revenue of Louis VII', *Speculum*, xlii (1967), 85–9.

[2] Pacaut, *Louis VII*, pp. 150–6, with the criticism by Benton, 'Revenue of Louis VII', 86–7.

[3] These estimates result from figures for *bladum*, *vinum*, and *avena* indexed by Lot and Fawtier, *Premier Budget*, to Brussel's transcription of the 'Compte général'. The price of grain averaged a little more than 60 s., that for wine, 12 to 16 s., and that for oats a little more than 20 s. per *muid*. Cf., for Normandy, Delisle, *Condition de la classe agricole*, p. 607, and J. R. Strayer, *The Royal Domain in the Bailliage of Rouen* (Princeton, N.J., 1936), pp. 25–8.

[4] *HF*, xxii, 740, 742, accounts of the *bailliage* of Paris in the 1250s; cf. xxi, 270.

[5] Luchaire, *Actes de Louis VII*, nos. 7, 111.

duchy, while the Capetian rulers settled for tallages on but two or three localities of the domain. This meant that even as the *parisis* superseded the other regional moneys to become a truly royal coinage, the taxes which assured its stability remained so limited in territorial incidence and rates of levy as to court obsolescence from the outset. With such defects, the advantage of being assessed on the staples of an expanding economy was lost. That there were no general exemptions as in Normandy betrays again the particularism of royal policy and the corresponding lack of any developed custom of the Île-de-France. The seigneurial aspect of these taxes stands out the more clearly when they are compared to the engagements Philip Augustus made to chartered Picard towns, at no such price, to maintain a stable coinage.[1] While the Capetian money-taxes cannot quite be interpreted as 'seignorial blackmail',[2] the original words 'redemption' and 'relief' are evocative of the lordly environment in which the king's people first asserted their interest in the state of the coinage.

Yet it may be questioned, in spite of these peculiarities, whether the Capetian money-tax developed independently of Normandy. Hostile though they usually were, the kings and dukes kept too closely in touch to be ignorant of one another's institutions. Nor would townsmen, particularly merchants, have failed to spread word of the imposition and its function. The Norman and French taxes seem to have been devised for similar if not identical purposes. Both were triennial, though this fact may signify common terms for minting rather than imitation; and there is some reason to think that the cyclic years of collections coincided.[3] On the chronology here set forth, the bare possibility remains that the institution of Capetian money-taxes preceded that of the *fouage* in Normandy. But it seems far more likely that Normandy had precedence. Louis VI's agreement with Orléans, which was quite unlike that with Compiègne some years earlier, was probably made in full knowledge of Norman practice, and was very possibly adapted from it.

[1] See below, pp. 149–50.

[2] Carl Stephenson's expression, *Borough and Town*, p. 100.

[3] Which would have been no great coincidence, to be sure. Cf. above, pp. 18–19 with p. 35.

IV

CONFIRMATIONS OF COINAGE
IN THE SOUTH

THE money-taxes of Normandy and the Île-de-France, the first of their kind (not counting the abortive one in England), were in one considerable respect also the last. Nowhere else do we find impositions to secure the coinage perpetuating themselves in so authoritarian a fashion. The most nearly comparable taxes were those of Aragon and Navarre, where they originated only after 1200; yet these, while they became institutionalized, remained in some degree subject to popular approval. And the only other money-taxes certainly imposed before 1200—those in the counties of Cerdanya, Nevers, and Vich—differed significantly from the Norman and Capetian institutions. What the counts received were not so much commutations of their profits from coinage as payments for their promises not to alter their currencies. With these events the emphasis shifts from commutation to the act of confirmation itself, an emphasis that in turn opens a whole new field of confirmations apparently unredeemed by taxes or payments. Characteristically, these confirmations gave expression to a restraining influence of the Church, and some of them, in their calculated solemnity, revealed a startling potential in political aggregations injured by arbitrary manipulations of coinage. The maintenance of coinage, no longer a local oddity, was becoming recognized as a major concern of Christian society.

A. *Aquitaine in the Eleventh Century*

Some time in the third quarter of the eleventh century, Duke Guilhem VIII of Aquitaine (1058–86) confirmed and stabilized his coinages at Niort and Saint-Jean-d'Angély on the standards then in effect at Poitiers. He granted 'perpetually to the Cluniac church' that the same coins, either deniers or *mailles*, should be struck simultaneously in the three places, and that any mutations at Poitiers should likewise be effected, 'without the help of any price', at Niort and Saint-Jean. His act, termed 'statute', was secured by an old-fashioned commination.[1]

---

[1] *Recueil des chartes de l'abbaye de Cluny . . .*, ed. Alexandre Bruel, 6 vols. (Paris, 1876–1903), iv, no. 3432: 'In nomine Patris . . . Ego Wilelmus gratia Dei Aquitanorum dux, confirmo et stabilio monetam Engeriacensem et Niortensem ac perpetualiter Cluniacensi aecclesie, que est constructa in honore beatorum apostolorum Petri et Pauli, stabiliendo

[cont. on p. 48]

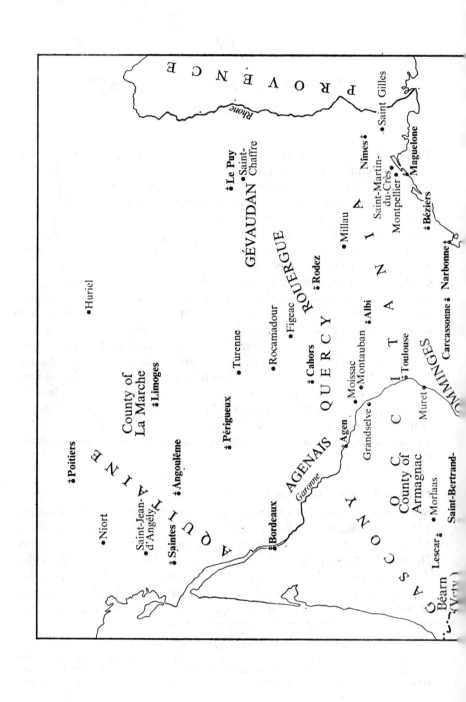

PROVENCE

Rhône

•Saint Gilles

‡Nîmes

Maguelone

•Le Puy
•Saint-
Chaffre

Saint-Martin-
du-Crès
•Montpellier
‡Béziers

GÉVAUDAN

Narbonne‡
Carcassonne‡

•Millau

•Huriel

ROUERGUE
‡Rodez

A
I
N
A
T
I

‡Albi

•Turenne
•Rocamadour
•Figeac
‡Cahors
QUERCY

‡Poitiers

County of
La Marche
‡Limoges

A
Q
U
I
T
A
I
N
E

‡Périgueux

Moissac•
Montauban•

C
C
O

•Toulouse

Muret•

•Niort

Saint-Jean-
d'Angély•
‡Saintes ‡Angoulême

•Agen
•Grandselve

County of
Armagnac

•Morlaas

Saint-Bertrand-

‡Bordeaux

Garonne

G
A
S
C
O
N
Y

Lescar‡

Béarn
(Vctv.)

MMINGES

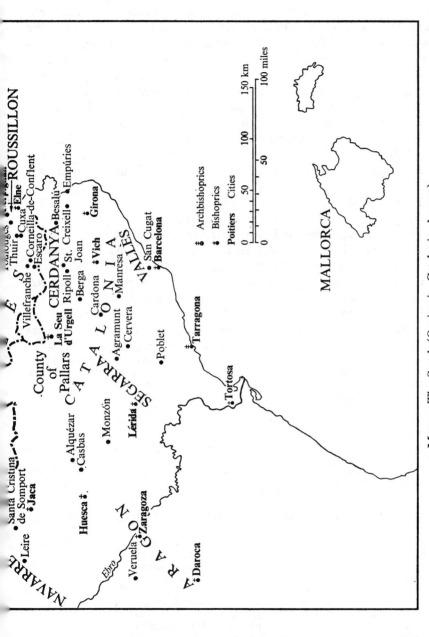

MAP 1. The South (Occitania, Catalonia, Aragon)

NAVARRE

ROUSSILLON

Toulouse •
Thuir •   ‡Elne
Villefranche • Cuxa ‡
• Corneilla-de-Conflent
•Escaro
County   • CERDANYA • Besalú
of   ‡ La Seu   Ripoll • St. Creixell • • Empúries
Pallars   d'Urgell   • Berga   Joan
CATALONIA   • Cardona   ‡ Vich   Girona ‡
SEGARRA   • Agramunt   • Manresa   VALLÈS
• Cervera   San Cugat •
Monzón •   Barcelona ‡
Alquézar •   • Poblet   Tarragona ‡‡
Casbas •
Lérida ‡
Santa Cristina
Leire •   de Somport
• ‡ Jaca
Huesca ‡
ARAGON
Veruela •   Zaragoza
Ebro   ‡ Daroca

‡ Tortosa

MALLORCA

‡ Archbishoprics
‡ Bishoprics
Poitiers   • Cities

0
0   50   100   150 km
0   50   100 miles

This text discloses the operations of a thoroughly traditional *moneta*. Nowhere had the Carolingian imprint been so tenaciously preserved as at Poitiers.[1] The mints at Niort and Saint-Jean, the revenues of which had been assigned to Cluny by charters of *c.* 1016–29 and *c.* 1043 (or before),[2] were expected to produce the same pieces as that at Poitiers,[3] much as Carolingian dies had been reproduced and distributed so as to promote an even supply of standard deniers over extended territories. As in the past, it was proving difficult to co-ordinate the work of moneyers whose minting was tied to local mercantile conditions; moreover, the duke himself must have been tempted to confine his minting to Poitiers, thereby frustrating his predecessors' concessions, for at Poitiers the only other hand in the till was that of the monks of Saint-Nicolas, who had a tithe on the coinage.[4] The monks of Cluny had every reason to want the decentralized and uniform coinage maintained.

These interests were perfectly consistent with what is known of the monetary circumstances. Abusive manipulations of coinage were still exceptional in Aquitaine. It is true that Count Aldebert II of Périgord (1032–?) tried to invalidate his father's coinage, but it is doubtful whether any debasement was involved in this case. His policy is said to have aroused the militant wrath of Géraud de Gourdon, bishop of Périgueux, but we are too poorly informed of the matter to determine whether any religious motive figured in the reaction and to what extent the bishop was defending a public interest.[5] Confidence in the prevailing coinages of payment

contrado, ut semper eo modo, eo tenore atque eodem pondere in supradictis locis feriatur, quo et Pictavis. Ita omnino, absque ulla exceptione, ut si quando Pictavis mutatur, et ibi mutetur, absque ullius pretii suffragatione; si quando vero ibi denarii fiunt, et ibi; si quando ibi medacule, et ibi. Si quis autem hoc nostrum statutum . . . Testes vero hujus donationis sunt: Hugo de Lisigniano, Girbertus.' My dating of this act follows that of Bruel (*c.* 1070), but I have been unable to confirm it; it appears to have been overlooked by Jacques de Font-Réaulx in his manuscript 'Catalogue des actes des ducs d'Aquitaine', in AD Vienne.

    [1] Poey d'Avant, *Monnaies féodales*, ii. 1–20; Dieudonné, *Manuel de numismatique*, iv. 334–6.

    [2] *Chartes de Cluny*, iii, no. 2737 (Font-Réaulx, no. 136); iv, no. 2855 (Font-Réaulx, no. 168). My thanks to Professor Olivier Guillot for verifying these probable dates.

    [3] I believe that Jacques Boussard, *Gouvernement d'Henri II*, p. 305, has misunderstood this point.

    [4] 'Cartulaire du prieuré de Saint-Nicolas de Poitiers', ed. Louis Rédet, *AHP*, i (1872), nos. 1, 4.

    [5] *Fragmentum de Petragoricensibus episcopis* . . . , ed. Philippe Labbé, *Novae bibliothecae manuscript[orum] librorum, tomus* . . . , 2 vols. (Paris, 1657), ii. 738: 'Iste verò Episcopus [Géraud de Gourdon] à mense Episcopali alienavit Castrum Agoniacum & Albam Rocham pro quadam guerra quam adversus Audebertum Cadenerarium Comitem habuit: deposuerat enim monetam Helianensem, quam Helias Comes pater eiusdem Audeberti iusserat fabricari.' According to Léon Dessales, *Histoire du Périgord*, ed. G. A. J. Escande, 3 vols. (Périgueux, 1883–5), i. 233–6, 390–1, the provocation was a debasement, but the sense of the verb *depono* seems to me more like 'depose' than 'debase'. In any case, the reliability of the source is questionable, for Labbé knew it only in sixteenth-century copies.

persisted down to the end of the eleventh century, although the supplies of coin were far from uniform;[1] and the fact that the *moneta pictavensis* was commonly stipulated once fears were aroused suggests that it had been the dominant money in the past.[2] Nor were the competing currencies—those of Angers, Angoulême, Limoges, Périgueux, and Turenne—visibly less reputable. Of these, too, reservations remained uncommon[3] and it is likely that most coinages in Aquitaine continued to be thought interchangeable for ordinary purposes. Only in the last years of the eleventh century, perhaps chiefly in consequence of the fears of ecclesiastical creditors over delayed repayments by pilgrims and crusaders, did anxiety about monetary stability begin to find expression in the charters.[4] Guilhem IX was an impoverished veteran of the First Crusade when he debased the money of Poitiers in 1103, an event that may have been heralded by some less conspicuous mutations in the south-west.

In the light of these facts, the interest of Duke Guilhem VIII's charter may seem limited. So far from protesting against mutations, the real concern of Cluny was probably to secure its rightful share of the proceeds of coinage, including those from mutations. There is no reason to infer that the monks were bringing popular fears for the coinage to the duke's attention; indeed, considering what was happening further south,[5] it is worth noting that the peace statutes of Aquitaine make no allusion to monetary problems. What was confirmed was not the standards, but the co-ordination of the standards, of the Poitevin coinage. The pressure was administrative and fiscal, the sort of constraint traditionally imposed upon Carolingian moneyers. At near-by Saintes the moneyers had been required

---

[1] 'Chartes et documents . . . de Saint-Maixent', ed. Alfred Richard, *AHP*, xvi (1886), nos. 95, 102, 108, 145, 167, 168; 'Cart. Saint-Cyprien de Poitiers', nos. 218, 321; 'Cart. Saint-Nicolas', no. 38; 'Chartes de l'abbaye de Nouaillé . . .', ed. P. G. de Monsabert, *AHP*, xlix (1936), nos. 140, 167; 'Chartes de Saint-Florent', no. 183; 'Le cartulaire de l'abbaye royale de Saint-Jean-d'Angély', ed. Georges Musset, *Archives historiques de la Saintonge et de l'Aunis*, xxx (1901), nos. 270, 319; xxxiii (1903), nos. 448, 450.

[2] 'Cart. Saint-Jean-d'Angély', xxx, nos. 90, 113, 260, 270, 319, 326; xxxiii, nos. 455, 476, 477; 'Chartes du Limousin antérieures au XIIIᵉ siècle', ed. Alfred Leroux, *Bulletin de la Société des lettres, sciences et arts de la Corrèze*, xxii (1900), no. 8; 'Cart. Saint-Nicolas', no. 30; 'Cart. Saint-Cyprien', nos. 66, 111, 394, 395; 'Chartes de Nouaillé', no. 169; 'Sancti Stephani cartularium', ed. Jacques de Font-Réaulx, *Bulletin de la Société archéologique et historique de Limousin*, lxix (1922), no. 95; and references above, p. 12 n. 2.

[3] 'Cart. Saint-Jean-d'Angély', xxxiii, Pièces annexes, no. 5; 'Chartes du Limousin', no. 8; 'Cartulaire de l'abbaye de Talmond', ed. Louis de la Boutetière, *Mémoires de la Société des antiquaires de l'Ouest*, xxxvi (1872), nos. 70, 108; 'Sancti Stephani cartularium', nos. 95, 125; *Cartulaire de l'église d'Angoulême*, ed. J. Nanglard (Angoulême, 1900), no. 131; 'Cartulaire du prieuré de Saint-Pierre de La Réole', ed. Charles Grellet-Balguerie, *Archives historiques de la Gironde*, v (1863), no. 100, §94; Dieudonné, *Manuel de numismatique*, iv. 248. (Plate I, nos. 8, 9.)

[4] 'Cart. Saint-Jean-d'Angély', xxx, nos. 90, 319; xxxiii, nos. 448, 450, 455; *Cart. Angoulême*, no. 119; 'Cart. La Réole', no. 104.

[5] See below, pp. 53–6.

in 1047 to swear fidelity to the abbess of Notre-Dame, whose nuns had been given the revenues of that mint.[1] If Duke Guilhem's statute may therefore be regarded as a precedented mode of confirmation, it was for that very reason in the public interest, and one realizes how easily the protection of proprietary right could be turned to social advantage. What is significant in this case is that the prince himself, not the moneyers, was taking solemn and explicit responsibility for the lawful operations of his mints. Given the terms, it would have been difficult to coin secretly or fraudulently. And the duke's renunciation of 'any price' on the occasion of mutations, even if merely intended to protect Cluny, would have provided the monks with a defence of local populations against exploitation.

That this concession had no known sequel in Poitou, despite the debasements of the early twelfth century, is a historical anomaly that cannot detract from its interest. Nowhere else have we so helpful a glimpse of the difficulty in maintaining the old *moneta* in a post-Carolingian principality, and of the sanction devised in response. But it is not far-fetched to imagine that the more overtly inhibitive enactments attested in other lands where coinages had been troubled may have been influenced or preceded by guarantees of proprietary right comparable to that of Guilhem VIII.

B. *Catalonia:* Cunctis pateat (*1118*) *and its Background*

A more consequential event was soon to occur in Catalonia. When the last hereditary count of Cerdanya died in 1117, his title and his mountainous domains passed to the dynasty of Barcelona.[2] Ramon Berenguer III (1086–1131) visited Cerdanya in the early spring of 1118. Whether this was his first visit in his new capacity is not clear,[3] but we know that the magnates and knights who gathered around him on this occasion did more than simply renew their professions of fealty and obligation. Upon their 'counsel and command' (*consilio et iussione*), Count Ramon Berenguer joined with the bishop of Elne, in a charter dated 4 April 'in the tenth year of King Louis', to establish a peace in the county of Cerdanya. This peace, drawing upon one of the oldest traditions in the Peace of God, was to secure plough animals and the men who worked with them. Cattle thieves were to incur

---

[1] *Cart. Notre-Dame de Saintes*, nos. 1, 77. The county was then held in fealty to the duke of Aquitaine by Geoffroy Martel, who was evidently seeking to restore a standard territorial coinage under solemn religious protection: the moneyers were convoked 'ex diversis civitatibus'.

[2] *Gesta comitum Barcinonensium* ..., ed. Louis Barrau Dihigo and J. J. Massó Torrents (Barcelona, 1925), p. 36; *Chronicon Rivipullense*, in *VL*, v. 246; Santiago Sobrequés Vidal, *Els grans comtes de Barcelona* (Barcelona, 1961), pp. 186–8, 211 n. 114.

[3] He may have become count as long as a year before, text of AC, La Seu d'Urgell, quoted incompletely by Joaquím Miret y Sans, 'Los vescomtes de Cerdanya, Conflent y Bergadà', *MRABLB*, viii (1901), 148–9; cf. Petrus de Marca, *Marca hispanica* ... (Paris, 1688), appendice, no. 361, and Sobrequés, *Els grans comtes*, p. 211 n. 114. The authority for the visit in 1118 is cited in next note.

the bishop's anathema, to make full restitution, and to pay a composition of 60 sous to the count, in the count's coinage. 'Wherefore', the charter continues,

the aforesaid count, with the counsel of all those mentioned above, establishes his coinage, which he has confirmed with his own hand, in the aforesaid county, as he has also established in his other counties, so that for as long as he lives, he will not change or lighten or debase the said coinage. In such a manner, moreover, that all men and women of the entire aforesaid county shall pay twelve deniers per yoke of oxen, and six deniers per man, and three deniers per plough implement. The aforesaid count, moreover, promises to God and all men of the said county that after the just-mentioned deniers shall have been paid to the above-named count, he shall never more request the said payment from the said men.

This peace was to be held secure even in the event of war involving the count or the magnates and knights of Cerdanya. And it was specified, finally, that the bishop was to have one-third of the judicial compositions arising from breaches of the peace. The count, the bishop Pere, and the scribe Bernat were the only signatories.[1]

With this singular charter, so nearly contemporary with events described in the preceding chapter, we feel ourselves, nevertheless, in a different world. Here is the local and archaic atmosphere of the early feudal county, where the magnates still sense the territorial solidarity that formerly found common expression in the count's court, but in which effective power now radiates from the castles held, in more or less nominal fealty, from the count.[2] Far from the king and close to the infidel, the contentious men of this rugged frontier found outlet for their best motives in the kind of all-encompassing co-operation with clergymen that had originated in the theocratic politics of Carolingian times and had been perpetuated in the peace movements and crusades. Here bishops could assemble and act, as co-rulers, in the most basic matters of constitutional order.

In such an environment it is hardly surprising that the coinage should have been assimilated by the peace. Disputes over the quality of money—whether between lords and tenants, buyers and sellers, or creditors and debtors—must sometimes have led to blows or acts of violent retaliation; and clipping and counterfeiting were troublesome crimes everywhere. Defenceless merchants and markets had very early come under the protection of the Peace of God. Indeed, there was precedent for including the

---

[1] ACA, Canc., Registro 4 ('Liber feudorum Ceritaniae'), fo. 50 (Appendix, no. 1); ed. Francisco Miquel Rosell, *LFM*, ii, no. 691. This text was included in the official compilation of the *Usatges* of Barcelona (art. 172 in edition by Abadal and Valls Taberner, cited below, p. 53, n. 2).

[2] We have the detailed but undated acts of fealty to the new count as sworn by fifteen castellan-vassals of Cerdanya, some perhaps in the assembly of spring 1118, *LFM*, ii, nos. 541–3, 548, 560, 569, 578, 614, 615, 644–5, 657, 672–4.

security of coinage among measures of peace, and not only in Catalonia. Edgar 'the Peaceful' had initiated legislation in England that received its fullest characteristic expression in the time of Cnut:

> And let us all take thought very earnestly about the improvement of the peace and the improvement of the coinage; about the improvement of the peace in such a way as may be best for the householder and most grievous for the thief; and about the improvement of the coinage in such a way that one coinage is to be current throughout all this nation without any debasement and no man is to refuse it.[1]

No such evidence is to be found in northern France, nor even, as we have seen, in Aquitaine, the later dukes being loath to share their regalian authority. What happened in Cerdanya in 1118 was most directly related to the experience of the contiguous Pyrenean domains, where the continental peace movement had penetrated early and where it flourished most vigorously.

The initiative in Catalonia, in this as in so much else, may be traced in the work of Oliba, abbot of Ripoll and Cuxa, bishop of Vich, and himself a native of Cerdanya. Oliba led not merely in introducing the peace statutes into the counties of the March but also, during the years 1027–33, in establishing the terms of comprehensive peace during fixed periods that became known as the Truce of God.[2] In an episcopal synod held at Vich in 1033, or shortly before, Oliba instituted a diocesan peace and truce, wherein the sanctions against violators were extended to those who abused the coinage. He urged clerical authorities at Ripoll to excommunicate, 'just as we have excommunicated', anyone who shall have been found to counterfeit or debase the episcopal coinage of Vich or to clip pennies, and likewise to punish patrons or protectors of such fraud. These censures were to be made public in Sunday services and Monday markets, 'so that through the many [they] can become known to the many'.[3] Apart from sheltering the coinage under the peace, this legislation hardly anticipated that in Cerdanya eighty-five years later. Its concern was primarily fraud outside the mint; Oliba was a saintly bishop and there is no record of arbitrary mutations during his pontificate (1018–47). Oliba did not mention laymen in his

---

[1] *Die Gesetze der Angelsachsen*, ed. Felix Liebermann, 3 vols. (Halle, 1903–16), i. 314–15 (II Cnut 8); for a convenient translation, see *English Historical Documents, c. 500–1042*, ed. Dorothy Whitelock (London, 1955), p. 420; cf. 408 (26.1), 397 (8).

[2] See generally Ramon d'Abadal i de Vinyals, *L'Abat Oliba, bisbe de Vic, i la seva època*, 3rd edn. (Barcelona, 1962), esp. pp. 215–42; Hartmut Hoffmann, *Gottesfriede und Treuga Dei* (Stuttgart, 1964), pp. 72–7.

[3] *VL*, vi. 308–9; *Jurisdiccions i privilegis de la ciutat de Vich*, ed. Eduard Junyent (Vich, 1969), no. 12; Eugen Wohlhaupter, *Studien zur Rechtsgeschichte der Gottes- und Landfrieden in Spanien* (Heidelberg, 1933), p. 24; Abadal, *Oliba*, p. 236; Hoffmann, *Gottesfriede*, p. 76; and Odilo Engels, 'Die weltliche Herrschaft des Bischofs von Ausona-Vich (889–1315)', *Gesammelte Aufsätze zur Kulturgeschichte Spaniens*, xxiv (1968), 1–9.

'synod',[1] which, if in fact restricted to the clerical order, must have been unusual among assemblies of the peace movement. His measure of *c.* 1033 was pastoral, administrative, not constitutional.

Somewhat later—just when, it is impossible to determine—the coinage of Barcelona also became associated with the peace. According to the *Usatges* of Barcelona (article *Moneta autem*), the money was to be preserved without increase in content of copper or diminution in gold, silver, or weight.[2] This provision, or its substance, conceivably originated toward the middle of the eleventh century together with the oldest material preserved in the *Usatges.* We know that gold as well as silver was minted in Barcelona at that time; also that the coinages, probably in both metals, were altered in the 1060s,[3] events that might have prompted some regulation of standards. Now the provision for a stable coinage is immediately preceded, in most if not all manuscripts of the *Usatges,* by articles relating to the peace, truce, and protection (*emparamentum*), and *Moneta autem* goes on to prescribe a common procedure against violators of the peace, truce, protection, and coinage. But it no longer seems possible to attribute these *usatges* concerning the peace to the time of Ramon Berenguer I, so that their conjunction with *Moneta autem* constitutes no presumption of the latter's antiquity. On the contrary, that conjunction points to a much later date, for the *usatges* in question represent a secular adaptation of the peace and truce to comital administration—what German scholars call the *Landfriede*—of a kind that now seems assuredly to have evolved more gradually, or to have occurred much later, than had formerly been supposed, the regulations perhaps not attaining the form they have in the *Usatges* until the time of Ramon Berenguer III or his successor. Moreover, as late as 1078 the *Forum judicum* was cited for penalties against counterfeiters in Catalonia, a fact that raises doubt whether *Moneta autem* yet existed.[4] Quite possibly,

[1] *VL,* vi. 308–9; cf. Hoffmann, p. 260; *VL,* vi. 320, for other peace assemblies at Vich.

[2] 'Moneta autem tam auri quam argenti ita diligenter sit servata ut nullo modo crescat in ere nec minuatur auro vel argento nec etiam penso.

Qui vero hec omnia vel unum ex hiis, scilicet pacem et treugam, emparamentum vel monetam fregerit, violaverit seu falsaverit, quia tale malum est et tale dedecus quod nemo redigere potest vel emendare ad principem, ita stabiliendo precipimus ut persone eorum cum omni honore et avere veniant in manu principis ad faciendam suam voluntatem secundum consilium et laudamentum ipsius curie . . .', *Usatges de Barcelona,* ed. Ramón d'Abadal i Vinyals and Ferràn Valls Taberner (Barcelona, 1913), p. 27 (art. 66); another text in *Cortes de los antiguos reinos de Aragón y de Valencia y principado de Cataluña,* 26 vols. (Madrid, 1896–1920), i: 1. 25 (art. 67); for other editions as well as a recent discussion of the origin of this code, see Carlo Guido Mor, 'En torno a la formación del texto de los "Usatici Barchinonae"', *AHDE,* xxvii–xxviii (1957–8), 413–32.

[3] Botet y Sisó, *Monedes catalanes,* i. 31–56, 84–5; 200–2 (mint contracts of 1056–66); see esp. citations at p. 41; Bonnassie, *Catalogne,* ii. 672. (Plate II, no. 10.)

[4] See José Balari y Jovany, *Orígenes históricos de Cataluña* (Barcelona, 1899), p. 677; 2nd edn., 3 vols. (Barcelona, 1964), ii. 708. I do not consider this evidence decisive.

therefore, the recognition of a stable coinage as an element of the peace in the county of Barcelona was contemporary with the charter for Cerdanya; it cannot presently be dated more precisely than *c.* 1060–*c.* 1150.[1]

No more than in the case of Vich does it appear that the regulation of Barcelona was directed against the ruler's monetary prerogative. *Moneta autem* betrays no suspicion that the count himself might be the perpetrator of a crime said to be so heinous that punishment can only be at the will of the prince, with the counsel and approval of his court. Yet in practice it must have proved awkward for the counts to engage in mutations that were likened to violations of the peace they were obliged to maintain.[2] The concession, such as it was, seems to have allayed any concerns the clergy and magnates might have felt. There is no allusion to coinage in the legislation extant from peace councils held in the diocese of Barcelona.[3] Nor was Oliba's measure reiterated in a confirmation of the peace and truce at Vich, although it was probably not forgotten.[4] The clerical fathers of the peace were dispensed from policing the coinage as the custom of Barcelona was extended to all the counties governed by its guardian.

As the peace movement attained its fullest popularity in the later eleventh and twelfth centuries, coinages became a means of propagating the ideal of peace. This point, having long been in controversy, must be treated with care. What we know is that in the counties of Roussillon and Toulouse and the viscounty of Béarn, symbols probably to be read as PAX (or PAS) replaced the traditional regal imprint on the coins. The reading seems least doubtful in the case of the famous 'morlans' of Béarn, where the device p^Ax originated toward 1100 and remained fixed during the next three centuries.[5]

---

[1] Valls Taberner assigned *Moneta autem*, along with articles relating to the count's peace, to *c.* 1060, reconstructing from the *Usatges* a 'Carta constitucional de Ramon Berenguer I (vers 1060)', *Obras selectas de Fernando Valls-Taberner*, 4 vols. in 6 tomes (Madrid–Barcelona, 1952–61), ii. 55–62; cf. 47. Subsequently, a commission of scholars rejected Valls Taberner's reconstruction of the *Usatges*; in their tentative view, the articles here in question assumed their permanent form perhaps in the time of Ramon Berenguer III: see Ramon d'Abadal i de Vinyals, *BRABLB*, xxviii (1959–60), 368–9; Ferran Soldevila, *Història de Catalunya*, 2nd edn. (Barcelona, 1963), pp. 107–8 n. 4. Cf. Wohlhaupter, *Studien*, pp. 44–6. On the basis of a thorough review of the problem, Pierre Bonnassie, *Catalogne*, ii. 711–28, arrives at agreement with Abadal's unpublished thesis that the *Usatges* were compiled under Ramon Berenguer IV; he doubts that *Moneta autem* antedates the mid-twelfth century. But there is little evidence for the minting of gold at Barcelona at that time, Botet y Sisó, *Monedes catalanes*, i. 53–7, 81–90, and it could be that the substance of the provision antedated its written form.

[2] *Usatges de Barcelona*, arts. 4, 63 (ed. Abadal and Valls Taberner, pp. 3, 25); criticisms by Abadal and Bonnassie.

[3] 'Cortes y usajes de Barcelona en 1064. — Textos inéditos', ed. Fidel Fita, *BRAH*, xvii (1890), 389–93; *Marca hispanica*, app. no. 268; cf. Hoffmann, *Gottesfriede*, pp. 77, 260–2.

[4] *VL*, vi. 320–3; cf. Wohlhaupter, *Studien*, pp. 30–1. See, too, below, p. 61.

[5] J.-Adrien Blanchet, *Histoire monétaire du Béarn* (Paris, 1893), pp. 53–6; Gustave Schlumberger, *Description des monnaies, jetons & médailles du Béarn* (Paris, 1893), pp. 1–2, and plate 1; Dieudonné, *Manuel de numismatique*, iv. 89–91. (Plate II, no. 12.)

At Toulouse a more schematic imprint $\approx + c$, believed to have been introduced in the time of Guilhem IX of Aquitaine (1097–9, 1114–19),[1] was perhaps the inspiration for the thoroughly questionable $\hat{r} \pm \text{⌀}$ that appeared on the coins of Roussillon, probably under its last hereditary count, Guerau II (1164–72).[2]

Assuming that 'peace' was denoted by these—or by some of these—legends, how is the term to be interpreted? Did it allude specifically to the programme known as the Peace of God or was it some more general motto or imperative, perhaps to be read in extension as PAX VOBISCUM?[3] Did it imply clerical participation in the coinage?—or serve to guarantee the quality of coinage? One has only to reflect on the psychology and literacy of the people who handled these coins to suspect that no one answer can be satisfactory by itself. The three coinages in question were of good repute, although not entirely immune from mutation; all were exploited by lay rulers, although in Béarn the Cluniac priory of Morlaas had a tithe of the profits from 1077.[4] Perhaps more significant is the fact that these were the coinages of regions where the peace movement was well known. The great men of Béarn and Armagnac swore a peace and truce in the presence of the bishop of Lescar in 1104,[5] not long after the device PAX appeared on their lord's coins. Roussillon was the homeland of the Truce of God and the observances established in the councils of Toulouges during the eleventh century cannot have been speedily forgotten.[6] And while Toulouse had no peace legislation of its own, its bishops had attended councils of the peace; and Guilhem IX—if indeed it was he who introduced the symbols read as PAX—surely understood why the peace movement had persisted in the

---

[1] Dieudonné, *Manuel de numismatique*, iv. 235; Georges Pierfitte, 'Monnaies des comtes de Toulouse', *RN*, 4th ser., xxxviii (1935), 48–59. (Plate II, no. 14.)

[2] Anatole de Barthélemy, 'Explication de quelques monnaies baronales inédites', *RN*, xi (1846), 288–90; Achille Colson, 'Recherches sur les monnaies qui ont eu cours en Roussillon', *Société agricole, scientifique et littéraire des Pyrénées-Orientales*, ix (1854), 47–8; Botet y Sisó, *Monedes catalanes*, i. 129–35. The Toulousan motif appeared on the coinage of Albi-Bonafos in the middle of the thirteenth century, and its influence may also be perceptible in Rouergue, Dieudonné, *Manuel de numismatique*, iv. 225–6. (Plate II, no. 13.)

[3] PAX VOBISCUM has been discerned on 'Una moneda inédita de Cervera', ed. Federico Udina Martorell, *Numisma*, iii (1953), 31–7. In my view, this coin can most plausibly be associated with the peace legislation of Cervera of September 1202, *Cortes de Cataluña*, i: 1. 86–7, and the charter of February 1203 (AM Cervera, pergamins) by which Queen Sancia, King Peter II, and Ramon de Cervera granted 'consulatum et conjuracionem inter se et contra illos qui non fuerint in eorum consulatu . . .', to the people of Cervera.

[4] *Cartulaire de Sainte-Foi de Morlaas*, ed. Léon Cadier (Pau, 1884), pp. 3–4; Dieudonné, *Manuel de numismatique*, iv. 89–90. Like Mme Castaing-Sicard, *Monnaies féodales en Languedoc*, pp. 12–14, I find no evidence that the bishops of Toulouse shared in the twelfth-century comital coinage; cf. Roger Limouzin-Lamothe, *La Commune de Toulouse et les sources de son histoire (1120–1249)* . . . (Toulouse, 1932), p. 195.

[5] Pierre de Marca, *Histoire de Béarn* (Paris, 1640), pp. 396, 397 n.

[6] Wohlhaupter, *Studien*, pp. 20–2, 36–9; Hoffmann, *Gottesfriede*, pp. 25–34, 72–6, 90, 98–102.

southern fringelands of Aquitaine.[1] Such people of these districts as took notice can have had little difficulty in thinking of their coinages as circulating in 'lands of peace' or in 'lands where peace reigns'. For the device PAX assumed the very place on the coins that had customarily been reserved for symbols of authority, such as the names of kings.[2] And the Peace of God was becoming the basis for a renewed public order toward 1100 not only in the county of Barcelona, but in all the old dioceses of the Pyrenees—including Roussillon and Béarn—where clerical and lay magnates had combined to institute the peace and truce or where oaths of the peace were collected.[3] In a sense the peace filled the void created by royal (and comital) impotence in the South; as Jean-François Lemarignier has suggested, the oaths of peace were sworn by men in fealty to God somewhat as their Carolingian forebears had sworn fealty to the king.[4] Still more fundamentally, the PAX of these coinages evoked the renewed penitential spirituality that found outlet in the monastic reforms and the crusade. Peace among Christians was an indispensable condition for recovering Jerusalem: the *visio pacis*, 'the true peace of which it is said "The peace of God surpasseth all understanding"'.[5]

In relating the coinage to the peace, the charter *Cunctis pateat* was at once traditional and timely. There remain some facets of that relationship to be examined. Yet it becomes clear that we must look beyond traditions of the peace movement for help in explaining what is most remarkable in the charter for Cerdanya. For thus far we have failed to find any very illuminating precedents for a ruler's sworn engagement to maintain his coinage intact nor any precedent whatever for an imposition to compensate for such a promise.

[1] Hoffmann, pp. 17, 94. Is the same remark, *mutatis mutandis*, applicable also to William the Conqueror, the last issue of whose English coinage bore the legend PAXS? See Brooke, *English Coins*, 3rd edn., plate 18, 8; Dolley, *Norman Conquest and the English Coinage*, pp. 15–21. On the circumstances at Toulouse, cf. J. H. Mundy, *Liberty and Political Power in Toulouse, 1050–1230* (New York, 1954), pp. 26–8 and n. 73.

[2] See Dieudonné, *Manuel de numismatique*, iv. 90–1; cf. 299, fig. 172; 325, figs. 192, 193.

[3] Evidence cited in nn. 4 and 5, p. 55 above; for Urgell, see AC, La Seu d'Urgell, 'Liber dotaliorum', 2 vols., i. 199ᵛ (203ᵛ); bishops of Comminges and Couserans had attended peace councils in the eleventh century, and the episcopal *patz* known in Comminges in the later twelfth century—*La Grande Charte de Saint-Gaudens (Haute-Garonne). Texte gascon du XIIᵉ siècle . . .* , ed. S. Mondon (Paris, 1910), p. 42; cf. below, p. 111—probably originated much earlier.

[4] Lot and Fawtier, *Hist. des institutions*, iii. 54; also Lemarignier, *Gouvernement royal*, pp. 39–42.

[5] See Roger Bonnaud-Delamare, 'Fondement des institutions de paix au XIᵉ siècle', *Mélanges . . . Louis Halphen*, pp. 19–26; Carl Erdmann, *Die Entstehung des Kreuzzugsgedankens* (Stuttgart, 1935), chs. 2, 8, 10. The quoted words—Saint Bernard's—are taken from Jean Leclercq, *L'Amour des lettres et le désir de Dieu . . .* (Paris, 1957), p. 58; and for the macrocosmic peace council summoned by a reformer pope in order to launch the First Crusade, see Robert Somerville, *The Councils of Urban II. i. Decreta Claromontensia* (Amsterdam: *Annuarium Historiae Conciliorum. Supplementum I*, 1972), pp. 69–82, and other versions of decrees there edited.

In fact, *Cunctis pateat* seems to have been most original in just these provisions. But the confirmation of the monetary standards, as distinct from the oath, can be traced back beyond the *Usatges* of Barcelona, beyond even the earliest manifestations of the Peace, to a charter of 'security and enfranchisement' granted to Cardona in 986. By this solemn privilege, following Al-Mansur's destructive invasion, Borrell II, count and marquis, confirmed concessions dating back more than a century to the foundation of this stronghold on the western border of the Christian settlements. And among many new provisions, he guaranteed 'honest business, a complete market and a single and genuine coinage without mutation and without any falsity, so that as it was at first, so may it always be, that it may always have firmness'.[1]

This curious clause forms the earliest known record of the confirmation of coinage in France and the Spanish March. For all its redundant verbosity, it distinguishes clearly between mutations and counterfeiting, and it expresses emphatically the intention of indefinitely securing the coinage. Moreover, the ceremonial form of the confirmation has already in this case the effect of stressing the ruler's responsibility. It is a text well worth pausing over.

Was there some immediate cause? Unfortunately, too little is known of economic conditions in the tenth-century viscounty of Cardona to demonstrate dissatisfaction with coinages in local use, nor do the fine series of archival pieces from the Vallès, Vich, and Urgell really compensate. Even in the domains of Sant Cugat del Vallès, transactions in coin seldom specified the silver money of payment in the later tenth century, perhaps an indication of continued confidence in the stability and convertibility of prevailing deniers; there, and doubtless even more so in the uplands, shortages of coin were frequent.[2] At Cardona, in any case, there is no evidence of a mint before 986, so that it is difficult to interpret the charter as a reaction against local manipulations.

The concessions can more plausibly be explained as an act of traditional

---

[1] *Cartas de población y franquicia de Cataluña*, ed. J. M. Font Rius, 1 vol. in 2 parts (Madrid–Barcelona, 1969), i: 1, no. 9. See also Botet y Sisó, *Monedes catalanes*, i. 185–6; and for the circumstances, Ferràn Valls Taberner, 'La primera dinastia vescomtal de Cardona', *Obras selectas*, iv. 207–10; J. M. Font Rius, *Orígenes del régimen municipal de Cataluña* (Madrid, 1946), pp. 52–6, 112–13; idem, *Cartas de población*, i: 2. 615–16; and Ramon d'Abadal i de Vinyals, *Els Primers Comtes catalans*, 2nd edn. (Barcelona, 1965), pp. 327–34.

[2] For some characteristic instruments from Solsona, see Domingo Costa y Bafarull, *Memorias de la ciudad de Solsona y su iglesia*, 2 vols. (Barcelona, 1959), ii. 611–16, nos. 3–10; see also *Cartulario de 'Sant Cugat' del Vallés*, ed. José Rius, 3 vols. (Barcelona, 1945–7), i, nos. 118, 124, 132–3, 138–40, 142–4, 146–7, 157, 171, 176–7, 180, 185; *El Archivo condal de Barcelona en los siglos IX–X . . .*, ed. Federico Udina Martorell (Barcelona, 1951), nos. 187–9, 191–3, 195, 196, 198–200, 202, 203, 205–9, 211. Bonnassie speaks of the years before 985 as the 'Âge archaïque de l'économie d'échanges', *Catalogne*, i. 364–71; see also ii. 885–908.

monetary administration. The coupling of market and coinage still manifests the precarious economy that had long depended on authoritarian regulation. What people chiefly feared was the abuse of coins by the public or the moneyers; they took refuge in the Roman insistence on an unadulterated coinage which had survived in Spain through the *Forum judicum*,[1] a text cited in the charter of Cardona, if not also through the old capitularies. The guarantee of immutability, having reference to the coin's quality and not to its imprint, and placing no other restriction on minting, effectively reiterated the conditions of Carolingian minting: because the standards were fixed, any deviation from them by the moneyers was a species of fraud against which the ruler's protection was needed. From this point of view the new emphasis on stability in 986 might be explained by the perceptibly accelerated diversification of monetary standards in the tenth century. One way of reversing that trend would have been to coordinate the issues of different mints in the count–marquis's power, a policy that would help to explain why no surviving deniers can surely be attributed to Cardona for at least another century;[2] the viscount—still very much a vice-count—may well have been obliged to bestow the same dies as were used by the comital moneyers at Vich or Barcelona.

For it is clear that the charter of Cardona marks a phase of political reconstruction on traditional lines. Stung by the collapse of his pro-Moorish policy, Borrell II acknowledged the tutelage of King Louis V and secured the testimonial support of the magnates in their official capacities. The confirmation of the sound coinage was in no way distinct from that of the other provisions, nor is there evidence of an oath; the religious sanctions were limited to comminations and signs of validation. Yet for all its formal archaism, the oathless confirmation was a representative act, affirmed by the marquis, his two sons, and the viscount Ermemir for themselves and for all the magnates, clerical or lay, as well as for lesser folk 'of all our realm'. The confirmed coinage thus makes its appearance as part of the ruler's concession for a loyal settlement on an embattled frontier, a settlement of urgent public interest.

Here, then, was a precedent for *Cunctis pateat* no less fundamental than the eleventh-century peace texts. In fact, it becomes clear that the emphasis on public tampering that persists even in *Moneta autem* derives from a Carolingian conception of monetary administration designed to maintain uniformity and protection; the Peace of God merely provided a new form for the expression of such guarantees or, more exactly, a new sanction for their enforcement within the old districts. If we could only know the circumstances in which *Moneta autem* was promulgated, it might be possible to trace a ceremonial tradition from 986 to 1118 in which the

---

[1] *Leges Visigothorum*, ed. Zeumer, pp. 252, 255, 309–11 (vi. 1. 4, 6; vii. 6. 1–5).
[2] Botet y Sisó, *Monedes catalanes*, i. 186–8.

stress on the ruler's responsibility for a confirmed coinage was progressively strengthened. By 1118, at any rate, the coinage is no longer one item among many but a central concern of the public order, its formerly indefinite confirmation now solemnly specified for life. The territory represented in 1118 is not the 'realm' (*regnum*) but the constituent county (*comitatus*), that is, the community most interested in the concession; moreover, the representation in 1118 is active rather than passively testimonial, expressed as the 'counsel and command of magnates and knights of the entire county of Cerdanya and Conflent'.[1] As in other assemblies of the peace, as before them in those of the *pagus*, the decisions affected all people of the land, even though few of them were present. The act implied the virtual identity of an administrative unit and the mass of its leading men, and it presumed the authority of such men, as lords, to speak for their non-noble tenants. The apparent assertiveness of these mountaineers causes us to wonder whether they were pressing an opportunity that had been missed in 1111 when the neighbouring county of Besalú was annexed by Ramon Berenguer III. Unfortunately, we do not know whether the assembly of 1118 was convoked for the purpose it happened to serve, and other aspects of the occasion are equally in doubt: whether clergy other than the bishop of Elne attended, even the whereabouts of the meeting.

Within this public setting, the form taken by the confirmation in 1118 was without known precedent in the South. Ramon Berenguer, in the curiously worded phrase of *Cunctis pateat*, 'has by his own hand confirmed' (*habet propria manu firmatam*) the coinage which he institutes in the county of Cerdanya. This can only be interpreted to mean an oath, of which the assembly was presumably witness and the bishop of Elne recipient and guarantor. The sacramental nucleus of the event, this oath must have been an outwardly familiar ritual, the count placing his hands on the gospels as he spoke. That his words went unrecorded, or at least were left out of the charter, may point to the novelty of this oath. Written oaths abound in the Spanish March and southern France; most of them were stereotyped forms of words, such as those sworn by eleven of the count's new vassals, some of them perhaps on this very occasion in 1118.[2] Moreover, *Cunctis pateat* appears to imply—though the passage is equivocal—that no confirmation had accompanied the institution of his coinage in other counties ruled by Ramon Berenguer III.[3]

---

[1] *LFM*, ii, no. 691.

[2] Texts cited above, p. 51 n. 2; see also *LFM*, ii, nos. 510, 840, and more than a hundred others, *passim*; cf. Botet y Sisó, *Monedes catalanes*, i. 202; and Auguste Molinier, 'Étude sur l'administration féodale dans le Languedoc (900–1250)', in *HL*, vii. 135–6.

[3] ACA, Reg. 4, fo. 42 (Appendix, no. 1; *LFM*, ii, no. 691): '. . . Qua propter predictus comes, consilio omnium supradictorum, mittit suam monetam quam habet propria manu firmatam in predicto comitatu, sicut et in ceteris suis comitatibus habet missam, ut omni tempore quandiu ipse superstes extiterit prephatam monetam non mutet vel minuet lege

The conceptual ancestry of the oath of 1118 is also elusive. Perhaps most nearly related were the engagements sworn by moneyers not to defraud the coinage, of which records from the archives of Ramon Berenguer I have survived.[1] The confirmation was a kind of extension of such an oath. Contemporaries might also have imagined an analogy with oaths to the peace and truce. Violations of the coinage were probably likened to breaches of the peace in 1118, as they certainly had been on other occasions in Catalonia, and the magnates of Cerdanya were undoubtedly familiar with conjurations of peace. Moreover, the peace oaths, unlike vassalic oaths, were sworn by lords as well as vassals.[2] Formally, however, there was little to differentiate the several kinds of ceremonial oath from one another: all were religious in basis, all were engagements—usually life-long—to some official function, all similarly worded. What chiefly distinguished the confirmation of the money in 1118 from most oaths of its day was that it established a constitutional obligation as well as a personal one. It was among the earliest inauguration oaths in the Spanish March.

The imposition on farm animals, implements, and persons was likewise an apparent novelty in 1118,[3] although it can hardly have been new in principle. Somewhat like a relief,[4] it was a payment for concessions by a new lord at his accession; the levy was not to be repeated but the concessions were to endure. The charter fails to make clear whether the levy was understood to secure the peace, the coinage, or both. But since the dispositive clauses, after describing the imposition, conclude with an allusion to the 'aforesaid peace' alone, it seems likely that the confirmed coinage was regarded as an element of the peace in Cerdanya. Accordingly, the levy can better be regarded as a species of 'peace-tax', a redemption of the peace, than as a money-tax. There is no evidence that Count Ramon Berenguer III betrayed his promises. In fact as well as intent, the levy was a fair payment, not the institution of a tax.

It would be hard to imagine a more thoroughly agrarian imposition. The peace of Cerdanya, a land inhabited almost exclusively by villagers in the early twelfth century, was 'a peace . . . of oxen and other plough animals and all men in touch with them or with the soil'.[5] These were the

---

uel penso . . .' The independent coinage of Besalú seems to have ceased with the death of Bernat III (1097–1111); cf. Botet y Sisó, *Monedes catalanes*, i. 110–21.

[1] *LFM*, ii, no. 838; Botet y Sisó, i. 202.

[2] A remarkable example for Pallars, c. 1100 (?), is preserved in AC La Seu d'Urgell, 'Liber dotaliorum', i. 199ᵛ. See also Marca, *Hist. Béarn* (1640), p. 397 n.

[3] Except so far as it resembled a tithe or rent. For a rent on oxen and horses in Cerdanya in 1027, see *Cartulaire roussillonnais*, ed. Bernard Alart (Perpignan, 1880), no. 32.

[4] For reliefs upon change of lordship, ancestors of the *joyeuses entrées*, see Molinier, in *HL*, vii. 148; Paul Guilhiermoz, *Essai sur l'origine de la noblesse en France au moyen âge* (Paris, 1902), p. 310 n. 159.

[5] ACA, Reg. 4, fo. 42 (*LFM*, ii, no. 691): '. . . mittimus pacem in predicto comitatu de

most settled elements of the population, more accessible, more numerous, and more vulnerable than the transient merchants and shepherds. The bucolic impression conveyed by *Cunctis pateat* is anticipated by the more detailed peace legislation of Vich dating, probably, from the later eleventh century, some injunctions of which may be read as a terrifying catalogue of the ravages feared by peasants of the Catalan plains.[1] It cannot be acciden-tal that the reform-minded bishop Berenguer of Vich (1075–99) minted a sound new currency described in texts of 1083 as the 'cattle coinage' and as 'the best coinage of Vich, where oxen are depicted'; surviving specimens, bearing the artful representation of a cowherd with a pair of oxen, per-fectly corroborate the contemporary description.[2] The security of cattle was a matter of enduring urgency in Catalonia. It became known in the twelfth century as *bovaticum*, a term that also designated the payment made to obtain it from the ruler. The imposition described in *Cunctis pateat* was in all but name the *bovaticum* (Cat.: *bovatge*) of later times.[3]

The main burden of the levy was therefore borne by peasants, especially the prosperous ones having animals and tools. If nobles and merchants joined in paying the sixpenny head tax, the larger share of peasants— averaging, at a guess, two sous or so on manses of the better valleys[4]— cannot have seemed an exorbitant price for the promise of improved security. More difficult to determine is the value of this composite impo-sition to the count who presumably collected it. If we assume that no men were exempt from the sixpenny tariff, that there were somewhat fewer assessable oxen than men, and that Berguedà was understood, as Conflent was said expressly, to be included in the county of Cerdanya[5]—plausible but undocumented assumptions—we must still estimate the population in order to arrive at a sum that can reasonably be imagined to have been collected. A calculation so blatantly speculative is best relegated to a foot-note. Estimating—with a wide margin of error—some 8,000 paying men

bubibus atque ceteris animalibus arantibus et omnibus hominibus tangentibus illos uel arantibus . . . .'

[1] *VL*, vi. 321.

[2] Botet y Sisó, *Monedes catalanes*, i. 168, 177–8 (nos. 149, 150), 182. And see above, Frontispiece.

[3] *Cortes de Cataluña*, i: 1. 67, arts. 17, 18; 80–1, art. 8 (allusions to *pax* 'bestiarum in usum laboracionis deditarum' and to *pax* 'bestiarum et instrumentorum aratoriorum', 1200); 88; Arxiu diocesà Girona, cartulary 'Carles Many', fo. 65; J.-A. Brutails, *Étude sur la condition des populations rurales du Roussillon au moyen âge* (Paris, 1891), pp. 276–7; Ferràn Soldevila, 'A propòsit del servei del bovatge', *AEM*, i (1964), 573–8.

[4] i.e. supposing such a manse to consist of one or two men at 6 d. apiece, a yoke of oxen at 12 d., and one or two *instrumenta aratoria* at 3 d. apiece.

[5] Berguedà, Conflent, and Cerdanya had long been the constituent *pagi* of the county of Cerdanya. See Miret y Sans, 'Vescomtes de Cerdanya, Conflent y Bergadà', 123, 148–9; a 'brevis de ipsos terminos de ipsa Marcha de Bergitano' survived in the early comital archives of Cerdanya, ACA, perg. Ramón Berenguer I, *sin fecha* 43; Registro 4, fos. 44–5 (*LFM*, ii, no. 696).

plus 2,500 pairs of oxen and an equal number of assessed implements, we obtain the figure of 7,125 s., or 356 l.[1] A sum of such proportions would have been unusually large in early twelfth-century Cerdanya, especially if any considerable part of it had been realized in coin. It would have been roughly double the ordinary revenues from Catalonian domains of comparable scope half a century later,[2] and would have compared well with the 411 l. borrowed by Ramon Berenguer from the cathedral church of Elne a year before, much the largest sum in specie mentioned in near contemporary local texts.[3] And it would have been over twice as much as the entire *moneta* of Girona was worth in 1131,[4] although, as we have seen, the levy detailed in *Cunctis pateat* cannot have been pegged to the returns of mints. It would have compared poorly, even had it been repeated, with the money-taxes of France and Normandy,[5] but these were much larger countries. For a count of the Spanish March deeply committed to the struggle against the infidel,[6] a collection on the scale we have estimated would have seemed a worthy compensation even for such considerable concessions as he made to the men of Cerdanya.

Why the latter were anxious about the stability of money is less clear. Specie was in short supply in the Catalan mountains; a high proportion of payments continued to be designated wholly or partly in kind long after 1100, and the recurrent allusions to deniers of unspecified mintage suggest no great sensitivity to intrinsic value or exchange rates.[7] Among coinages likely to have trickled into Cerdanya—those of Roussillon, Besalú, Empúries, Vich, and Urgell; that of Melgueil was becoming known at least for purposes of account—no two seem to have been exactly equivalent in standards and none had been notoriously unsteady in the time of Ramon

[1] There were some ninety inhabited places in Cerdanya alone in the later thirteenth century, according to Lluis Solé i Sabaris *et al.*, *Geografia de Catalunya*, 2 vols. (Barcelona, 1968), ii. 217; and some 1,852 hearths were recorded in the inventory of 1359, *DI*, xii. 84–91. Estimating four persons to the hearth and allowing for a considerable increase in population since the early twelfth century, I obtain the figure of 6,500 persons, or 2,000 adult males. I allow for populations 50 per cent larger in Conflent and Berguedà—cf. *Geografia*, ii. 256–7, 190–3—or some 6,000 adult males. (The rates, again, were 6 d. per man, 12 d. per yoke of oxen, 3 d. per implement.)

[2] A provisional estimate based on studies forthcoming in my edition of 'Fiscal Accounts of Catalonia under the Early Count–Kings (A.D. 1151–1213)'.

[3] *Marca hispanica*, app., no. 361; cf. *LFM*, ii, no. 695.

[4] *Marca hispanica*, app., no. 381; col. 1273.

[5] Cf. above, pp. 26, 42.

[6] Sobrequés, *Grans comtes*, pp. 174–86.

[7] *LFM*, ii, nos. 555, 695; AC La Seu d'Urgell, 'Liber dotaliorum', i. 7, 206ᵛ (210ᵛ); *Cart. roussillonnais*, nos. 37, 42, 47, 49, 55, 58, 60; Biblioteca Central, Barcelona, cartulary of Gerri (MS. 1619), nos. 13, 19, 43, 58, 65; *El Cartulario de Tavernoles*, ed. Josefina Soler García (Castellón de la Plana, 1964), nos. 32, 35, 39, 40, 49, 53, 55, 58, 61, 69; Francisco Monsalvatje y Fossas, *Noticias históricas*, 26 vols. (Olot, 1889–1919), ix, nos. 24–6; xi, no. 376. See also Brutails, *Populations rurales du Roussillon*, pp. 44–8; and cf. Bonnassie, *Catalogne*, ii. 907–9, who, however, has no statistical series for upper Catalonia.

Berenguer III.[1] Nor were the latter's coinages of Barcelona and Girona disreputable.[2] Bullion clauses, providing for alternative forms of repayment in case of debasement, did not yet occur, although payments in weights of precious metal were not uncommon.[3] Moreover, revenues and fixed dues were commonly paid in kind,[4] a circumstance that would seem to have protected churches and lay lords from the depreciation of coinage. Appearances, however, may be misleading. Texts relating to Cerdanya are far from plentiful, and it is not unlikely that local barons, having lately become more enterprising and mobile, were increasingly in need of liquid exchange.

That as long as a century before this the maintenance of coinage had already been a matter of public concern in the plain of Vich and the vicinity of Barcelona is easier to understand. Specie was more useful and more abundant in lower Catalonia than in the mountains. Around Barcelona it had become fundamental to a diversified economy as early as the year 1000.[5] This was an age of reconstruction after the destructive invasion of Al-Mansur; Muslim gold flowed in to supplement the local moneys, and the supply of gold was sustained when the Catalans took the offensive against the Muslims early in the eleventh century.[6] The monks of Sant Cugat paid wages in coin for construction of their cloister and other works.[7] Prevailing monetary values were known even where, as in the hinterlands of Tarragona and Barcelona, it remained convenient to transact in kind. The common provision for alternatives to cash payments in this fertile region may point to a growing economy as much as to absolute shortages of specie.[8] The most significant fact, however, is that in lower Catalonia people were conscious of the intrinsic value of coins and of differences

---

[1] Monsalvatje, *Noticias históricas*, xi, nos. 367, 375, 423; *Cart. Tavernoles*, no. 119; *LFM*, ii, no. 695; Botet y Sisó, *Monedes catalanes*, i. 113, 127–8, 136–45, 153, 159–60, 168–84. There may have been a comital money of Cerdanya, Botet y Sisó, i. 122–4, but if so it was never minted in large amounts.

[2] Botet y Sisó, i. 38–43, 47–63, 73–7, 87–9, 90–110. The coinages of Girona, however, were unusually small and light; I find no mention of them in Cerdanya.

[3] Monsalvatje, *Noticias históricas*, ix, no. 26; *Marca hispanica*, app., no. 361; *LFM*, ii, no. 695; BN, Collection de Baluze, cviii, fos. 339^v–340, 100^{rv}; *Cart. Tavernoles*, nos. 40, 49, 54.

[4] *LFM*, ii, no. 695; *Cart. roussillonnais*, no. 32; AC La Seu d'Urgell, 'Liber dotaliorum', i. 7, 226^v (230^v); *Cart. Tavernoles*, nos. 5, 55.

[5] Pierre Bonnassie, 'Une famille de la campagne barcelonaise et ses activités économiques aux alentours de l'An Mil', *Annales du Midi*, lxxvi (1964), 270–7 (abridged translation by S. L. Thrupp, *Early Medieval Society* [New York, 1967], pp. 107–11); idem, *Catalogne*, i. 363–433; ii. 895–930.

[6] Bonnassie, 'Une famille', 275 n. 58; Sobrequés, *Grans comtes*, pp. 16–34.

[7] *Cart. 'Sant Cugat'*, ii, nos. 481, 482, 606; cf. no. 456.

[8] *El 'Llibre Blanch' de Santas Creus (cartulario del siglo XII)*, ed. Federico Udina Martorell (Barcelona, 1947), nos. 4–6, 8, 13, 54; *Cart. 'Sant Cugat'*, ii, nos. 359, 362, 401–2, 409, 417, 420, 443, 514–15, 528, 535, 537, 539, 551, 567, 623, 633, 637, 659, 661, 664, 688, 727, 747, 775 (etc.; these acts span the whole eleventh century, and are no less common toward 1100 than before).

between the diverse gold and silver pieces then in local circulation. In contrast to the practice prevailing in the uplands, they often specified 'good coin', or money of 'legitimate weight', or mancuses 'of the best gold', or the like. A certain concentration of such references toward the middle of the eleventh century has already been suggested as a reason for placing the *usatge Moneta autem* in that period, but sensitivity to the weight and alloy of coin was not altogether new even then.[1]

The economic interest in sound money is not likely to be underestimated as a cause for the Catalonian measures we have examined. But its influence and novelty were blunted in a social environment in which profit still mattered very little. The 'new men' of the story were not (as far as we know) freshly hatched businessmen of Barcelona but reformer bishops. Prelates shared with counts the old protectorate over local markets in a persistently disjointed rural economy; and none of the coinages they minted for use in regional exchange seems to have attained the popularity that might have established it as a major fiscal resource. Of incipient conflict over the money we find no trace. The measure *Cunctis pateat*, while constitutional in form, was nevertheless co-operative and prudential in spirit, maintaining the tradition of comital and synodal legislation against monetary fraud. A peculiar conjunction of circumstances religious, political, and economic, the Pyrenean setting in which coinages were first secured by counsel and by oath was as much a *prolongement carolingien* as a harbinger of the future.

c. *Melgueil in the Twelfth Century*

Two generations were to pass before men of the Spanish March again expressed much concern about the state of their coinages. In the meantime the scene of interest shifts to the coast of Languedoc, where the earliest public guarantees as to the stability of a coinage date from the decade after *Cunctis pateat*. The money of Melgueil, in negotiations extending over many years, was to be repeatedly confirmed under oath; moreover, the reformed papacy was to have its first occasion in this matter to lend its prestige to the cause of good money. And of these events, for once, we are comparatively well informed. What has survived, indeed, is virtually an archive of the coinage, and the preservation of these documents not only points to the exceptional local importance of their subject but provides us with a diverting glimpse into the play of personal ambition, rivalry, and piety in Languedoc during the early crusading period.[2]

---

[1] '*Llibre Blanch*' *de Santas Creus*, nos. 11, 12; *Cart. 'Sant Cugat'*, ii, nos. 440, 450, 458, 461, 554, 581, 638, 642, 644, 649, 656, 689, 760, 777; Botet y Sisó, *Monedes catalanes*, i. 38–43, 49–52; cf. 28–9, 32–3. Most of these references relate to gold.

[2] The monetary texts were preserved chiefly in two local collections: that of the cathedral of Maguelone, whose bishops were closely associated in the affairs of Melgueil and Montpellier, and that of the lords of Montpellier. These archives would doubtless have

The money minted by the counts of Melgueil, in their little *castrum* not far east of Maguelone and Montpellier, was riding a flood-tide of success in the early twelfth century. With its distinctive and stable imprint, it dominated an expanding and diversified local economy. It overwhelmed the coinage of Narbonne, which it somewhat resembled (whose design, indeed, it had appropriated), and reached Catalonia in the purses of knights, clergymen, and merchants by the close of the eleventh century.[1] Count Raimond II (*c.* 1087–*c.* 1120) was already minting it in large amounts when, in the first years of the twelfth century, he made its profits the security for a debt of 3,000 s. Upon taking the Cross not long afterward he drew from the mint in providing for a dowry of 10,000 s. when his daughter should marry, as well as for bequests totalling 140 s.[2]

The coinage of Melgueil was much the greatest fiscal resource of its proprietor. That fact rather than its instability was what first brought it into the political arena. In 1121, when Count Bernard IV (*c.* 1120–*c.* 1132) married the daughter of his powerful vassal, Guillem V of Montpellier, he pledged the coinage for his good faith in conventions over the dowry.[3]

been lost (like those of Melgueil) had they not been transcribed in cartularies. For the subject of this section, two old works by Alexandre Germain remain useful: 'Étude historique sur les comtes de Maguelone, de Substantion et de Melgueil', *MSAM*, iii (1850–4), 523–640; 'Mémoire sur les anciennes monnaies seigneuriales de Melgueil et de Montpellier', ibid., 133–255. See also Jean Baumel, *Histoire d'une seigneurie du Midi de la France. Naissance de Montpellier (985–1213)* (Montpellier, 1969), ch. 3, esp. pp. 109–20; other recent works are cited in notes below.

[1] Poey d'Avant, *Monnaies féodales*, ii. 290–2; J.-F. Chalande, 'Monnaies baronales & épiscopales de la province de Languedoc', *HL*, vii (1879), 407–8; Dieudonné, *Manuel de numismatique*, iv. 240–3; Castaing-Sicard, *Monnaies féodales en Languedoc*, pp. 29–36. For the economy, see Alexandre Germain, *Histoire du commerce de Montpellier . . .*, 2 vols. (Montpellier, 1861), i. 2–6, 16–25, 44 n., 76, 91–107, 179–89; ii. 25–30, and see also below, pp. 67–8. For early evidence of Melgorian money in Catalonia, see *LFM*, ii, no. 695; Botet y Sisó, *Monedes catalanes*, i. 128. For purposes of account, at least, the Melgorian coinage may have been known in Cerdanya as early as 963, *Marca hispanica*, app., no. 102, but the text (a donation to Cuxa) is not above suspicion. (Plate II, no. 15.)

[2] *Cart. Maguelone*, i, no. 32.

[3] Ibid., no. 43; *Liber instrumentorum memorialium. Cartulaire des Guillems de Montpellier*, ed. Alexandre Germain (Montpellier, 1884–6), no. 59. These texts, and others following in both cartularies, speak of Raimond rather than Bernard. But Bernard IV certainly married the only daughter of Guillem V whose name was Guillemette (Latin: Guillelma; see e.g. *Cart. Guillems*, nos. 67, 71; cf. pp. xxxviii–xxxix, xli), and if he had married her only after his late father (or brother?) had done the same, there would probably have been some record of an event so irregular. Dom Vaissete long ago suggested, *HL*, iv (new edn.), 176–7, that a copyist's misreading of initial B's for R's accounts for the confusion; and while it is singular that this should have happened in documents copied independently into different cartularies, no better explanation has been found. See Germain, 'Étude sur les comtes', 535 n., 546, 623; *Cart. Guillems*, p. 100 n. Germain, followed by recent scholars, assumed that Ermessinde, Guillemette's mother, was the daughter of Count Pere of Melgueil (d. *c.* 1087). If so, Bernard and Guillemette would have been first cousins, and it would seem astonishing that no record of ecclesiastical opposition to, or dispensations for, such a marriage survived; but Dom Vaissete had cast doubt on the

This agreement did not immediately cost the count his control of the money, but it revealed an ominous dependence on his vassal which the latter's successor was to exploit. Guillem VI of Montpellier (1121–49) promptly trespassed upon the milling rights of another vassal of his brother-in-law, and when Bernard took his lesser vassal's part, a war broke out in which 'almost all the countryside was destroyed'. Reconciliation came in a detailed compromise (9 May 1125) imposed by papal judges-delegate, including the bishop of Maguelone, who had initiated the arbitration. This document, while granting redress to Bernard's minor vassal, showed that much more than a mill was at issue. Among settlements relating to jurisdiction, fiefs, castles, and the fealty owed by Guillem to Bernard, the coinage figured in two provisions: (1) the men of Montpellier were forbidden to clip coins; and (2) the count of Melgueil confirmed his coinage at an alloy of 5 d. fine and a weight of 24 d. to the ounce.[1]

These monetary settlements look like a quid pro quo between the count and the lord, but both were so obviously in the public interest that we may suspect the influence of some more general sentiment. Taken together they recall *Moneta autem* and the measures at Cardona and Vich; as in Catalonia, as indeed in contemporary Normandy and England, the coinage had to be protected from its users as well as its makers. And here, again as in Catalonia although not this time in connection with the Peace, the bishop's intervention was critical. It is not far-fetched to speculate that Gualter of Maguelone (1104–29) may have known of the confirmation sworn before Pere Bernat of Elne (1113–c. 1130) in Cerdanya just seven years before; the two prelates were experienced provincial colleagues, both having served on papal commissions, and they had long known one another.[2] But whereas *Cunctis pateat* obliged us to imagine how the confirmation of the coinage was sworn, the agreement of 1125 provides the first explicit record of such an oath. On the altar of Saint-Martin du Crès—a village church in the episcopal domain—the count of Melgueil confirmed 'to God and all faithful Christians by an oath in the hand of the bishop of Maguelone' that he would maintain the coinage in its designated weight and alloy. The public, indeed universal, address of this oath is worth especial note; otherwise, the ceremony must have resembled those in which Bernard IV and Guillem VI swore to each other, on the same altar, to preserve the agreements; a number of vassals of each lord ratified the pact by their oaths, and the whole

relationship, suggesting that the unnamed daughter of Pere who married a Guillem de Montpellier about 1080 was not Ermessinde, wife of Guillem V. Cf. *HL*, iv. 176, 178, 181–2, 184, with 180; Germain, 'Comtes de Maguelone', 546; and *Cart. Maguelone*, i. 90 n.

[1] *Cart. Guillems*, no. 61; see also no. 62. On the standards, see Paul Guilhiermoz, 'De la taille du denier', *BEC*, lxxxiv, 268–70; Dieudonné, 'Le melgorien', *RN*, 4th ser., xxxv, 31–5.

[2] *Gallia christiana*, vi. 745–7, 1045; *Thesaurus novus anecdotorum*, ed. Edmond Martène and Ursin Durand, 5 vols. (Paris, 1717), iii. 131.

of the *pax et concordia* was witnessed by still other men representative of the two sides, including a moneyer. Vassalic in modes of solidarity, clerical in inspiration and testimonial procedure, this settlement of 1125, especially in its multiplication of oaths, was not altogether unlike the simpler conventions of the peace then common to the west. The curiously rambling yet correct and explicit text, recording ratifications as well as the terms themselves, is characteristic of meridional diplomatic in the age of the reformed Church.[1]

Count Bernard's confirmation was no idle gesture. The alloy of Melgorian deniers had declined from about 8 d. fine in 1097 to 5 d. in 1125, most if not all of this debasement having occurred by 1116.[2] Because the weight of the coins remained nearly constant, the motive of these mutations may have been not so much to secure profits—the normal *seigneuriage* on such a coinage being satisfactorily lucrative—as to bring the melgorian closer to parity with neighbouring moneys. The near equivalence of melgorians with deniers of Béziers or Narbonne recorded in 1097, or with those of Roussillon in 1128,[3] suggests such a policy, while the existence of determined exchange rates is a clear sign of an active money market in lower Languedoc. Transactions in coin were relatively frequent as compared with those in kind, and the brand of coinage was commonly specified.[4] Agrarian products were evaluated in money,[5] as were various goods fetching tolls or marketed in the lowlands west of the Rhône.[6]

Not surprisingly, therefore, the men of this region became sensitive to fluctuations in the intrinsic value of coins. Clauses providing for repayments in fixed weights of fine silver in case melgorians were debased begin

---

[1] *Cart. Guillems*, no. 61.

[2] *Cartulaire de Béziers. Livre noir de Béziers*, ed. J.-B. Rouquette (Paris–Montpellier, 1918), nos. 101, 116; Germain, 'Monnaies seigneuriales de Melgueil', 175–80; Dieudonné, 'Le melgorien', 34; Émile Bonnet, 'Des variations de valeur de la monnaie melgorienne', *Bulletin archéologique du Comité des travaux historiques et scientifiques* (1903), 496–8. Cf. *Cartulaire du chapitre d'Agde*, ed. Odile Terrin (Nîmes, 1969), no. 247.

[3] *Cart. Béziers*, no. 101; Botet y Sisó, *Monedes catalanes*, i. 128, or AD Pyrénées-Orientales, B 58.

[4] *Cart. Maguelone*, i, nos. 10, 12–15, 17, 21–2, 34, 39–40, 45–6, 60, 79; cf., for same period (1079–1150), nos. 23, 33, 40–1, 51, 61; see, too, no. 30. Also *HL*, v, nos. 236, 238, 251, 253–4, 258ii, 329x, 333, 337, 353i, 381, 387, 391ii, 426, 430ii, 456vi, 469, 479ii, 483vi, 489vii, 489viii, 523, 535ii, 546, 559i, 559ii, 559iv, 567ii, 576; *Cart. Béziers*, nos. 83–5, 98, 104–5, 114, 122, 128, 135; *Cart. Agde*, nos. 23, 30, 38, 41, 189, 198 and *passim*. The economy of money was less developed in the upper Hérault valley and in the vicinity of Nîmes; see *Cartulaire du chapitre de l'église cathédrale Notre-Dame de Nîmes*, ed. Eugène Germer-Durand (Nîmes, 1874), nos. 128–211, *passim*; but see also nos. 149, 150, 154, 159, 170, 186, 189, 202, 204–11; *Cartulaire de Gellone*, ed. Paul Alaus, l'Abbé Cassan, and Edmond Meynial (Montpellier, 1898), nos. 232, 435, 449, 303–4, 344, 351, 346, 361, etc.; cf. no. 482.

[5] *Cart. Maguelone*, i, nos. 23, 33; *HL*, v, nos. 432ii, 524iii; *Cart. Nîmes*, nos. 130, 137, 196, 200, 210.

[6] See *Cart. Maguelone*, i, nos. 6, 10, 15, 32, 42, 53; *Cart. Guillems*, nos. 245, 275.

to appear during the generation before 1125,[1] doubtless as a result of mutations, and they become commonplace in the second quarter of the twelfth century.[2] Apart from these bullion clauses, revealing the anxiety of lenders, we know little about the impact of mutations of the Melgorian money. In 1130 Bernard IV alluded to the injury caused by a debasement to Guillem VI and his 'men',[3] which may mean that burghers of Montpellier as well as rural tenants felt the pinch, but there is no direct evidence of merchants complaining in 1125 or thereafter. It seems probable that the people most vulnerable to debasements were landlords drawing fixed incomes from dues, rents, and tolls. This would account for the concern expressed by the bishop of Maguelone and the lord of Montpellier in 1125 and later. Both rulers had important domains which they were beginning to exploit methodically: domains more extensive and better administered, it appears, than those of the count of Melgueil.[4]

In the years after 1125 Bernard IV and Guillem VI were caught up in the projects of the outer world. Both were the sons of crusaders.[5] The count was a vassal of the Holy See[6] and a nephew of the controversial abbot Pons of Cluny (1109–22, d. 1125); he cannot have forgotten a visit to Melgueil by the ailing pope Gelasius II, attended by Pons, in 1118, when he would have been impressed by news of the reconquest of Zaragoza among other events on the crusading frontiers.[7] Guillem VI doubtless felt personally committed to the Christian cause in Spain. His father had fought beside Ramon Berenguer III in the crusade against Mallorca, and he himself was to be enfeoffed with the city of Tortosa in reward for services against the Almorávides of the Ebro valley.[8] It is possible that Guillem VI sojourned

[1] *HL*, iv. 405; Bonnet, 'Des variations de valeur de la monnaie melgorienne', 498–507; *Cart. Agde*, no. 190.

[2] *LFM*, ii, no. 764; *HL*, v, nos. 515ii, 582, 602ii; *Cart. Guillems*, nos. 141, 220, 226, 231–3, 261, 488, 540; *Cart. Maguelone*, i, no. 87. For the specifying of 'good' melgorians, coin of stated standards, and the like, see *HL*, v, nos. 354, 359, 489viii–xi, 515ii, 567ii, 571iv, 591v, 593, 604iii; *Cart. Guillems*, nos. 222, 349.

[3] *Cart. Maguelone*, i, no. 55; *Cart. Guillems*, no. 66: 'pro dampno quod tu, Guillelme Montispessulani, filius Ermesendis, et tui homines habebatis in hac presenti minoratione Melgoriensis monete . . .'

[4] *Cart. Maguelone*, i, nos. 6, 11, 15, 17, 19, 21, 29, 30 (pp. 63–4), 34, 38–9, 42, 44, 51, 52, and esp. 49; *Cart. Guillems*, nos. 94, 247–60, etc. (see pp. 801–2). We have no cartulary of Melgueil, which may or may not be significant; but cf. Raimond II's testament of c. 1109, *Cart. Maguelone*, i, no. 32, with Guillem V's of 1114, no. 38.

[5] Guillem V was an illustrious participant in the First Crusade, *HL*, iii. 482, 492, 503, 512, 515, 521, returning to the Holy Land about 1105, 577–8, and later serving in the expedition against Mallorca, 620–2; for Raimond II of Melgueil, see 580–1.

[6] Since 1085, *Cart. Maguelone*, i, no. 14.

[7] *HL*, iii. 633, 635–7; *JL*, i, nos. 6657–63; Marcelin Defourneaux, *Les Français en Espagne aux XIᵉ et XIIᵉ siècles* (Paris, 1949), p. 156.

[8] Defourneaux, *Français en Espagne*, pp. 151–2, 155–6; cf. p. 169, where it is asserted that the lord of Montpellier was not yet a vassal of Aragon-Catalonia in the twelfth century. For proof that he was, as early as 1136, see pp. 174–5, and *Cart. Guillems*, no. 152. See also André Dupont, *Les Relations commerciales entre les cités maritimes de Languedoc et les cités méditerranéennes d'Espagne . . .* (Nîmes, 1942), pp. 73–89.

in Spain as early as 1126 or 1127, and quite certain that he went to the Holy Land some time before 1130.[1] Bernard IV may have undertaken such expeditions himself, perhaps in company with his vassal.[2] Both men were known for their piety; both were to end their days as monks, Bernard IV at Saint-Chaffre (*ord. clun.*) as early as 1132, and Guillem VI at Grandselve (*ord. cist.*) in 1149.[3]

Bernard's enterprises badly exceeded his means, and in the course of renewed negotiations beginning in 1128 he lost whatever freedom he still had to exploit the coinage. In July 1128 he borrowed 13,000 s. of Melgueil from Guillem VI, who was authorized, in return, to collect 6 d. per l.— which was one-half of the comital *monedatgue* (*sic*)—until the debt was discharged.[4] By April 1130 the debt had grown to 18,000 s.; the count at that time debased the coinage, and in a new accord Bernard assigned to Guillem *and his successors*, indefinitely, a fief of 3 d. upon every 20 s. minted.[5] The latter agreement seems to have superseded that of 1128.

Of especial interest, from our point of view, is the constitutional aspect of these concessions. In the convention of April 1128 the count confirmed the coinage at the same standards that had been fixed in 1125, but he added this new clause to the declaration: 'nor shall I cause it [the money] to be made otherwise, unless with the counsel and consent of Guillem, lord of Montpellier, and of my good men'.[6] Evidently the count could not afford to renounce entirely his right to manipulate the coinage, his confirmations to the contrary. And his vassals, for their part—the more easily because they included the powerful Guillem VI—had arrived at a perception of their common interest in a stable coinage. This was not the first indication that vassals were gaining the right to be consulted in the vicinity of Montpellier;[7] but the reservation of consent as well as counsel in the matter of coinage went beyond any such rights known to have been in effect, save only, perhaps, those of the chapter relative to the bishop of Maguelone.[8] The count's oath, however, was not directed to his vassals,

---

[1] No act in Guillem's name or presence from spring 1125 to July 1128 is to be found in the *Cart. Guillems*. Archbishop Olleguer of Tarragona was one of the papal judges-delegate in the case settled in 1125. The trip to the east is mentioned in a local charter of January 1129–30, *Spicilegium*, iii. 483.

[2] Cf. Frédéric Fabrège, *Histoire de Maguelone*, 2 vols. (Paris–Montpellier, 1894–1900), i. 229.

[3] *HL*, v, no. 520; iv. 182; also *Cart. Maguelone*, i, nos. 54, 58; *Cart. Guillems*, pp. vi–vii, ix.

[4] *Cart. Maguelone*, i, no. 47; *Cart. Guillems*, no. 65.

[5] *Cart. Maguelone*, i, no. 55; *Cart. Guillems*, no. 66.

[6] *Cart. Maguelone*, i, no. 47; *Cart. Guillems*, no. 65.

[7] See e.g. *Cart. Guillems*, no. 94; Guillem V's daughters, by his will of 1121, were not to be married without the counsel of his heir to the lordship of Montpellier 'et absque consilio nobilium virorum Montispessulani'. For a marriage contract 'consilio maximae partis Melgoriensium Militum', see *Spicilegium*, iii. 483.

[8] Cf. *Cart. Maguelone*, i, nos. 19, 33, 58.

some of whom were present, nor did it pertain only to the coinage, as had one of the oaths in 1125; a personal engagement to his creditor, it secured all of the agreements, including the confirmation, comprehensively.[1] Neither the bishop nor the papal legate took part in the proceedings. For all of these differences, the agreement of 1128 resembled that of 1125, notably in its forms of ratification and testimony. The leading men of Melgueil and Montpellier were groping toward a stable balance of authority using diplomatic models still highly flexible.

The debasement of 1130 was probably in conformity with the principles laid down in 1128. That we do not hear of the count's vassals giving their consent does not mean that they had not consented; and the approval of the greatest of them was implicit in Guillem VI's acceptance of a fief on the coinage. The newly lowered standards were accompanied by a new declaration of confirmation, but not this time by any reservation of counsel and consent in case further mutations became necessary. This omission, given the circumstances, can hardly be interpreted as trickery. The count was in no position to impose on his vassals, and having associated the lord of Montpellier in his prerogative he would have found it impossible to alter the standards before such an intention became generally known. It seems clear that Bernard IV now meant to renounce definitively his (and his successors') right to alter the coinage. Moreover, a new clause provided that if moneyers should be charged with violating the standards, they should be tried in the count's court 'with the counsel of Guillem of Montpellier and of the good men of [the county of] Substantion'.[2]

The oaths of confirmation in 1130, like earlier ones, can be understood only in the full context of the settlement. Not only did the count alienate rights on the coinage, but he also granted his great vassal considerable powers of tutelage and wardship in the event of an early succession to the county. The conveyance was approved by the countess, Guillem's sister; approved and witnessed by Archbishop Arnal of Narbonne acting as papal deputy; and witnessed by vassals of both parties. In the principal text or 'oath charter' (*carta sacramentalis*), Bernard IV swore to execute all his intentions faithfully;[3] but more than this was required to satisfy his creditor. Another charter recorded a pledge of domain revenues for the count's good faith,[4] and in still another, Bernard swore to maintain Guillem faithfully in his new fief of proceeds from the coinage. The latter text, in vernacular, seems to have been carried to at least two churches of the

---

[1] *Cart. Maguelone*, i, no. 47; *Cart. Guillems*, no. 65: 'Et insuper ego Bernardus, Melgorii comes, juro sacramento tibi Guillelmo de Montepessulano, quod hec omnia predicta, sicut ex parte mei dicta sunt, ego firmiter ac inviolabiliter in perpetuum tenebo et observabo, sine tuo tuorumque successorum enganno, per aquest sanz.'
[2] *Cart. Maguelone*, i, no. 55; *Cart. Guillems*, no. 66.
[3] Cited in preceding note.
[4] *Cart. Maguelone*, i, no. 57; *Cart. Guillems*, no. 67.

county, where it received the sworn ratification of the count's vassals and the testimony of local witnesses.[1] On the other side, the lord of Montpellier swore that he would neither mint another coinage in the region nor counterfeit that of Melgueil. This act, in yet another charter, was rightly entitled 'oath of fealty . . . concerning the coinage' by a rubricator.[2] Its wording conformed to the common formulas of meridional oaths of fealty, and the same may be said of the count's vernacular engagement. For all the familiar verbiage about good faith 'from this hour forward', summonses, and amends within forty days, the coinage might almost have been a castle; and in squeezing in a stipulation as to the monetary standards, the scribe who drafted the count's oath could do no better than refer to the principal *carta del sacramental*.[3]

In short, the sworn *confirmatio monetae* at Melgueil had failed to disengage itself from the vassalic formularies of local scribes. The oaths of 1128 and 1130, so far as they are revealed by these texts, were not oriented ceremonially toward assemblies, nor even perhaps toward the witnesses who attended them; they were inwardly directed—the mutual engagements of individual lords in a setting more domestic than public. By contrast, the solemn confirmation in 1125 'to God and all faithful Christians' stands out as a more nearly public and political event. And this settlement, alone among those we have examined, was the work of prelates, of men whose religious formation may have disposed them to take a less proprietary view of the coinage. It should not be forgotten that these prelates were papal judges-delegate and that a papal deputy approved the settlement of 1130. For we have now to notice another and more direct intervention by the pope in the negotiations over the coinage of Melgueil.

On 23 May of a year necessarily between 1125 and 1129, Honorius II wrote firmly to Bernard IV, addressing him as a 'special son of Saint Peter'. The pope ordered that Melgorian money be made only at Melgueil, but admonished the count to preserve this money without 'falsity', as it had been minted in the time of Pope Calixtus II (1119–24). Should he presume to do otherwise, the count was told, he would lose the pope's support of his

---

[1] *Cart. Guillems*, no. 69. This act, a *convenientia*, bears a generic and verbal resemblance to *HL*, v. 824–825ii, a defensive convention between the viscount of Béziers and a vassal of the count of Foix (*c.* 1112). Equally suggestive is the parallelism between *Cart. Guillems*, no. 68 (monetary convention of 1130) and *HL*, v, no. 428.

[2] *Cart. Guillems*, no. 68, and—without the rubric—*Cart. Maguelone*, i, no. 56.

[3] *Cart. Guillems*, no. 69: '. . . E sobre tot aizo, s'il coms o altre, om o femna, la moneda de Melgor de la lei o del pes, que faita deu esser, si con es escrit en la carta del sacramental del comte, amermava, ad aquel ajudaire ni consellaire non serai . . .' Cf. this text and ibid., no. 68, with nos. 84, 316–22, 390–2, 405–7, 422–4; *HL*, v, nos. 428, 441ii, 447, 483iii, 509i, 509ii, 509iv, 532i, 532iv–xii; and (chosen at random) *LFM*, i, nos. 238, 239; ii, nos. 539–44, 554, 560. The formula is no less common in the 'Cartulaire des Trencavel', Société archéologique de Montpellier, MS. 10, e.g. fo. 79ᵛ. For the Carolingian origins of the basic formulas, see Elisabeth Magnou-Nortier, 'Fidélité et féodalité méridionales d'après les serments de fidélité . . .', *Structures*, pp. 116–19.

mint rights.[1] What lay behind this letter is harder to guess than might at
first sight appear. Had the count appealed for permission to debase his
coinage? If so, why did the pope begin by confirming the mint rights?—
and why was there no allusion to the oath of 9 May 1125, from which the
count would presumably have requested dispensation? The latter question
could be answered satisfactorily only if the papal letter could be placed in
the year 1125. But the letter surely dates from a later year, for it answered
to requests of a sort that are not likely to have been made at the very time
when a papal commission was preparing a settlement of controversies over
the coinage among other matters. A situation in keeping with the letter's
contents can better be imagined in the years 1127–9, and most likely in
1129. Word had reached the pope—from what quarters, it seems useless to
speculate—of threats to his vassal's monetary prerogative. These threats
may have been represented as the response to fears that the count might
debase the coinage; they may even have coincided with an appeal to
authorize such a debasement, for Bernard IV must have been in financial
trouble as he returned from the Holy Land (as he had been before bar-
gaining with Guillem VI in July 1128). Whatever its date, the pope's
intervention helps to explain why the count was obliged to negotiate with
the lord of Montpellier and why the latter, in his oaths of 1130 and later
years, pledged not to make any money other than the Melgorian in his
lordship and the county.

The pronouncement by Honorius II was in the spirit of the reformed
papacy. While it rested upon the pontifical suzerainty over Melgueil, its
more fundamental support was the moral jurisdiction of Saint Peter. It
reflected a vassalic structure of authority, in keeping with the feudalistic
oaths of 1130 and with general notions espoused by Rome at the time, yet
its language was unequivocally religious. 'The holy Church defends what
is irreprehensible', the letter began, and Honorius centred his warning
upon 'falsity' in coinage.[2] He could well have been thinking of mutations
as a species of falsification, for the fathers of the First Lateran Council
(1123) had lately commanded that the makers and knowing users of 'false
money' be excommunicated.[3] Of specific situations in which the stability of

[1] *Bullaire de l'église de Maguelone*, ed. J.-B. Rouquette and Augustin Villemagne,
2 vols. (Montpellier, 1911–14), i, no. 24 (JL, i, no. 7345; text also in *Cart. Guillems*, no. 3;
HF, xv. 265; *PL*, clxvi. 1268). Alexandre Germain argued for 23 May 1129, 'Anciennes
monnaies de Melgueil', 137, supposing that the pope was alluding to the debasement
mentioned in April 1130. But the papal letter does not refer to any specific debasement;
it warns against the falsification of coins. Baumel, *Naissance de Montpellier*, p. 115, was
also misled about the date.

[2] *Bull. Maguelone*, i, no. 24: 'Quod irreprehensibile est sancta defendit Ecclesia . . . .
Tua interest, ut si protectionem nostram habere desideras, in fabricanda moneta nichil
falsitatis admisceas, et ne aliter quam tempore predecessoris nostri felicis memorie pape
Calixti constitutum est, eam de cetero facias fabricari. . . .'

[3] *Conciliorum oecumenicorum decreta*, ed. Josephus Alberigo *et al.*, 3rd edn. (Bologna,
1973), pp. 192–3, c. 13.

a local coinage was at issue, that of Melgueil seems to have been the first to arouse the active concern of the Holy See.

The politics of the Melgorian money fell into a lock-step after 1130. Although the debt of 18,000 s. disappeared with the death of Bernard IV two or three years later, the fief of 3 d. per l. of minted coin was to be the cause of further conventions between successive counts and Guillem VI in which the coinage was repeatedly confirmed upon the standards established in April 1130. The confirmations sworn by Alfons-Jordan of Toulouse about 1132,[1] by Berenguer-Ramon of Provence soon afterward,[2] and by Béatrix and Bernard-Pelet in 1146 resembled that of Bernard IV both in form and substance.[3] It is true that the agreement of 1146 was based primarily on that of 1125, but since the monetary standards of 1125 had become obsolete, neither they nor the emphatically ceremonial terms of their religious confirmation in 1125 were included in the pact between the ageing Guillem VI and the countess and her new husband.[4]

By mid-century the house of Melgueil seems to have recovered its financial stability. If this was one reason for its maintaining a stable currency, another must have been the continued prosperity of the mint. That the coinage was normally producing revenues of several thousand sous a year in the later twelfth century[5] goes far to explain why there was no money-tax—that is, none other than the *monedatgue* from the mint—in the county of Melgueil. The long-term maintenance of the monetary standards and types[6] did not dissolve a prudent vigilance in the money market, however. Clauses guaranteeing alternative repayments in fine silver occurred repeatedly in the second half of the twelfth century.[7] These clauses show that creditors feared deterioration of the coinage as much as debasement,[8] fears

---

[1] *Cart. Guillems,* no. 80. On the dynastic background of this convention and of the others to 1146, see Germain, 'Comtes de Maguelone', 557–68.

[2] *Cart. Guillems,* nos. 71, 72 (*Cart. Maguelone,* i, no. 62). It is probable, but not clear, that these engagements were made under oath. Guillem's declaration of fealty in 1135, *Cart. Guillems,* no. 73, though on the form of an oath and comparable to his oath of 1130, was not sworn.

[3] *Cart. Guillems,* no. 76. Cf. no. 66. For Guillem's oath in 1146, see no. 77 (*Cart. Maguelone,* i, no. 71).

[4] *Cart. Maguelone,* i, no. 73; see also nos. 71, 72, 74; *Cart. Guillems,* no. 74; see also nos. 75–7.

[5] See *Cart. Maguelone,* i, no. 155, countess Béatrix reserves a pension 'quamdiu vixero, in ipsa moneta Melgorii, singulis annis, de primis denariis qui de moneta provenerint, tria milia solidorum, ita ut, si de moneta non provenirent, de aliis reditibus Melgorii ... complecterentur'. Cf., for the early thirteenth century, ibid., ii, no. 315.

[6] No change in either from 1130 to 1174, Dieudonné, 'Le melgorien', 34; Poey d'Avant, *Monnaies féodales,* ii, plate 85, nos. 17–19.

[7] *Cart. Maguelone,* i, nos. 87, 121, 140, 212, 216, 222, 230, 247; *HL,* v, nos. 602ii, 604i, 623; viii, nos. 23, 58, 67, 68; *Cart. Guillems,* nos. 141, 197, 237, 261, 340, 343, 345, 435, 472, 474–5, 482, 488; *Cart. Agde,* nos. 29, 66, 170, 183.

[8] See e.g. *Cart. Guillems,* no. 141 (1157): '... reddam vobis, vel vestris, CL solidos

that were surely justified. The longer the money remained unchanged, the more the people must have been tempted to pay dues and debts in worn or damaged deniers. In 1160 the count of Toulouse had occasion to acknowledge receipt of 2,000 s. of Melgueil 'in new coin', by which he can only have meant freshly minted money on the old standards.[1]

When the daughter of Béatrix and Bernard-Pelet married Count Raimond V of Toulouse in 1172,[2] the dependency of Melgueil upon Montpellier was ended. Raimond V, as count of Melgueil, maintained Guillem VII of Montpellier in his fief on the money,[3] but Raimond did not himself confirm the coinage, not at least in the customary way. On the contrary, in 1174 he carefully redefined the standards, reducing the weight of the coins slightly. The new standards were promulgated in a *stabilicio et conventio* with the moneyers, not with the lord of Montpellier nor in the presence of an assembly; on the basis of this regulation the Melgorian coinage was to be administered during the rest of the twelfth century and far into the thirteenth.[4] So it happened that the public and sworn confirmation of coinage, reaching an early climax at Melgueil, lapsed after 1125 into more conventional and perhaps less solemn forms. The observance of these promises was little more than deflected under the relatively strong dynasty of Toulouse. Neither rural vassals nor burghers gained much influence over a coinage, still thoroughly seigneurial, that was too popular for its proprietors to risk abusing.

D. *Aragon and Catalonia (1155–1213)*

By the third quarter of the twelfth century, the Melgorian coinage was in common use throughout Occitania and Catalonia. The adjustment of its standards in 1174 cannot have been independent of monetary policy elsewhere. In fact, we hear of recoinages or changes of standard quite generally during the 1170s: in the kingdom of Aragon, the counties of Barcelona, Provence, and Toulouse, the bishopric of Vich, even in the west Spanish realms, as well as at Melgueil. Moreover, several of these mutations occurred in 1174, two of them probably within a few weeks of the adjustment of the melgorian; and their result was to establish or confirm the

---

melgorienses, sine dolo, vel argentum finum, ad rationem marche, que valet L solidos, si hec moneta habatuda fuerit, vel deteriorata.' The phrase is routine in texts cited in preceding note.

  [1] *HL*, v, no. 634i; cf. *Cart. Agde*, no. 30 (1139). For other allusions to 'good' and 'current' coin, see *HL*, v, nos. 567ii, 571iv, 593, 604ii, 604iii, 623; viii, nos. 4, 58; *Cart. Maguelone*, i, nos. 87, 247; *Cart. Agde*, nos. 40, 51–4, and *passim*.
  [2] *HL*, viii, no. 15; *Cart. Maguelone*, i, no. 155; Germain, 'Comtes de Maguelone', 574–80.
  [3] *Cart. Maguelone*, i, no. 156.
  [4] Ibid., no. 161; Germain, 'Anciennes monnaies de Melgueil', 139–46.

silver of Jaca, Barcelona, Vich, and Melgueil in close parity, at 4 d. fine and about 216 d. to the mark.[1]

Among the earliest of these events was a public recoinage in Aragon which coincided with the marriage and knighting of King Alphonse II (1162–96) on 18 January 1174.[2] It is not unlikely that the directive was attended by a confirmation of the money, for pledges and sales were soon stipulating coinage confirmed by the king.[3] Such a ceremony, having no warrant in the old *fueros*, could well have been the first of its kind in Aragon, but we have no record of it in 1174. The *iaccensis moneta nova* is required as early as June 1174,[4] and comparable references become common in texts dated after February 1175.[5] There are indications that the recall of old coin was incomplete, if indeed it had been undertaken at all. Nominally, the mutation of 1174 was merely a change of types: the new king replaced his inherited Jaca coin with another bearing his own insignia, but at the same alloy (4 d. fine).[6] The *iaccensis*, having long enjoyed exclusive legal currency in Aragon, had been a quaternal money since 1135 or before. We hear of recoinages in 1128 and 1135, for which reason, among others, it has been supposed that the coinage of Jaca was issued thereafter at intervals of seven years. Yet there is no evidence of public recoinages between 1135 and 1174, and Alphonse's in the latter year, a year out of phase with the septennial cycle 1128–35, was quite surely the first since his accession in 1162. While the *iaccensis* retained a better reputation than the Christian silver of Catalonia, worn pieces must have been circulating by this time, and minor alterations may have occurred. The price of the

---

[1] These facts are documented below. The debasement at Toulouse occurred on an uncertain date probably later than May 1175 and certainly before April 1178: cf. AD Haute-Garonne, H Malte, Caignac no. 31 (liasse 3, no. 1) with AN, J 321, no. 28 (*LTC*, i, no. 286). See also AD Haute-Garonne, E 508, no. 1, text dated 'mense marcii feria .iii. anno ab incarnatione Domini .m.c.lxx.viii', i.e. a Tuesday in March of 1179 (or possibly 28 March 1178); cf. Castaing-Sicard, *Monnaies féodales en Languedoc*, p. 16. For Provence, see Henri Rolland, *Monnaies des comtes de Provence, XIIᵉ–XVᵉ siècles . . .* (Paris, 1956), pp. 109–10 (but the date of the concession of 'moneta comitatus Prouincie quam ibi de nouo fieri constituo [Alfonso II]' is 31 October 1173, not 1174). For Castile and Leon, see Claudio Sánchez-Albornoz, 'La primitiva organización monetaria de León y Castilla', *AHDE*, v (1928), 334–8; idem, '¿Devaluación monetaria en León y Castilla al filo del 1200?' *Homenaje a Jaime Vicens Vives*, 2 vols. (Barcelona, 1965), i. 607–8; and Octavio Gil Farrés, *Historia de la moneda española* (Madrid, 1959), p. 200.

[2] 'Documentos para el estudio de la numismática navarro-aragonesa medieval (2.a serie)', ed. Ubieto, *PSANA*, ii (1953), 95, no. 33, donation to Santa Cristina del Somport (November 1174): '. . . Facta carta mense novembris, era M.ª CC.ª, in anno quando rex Ildefonsus fuit milite facto et ipso die presit mulier illa regina et mutavit illa moneta Iachesa'; ACA, perg. Alfonso I, 146, indicated by Jaime Caruana, 'Itinerario de Alfonso II de Aragón', *EEMCA*, vii (1962), 145–6.

[3] e.g. *Col. dipl. Huesca*, i, nos. 379, 393, 394, 397, etc.; but cf. below, pp. 83–5.

[4] 'Documentos (2.a serie)', ed. Ubieto, 94, no. 32.

[5] *Col. dipl. Huesca*, i, nos. 310, 314, 320, 325, 348.

[6] See ibid., nos. 306, 308, 316, 322, etc.; Heiss, *Monedas hispano-cristianas*, ii. 6–11; Beltrán, 'Dineros jaqueses', 86–7. (Plate II, nos. 16, 17.)

morabetin varied between 6 s. 3 d. *iacc.* and 7 s. 2 d. from 1167 to 1174, nor is this the only evidence of uneasiness about the intrinsic value of the denier of Jaca during the years just preceding Alphonse's recoinage.[1]

Our record of the recoinage of Barcelona takes quite a different form, being at once more explicit and more doubtful. What we have is an undated declaration, in the form of a charter, ordaining the standards of the mint, the count–king's confirmation of the money, and penalties for violations of the ordinance. 'I make and establish', says Alphonse, 'a new money of Barcelona, good and legal, which shall circulate through my land all the days of my life'; this coinage is to be at 4 d. fine and 18 s. to the alloyed mark (with *medalie*, corresponding to obols, at 3 d. and 20 s. respectively). 'The aforesaid money, moreover, I wish and make firm [*firmam*] and stable in the aforesaid weight and alloy for all the days of my life without any fraud and without bad will and without any deceit, so that it will not be altered or changed or debased.' Violators of these terms, including counterfeiters, were to be in the king's mercy. The motive for so ordaining, it was added, is 'to provide for the common utility of my whole people and land'.[2]

Lacking marks of validation—there appear neither date nor subscriptions—this text inevitably arouses suspicion. Yet it survives in the king's archives in at least two copies of different date, and its contents are altogether plausible. All that can be said against it is that the decision to confirm a new coinage publicly, for which the existence of the document is sufficient evidence, was apparently not implemented. Two substantive defects may help us to understand why it was not. For one thing, Alphonse's charter lacks any real quid pro quo; second, it makes no reference to an oath. So drafted, it must naturally have been queried in the king's counsels, and since its contents were not such as to require formal promulgation, it may simply have been buried.

The circumstances point strongly, if not quite conclusively, to a date in 1174. Botet y Sisó has shown that a Barcelona coinage on the standards recorded in Alphonse's pseudo-declaration was minted in the later seventies, and it is known that in 1175 the mint of Barcelona was not only active but producing 'new' deniers.[3] A new coinage for Provence had been esta-

---

[1] Beltrán, 'Dineros jaqueses', 80–6; 'Documentos para el estudio de la reconquista y repoblación', ed. Lacarra, no. 56; 'Documentos (1.a serie)', ed. Ubieto, nos. 4, 9; 'Documentos (2.a serie)', nos. 26–31, 34; *Col. dipl. Huesca*, i, nos. 158–298 (*passim*), 249, 299; texts cited by Joaquím Miret y Sans, *Les Cases de Templers y Hospitalers en Catalunya . . .* (Barcelona, 1910), pp. 137–8. See generally Octavio Gil Farrés, 'Consideraciones acerca de las primitivas cecas navarras y aragonesas', *Numario hispánico*, iv (1955), 5–36.

[2] ACA, perg. Alfonso I, extrainv. 2602 (Appendix, no. 3 below). The piece was printed by Botet y Sisó, *Monedes catalanes*, iii. 240 from a copy in ACA, Reg. 2, fo. 47; but the former text is much the earlier and was probably the exemplar from which the latter was copied.

[3] Botet y Sisó, *Monedes catalanes*, ii. 25–8; AC Barcelona, 'Libri antiquitatum', i, fo. 191

blished by Alphonse II as early as October 1173; but the recoinage of Aragon can be placed early in 1174, as we have seen, and it seems reasonable to suppose that the king saw fit to synchronize his Spanish emissions, for which the standards must have been nearly the same. Moreover, when we find Bishop Pere of Vich in the king's company in January 1174 at the festival where the new money of Aragon was proclaimed, and then again in the following December a few days after issuing his own charter-confirmation which specified standards identical with those of Barcelona and which in no way interfered with the circulation of Barcelona silver outside of the city markets of Vich,[1] the near coincidence between the episcopal and royal declarations in Catalonia becomes probable. The Catalonian ordinances, for their part, closely correspond to the regulation of the melgorian, which we know took place on 1 November 1174; and it appears significant in this connection that in the same month Alphonse set off for Languedoc to confer with his rival Raimond V.[2] On these grounds, his Catalan recoinage may be dated most plausibly toward the end of the year 1174.

What is known about the economy and coinage of Barcelona in the middle decades of the twelfth century is consistent with this dating of Alphonse's act and helps to explain it. The young king seems to have continued minting his father's coinage, there as in Aragon, while allowing—and doubtless profiting from—minor alterations.[3] He had inherited a confused finance together with ambitious and costly Provençal politics[4] for which

(no. 517), ed. Botet, iii. 239; *Cartulari de Poblet* . . . , ed. Joan Pons i Marquès (Barcelona, 1938), no. 309, donation-sale of property to Poblet for 100 'solidos barchinonensium novorum et unam mulam que valebat sine dubio c. solidos barchinonensium . . . '. See also *'Llibre Blanch' de Santas Creus*, no. 187, will of 2 June 1175: '. . . et iamdictus frater meus [i.e. of Ramon de Miralpeix] persolvat Salomoni de Regina CLXX. solidos, secundum rationem quod tunc temporis erant denarii'; ACA, Monacales, perg. St. Benet de Bages, 501, 504, 506. (Cf. Plate III, no. 19.)

[1] Caruana, 'Itinerario de Alfonso II', 146, 152; ACA, perg. Alfonso I, 160; cf. below, pp. 78–80. The bishop had also attended the king at Lérida in October 1173 when the new coinage of Provence was ceded, although he did not subscribe that diploma; see Caruana, 'Itinerario', 144–5; AM Lérida, Privilegios, no. 5, ed. Concepción Pérez Pérez, 'Comentarios a los privilegios dados por Alfonso II el Casto a la ciudad de Lérida', *VII Congreso de Historia de la Corona de Aragón*, ii (Barcelona, 1962), 251.

[2] Texts cited by Caruana, 'Itinerario de Alfonso II', 151–2; see generally Jordi Ventura Subirats, *Alfons 'el Cast', el primer comte-rei* (Barcelona, 1961), pp. 160–4, 213–14.

[3] Botet y Sisó, *Monedes catalanes*, i. 73–90; ii. 23–31. For stipulations of good Barcelona coin, or reservations in case of mutation, see Joseph Mas, *Notes històriques del bisbat de Barcelona*, 12 vols. (Barcelona, 1906–15), xi, no. 1962, cf. nos. 1850–1961; *Cart. 'Sant Cugat'*, iii, nos. 1037, 1046, 1053; *'Llibre Blanch' de Santas Creus*, nos. 76, 134, 138, 170–1; ACA, perg. Alfonso I, 65, 108; Arxiu de Montserrat, perg. Sant Cugat, pieces dated 28 November twenty-sixth of Louis VII, 29 March thirty-seventh of Louis VII; AHN, Clero, Poblet, carpeta 2019, 1; AC Vich, cal. 6, 1926.

[4] The finance of Alphonse II has not yet been adequately studied. For some suggestive documents, see ACA, perg. Ramón Berenguer IV, 8 apéndice; perg. Alfonso I, 13, 46–8,

Saracen tribute could not altogether compensate; significantly, his preferred money of account in Catalonia was the gold morabetin, while the denier of Barcelona, now circulating throughout his Catalan domains, could not yet be securely valued in gold or silver.[1] Alphonse's 'new money' in 1174, on which REX was added to the legend, perpetuated the old comital types, which themselves resembled the melgorian (and not the *iaccensis*). To 'stabilize' it and make it 'good and legal' was to try to restore its reputation, to render it competitive with the rival melgorian in the Mediterranean.[2]

Our evidence for the recoinage of Vich is most explicit and least complicated. On 13 December 1174 Bishop Pere de Redorta (1146 or 1147–85) declared in a lengthy charter that he

makes and restores [*facio et restauro*] the money of Sant Pere of the See of Ausona by counsel of all the canons of the same church and of Ramon de Montcada and of many good men of both the town and diocese of Vich. I make this coinage at an alloy of 4 deniers of pure silver and at legitimate weight, such that 18 sous of deniers issue from the mark. And in order that this coinage be observed firmly, and held in the aforesaid alloy and weight, I the present bishop Pere agree, in word of truth and purity of faith, and cause to swear at the peril of my soul through two canons, namely Pere de Tavertet and Ramon de Malla, and through two noble and eminent men, namely Ramon de Montcada and Pere de Lluçà: and I affirm that the aforesaid money not be changed in all my life; let it not be diminished either in alloy or weight by my counsel or ruling or will. If anyone should lessen it in any way, I have the right to punish by counsel of my good men . . ..

The text goes on to paraphrase the oaths sworn by the deputy canons and nobles, with the words of the latter—'we, moreover, the aforesaid Ramon . . . and Pere . . . swear likewise'—breaking through the surface of indirect discourse. Here the charter ends with the *Actum* and date, only to resume in the bishop's formal voice of statutory declaration: 'Moreover we

---

55, 56, 60, 62, 94; see also Soldevila, *Hist. Catalunya*, 2nd edn., chs. 6–9, esp. pp. 189–93, 198–208; Ventura, *Alfons 'el Cast'*, chs. 6–12, 15, 16, 18–21.

[1] An impression derived from ACA, pergs. Ramón Berenguer IV and Alfonso II; '*Llibre Blanch*' *de Santas Creus*, nos. 45–181; see also Josef Salat, *Tratado de las monedas labradas en el principado de Cataluña . . .* , 2 vols. (Barcelona, 1818), i. 97.

[2] See Plate III, no. 19, Plate II, no. 11. My argument for the date of Alphonse's draft-declaration is in conflict with that of Jaime Lluis y Navas (in collaboration with Salvador Clotet Madico), 'La moneda "nova" barcelonesa de Alfonso I', *Numario hispánico*, x (1961), 123–6. They argue, on the basis of a single, poorly legible obol whose type anticipates that of Peter II's coinage, that the 'new money' associated with the declaration must date from 1194–6. In so arguing, they overlook three facts: (1) there need not—indeed, cannot—have been a single 'new' coinage in the reign of Alphonse; (2) a recoinage about 1174 is attested in dated texts (see p. 76 n. 3 above), unlike that claimed for 1194–6; (3) the standards specified in the draft-confirmation were quite as consistent with the monetary circumstances of 1174 as with those of twenty years later. The texts, as Botet y Sisó knew, constitute the only reliable evidence for the monetary history of Alphonse II and his son.

establish [*statuimus*] that if anyone in the town of Vich should sell or buy anything with any other money than the aforesaid, let him pay 10 sous in justice if he be a good man [*probus homo*]'; if such violator be a *mediocris*, the text continues, let him pay 5 sous; and if of the lower class, let him draw the water on market-day, or if it happen during the week, let him enter the pillory. Further penal regulations ensue. The subscriptions are those of the bishop and the four jurors.[1]

This document reads like an elaborated version of Alphonse's contemporary draft-charter, a fact that strengthens our suspicion that the two texts were related. But *how* were they related? Was the bishop setting an example for a reluctant king by having his confirmation sworn before his assembled people? Was the king's failure to execute the constitutional formalities a betrayal? These are no better than plausible speculations, to which we shall return; they must not be allowed to obscure the immediate circumstances of the Vigatan text. Awkward and verbose, it reveals again the confusion of local scribes facing new situations. It recalls *Cunctis pateat* in its vague and formulaic reference to assembled notables and in its account of the oaths, yet it cannot otherwise be traced to local or Catalonian models. What now preoccupied the bishop and his subjects was not the peace, not even primarily the countrysides, but the market-place, already in 1174 showing the diversity and vigour for which Vich was to be noted.

The episcopal currency was ageing and unreliable,[2] its differently worn pieces confusing local trade and the exchange with better coinages. Contemporary acts betray a preference for morabetins and deniers of Barcelona in the plain of Vich, while the old money of Besalú held out in the valley of Sant Joan to the north. A distinct tendency in these regions to stipulate 'good' or 'best' coin of whatever mint (or of none in particular) points to suspicion of the bishop's money along with the rest.[3] Accordingly, what was lacking in the king's draft-charter—a fair exchange—was secured at Vich in 1174: the bishop promised to 'restore' the coinage, meaning that his mutation would take the form of a recoinage on standards now openly defined though probably not very different from those previously in nominal effect; while the people through their notables agreed to use none but

---

[1] ACA, perg. Alfonso I, 160 (original, or original copy); Junyent, *Jurisdiccions i privilegis de Vich*, no. 39. The piece was edited from an original in AC Vich (now lost if not identical with perg. Alfonso I, 160) by Villanueva, *VL*, vi. 241–3; and subsequently, from the text in ACA, by Joseph Gudiol y Cunill, *Les Monedes episcopals vigatanes* (Vich, 1896), pp. 20–1; and by Botet y Sisó, *Monedes catalanes*, i. 211–12. The background is usefully indicated by Jaime Lluis y Navas Brusi, 'Le droit monétaire dans la région de Vich pendant la reconquête espagnole . . .', *RN*, 5th ser., xviii (1956), 209–32, a work which is not always reliable in detail.

[2] See Botet y Sisó, *Monedes catalanes*, i. 178–80, nos. 151–6; pp. 183–5.

[3] AC Vich, cal. 6, 25, 28, 29–31, 368, 373, 384, 394, 402, 1659, and *passim*; Arxiu de Sant Joan de les Abadesses, pergs. s. XII. It does not seem possible to document increasing dissatisfaction toward 1174, although a bullion clause appears, exceptionally, in a local pledge dated 2 May 1173, AC Vich, cal. 6, 2404.

the episcopal money in the city. The latter provision must be interpreted in a fiscal light. What the bishop wanted was to ensure demand for his money in the busiest and most easily supervised markets of his domain and to profit from violations, not to insist on his obsolete monopoly of the comital money of Ausona.[1]

The restoration of the coinage at Vich was characteristic of Pere de Redorta and his capable canons. His pontificate was a prosperous time for the church of Sant Pere, while he himself entered vigorously into the public affairs of Catalonia.[2] In 1176 he reformed the administration of the canonry, instituting the monthly provostships which were then being established in other Catalan chapters as well; and in the first distribution of assignments, Pere de Tavertet and Ramon de Malla, deputy jurors of the coinage in 1174, were associated in the *prepositura* of June.[3] Only weeks before, in a text which further illuminates the personal involvements in the restoration of 1174, the bishop's moneyer had attested how the proceeds of the mint were rightfully apportioned.[4] We learn with interest that the bishop who took full responsibility for the quality of coinage then collected but half of its revenues; the other half was divided in shares held by the moneyer in fief from the bishop, by the sacristan (none other than Pere de Tavertet, on the threshold of a brilliant career),[5] by Guillem Ramon de Montcada (seneschal of the county of Barcelona and co-lord of Vich), and by the viscount of Cardona. Pere de Lluçà, who had sworn together with the lord of Montcada in 1174, had inherited the right to coin one pound of alloyed silver per week for himself, a fact that not only explains the most obscure name among the jurors of 1174 but also suggests that the episcopal mint,was very active in the time of the restored coinage. As for the new money, it can be identified with a specimen bearing the name PETRUS in its legends, and it probably continued to be struck well into the thirteenth century.[6]

---

[1] Cf. *VL*, vi. 296, reference in 1038 to the (bishop's) 'monetam publicam suae regionis', with *PU Spanien. Vorarbeiten zur Hispania pontificia*, ed. Paul Kehr, 2 vols. (Berlin, 1926–8), i (*Katalanien*), part 2, no. 56, Pope Eugene III's confirmation of episcopal rights at Vich in 1150, which speaks of 'monetam quoque tuę ciuitatis'.

[2] ACA, perg. Alfonso I, 126, in June 1172 the king pledges 150 s. on his *questa* at Moià to the bishop and canons of Vich in exchange for their loan of 33 marks and 100 morabetins. On Pere de Redorta (bishop 1146 or 1147–85), see Juan Luís de Moncada, *Episcopologio de Vich . . .*, ed. Jaime Collell, 3 vols. (Vich, 1891–1904), i. 449–504; or *VL*, vii. 3–11; and ACA, perg. Alfonso I, 60, 67, 146; *LFM*, i, no. 240.

[3] *VL*, vi. 255–7.

[4] ACA, perg. Alfonso I, 194; Junyent, *Jurisdiccions i privilegis de Vich*, no. 40; ed. Botet y Sisó, *Monedes catalanes*, i. 211. Cf. this arrangement with that recorded in 1104, *Jurisdiccions*, nos. 23–4.

[5] On this personage, see Moncada, *Episcopologio de Vich*, i. 517–53. From a village north of Vich, he became a canon in 1157; his brother's son was to be bishop (1195–1233), while he himself became closely associated with the kings Alphonse II and Peter II.

[6] Junyent, *Jurisdiccions i privilegis de Vich*, no. 24; Botet y Sisó, *Monedes catalanes*.

Whatever their differences and novelty, the episcopal confirmation of 1174 and Alphonse II's declaration (as we have it) share elements indicative of a growing tradition in Catalonia. Their penal injunctions against counterfeiters and debasers recall very similar provisions in the early peace legislation of Vich and Barcelona.[1] More significantly, their confirmation for a lifetime corresponds exactly to the engagement made in Cerdanya in 1118.[2] Nor is that all: for the provisions for punishment of violators and for lifelong stability likewise appear together in a somewhat enigmatic text of 1155 which reveals the cause of good money persisting in the Catalan peace movement. To some regulations about the Truce, prelates assembled in a council at Lérida—among them, almost certainly, Bishop Pere of Vich—appended the directive that the 'emperor' (*imperator*), for the sake of God and his own salvation, should establish whatever coinage he has at good weight and 4 d. fine 'without any price', to preserve it unchanged during his lifetime and even to 'confirm it to remain so'. Counterfeiters are to be excommunicated and to undergo corporal punishment, with the bishops receiving the tithe of confiscated coin and chattels from the ruler.[3]

Why should a council meeting on the border of Aragon and Catalonia have enjoined an emperor? Can we interpret the provision as having reference to Ramon Berenguer IV, then ruling Aragon as *princeps* and Catalonia as count? The unspecific 'whatever coinage' (*monetam quid-quam*) is consistent with this view, for we know that this ruler had coinages, nominally of the required alloy, in both realms. Moreover, the recommended renunciation of 'any price' (*sine omni precio*) looks like a reaction against an imposition with recent precedent in Catalonia. Yet Ramon

---

i. 184–5. On the interests in the coinage, see also Engels, 'Weltliche Herrschaft des Bischofs von Ausona-Vich', 15–20.

[1] Compare these texts (cited again next note) with *VL*, vi. 308–9, and *Moneta autem*, ed. Abadal and Valls Taberner, *Usatges de Barcelona*, p. 27 (art. 66). The bishop's engagement to punish with counsel corresponds significantly to *Moneta autem*. These injunctions probably derive ultimately from the *Forum judicum*, ed. Zeumer, *Leges Visigothorum*, pp. 309–11 (vii. 6 *De falsariis metallorum*).

[2] ACA, perg. Alfonso I, extrainventario 2606: '. . . Predictam monetam uolo et facio [Alphonse II] firmam et stabilem in predicto penso et lege cunctis diebus uite mee sine omni fraude . . .'; perg. Alfonso I, 160: '. . . Conuenio [Bishop Pere of Vich] etiam quod prescripta moneta non mutetur in omni uita mea, nec in lege nec in pondere minuatur . . . .' Cf. *LFM*, ii, no. 691: '. . . predictus comes [Ramon Berenguer III] . . . mittit suam monetam quam habet propria manu firmatam in predicto comitatu . . . ut omni tempore quandiu ipse superstes extiterit prephatam monetam non mutet vel minuet lege vel penso . . . .'

[3] Biblioteca Central (Barcelona), MS. 193, text (which I was unable to find in the cited MS. in 1972) printed by Ferràn Valls Taberner, 'Ein Konzil zu Lerida im Jahre 1155', *Papsttum und Kaisertum: Forschungen . . . Paul Kehr zum 65. Geburtstag dargebracht*, ed. Albert Brackmann (Munich, 1926), p. 368: 'Monetam quidquam bene pensatam et quatuor denariorum argenti mittet imperator sine omni precio propter Deum et anime sue salutum [*sic*] nunquam in diebus suis mutandum, sed eam ita mansuram firmat. . . .' Valls Taberner was unaware of the text subsequently published by Paul Kehr, *PU Spanien*, ii. *Navarra und Aragon*, part 2, no. 76 (published in 1928) which not only suggests the presence of Pere de Redorta, but proves that Jacintus presided.

Berenguer IV did not style himself 'emperor', and to refer to him as such at a time when his vassalage to the emperor Alphonse VII of Castile-Leon was acknowledged[1] would have been oddly mistaken. Whether Ramon attended this council or not (and he can hardly have been ignorant of its proceedings), it seems much more likely that the monetary injunction was directed toward Alphonse VII and his successors.

In fact, the council of Lérida addressed itself generally to conditions in Spain. Celebrated by the cardinal-legate Jacintus, who had been travelling in Castile and Navarre, it reiterated provisions of the second Lateran Council.[2] Alphonse VII, who surely did not attend, had several coinages to which the ruling might have applied; to speak of him as 'emperor' was not only flattering (and customary), it was also efficient.[3] And since he least of all can have admitted Ramon Berenguer to be so designated, we are entitled to suspect the latter's interest, if not influence, in the measure. What was envisaged in 1155 was a type of confirmation, albeit in uncompensated form, known in Catalonia but not yet elsewhere in Spain. Whether or not Ramon himself had already made such an engagement, it can be assumed that he would have resisted an attempt to have the obligation incorporated in the standing legislation of the regional church. On the other hand, as an accomplished champion of the clergy, he or his supporters were well placed to parry the monetary injunction in the direction of the west Spanish realms.

However that may be, the legislation of 1155 suggests strongly that the regulations of the 1170s derived in part from a standing ecclesiastical programme.[4] Nor was parity at 4 d. fine silver a new idea in 1174. If public regulation was generally delayed until then, it was because the moral influence of the Church (by no means enhanced by its fiscal interest) was less efficacious than political and economic realities. Not until the 1170s were the lay rulers of Catalonia, Aragon, Castile, and Leon old enough to establish policies of their own. Moreover, the moneys then regulated or reissued were precisely the most widely useful and prosperous ones, while of lesser coinages—those, for instance, of Béziers, Narbonne, Roussillon, Girona, and Urgell—the records say nothing. In Catalonia Alphonse II understandably allowed his coinages of Besalú and Girona to lapse; he

---

[1] Soldevila, *Hist. Catalunya*, 2nd edn., pp. 176–8, 186–8; H. J. Hüffer, *La Idea imperial española* (Madrid, 1933), pp. 30–43; Ramón Menéndez Pidal, *El Imperio hispánico y los cinco reinos* . . . (Madrid, 1950), pp. 168–71.

[2] Valls Taberner, 'Ein Konzil zu Lerida', pp. 364–8; Hüffer, *Idea imperial*, p. 41; Kehr, *PU Spanien*, ii. *Navarra und Aragon*, part 2, nos. 69–75. Its language echoed that of the council of Valladolid, likewise celebrated by Jacintus, January 1155, text in Carl Erdmann, *Das Papsttum und Portugal im ersten Jahrhundert der portugiesischen Geschichte* (Berlin, 1928), pp. 55–8.

[3] Heiss, *Monedas hispano-cristianas*, i. 7–14; Gil Farrés, *Moneda española*, pp. 196–8; Sánchez-Albornoz, 'La primitiva organización monetaria', 314–34.

[4] For discussion of this point see below, pp. 102–4.

likewise discontinued the money of Roussillon upon assuming the comital title there in 1172.[1] The result was to secure for his deniers of Barcelona the kind of superiority in Catalonia which his silver of Jaca had long enjoyed in Aragon. His promotion of these coinages, which may have been influenced by his awareness of the sovereign monopolies of coinage in Castile, Leon, and Navarre, corresponded to the equally decisive emphasis on the currency of Paris by his Capetian contemporaries.[2]

The *conjoncture* of the 1170s has its related economic significance. Over regions extending from Portugal to Provence, the trades in produce and money alike had become integrated and stable enough to render urgent some co-ordination in the issuance of coinages. From this time on, popular sensitivity to the relative values of coinages, so far as it can be measured at all in the increasingly formulaic clauses of written instruments, is so constant a factor as to lose its utility as a measure for distinguishing between meridional economies. It is true that the supply of specie tended to lag behind demand more often in some places than in others—so, for example, the upland Segarra has been found to contrast perceptibly with the bustling environs of Poblet toward 1200[3]—but everywhere it became exceptional to designate payments in unspecified deniers or sous.[4] Meanwhile, the gold morabetin, openly minted by the king of Castile from 1172 but long since handled in tributary payments and Mediterranean commerce, established itself as a standard for evaluating, or accounting in, silver throughout the Spanish kingdoms.[5]

People seldom recognize their good fortune until it is past. If the recoinages and confirmations of the 1170s seemed at the time to promise monetary stability, the satisfaction must soon have given way to disillusionment. For the new generation—it was that of the rise and collapse of the first Aragonese empire and the early Albigensian crusades—saw renewed mutations of coinage; and these manipulations, more shocking than in the recent past, were followed by negotiations in which the price of confirmation was

[1] See Botet y Sisó, *Monedes catalanes*, i. 90–121, 124–35; cf. ii. 23–31.

[2] Cf. above, p. 44.

[3] Agustí Altisent, 'Un poble de la Catalunya nova . . .. L'Espluga de Francolí de 1079 a 1200', *AEM*, iii (1966), 148; idem, 'Notícies socials i econòmiques de Montblanc, la Guàrdia dels Prats i la Riba, pels voltants del 1200 . . .', *VIII Assemblea intercomarcal d'estudiosos: Montblanc, 1966* (Montblanc, 1967), pp. 56–7.

[4] The most typical exceptions occur in memorials of small seasonal renders in coin or of small bequests, e.g. *Col. dipl. Huesca*, i, nos. 268, 283, 289, 377, 384; '*Llibre Blanch*' de *Santas Creus*, nos. 122, 157, 158.

[5] Felipe Mateu y Llopis, *La Moneda española (breve historia monetaria de España)* (Barcelona, 1946), pp. 163–7; Gil Farrés, *Moneda española*, pp. 136–7, 158, 164–5, 198–9; Jean Gautier-Dalché, 'L'histoire monétaire de l'Espagne septentrionale . . .', *AEM*, vi (1969), 59–65; and see generally collections such as the *Colección diplomática de Irache*, ed. J. M. Lacarra, 1 vol. to date (Zaragoza, 1965); or cartularies such as those of Santes Creus or Sant Cugat.

steeply increased. Or, rather, transformed: for when a new order emerged in the thirteenth century, many people in Christian Spain were paying taxes to secure the stability of their money.

How this came about in the Pyrenean realms is almost as obscure as the stories of the incipient money-taxes in Normandy and the Île-de-France. Here again some critical phases are undocumented, although our ignorance of the southern development is relieved not only by more surviving texts but also by allusions to lost ones. Among the latter, a record (or records?) dating from 1205 and summarized by Zurita is of outstanding importance. This is the famous proclamation of the *monedaje* by Peter II (1196–1213): the chronicler specifies the incidence of this money-tax in Aragon and Catalonia, and associates the levy with Peter's fiscal desperation.[1] Zurita's account poses problems, as we shall see, but it is so plausible and so fully descriptive of the famous Spanish institution known from later sources that modern historians without exception have regarded it as marking a *terminus a quo*. Yet the imposition described for us plainly evoked the tradition of confirming the coinage, however singular its place in that tradition, and it was heralded by recent precedents not only in the Crown of Aragon but also in Leon. Like other bold acts, it was a culmination as well as a departure.

On its face, Peter's proclamation of 1205 draws our attention to Aragon. Zurita says that it took place in November at Huesca, where the king is known to have had a mint and the cathedral chapter a share in the proceeds of the *iaccensis*.[2] Now public proclamations of coinage or recoinage had been customary in Aragon for generations.[3] In the years after the new coinage of 1174, this custom appears to have been tested and reaffirmed. Some time before 1187, and most likely toward 1180–1, Alphonse II debased his money of Jaca,[4] doubtless so as to create a favourable exchange

---

[1] Gerónimo Zurita y Castro, *Anales de la Corona de Aragón*, 6 vols. (Zaragoza, 1578–85; also 4 vols., 1668–70), book 2, ch. 52 (ed. Antonio Ubieto Arteta *et al.*, 4 vols. to date [Valencia, 1967–72], ii. 144–5, 319). For other accounts, see Ignacio de Asso y del Rio, *Historia de la economía política de Aragón* (Zaragoza, 1798; ed. José Manuel Casas Torres, Zaragoza, 1947), p. 293; Salat, *Tratado de las monedas*, i. 17; Víctor Balaguer, *Historia de Cataluña*, 11 vols. (Madrid, 1885–7), iii. 143; Antonio Rovira i Virgili, *Història nacional de Catalunya*, 7 vols. (Barcelona, 1922–34), iv. 460–1; Luis García de Valdeavellano, *Historia de España . . .*, 5th edn., 1 vol. in 2 parts (Madrid, 1973), part 2, p. 593; cf. pp. 577–9. Neither J. C. Russell, 'The Medieval Monedatge of Aragon and Valencia', *Proc. Amer. Philos. Soc.*, cvi (1962), 483–4, nor Felipe Mateu y Llopis, '*Super monetatico o morabetino . . .*', *Mélanges offerts à René Crozet . . .*, 2 vols. (Poitiers, 1966), ii. 1115, advance beyond Zurita's knowledge of the origins of the *monedaje*.

[2] *Col. dipl. Huesca*, i, no. 301; ii, nos. 576, 713.

[3] For the old *fuero* of Jaca, see above, p. 10. Is it coincidental that of public regulations of the *iaccensis* known for 1128, 1135, 1174, 1197, and 1205, all but one (possibly two) date from November? See 'Documentos', ed. Lacarra, *EEMCA*, ii, no. 56; 'Documentos (1.a serie)', ed. Ubieto, no. 4; '. . . (2.a serie)', no. 33; *Jaca: Documentos municipales, 971–1269*, ed. Antonio Ubieto Arteta (Valencia, 1975), no. 25; Zurita, *Anales*, book 2, ch. 52.

[4] *Cartulario de San Pedro el Viejo*, fos. 101ᵛ, 145ᵛ, cited by Ricardo del Arco, *Huesca en*

for the mint. The protests that resulted led to an accommodation whereby the king confirmed the new coinage under oath, at the reduced alloy of 3 d. fine, for life. By April 1183 scribes at Huesca were stipulating *confirmed* money of Jaca in instruments of pledge or sale; and this requirement, in several variants—*moneta firma regis, moneta bona et firmata, moneta que firmata erit a domino rege in Aragone*—henceforth becomes commonplace.[1]

Some time later Alphonse came to regret this engagement so much that he decided to revoke it. To this end he did what no Spanish ruler had yet done in the matter of coinage: he appealed to the pope. In a letter dated 4 September 1191, Celestine III responded by authorizing the king to restore the quaternal money of Aragon, on the conditions that he 'promise again' to hold that coinage inviolate in future, neither weakening nor strengthening it, and that a tenth of the profits of minting be reserved for the Templars in support of their work in the Holy Land.[2] Probably Alphonse acted upon this dispensation, although we have no record of what must necessarily have taken the form of a proclamation or charter. To judge from Aragonese texts of 1192–6, confirmations were then coming to be expected frequently;[3] and another papal record states unequivocally that the money of Jaca was debased once again at the end of Alphonse's reign (?1195–6).[4] So it seems that the restoration of quaternal coinage was a convenient prelude to the repetition of lucrative debasements. The manipulations were the easier to manage as they entailed no change of type.

---

el siglo XII (*Notas documentales*) (Huesca, 1921), pp. 111–12; *Col. dipl. Huesca*, i, nos. 357, 359, 361, 368, 370; cf. nos. 379, 393, etc. Also ACA, perg. Alfonso I, 442, in an account of 1187 for Lérida, the bailiff is responsible for 1845 s. *iacc.* paid 'eo tempore quo moneta uilescerat', and perg. Alfonso I, 478, account of March 1188 which refers to 'cambium nouorum denariorum [iaccensium]'. These facts were overlooked by Beltrán, 'Los dineros jaqueses', 87, who places the debasement in 1191.

[1] *Col. dipl. Huesca*, i, nos. 379, 393–4, 397, 399, 403; ii, no. 486, 653, 655, 656.

[2] ACA, Canc., Reg. 309, fo. 11 (also ed. Kehr, *PU Spanien*, i. *Katalanien*, part 2, no. 238): 'Celestinus episcopus seruus seruorum Dei dilecto filio illustri regi Aragonensi[?um] salutem et. . . . Cum utilitas publica compendiosa pietate seruatur ut populi terrene potestati subditi publicis beneficiis obligentur et rationi consentaneum creditur et . . . , inde est quod regie deliberationis propositum favore debito amplectentes quo licentiam auctoritatem apostolicam in comutanda moneta Aragonensi humiliter postulauit, ut, quomodo de tribus constat denariis, augmentum recipiat quod de quatuor denariis de cetero componatur, ita ut sub religione iuramenti regia eminentia repromittat quod eadem moneta futuris temporibus inuiolabilis obseruabitur et diminutionem in se non recipiat uel etiam ingrementum, decima parte lucri fratribus militie Templi conferanda ut laborantibus ultra mare necessaria subuentione transmittitur ac illud iuxta regiam comendababilem [*sic*] uoluntatem libere tua celsitudo inpleat plenam auctoritatem duximus concedendam . . . .' The Templars had been entitled to a tithe on all royal revenues since 1143, *DI*, iv. 95, and Kehr, *PU Spanien*, i. *Katalanien*, part 2, no. 182; but that on coinage had not previously been reserved explicitly.

[3] 'Documentos (1.a serie)', ed. Ubieto, no. 18: 'vos convenimus XXVIII sol*idos* optime monete [Iaccensis] . . .' (April 1192); also no. 19; *Col. dipl. Huesca*, ii, no. 486, repayment to be 'monete que tunc erit firmata a domino rege in Aragone', and no. 512.

[4] See next note.

Peter II pursued a similar course. According to the letter *Quanto personam tuam*, issued on his appeal by Pope Innocent III on 5 April 1199, the young Peter, only weeks after his accession, had indiscreetly sworn confirmation of his late father's recently debased coinage, only to find that currency too disruptive to be tolerated. He was therefore dispensed from his oath and ordered to mint a new coinage on the standards of his father's 'best coinage', without recalling the undebased pieces still in circulation.[1]

For all its interest in other respects,[2] this celebrated text has the immediate importance of illuminating the process of confirmation in Aragon. It was the cunning of 'your counsellors, nay rather deceivers', the pope told Peter, 'that induced you to swear, without asking the people's assent, to conserve your father's coinage for a certain time'.[3] Clearly the oath had become the centrepiece of the Aragonese *confirmatio monetae*, as it had also in the Catalan; but whose influence was to determine its substance? Very likely the pope's words echoed those of the king's presumably tendentious appeal, for it is plausible that the young ruler should have been groping for wider support as he assumed political responsibility. Peter's reaction was surely evident in the support of his appeal by 'prelates' and 'many others in your kingdom', as the pope put it, and it can possibly be traced back as far as November 1197. In a significant charter issued 'upon full deliberation with my wise barons at Jaca', the king decreed that his own money of Jaca was henceforth to have exclusive currency in Aragon; further, he enjoined his own officials against alienating royal lands to *infançones*, churches, or persons other than his own men who will do service for them.[4] This *stabilimentum*—so called by Peter himself—represents the king as in a position of strength. Could he have ventured so firm and public a declaration concerning a coinage in bad repute had he not already committed himself to remedy his *faux pas*? Since only sixteen months elapsed between the legislation of Jaca and the letter *Quanto*, it seems most likely that the former presupposed the restored quaternal coinage requested of the pope.[5]

---

[1] *La Documentación pontificia hasta Inocencio III (965–1216)*, ed. Demetrio Mansilla (Rome, 1955), no. 183; also in *PL*, ccxiv. 558–9, and *X* 2. 24. 18; registered in Po, i, no. 656; original text in Appendix, no. 6. The date of Peter's confirmation is determined by the pope's allusion to the campaign with the king of Castile against the Moors; see also Mansilla, no. 184, and cf. Zurita, *Anales de la Corona de Aragón*, book 2, ch. 48 (ed. Ubieto, ii. 132). A probable indication of the value and repute of the debased *iaccensis* may be found in a pledge dated 18 April 1197 which stipulates alternative repayment—'si forte tunc moneta ista fuerit peiorata uel cambiata'—in morabetins evaluated at 9 s. apiece, Barcelona, Biblioteca Central, pergs. Miret y Sans, 4000.

[2] See below, pp. 104, 166–72.

[3] *Documentación pontificia*, ed. Mansilla, no. 183; *PL*, ccxiv. 558 (Appendix, no. 6).

[4] *Jaca: Documentos municipales*, no. 25.

[5] Moreover, Innocent III was on good terms with Peter in September 1198, ACA, Bulas, Inocencio III, leg. 3, no. 1. Against this view it may be argued that, since only ten barons are named as witnesses, the text displays the partisan king promoting the weakened money; cf. Dámaso Sangorrín y Diest-Garcés, *El Libro de la Cadena del concejo de*

Whether the 'full deliberation' with the 'wise barons' answered to the papal notion of popular assent or was merely factional is less clear. Certainly the king (or his adviser–tutors) sought to avoid the appearance of acting arbitrarily. Their enactment was consistent with the publicity customarily given to proclamations of coinage in Aragon.

Presumably Peter II re-established the quaternal coinage, but he may not otherwise have heeded the papal directive. An interpolation in the original of *Quanto personam tuam* arouses the suspicion that he recalled or invalidated his father's undebased coinage.[1] We hear no more of mutations of standard or confirmations in Aragon until the proclamation of 1205. In the meantime, perhaps on the occasion of his coronation at Rome in 1204, Peter introduced a new type bearing a crowned portrait.[2] And he was occupied with the silver coinage of Barcelona in ways that must now be examined.

Alphonse II is not known to have confirmed his money of Barcelona after 1174 (if he did so then), but there are indications of a slightly enlarged coin—its ratio to the alloyed mark falling from 54 s. to 44—toward 1183–4.[3] This coinage, normally evaluated, as was the *iaccensis*, at 7 s. to the morabetin,[4] seems to have corresponded better than its predecessor to the *iaccensis*. The quaternal silver of Barcelona continued under Peter II, who merely altered the legend; it was debased in 1209 and after, perhaps more than once, and restored in March 1213, only to be debased again a few years later.[5] It will be necessary to investigate the relation between these

---

Jaca . . . (Zaragoza [1921]), p. 176 n., who believes that Peter was acting as a minor, in accordance with his father's will; and Beltrán, 'Los dineros jaqueses', 87, who interprets the text as a kind of confirmation of Alphonse's debased money. Probably this text corresponds to the 'Privilegio del rey Pedro II dando facultad a Jaca para labrar moneda', dated 1197, in AM Jaca, cited by Ricardo del Arco, 'Archivos históricos del Alto Aragón', reprint from *Universidad* . . . (Zaragoza, 1929), p. 55.

[1] Cf. *Documentación pontificia*, ed. Mansilla, no. 183, with text below, p. 204, at n. a; and see T. N. Bisson, '"Quanto personam tuam" (*X* 2. 24. 18): its Original Significance', *Proceedings of the Fourth International Congress of Medieval Canon Law* . . . (Vatican City, 1976), p. 239.

[2] See Heiss, *Monedas hispano-cristianas*, ii. 12, and plate 71; Beltrán, 'Los dineros jaqueses', 89–90. On the coronation and its background, Soldevila, *Hist. Catalunya*, 2nd edn., pp. 219–24. (Plate II, no. 18.)

[3] Botet y Sisó, *Monedes catalanes*, ii. 26–7; '*Llibre Blanch*' de Santas Creus, nos. 271, 278; *Cart*. '*Sant Cugat*', iii, nos. 1152, 1159; ACA, perg. Alfonso I, 408. This evidence seems to me decisive against Octavio Gil Farrés, 'The Billon Dineros of Barcelona . . .', *Seaby's Coin and Medal Bulletin* (1957), p. 292, who holds for a single standard under Alphonse II; and against Lluis y Navas (see above, p. 78 n. 2) who proposes a different chronology for the mutations under Alphonse II.

[4] Botet y Sisó, ii. 26, 28; Arxiu Ripoll, text of 1180 (*corr.* 1189), cited by Salat, *Tratado de las monedas*, i. 77; '*Llibre Blanch*' de Santas Creus, no. 259; ACA, pergs. Alfonso I, 417, 567. Cf. p. 86, n. 1, above.

[5] *Chronicon Barcinonense*, ed. Henrique Florez, *España sagrada* . . . , 58 vols. (Madrid, 1747–1918), xxviii (1794), 332–3; *Cart*. '*Sant Cugat*', iii, nos. 1200, 1214, 1237, 1280; ACA, pergs. Pedro I, 13, 64, 76, 164, 320, 377, 381, 382, 384; ACA, Gran Priorato

manipulations and the money-tax established (for Catalonia as well as Aragon) in 1205. But we have first to notice that if the *monedaje* was an innovation in Aragon in 1205, it was not so in Catalonia, where it had recent and unpopular precedents.

On 22 March 1205 at Girona, or so it appears, Peter II issued a comprehensive charter of privileges for Catalonia, acknowledging and renouncing novel exactions—tolls and tallages—and promising to reform the royal administration.[1] Among further provisions is the following: 'Likewise, I promise that I shall not change the coinage of the Barcelonans in all my life, nor allow it to be worsened, nor shall I cause it or the *bovaticum* afterwards to be redeemed. Moreover, I wish and direct [*instituo*] that after my death this coinage shall endure and persevere in the same state and value and shall remain unchanged for one year.' The king's faithful renunciation of the impositions on salt, coinage, and *bovaticum* is apparently secured by the oaths of his Catalan barons Gaufred de Rocabertí and Ramon Galcerà de Pinós.[2]

The interest of this text—a veritable Great Charter for Catalonia—is equalled, unfortunately, by its doubtfulness. It survives only in cartularies of the cathedral church of Girona. Had it gone into general effect, even briefly, it would surely have left some traces in other ecclesiastical collections, if not also in regional custom. Yet it is not likely to have been forged; for while its contents accord perfectly, in some ways exclusively, with its purported date, the fabrication of so comprehensive an act would have been hopeless in Peter's lifetime and for some time thereafter. Conceivably the text records an actual engagement on the part of the king, which was promptly suppressed through destruction of the originals; but more likely, what we have is the copy of a finished draft that was repudiated, much as that of 1174 seems to have been.

Either way the text may be held to demonstrate: (1) that the Catalonian tradition of a sworn *confirmatio monetae* for life remained current, although

... de San Juan, Sección 1, Arm. 17, 321; AC Barcelona, Diversorum C, capsa 20, 2350 (1211); Arxiu Sant Joan de les Abadesses, pergs. s. XIII, 8 ides May 1213 (edition cited below, p. 92, n. 6); Botet y Sisó, ii. 31–5. Cf. Gil Farrés, 'Billon Dineros of Barcelona', pp. 293–4. (Plate III, no. 20.)

[1] Arxiu diocesà Girona, cartulary 'Carles Many', fo. 65 (another copy in AC Girona, MS. 7 ['Llibre verd'], fo. 213ᵛ); text indicated by Villanueva, *VL*, xiii. 158; Joaquím Botet y Sisó, 'Cartoral de Carles Many: index cronológich . . .', *BRABLB*, iv (1908), 322, no. 346; edited and discussed critically by T. N. Bisson, 'An "Unknown Charter" for Catalonia (A.D. 1205)', *Album Elemér Mályusz; Szekesfehérvár-Budapest, 1972* (Brussels, 1976), pp. 61–76.

[2] Arxiu diocesà Girona, 'Carles Many', fo. 65 (Bisson, '"Unknown Charter"', 76): '. . . Promitto similiter quod monetam barchinonensium in tota uita mea non mutem, nec deteriorari permittam, nec faciam ipsum uel bouaticum deinde redimi. Volo etiam et instituo quod post obitum meum hec moneta duret et perseueret in eodem statu et ualore et non mutetur per unum annum. Sciendum tamen est quod hoc instrumentum facio iurare Gaufridum de Rochabertino, R. Gaucerandi super animam meam in salinis tantummodo et in moneta et bouatico . . ..'

it may have been resisted by the count–king; (2) that, accordingly, a ruler's death had become the signal for arbitrary mutations; and (3) that efforts had been made, presumably by Peter himself, to 'redeem' the coinage— that is, to exact payments instead of altering the coinage. On all of these points (and not alone on these) we are carried back to *Cunctis pateat*, whose echoes in 1205 suggest that that text had already found its place in the custom of Catalonia. In 1118, it will be remembered, Count Ramon Berenguer III had sworn his lifetime confirmation of the coinage upon assuming power in Cerdanya (cf. points 1 and 2); and he had spoken of that confirmation, explicitly, as the justification for imposing a payment for that one time only (cf. points 2 and 3).[1] Now if *Cunctis pateat* could have been interpreted as excessively restricting royal rights of coinage, one good reason for Peter's objection to the terms of confirmation recorded in 1205 becomes apparent. But there is yet another parallel between *Cunctis pateat* (or the practice therein specified) and the charter of Girona. Bearing in mind that in 1118 the stable coinage was comprised in the peace, that indeed that imposition was associated with the 'peace of oxen'—which was, precisely, the original meaning of *bovaticum*[2]—it cannot seem accidental that the charter of 1205 renounces the redemption of *moneta* and *bovaticum* in the same clause.

In fact, the only element of the monetary provisions of March 1205 that has no correspondence in *Cunctis pateat* is their use of the word *redimere* (to redeem, ransom, repurchase). In a sense, this discrepancy must be superficial, for it seems manifest that the imposition of 1118 was a purchase of monetary stability in much the same way as the *redempciones monete* (so-called) at Orléans and Étampes in 1137 and 1138. But the term *redimere* probably bore a slightly different, or additional, signification in 1205, one which serves to connect the text in which it appeared with the recent past and serves even to identify an unnoticed levy of a money-tax. One has only to attend to the words, quoted above, and to the syntax of Peter's promise— not to change the coinage for life, nor to allow it to be debased, nor 'to cause it *afterwards* [*deinde*] to be redeemed'—to be reminded of the events under Alphonse II and Peter II. All that is lacking from our previous account to render the correspondence perfect is explicit testimony of recent impositions to secure the coinage, although such exactions might almost be deduced from the language of 1205. As it happens, no deduction

---

[1] *LFM*, ii, no. 691; cf. above, pp. 50–61.

[2] See *Cortes de Cataluña*, i: 1. 67 (Girona, 1188), art. 18: '... promittimus quod de cetero non aliquid exhigamus occasione bovatici vel constitute pacis ab aliquibus hominibus constitutis a Salsis usque Ilerdam et Tortosam et in suis finibus' (i.e. in Catalonia). (See also arts. 5, 6, on *pax bestiarum*.) Was this renunciation, which was not repeated until 1205, in conflict with *Cunctis pateat*? Cf. Soldevila, 'A propòsit del servei del bovatge', 576; and for a fuller discussion, T. N. Bisson, 'Sur les origines du *monedatge*: quelques textes inédits', *Annales du Midi*, lxxxv (1973), 91–8.

is necessary. For there is evidence that in March 1197, alleging the urgent necessity of the Saracen war, Peter had collected a *redemptio monete* in the town of Vich.[1] Now it seems impossible to explain this except as an allusion to a money-tax. Both the verbal context and the political circumstances require this interpretation. Peter had made his accession to the county of Barcelona the occasion for a 'ransom of the coinage': that is, he had claimed the right to a profitable debasement, and then promised to secure the money in exchange for payments such as at Vich. It was as if he were strengthening the coinage for a fee after having debased it; the capability of profiting by strengthening or securing the money *as well as* by debasing it largely explains the Catalan grievance of *redemptio monetae* in 1205. The identity of language and situation virtually proves that those who drafted the charter of Girona had the precedent of Vich in mind. It seems unlikely that the exaction of 1196 or 1197 was confined to Vich, although the bishop and canons of that town may alone have had the discretion to demand a charter of non-prejudice, our only record of the tax, in return. A *bovaticum* at Peter's accession was collected not only in the diocese of Vich but also in neighbouring districts, a fact which likewise helps to explain the charter of 1205.[2] But if the foregoing analysis is correct, we may suppose that the words 'monetam . . . redimi' were used in two slightly different senses in 1205: to denote the sale either of a good or improved coinage at will, or of a lifetime confirmation upon accession. In the first of these senses the imposition was novel and, therefore, unjustified; in the second it had precedents both Catalan and French, including a very recent one. Once again, *Cunctis pateat* springs to mind: was it to be regarded as recording an incident, a precedent, or a custom? Could the people of Catalonia insist on the confirmation of coinage without paying a price? The events of 1196–1205 constituted the test.

In the provisions of Huesca (November 1205), Peter II resolved the issue for his own time by imposing the money-tax in Catalonia and Aragon. He had reserved this prerogative not only by failing or refusing to

---

[1] ACA, perg. Pedro I, 26; ed. Bisson, 'Sur les origines du *monedatge*', 99–100, no. 1, confirmation charter for the church of Vich: '. . . Sciendum autem uolo esse preterea presentibus et futuris quod redemptionem hanc monete quam in uilla Uici inpresenciarum accepi propter ingruentem necessitatem exercitus sarracenorum numquam amplius in casu consimili exigam uel exigere faciam, nec a meis successoribus unquam aliquo tempore uobis aut uestris successoribus exigatur uel demandetur . . ..' If I am not mistaken, the significance of this passage has eluded the writers who have noticed it, e.g. Joaquín Miret y Sans, 'Itinerario del rey Pedro I de Cataluña, II en Aragón (1196–1213)', *BRABLB*, iii (1905–6), 85–6; Botet y Sisó, *Monedes catalanes*, i. 170–1; and Lluis y Navas Brusi, 'Droit monétaire', 227–8. Clearly the king was neither seizing nor confirming the coinage of Vich (Botet y Sisó) nor appropriating its profits (Lluis y Navas). Already in the seventeenth century Moncada, *Episcopologio de Vich*, ed. Collell, i. 521, had rightly read the passage as alluding to a tax, but without recognizing the nature of the tax.

[2] AC Vich, Mensa episcopal, 'Variarum rerum', no. 30; cf. *Cortes de Cataluña*, 1: 1, 84, art. 16.

promulgate the charter of Girona eight months earlier, but also by exclud-
ing the *confirmatio monetae* from the peace legislation; and fiscal urgency
now obliged him to establish generally what had previously been requested
locally and occasionally. Here let us observe that the foregoing discussion
of precedents for the money-tax is not inconsistent with Zurita's account.
What Zurita says is that Peter introduced 'new exactions and tributes',
including the *monedaje*, and that *provisiones* for the latter were made in
November 1205. Now his word *monedaje* obviously translates the Latin
monetaticum; and we have seen that a money-tax called *redemptio monete*
had already been levied in Catalonia. May we assume that these were
simply two expressions for the same imposition? If not, how did they
differ?—and did Zurita mean that the *monedaje*, so called, antedated 1205?

Monetaticum (or *monedaticum*) was not a new word in the Spanish March
in 1205. It designated the ruler's profit from the mint;[1] and just as in
Normandy its application to an imposition surely represented an extension
of its original meaning. Yet it is hard to find it in reference to a tax before
1205. A dispensation from *monetage* at Alquézar (Aragon) in 1083 evidently
has to do with the *montagium*, which is a toll, not the money-tax.[2] Equally
doubtful are the allusions to *monetaticum* (with *bovaticum*) in the exemption
clauses of Catalonian charters dated 1155 and 1203, and to the renunciation
of *monetaticum* in an Aragonese charter of 1179. Of these texts, the first, a
grant by Ramon Berenguer IV to the bishop of Tortosa, is suspect both
internally and externally: the mention of *bovaticum* in 1155 would have
been no less irregular than that of *monetaticum*, nor do these terms normally occur conjointly before the thirteenth century; moreover, the text
comes down to us in a late copy.[3] Alphonse II's charter for the nunnery of
Casbas (1179), which survives in an informal copy of the later thirteenth
century (when the exemption had become valuable), renounces *monetaticum* in a clause to which the word might have been added without com-
punction by a copyist noting the phrase 'nor any obligations which pertain
to the royal majesty' which follows.[4] Finally, the exemption from *monetaticum* and *bouaticum* at Escaro (Conflent) dated Perpignan, 6 January 1203,
although plausible in itself, occurs in a charter of Peter II whose presence

---

[1] See e.g. Count Bernat of Besalú's donation to Santa Maria of Besalú of 'decimam de
ipsa moneta quae fuerit facta in praedicto Bissuldono amodo et usque in sempiternum,
tam de auro quam de argento quam in monetatico et in capite . . .', ed. Marca, *Marca
hispanica*, app., no. 283 (numerous other editions). See also J. F. Niermeyer, *Mediae
latinitatis lexicon minus* (Leiden, 1954–76), p. 703.

[2] *Col. dipl. Huesca*, i, no. 48 ('trasunto del s. XIV'). The exemption of Santa Cilia from
moravetinus (a late term for certain money-taxes) occurs in a manifestly forged privilege
dated August 1098, *Colección diplomática de Pedro I de Aragón y Navarra*, ed. Antonio
Ubieto Arteta (Zaragoza, 1951), no. 52. See also Archivo de Casbas, cajon 10, no. 16.

[3] AM Tortosa, cal. Bisbe y Capitol, 78, no. 8.

[4] Archivo de Casbas, legajo no. 1; ed. (uncritically) by Agustin Ubieto, *Documentos de
Casbas* (Valencia, 1966), no. 8.

in Perpignan at the required time seems doubtful.[1] Yet this charter, whose date as we have it (once again in late copies) may be mistaken, surely post-dates the redemptions of coinage and peace known to have been levied in the diocese of Vich after 1196, one or both of which could well have been collected in Roussillon too. Nevertheless, there is no evidence of the *monetaticum* as such having been collected before November 1205.[2] Even if one or more of the questionable allusions are genuine, it must have been extraordinary to refer to the money-tax as *monetaticum* prior to the provisions of Huesca. The first unequivocal allusion occurs in an account which shows that *monetaticum* was being collected in Catalonia some time before late October 1207,[3] and it is renounced in a charter of franchise dated 5 December 1207.[4] Thereafter it figures very often in privileges, although not all recipients obtained, or thought to insist upon, this right or exemption.[5]

Meanwhile, the term *redemptio monete* (or its variants) fades away. The earliest records of collections, like the privileges, speak only of *monetaticum*.[6] If royal officials preferred this word, their reason, conceivably, was that it connoted a justified profit of coinage while seeming less evocative of recent unpopular exactions. It was better suited to the effort to turn an occasional levy into a general tax in Aragon as well as Catalonia. Yet if the new usage attached to a new institution in or about 1205, the *monetaticum* did not altogether lose the character of a ransom or purchase of the coinage. In Catalonia it remained closely associated with the *bovaticum*, which continued to be thought of as an accession tax.[7] Unfortunately, Zurita's

[1] AD Pyrénées-Orientales, B 8 (from a copy of a copy dated 21 December 1246); an eighteenth-century copy in J 20D, i, no. 170, is said to have been made from the original. Miret y Sans, 'Itinerario del rey Pedro I', 269–70, found nothing 'sospechoso' in this charter, although his evidence showed the king at Tarragona late in December 1202 and again on 13 January 1203.

[2] Nor is there evidence of exemptions in charters known to me. Mateu y Llopis, '*Super monetatico*', 1118, cites an exemption 'en 1196 en Aragón a favor del comendador de la casa de Nuestra Señora de la Merced', but he has misread ACA, Reg. 340, fo. 160. Johannes Vincke, *Staat und Kirche in Katalonien und Aragon während des Mittelalters* (Münster, 1931), p. 98, asserts that Alphonse II freed the abbey of Veruela from *monetaticum*, but I do not find support for this in his cited source, ACA, Reg. 2, fo. 170.

[3] ACA, perg. Pedro I, 271.

[4] ACA, perg. Pedro I, 274.

[5] ACA, pergs. Pedro I, 315, 416, 434–5; Reg. 310, fos. 37, 69; Cart. '*Sant Cugat*', iii, nos. 1275, 1278; Barcelona, Biblioteca Central, MS. 729, ix. 148–9; *Cartas de población*, ed. Font Rius, i: 1, no. 238; Costa y Bafarull, *Memorias de Solsona*, ii. 651; AC Tortosa, perg. priv. reg., 41; AHN, Clero, Poblet, carpeta 2109, 11.

[6] See ACA, perg. Pedro I, 271; AC Barcelona, Div. C, capsa 9, 315 (17 III 1212); Arxiu Sant Joan de les Abadesses, pergs. s. XIII, 8 ides May 1213, ed. Bisson, 'Origines du monedatge', 102–4, no. 4. For the identity of *bovaticum* and *monetaticum*, see below, p. 94.

[7] See privileges cited above, n. 5; also ACA, perg. Pedro I, apéndice 3 (ed. Bisson, 'Origines du *monedatge*', 101, no. 3); and Soldevila, 'A propòsit del servei del bovatge', 573–7. In fact, the expression *redempcio monete* sometimes recurred, as in 1222, *Documentos de Jaime I de Aragón*, ed. Ambrosio Huici Miranda and María Desamparados Cabanes Pecourt, 2 vols. to date (Valencia, 1976), i, no. 33.

account of the provisions of Huesca does not make clear how the *monedaje* was justified. Was it represented as the price of a confirmation for life, in accord with Catalan precedent? Or did the king agree to desist from minting money at all for some fixed term, as was later to be done in Aragon?[1] In the latter case (or some form thereof, for there are other possibilities), the notion of *redemptio* would have subsisted. Moreover, there was a remarkable recent precedent for such an enactment, of which Peter and his officers cannot have been ignorant. In (or possibly before) the *plena curia* celebrated at Benavente on 11 March 1202, Alphonse IX of Leon had relinquished his right to mint for seven years in exchange for the payment of one morabetin per head; and while the transaction was described as a sale—'the lord king sold his money to the peoples of the land'—the payment or imposition was labelled a purchase (*emptio monete*).[2] To 'sell the coinage' was not merely to forgo mutations but even the temptation to manipulate.

Yet Peter II did not simply follow the example of Alphonse IX. His mints, in both Aragon and Catalonia, remained active after 1205, and his silver of Barcelona was altered as early as 1209.[3] In fact, the provisions of Huesca, whatever their justification, cannot have been fully implemented. Zurita remarks that the *monedaje* antagonized nobles and townspeople in Aragon, and it may be that this opposition stifled the imposition there for a while. Next to nothing is said of *monetaticum* in Aragonese texts, including privileges,[4] during the rest of Peter's reign. Nevertheless, the quaternal *iaccensis* was kept unaltered, a policy which, if not somehow compensated, must have betrayed blatant partiality for Aragon. For in Catalonia it was very different. There we hear not only of manipulations, but of collections of *monetaticum*: one or more before October 1207, another which must have nearly coincided with the debasement of 1209, followed by yet another levy in 1213 before Peter's untimely death.[5] But it

[1] See below, pp. 116–17; and cf. next note.

[2] *Córtes de los antiguos reinos de León y Castilla*, 5 vols. (Madrid, 1861–1903), i. 43–4: '. . . cum dominus rex vendidit monetam suam gentibus terre a Dorio usque ad mare, VII annis de singulis pro emptione ipsius, singulos recipiens morabetinos similiter eodem anno, et tempore simili eorum empta fuit moneta in tota Extremadura.' Consult generally Sánchez-Albornoz, 'La primitiva organización monetaria de León y Castilla', 334–42.

[3] *Col. dipl. Huesca*, ii, no. 713; Salat, *Tratado de las monedas*, ii, inst., no. 3; *Chron. Barcinonense*, *España sagrada*, xxviii. 332.

[4] Of five exceptions I have noted in privileges, all from 1210–12, at least three appear to have reference to Catalonia as well as Aragon: *Cartulaire général de l'ordre des Hospitaliers de S. Jean de Jérusalem (1100–1310)*, ed. Joseph Delaville le Roulx, 4 vols. (Paris, 1894–1901), ii, nos. 1325, 1357; Maria Luisa Ledesma Rubio, *La Encomienda de Zaragoza de la Orden de San Juan de Jerusalén en los siglos XII y XIII* (Zaragoza, 1967), apéndice, no. 106. See also ACA, pergs. Pedro I, 434, 435.

[5] ACA, perg. Pedro I, 271; Bisson, 'Origines du *monedatge*', 101–4, nos. 3, 4; AC Barcelona, Div. C, capsa 9, 315 (17. III. 1212); *Privilegis i ordinacions de les valls pirenenques*, ed. Ferran Valls Taberner, 3 vols. (Barcelona, 1915–20), iii. 408–9; ACA, perg. Jaime I, no. 35.

is hardly easier to connect these impositions with Zurita's account of the establishment in 1205 than with the evidence of the coinage itself.

According to Zurita, the taxation instituted in 1205 was imposed upon the property of all except armed knights at the rate of 12 d. per l. of moveables.[1] How land or dwellings were assessed is not made clear, nor is anything said about the term of the imposition, so that it would be difficult to estimate its fiscal importance even if we could reliably estimate the population of payers. What can be said is that the contemplated imposition bore some resemblance to that designated by *Cunctis pateat* in 1118, which included a 12 d. assessment on each pair of oxen; and that (so far as Zurita's description goes) it corresponds precisely with the tariff for the *bovaticum* ordered by Peter III in 1277.[2] These similarities are probably not accidental. For it is quite clear that the earliest Catalonian *monetaticum* of which we have good evidence, just like the tax stipulated in 1118, took the form of a *bovaticum*: meaning, presumably, that it was assessed at least partly on farm animals. Late in 1210, one Ramon de Manresa presented his accounts for a collection of *bouaticum* or *monetaticum*—these terms are employed interchangeably—in Cerdanya, Conflent, and Roussillon during 1209.[3] This levy, having been preceded by a *monedaticum* of uncertain location within Catalonia in 1206 or 1207,[4] probably represented the belated application of the directives of 1205. Moreover the levy contemplated in 1213 was termed *bouaticum et monetaticum*,[5] an expression which, again, appears to designate a single imposition with alternative names. If confusion there was, it must have arisen partly from the circumstances of 1118, but the matter may be more complicated than that. For whereas,

---

[1] Zurita, *Anales de la Corona de Aragón*, book 2, ch. 52, ed. Ubieto, ii. 144–5: 'Este servicio se impuso en Aragón y Cataluña, y se repartió por razón de todos los bienes muebles y raíces que cada uno tenía, sin eximir a ninguno, aunque fuese infanzón o de la orden del Hospital, o de la caballería del Temple, o de otra cualquiere religión. Y tan solamente se eximían los que eran armados caballeros, porque en aquellos tiempos se preciaban más los reyes y grandes señores de la regla y orden de caballería. Pagábanse por los bienes muebles a razón de doce dineros por libra, exceptuándose ciertas cosas. Y era muy grave género de tributo.'

[2] *VL*, xvii. 260–1, text of 24 February 1277 entitled *Modus colligendi bovaticum in tota Cataloniä*: '... Dentur nobis pro pare bovum octo solidi .... Pro exaderiis et bordariis vel scimplicibus ministralibus unusquisque det duos solidos .... De rebus mobilibus duodecim denarii pro libra ...'; cf. *LFM*, ii. 691.

[3] ACA, perg. Pedro I, apéndice 3 (ed. Bisson, 'Origines du *monedatge*', 101–2, no. 3): '... recepi [the king's notary] computum de Raimundo de Minorisa ... de omnibus que receperat pro facto taridarum et de bouatico Cerritanie, Confluentis et Rossilionis quod dictus Raimundus de Minorisa collegit et recepit pro domino rege anno m⁰ cc⁰ nono et de quinque milibus solid⟨is⟩ quos recepit de questia Gerunde et de mille ducentis solidis ... de justiciis Ville Franche Confluentis et de Tuhir ... facta itaque computatione diligenter de taridis et monetatico et denariis Gerunde et Ville Franche et de Tuhir....' This *bovaticum* evidently corresponds to that described by Zurita, *Anales*, book 2, ch. 69 (ed. Ubieto, ii. 210), as the first to be imposed in the Crown of Aragon, and associated with the marriages of Peter's sisters in 1209.

[4] ACA, perg. Pedro I, 271.

[5] Text cited and quoted in n. 2, p. 95.

conceivably, the money-tax was understood to secure the peace of coins just as the cattle-tax secured the *pax bestiarum*, the word *bovaticum*, unlike *monetaticum*, might refer to the mode as well as the object of the levy. Could it be that Peter II sought to disguise, or to justify, his new imposition as a *bovaticum* where, as in the Pyrenees, the interest in rural security persisted among people whose animals were still primary assets, while reserving the word *monetaticum* for those whose interest in coinage and wealth in urban property he now wished to exploit? More probably, the tax was everywhere advertised as purchasing two goods for the price of one, as in 1118. For it seems unlikely that the same people can have been expected to pay two different taxes in 1213, and it is impossible to construe the record of 1210 in that way.

The accounts summarized in the latter record have the importance of furnishing the first solid evidence of receipts for a money-tax in the South. With deductions for a tallage at Girona and for profits of justice at Villefranche-de-Conflent and Thuir, the collector reported a total of 107,774 s. 3 d. for the *bouaticum* or *monetaticum* of Cerdanya, Conflent, and Roussillon.[1] What are we to make of this figure? Three problems are posed: the incidence and *per capita* weight of the tax, the relation of the sum collected to current proceeds of coinage, and its relation to ordinary royal revenues in Catalonia. On the first of these problems, our ignorance of the full terms of assessment in 1205 and 1209, to say nothing of defects in the data of early Catalan demography, precludes any very satisfactory answer. Nevertheless, it can be said that the tax of 1209, and, indeed, its predecessor of 1206–7, probably fell upon freeholders and lords' and king's tenants alike, with exemptions, if any, quite limited, as laid down in 1205. No seigneurial barriers impeded the circulation of the coinage of Barcelona in Catalonia; moreover, the *monetaticum* envisaged in 1213 was to be collected from tenants of the abbot of Sant Joan de les Abadesses.[2] It also seems clear that the tax of 1209 was heavier, probably much heavier, than the agrarian imposition recorded for Cerdanya in 1118. It would have been an exceptionally large and wealthy peasant household that paid more than $2\frac{1}{2}$ or 3 s. in 1118; but when the proceeds of 1209 are divided by the (roughly) estimated total of hearths in Cerdanya–Conflent–Roussillon for that date—some 10,500[3]—there results a figure of 10 s. as the average

---

[1] ACA, perg. Pedro I, apéndice 3 (Bisson, 'Origines du *monedatge*', 101–2, no. 3).

[2] The abbot of Sant Joan was authorized to recover his loan to Dalmau and Guillem de Creixell (royal commissioners) 'de denariis primis bouatici et monetatici, sicut colligere et recuperare uolueritis ad uestram uoluntatem et amonicionem', Bisson, 'Origines du *monedatge*', 103, no. 4.

[3] This figure is based on *DI*, xii. 84–91, 115–29, which enumerates some 12,336 hearths for Cerdanya, Conflent, and Roussillon in 1359; and on the assumption, possibly supported by ACA, perg. Ramón Berenguer IV, 233 (inventories of comital domains in 1151) that the upland population in these areas increased during the later twelfth and

yield per hearth of Peter II's money-tax. This does not necessarily mean that the agrarian assessment—the *bovatge*, strictly speaking—was much heavier in 1209 than in 1118. More likely, the difference lay in a new and more comprehensive property assessment, such as was mentioned by Zurita, devised to tap the prosperity of Perpignan, Villefranche, and other market-towns of these regions. On the other hand, a figure of 10 s. is perfectly conceivable as a hearth tax—even as a tax on rural hearths—as well as an average per hearth in 1209. For in October 1207 some prelates in Old Catalonia had agreed to allow the king to tax their tenants at precisely that rate,[1] and this levy—one of the earliest royal *fogatges*—was surely well known to collectors and inhabitants in the adjoining Pyrenean lands a few months later. Could it be that the *monetaticum* accounted in 1209–10 was itself imposed on hearths alone? Possibly; but the startling identity of assessment rate in 1207 and presumable average yield in 1209, resting as it does upon a questionable estimate of the number of hearths, does not constitute proof.[2] Both the provisions of Huesca and the usage *bouaticum* in 1209 point to a levy on property, or primarily on property, rather than on hearths alone. Our average figure per hearth has only the value of an indicator of magnitude.

To relate the receipts of *monetaticum–bovaticum* in 1209–10 to revenues of coinage is equally baffling. Probably the levy in Cerdanya, Conflent, and Roussillon was conceived as the regional share of a subsidy to be collected throughout Catalonia, for the coinage it was supposed to secure was used by all Catalans. But we do not know what monetary prerogatives were renounced, nor for how long, so that even if an estimate of receipts (actual or anticipated) for all Catalonia could be extrapolated from the figures for Cerdanya–Conflent–Roussillon, we should not know how to interpret it. What does seem likely is that the renewed mintings and manipulations in 1209 represented a breach of understanding: the taxation of Catalonia was not yet complete, nor is there evidence of Catalonian (or Aragonese) periods of recoinage as short as three or four years. For the new coinages, some records have luckily survived. One of these suggests that the king's receipts from the mint averaged 21,051 s. per year between 1209

thirteenth centuries. Perpignan must have been growing rapidly toward 1200, although the evidence is unsatisfactory; see *LFM*, ii, no. 793, and R. W. Emery, *The Jews of Perpignan in the Thirteenth Century* ... (New York, 1959), p. 12.

[1] ACA, pergs. Pedro I, 265–8; Arxiu diocesà, Girona, 'Carles Many', fos. 51–2; AC Vich, cal. 37 (Privilegis i Estatuts, iv), no. 68. Moreover, as I hope to show elsewhere, there is reason to infer that the proceeds of the *bovaticum* accounted in 1200 averaged around 8 to 10 s. per hearth.

[2] One of those who consented in October 1207 was the prior of Corneilla-de-Conflent (perg. Pedro I, 268), which suggests the possibility of some identity of hearth tax and *bovaticum–monetaticum*. But there is nothing else in the texts cited above, n. 1, to confirm this. It may be that the tenants of Corneilla were spared when the collectors of *bovaticum* appeared, or that the prior's consent was only then redeemed.

and 1212.[1] Now this amount, itself probably exceptionally large, was less than one-fifth the returns from the *bovaticum* or *monetaticum* of Cerdanya, Conflent, and Roussillon. If proceeds of the money-tax elsewhere were at all comparable, then the new imposition must have been worth far more— indeed, disproportionately more—than the cumulative revenues of coinage over a long period of years. So, notwithstanding the defects of our evidence and calculations, it appears that the earliest known *monetaticum*, like the *monetagium* and *tallia panis et vini* in the North, cannot have been pegged very closely to the normal profits of mints. But the discrepancy in Catalonia was of a different sort, for there the mint revenue and money-tax alike seem to have formed a more significant proportion of royal revenues than they did in Normandy or France.

Even for this critical computation, we are reduced to conjecture. No study of the revenues of Alphonse II or his son has yet been made, nor is it likely that the abundant records, when systematically examined, will yield very reliable figures of over-all receipts.[2] Yet there is reason to suppose that a levy on Catalonia on the scale of returns known for its east Pyrenean corner might have approximated, if it did not greatly exceed, a year's revenue from royal domains, rights of lordship, tallage, and coinage. To make the point more reservedly and securely, the receipts from Cerdanya– Conflent–Roussillon alone—over 107,000 s.—must have represented a very substantial proportion of the over-all royal income of Catalonia in 1209 or 1210. Moreover, the average of proceeds from the mint of Barcelona during 1209–12 was far larger than the revenues from any single bailiwick or other fixed domain resource.[3]

These estimates are consistent with evidence that the count–kings relied more heavily on their coinages in times of fiscal urgency than did their northern contemporaries. Zurita connected the settlement of the *monedaje* with the king's insolvency, as we have seen. It is true that Peter II travelled incessantly during the years 1203–5; he married Maria de Montpellier, planned an invasion of Mallorca, and was crowned at Rome, where he promised to pay the pope 250 mazmudins a year.[4] But these enterprises, once the invasion was given up, were only routinely beyond his means, so to speak, nor was the money-tax yet available to pay for them. His paramount special resources in these years were a loan of 150,000 s. *melg.*,

---

[1] ACA, perg. Pedro I, 436; the Templar's tithe 'ex lucro monete Barchinone' amounted to 8,870 s. for the period 2 February 1208–25 November 1212; see also pergs. Pedro I, 445, 455.

[2] There survive accounts for individual domains and collections, but no comprehensive annual statements (for which the king probably had little use); see my forthcoming edition of 'Fiscal Accounts of Catalonia . . . (1151–1213)'.

[3] Cf. ACA, perg. Pedro I, 436, with pergs. Alfonso I, 435, 568, for example. These estimates are based on studies to be published in 'Fiscal Accounts of Catalonia'.

[4] Miret y Sans, 'Itinerario del rey Pedro I', 270–84, 365–74; *Documentación pontificia*, ed. Mansilla, no. 306; Soldevila, *Hist. Catalunya*, 2nd edn., pp. 221–8.

secured on Millau and other places in Rouergue and Gévaudan, by Raimond VI of Toulouse in April 1204;[1] his acquisition of Montpellier a few weeks later;[2] and a gift of 42,000 s. *barc.* from the bishop and townsmen of Vich in April 1205.[3] In fact, Peter seems to have been in better financial condition just before the provisions of Huesca (November 1205), which were not hurriedly or completely put into effect, than during his first years as king. His father's will had seriously entangled the revenues of domains for payments, alms, and foundations, amounting to some 100,000 s. in Catalonia alone;[4] and debts of Alphonse were still outstanding in 1200, if not, indeed, much later.[5] Peter was able to capitalize on his own novelty by selling his confirmations of privilege or renunciations of right;[6] but these sales cannot have fully compensated for the suspension of so much of his ordinary revenue. Fortunately, his proceeds of coinage were intact, and it is precisely at his accession that the new money-tax is first attested. If the *redemptio monete* of Vich was also collected elsewhere (and *a fortiori* if it was identical with the concurrent *bouaticum*), its proceeds must have constituted the young king's chief extraordinary resource.

That Alphonse II had reserved the revenues of coinage was not accidental. For him, too, they had been a mainstay; and the frequent manipulations of his later years, which still echoed in the general charter of 1205, could probably be associated with extraordinary expenditures if they could be dated more exactly. The debasement of the *iaccensis* in his last year or so apparently coincided with the expedition to Compostella through which Alphonse aspired to leadership in a new Hispanic coalition against the Moors.[7] But to alter or redeem the coinage was merely to exceed the ordinarily lucrative revenues of the mints. In March 1175, 'impelled by necessity'—possibly the financing of an expedition to Navarre—Alphonse had obtained the bishop's tithe of the coinage of Barcelona for nine months,[8] just the period, presumably, when the new coinage would have been most abundantly produced. Now a revenue whose tithe can have

---

[1] *HL*, viii, no. 128 (or *LTC*, i, no. 756, with date corrected; cf. Miret y Sans, 'Itinerario', 273–6).   [2] *LTC*, i, nos. 717, 718, 721.

[3] AC Vich, cal. 37 (Privilegis i Estatuts, iii), 57 *bis* (Junyent, *Jurisdiccions i privilegis de Vich*, no. 57); see also Bisson, 'An "Unknown Charter" for Catalonia'.

[4] *DI*, iv. 395–411.

[5] ACA, perg. Pedro I, 84. The early *monetatica* of James I were used to redeem pledges, *Colección diplomática del concejo de Zaragoza*, ed. Angel Canellas Lopez, 2 vols. (Zaragoza, 1972), i, no. 52.

[6] *LFM*, ii, nos. 797, 801, 802; AD Pyrénées-Orientales, J 20 D, i (cartulary of Arlessur-Tech), no. 43; cf. *Privilèges et titres . . . de Roussillon et de Cerdagne*, ed. Bernard Alart (Perpignan, 1874), p. 84; *Cartas de población*, ed. Font Rius, i: 1, no. 207; ACA, perg. Pedro I, 26.

[7] Antonio Ubieto Arteta, 'La peregrinación de Alfonso II de Aragón a Santiago de Compostela', *EEMCA*, v (1952), 438–52; Ventura, *Alfons 'el Cast'*, pp. 260–5.

[8] AC Barcelona, 'Libri antiquitatum', i, fo. 191 (no. 517; Mas, *Notes històriques*, xi, no. 1992).

helped to meet a king's necessity was no negligible amount, something which Peter II likewise understood when in 1211 he repeated his father's agreement with the bishop of Barcelona.[1] At that time, the tenth on the mint of Barcelona was running around 2,340 s. per year.[2] As far back as 1148, Ramon Berenguer IV had reserved the *moneta* and justice when pledging practically all his income from Barcelona for a loan to meet military expenses.[3]

It is easier to demonstrate the fiscal importance of the count–kings' coinages (or, at least, of that of Barcelona) than to explain it. But several factors seem pertinent. First, the circulation of coined money was surely more swift and voluminous in many parts of Catalonia and Aragon than in the Capetian homelands. While tribute from the Saracen border-realms was declining, Alphonse II exploited silver mines in Aragon and, probably, Catalonia.[4] Money markets and capital enterprise could found be at Tarragona, Lérida, Barcelona, and Vich, to name no other places, by the end of the twelfth century.[5] Second, the comital–royal demesnes were less lucrative than those of Normandy or the Île-de-France. As new frontiers were opened to the west and south, the grasp on peasant tenancies in Old Catalonia, never heavily burdened, was relaxed for a time.[6] It is true that the count–king's protectorate over free peasants expanded,[7] but obligations continued moderate and subjection light in comparison with conditions prevailing on the great northern farmlands. Third, and doubtless in significant correlation with this second factor, the count–kings were slow to improve their administrative methods. One has only to examine their fiscal

[1] AC Barcelona, 'Libri antiquitatum', i, fo. 191 (Mas, xii, no. 2450). Both in 1174 and 1211, the bishop was allowed 4 d. per mark. In April 1213, Peter felt obliged to ask for the bishop's tithe of coinage for life, agreeing, however, to raise the episcopal allowance to 6 d. per mark, 'Libri antiquitatum', i, fo. 192 (Mas, xii, no. 2532).

[2] Calculation based on ACA, perg. Pedro I, 436.

[3] Text from AC Barcelona, quoted by Joaquím Miret y Sans, 'Los ciutadans de Barcelona en 1148', *BRABLB*, ix (1921), 137–9.

[4] Ramón de Huesca, *Teatro histórico de las iglesias del reyno de Aragón*, 9 vols. (Pamplona, 1780–1807), ix. 491–2, cited by Caruana, 'Itinerario de Alfonso II', 210; *LFM*, i, no. 22; cf. Miret y Sans, 'Itinerario del rey Pedro I', 85; Salat, *Tratado de las monedas*, i. 5–6.

[5] Agustí Altisent, 'Comerç marítim i capitalisme incipent. Episodis de la vida econòmica d'un matrimoni tarragoní (1191–1203)', *Miscel·lània històrica catalana* . . . (Poblet, 1970), 161–80; idem, 'Una societat mercantil a Catalunya a derreries del segle XII', *BRABLB*, xxxii (1967–8), 45–65; Josep Lladonosa i Pujol, *Història de Lleida*, i (Tàrrega, 1972), 253–79; A.-E. Sayous, 'Les méthodes commerciales de Barcelone au XIIIe siècle . . .', *Estudis universitaris catalans*, xvi (1931), 155–98; Arcadi García, 'Origens del mercat de Vich', *Ausa*, v (1964–7), 129–34.

[6] See ACA, pergs. Ramón Berenguer IV, nos. 233, extrainventario 2502; cf. Joaquím Miret y Sans, 'Pro sermone plebeico', *BRABLB*, vii (1913), 163–4; Eduardo de Hinojosa, *El Régimen señorial y la cuestión agraria en Cataluña durante la edad media* (Madrid, 1905), pp. 80, 86–8, 91–2, and ch. 5; Pierre Vilar, *La Catalogne dans l'Espagne moderne* . . . 3 vols. (Paris, 1962), i. 381–92.

[7] e.g. *LFM*, i, no. 396; *Cartas de población*, ed. Font Rius, i: 1, no. 230.

records to discover what 'necessities' impelled them to exploit the coinage (among other devices). Lacking central receipts or treasury, they borrowed freely for immediate needs, often assigning exploitations of land and revenue toward repayment, and they relied on local surpluses and exchanges to meet routine expenses.[1] It was symptomatic that the very collector who accounted for 107,774 s. in *bouaticum–monetaticum* in 1210 also reported expenditures amounting to 112,231 s. So domestic a finance, confusing and wasteful, was congenial to rulers noted for their courtly probity and largesse. It was viable because the fisc was not only ample, but expanding: Alphonse II's resumption of Roussillon (1172) and Pallars Jussà (1192), for example, was matched by Peter II's acquisition of Montpellier (1205) and Urgell (1209).

Nevertheless, the intensified exploitation of coinages and the initiation of money-taxes plainly manifested a more systematic effort to meet increasing fiscal need. Some of the pressures were not peculiar to Aragon–Catalonia: more costly military operations, expanded entourages, probably some increase in prices. For all his ambitions, Peter II could not match the success of Philip Augustus. But Peter's *monedatges*, assigned like the *bovatges* to vicar-collectors who worked with inventories of domain and accounted in writing, opened the way to exploiting new resources. Tallages became more frequent and more comprehensive;[2] charters of non-prejudice, which were seldom gratuitous, more numerous.[3] It was no fault of the improved method that Guillem Durfort's balance for *monedaticum* in October 1207 showed such a deficit as to make it necessary to negotiate new hearth taxes.[4] The Templars, having long enjoyed a tithe on the count–king's revenues, were by now much engaged in royal fiscal administration, and the survival of their accounts for the coinages of 1208–12 shows that the mint of Barcelona was then being supervised with care. Peter's spectacular last years—his expeditions to Valencia (1210), Las Navas de Tolosa (1212), and Muret (September 1213)—certainly strained his resources. The debased billon of 1209, while not replacing the old quaternal issues, must have obliterated the *confirmatio monetae* at Barcelona; not only ternal but even 'double' (*duplenus* or *doblench*) issues are attested for these years.[5]

[1] e.g. ACA, pergs. Ramón Berenguer IV, apéndice 6 and 9; pergs. Alfonso I, 59, 126; Pedro I, 201, 271.

[2] See e.g. ACA, pergs. Ramón Berenguer IV, 233; Alfonso I, 303; Bisson, 'Origines du monedatge', 101–2, no. 3; *DI*, iv. 403.

[3] See e.g. texts cited above, p. 98 n. 6.

[4] ACA, Pedro I, 271; the urgency was undoubtedly evident before the date of this account (31 October 1207): see *Privilèges de Roussillon*, ed. Alart, pp. 91–2; ACA, pergs. Pedro I, 265–8.

[5] See Bisson, 'Origines du *monedatge*', 103, no. 4, and p. 97 n. 30; AC Barcelona, Div. C, capsa 14, 1264 (6 XII 1212); ACA, pergs. Pedro I, 164, 200, 320. In fact, it was normal to mint coins of less than full weight or alloy with the rest: see above, p. 76; Botet y Sisó, *Monedes catalanes*, ii. 29–30; and for 'boconaylla', or billon, see *Col. dipl. Huesca*, ii, no. 576; *Chron. Barcinonense, España sagrada*, xxviii. 332.

These were accompanied by measures intended to maximize revenues of the mint,[1] by vast loans, including one from mint-men at Jaca,[2] and by new subsidies from churches and towns.[3] In March 1213 the quaternal silver was re-established, together with talk of a compensatory tax to follow;[4] three weeks later, on what was to be his last visit to Barcelona, the king was obliged to revise his minting agreement with the bishop on the latter's terms;[5] and on the eve of Peter's fatal expedition, the profits of coinage seem to have been declining.[6]

It may seem difficult to attribute constitutional significance to these monetary events in Catalonia and Aragon. Was it not a story of haughty prerogative merely exacerbated by fiscal urgency? The provisions of Huesca can hardly have sprung from 'full deliberation', as did the pro-clamation of Jaca in 1197, if they encountered the Aragonese opposition mentioned by Zurita; while of extant charters of confirmation, two of those designed for the count–kings were apparently shelved. But the tide was running against the kind of arbitrariness that marked Peter's later years. His behaviour in Aragon at the start of his reign was such as to acknowledge the right of the magnates to be consulted on the coinage. In Catalonia, while neither Peter nor his father admitted the monetary customs to their constitutions of the peace and truce, they must have found it hard to reconcile the repeated ransoms of coinage or *bovatge* with the *Usatges*. If nothing more, the baronial scheme of 1205 showed that Catalans had not given up the hope of achieving a stabilized coinage gratis in keeping with *Moneta autem* and the programme of Lérida (1155); and even if *Cunctis pateat* could be interpreted otherwise, it unquestionably limited the royal monetary prerogative. Popular discontent with redemptions of coinage, explicit in the charter of February 1205, may probably be discerned in other royal privileges renouncing exactions in general terms.[7] Moreover,

---

[1] AC Barcelona, 'Libri antiquitatum', i, fo. 191 (Mas, *Notes històriques*, xii, nos. 2448, 2450); cf. perg. Div., A, 1115 (26 XII 1211).

[2] ACA, pergs. Pedro I, 316, 325, 361, 377, 441; Beltrán, 'Dineros jaqueses', 90; the Templars' share in the coinage of Jaca was regulated at Toledo, 15 June 1212, AHN, Cod. 597B, fo. 221, indicated by Manuel Magallón, 'Los Templarios de la Corona de Aragón. Índice de su cartulario . . .', *BRAH*, xxxii (1898), 458, no. 45.

[3] AM Tarragona, pergs. (Lérida, 10 kal. February 1208–9); AM Cervera, pergs. (same date); AC Vich, cal. 37 (Privilegis i Estatuts, ii), 38 (Toulouse, 24 January 1213). A flurry of privileges for Catalan churches issued from Lérida in the third week of March 1211 points to some financial consideration: *VL*, v. 273–5; AC Tarragona, cartulary-roll; *Marca hispanica*, app., no. 498 (cf. ACA, perg. Pedro I, 385); AC Girona, Privilegis reials, 7.

[4] *Chronicon de rebus alibi notis*, *VL*, viii. 230; and texts of 17 March 1213, ACB, Div. C, cap. 9, 315 (17 III 1212), and 8 May 1213 as quoted above, p. 95 n. 2.

[5] AC Barcelona, 'Libri antiquitatum', i, fo. 193 (Mas, *Notes*, xii, nos. 2532, 2533).

[6] ACA, perg. Pedro I, 445, 455.

[7] See e.g. AC Vich, cal. 9, charter of (Perpignan) April 1196 (Junyent, *Jurisdiccions i privilegis de Vich*, no. 48), AM Vich, Privilegis, ix, no. 172 (Junyent, no. 57); AM Tarragona, pergs. (Lérida, 10 kal. February 1208–1209).

the coinages of Jaca and Barcelona were becoming more fully public institutions. In Aragon scribes allude to the king's money in formulas—such as *moneta bona et firmata*—that signify legitimacy and quality; while in Catalonia, where the work of the moneyers was being better protected and better supervised, notaries were required to inscribe the value of sous of Barcelona in terms of the mark in instruments relating to monetary transactions.[1] But it is the solemn charters, whether enacted or not, that most remarkably disclose the enlarging sphere of associative interest in coinages of the Spanish March. The publicity and sworn confirmation of 1118 survived not only in the recommendations of 1155, 1174, and March 1205, but also in the solemn engagement effected in the bishop's name before a diocesan assembly at Vich in 1174; moreover, the terms on which the restored coinage of Vich was exploited were made public in the charters of 1174 and 1176. Nor did the count–kings, after all, make a perfect record of opposition to such engagements. Whatever may have happened in the past, it is certain that in 1210, when he was not only minting debased silver at Barcelona but also collecting a money-tax, Peter II confirmed the coinage of Agramunt (the comital money of Urgell). The king's acquisition of Urgell in 1209, by cession of its widowed and threatened countess, was a windfall, so that Peter could be satisfied with the ordinary revenues of this reputable coinage, apparently then at parity with his quaternal currencies,[2] among the other fiscal rewards. Sworn for life (along with other provisions) by two barons on behalf of the ruler, the confirmation was worded in language very reminiscent of the earlier Catalonian charters. It was an engagement to conserve the present coinage and to mint no other unless of the same standards.[3]

Clearly, the confirmation of coinage had become the norm, a moral imperative if not quite the law, in Catalonia and Aragon. This was not merely in the interest of the church, it was probably the result of clerical urging. While the ecclesiastical impulse in this matter was popular, it does

---

[1] Salat, *Tratado de las monedas*, ii. 2–3; *Chronicon de rebus alibi notis*, *VL*, viii. 230; *Chronicon Barcinonense*, in *Marca hispanica*, col. 755: 'XI. Kal. Madii anno MCCXIII. fuit injunctum omnibus Notariis Barchinonae quòd ponerent in cartis ad XLIV ff. marcham argenti.'

[2] See e.g. ACA, perg. Pedro I, 155.

[3] ACA, perg. Pedro I, 355 (*DI*, viii. 106–9): '... uobis uniuersis hominibus Acrimontis ... Conuenimus etiam uobis quod monetam acrimontensem non mutemus nec uiciemus nec mutari nec uiciari sinamus in aliquo nec cudamus nec cudi permittamus unquam quandiu nobis fuerit uita comes nisi sub ea lege et pondere in quibus modo eam consistere constat.' See also Botet y Sisó, *Monedes catalanes*, i. 148, 150; and for the coins, pp. 160–1. The coinage of Agramunt, which had not enjoyed exclusive circulation in Urgell, seems to have occasioned little anxiety among persons negotiating through instruments; see e.g. AC La Seu d'Urgell, 'Liber dotaliorum', i. 255 (259)[r]; pergs. 7 ides June 1185, 8 ides June 1187, 17 kal. April 1176–7; *Cart. Tavernoles*, no. 74; AHN, Clero, Poblet 2040, nos. 9, 19; and, for an exceptional reservation of the 'best coinage' current in the county of Urgell in case of mutation of the money of Agramunt, Barcelona, Biblioteca Central, pergs. Miret y Sans, 3170.

not appear that prelates were yet much concerned about counsel or consent in monetary matters. Their interest, very like the clerical influence on the monetary regulations at Melgueil a generation earlier, lay in legitimacy, publicity, and oaths of confirmation. Nor does the parallel end there. For just as had happened in Languedoc, so now in Pyrenean Spain the conservation of coinage came into the purview of popes as well as bishops. This development was foreshadowed during the first Spanish legation of the cardinal–deacon Jacintus (1154–5), who presided over the council of Lérida which sought to impose a lifetime confirmation of coinage upon Alphonse VII.[1] Jacintus returned to Spain, as an aged man, in 1172, and in the following year he held another council at Lérida, whence many of the statutes of 1155 were reissued.[2] The monetary provision, having become obsolete, was among those dropped, but since it could easily have been recast to fit the altered circumstances and since, moreover, meridional coinages were then coming to be quite generally regulated, the decision to omit it probably followed some discussion of the *confirmatio monetae*. If we could be sure—and it is at least very likely—that Bishop Pere attended this legatine council in 1173, as he all but certainly did that of 1155, then we could plausibly relate his charter of Vich (December 1174) to a moral–constitutional discussion in which he had been repeatedly associated with a legate, the same legate, of the Roman Church. For if that discussion took place at Lérida in 1173, it must have continued at Zaragoza in January 1174, where not only Pere de Redorta (and most of the other bishops of Catalonia) but the cardinal–legate himself attended the young king as he married and proclaimed a new coinage. The significance of this juncture now becomes very clear. Yet the ecclesiastical position remains as obscure to us as it was conceivably critical in 1174. Was it the failure—or the restraint—of the fathers at Lérida that emboldened Alphonse to avoid confirming his new *iaccensis* and then to scrap his draft-confirmation for Catalonia? What was Jacintus's role?[3] At the very least he must have sympathized with the sentiment that culminated in Bishop Pere's

---

[1] Above, p. 82.

[2] The text may be read in *España sagrada*, xlviii. 301–7; see also ibid., xlvii. 150–2; Johannes Leineweber, 'Studien zur Geschichte Papst Cölestins III' (diss., Jena, 1905), pp. 26–32; Gerhard Säbekow, 'Die päpstlichen Legationen nach Spanien und Portugal bis zum Ausgang des XII. Jahrhunderts' (diss., Berlin, 1931), pp. 48–51, 53–5 (but Säbekow does not mention the council of 1173); Piero Zerbi, *Papato, impero e 'respublica christiana'*, *dal 1187 al 1198* (Milan, n.d. [1955]), p. 75; and Paul Kehr, *Das Papsttum und die Königreiche Navarra und Aragon bis zur Mitte des XII. Jahrhunderts* (Berlin, 1928), p. 52 (Spanish translation, *EEMCA*, ii. 173–4). Although its date has not been precisely determined, this council almost certainly antedated the festival at Zaragoza of 18 January 1174.

[3] Conceivably, the legate (if not the pope) regarded the exhortation realistically as incapable of being enforced and likely to antagonize the king. In June 1174, Alexander III appealed to Alphonse to make restitution to San Salvador de Leire, including 1,000 s. (of revenue?) granted by Peter I, *PU Spanien*, ii. *Navarra und Aragon*, part 2, no. 136.

confirmation-charter eleven months later. Certainly, neither king nor legate can have forgotten the circumstances of 1173–4, for when Alphonse appealed, many years later, for a pontifical dispensation to restore his quaternal coinage in Aragon, the pope who responded was none other than the former legate Jacintus, recently elected as Celestine III, although nearing ninety. Anxious about reconciling a new mutation with a past confirmation, the king must have contacted Celestine, as an old acquaintance, almost at once upon hearing of his election. The pontifical letter of 1191, in authorizing the sworn confirmation of a quaternal coinage, probably gave expression to one of Celestine's old-standing recommendations in Spain; it also revealed his renewed solicitude for the Templars and the crusade.[1] Yet the initiative remained with the monarchs. Alphonse's *iaccensis* was again debased at the time of his death, and there is no evidence that the pope knew or noticed this until Peter II sought dispensation from his hasty confirmation of the weakened money. The pontifical jurisdiction over oaths formed the basis of *Quanto personam tuam* as well as of Celestine III's letter; where Innocent III's text significantly differed was in its reference to faithful counsel, with its implication that the 'assent of the people' was required for confirmations of coinage. Of notions then current in the Pyrenean realms, only the precedent echoing from *Cunctis pateat* could approach such a doctrine. But it was not Innocent's purpose to advocate a popular restraint on monetary prerogatives; *Quanto* was consistent with former papal utterances on confirmation without, as we shall see, going beyond them. Ironically, the immediate effect of the letter was to free Peter II to do as he pleased with his coinage, and he was not again to furnish occasion for papal direction on monetary matters.

E. *Toulouse and Quercy (1205–1212)*

As time passed, Peter II's ambitions were fatefully woven into the destiny of Occitania. And there, too, the confirmation of coinage found new expression, first at Toulouse on the eve of the Albigensian Crusade, and then at Cahors in the aftermath of its first fury. Were these events the reverberation of recent experience in the Spanish March?

In July 1205 Count Raimond VI of Toulouse (1194–1222) confirmed his *septena* coinage, under oath, for his lifetime. His promise not to alter or diminish in alloy or weight the coinage that had been established at the time of his father's mutation was expressed in a charter of cession and

---

[1] See above, p. 85 n. 2. The aged legate had made at least one more trip to Spain in the years just preceding his election, Leineweber, 'Studien', p. 32. Pope Celestine's confirmation to the Templars of San Juan de Monzón was dated 27 August 1191, about a week before the dispensation to the king, *PU Spanien*, ii. *Navarra und Aragon*, part 2, no. 185. See generally Zerbi, *Papato, impero e 'respublica christiana'*, pp. 148–67.

donation to all the churches of Toulouse, all the consuls and all inhabitants within and without the walls of the city. The ceremony took place in the cloister of Sainte-Marie de la Daurade in the presence of the consuls and many notables of the town.[1]

Merely to describe this act is to recognize that it constitutes something dramatically new in our story. Written by order of the elected consuls of Toulouse, it was preserved in a consular cartulary which itself, perhaps significantly, was initiated in 1205.[2] By notarial custom, it listed the consuls, somewhat as Aragonese royal scribes listed the territorial lords, as if to define the structure of operative authority. Obviously, the consuls acted in collaboration with the local clergy. The churches of Saint-Étienne, the Daurade, and Saint-Sernin had pride of place among the beneficiaries, and the religious solemnity of the count's ritual oath is duly clear. Yet there is nothing to suggest that the bishop participated in a rite which was elsewhere of especial interest to the reformed episcopate, nor is this surprising in view of the failings of the incumbent Raimond de Rabastens, who was about to be deposed.[3] While the legend PAX continued to appear in the immobilized types,[4] the coinage did not figure in local conciliar legislation at the turn of the thirteenth century. The confirmation of the Toulousan money was the work of a new patriciate that had come to power in 1202, imposed itself on the surrounding countrysides by force of arms, and assumed virtual control of municipal and commercial regulation.[5] It

---

[1] AM Toulouse, AA 1 ('Cartulaire du Bourg'), no. 72, ed. Limouzin-Lamothe, *Commune de Toulouse*, pp. 403-4: 'Notum sit omnibus hominibus hanc presentem cartam legentibus vel audientibus, quod ego Raimundus ... propria ac spontanea voluntate, concedo et confirmo et ... dono ecclesie sancti Stephani et ecclesie beate Marie et ecclesie sancti Saturnini ceterisque omnibus tolosanis ecclesiis et consulibus et omnibus urbanis et suburbanis Tolose, tam presentibus quam futuris, et omni populo tolosano, quod ego nec aliquis nec aliqua in vita mea illam monetam septenam tolosanam, quam dominus comes Ramundus, pater meus qui fuit, constituit tunc temporis, quando monetam tolosanam mutavit, illam videlicet quam Ildefonsus, pater eius qui fuit, constituerat, nunquam mutem nec minuam eius legalitatem nec pondus ullo modo. Et ut hoc ita firmiter habeatur ... hec omnia per fidem meam affirmo et, tactis sacrosanctis Evangeliis, corporaliter iuro. Hoc autem mandavit et confirmavit prefatus dominus comes Ramundus, mense Iulii, in claustro beate Marie, regnante Philippo rege Francorum et eodem Ramundo tolosano comite et Ramundo episcopo, anno M°CC°V . . . . Erant autem tunc consules Willelmus Arnaldus de Montetotino . . . . Huius tocius rei sunt testes ipsi prenominati consules et . . . [18 notables are named] et plures alii qui ibi aderant et Petrus Sancius qui, mandato consulum, cartam istam scripsit.

[2] Limouzin-Lamothe, pp. 3-4; and text quoted in preceding note. The record plainly post-dates the enactment of July 1205 that it memorializes (*concedo . . . confirmavit . . . in claustro*), although there is no good warrant for the date 1207 given in the (incomplete) copy of *HL*, viii, no. 135, from an unidentified source.

[3] Guillaume de Puylaurens, *Chronique*, ed. Jean Duvernoy (Paris, 1976), cc. vi, vii, pp. 40-4.

[4] Dieudonné, *Manuel de numismatique*, iv. 235; Pierfitte, 'Monnaies des comtes de Toulouse', 56-9.

[5] AM Toulouse, AA 1, ed. Limouzin-Lamothe, nos. 9, 21, 16-18, 13, 23, 29, 59, 60, 38-41, 30, 24, 57, 62, 64, 67, 65, 61, 68, 66, 63, 70, 69, 53, 52; Mundy, *Political Power in*

was among the climactic events in a surge of civic initiative that had all but overwhelmed the count.

Nevertheless, it was less important in practice than in law. If the consuls and people paid nothing for it, as seems certain in the circumstances, it cannot have cost Raimond VI much either. For the counts of Toulouse had traditionally held their coinage in better respect than some contemporaries elsewhere. The *septena* established in the later 1170s not only remained intrinsically superior to the regional currencies regulated at about the same time, but was held steady even as those in Aragon and Catalonia were fluctuating. While concerned as in many parts of the South to stipulate coinages in general use, people of the county of Toulouse betrayed little anxiety about the stability of their lord's money toward 1200.[1] By that time the count no longer had full control of the mint; at least a quarter of its proceeds was in other hands, and probably had long been so, a situation in which he might have found it difficult to manipulate the coinage, even had he wished, for many years before the confirmation of 1205.[2]

In all this there is little to remind us of the Catalonian experience. Neither in its verbiage nor in its allusion to the assembly does the charter of 1205 seem very familiar. The assertiveness of the consuls was clearly exceptional. Yet for all its originality, this impressive event at Toulouse cannot safely be dissociated from its Pyrenean setting. As at Vich in 1174, as also at Agramunt in 1210, the interest of the county was represented in some sense in the assembly at Toulouse.[3] That the scribal forms differed from those used elsewhere may simply reflect the independence of a proud new corps of notaries in these years.[4] In its substance—the securing of the coinage in weight and alloy for life—the Toulousan enactment conforms perfectly to the Catalonian programme; so too, of course, does the oath, even if Raimond VI, unlike the count–kings, was willing or obliged to perform it himself. On the other hand, there is no specific correspondence with the act of 1190 by which Guillem VIII of Montpellier promised his

Toulouse, chs. 4–6, and pp. 108–9. Castaing-Sicard, *Monnaies féodales en Languedoc*, pp. 11–17, gives a good account of the use of Toulousan money, but is misled about the date of the confirmation and (I believe) about its explanation.

[1] *HL*, viii, nos. 44, 119ii, 126; *LTC*, i, nos. 292, 305, 365, 395, 396, 404, 406, 413, 419, 426, 443, 452, 457, 459, 464, 466, 468, 477, 517, 572, 574, 576, 614, 616, 640–3, 667, 695, 699, 701, 711, 754–5; nos. 649 (A.D. 1202) and 859 (1208) show *tolzas* evaluated at two melgorians; *Travaux pratiques d'une conférence de paléographie à l'Institut catholique de Toulouse*, ed. Célestin Douais (Toulouse–Paris, 1892), nos. 5, 6, 8, 9, 11–14. BN, MS. lat. 9994 (cartulary of Grandselve), fos. 53ᵛ–79ᵛ, shows increasing reliance on Toulousan money for account, 1175–82.

[2] AD Haute-Garonne, H-Malte, Toulouse 1, 100, cited by Mundy, *Political Power in Toulouse*, p. 243 n. 3; E 501 (21 March 1199), ed. Georges Boyer, 'Un texte inédit du XIIᵉ siècle sur l'atelier monétaire de Toulouse', *Annales de la Faculté de droit d'Aix*, new ser., no. 43 (1950), 38–9; see also pp. 43–4, and Mundy, pp. 52–3, who also prints the text (pp. 203–4).   [3] Cf. above, p. 102.

[4] See Mundy, pp. 118–21, on the early consular notariate at Toulouse.

lord Raimond IV of Melgueil (who was Raimond V of Toulouse) not to counterfeit or obstruct the Melgorian coinage as long as it was maintained in its established weight and alloy;[1] this quasi-confirmation in the Melgorian tradition was not strengthened under Raimond VI, who seems to have taken little interest in the monetary rights which, together with his title to Melgueil, he lost by papal decree in 1212.[2]

Other, more general circumstances argue for connecting the Toulousan event with Catalonia. The homeland of *Cunctis pateat* was no further from Toulouse than from Barcelona. When the legend PAX appeared on the Toulousan coins, the stability of money was of manifest concern to the Pyrenean peace movements; and for a time around 1100 the counts of Toulouse seem to have imitated Aragonese coin types.[3] There were 'Spaniards' at Toulouse about 1200,[4] and 'Toulousans' (*de Tolosa*) at Lérida, where their forebears had taken part in the reconquest.[5] The *Ispanoli* brothers had shares in the mint rights of Toulouse until 1199;[6] a Pere Sanz was the consular notary who wrote the charter of 1205;[7] and one has only to think of Pere Vidal or Folquet de Marseille—the latter successively troubadour of Alphonse II, Cistercian reformer, and (from 1206) bishop of Toulouse—to recall that the culture common to the courts of Toulouse and Catalonia–Aragon–Provence was not only commercial.[8] Peter II was on close terms with Raimond VI in 1204, when the count not only made him a vast loan but attended him at Montpellier after his wedding;[9] nor were the consuls of Toulouse incapable of communicating directly with the king of Aragon.[10] Such is the evidence: inconclusive surely, yet suggestive. If it does not prove the influence, or diffusion, of a ceremony incubated in Catalonia, it suffices to place the Toulousan confirmation of 1205 within a distinctively southern mode of restriction upon monetary rights.

[1] *Cart. Guillems*, no. 87; cf. above, pp. 73–4. [2] *HL*, vi. 376–7.
[3] Above, p. 54; Pierfitte, 'Monnaies des comtes de Toulouse', 54–8; Dieudonné, *Manuel de numismatique*, iv. 235; cf. Pierfitte, plate iii, 12, 13, with Heiss, *Monedas hispano-cristianas*, ii, plate 71. Both Pierfitte and Dieudonné assimilate Pierfitte, plate iv, 2, 3, coin of Bertrand (1105–12), to other Aragonese types, much less plausibly, in my view.
[4] See e.g. Mundy, *Political Power in Toulouse*, pp. 203–4, cf. pp. 52–4, 99, and notes; cf. the cautious assessment by Charles Higounet, 'Le peuplement de Toulouse au XIIe siècle', *Annales du Midi*, lv (1943), 493.
[5] See e.g. José Lladonosa i Pujol, 'Marchands toulousains à Lérida aux XIIe et XIIIe siècles', *Annales du Midi*, lxx (1958), 223–6; idem, *Hist. Lleida*, i. 132, 154, 158, 198.
[6] Mundy, pp. 203–4, 242; their father was the vicar Espanolus.
[7] Limouzin-Lamothe, *Commune de Toulouse*, p. 404; his acts (1201–5) are cited on p. 44.
[8] Stanisław Stroński, *Le Troubadour Folquet de Marseille. Édition critique* . . . (Cracow, 1910), pp. 4*–12*, 52*–53*, 87*–91*, 113*; Martín de Riquer, 'La littérature provençale à la cour d'Alphonse II d'Aragon', *Cahiers de civilisation médiévale*, ii (1959), 179–80, 187–8. [9] *LTC*, i, no. 756 (cf. above, p. 97).
[10] Letters of the consuls to Peter II, dated 1211 and 1213, cited by Mundy, *Political Power in Toulouse*, pp. 121, 337. See also ACA, Canc., perg. extrainv. 3235.

A few years later came the turn of the coinage of Cahors. According to a lost text quoted by the antiquary Lacroix, who dated it 1211, the bishop Guillem IV de Cardaillac (*c.* 1208–34) agreed with the citizens of Cahors to mint a coinage at 4 d. fine which he promised not to alter nor diminish in weight or alloy during his lifetime.[1] This understanding, at least as regards the alloy, lasted barely a year. It was superseded in July 1212 by a lengthy charter wherein the bishop committed himself to mint on a standard of 3 d. fine and 20 s. 6 d. to the mark, promising not to alter this coinage in weight or alloy during his episcopate, but reserving the right of his successors to a single mutation. The new coinage was in satisfaction of appeals to the bishop from barons of Quercy and burghers of Cahors; 'and through their prayers and for 10,000 sous which the burghers have given us,' said the bishop, 'we have caused [it] to be done'.[2]

With these remarkable texts, yet another scene on the familiar stage is illuminated. It is true that we know less about the contemporary *caorcencs* than about most of the other coinages heretofore considered.[3] Yet the evidence from Quercy suffices to suggest that the enactment of 1211 constituted a mutation whereby the coinage Bishop Guillem had inherited, traditionally stable and at least roughly ternal in standard, was strengthened in alloy to 4 d.[4] Whether this mutation caused dissatisfaction for reasons other than its novelty is less clear. Was it partial to prelates (who took no part in the act of July 1212) with incomes in fixed payments? Conceivably the new rates of exchange upset a convenient ratio with the coinage of Rodez[5] and otherwise disfavoured those in possession of the old coin, which must have been outstanding in large amounts, for it is harder to imagine 10,000 sous being paid simply for the convenience of maintaining the traditional coinage. However that may be, the act of 1212 effectively countermanded the recoinage of 1211, which was aborted if it occurred at

[1] Guillaume de Lacroix, *Series & acta episcoporum cadurcensium* . . . (Cahors, 1617), p. 87: 'Monetam istam non mutabimus, nec minuemus de pondere & lege omnibus diebus vitae nostrae, & istam Monetam faciemus operari ad quatuor denarios argenti & c.'

[2] BN, Collection de Doat, cxviii, fos. 7–8ᵛ, or Lacroix, *Acta episcoporum cadurcensium*, p. 88; independent copies of a lost parchment. Text (from Doat) in Appendix, no. 8; excerpts in notes following.

[3] See Dieudonné, *Manuel de numismatique*, iv. 223–4; Castaing-Sicard, *Monnaies féodales en Languedoc*, pp. 47–50. (Cf. Plate III, no. 21.)

[4] *Les Plus Anciennes Chartes en langue provençale* . . ., ed. Clovis Brunel (Paris, 1926), nos. 228, 244, 258, 273, 299; *LTC*, i, nos. 476, 719, 851 (the latter two pieces, dated respectively June 1204 and June 1208, are exceptional in specifying 'good caorsins'). The new standard of 1212 would have restored the coinage to near equivalence with that specified in AD Tarn-et-Garonne, G 998 (1206) and AN, J 318, no. 15 (1208; = *LTC*, i, no. 851), with silver at 60 s. to the mark fine, cited by Castaing-Sicard, *Monnaies féodales en Languedoc*, p. 48 n. 213. A smaller coinage of Cahors was also circulating, for the charter of 1212 prohibited the use of 'obolos veteres Caturcenses' save to exchange them.

[5] BN, Doat, cxviii, fos. 7ᵛ–8: 'Et burgenses Caturci mandaverunt et convenerunt nobis quia de caetero non acciperent denarios Ruthenenses nec obolos veteres Caturcenses nisi ad cambium . . ..'

all. The bishop's initial motive is likewise inexplicit. Possibly it was as much political as fiscal, although we may conjecture that even a strengthening of the coinage would have been so devised as to ensure some profit. But the terms of 1212 suggest strongly that Guillem IV, like Pere de Redorta at Vich in 1174, was seeking to reduce the concurrency of other moneys in Quercy and to establish a good coinage of his own in exclusive circulation at Cahors. The fines specified for using coin of Rodez or 'old obols of Cahors' —7 s. and loss of the pieces—were very comparable to those instituted at Vich.[1] Moreover, Bishop Guillem could well have been caught in a disagreement among his burghers themselves, for their assent to both acts is indicated. Would not some local merchants with wide connections—this was, after all, the home of the 'cahorsins'—have seen advantage in establishing parity with the quaternal coinages now prevailing not only in the Midi but also in the Île-de-France?[2] Such an outlook would doubtless have found sympathy in the bishop himself, for reasons to be set forth in a moment. Nevertheless, the alteration sat badly with the great men of Quercy, including burghers of Cahors. The settlement of 1212 was not without some appearance of provinciality. For as we turn from its monetary to its constitutional aspect, how familiar, how characteristically meridional, it all seems!

Was it not, after all, virtually the Catalonian *confirmatio monetae* in its early, Pyrenean form? The bishop confirms his coinage for life, for a fee that is said explicitly to compensate him for giving up a mutation, and he obtains recognition of his successors' right to one mutation. If we leave out the fee and include the penalties for illicit use of foreign coinages, we find astonishing parallelism with the charter of 1174 for Vich, where—again as at Cahors—the bishop was regulating a comital–diocesan coinage with especial reference to its use in his city.[3] That the charter of 1212 does not speak expressly of assembled barons and citizens is unimportant, for their intervention is otherwise recorded even more emphatically than in the Vigatan text.[4] To be sure, there were enough differences in 1212 to disprove any immediate conformity to a known Catalonian model. The charter, structurally, is even less formulaic, more directly narrative, than the experimental Catalonian records; substantively, the bishop's *assecuracio* is not stated to have been sworn, while the 'right to change the coinage once' does not precisely correspond to the mutation-at-accession that is implied

---

[1] See preceding note; and cf. Appendix, no. 8, with pp. 78–9, above.

[2] e.g. the coinages of Barcelona, Melgueil, Tours, and Nevers. Cf. citations below, p. 110 n. 4.

[3] Cf. above, pp. 78–81.

[4] BN, Doat, cxviii, fos. 7–7ᵛ: '. . . volumus [the bishop] facere monetam in Caturcinio ad quatuor denarios et barones Caturcenses et burgenses Caturci rogaverunt nos quia faceremus eam ad tres denarios et per preces eorum et per decem milia solidorum quos dederunt nobis burgenses nos fecimus fieri . . ..' See also quotation in p. 108 n. 5 above.

or explicit in Catalonia. Yet one of the ways in which the confirmations at Cahors differ from their Pyrenean antecedents is in their allusion to civic initiative,[1] a point on which the parallelism with the Toulousan confirmation becomes striking in its turn. The similarities between the confirmations of Cahors and these other ones in the Midi are less likely to be accidental than the differences. Again we must take account of the associations through which the men of Occitania and the March could have become familiar with each other's institutions.

That Catalans frequented Quercy as well as Toulouse is quite certain. The shrine of Rocamadour, in the north of Quercy yet within the limits of southern speech, had been favoured by Alphonse II in his will of 1194, and was further endowed by Peter II in 1207.[2] The Arnal de Lérida settled at Montauban in these years[3] surely came of a Catalan family; while the Pere de Caors living at Lérida in 1200 can hardly have been the only one of his wandering compatriots to venture into Catalonia.[4] The diocese of Cahors, like upland Comminges to the south, had peace-keeping operations remarkably analogous to those in effect in Catalan dioceses at the turn of the thirteenth century.[5] Perhaps more significant, if still circumstantial, the bishop and notables of Cahors remained in direct touch with their Toulousan neighbours. The bishop was a vassal of the count, and both Guillem IV and his predecessor had formally acknowledged the lordship of Raimond VI.[6] The latter had issued a privilege of safe-conduct for the burghers of Cahors as late as 1203,[7] and he passed through Montauban and Moissac early in 1211 hoping to rally support for his failing cause.[8] Moreover, the consulate of Cahors was taking form just when that of Toulouse was riding

[1] The preponderant role of the men of Cahors may be inferred from Lacroix's allusion to agreement with the *cives* in 1211, *Acta episcoporum*, p. 87; from the charter of 1212 as quoted above, p. 108 n. 5 and p. 109 n. 4, but above all from the fact that they—the *burgenses*—paid the fee.

[2] *DI*, iv. 402; ACA, Canc., perg. Pedro I, 226 (Miret y Sans, 'Itinerario del rey Pedro I', 375–6). For the increasing fame of Rocamadour toward 1200, see Guillaume Lacoste, *Histoire générale de la province de Quercy*, 2nd edn. by Louis Combarieu and François Cangardel, 4 vols. (Paris, 1968), ii. 128, 138.

[3] *HL*, viii, no. 143; *LTC*, i, no. 533. Guillem de Tudela, who came from Navarre to settle in Montauban in 1210, as he says at the start of his *La Chanson de la croisade albigeoise*, ed. Eugène Martin-Chabot, 3 vols. (Paris, 1931–61), i, c. 1, leaves no doubt in his early pages that the roads across the Pyrenees were busy; and for the evidence in general, see Charles Higounet, 'Mouvements de population dans le Midi de la France du XIe au XVe siècle d'après les noms de personne et de lieu', *Annales: Économies, Sociétés, Civilisations*, viii (1953), 1–19.

[4] Lladonosa i Pujol, *Hist. Lleida*, i. 154, 296; see Philippe Wolff, 'Le problème des cahorsins', *Annales du Midi*, lxii (1950), 231–2, 235–8, and (cited by Wolff) *Cahors: inventaire . . . des archives municipales. Première partie . . .* ed. Edmond Albe (Cahors, n.d.), nos. 63, 113.

[5] Bisson, *Assemblies in Languedoc*, pp. 103, 124–7; *Cortes de Cataluña*, i: 1. 69–70.

[6] *HL*, viii, no. 160.

[7] BN, Doat, cxviii, fo. 1; indicated by Albe, *Cahors: inventaire des archives*, no. 1.

[8] *Chanson de la croisade*, i, cc. 59, 60 (146, 148).

its crest of success; the former is first revealed to us in an act of August 1207, passed at Toulouse, by which the consuls of the two towns settled differences over the practice of *marque* and reprisal.[1] And we know, in any case, that the *septena* money of Toulouse circulated in lower Quercy, as in other regions bordering on Toulousain.[2] Given these circumstances, it is most improbable that the people of Quercy were ignorant of the confirmation at Toulouse in 1205, or indifferent to it.

But the changing times were creating another horizon. When Raimond VI was condemned, Bishop Guillem IV did homage to Simon de Montfort for the county of Cahors (20 June 1211).[3] Significant in itself and consistent with the bishop's early resolve to support the crusade, this event was soon eclipsed by a profoundly symptomatic political decision: Guillem went to France and rendered liege homage and fealty to King Philip Augustus. The ceremony was recorded in a charter, dated Paris, October 1211, issued together with the king's grant of safe-conduct to a burgher of Cahors.[4] To Guillem IV—a prelate of the borderlands nurtured in a baronial family of Quercy[5]—the crusade had revealed the power of the North. And he and his companions must have handled the quaternal money of Tours in the very year when he instituted one of his own at Cahors.

What all of these acts—homages and consular accords, safe-conducts and confirmations—reveal alike is the impulse, widely shared, to remedy the insecurities of the turbulent southlands.[6] In this sense, the 'money in Quercy' (as the charter of 1212 spoke of it) was like the peace in Quercy, a diocesan interest in which the collaboration with knights and townsmen was as much to the advantage of the bishop as to that of his people. Already before 1200 the bishop was convoking men of Quercy, on occasion, to 'swear the peace' in his presence. Moreover, it had become customary for barons and notables from the towns to assemble and institute taxation— the *comune*—when the bishop saw fit to call out the militia of the peace. Money was collected in the parishes and deposited at Figeac and Cahors.[7] Neither the *comune* nor the *patz*[8] of Quercy seems to have been explicitly connected with the coinage, as happened in the case of the Catalan *bovatge*.

---

[1] BN, Doat, cxviii, fo. 3; *Cahors: inventaire des archives*, ed. Albe, no. 2.

[2] Brunel, *Chartes en langue provençale*, no. 326; Castaing-Sicard, *Monnaies féodales en Languedoc*, p. 22, and map 1.   [3] *HL*, viii, no. 160.

[4] *Rec. des actes de Philippe Auguste*, iii, nos. 1206, 1207; *Cahors: inventaire des archives*, ed. Albe, no. 4 and p. 10 n. 2. The exceptional terms, *Actes*, iii, no. 1206, in which the king accepted the bishop's proffered submission underline the significance of the occasion.

[5] For the Cardaillac, materials may be found in AD Lot, F 349–53.

[6] See Bisson, *Assemblies in Languedoc*, pp. 102–3.

[7] AN, J 896, no. 33; ed. Albe, *Cahors: inventaire des archives*, no. 46 (pp. 46–50). The interest of this evidence for the history of consultation is discussed in *Assemblies in Languedoc*, pp. 124–6.

[8] For the provision *De patz segre*, see Émile Dufour, *La Commune de Cahors au moyen âge* (Cahors, 1846), pp. 202–4; *Le 'Te Igitur'*, ed. Paul Lacombe and Louis Combarieu (Cahors, 1874), p. 160.

But it looks as if the collective influence on the coinage was characteristic, an easy enlargement of a sphere of associative interest in Quercy that was already well defined by 1211–12, when the barons took a direct interest in the transfer of their overlordship as well as in the coinage.[1] And the offer of a compensatory levy in 1212 certainly sprang from local experience with consented taxation.

Nevertheless, the grant in 1212 was not perfectly analogous to the *comune*. For it was the burghers of Cahors alone who paid it, having presumably assessed it upon themselves and their tenants.[2] In its relation to the coinage, their payment had the character of a ransom, not a commutation. This is not to say that the bishop saw no connection between the 10,000 sous and his profits of coinage; by estimates from evidence of the year 1224, the grant might have been roughly ten years' earnings of the *moneta*.[3] But what the bishop was selling in 1212 was not the coinage, merely a mutation, and his enactment was altogether comparable to the redemption of the stable coinage in Cerdanya nearly a century before.

F. *Toward a Parliamentary Custom of the Confirmed Coinage*

The diffusion of the *confirmatio monetae* was not at an end in 1212. What had happened at Cahors was soon to happen in the neighbouring diocese of Agen; the confirmation by Raimond VI in 1205 was to be repeated by his son at his accession seventeen years later as the consuls of Toulouse tried to turn the precedent into a custom;[4] and there were to be similar enactments elsewhere in Gascony and Languedoc even as the money-tax spread through the realms of the Spanish March. But the foundations were in place by the early thirteenth century. In the course of some two hundred years, the arbitrary exercise of monetary prerogatives had come to be mitigated or commuted in characteristic ways among peoples settled in lands extending from the Massif Central to the Ebro.

The first impulses can be traced in comital and synodal legislation dating from the heroic age of the principality of Barcelona. There, as also in eleventh-century Aquitaine, the idea of confirming the coinage was built upon early medieval regulations intended to protect ruler and public alike

---

[1] Pierre des Vaux-de-Cernay, *Hystoria albigensis*, ed. Pascal Guébin and Ernest Lyon, 3 vols. (Paris, 1926–30), i. 245–6 (c. 246); cf. *Chanson de la croisade*, i, c. 85 (202).

[2] It seems useless to speculate about the relation of these 10,000 s. to the paying population. They could, after all, have been collected partly from men outside the city. The money-tax in Agenais, first attested in 1232, was a *fogatge*, below, p. 117.

[3] AM Cahors, DD 1; ed. (unreliably) by Lacroix, *Acta episcoporum cadurcensium*, pp. 89–90.

[4] AM Toulouse, AA 1, no. 82; ed. Limouzin-Lamothe, *Commune de Toulouse*, pp. 421–2. In address, content, ceremony, even in the form of attendance, this act was substantially the same as that of 1205. Not remedy but reassurance was the Toulousans' need. For the circumstances, see Mundy, *Political Power in Toulouse*, pp. 88–9; Bisson, *Assemblies in Languedoc*, pp. 52–4.

from the abuse or counterfeiting of coins. Sworn engagements to maintain the coinage unaltered, occurring first in Catalonia and then at Melgueil early in the twelfth century, placed rulers under a new obligation. What may be called the normal southern form of this practice—the ceremonial oath to preserve the money for life in weight and alloy—appears in the charter for Cerdanya (1118); it recurs half a century later at Vich, when it was certainly known also at Barcelona, and spreads thereafter to Toulouse, Urgell, Cahors, the Agenais (by 1232 at latest),[1] and Narbonne (by 1265).[2] The ceremonies at Toulouse and Cahors were not without significant peculiarities, while the tradition of confirmation at Melgueil was associated with vassalic engagements in a quite distinctive mix. It would be mistaken to exaggerate the constancy of meridional solutions to the problems caused by unstable currencies. Among vast numbers of formulaic notices and charters surviving from this 'written civilization', the charters of coinage, no two of which are identical, stand out as the work of scribes stumbling on unfamiliar ground. Yet the resemblances of the confirmations—in circumstance, content and written form, even in the taxes associated with some of them—are strong: strong enough, indeed, to define an original southern family of Pyrenean ancestry.

An imposition to compensate for the secured coinage is first attested in 1118 in Cerdanya, where it likewise bought the peace; and the assimilation of the coinage in the Peace of God persisted until the statutes of peace and truce became an expression of the ruler's will in the time of Alphonse II. A co-ordinated regulation of monetary standards becomes perceptible in the 1170s, when several coinages were altered or publicly confirmed so as to be equivalent or conveniently convertible. By that time, the demands and supplies of coined money, despite regional variation, were generally sufficient to create widespread agreement about the prices of coinages in terms of silver and gold, and the frequent stipulation of such values betrays a heightened anxiety about unexpected mutations.

The anxiety was not allayed by the subsequent policies of the count–kings. Alphonse II and his son both resisted confirmations of coinage urged upon them in Catalonia; in their mounting financial difficulties, they both manipulated their coinages; and Peter II, if not also his father, collected ransoms of monetary stability well before instituting the *monedaje* in 1205. Both the coinages and the derivative taxes were of relatively greater fiscal value in Catalonia than in Normandy or the Île-de-France. These factors—the renewed mutations and the importance of the money-taxes—helped to make Peter II's reign one of crucial constitutional significance. While the peoples remained fearful, the rulers were tempted to

[1] See below, p. 117.
[2] AM Narbonne, AA 109, fo. 34; see T. N. Bisson, '*Confirmatio monete* à Narbonne au XIIIe siècle', *Narbonne. Archéologie et histoire*, 3 vols. (Montpellier, 1973), ii. 55–9.

exploit their fear, and in the early years of James I, with the fiscal crisis unresolved, the confirmation of coinage became the ruler's concession for the consent of his magnates and towns to taxes. Such is all but certainly the explanation for the four spectacular *confirmationes monetae* celebrated by the young king in courts-general of Aragon in 1218, 1221, 1223, and 1236;[1] the *monetatica* granted on these occasions amounted to his principal extra-ordinary resource at those times. But to confirm the coinage whenever money was needed was to make a mockery of the Catalonian principle. Had not the lifetime confirmation been introduced into Aragon long before? The truth is that we do not surely know. Even if it had—if, for example, Peter II had sworn in like terms in Aragon and Catalonia upon his acces-sion—it was apparently repudiated in both realms when the money-taxes were decreed or imposed in 1205 and after. Fiscal necessity was closing in. As early as 1196 Peter could make the coinage his excuse for collecting a war subsidy, and no such imposition can have been collected without consent. Moreover, Peter and his ancestors had sworn the solemn con-firmation often enough to encourage the idea that such acts, however they might be violated, were sanctioned by custom. That they felt obliged to take their confirmations seriously is proven by their appeals to popes for dispensations. And their exposure to prelates like Jacintus and Pere de Redorta can only have sharpened their awareness of the moral and political dangers of ignoring popular sentiment.

The representation of that sentiment remained variable well into the thirteenth century. Publicity and Christian solemnity were the only in-dispensable requisites for the confirmation of coinage and no written law prescribed the appropriate assembly. Yet almost everywhere it came up in the South, the matter was recognized to be an interest of the traditional territorial community. The assemblies known to us tended to be juris-dictional, not narrowly tenurial: it was as barons of their region rather than as episcopal vassals that the great men of Quercy acted in 1212, much as the 'magnates and knights of the whole county of Cerdanya and Conflent' had intervened to secure the confirmation of another coinage almost a cen-tury before. It was the same at Vich (1174), where, however, as more emphatically in the instances of Toulouse (1205, 1222), one senses the preponderance of the city over the hinterland. These coinages had retained their age-old attachment to the county.

That is why the assemblies that dealt with them were representative. They were gatherings of regional élites, of those who worried about the instability of coinage (although not the only ones afflicted by it): officers of the counties, in early times; later the custodians of the peace, barons, knights, and merchants and magnates of leading towns; but not delegates

---

[1] *Col. dipl. Zaragoza*, i, nos. 48, 49, 52; ACA, Reg. 22, fos. 105–106ᵛ (the best among mediocre editions is Botet y Sisó, *Monedes catalanes*, iii. 252–6).

or experts in coinage. They easily presumed to deal with a matter of common concern. But in the second half of the twelfth century two factors were interacting in some regions to render this traditional mode of representation inadequate. First, coinages like those of Jaca and Barcelona, having become institutions of their realms, could no longer be regarded the appropriate interest of any single district or county.[1] Second, the growth in size and social importance of hinterland towns and villages meant that, even where the county retained its coinage (so to speak), the barons and citizens could no longer claim sole custody of the pertinent regional custom. Accordingly, it began to seem desirable to deal with the coinage in those larger, more representative ceremonial assemblies known as 'full' or 'general courts' (*plena curia, curia generalis*).[2] In Leon and Castile this change was so conspicuous that Claudio Sánchez Albornoz has seen in the coinage a principal cause for the introduction of urban deputies in the *Cortes* of those realms.[3] For the regions of interest to us the evidence, unfortunately, is more problematical.

In the case of Aragon, the four confirmations of coinage by James I already mentioned were celebrated in plenary courts attended by prelates, barons, and (in 1223 and 1236) the leading men of the towns:[4] was that of 1218 the first occasion of this kind? Quite possibly, for the minority of James and the reaction against Peter certainly encouraged a less arbitrary royal administration; yet it must be remembered that Peter had confirmed the *iaccensis* at least once and perhaps twice soon after his accession, that the lack of *assensus populi* was alleged by that king as a reason for invalidating the first of these acts, and that the direct evidence for his decree at Huesca (1205) has likewise disappeared. If by 1205 the customary sentiment of the Aragonese was already that the king's coinage should be confirmed at accession, as seems likely, then it is very conceivable that the appropriate occasion was already thought to be the 'full court', and perhaps even one of that sort to which, as early as 1164, the notables of five

[1] For the peculiar structural characteristics of the kingdom of Aragon, see J. M. Lacarra, '"Honores" et "tenencias" en Aragon (XIe siècle)', *Structures*, pp. 143–74.

[2] In saying that such bodies were 'more representative', I do not simply mean that deputies from local communities began to appear in them (although that is part of it). The point is that they were specially convoked to provide fuller contact with the larger territorial aggregate of magnates and settlements. There are no adequate studies of the early 'full courts' of Aragon and Catalonia, although the following are useful: Ferràn Valls Taberner, 'La cour comtale barcelonaise', *RHDFE*, xiv (1935), 662–82; E. S. Procter, 'The Development of the Catalan *Corts* in the Thirteenth Century', *Homenatge a Antoni Rubió i Lluch . . .*, 3 vols. (Barcelona, 1936), iii. 525–46; and cf. now *English Historical Review*, xcii (1977), 107–24.

[3] Claudio Sánchez-Albornoz, *La curia regia portuguesa. Siglos XII y XIII* (Madrid, 1920), pp. 154–8; idem, 'La primitiva organización monetaria', 338–41. The contention is withdrawn in his 'Devaluación monetaria', 617.

[4] Among these towns were Lérida and Tortosa, in the Catalonian borderlands where the *iaccensis* circulated; Lérida was invariably the meeting-place for courts of the two realms together.

Aragonese towns had been convoked to swear the peace.[1] What is clear, in any case, is that when the *fueros* of Aragon were put in writing in the thirteenth century, their compilers retained no evidence earlier than that of the 'general court' of Monzón (1236) to justify plenary consultation for the confirmation of coinage.[2] Whatever the earlier precedents, the parliamentary custom dated only from the early years of James I.

In Catalonia it was quite different—or so it appears. There we hear nothing, in James's reign, of a confirmation of the *barchinonensis* until 1253;[3] only in 1258 was it stipulated that the rulers of Catalonia should henceforth swear 'publicly' upon accession to maintain the coinage unaltered;[4] not until 1292 do the statutes of an inaugural court bear unequivocal witness to a sovereign's recognition of this privilege.[5] But these facts may be misleading. Many Catalans doubtless thought of the inaugural oath to uphold the coinage as a venerable custom enshrined in the *Usatges*, and if the precedent of *Cunctis pateat* had been followed in 1162 or 1196, the oath would surely have been celebrated in an assembly. To follow a precedent, however, was not necessarily to admit a custom; moreover, Peter II, having certainly redeemed the coinage and the peace in his first years, found it expedient to renounce a principle that limited his exploitation of the coinage thereafter. The arbitrariness of his monetary policy after 1205 must have antagonized the Catalonian magnates and townspeople. It is puzzling to find no evidence of reaction to that policy at his death.

What happened in the great inaugural court at Lérida in 1214 is the crux of the matter. It should be said at once that our evidence of that occasion is very incomplete.[6] Nevertheless, we do know that it was an unusually solemn gathering of the prelates, barons, knights, and deputy townsmen from both of the child-king's realms, and that these men swore fealty to James[7] (an unprecedented act, according to a contemporary observer).[8] In the circumstances, it is hard to believe that such a submission—by the Catalans, at least—could have been made without some compensating concession by the ruler. And would not the confirmed coinage have figured prominently in any such quid pro quo? Yet, it is improbable that an oath of confirmation was sworn at Lérida, and quite certain that no

[1] *DI*, viii, no. 10.

[2] *Los Fueros de Aragón según el manuscrito 458 de la Biblioteca nacional de Madrid*, ed. Gunnar Tilander (Lund, 1937), vii, c. 266 (pp. 154–8).

[3] Salat, *Tratado de las monedas*, ii. 3–4.   [4] *DI*, vi. 141–4.

[5] *Cortes de Cataluña*, i: 1. 157, art. 10.

[6] It is discussed critically by Ferran Soldevila, *Els Primers Temps de Jaume I* (Barcelona, 1968), pp. 67–82; Soldevila reprints, from the copy by Miret, the remarkable contemporary list of the barons, knights, and townsmen who attended, pp. 83–4. (This document is now ACA, Canc., extrainv. 3131.)

[7] *Libre dels feyts*, ch. 11; ed. Ferran Soldevila, ... *Les Quatre Grans Cròniques* (Barcelona, 1971), p. 7.

[8] Zurita, *Anales de la Coróna de Aragón*, book 2, ch. 66; ed. Ubieto, ii. 200.

such act could then have been based on the tradition of *Cunctis pateat* nor, indeed, put in writing at all. For there is no evidence of a new *monedatge* in Catalonia thereafter; moreover, in 1222 the coinage of Barcelona was changed without reference to any prior restraint or appeal for dispensation.[1] Conceivably, the matter of a confirmation was simply postponed in 1214: this would explain why the *bovatge* was approved only in 1217 by the Catalonian prelates and barons,[2] and why the *iaccensis* was confirmed (and redeemed!) only in 1218 in a second plenary court of both realms at Lérida.[3] But if the Catalans were still lacking the confirmation, why should they not have obtained theirs, too, in this court? The most plausible conjecture is that they refused, this time, to grant the *monedatge*. In so doing they could well have revived the abortive baronial programme of 1205, according to which their coinage should be confirmed without redemption, and they would have been holding out for a concession that they were to win at last in the privilege of 1258. If this analysis is correct, our conclusion must be that the *confirmatio monetae* was slow to attain parliamentary status in Catalonia because the magnates of that realm, at a critical time in their history, clung tenaciously to one of their oldest customs of the coinage: that 'it be diligently conserved', in the words of *Moneta autem*, without cost to the people.

In the Agenais, finally, we have our clearest example. In 1232 Bishop Géraud, newly appointed to the see of Agen, confirmed his coinage for life 'with the consent of the barons and the knights and the burghers and the general court of Agenais', receiving in return the grant of 12 d. per hearth in the diocese.[4] Two years later his successor also confirmed the money of Agen, acting on the 'common instance' of citizens of Agen and of barons and knights of the diocese; that this event so described likewise occurred in a 'general court' is made all but certain by subsequent notices of bishops' inaugural confirmations in such assemblies of Agenais, a practice said to be customary in 1263.[5] Now there is no reason to suppose that this parliamentary interest in the coinage was new in 1232, for the general court of Agenais, as a body including elected citizens and villagers, is attested in the custom of Agen, written down after 1221, but reflecting traditional practice.[6] And by analogy with Pyrenean experience, it is of interest that

---

[1] AM Perpignan, AA 9, fo. 2ʳ. After his confirmation of 1253, James I obtained a papal dispensation to alter the coinage of Barcelona, Salat, *Tratado*, ii. 4–5.

[2] Zurita, *Anales*, book 2, ch. 69; ed. Ubieto, ii. 210.

[3] *Col. dipl. Zaragoza*, i, no. 48; cf. no. 52 (p. 147): in the court of Daroca (March 1223), James added: 'Confitemur etiam nos tria monetatica cum isto quod modo a vobis accipimus pro confirmationibus eiusdem monete accepisse . . . .'

[4] AD Lot-et-Garonne, new G 2, no. 1, quoted in T. N. Bisson, '. . . The General Court of Agenais in the Thirteenth Century', *Speculum*, xxxvi (1961), 275–6, n. 129.

[5] Ibid., 275–6; *LTC*, iv, no. 4883.

[6] Henry Tropamer, *La Coutume d'Agen* (Bordeaux, 1911); quoted in my 'General Court of Agenais', 262 n. 59.

the general court of Agenais was fundamentally an association for the maintenance of the regional peace. It was characteristic of the rolling lands sloping down from either side of the Pyrenees that the stabilized money and the peace should have been perceived as the common concerns of incipient regional communities.

Even as it achieved customary or parliamentary standing, the meridional conservation of coinage remained faithful to ancient tenets of public monetary vigilance; that, indeed, was one reason for its vitality. What good to prohibit mutations if counterfeiters and clippers went unpunished? The bishops of Vich and Cahors used the public occasions of their confirmations to provide for the protection of their threatened coinages in local exchange. If in 1214 James I's confirmation was omitted in his inaugural assembly, his sanction against public monetary abuse certainly was not.[1] The obligations of moneyers were becoming better regulated, to the mutual advantage of ruler and society. At Melgueil, where the prospering minters still paid the only money-tax, the old confirmation was renewed in 1215 in a charter which admitted the consuls of Montpellier to a share in the coinage.[2] Elsewhere, the mints were slower to come under communal surveillance; but at Barcelona, where the Templars continued to regulate the *moneta* under James I the accounts of 1222 suggest that the royal profits of coinage by no means suffered under open and orderly management.[3] Furthermore, even the untutored men who demanded the oaths were awakening to the economic complications of the unconditional confirmation.

In the South it had long been customary to reckon the value of deniers in relation to the mark of silver, and since the 1170s, when the stable morabetin had become widely current in the Pyrenean kingdoms, the pricing of silver in terms of gold was common there. As market rates fluctuated, as supply in addition to intrinsic quality became influential, rulers must have been urged or tempted to ordain the price of circulating specie. Peter II issued such decrees in 1213;[4] and his son carried the practice a step further in 1222, when he confirmed an ordinance of the vicar of Barcelona requiring that the new *doblench* coinage be overvalued by 25 per cent in relation to the old quaternal deniers—this 'even though', the king admitted, 'it may seem to some that . . . some people are unjustly troubled'.[5] That people in Aragon had already been troubled by such mutations of

[1] *Cortes de Cataluña*, i: 1, 94, art. 18.

[2] Germain, 'Anciennes monnaies de Melgueil', 231–2. Cf. next note.

[3] ACA, perg. Jaime I, 207, ed. Botet y Sisó, *Monedes catalanes*, iii. 240–3. In 1218 James, or the consuls of Montpellier on his behalf, paid 20,000 s. to Bishop Bernard of Maguelone, count of Melgueil, for a fief of 4 d. per l. on the coinage of Melgueil, Germain, 'Anciennes monnaies', 233–4.

[4] *VL*, viii. 230. In 1218 a reservation of the 'good quaternal money' of Barcelona referred to mutations 'dargento uel de ualore', ACA, perg. Jaime I, 106.

[5] AM Perpignan, AA 9, fo. 2ʳ; Botet y Sisó, *Monedes catalanes*, ii. 38–9.

imposed value is suggested by the terms on which James confirmed the *iaccensis* in the general court of Huesca in 1221. He renounced not only its diminution in weight and alloy but also its mutation or reinforcement 'in number'.[1] Moreover, in all of these Aragonese confirmations by the young king, it was stipulated that the final coinage of Jaca minted by his father should circulate until Michaelmas 1228 with its *value* unchanged.[2] Does this clause also imply that the Aragonese magnates had come to recognize the economic impracticality of an unlimited or lifetime confirmation? More likely, the limited term was at the king's insistence, for as late as 1258 the Catalans wanted, and won, the old indefinite confirmation of their coinage. But lest the traditional prohibition seem ambiguous, that charter made explicit allowance for the necessity that might, from time to time, require the minting of new coins on the fixed standards.[3]

---

[1] *Col. dipl. Zaragoza*, i, no. 49: '. . . nec istam [monetam] mutabimus vel augebimus numero aut diminuemus penso vel lege . . ..' See also no. 52, the same language in the confirmation at Daroca in 1223.

[2] Ibid., no. 48: '. . . usque ad finem prefati temporis inviolabiliter et irrefragabiliter in suo valore consistat'; cf. nos. 49, 52.

[3] *DI*, vi. 141–4. It is made clear that the citizens of Barcelona received this privilege on behalf of the king's subjects of Catalonia.

V

CONFIRMATIONS OF COINAGE
IN THE NORTH

POPULAR dissatisfaction with unstable coinages was not confined to the South. It can be discerned in the royal charters (already discussed) for Compiègne, Étampes, and Orléans, whatever the consequences of those charters. Can we suppose that the people of Normandy would have settled so quietly for repeated payments of the *fouage* if that tax had not been understood at first to be a fair price for a secured coinage? So in Capetian France, and perhaps also in Normandy, the rulers exploited conservationist sentiment by effectively selling their confirmations of coinage; and much the same thing happened in the county of Nevers in 1188. Concerned more with the coinage than its Capetian cousins, the charter for Nevers may be regarded as the classic expression of the *confirmatio monetae* as it developed in the North. Yet it was neither the only nor the earliest such expression in northern baronial domains, nor was it very typical of northern responses to monetary problems in the later twelfth and early thirteenth centuries. Those problems were unfolding somewhat diversely in the provinces bordering on the Île-de-France; and if the conservation of coinage remained a dominant social concern, it began to weaken here and there as alternative interests or pressures arose.

A. *Burgundy* (*1101–1203*)

In 1101 Duke Eudes I of Burgundy confirmed to the chapter of Saint-Bénigne a half-share in the coinage of Dijon that had been ceded by his brother Hugues I a generation before. It was stipulated that the money should not be weakened, strengthened, nor alienated without permission of the abbot and monks; and 'so that all may know that I have decreed this faithfully', the duke caused his moneyer Jean to swear to his concession before the monks. Together with other provisions, the confirmation and the oath were witnessed by the duke's son and by other great men of the duchy.[1]

---

[1] *Chartes et documents de Saint-Bénigne de Dijon* . . ., ii, ed. Georges Chevrier and Maurice Chaume (Dijon, 1943), no. 398; and at p. 176: '[IX] Medietatem Divionensis monetę, de qua multotiens fraus monachis illata est, ita amodo sancto Benigno concedo, sicut [*348*] eam illi prefatus frater meus, Hugo dux, noscitur concessisse, ut eadem moneta

This regulation does not seem to have been directed against manipulations of the coinage *per se*. On the contrary, mutations were envisaged as among the normal incidents of a *moneta* in which the right of the abbot and monks was secured. There is no indication that the latter's permission to alter the coinage might be affected by moral as well as by fiscal considerations, nor do other Burgundian texts help us much on this point. Toward 1100 the *digenois* was not yet commonly distinguished in charters from other concurrent coinages, although it was probably becoming more plentiful; and its intrinsic value or variability was not yet subject to frequent reservation in charters.[1] Nothing in the known economic circumstances would cause us to imagine a popular impulse behind this Burgundian monetary regulation.

Yet it would be equally mistaken to exaggerate the lordliness of an agreement whose significance, in fact, is not so much constitutional as religious. Duke Eudes was making amends to Saint-Bénigne on the occasion of his penitential pilgrimage to Jerusalem. With the coinage as with other issues it was 'right' in the usual sense of the clerical reformers that concerned him and the monks; and just as in eleventh-century Barcelona the moneyer's oath served to protect these lords from fraud in their own mint.[2] A rightly administered coinage probably sufficed to satisfy the regional interest as it was represented by the assembled magnates in 1101.

No more demanding standard was forthcoming for many decades in Burgundy. The monetary agreement of 1101 was confirmed by Hugues III in 1177 in terms that prove its continued importance to the duke and the abbey.[3] Moreover, a comparable provision appears in the convention of 1185 by which the same duke and the bishop of Langres established the moneys of Dijon and Langres in exclusive currency in their co-seigneury

ab[s]que permissu abbatis aut monachorum Divionensium non minuatur, non augmentetur, non alio transferatur; et, ut noverint omnes hoc ipsum me fideliter decrevisse, ipsum monetarium nomine Johannem, hanc eandem concessionem in manu monachorum sub sacramento firmare feci'; cf. no. 348 (1076–9). These acts were catalogued by Ernest Petit, *Histoire des ducs de Bourgogne de la race capétienne* . . ., 9 vols. (Dijon, 1885–1905), i. 191, 427 (no. 112).

[1] *Chartes de Saint-Bénigne*, nos. 218, 229, 241, 242, 287, 290, 311, 358, 360, 366, 439; *Les Chartes de Saint-Étienne de Dijon* . . ., i: 2, ed. Adrien Bièvre-Poulalier (Dijon, 1912), nos. 3 *bis*, 12, 21, 47; also no. 2, as exceptional as it is illuminating: a *cens* of 5 'solidos monetae Divionensis aut in castro Divione aeque valentis'. The numismatic history of early ducal Burgundy remains obscure: see generally Dieudonné, *Manuel de numismatique*, iv. 113–15, and Richard, *Ducs de Bourgogne*, pp. 369–70. For the quite different situation in the Mâconnais from *c.* 1080, see Georges Duby, *La Société aux XIᵉ et XIIᵉ siècles dans la région mâconnaise* (Paris, 1953), pp. 357–9; new edn. (Paris, 1971), pp. 281–2.

[2] Cf. above, p. 6.

[3] AD Côte-d'Or, 1H 14, no. 1, printed by Urbain Plancher, *Histoire générale et particulière de Bourgogne* . . ., 4 vols. (Dijon, 1739–81), i, *preuves*, no. 91 (Petit, *Ducs de Bourgogne*, ii. 389, no. 612).

Archbishoprics

Bishoprics

Poitiers Cities

0   50   100   150 km

0   50   100 miles

Fécamp

Lillebonne

JERSEY

⚜ Caen

N O R M A N D Y

• Mortain
• Domfront
• Saint-James

Alençon

B R I T T A N Y

Bellême

M A I N E

⚜ Angers

Loire

P O I T O U

Poitiers ⚜

MAP 2.

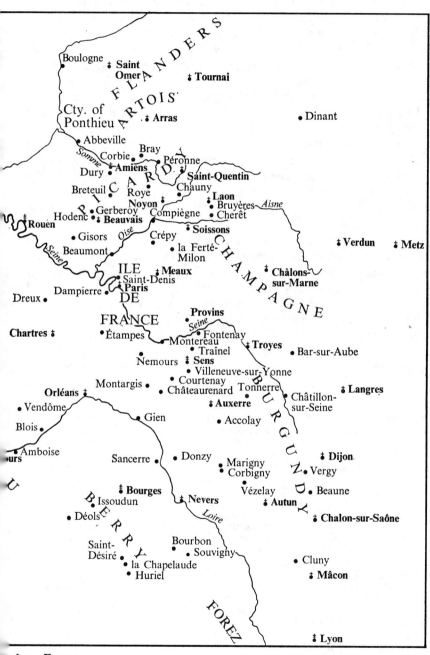

Boulogne

Saint Omer

FLANDERS

Tournai

ARTOIS

Cty. of Ponthieu

Arras

Dinant

Abbeville

Somme

Corbie   Bray

Péronne

Dury   Amiens

Saint-Quentin

PICARDA

Breteuil   Roye   Chauny

Gerberoy   Noyon   Laon

Hodenc   Beauvais   Compiègne   Bruyères   Aisne

Rouen   Cherêt

Oise

Gisors   Crépy   Soissons

Seine

Beaumont   la Ferté-Milon

CHAMPAGNE

Verdun   Metz

Dreux   Dampierre

ILE   Meaux

Saint-Denis

Paris   Châlons-sur-Marne

DE

FRANCE   Provins

Chartres   Étampes   Seine

Fontenay

Montereau   Troyes

Traînel   Bar-sur-Aube

Nemours   Sens

Villeneuve-sur-Yonne

Montargis   Courtenay   Tonnerre   Langres

Châteaurenard

Orléans   Auxerre   Châtillon-sur-Seine

Vendôme

Gien   Accolay   BURGUNDY

Blois

Amboise   Sancerre   Donzy   Dijon

urs   Marigny   Vergy

Corbigny

Bourges   Vézelay   Beaune

BERRY   Issoudun   Nevers   Autun

Déols   Loire   Chalon-sur-Saône

Saint-Désiré   Bourbon

la Chapelaude   Souvigny   Cluny

Huriel   Mâcon

FOREZ

Lyon

of Châtillon-sur-Seine. Hugues promised not to alter the coinage of Dijon in weight or alloy without the bishop's approval.[1] Yet this concession itself, and in a general way the entire charter, pointed to changed circumstances. The promise not to alter the *digenois* was to hold for life (*in vita mea*), a specification that suggests that arguments against the free mutation of coinage such as had already arisen in the Île-de-France (and in Catalonia) were now becoming known, and being countered, in Burgundy. As we shall see, this inference is supported by other, more explicit testimony. It is also consistent with the principle of the same agreement that foreign moneys should be received at Châtillon only for conversion into the statutory coinages *secundum valorem earum*. If the control of monetary exchange had become so profitable as to recommend such an emphatic exercise of lordship as this, can it be doubted that the inhabitants of this place hard by Champagne had become sensitive to the intrinsic value and stability of their deniers?

Nevertheless, this awareness had manifested itself more slowly, and perhaps less pervasively, in Burgundy than in Occitania. As in the Île-de-France, it was not until the second half of the twelfth century that instruments of central Burgundy commonly specified the coinage in which local transactions were accounted, nor was the pace in the Mâconnais very much faster.[2] A number of fairly reliable coinages in rough parity with one another had been circulating in diversified rural economies strengthened, in the South, by the income and enterprise of Cluny.[3] In censives donated to Fontenay about mid-century, the values were defined in 'sous of Provins money or of that which will circulate without exchange at Rouge-

---

[1] Plancher, *Hist. Bourgogne*, i, *preuves*, no. 104 (Petit, iii. 262, no. 732): 'Ego Hugo Dux Burg. omnibus notum facio conventionem talem factam esse inter me & Dominum Manassem Lingon. Episcopum super cursu monetarum apud Castellionem super Sequanam, quod nullae aliae monetae ibi currant nisi Divionensis & Lingonensis ad scambium, secundum valorem eorum [*sic*]; concessi etiam quod monetam Divionensem nec à lege nec à pondere mutabo in vita mea absque assensu Lingonen. Episcopi . . ..'

[2] *Chartes de Saint-Étienne de Dijon*, i: 2, nos. 64, 72, 73; i: 3, ed. P. Bourrier (Dijon, 1912), nos. 2, 3, 24; i: 4, ed. Georges Valat (Dijon, 1907), nos. 19, 24, 32, 43, and cf. nos. 102, 107; Petit, *Ducs de Bourgogne*, ii, *p.j.*, nos. 244, 282–3, 296, 304, 342, 364, 383–4, 395, 464, 592, 616; 'Cartulaire du prieuré de Jully-les-Nonnains', ed. Ernest Petit, *Bulletin de la Société des sciences historiques et naturelles de l'Yonne*, xxxiv (1880), 261–82; AD Côte-d'Or, 15H 13 (cartulary of Fontenay), fos. 1–32; *Cartulaire de Saint-Vincent de Mâcon . . .*, ed. Camille Ragut (Mâcon, 1864), nos. 18, 19, 24, 30, 34, 511, 531, 535–6, 537, 552, 554, 568, 574, 577, 578, 584–5, 596, 600, 602, 604, 627; *Chartes de Cluny*, v, nos. 3660, 3665, 3703, 3712, 3714, 3716, 3734, 3754, 3758, 3760, 3790, 3828, 3914, 3951, 3966, 4012, 4053, 4054, 4132, 4133 and acts following.

[3] The currencies mentioned in the texts cited are chiefly those of Dijon, Chalon-sur-Saône, Cluny, Mâcon, and Lyon. See generally Fournial, *Villes et l'économie d'échange en Forez*, pp. 496–500; Duby, *Société dans la région mâconnaise*, pp. 349–63; new edn., pp. 275–85, and idem, 'Économie domaniale et économie monétaire: le budget de l'abbaye de Cluny entre 1080 et 1155', *Annales: Économies, Sociétés, Civilisations*, vii (1952), 155–71.

mont'.[1] Under Hugues III (1162–92), however, the situation changed. His ambitious projects as ruler and crusader exceeded his resources and caused him, among other measures, to debase the *digenois* steeply some time between 1174 and 1185.[2] This can hardly have pleased landlords possessed of fixed revenues in specie (although there is little evidence for renders being stipulated in specific currencies in the vicinity of Dijon), but the *digenois* had probably been too strong for easy convertibility and sustained currency. When the duke thereupon moved to restore the good money, some townsfolk complained. And in his charter of 1187, Hugues III promised the people of Dijon that he would mint his local coinage at an alloy no stronger than 5 d. fine.[3]

So for the first time a Burgundian coinage came under public restraint. The men of Dijon had surely taken, or shared in, the initiative, for this concession does not figure in the charter of Soissons upon which that of Dijon was based. Yet the terms make no reference to local circumstance, conceivably because the money minted at Dijon enjoyed quite extended currency. In 1203 the same provision was to be incorporated in the charter for Beaune,[4] a fact that suggests that the policy had been recognized and approved throughout the duchy. Monetary confusion persisted during 1188–9, when a light and a 'strong money' of Dijon were circulating together and when coin of Provins was preferred even at Dijon; but order was then restored.[5]

Did the provision of 1187 amount to a confirmation of the coinage? It was expressed in the first person, which implies a lifelong engagement, and as so often elsewhere, it appeared in a charter; moreover, the terms of the charter were secured by the oaths of the duke, his son, and some of his barons. Nevertheless, the monetary concession was singularly limited. It left the duke free to alter the coinage within a range itself ill determined, since there was no reference to the permissible weight (or size) of the coins. Were it not for this vagueness, it would be tempting to credit the burghers

---

[1] AD Côte-d'Or, 15H 13, fos. 9–10: 'Census autem annualis est quinque solidi prouiniensis monete uel illius que sine scambio apud Rubeum Montem curret . . ..'

[2] Petit, *Ducs de Bourgogne*, ii. 178–205, and *p.j.*, nos. 484, 500, 518, 519, 522, 525, 532, 552, 655, 672, 674; iii. 1–75, and *p.j.*, no. 709; *Chartes de commune et d'affranchissement en Bourgogne*, ed. Joseph F. Garnier, 4 vols. (Dijon, 1867–1918), i. 2–4, 14–15. The debasement is attested indirectly in texts cited by Richard, *Ducs de Bourgogne*, p. 371 n. 1, and Auguste Carlet, 'Archéologie et histoire monétaire. Monnaies dijonnaises de la fin du XIIᵉ siècle', *Annales de Bourgogne*, xi (1939), 24–8. In my view, the agreement by which the bishop of Langres obtained the right to be consulted when the *digenois* was altered (above, p. 124) establishes 1185 as the *terminus ad quem* for the principal debasement. (Cf. Plate III, no. 22.)

[3] AM Dijon, B 1, ed. Garnier, *Chartes de commune*, i. 12: '[36.] Monetam vero meam divionensem non possum fortiorem facere quam ad legem .v. denariorum.' For the background, see Petit, *Ducs de Bourgogne*, iii. 1–34; and for the peculiar role of the king in founding this nominally ducal commune, Petit-Dutaillis, *Communes françaises*, pp. 103–5.

[4] Garnier, *Chartes de commune*, i. 211, art. 35.

[5] Carlet, 'Monnaies dijonnaises', 28–30; cf. Richard, *Ducs de Bourgogne*, p. 371.

with precocious economic realism in allowing some discretion for mutation. All things considered,[1] the promise of 1187 looks like a compromise. The duke maintained his monetary prerogative for practical purposes; the burghers gained protection against an overvalued currency. No price attached expressly to the concession regarding the coinage, but for the charter as a whole the duke, in his urgent need, was to receive 500 marks silver from the men of Dijon.[2]

The political background of these events will presently concern us further. But it should be clear already that the reactions of 1185–7 against recent debasement owed little or nothing to older traditions of monetary regulation at Dijon. The coinage had now to be protected from its proprietor as well as its maker, by measures in which secular impulses appear to have gained at the expense of religious ones. And the settlement of 1187 together with the restoration of an acceptable coinage (at an alloy of 5 d. fine, or less) served to re-establish a monetary equilibrium in ducal Burgundy. Hugues III was soon succeeded by his son Eudes III (1193–1218), who not only adopted the provision of Dijon for his charter to Beaune (1203) but also confirmed the charter of Dijon, and the monetary treaties with the chapter of Saint-Bénigne and the see of Langres.[3] And although Eudes certainly changed the legend of the *digenois* while holding, like his predecessors, to a traditional type, there is no evidence that he altered the coinage in weight or alloy.[4]

B. *Blois and Champagne (1165–1224)*

For the domains of the House of Blois we are likewise dependent on the testimony of scattered charters. One of these is a veritable curiosity. Preserved in an antiquary's copy of a lost portal inscription at Blois, it records a concession by Thibaut V, count of Blois and seneschal of France (1152–91), and the countess Alix 'to the men of this land'. The lords limit their own rights of requisition while reserving certain amends; and they promise not to debase the coinage nor to exact the *cornagium*. The text concludes with a ponderous commination in keeping with the pious motive expressed in the preamble.[5]

---

[1] Cf. below, pp. 136–8, 149–51, for provisions in Nevers (1188) and Picardy (1195).

[2] Garnier, *Chartes de commune*, i. 13, art. 45; cf. art. 46.

[3] Ibid., nos. 9, 124 (art. 35), 184 (art. 27). Anatole de Barthélemy, 'Notice sur les monnaies ducales de Bourgogne . . .', in Petit, *Ducs de Bourgogne*, v. 348, is my authority for the confirmation to Saint-Bénigne, but he does not cite his source. In a new charter (1194), Eudes confirmed the local currency of the episcopal *hyilenses* of Autun, *Cart. Autun*, part 2, no. 26.

[4] Barthélemy, 'Monnaies ducales de Bourgogne', 343–8. (Plate III, no. 23.)

[5] Jean Bernier, *Histoire de Blois . . .* (Paris, 1682), p. 301; his facsimile is reproduced in Plate X. Unfortunately, Bernier did not provide his own transcription, which resulted in confusion not entirely dispelled by Jules Quicherat, *BEC*, ii (1840), 305, and Étienne Cartier, 'Recherches sur les monnaies au type chartrain . . .. Septième article', *RN*, xi

Despite some suspicious aspects of its tradition, this enactment must be accepted as authentic. What was inscribed, in necessarily truncated verbiage, was the gist of an act of which no full manuscript survived and which can only be dated 1164–91—probably soon after 1164.[1] Both the substance and the language are more appropriate to its purported time than to any later century. In fact, the dispositive expression 'perdonavervnt hominibvs istivs patrie' appears to have been borrowed verbatim from another portal inscription, this one dating from the end of the eleventh century, and likewise our only evidence of a dispensation to the *blésois* by their count and countess.[2] It cannot very well be argued that these were authentic 'lapidary charters', that is, instruments in uniquely lapidary form.[3] But the inscriptions were appropriate memorials for a community still lacking corporate identity and they must have been almost as old as the acts they record. Those acts found no place in the archives of Blois, although the earliest manuscript privilege (June 1196) not only employs the term *patria* but alludes to one custom mentioned in the concession of Thibaut V and Alix.[4] The inscription of their concession is very imperfect, whether because of Bernier's errors or because of defects or decay in the original, it is difficult to decide.

(1846), 37–9. Bernier's facsimile may be read, with minimal emendation, thus: 'Francie senescalvs comes Teobaldvs et Aaliz comitissa pro amore Dei et pro animabvs antecessorvm svorvm perdonanervnt hominibvs istivs patrie captionem eqvorvm et telarvm in qvibvs mandvcabant necnvn vineas et prata et viridarios et alberetas in manv cepit ita qvod comes habeebit in forisfacto vinearvm x so et [*Bern.*: x so x] abebit avrem etiam hominis forisfaceintis nisi potetrit x solidos redtere. Habebit in forisfacto pratorvm et de vaca vi denarios et de porco et ove i denarivm. Perdonavervnt etiam qvod monetam minvs valentem n[on] facient nec cornagivm vltra capient. Divine igitvr potencie svplicamvs vt qvicvmqve sacram permaginam et qvod sancgitvm est violare vel vllatenvs infirmare presvmpserint aeterna malediccione et Dei vltionvm ira feriantvr implacabili.'

[1] See Bernier, *Hist. Blois*, pp. 300–1; Éloi Johanneau, *Mémoire sur deux inscriptions latines de la ville de Blois, du XIe et du XIIe siècles* (Blois, 1840); Augustin Deloye, 'Des chartes lapidaires en France', *BEC*, viii (1846), 32 n. Neither the town nor (*a fortiori*) the *patria* of Blois yet had corporate identity or archives. The extreme dates of the text are determined by the marriage and death of Thibaut V. My argument for a relatively early date within this period depends on: the pre-existence of a related inscription (see below), the confirmation of the coinage in Champagne in 1165 (below, pp. 130–3), and circumstances of Thibaut's career, for which see Le Père Anselme de Sainte Marie, *Histoire généalogique et chronologique des grands officiers de la Couronne*, 9 vols. (Paris, 1726–33), ii. 845–6; Pacaut, *Louis VII et son royaume*, pp. 172–4, 181–2, 186, 189, 195; 'Cart. Sainte-Croix d'Orléans', nos. 51, 53, 58, and esp. 59.

[2] Bernier, pp. 293, 301; his facsimile of the earlier charter is reproduced and transcribed in the *Nouveau Traité de diplomatique . . . par deux religieux bénédictins*, 6 vols. (Paris, 1750–65), ii. 652, 654.

[3] See Arthur Giry, *Manuel de diplomatique . . .* (Paris, 1894), p. 500: 'en réalité, les inscriptions de cette espèce ne sont que des copies, souvent abrégées, dont les originaux étaient écrits sur parchemin.' The inscription of 1164–91 refers explicitly to 'parchment' (*permaginam* [*sic*]).

[4] 'Cartulaire de la ville de Blois (1196–1493) . . .', ed. Jacques Soyer and Guy Trouillard, *Mémoires de la Société des sciences et lettres du Loir-et-Cher*, xvii (1903–7), introduction, and no. 10; see also art. 11 (p. 53).

In its monetary clause, the facsimile runs: 'Perdonavervnt etiam qvod monetam minvs valentem ent / n[?] facient nec cornagivm vltra capi / ', a manifestly corrupt reading. But one has only to juxtapose the final 'ent' with 'capi' of the line below to recover the plain sense of the passage: 'monetam minvs valentem / n[on] facient nec cornagivm vltra capient.'[1] And to do this is to notice how closely the last three words governed by 'nec' are bound up with the comital engagement not to weaken the coinage. Was the *cornagium* of Blois, then, a money-tax? There seems to be no other mention of any comital exaction so called in extant texts of the twelfth century from Blois and its vicinity,[2] which suggests that it had, indeed, been levied *de novo*. Like the *cornagium* later attested in neighbouring Berry, it must have applied to horned beasts in some way,[3] must therefore have been borne by wealthy peasants and other proprietors. And a new exaction of this sort clearly bore some resemblance to the *bovatge* through which a Catalonian coinage had been secured a generation before; moreover, it should be remembered that extant allusions to the early money-taxes elsewhere, apart from those in constitutive charters, are exceedingly rare. While inconclusive in themselves, these circumstances taken together with the suggestive, almost compelling context make it seem very possible that the *cornagium* of Blois had been levied as a compensation for the restoration of a good or a stable coinage.

However that may be, Thibaut and Alix were evidently responding to complaints about debasements. The numismatic evidence points to a characteristic slippage of standard in the eleventh and twelfth centuries,[4] but there is no explicit testimony either of abrupt mutations or of anxiety about the local coinage. First specified in instruments of the later eleventh century, the *blesensis* does not seem to have been overly plentiful, or else its supply lagged behind the needs of a growing economy.[5] Nor was it notably preferable in its homeland to neighbouring coinages, one of which, the *carnotensis*, was exploited by the same ruler.[6] Lords with customary revenues stipulated in coin of Blois—such as Hugues d'Amboise—cannot have approved of debasements, but such stipulations seem to have been less common in local charters than mentions of amounts in unspecified

---

[1] See p. 126 n. 5 above, and Plate X.

[2] However, a *coruagium* (*sic*) was among the exactions upon tenants of Saint-Lomer usurped (from the abbot and monks?) by Count Jean of Vendôme some time before 1180, *Joannes Saresberiensis . . . opera omnia*, ed. J. A. Giles, 2 vols. (Oxford, 1848), ii, no. 327; and since the word *coruagium* seems to be attested only by this letter, for which we have no early manuscript, there is strong reason to amend the reading to *cornagium* (my thanks to Professor Christopher Brooke and Sir Richard Southern on this point).

[3] Du Cange, *Glossarium*, s.v. *cornagium*.

[4] Dieudonné, *Manuel de numismatique*, iv. 314–15; Poey d'Avant, *Monnaies féodales*, i. 231–3. (Plate III, no. 24.)

[5] As late as 1196 the count was careful to reserve his right to buy food on credit, Soyer and Trouillard, 'Cart. Blois', no. 10, art. 14 (p. 54).

[6] *Marmoutier. Cartulaire blésois*, ed. Charles Métais (Blois, 1889–91), nos. 48, 62, 66

currencies.[1] The most we can say, therefore, is that the coinage of Blois had failed to distinguish itself.

Thibaut's charter betrays no specifically *bourgeois* impulse, although the unenfranchised men of Blois undoubtedly shared with rural tenants the concern to be rid of arbitrary exactions. The concession was advisedly addressed to men of the *patria*, by which, however, something less than the whole county was probably intended. The privilege of 1196 likewise referred to the *patria* in chartering 'all men of Blois and those living within the *banlieue* of Blois'.[2]

No trace of the attendant ceremony figures in our starkly reticent charter. Nevertheless, the preamble and commination suffice to place its motivation within the older tradition of Benedictine piety. Conjecturally, the local houses of Saint-Lomer and Bourgmoyen, if not also Vendôme and Pontlevoy, had some part or interest in the discussions that surely accompanied the enactment.[3] Once again, the comparison with the privilege of 1196 may help, for that document—also expressly pious and approved by the then widowed countess mother—occasioned a public assembly in the count's *curia* at Blois. Moreover, that privilege received the solemn oaths of the count and his barons and of the townspeople there gathered.[4] On the other hand, it is not unlikely that Thibaut V and his wife had acted in knowledge of his elder brother's confirmation of the money of Provins in 1165, or of her father's confirmations of the moneys of Étampes and Orléans in 1137–8, of which the two former were likewise sworn.[5]

Thus, for all its obscurity, the lapidary charter of Blois can be

69, 73, 77, 78, 122, 152; cf. nos. 34, 38, 41, 46, 49, 51, 52, 63, 68, 70, 76, 87, 120–1, 127, 134, 137–8, 144, 155–6, 178; *Cartulaire de Marmoutier pour le Dunois*, ed. Émile Mabille (Châteaudun, 1874), nos. 83, 152, 157, 159; *Cartulaire de l'abbaye cardinale de la Trinité de Vendôme* . . . , ed. Charles Métais, 5 vols. (Paris, 1893–1904), ii, nos. 361, 408, 426, 454, 520, 535; cf. nos. 327, 444, 527, 529, 549, 559, 599; *Gallia christiana*, viii, *inst.*, 419–20, no. 7; AD Loir-et-Cher, 46H 3, no. 30. See generally André Chédeville, *Chartres et ses campagnes (XIᵉ–XIIIᵉ siècles)* (Paris, 1973), pp. 431–6.

For evidence of exchange and prosperity around Blois in the time of Thibaut V, see also BN, MS. n. a. fr. 6278, fos. 168ʳ–170, 203ʳ; Bernier, *Hist. Blois, preuves*, pp. iii, vi, vii, xi; AD Loir-et-Cher, 3H 66, no. 1; 3H 110; *Cart. Vendôme*, ii, no. 560; *Gallia christiana*, viii, *inst.*, 426, no. 15.

[1] *Cart. Vendôme*, ii, no. 454; cf. no. 520, and nos. 483, 506, 551; *Marmoutier. Cart. blésois*, nos. 104, 144, 154; AD Loir-et-Cher, 11H 128, p. 40.

[2] 'Cart. Blois', no. 10; cf. Count Thibaut's endowment-charter for Saint-Sauveur (Blois, 1188), which likewise alludes to the *banlieue* as a jurisdictional unit, *Gallia christiana*, viii, *inst.*, 426. See also Alexandre Dupré, 'Étude sur les institutions municipales de Blois', *MSAHO*, xiv (1875), 442–6; and cf. Robert Chazan, 'The Blois Incident of 1171: A Study in Jewish Intercommunal Organization', *Proc. Amer. Acad. for Jewish Research*, xxxvi (1968), 21.

[3] See *Gallia christiana*, viii. 1355–7, 1368–71, 1382–3, 1390.

[4] 'Cart. Blois', no. 10, pp. 55–8; also nos. 20, 21; cf. of the latter, the notification by the count's aunt Marie de France, it was said that, in addition to many others, upon her nephew's order, 'Hoc etiam juravit communitas terre Blesis'.

[5] See below, pp. 131–3; above, pp. 29–31.

characterized with some assurance. It was, in fact, like its ancestor, an early specimen of the 'land-charter', providing remedies for disorder in a jurisdictional area extending from the streets of the *castrum* to the houses and fields of the adjacent countryside. It dealt with the coinage as a public and moral issue, not unlike certain engagements to the peace elsewhere. The monetary provision was solemn and (apparently) innocent. Immediate and unusual in its provocation, aristocratic in its initiative, and probably secured under oath, that provision simply forbade debasements. One could argue that its wording was cynically contrived to favour the landlords, but that seems improbable. The general expectation—in conformity with the prevailing motive—must have been that the coinage would be indefinitely (and gratuitously) secure from alteration. And, so far as we can tell, that expectation was not frustrated. No confirmation of coinage (and no dispensation from *cornagium*) appear among the numerous franchises granted in 1196, nor, on the evidence, was any confirmation then needed.[1] For a Christian people accustomed to lapidary reminders of its rights, the freshly chiselled words over the portal of Saint-Fiacre, associated with the happy memory of late distinguished lords, must have retained all their moral force.

Meanwhile, events had taken a course at once symmetrical and distinctive in the domains of Henri I le Libéral (1152–80), who was even more celebrated than his younger brother.[2] Among several coinages in Champagne, those of Provins, Troyes, Meaux, and Châlons-sur-Marne had especial importance in this age of the expanding fairs. Count Henri I exploited the first two of these himself and the third jointly with the bishop of Meaux; these currencies appear to have been issued in intrinsic parity with one another while the episcopal coinage of Châlons came to be recognized as stronger by one-fifth (15 d. *pruv.* = 12 d. *cat.*). As was so common in the North, regional instruments of the early twelfth century were slow to stipulate or specify the money of payment or account, and just as in Burgundy, a preference for concurrency *sine scambio* is perceptible in the comital domains.[3] The growth of trade probably encouraged

[1] See generally, *Marmoutier. Cart. blésois*, nos. 173–89; *Cart. Vendôme*, ii, nos. 577–636; 'Cart. Blois', nos. 10, 22, 31.

[2] See generally, Henri d'Arbois de Jubainville, *Histoire des ducs et des comtes de Champagne*, 6 vols. in 7 (Paris, 1859–67), iii; Dieudonné, *Manuel de numismatique*, iv. 131–41; Elizabeth Chapin, *Les Villes de foires de Champagne des origines au début du XIVᵉ siècle* (Paris, 1937); Bautier, 'Les foires de Champagne'; and Michel Bur, 'Remarques sur les plus anciens documents concernant les foires de Champagne', *Les Villes . . .* (Reims, 1972), 45–60. Professor John F. Benton generously put at my disposal his unpublished 'Recueil des actes des comtes de Champagne, 1152–1197', from which my citations marked with an asterisk (*) are drawn; numerals in parentheses following citations refer to comital acts in Arbois de Jubainville, iii, 'Catalogue des actes d'Henri le Libéral, comte de Champagne, de Marie, sa femme, et d'Henri II, son fils aîné'.

[3] *Cartulaire de l'abbaye de Saint-Loup de Troyes*, ed. Charles Lalore (Paris, 1875), nos. 8, 9, 12, 15–17, 19, 21, 23, 25, 28 (58), 36, 41, 51 (260); *Cartulaire de l'abbaye du*

the tolerance of diverse coinages; tolls seem to have been especially lucrative in Champagne even before the cyclic fairs matured[1] and it must have been impractical to insist on payments in local money by travelling merchants. Nevertheless, the stability of the regional currencies had not escaped suspicion. The coinage of Châlons was tested in connection with a payment of eleven *sous* in 1116;[2] and the *provinois*, which had in fact declined in value, circulated in 'strong' pieces together with weak during the early years of Henri le Libéral.[3]

It was just then that the latter moved to recover the regalian prerogative in the mint of Meaux that had slipped away during the eleventh century. When the bishop complained, Count Henri settled the issue in a remarkable charter given in his palace at Provins in 1165. He acknowledged that he had imitated the (episcopal) money of Meaux in his own lands, meaning perhaps at Provins and Troyes, in issues that had deteriorated from the bishop's own standards. 'Wishing to correct the fault', Henri swore upon holy relics to stop minting money of Meaux, whether good or false; he would henceforth preserve the existing coin undiminished, give it currency and parity with his coinages of Provins and Troyes, and do justice upon those who violate or falsify the bishop's coinage. There follows a restatement, almost verbatim, of what had just been promised, preceded by the emphatic words: 'This, however, I wish to make clear, that I neither ought nor should alter or lighten the coinage of Meaux.' The count's faith was pledged by his barons Anseau de Traînel the butler, Hugues de Plancy, and Eudes the constable—no minor detail, for these were men of exceptional importance and of tried fidelity to Henri. The charter concluded with a list of witnesses whose names were omitted by the thirteenth-century scribes whose copies we have, and it received the comital seal.[4]

Paraclet, ed. Charles Lalore (Paris, 1878), nos. 54, 58 (82), 59, 61 (189), 68; *AD Marne, H 585 (1161); *'Chartes de l'abbaye de Mores (Aube)', ed. Charles Lalore, *MSAA*, xxxvii (1873), 53–4; É.-A. Blampignon, *Bar-sur-Aube* (Paris, 1900), *chartes*, nos. 13, 15; *Gallia christiana*, iv, *inst.*, 176–7 (73); *Louis Chantereau Le Febvre, *Traité des fiefs . . .* (Paris, 1662), *autres preuves*, p. 4 (53); Arbois de Jubainville, *Comtes de Champagne*, iii, *p.j.*, nos. 102, 105; BN, MS. lat. 17098, fo. 35ʳ (235); MS. lat. 5528, fo. 2ʳᵛ (131); AD Côte-d'Or, 15H 13, fo. 43. (Plate III, no. 25.)

[1] See e.g. Auguste Harmand, 'Notice historique sur la Léproserie de la ville de Troyes . . .', *MSAA*, xiv (1848), 519–20; Bur, 'Foires de Champagne', 49–50, 59.

[2] Raymond Serrure, 'L'atelier monétaire de Châlons-sur-Marne', *Bulletin de numismatique*, viii (1900), 27.

[3] *Cart. Longpont*, no. 7; AD Côte-d'Or, 15H 13, fo. 43; Arbois de Jubainville, *Comtes de Champagne*, iii. 247; BM Meaux, MS. 63, fo. 129 (text of 1161); Félix Bourquelot, 'Études sur les foires de Champagne . . .', *Mémoires présentées . . . à l'Académie des inscriptions et belles-lettres . . .*, v (1865–6), 50. Cf. Anatole de Barthélemy, 'Monnaie', in Arbois de Jubainville, iv: 2. 770–1, who asserts, without citing evidence, that the 'strong coin of Provins' dates from the reign of Thibaut II (1125–52). Dr. Michel Bur kindly informs me that he finds no such evidence prior to 1161 (text of Meaux cited above).

[4] BN, MS. lat. 5528, fo. 2ʳᵛ (ed. Edmond Martène and Ursin Durand, *Veterum*

Henri le Libéral thereby admitted the bishop's right to exploit a coinage concurrent with comital coinages, only reserving jurisdiction over violators. On such terms it is hard to see why the count went on to forswear debasing the money of Meaux. Yet, redundant or not, the clause to that effect cannot have been regarded lightly, for it was reproduced as if the substance of the count's concession in a notice of ratification issued by Henri's brother Étienne, count of Sancerre.[1] In some sense, therefore, the settlement of 1165 was regarded as a confirmation of the coinage; the bishop, perhaps because he lacked control over all the dies, required the count's sworn assurance as to coinage bearing the imprint of Meaux. Moreover, the coinage of Meaux so restricted was to circulate in the counties of Provins and Troyes together with, and at the same alloy and weight as, the moneys of those counties, which implies that the confirmation extended to those other coinages as well, or at least that the principle of an indefinitely stable currency was being admitted throughout the comital domains. On either view, this suggestive equation of coinages imparts to the text in which it appears an enlarged territorial significance. Unlike the king in his confirmation at Étampes in 1137–8, or Thibaut V in his at Blois some years later—Thibaut, to draw the parallel, having said nothing of his coinage of Chartres—Count Henri appears to have been thinking of currencies nearly uniform throughout Champagne. It is all the more striking, therefore, that the count made his solemn engagement to the clergy of Meaux alone, although in the circumstances the right of that church may have been identified with the public preference for stabilized currencies. The charter was least unusual in its sworn ratification by barons

---

scriptorum et monumentorum . . . amplissima collectio, 9 vols. [Paris, 1724–33], i. 873): 'Ego Henricus Trecensis palatinus comes uniuersis . . . notum facio quod orta discordia inter me et dominum Meldensem episcopum monetam meldensi monete similem feci in terra mea, vnde ipsa meldensis moneta deterior et uilior facta est, in quo cum me errauisse cognouissem, erratum uolens corrigere super sanctas reliquias iuraui quod meldensem monetam nec bonam nec falsam deinceps fieri faciam aut fieri permitam nec aliquo modo deteriorabo uel deteriorari sustinebo in posse meo, set cum pruuinensi et trecensi moneta eadem lege et eodem pondere per comitatum pruuinensem et trecensem et in toto posse meo ut currat et omnino sine cambio accipiatur faciam . . . . Hoc autem manifestum esse uolo quod meldensem monetam nec debeo nec possum mutare aut alleuiare set cum predictis monetis meis eadem lege sicut dictum est et eodem pondere per comitatum pruuinensem et trecensem et in toto posse meo ut currat et omnino sine cambio accipiatur facere debeo. Iurauerunt etiam ex mandato meo tres barones mei, videlicet . . ..' The barons who swore with Henri can be traced in comital acts from the start of the reign, *LTC*, i, no. 118 (1); *AD Marne, H 551 (5); Eudes the constable disappears in the later 1160s, but Anseau and Hugues continued to serve the countess Marie after Henri's death in 1180, *BM Provins, MS. 85, no. 22 (324). See also below, p. 162.

[1] BN, MS. lat. 5528, fo. 3ʳᵛ: 'Ego Stephanus . . . notum facio quod sicut dominus et frater meus comes Henricus in litteris suis ius ecclesie meldensis recognovit, hoc scilicet quod meldensem monetam nec mutare nec alleuiare nec aliquo modo deteriorare debet, set cum monetis suis [of Provins and Troyes] . . . ut currat et accipiatur facere debet, sic et ego recognosco . . ..'

of the household, a procedure reminiscent of the confirmation of Étampes sworn by Luc de Male on behalf of the king whose daughter Henri later married.[1]

Such as it was, the security of coinage affirmed in 1165 remained in effect for two generations thereafter. These were times of grand and increasing prosperity in Champagne.[2] Transactions or renders in food-stuffs, not counting tithes, continued frequent,[3] yet there seems to have been no shortage of specie. Neither the bishops of Meaux nor the counts of Troyes were disposed to manipulate reputable coinages then being minted in large amounts.[4] Even the clippings from the mint of Troyes were a considerable revenue for the count toward 1180.[5] The real problem was how to maintain some control over the mint-men, how to hold them to their agreements. Count Thibaut III (1197–1201) became so suspicious

[1] Cf. above, p. 30.

[2] For revenues of tolls and of fairs, see e.g. *Cart. Paraclet*, nos. 75 (349), 93 (444); Arbois de Jubainville, *Comtes de Champagne*, iii, 'Catalogue des actes . . .', no. 221; BN, MS. lat. 17098, fos. 35ᵛ (316), 58ᵛ–59 (616), 61ᵛ–62, 150ᵛ, 164; Harmand, 'Notice sur la Léproserie de Troyes', 525–7 (196, 246, 309); Chapin, *Villes de foires*, *p.j.*, pp. 279–86, nos. 1–2 (47, 124), 3–4; *AD Aube, 20H 9; *BM Provins, MS. 85, no. 5 (137); MS. 92, fos. 227–9 (25); Victor Carrière, *Histoire et cartulaire des Templiers de Provins . . .* (Paris, 1919), pp. 103–4, 110 (65); *Cartulaire général de l'Yonne . . .*, ed. Maximilien Quantin, 2 vols. (Auxerre, 1854–60), ii. 118–19 (82); *AN, K 192, no. 312 (155); *AD Yonne, G 510; *Blampignon, *Bar-sur-Aube*, pp. 406–8 (78; faulty edition of charter of 1170); *BN, MS. lat. 5993, fo. 122 (218); *Coll. Dupuy, ccxxvi, fo. 52ʳᵛ.

[3] *Cart. Saint-Loup de Troyes*, nos. 2, 3, 43 (181), 46; *Cart. Paraclet*, nos. 6, 15, 21, 53, 63–5, 67, 69, 71, 88; *Cartulaire de l'abbaye de La Chapelle-aux-Planches . . .*, ed. Charles Lalore (Paris, 1878), nos. 15, 16, 17 (48), 18, 24, 26 (27), 44; *AN, K 192, nos. 202 (59 *bis*), 260 (43 *bis*); *Monuments historiques . . .*, ed. Jules Tardif (Paris, 1866), pp. 290–1 (64); *Blampignon, *Bar-sur-Aube*, pp. 406–8; *AD Marne (Reims), H 318 (A.D. 1163), H 1384 (120; A.D. 1164); *BM Provins, MS. 92, fo. 52 (145); *Toussaint du Plessis, *Histoire de l'église de Meaux . . .*, 2 vols. (Paris, 1731), ii. 57 (157), 59 (176); *LTC*, i, no. 271 (253); *A.-L. Paris, *Histoire de l'abbaye d'Avenay*, 2 vols. (Reims, 1879), ii. 85–6; Harmand, 'Notice sur la léproserie de Troyes', 521–2, 525 (196), 527, 528–9, 533 (438), 536–7, 539, 555–6 (1715). The count's *salvamentum* came to be accounted or stipulated in oats, e.g. *AD Marne, H 714 (15 August 1156); Arbois de Jubainville, *Comtes de Champagne*, iii, *p.j.*, nos. 130, 154 (159, 362); BN, MS. lat. 17098, fos. 32ᵛ–35 (212); *AD Aube, G 2857 (A.D. 1176, 1178, 1186). That monetary values could easily be assigned to the land and its produce appears from a settlement between the abbeys of Larrivour and Montiéramey in 1174, *AD Aube, n. a. 524 (227); see also *BM Provins, MS. 85, no. 24 (435). In 1185 the countess Marie gave in alms 'modium frumenti de preposito meo de Brayo [Bray] singulis annis usque ad mediam Quadragesimam de primo proventu bladorum meorum qui ea dem prepositura exibunt recipiendum', *AD Yonne, H 488.

[4] The local mints certainly continued active while the work of the changers grew: Arbois de Jubainville, *Comtes de Champagne*, iii. 231, 245–6, *p.j.*, no. 144 (223); 'Catalogue des actes . . .', nos. 23, 137, 180, 303, 309; Michel Veissière, *. . . Saint-Quiriace de Provins (XIᵉ–XIIIᵉ siècles)* (Provins, 1961), *p.j.*, no. 13 (91); *BM Provins, MS. 92, fos. 227–9 (25); BN, MS. lat. 17098, fos. 32ᵛ–35; *AD Marne, 18H 33, no. 2. There was a persistent concern with intrinsic value, however; perhaps not merely legalistic, for the sou of Troyes was said to be at 44 to the mark in 1190, that of Provins at 50 in 1197, Petit, *Ducs de Bourgogne*, iii, *p.j.*, no. 1444 (478–9); Arbois de Jubainville, iii. 248.

[5] Harmand, 'Notice sur la léproserie de Troyes', 526 (original, *BN, Coll. Champagne, lviii, fo. 127).

of the moneyers at Meaux that he forcibly restrained them from entering the bishop's house where they worked.[1] The resulting litigation was settled on terms of which we are ignorant; and in 1208 the countess Blanche entered into a pact (*societas*) with the bishop providing for their joint minting at Meaux, Provins, and Troyes for three years, and allowing the bishop one-third of the proceeds.[2] This agreement effectively confirmed the tendency first visible in 1165 to standardize the coinages of the county; whether the pact expired in 1211 is not clear, but it was certainly renewed by Bishop Guillaume in 1214.[3]

None of these events was perfectly analogous to the confirmations of coinage elsewhere for which ransoms or taxes were sometimes paid. But the text of the 'society' of 1208 refers to revenues 'from all *monetagium* and from all service [*seruitium*] which will be done for the money',[4] and at least one scholar has interpreted this *monetagium* as a money-tax.[5] On its face, however, the meaning would seem rather to be *seigneuriage*, and most historians who have passed this way have followed Du Cange in this reading.[6] In support of the prevailing view is the perfect silence of abundant local texts regarding the money-tax; if there was one in Champagne, it cannot have been pegged to the confirmation of coinages. And yet, some doubt lingers. Were the *monetagium* and *servitium* two words for the same thing? If not, how did their meanings differ?

A text of several years later suggests an unexpected answer: namely, that the terms did mean different things, that the *monetagium* probably was, indeed, *seigneuriage*, but that the *servitium* was a sort of money-tax. In 1224 Count Thibaut IV (1201–53) made known the terms on which the moneyers in the three mint towns were obligated to the bishop of Meaux for the next three years. The moneyers were to pay the bishop 'for the service of his coinage of Meaux which they have to mint with my coins of Provins and Troyes 433 l. 6 s. and 8 d.' of Provins in six-monthly terms coinciding with the fairs of Saint-Ayoul (Troyes) and of Bar. Now this 'service' (*seruitium*) was certainly not *seigneuriage*; the latter was

---

[1] BN, MS. lat. 5528, fos. 3ᵛ–4; Barthélemy, 'Monnaie', in Arbois de Jubainville, iv: 2. 772–3. The bishop of Meaux was having difficulties with his hereditary moneyers as early as *c.* 1133, BN, MS. lat. 5528, fos. 2ᵛ–3.

[2] BN, MS. lat. 5993, fos. 28ᵛ–29; *Gallia christiana*, viii, *inst.*, 558, no. 10 (Arbois de Jubainville, 'Catalogue des actes . . .', *Comtes de Champagne*, v, no. 695).

[3] BN, MS. lat. 5993, fo. 30ʳ (Arbois de Jubainville, v, 'Catalogue', no. 862).

[4] BN, MS. lat. 5993, fo. 28ᵛ (*Gallia christiana*, viii, *inst.*, 558, no. 10): '. . . tali modo scilicet quod ubicumque fuerit fabricatum, siue Trecis siue Pruuini siue Meldis, dicta comitissa de omni monetagio et de seruitio quod fiet pro moneta, et de omnibus prouentibus qui inde prouenient quocumque modo proueniant duas partes habebit et nos terciam habebimus.'

[5] See [?Alfred] Hiver, 'Considérations sur les monnoies du comté de Champagne', *RN*, iv (1839), 35.

[6] Du Cange, *Glossarium*, s.v. *monetagium*; cf. Brussel, *Nouvel Examen des fiefs*, i. 195; Adrien de Longpérier, 'Recherches sur les monnaies de Meaux', *RN*, v (1840), 128.

calculated separately as 6 d. to the pound of 22½ s., or just over 2 per cent.[1] On the other hand, the designated *servitium* was no rough sum, let alone the arrears from some incomplete share or collection: it was precisely one-third of 1,300 l., which can only mean that it was the same share of the revenues of the mint that had been assigned to the bishop in the charter of 1208. What had become of the count's two-thirds of *servitium* in 1224 is not evident—perhaps that required a separate charter now lost—but it was agreed that of the 6 d. per l., the count was to have 4 d. and the bishop 2 d.

In short, the moneyers had to pay a predetermined fee, a very large fee, for the right to exploit the coinages. That they were willing to do so is striking evidence of the prosperity of the mints and it suggests a reason why no such money-tax as had developed elsewhere was imposed in Champagne. From the seigneurial point of view, the *servitium* had all the advantages of the money-tax without its defects. Much easier to collect and not much less rewarding, it entailed no restriction on the prerogative to alter the coinage. In fact, it was in the new money of Provins that the moneyers were to pay the *servitium* in 1224, and the bishop was changing the coinage of Meaux at about the same time.[2] Was that fee, then, wholly lacking conceptual analogy to the money-tax or *monetagium*? To decide that, we should have to know how the figure of 1,300 l. had been arrived at. Was it some approximation of the profits of mints additional to *seigneuriage* plus reasonable return to the minters, some kind of farm, or 'second *seigneuriage*'? Or was it merely the competitive price for a lucrative concession? We do not know. But it may be significant that these agreements documented between 1208 and 1224 retained the three-year minting terms that had been clearly associated with the money-tax in Normandy and the Île-de-France.

c. *Nevers: the Charter of Corbigny (1188)*

'In his time'—the allusion was to Bishop Guillaume (de Toucy) of Auxerre (1167–81), in the voice of one whose memory was fresh—'the counts of Nevers changed frequently, whence arose countless tribulations and troubles . . . for his church and for others.'[3] Very likely the mutation of coinage was among the troubles of this *comitum mutatio*, as we shall see;

---

[1] BN, MS. lat. 5528, fo. 4ʳᵛ (ed. Barthélemy, in Arbois de Jubainville, *Comtes de Champagne*, iv: 2. 771–2; 'Catalogue des actes', ibid., v, no. 1639): the moneyers 'recognouerunt se debere venerabili patri P. Meldensi episcopo pro seruicio monete sue meldensis quam ipsi habent ad cudendum cum monetis meis pruuinensibus et trecensibus quadrigentas et trigintas tres libras et sex solidos et octo denarios pruuinensium nouorum soluendas per tres annos . . .'.

[2] See preceding note; also *HF*, xxii. 82, and *LTC*, ii, no. 1704.

[3] *Gesta pontificum Autissiodorensium*, ed. L.-M. Duru, *Bibliothèque historique de l'Yonne* . . ., 2 vols. (Auxerre, 1850–63), i. 422.

but the clergy who complained had worse things in mind. While the sons of Thibaut the Great had upheld their father's reputation in Blois and Champagne, the descendants of Count Guillaume II of Nevers (1095–1147)—himself a crusader and renowned for his justice, a man who ended his days a Carthusian monk—had lapsed all too often into violence against Vézelay abbey and other churches.[1] In 1181 the comital dynasty of Nevers failed in the male line, an event promptly exploited by the young Philip Augustus, to whose first cousin, Pierre de Courtenay, the heiress Agnès was married in 1184; having in the meantime administered Nevers directly, the king obtained from Pierre, 'for the increase of the Crown', the fief of Montargis.[2] According to the canons of Auxerre, Pierre de Courtenay persisted in the abuse of churches for which his wife's family was notorious. He was, they recalled, 'a man . . . of immense power, but incautious of mind and prone to dreadful violence'.[3] This impression is confirmed by the charters and letters,[4] most of which, however, tell a different—and equally tendentious—story.[5] What seems clear is that Pierre, like his predecessors in Nevers, was an impulsive man for whom the crusade afforded the best means of reconciling ambition with piety. It was the mobilization of the Third Crusade that occasioned the incident that is of interest here.

In 1188 Pierre de Courtenay and Agnès acted in the old abbey-town of Corbigny, upon the counsel and consent of bishops, abbots, and barons of the county of Nevers, to establish a coinage at 4 d. fine silver and 16 s. 8 d. to the mark of Troyes. The count and countess swore to maintain this coinage 'perpetually' in its newly instituted weight and alloy, giving assurance that their posterity would swear likewise. Any fraudulent

[1] René de Lespinasse, *Le Nivernais et les comtes de Nevers*, 2 vols. (Paris, 1909–11), i. 261–396.

[2] *Rec. des actes de Philippe Auguste*, i, no. 106; Lespinasse, *Nivernais*, i. 396–9; Alexander Cartellieri, *Philipp II. August, König von Frankreich*, 5 vols. (Leipzig, 1899–1922), i. 108, 110, 236–7.

[3] *Gesta pontificum*, ed. Duru, i. 440–1; also 442–4. See also, on Pierre de Courtenay (the future Latin Emperor of Constantinople) and Agnès, Jean Du Bouchet, *Histoire généalogique de la maison royale de Courtenay . . .* (Paris, 1661), pp. 29–42; Anselme, *Officiers de la couronne*, i. 475–6.

[4] *Chartes de Cluny*, v, no. 4312; *Cartulaire du prieuré de La Charité-sur-Loire . . .*, ed. René de Lespinasse (Nevers, 1887), nos. 8, 80; *Epistolae pontificum Romanorum ineditae*, ed. Samuel Loewenfeld (Leipzig, 1885), no. 389.

[5] 'Les chartes de Saint-Étienne de Nevers', ed. René de Lespinasse, *BSN*, 3rd ser., xii (1908), 93 (no. 16; also in *Chartes de Cluny*, v, no. 4297); *Cartulaire de Saint-Cyr de Nevers*, ed. René de Lespinasse (Nevers, 1916), no. 102; Jean Lebeuf, *Mémoires concernant l'histoire civile et ecclésiastique d'Auxerre . . .*, ed. Ambroise Challe and Maximilien Quantin, 4 vols. (Auxerre, 1848–55), iv, nos. 80, 81; *Chartes de Cluny*, v, nos. 4344, 4364; *Cart. Hospitaliers*, i, nos. 716, 965; 'Cart. Jully-les-Nonnains', 276–7; *Cart. Yonne*, ii, nos. 375, 441, 442, 450; *Droits et privilèges de la commune de Nevers*, ed. Henri Crouzet (Nevers, 1858), pp. 106, 154; 'Chartes inédites relatives à la famille de Courtenay et à l'abbaye des Écharlis (XIIᵉ–XIIIᵉ siècles)', ed. Henri Stein, *Annales de la Société historique & archéologique du Gâtinais*, xxxvi (1922), nos. 3, 10.

departure from these standards, whether by the count or by his moneyers, would dispense 'ecclesiastical persons and barons of our land' from the obligation of using the count's coinage; the bishops of Auxerre and Nevers were to have jurisdiction over violations of these terms. In order to prevent 'debasement or counterfeiting', there was to be 'more frequent' supervision by money-changers and men skilled in matters of silver and weight, and prelates and barons themselves might investigate when they saw fit. Moreover, 'for the perpetuity of this coinage and for the journey to Jerusalem, it pleased the ecclesiastical persons and barons of our land' that the count and countess might collect twelve deniers from every house 'having its own residence and hearth, in this year only, through the cities and castles and *bourgs* and villages in which our coinage has rightful currency'. Lest the willing grant of this tax become a precedent, the churches and barons were to receive patent letters incorporating the provisions of Corbigny, which were themselves published as a solemn charter bearing the seals of Pierre I and Agnès of Nevers.[1] In the same year their charter was reissued in the king's name at Paris.

Perpetuitas monete!—the notion of conserving the coinage could hardly have been put more extremely. No mere confirmation of the coinage, the charter of Corbigny was a concession to the magnates of Nevers so sweeping that it can only be explained as a reaction against the arbitrariness for which the counts were noted. Pierre and Agnès practically relinquished control of their coinage, reserving (presumably) only their *seigneuriage*. They forswore not only mutations but the very privacy of minting through which they had exercised a quasi-proprietary right. Taken literally, the provision that prelates and barons might cease to honour the comital money in the event of violation seems to have been intended to apply only through a second generation: if such was indeed the meaning, the implied rebuke to Pierre I was thereby underscored. The projected hearth-tax was not effectively compensatory, since it was to be levied only once;

---

[1] AD Nièvre, 2G 11 (formerly B 1 and G 64; but I am informed that the document has been missing from the archives for many years), ed. Maurice Prou, 'Recueil de documents relatifs à l'histoire monétaire', *RN*, 3rd ser., xiv (1896), 286–8 (Prou's transcription reproduced below, Appendix, no. 4). The royal version, which was preserved in a cartulary of Auxerre long since lost, is known only through the edition by the Abbé Lebeuf, *Mémoires concernant l'histoire d'Auxerre* (1743); ed. Quantin, iv, no. 78. This version has misled more than one scholar—e.g. Georges de Soultrait, *Essai sur la numismatique nivernaise* (Paris, 1854), p. 39; Henri Sarriau, 'Numismatique nivernaise', *BSN*, 3rd ser., vi (1896), 42; and Lespinasse, *Nivernais*, i. 401–2 (the two latter overlooked Prou's publication). My own reconstruction of events—below, pp. 138–42—supports Prou's assertion that the royal text was a 'diplôme confirmatif': it was that in fact, at least, if not in form. It was probably solicited by the bishop of Auxerre, for his clergy not only copied it but cited it in subsequent disputes over the money at Auxerre (below, p. 143). It seems above suspicion. The clergy of Auxerre would not have replaced the words *moneta nostra* in the charter of Corbigny with the ambiguous *moneta Nivernensis*, language that could almost have invited the counts to pretend that the coinage of Auxerre was exempt from the confirmation.

significantly, it was labelled *beneficium*, or 'favour'—not *monetagium* or *redemptio*. Moreover, the sworn confirmation of the money could not alone justify the grant. The favour offered by the assembled *nivernais* was to provide for the need of a ruler who was taking the cross. To obtain a subsidy for crusade such as was then being freely, if not always happily, granted in northern France, a Pierre de Courtenay had to renounce an ordinary revenue. Later counts of Nevers were understandably dissatisfied with this agreement, which had, indeed, no parallel in France.[1]

The confirmation of coinage seems to have been unknown in Nevers before 1188. It is believed that the comital money remained relatively good and strong down to the middle of the twelfth century or a little later.[2] But the quality and attribution of extant coins are too doubtful to admit of certainty on this point. All that can be said is that the weight specified in 1188 was significantly lower than the best weights of earlier deniers. The new coinage, corresponding to the *parisis* in weight although a little weaker in alloy,[3] was a relatively good coinage; quite likely the same standard had been in effect or was then introduced in the mints of Auxerre and Tonnerre, which were also the preserve of the counts of Nevers.[4] As for the evidence of texts, that too is problematical. It does suggest anxiety about the stability of coinages circulating in the vicinity of Nevers beginning in 1165,[5] and it shows that the money of Nevers had strong competition from those of Gien, Provins, and Souvigny, as well as from the concurrent deniers of Auxerre.[6] In 1164 Count Guillaume IV

---

[1] See below, pp. 140, 143, 190.

[2] Caron, *Monnaies féodales*, pp. 104–5; Sarriau, 'Numismatique nivernaise', 31; Dieudonné, *Manuel de numismatique*, iv. 299–301.

[3] Sarriau, 'Numismatique nivernaise', 42; Dieudonné, *Manuel de numismatique*, ii. 219; iv. 301. In 1230 the 'strong' money of Nevers was regarded equivalent to the *parisis*, 'Chartes de l'abbaye de Corbigny', ed. Anatole de Charmasse, *Mémoires de la Société éduenne*, new ser., xvii (1889), 22–3. Sarriau asserts that the standards of 1188 were never put into effect, on the ground that the surviving deniers weigh less than required.

[4] Dieudonné, *Manuel de numismatique*, iv. 108–9, 138. The deniers of Auxerre were already at 50 s. to the mark in 1174, and their alloy was 4 d. in 1194, *Cart. Yonne*, ii, no. 232, and nos. 45, 450; these standards correspond to the stipulations of 1188.

[5] Lebeuf, *Mémoires concernant l'histoire d'Auxerre*, iv, nos. 57, 67, 68; BM Auxerre, MS. 161, fos. 56–61; 'Chartes de Corbigny', 16; *Cart. Yonne*, ii, no. 179, recognition of a pledge to the bishop of Auxerre for 60 l. in a coinage not specified, *c.* 1167–80: 'Sciendum autem quod tempore illo, quo hec facta sunt, marcha argenti XL et duos solidos comparabatur, ad cujus valenciam predicta pecunia reddetur, si tamen aliqua occasione contingeret monetam mutari.'

[6] *Cart. Yonne*, ii, nos. 84, 98, 114, 190, 219, 298, 304, 306–7, 316, 339, 341–2, 347, 371, 381, 384; 'Chartes de Corbigny', 16; 'Titres du prieuré de Mêves-sur-Loire (XIIᵉ, XIIIᵉ siècles)', ed. René de Lespinasse, *BSN*, 3rd ser., vii (1899), 206, 210; 'Chartes de Saint-Étienne de Nevers', *BSN*, 3rd ser., xii, no. 21; *Cart. Saint-Cyr*, no. 106. Indeed, the texts suggest that the coinage of Nevers was in relatively short supply; see also BM Auxerre, MS. 161, fo. 73ʳ, mention in 1196 of a *cens* of Saint-Germain 'illius monete que in comitatu Nivernensi cucurrunt'; and the remarks of Adrien Blanchet in *RN*, 5th ser., i (1937), 327. On the other hand, a hoard buried at Accolay (arr. Auxerre, cant. Vermenton) soon after 1193 included at least 1380 deniers from Nevers and Auxerre, and

had to admit that an occasional tallage in the *bourg* Saint-Étienne (Nevers) might be paid in that 'money which then will be'.[1] Possibly the supply of local deniers had lagged behind the requirements of an economy in which markets and pecuniary exchange were themselves sluggish until around the middle of the twelfth century.[2] In that case one could easily imagine a policy of traditional, limited minting being drastically changed by needy rulers determined to exploit their mints for profit. And if the prevailing form of their manipulation was demonetization and debasement, as it seems to have been, one could have expected complaints from landlords, who were not the only ones, however, to be concerned about coinages in a region where revenues were becoming fixed in custom.[3] By 1188 the count of Nevers must have been promoting or requiring the use of his coinage, for the magnates were to be allowed their choice of the currency of receipt only in case the comital money were altered.

If the confirmation of the coinage was a novelty, in other respects the charter of Corbigny was less original. The counts of Nevers were used to sanctioning charters under oath. In 1164 Guillaume IV had not only sworn to uphold his privilege for Saint-Étienne, but had promised to secure his brother Gui's oath when Gui came of age;[4] and pursuant to that form of stipulation this charter was confirmed by successive counts.[5] In 1185 the customary reconfirmation took a form that anticipated Corbigny in another respect as well: for besides providing for subsequent sworn confirmations, the count and countess appointed the bishops of Auxerre and Nevers as guarantors.[6]

So, too, with their fiscal enactment. The twelvepenny hearth-tax—which, to be sure, cannot have been very novel anywhere by the later twelfth century—had formed part of the *salvamentum* collected by the counts of Nevers in their lordship of Marigny (-sur-Yonne) about 1112.[7]

only a scattering of deniers from Tonnerre, Souvigny, Gien, Provins, Chalon, Sancerre, and Paris, Maximilien Quantin, 'Note sur une trouvaille de monnaies du moyen-âge faite à Accolay', *Bulletin de la Société des sciences historiques et naturelles de l'Yonne*, xxxix (1885), 226–33; Émile Caron, 'Monnaies féodales', *Annuaire de la Société française de numismatique et d'archéologie*, vi (1882), 184–9.

[1] 'Chartes de Saint-Étienne de Nevers', no. 9.

[2] See evidence cited in p. 138 n. 6; and for the rural economy, markets, and exchange, see Hugues de Poitiers, *Historia Vizeliacensis monasterii*, ed. Luc d'Achery, *Spicilegium*, 2nd edn., ii. 520; *Gesta abbatum S. Germani Autissiodorensis*, HF, xii. 307; 'Chartes de Corbigny', 6–7; *Cart. Saint-Cyr*, nos. 55, 76, 87, 93, 101; 'Chartes de Saint-Étienne', no. 6; 'Titres de Mêves-sur-Loire', 201–5; *Cart. La Charité*, no. 65; *Cart. Yonne*, ii, nos. 149, 200, 360, 500, and *passim*; *Ordonnances*, xi. 217–19; Lebeuf, *Mémoires concernant l'histoire d'Auxerre*, iv, nos. 80, 81, 132; Petit, *Ducs de Bourgogne*, iii, *p.j.*, nos. 753, 875, 876; *Chartes de Cluny*, v, no. 4344; *Cart. Hospitaliers*, i, no. 716.

[3] *Cart. Yonne*, ii, nos. 253, 431.   [4] 'Chartes de Saint-Étienne', no. 9.

[5] Ibid., nos. 12, 16, 23.

[6] Ibid., no. 16; this charter also anticipated that of Corbigny, although perhaps less significantly, in being submitted to the king for his ratification; see below, p. 142.

[7] *Cart. Autun*, part 2, no. 6.

The occasional aid probably dated from the same epoch in Nivernais; that for crusade figures in the settlement of 1164 by which Guillaume IV gave up his arbitrary *questa* on the men of the *bourg* of Saint-Étienne in return for the grant of 3,000 sous (in specie not specified!) when the usual feudal contingencies arose.[1] As we have seen, this agreement was repeatedly confirmed. In the confirmation by Pierre and Agnès in 1185, the levy on the occasion of ransom was remitted, leaving only those for the eldest daughter's marriage and for the crusade.[2] Now if we can assume that the occasion of crusade was invoked at Nevers in 1188, we may wonder whether the people of Saint-Étienne were doubly liable under terms of the old charter of Nevers and the new charter of Corbigny. This question must have arisen, for in addition to the concern of the bishops of Auxerre and Nevers with both agreements, the older charter remained subsequently in effect. There were complaints in 1187 that Pierre had violated the 'liberty of the *bourg* of Saint-Étienne';[3] and while the aid of crusade may not yet have been at issue there, it most probably figured in a complaint of 1190 by the monks of Saint-Germain of Auxerre, who appealed to Count Henri II of Troyes to free them from a 'tithing' by Pierre de Courtenay.[4]

Conceivably, therefore, the canons of Auxerre had Pierre's fiscal prowess in mind when they spoke of his 'immense power'. The count tried to improve the ordinary as well as the extraordinary resources of an estate that had been in difficulty as lately as 1174;[5] and his successor, Hervé de Donzy, was to pay a relief valued at 3,000 marks—not very much less than the relief for Flanders in 1192—when he won the county of Nevers in 1199.[6] In these circumstances, the renunciation by Pierre and Agnès was probably less damaging, although not less shortsighted, than on first sight it seems. Their mints cannot have matched those of Champagne in productivity or value, so that to abandon the uncertain returns of manipulating may have seemed tolerable compensation for a levy that must have

[1] 'Chartes de Saint-Étienne', no. 12. But the notion of subsidy on justifiable occasions was not specifically feudal: in 1158 the count of Nevers authorized the canons of Saint-Nazaire, Autun, to collect from men at Marigny-sur-Yonne, not 'quibuslibet occasionibus, sed manifesta ecclesie sue necessitate, velud terrarum emptione, vel famis urgente incommodo, vel apostolica seu regia procuratione', *Cart. Autun*, part 2, no. 11.

[2] 'Chartes de Saint-Étienne', no. 16.

[3] *Epist. pontif. Rom.*, ed. Loewenfeld, no. 389; cf. *Chartes de Cluny*, v, no. 4312; *PU Frankreich. v. Berry, Bourbonnais, Nivernais und Auxerrois*, ed. Wilhelm Wiederhold (Berlin: *Nachrichten von der königlichen Gesellschaft der Wissenschaften zu Göttingen, Philologisch-historische Klasse*, 1910), no. 130.

[4] BM Auxerre, MS. 161, fo. 82ᵛ.

[5] *Gesta pontificum*, ed. Duru, i. 422–3; *Brevis chronicon Altissiodorensis*, HF, xii. 299–300; Lebeuf, *Mémoires concernant l'histoire d'Auxerre*, iv, no. 67; Petit, *Ducs de Bourgogne*, iii, *p.j.*, nos. 875, 876; *Cart. Saint-Cyr*, no. 102; *Cart. La Charité*, no. 8; *Cart. Yonne*, ii, no. 450; Lespinasse, *Nivernais*, i. 375, 381, 390, 395.

[6] *LTC*, i, no. 502; René de Lespinasse, *Hervé de Donzy, comte de Nevers* (Nevers, 1868), pp. 5–17; idem, *Nivernais*, i. 407–10.

been expected to bring in enough money—perhaps 350 to 500 marks[1]—to support the count and his entourage on crusade.

The charter of Corbigny was thus a product of local circumstances: of traditional forms of privilege and taxation, of the immediate necessity of crusade, of anxiety about a coinage no longer reliable. But these circumstances were not all peculiar to Nevers, nor was the charter altogether immune from external influence. As we have seen, a somewhat parallel evolution in Burgundy had resulted in a charter for Dijon in 1187 in which Duke Hugues III secured his coinage at a maximum of 5 d. fine. Now that charter, which cannot have pleased landlords as much as townspeople, was to cost the inhabitants of Dijon 500 marks yearly, a revenue that helps us to understand why we hear of no such subsidy for crusade in Burgundy as in Nevers.[2] The immediate cause of that charter, however, was not the crusade but a costly settlement with the king following the duke's defeat in the war of Vergy. Hugues had come to terms with Philip Augustus during the latter's sojourn at Tonnerre in the early spring of 1187, and the revised charter for Dijon received the royal confirmation at that time.[3] These events were well known to the rulers of Nevers, themselves protégés of the king, and the relatives of both parties in the issue. Tonnerre belonged to Agnès's mother Mathilde of Burgundy, who probably tried to mediate.[4] Is it far-fetched to speculate that a resolution of the monetary problem in Nevers like that being effected in Burgundy was first contemplated on this occasion? Surely the king then heard of the complaints against Pierre that the clergy had prudently directed to the pope.[5] More specifically, it will be remembered that the king had reserved his triennial tallage 'for the stability of the money' at Orléans as recently as 1183.[6] That charter, of which Pierre de Courtenay may have heard through his own

---

[1] This assertion is based on speculative assumptions about population and reasonably secure comparisons of crusading finance. The elements of the estimate will be found in Ferdinand Lot, 'État des paroisses et des feux en 1328', *BEC*, xc (1929), 86; Georges de Soultrait, *Dictionnaire topographique du département de la Nièvre* (Paris, 1865), pp. v–ix; Petit, *Ducs de Bourgogne*, iii, *p.j.*, 312–13, nos. 863, 864 (cf. Geoffroy de Villehardouin, *La Conquête de Constantinople*, ed. Edmond Faral, 2nd edn., 2 vols. [Paris, 1961], i. 22–4, 32–4); Rigord, *Gesta Philippi Augusti*, c. 72, ed. H.-Fr. Delaborde, *Œuvres de Rigord et de Guillaume le Breton*, 2 vols. (Paris, 1882–5), i. 106–7.

[2] Above, pp. 120–5; text cited p. 125 n. 3. It is true that the duke was compelled to make amends to despoiled churches amounting to 30,000 l. *paris.*; but there are good reasons for doubting that this indemnity was enforced against the man who now became the king's trusted leader on crusade, Petit, *Ducs de Bourgogne*, iii. 37–71; Richard, *Ducs de Bourgogne*, p. 187. According to Rigord, *Gesta Philippi Augusti*, c. 36, ed. H.-Fr. Delaborde, i. 53, Philip Augustus ceded a fief pertaining to Vergy to Hugues to help the latter pay the indemnity; but Rigord also says that the king promptly restored 'tria castra optima' that he had taken in pledge; see also Rigord, c. 72, p. 106.

[3] Petit, *Ducs de Bourgogne*, iii. 1–36; Richard, *Ducs de Bourgogne*, pp. 157–74, 178–87.

[4] Petit, iii. 32–3.

[5] *Chartes de Cluny*, v, no. 4312; *Epist. pontif. Rom.*, ed. Loewenfeld, no. 389; 'Chartes de Saint-Étienne', no. 20.　　　　　　　　　　　　　　　[6] Above, pp. 35–6.

contacts,[1] bore the sign of Thibaut, the king's seneschal, who as count of Blois had once confirmed a coinage himself; and it is interesting to find that Thibaut V also attended the king in his ratifications of the charters for Dijon in 1187 and for Nevers in 1188.[2] In his presence was linked the experience of an older generation of confirmations and redemptions of coinage and that of renewed monetary fluctuations in times of heightened fiscal stringency. Toward the end of the year 1187, word reached France of the fall of Jerusalem, a disaster which nearly coincided with the appointed lapse of the general pecuniary aid for the Holy Land.[3] Early in 1188 Philip Augustus resolved to make the crusade on which both Pierre de Courtenay and Hugues III were to accompany him. In March he ordained a new subsidy, the 'Saladin tithes', in terms that encouraged the lords of communes and territories to make their own collections.[4] The *fouage* of Nevers appears to have been one response to that ordinance.[5]

Yet for all this wider involvement, the charter of Corbigny remained a parochial event. Unlike *Cunctis pateat*, which in some other respects it resembled, it was to have constitutional influence only in its county of origin. But that influence was considerable. The royal protectorate notwithstanding, the king's moneys were slow to penetrate Nivernais,[6] where the comital coinages were confirmed in their currency. On the other hand,

---

[1] 'Cart. Sainte-Croix d'Orléans', no. 102; cf. *Rec. des actes de Philippe Auguste*, i, no. 128, the king confirms Pierre's father's concession to the nuns of the hospice of Orléans, in an act attested by Thibaut V.

[2] Garnier, *Chartes de commune en Bourgogne*, i. 19–20; Lebeuf, *Mémoires concernant l'histoire d'Auxerre*, iv, no. 78.

[3] M. W. Baldwin, in K. M. Setton, *A History of the Crusades*, 4 vols. to date, 2nd edn. (Madison, 1969–77), ii. 608–18; *Rec. des actes de Philippe Auguste*, i, no. 123; F. A. Cazel, Jr., 'The Tax of 1185 in Aid of the Holy Land', *Speculum*, xxx (1955), 385–92.

[4] Rigord, ed. Delaborde, i. 81–90 (cc. 53–9; cc. 58–9 = *Rec. des actes de Philippe Auguste*, i, nos. 228, 229). Some of the difficulty encountered upon renewal of the subsidy is reflected in the diatribe by Peter of Blois, *PL*, ccvii. 74 (paraphrasing Luke 2: 1): 'Sane, sicut audivimus, exiit edictum a Philippo rege, ut describeretur Gallicus orbis, et oneraretur Ecclesia decimationibus recidivis. Sic paulatim transibit decimatio in consuetudinem et praesumpta semel abusio ignominiosam Ecclesiae servitutem infliget.' The sentiment at Corbigny, although expressed more soberly, was substantially the same. See also Cartellieri, *Philipp II. August*, ii. 69–85.

[5] Against this view it could be held that the hearth-tax of Nevers did not answer to the royal imposition of tithes (*decimationes*) on movables and property; and it is true that there was talk in 1190 of a *decimatio* by the count of Nevers at Auxerre, BM Auxerre, MS. 161, fo. 82ᵛ. But that tithe was resisted, and there is no other evidence of a crusading subsidy for the count of Nevers except the *beneficium* granted at Corbigny. The royal ordinance itself, *Rec. des actes de Philippe Auguste*, i. 280, art. 9, spoke of *tallia vel decima* in one clause. Possibly the 12 d. per hearth, easier to levy than the tithe, was regarded an approximation of the tithe for the masses of paying men. The *decimationes* around Sens took the form instituted by the king and aroused the anxiety alluded to by Peter of Blois, *Cart. Yonne*, ii, no. 385.

[6] Allusions to the money of Paris in the count's domains remain exceptional down to 1200; see e.g. *Cart. Hospitaliers*, i, no. 716; *Cart. Yonne*, ii, no. 378, a comital toll at Châteaurenard; no. 386, a pension at Villeneuve-sur-Yonne; nos. 403, 424, 455, revenues at Sens.

the insistence on the use of the deniers of Nevers could not be maintained, given the rigid determination of their standard in near parity with the abundant and reputable *provinois*;[1] the counts and the minters had lost the means of exploiting the markets in money and silver. As a result foreign currencies continued to flourish in the counties of Nevers, Auxerre, and Tonnerre, especially for large payments and accounting.[2] Hervé de Donzy (count of Nevers, 1199–1222) altered his coinage, probably soon after his accession, only to arouse the protest of the bishop of Auxerre.[3] It became necessary to stipulate obligations in 'strong sous of Nevers money'.[4] At Auxerre Pierre de Courtenay probably went on minting the statutory coinage until 1215,[5] but his successor Gui de Forez (1226–41) issued a 'new money' of reduced weight (18½ s. to the mark and 4 d. fine), which soon brought him, in turn, into conflict with the bishop and cathedral clergy. In arguments adjudged by the archbishop of Sens, the count appears to have claimed that the charter of 1188 made no reference to the money of Auxerre and that he was not the first count to depart from the sworn standards, but the bishop and canons clung to the letter of their charter and won the case.[6] Not for another generation were the terms of 1188 modified to a count's satisfaction.[7]

So it may be said that the instituted conservation of coinage came as close to realization in the practice of Nevers and Auxerre as was possible in the economic circumstances of the early thirteenth century. The interest of rural lords, led by the clergy, continued to prevail.[8] That the counts could

---

[1] Above, p. 133 n. 4, coinage of Provins, like that of Nevers, at 50 s. to the mark in 1197; cf. above, pp. 131, 138. An account of about 1219 shows the money of Auxerre evaluated at a shade less than that of Provins (320 l. *autiss.* = 310 l. *pruv.*), Lebeuf, *Mémoires concernant l'histoire d'Auxerre*, iv, no. 142. For *provinois* money in Nevers and Auxerre, *Cart. Yonne*, ii, nos. 420, 504; Lebeuf, iv, nos. 99, 119, 132. The coin of customary renders continued to be unspecified in many cases: 'Chartes de Saint-Étienne', no. 22; *Gallia christiana*, xii, *inst.*, 347 (no. 57); Lebeuf, iv, nos. 80, 82, 84, 100; *Cart. La Charité*, nos. 77, 90; cf. BM Auxerre, MS. 161, fo. 73ʳ, quoted above, p. 138 n. 6.

[2] 'Chartes de Corbigny', 16; 'Chartes de Saint-Étienne', no. 21; *Cart. Saint-Cyr*, no. 106; 'Titres de Mêves-sur-Loire', 210; *Cart. La Charité*, nos. 43, 85, 90; *Inventaire des titres de Nevers de l'Abbé de Marolles . . .*, ed. Georges de Soultrait (Nevers, 1873), c. 262; Lebeuf, *Mémoires concernant l'histoire d'Auxerre*, iv, no. 132.

[3] *Gallia christiana*, xii, *inst.*, 149 (no. 69); see also Poey d'Avant, *Monnaies féodales*, i. 314–15, and Sarriau, 'Numismatique nivernaise', 43–4. (Plate III, no. 26.)

[4] 'Titres de Mêves-sur-Loire', 211–12; 'Chartes de Corbigny', 22–3; *Le Chartrier ancien de Fontmorigny . . .*, ed. Albert Huchet (Bourges, 1936), no. 250; *HF*, xxiii. 633.

[5] Lebeuf, *Mémoires concernant l'histoire d'Auxerre*, iv, no. 132. In 1231, it is true (ibid., no. 163), mutations of the coinage of Auxerre were said to have occurred since 1188, but the assertion did not apparently carry weight, and evidence from 1219 (ibid., no. 142) suggests that no alteration of significance had yet occurred.

[6] Ibid., no. 163; the meaning of the text, in Lebeuf's incomplete copy, is not clear on all points.

[7] 'Recueil de documents relatifs à l'histoire monétaire', ed. Prou, *RN*, 3rd ser., xiv. 288–91, no. 2.

[8] As usual, our perspective is distorted for lack of secular archives; but in addition to

muster no perceptible support for a more flexible policy points to a sufficiency of specie in the market towns, perhaps also to the irrelevance of the issue to the townsmen. The men of Auxerre, where the wine trade was flourishing well before it aroused the exclamation of Salimbene (1245),[1] were content to see operations suspended in the local mint for a period of six years beginning in 1215 or 1216.[2] And the burghers could share in the satisfaction of all people that their purchase of a stable coinage had not become a precedent. The counts were the losers. They could not even risk, or bother, changing the types, almost the only monetary pre-rogative left to them. From the age of the changing counts far into the thirteenth century persisted the sickle-type descended from the degenerate R$_X$E on the coins of Nevers and the both-side short crosses on those of Auxerre and Tonnerre—devices of an anxious rural society.[3]

D. *Picardy* (c. *1080–1215*)

Our scene shifts northward—to the 'fertile and agreeable country covered with vineyards, where the cultivation of wheat flourishes';[4] to the flatten-ing grainlands, less wooded, stretching beyond the zones of viniculture through Artois toward Flanders; to the towns of the Aisne, Oise, and Somme.[5] Here again the coinages were very numerous, but they were less irregular and more nearly autonomous than those of domains to the north and the south-east. Even in the twelfth century they were mostly minted in cities by counts or bishops who had resisted political integration by would-be princes and whose grasp of regalian prerogatives had been less shaken by seigneurial usurpation than elsewhere.[6] More novel and equally character-

---

texts cited above, pp. 137 n. 1, 138 n. 6, and 143 n. 2 to this chapter, see also Lebeuf, iv, no. 163.

[1] Ibid., nos. 94, 112, 127; *Cart. Yonne*, ii, no. 450; Roger Dion, *Histoire de la vigne et du vin en France des origines au XIXe siècle* (Paris, 1959), 245–6.

[2] Lebeuf, *Mémoires concernant l'histoire d'Auxerre*, iv, no. 132.

[3] See Sarriau, 'Numismatique nivernaise', 35–46, and plate 2; Poey d'Avant, *Monnaies féodales de France*, i, nos. 2105–40, and plate 46 (types of Nevers undergo minimal altera-tion from the early twelfth to mid-thirteenth century); for Auxerre and Tonnerre one cannot even distinguish the reigns, Poey d'Avant, iii, nos. 5880–97 and plate 136; nos. 5855–8, and plate 135 (nos. 18–20).

[4] From Ratbod's description of the Noyonnais (eleventh century), *De vita sancti Medardi*, *PL*, cl. 1507, cited by Abel Lefranc, *Histoire de la ville de Noyon et de ses in-stitutions* . . . (Paris, 1887), p. 27.

[5] The denomination 'Picardy', linguistic or cultural rather than geographical and attested from the twelfth century, is used here for want of a single convenient term for the *pays* extending from the Île-de-France (Beauvaisis, Soissonnais) to Ponthieu, Artois, and the Cambrésis. See Robert Fossier, *La Terre et les hommes en Picardie jusqu'à la fin du XIIIe siècle*, 2 vols. (Paris, 1968), i. 103–7.

[6] For the coinages, see Dieudonné, *Manuel de numismatique*, iv. 325–33; for the political circumstances, Pierre Feuchère, 'Une tentative manquée de concentration territoriale entre Somme et Seine: la principauté d'Amiens-Valois au XIe siècle . . .', *Le Moyen Âge*, lx (1954), 1–37; K. F. Werner, 'Königtum und Fürstentum', 189–91.

istic was the rise of an influential class of townspeople in this land of communes; yet the municipal coinages to be explained in this way were few and temporary,[1] nor were the burghers south of Arras yet very distinct from lords and peasants in their economic pursuits. While the favoured coinages of Châlons, Meaux, Provins, and Anjou found their way into Picard markets from the east and south, and the deniers of Arras (the 'money of Flanders') from the north,[2] most people paid or accounted in their local moneys of Amiens, Beauvais, Boulogne, Corbie, Laon, Noyon, Péronne, Ponthieu, Saint-Quentin, and Soissons.[3] This particularism did not long survive the pressure of Philip Augustus, who annexed the counties, and terminated or replaced the coinages of Amiens (1186), Péronne (1191), Boulogne (1212), and Saint-Quentin (1214),[4] and whose *parisis* attained general currency toward 1190 even around towns whose lords preserved their coinages.[5]

[1] Even the clearest case for Picardy, the coinages of Amiens inscribed PAX and MONETA CIVIUM, is difficult to affirm; see Dieudonné, *Manuel de numismatique*, iv. 325–7. For Saint-Omer, see Claude Richebé, *Les Monnaies féodales d'Artois du Xe au début du XIVe siècle* (Paris, 1963), pp. 83–6.

[2] 'Cartulaire du chapitre de la cathédrale d'Amiens', ed. Edmond Soyez and Joseph Roux, *MSAP, Documents inédits . . .*, xiv (1897), no. 61; 'Le cartulaire de l'abbaye de Sélincourt (1131–1513)', ed. Georges Beaurain, *MSAP*, xl (1925), nos. 18, 91, 124; L.-C. Douët-d'Arcq, 'Recherches historiques et critiques sur les anciens comtes de Beaumont-sur-Oise . . .', *MSAP, Documents inédits . . .*, iv (1855), no. 197; 'Cart. Saint-Vincent de Laon', no. 37; Luchaire, *Louis VI*, p. 337 (no. 435); AD Oise, G 1984, fos. 187, 33, 81ᵛ, 91–2, 105 (and 177), 166; AD Nord, 28H 46, *pièce* 1196; AD Somme, H 16, no. 1, p. 181; *Cartulaire de Héronval publié par le Comité archéologique de Noyon* (Noyon, 1883), nos. 12–14; 'Cartulaire de l'abbaye de N.-D. d'Ourscamp . . .', ed. Achille Peigné-Delacourt, *MSAP, Documents inédits . . .*, vi (1865), nos. 340, 51, 337, 72, 403, 303, 318; *Recueil des actes des comtes de Pontieu (1026–1279)*, ed. Clovis Brunel (Paris, 1930), nos. 27, 41, 101, 109 (art. 32), 112.

[3] 'Cart. Amiens', nos. 16, 17, 23, 24, 31, 40, 41, 82, 95; 'Cart. Sélincourt', nos. 31–3; Douët-d'Arcq, 'Comtes de Beaumont', nos. 9, 10, 18, 29, 31, 80; *Cartulaire de l'Hôtel-Dieu de Beauvais . . .*, ed. Victor Leblond (Paris, 1919), nos. 7, 29, 34; *Cartulaire de la Maladrerie de Saint-Lazare de Beauvais . . .*, ed. Victor Leblond (Paris, 1922), nos. 7–9, 20; Maurice Prou, 'Essai sur l'histoire monétaire de Beauvais à propos d'un denier de l'évêque Philippe de Dreux', *MSAF*, lvi (1897), 70–1 n. 2; BN, MS. lat. 17758, fos. 89ʳᵛ, 92ᵛ–93ʳ, 159ʳᵛ; *Recueil de documents inédits concernant la Picardie . . .*, ed. Victor Beauvillé, 4 vols. (Paris, 1860–82), ii, nos. 14, 17; iv, no. 19; 'Cart. Saint-Vincent de Laon', nos. 38, 39; 'Cartulaire de Tinselve', ed. L.-V. Pêcheur, *BSS*, 2nd ser., v (1875), 224–5; *Cart. Hospitaliers*, ii, no. 1133; W. M. Newman, *Les Seigneurs de Nesle en Picardie (XIIe–XIIIe siècle) . . .*, 2 vols. (Philadelphia–Paris, 1971), ii, nos. 5, 74; AD Oise, G 1984, fos. 33ʳᵛ, 66ᵛ, 74–5, 77–8, 98ᵛ–99, 105, 116ᵛ–117, 177ᵛ–178; BN, Coll. Moreau, lxxi. 185; lxxx. 32ʳᵛ; Coll. Picardie, ccii. 70ʳ; *Cart. Héronval*, nos. 2, 18; 'Cart. Ourscamp', nos. 94, 199, 364; *Rec. des actes des comtes de Pontieu*, nos. 17, 116; AN, LL 985B, fos. 226ʳᵛ, 234ᵛ–235; BN, MS. lat. 11070, fo. 86ʳᵛ; 'Cartulaire de l'abbaye de Saint-Léger de Soissons (1070–1666)', ed. L.-V. Pêcheur, *BSS*, 2nd ser., ii (1870), nos. 19, 27, 38, 46–7, 51–2, 54, 62, 66.

[4] L. L. Borrelli de Serres, *La Réunion des provinces septentrionales à la couronne par Philippe Auguste . . .* (Paris, 1899); Dieudonné, *Manuel de numismatique*, iv. 79, 325–33; Lafaurie, *Monnaies des rois de France*, pp. 21–2. Philip Augustus minted *parisis* at Péronne, Arras, and Saint-Omer from 1191, if not before.

[5] e.g. at Corbie, where the abbot was required to admit the king's money of Paris, but clung to his own monetary rights, *Rec. des actes de Philippe Auguste*, i, no. 162; in Ponthieu,

By that time popular uneasiness about the value or stability of the money was an old story in Picardy. The use and supply of coin were already well restored by the first decade of the twelfth century, when alarming mutations seem to have occurred at Amiens as well as at Laon.[1] In 1129 Louis VI had seen fit to stipulate that payments to the king by the men of Bruyères-en-Laonnais be in 'good money'.[2] Such indications were frequent thereafter for petty renders or rents as well as for compensatory payments.[3] The same caution shows in the preference for white deniers,[4] perhaps equivalent to *bona moneta*, as opposed to the black pieces (*nigri*) of Laon, Noyon, and Soissons.[5] Fossier finds suspicion of coined money decreasing after about 1150, but reservations of alternative coinages for repayment continue to turn up—around Noyon, for example, in fear for the local coinage (1187) and for that of Laon (1191).[6] At Laon the abbot and canons of Saint-Martin, in renting a valuable local tenure in 1193 for 60 l. *laud.*, were careful to distinguish between negligible variations in the deniers of payment and a real mutation; in the latter case, the settlement was to be according to the original evaluation of the currency in terms of silver.[7] If confidence was increasing and reservations persisting, one reason may have

Rec. des actes des comtes de Pontieu, nos. 138, 139, 143, 154, 165–7; in Beauvaisis, *Cart. Hôtel-Dieu*, nos. 47, 62; *Cart. Maladrerie*, nos. 6, 36, 38; Eugène de Buchère de Lépinois, 'Recherches historiques et critiques sur l'ancien comté et les comtes de Clermont en Beauvoisis . . .', *MSO*, x: 1 (1877), *p.j.*, nos. 1, 5, 35, 39, 45, 62, 70; and at Noyon, AD Oise, G 1984, fos. 116^{rv}, 119^v, 122^{rv}. In the *Scripta de feodis* . . . for Crépy, Chauny, and La Ferté-Milon, written probably toward 1214 (Newman, *Seigneurs de Nesle*, i. 44–5), it was necessary to specify the local black moneys in order to represent customary payments accurately, *HF*, xxiii. 650–5. See also below, pp. 151–3; and Fossier, *Picardie*, ii. 733, n. 2.

[1] Guibert de Nogent, *De vita sua*, iii, c. 7, ed. Bourgin, p. 159; tr. Benton, p. 169. Guibert's allusion to the 'Ambianenses obolos, corruptissimum etiam quiddam' is more expressive than lucid; but cf. BN, MS. lat. 17758, fo. 48, ed. Maurice Prou, 'Essai sur l'histoire monétaire de l'abbaye de Corbie', *MSAF*, lv (1895), 86, which shows that the deniers of Amiens were at 7 d. fine about 1080, and the obols probably at 6 d. See generally Fossier, i. 237, 246; ii. 565; and *Miracula S. Marculfi*, in *Acta sanctorum*, 70 vols. (Antwerp, etc., 1643–1940), Mai, vii. 530B.

[2] AD Aisne, G 39; see Luchaire, *Louis VI*, pp. 201–2, 337 (no. 435); p. 340 (no. 497).

[3] *PU Frankreich. Neue Folge*, iv. *Picardie*, ed. Johannes Ramackers (Göttingen: *Abh.*, 3rd ser., xxvii, 1942), nos. 40, 46, 48, 73, 118, 138; BN, MS. lat. 11070, fo. 86^{rv}; AD Aisne, G 1850, fo. 193^v; 'Cart. Saint-Vincent de Laon', no. 34; Amadée Piette, 'Histoire de l'abbaye de Thenailles . . .', *BSS*, 2nd ser., viii (1878), 222, no. 6; 223, no. 8; *LTC*, i, no. 279; *Rec. des actes de Philippe Auguste*, iii, no. 1113.

[4] Newman, *Seigneurs de Nesle*, ii, no. 69; *Rec. des documents*, ed. Beauvillé, iv, no. 29.

[5] See e.g. AD Oise, G 1984, fos. 33^{rv}, 105; 'Cart. Saint-Léger de Soissons', nos. 45, 51, 73, 75.

[6] AD Oise, G 1984, fos. 187^{rv}, 105, 177.

[7] *Rec. des documents*, ed. Beauvillé, iv, no. 19: '. . . Solutio autem memorate pecunie fiet ex Laudunensi moneta nunc temporis currente et hac quamdiu curret, sive melior fuerit, sive pejor tenebitur. Quod si eadem forte ceciderit, solutio fiet secundum eam estimationem argenti juxta quam eadem moneta et argentum nunc inter se commutantur . . . .' For Peter the Chanter's similar resolution of a similar problem, see below, pp. 174–5.

been that rates of exchange were becoming better determined and more widely recognized in the later twelfth century.[1] The diversity of standard prevailing until then helps to explain why stipulations of preferred coinage seem to have been more common in this region in the first half of the century than in Champagne.[2]

In view of these facts, it is worth remark that we do not find charters confirming the coinage in Picardy. Yet there as elsewhere people must have thought it right for a coinage to be held firm during its proprietor's lifetime. That notion is implicit in the agreement of about 1080 between the abbot of Corbie and his moneyers, even though the purpose of that agreement— much as in contemporary Barcelona—was not to safeguard any popular interest as such but to secure the ruler from malfeasance in the mints.[3] Expressions of public concern were to be formulated gradually out of recognition of the threat to fixed revenues posed by fluctuating coinages.

At Saint-Quentin the *communards* put it this way in their aggressive *Establissement* dated about 1151: 'And if anyone owes rent [*chens*] to his lord—for land or for house or for meadow or for wood, or for whatever inheritance—he shall render the rent at first established; and if the lord insists on having a better money than this, he shall not be able to do it lawfully in any way, but he shall pay him in that money and amount that he agreed upon with him.' By a further provision (possibly slightly subsequent to the original text), lords were required to content themselves with the 'money which [was] established and minted in the county, and anciently accustomed', while their tenants were to render 'denier for denier without any exchange'.[4] This extraordinary text not only makes clear why the coin of Saint-Quentin was designated in local charters for customary payments, but also illuminates other testimony that lords hedged against loss by stipulating the very kinds of alternative or exchange to which the men of

---

[1] See e.g. 'Un cartulaire de l'abbaye de Saint-Vaast d'Arras . . .', ed. A. Guesnon, *Bulletin historique et philologique du Comité des travaux historiques et scientifiques* (1896), 274, act of 1152: '. . . solventes pro relevagio tres solidos monete Ambianensis vel Corbeiensis . . . .' With few exceptions—e.g. Prou, 'Essai sur l'histoire monétaire de Corbie', 86; AD Oise, G 1984, fo. 75—the monetary equivalences noted in texts date from after 1150, and mostly after 1180; see below, p. 152.

[2] 'Cart. Amiens', nos. 8–31; AD Oise, G 1984, fos. 66ᵛ, 75; BN, Moreau, lxxi. 185; 'Cart. Ourscamp', nos. 83, 303, 318; *Rec. des actes des comtes de Pontieu*, nos. 17, 41. But the general differentiation between 'good money' and 'black' was already tending toward the pattern of equivalence that was defined in the later twelfth century (references above, p. 146 nn. 2, 3, 4).

[3] BN, MS. lat. 17758, fo. 48ʳ (ed. Prou, 'Essai sur l'histoire monétaire de Corbie', 86): 'Gracia Dei Everardus abbas Corbeye. Scriptis uolumus retinere qualis moneta Corbeye nostris temporibus agenda sit quantaue firmitate nobis uiuentibus sit tenenda. Constituimus . . .'; cf. above, p. 6.

[4] *Archives anciennes de la ville de Saint-Quentin*, ed. Emmanuel Lemaire, 2 vols. (Saint-Quentin, 1888–1910), i. lxxx, arts. 41, 43 (reproduced in Appendix, no. 2). This text survives only in a fourteenth-century copy in the *Livre Rouge* of Eu. Arthur Giry's classic exposition of the circumstances is in *Archives anciennes*, i. v–xvi.

Saint-Quentin were opposed.[1] What is harder to determine is how this tension was related to prices. On Fossier's evidence, livestock was the only considerable commodity that became more costly in later twelfth-century Picardy; prices of land did not increase perceptibly before the 1220s, while rents declined, if anything, between 1180 and 1220.[2] To this last development the progressive substitution of the relatively strong *parisis* for depreciated local moneys may have contributed as well as the accelerated disposal of troubled fortunes.

The monetary provisions of the *Establissement* of Saint-Quentin afford a rare glimpse of anti-seigneurial sentiment. Over against arbitrary remedies for ageing and slipping silver, the people of the commune proclaimed the immutability of rents. Moreover, they expressly rejected the fraudulent tests by which covetous lords could represent themselves as short-changed.[3] But it is important to notice that these provisions do not explicitly reject the mutation of minted deniers.[4] The implied complaint against Raoul I of Vermandois (*c.* 1120–52) was not that he had altered the coinage, but that he (and other lords?) had abused the usual devices of exchange. Does this mean that the coinages of the turbulent Raoul were above reproach? Or that the *communards* already understood the futility of trying to prevent any mutation? Allusions to the local money in other texts are too few to be conclusive, but they are none the less suggestive. In 1141 the *viromandensis moneta* was rated stronger than the coinage of Meaux by one-third, and in 1152 a render of one obol seemed worth reserving in the coin of Vermandois.[5] In 1143 the 'best money' and in 1153 the 'good money' of Vermandois was designated.[6] It looks as if at least two coinages of Saint-Quentin were current when the *Establissement* was drawn up, of which the stronger may have been initiated in the early years of Raoul I. If the latter had forcibly revoked the good money upon minting the weakened, or had mis-represented the debased issue—if, indeed, he had ransomed a coinage as he himself, the king's seneschal, had seen the young Louis VII do—then one should have expected some more pointed reaction than what has come down to us. Raoul de Vermandois, for all his 'incomparable avarice', did not simply debase his money.[7]

---

[1] BN, Moreau, lvi. 222; AD Oise, G 1984, fos. 75, 77.

[2] Fossier, *Picardie*, ii. 576–82.

[3] *Archives anciennes*, ed. Lemaire, i. lxxx, art. 42 (Appendix, no. 2).

[4] The interpretation of Lemaire, *Archives anciennes*, i. ci, therefore seems to me mis-taken: 'La monnaie en usage est proclamée immuable et toutes précautions sont prises contre le seigneur qui voudrait, par des altérations ou une refonte, se procurer un gain au préjudice des membres de la commune.'

[5] AD Oise, G 1984, fos. 75, 77–8.

[6] BN, Coll. Picardie, ccxxxv. 171; MS. lat. 11070, fo. 86[rv].

[7] According to Lambert de Waterlos, ed. G. H. Pertz, *MGH, Scriptores*, xvi (1859), 522, 'Is [Raoul] terram bene tenuit, sed avaritia incomparabilis fuit.' Cf. Petit-Dutaillis, *Communes françaises*, p. 78: 'Raoul Ier . . . a dû sans doute . . . faire de la mauvaise monnaie.'

The coinage of Vermandois was certainly altered toward 1164–7 when Philippe d'Alsace (count of Flanders) came to power in right of his wife. His type retained a design which slightly and accidentally resembled the obverse type of the *parisis*; and the coinage of the countess Aliénor (1183–1214) intentionally sharpened this resemblance.[1] The values of these coinages are poorly known, but they were most likely fixed in approximate parity with the *parisis*.[2] Records of this period betray no uneasiness about the stability of the deniers of Saint-Quentin.[3] Aliénor had married Count Mathieu de Beaumont, chamberlain to the king of France (1151–74), and the townspeople of Saint-Quentin evidently favoured her alliance with Philip Augustus against the count of Flanders. Her charter for Saint-Quentin (1191–2), which survives incomplete, expressly confirmed the 'usages and customs' of the time of her father Raoul I, although it consisted mainly of articles that do not appear in the *Establissement* as we have it;[4] and Philip Augustus confirmed her charter in 1195.[5]

Now this royal confirmation contains a provision of the highest interest to our inquiry. It reads as follows:

[39.] We cannot manipulate [*divellere*] the coinage nor mint another unless by the consent of the mayor and sworn men; but if, upon necessary investigation, we should find it insufficient in quantity, we shall be able to increase the same [money] by renewal; and we shall not permit a lighter [money] to be made and we shall cause the old to circulate with the new.[6]

---

[1] Poey d'Avant, *Monnaies féodales*, iii. 384–5; Caron, *Monnaies féodales*, p. 379; Dieudonné, *Manuel de numismatique*, iv. 329–30, figs. 197, 198; cf. Lafaurie, *Monnaies des rois de France*, p. 21. For the political background, see Borrelli de Serres, *Réunion des provinces septentrionales*, pp. xiii–xxxv. (Plate III, no. 27.)

[2] As was Philippe's money of Arras; see e.g. 'Cart. Amiens', no. 61, a pledge at Dury (arr. Amiens, cant. Boves) 'pro XXXa libris attrebatensium sive parisiensium' some time before an uncertain day in 1180. I think it improbable that the reference here was yet to a royal coinage at Arras; but cf. Richebé, *Monnaies féodales d'Artois*, p. 142; Fossier, *Picardie*, ii. 733 n. 2.

[3] F. van de Putte, communication in *Revue de la numismatique belge*, 4th ser., iv (1866), 282; AN, LL 985B, fos. 234ᵛ–235; Richebé, p. 152.

[4] *Le Livre Rouge de l'Hôtel de Ville de Saint-Quentin*, ed. Henri Bouchot and Emmanuel Lemaire (Saint-Quentin, 1881), no. 200. The charter may have helped to secure support for the countess in a local war, *Chronicon anonymi Laudunensis canonici*, HF, xviii. 710.

[5] Arthur Giry, 'Étude sur les origines de la commune de Saint-Quentin', in *Archives anciennes*, i. xvi; Lemaire, ibid. xcv, cii; and Petit-Dutaillis, *Communes françaises*, pp. 78–80, who cites with approval Vanderkindere's reinterpretation of Philippe d'Alsace's communal policy. Cf. Henri Pirenne, *Histoire de Belgique*, 6 vols., i, 5th edn. (Brussels, 1929), 206–8, 218–24. For the royal charter, see next note.

[6] *Rec. des actes de Philippe Auguste*, ii, no. 491: '[39.] Nos monetam non possumus divellere nec aliam facere nisi assensu majoris et juratorum; sed si eam prout necesse sit non sufficere sciverimus, eandem renovando augere poterimus nec leviorem fieri permittemus veteremque cum nova currere faciemus.' The faulty text given by Félicien de Saulcy, *Recueil de documents relatifs à l'histoire des monnaies . . .*, 4 vols. (Paris, 1879–92), i. 116–17, based on that in *Ordonnances*, xi. 230, is followed by Guilhiermoz and Dieudonné, 'Chronologie des documents monétaires de la numismatique royale . . .', RN, 4th ser., xxxiii (1930), 214, no. 32.

This language is clear enough, on the whole. The uncommon verb *divellere* recurs in this provision in charters based on that of Saint-Quentin, except in the charter of Roye, where it is replaced by *mutare*.[1] Possibly the word *divellere* had been carefully chosen at Saint-Quentin in order to incorporate the older prohibition of mutilation in the new injunction against mutation.[2] For there can be no doubt that this monetary regulation first attested to us in 1195 had grown out of recent experience at Saint-Quentin. The lords vying for favour with the powerful men of the commune after about 1167 could not very well have imposed their new coinages without seeking approval or, alternatively, arousing discontent; and the apparent respectability of those coinages points to publicity or consensus of the very sort envisaged by article 39 in 1195. What is more, that part of the royal charter was probably no more novel in 1195 than articles 1–18, which simply reiterate the countess's charter of 1191–2 to the point where the latter breaks off. Neither in 1195 nor soon thereafter did the king mint at Saint-Quentin, where his lordship remained indirect; and the monetary provision was to reappear only in royal charters patterned on that of Saint-Quentin. In its earliest form that provision most likely figured among the lost articles of the earlier charter, a result of discussion between Countess Aliénor and the commune.

It is a curiously original provision. Formally, it bears hardly more resemblance to the sworn confirmations of coinage elsewhere than did the old contract of Corbie. On the other hand, it holds substantially to the principle of conserving the coinage. Debasement is expressly prohibited and mutations of any sort are limited to the exceptional occasions of urgent shortage. Yet the venerable principle has been compromised this time by the frank recognition that occasions for mutations do, in fact, arise: that a circulating coinage wears out and becomes scarce. To the traditional prohibition of arbitrary mutations was added a new safeguard against the obligatory exchange of old deniers when the renovation of the money was decreed.

Equally significant was the procedural innovation. For the first time in France, a townsfolk assumed a statutory role in monetary issues of public interest. But it does not follow that the mayor and sworn men of Saint-Quentin, in whom this right was vested, would necessarily represent popular ideas about coinage. On the contrary, to judge from the only clue in our text—the declaration that the money will not be reduced in weight— it appears that the charter tended to favour proprietors or lords. In

---

[1] *Rec. des actes de Philippe Auguste*, ii, no. 539, art. 7; no. 540, art. 35 (Roye, 1196; the year-date 1183, given in *Ordonnances*, xi. 228, and consequently by Saulcy, *Rec. de documents*, i. 116, has no warrant); *Rec. des actes de Philippe Auguste*, iii, no. 1295, art. 38 (Chauny, 1213); no. 1389, art. 25 (Crépy, 1215).

[2] Nevertheless, the early thirteenth-century translation in the *Livre Rouge de Saint-Quentin*, p. 433, begins: 'Nous ne poons le monnoie abatre, ne autre faire ...'.

Burgundy, by contrast, the people of Dijon had lately secured the assurance that their coinage would not be *strengthened* beyond a certain point.[1] But it would be mistaken to press the implications of this difference, which may have had more to do with conditions of exchange in the two regions than with differing social interests.

As the trickle of Parisian deniers became a flood in the 1190s, the old anxiety over the value of rents revived in Picardy. Everywhere obligations formerly paid in local currencies were being settled or accounted in *parisis*.[2] Around Beauvais this tendency was favoured by proximity to the Capetian demesnes, preferment of the king's relations to the episcopal see, and the persistence of a relatively strong money minted by the bishop–count in near parity with the *parisis*.[3] Philippe de Dreux (1175–1217), first cousin to Philip Augustus, having begun by issuing a distinctively new coinage, failed to replenish it adequately or to promote its currency throughout the diocese. As a result, so it was said toward 1212–14, 'the *parisis* and *beauvaisis* are now received indifferently in all transactions'.[4] The trouble with this practice was that the deniers of Beauvais were fractionally stronger

[1] Above, p. 125.

[2] A.-L.-A. Trudon des Ormes, 'Étude sur les possessions de l'ordre du Temple en Picardie', *MSAP*, xxxii (1894), 313, 325; AN, S 4195, no. 21; 'Cart. Amiens', nos. 61, 76, 82, 95–6, 100, 108, 117; Douët-d'Arcq, 'Comtes de Beaumont', *preuves*, nos. 9, 10, 13, 15, 18, 26, 28–32, 34, 44, 47, 56; *Rec. des actes de Philippe Auguste*, i, no. 145; AD Oise, G 1984, fo. 119vb; *Cart. Héronval*, nos. 18, 25, 28; 'Cart. Ourscamp', nos. 316, 324, 364, 149, 397, 395, 250, 902, 453, 67, 224, 431, 254, 711, 368, 108, 456, 624, 61; and citations on p. 145 n. 5. Moreover, the Parisian standard was adopted or imposed at Péronne and Arras, whose currencies continued to be designated, e.g. AD Oise, G 1984, fo. 166; BN, MS. lat. 9930, fo. 29^v; Richebé, *Monnaies féodales d'Artois*, pp. 124–6. At Soissons, where the *parisis* was most likely among the *fortes* distinguished from *denarii nigri* by 1190, a rent of 50 *solidi nigrorum* was sold in 1233 for 400 l. *fortium*, 'Cart. Saint-Léger de Soissons', nos. 51, 75.

[3] *Gallia christiana*, ix. 723–40; Newman, *Seigneurs de Nesle*, i. 225–7; L.-H. Labande, *Histoire de Beauvais et de ses institutions communales* . . . (Paris, 1892), pp. 62–8; and texts cited on p. 152 n. 1. Early in the twelfth century (*c.* 1100–23) the denier *belv.* was rated one-third stronger than that of Paris, Ch.-A.-A. de Manneville, 'De l'état des terres et des personnes dans la paroisse d'Amblainville (Vexin français) . . .', *MSO*, xiii:2 (1887), 523, see also 527, 529–30.

[4] Antoine L'Oisel, *Mémoires des pays, villes, comté et comtes, évesché et évesques . . . de Beauvais* (Paris, 1617), p. 277, as quoted by Prou, 'Histoire monétaire de Beauvais', *MSAF*, lvi. 63, n. 1: 'Dominus Belvacensis comes est et episcopus, et moneta belvacensis ipsius est eo modo quod in tota diocesi praeterquam in domo episcopi et intra portas ejus non potest formari moneta; ipse enim cuneos tradit monetariis, et de singulis libris monetatis habet denarios IV. Materia monetae talis est: duae partes sunt de argento examinato et III de cupro vel circa. Materia parisiensis monetae talis est: in duodecim denariis sunt V partes de argento examinato et VII de cupro vel circa. Et nunc indifferentur recipiuntur in omnibus venalibus parisienses et belvacenses, tam propter paucitatem belvacensis monetae, tum qui[a] cursum debitum non facit episcopus habere monetam suam, cum alii episcopi obtinuerint et ipse multo tempore obtinuerat quod moneta belvacensis cursum publicum habet per totam diocesim.' That this text displays the point of view of the canons, if it was not, indeed, their work, is strongly suggested by the record of discussions between the canons and the bishop relating to *cens* of the chapter late in 1214, Labande, *Hist. Beauvais*, pp. 277–9; and by texts cited on p. 152 n. 1 below.

than those of Paris. The difference was too slight to affect petty exchange very much, but it was sufficient to worry the greater landlords. Accordingly, the canons of Beauvais sought an accommodation with the king, who ordained in 1215 that the bishop, dean, and chapter might count 12 d. *belv.* as equivalent to 13½ s. *paris.* in the receipt of rents.[1] This was a profoundly conservative agreement. Given the success of the *parisis*, some might have preferred to see the money of Beauvais reduced so as to correspond with that of Paris. But how could such a mutation have been carried out without prejudice and economic disorder? To Philippe de Dreux, who had all but given up the episcopal coinage in favour of the king's and who perhaps retained some respect for immutability in principle, that alternative did not seem worth the bother. In his last years the local mint was inactive, and in 1220, only three years after his death, the *moneta belvacensis* was regarded as a thing of the past.[2]

The commune of Beauvais seems to have taken no part in the settlement of 1214, which perhaps simply extended to rents an understanding already in effect for credit and exchange. At Noyon, however, there had been more urgent reason for concern because the local black money was so much less valuable than the moneys of Beauvais or Paris that there could be no question of its receipt 'indifferently' with the *parisis*. The mayor and sworn men of Noyon joined the clergy in petitions alleging injury to the church and all the people 'on account of the uncertain currency of money', with the result that in November 1197 Bishop Étienne de Nemours (1188–1221) decreed as follows. The deniers of Paris were to have lawful currency at Noyon 'so that rents owed within the boundaries of the commune should be paid in Parisian money, counting 12 *parisis* to 18 black [deniers] henceforth'. It was stipulated that in case this bishop or any of his successors should issue a coinage stronger than 3½ d. alloy, then all rents were to be paid in *parisis*. The *teloneum*, however, and most other *consuetudines* were to be paid in any coinage current at Noyon.[3]

Here already, in an episcopal ordinance years before the royal decree at Beauvais, loomed the shadow of the king. To prelates rewarded by the

[1] It is probable that the ratio was 6 s. *paris.* to 5 s. *belv.* in 1179, Prou, 'Histoire monétaire de Beauvais', 70–1 n. 2, although that scholar was justifiably cautious about that interpretation of an inexplicit text; but Prou overlooked the text of *c.* 1100–23 cited above, p. 151 n. 3. In the 1190s the mark was accounted at 36 s. *belv.* (BN, MS. lat. 5471, fo. 278; cf. fo. 279), which suggests a narrowing ratio of 10 s. *paris.* to 9 s. *belv.* The ordinance of 1215 is known from *mandements* printed by Prou, ibid., 74 n. 1, 77 n. 1; newly ed. Monicat and Boussard, *Rec. des actes de Philippe Auguste*, iii, nos. 1358 (without citation of Prou, who established the date), 1367.

[2] '... octo libras parisiens. vel belvacens., si belvacensis moneta in usum redierit', quoted by Labande, *Hist. Beauvais*, p. 68 n. 4, from BN, Coll. Picardie, clxii. 32.

[3] AD Oise, G 1984, fos. 116ᵛ–117ᵛ (the bishop's ordinance and the patent notification by the mayor and sworn men; ed. Lefranc, *Hist. Noyon*, pp. 204–5); the former text in Appendix, no. 5. The coinage of Abbeville (Ponthieu) had also been evaluated at 3:2 in relation to *parisis*, AN, JJ 26, fo. 273ᵛ.

licensed operations of ten tables of exchange,[1] it no longer made economic sense to insist on their own currency, which lagged behind the *parisis* in quantity as well as quality. The black deniers were still 'legal tender', as we might say, save for renders of less than a denier's worth—these must henceforth be paid in obols of Paris—but the *parisis* now became the statutory money of account. Disputes between those having to transact in a mix of deniers of Paris and Noyon would have been eased by acceptance of the simple ratio 2:3. Less clear in meaning, but perhaps even more significant, were the clauses relating to the contingencies of recoinage by the bishop. What may be inferred is that an alloy of $3\frac{1}{2}$ d. fine was thought tolerably equivalent to that of the circulating black money (although possibly, in fact, a trifle stronger), which might therefore be replenished without prejudice to the instituted rate of exchange; but that to strengthen the alloy of fine silver to 4 d. or more would effectively disqualify such a coinage from the fixed ratio with the established *parisis*. Because a coinage at 5 d. would have corresponded to the popular *parisis*,[2] the issuance of deniers stronger than that could not realistically have been contemplated. In effect, therefore, the bishop was admitting severe restrictions on his monetary prerogative; his coinage was stabilized in dependence on a royal currency that was winning acceptance as a superior standard for the evaluation of customary payments. Tolls and other occasional payments, however, required no such regulation at Noyon, where the trade in money as well as in grain and wine was prospering.[3]

So at Noyon as at Saint-Quentin the townspeople were demonstrably interested in monetary policy during the 1190s. But it would be erroneous to characterize these impulses as peculiarly communal or *bourgeois*, for the situation had changed since the turbulent days of the *Establissement* of Saint-Quentin. The overriding economic concern was now to get the languishing local currencies into acceptable and recognized ratios with the stabler and more abundant moneys carried into Picardy from the borderlands; it was a concern that the mayor and sworn men of Noyon shared with the landowning canons, and it may be doubted whether the situation was very different at Saint-Quentin in 1195, or even at Beauvais, a few years

[1] Lefranc, *Hist. Noyon*, pp. 193–4, an episcopal statute 'communi assensu et consilio hominum nostrorum, majoris etiam et juratorum tociusque urbis et communie' dated 1180.

[2] Just when the *parisis* was fixed at 5 d. is not known, but that alloy may be deduced already from the agreement of 1197 at Noyon, as Prou showed, 'Histoire monétaire de Beauvais', 71–3; it was certainly the standard by *c.* 1212–14, text quoted in p. 151 n. 4 above.

[3] But the sense of the final clause is admittedly unclear. My supposition is that the petty customs were to continue to be paid in usual amounts of coin, not values of account. In 1201, e.g., we hear of 'quatuor nummos . . . pro dolio' of wine, Lefranc, *Hist. Noyon*, p. 207; and cf. pp. 167–8. For evidence of enterprise and prosperity in the later twelfth century, see Lefranc, pp. 160–76, 190–6, 201–4; Charles Seymour, Jr., *Notre-Dame of Noyon in the Twelfth Century* . . . (New York, 1968), pp. 25–9.

later, where nothing was said of communal intervention.[1] In few of the
Picard towns do the moneyers stand out as individuals or as a class, in
marked contrast to their evident prosperity in Artois and Flanders.[2] No
special need of monetary expertise can have been felt when the mayor and
sworn men were designated as consultants at Saint-Quentin. Nor should
the reiteration of the regulation of Saint-Quentin in the royal charters for
Roye (1196), Chauny (1213), and Crépy (1215) be understood to imply that
an urban estate was forming around the issue of a stable money.[3] In none
of these places were there active mints when the king made these grants
and in none did the king institute mints.

Nevertheless, the regulation of Saint-Quentin (1191–5) together with
the monetary agreements at Noyon and Beauvais in the years thereafter were symptomatic of a reviving general awareness of coinage as
an economic utility. In the background lay uncertainty in exchange
owing to natural depreciation and localism rather than arbitrary manipulations. The mutations attested in the later twelfth century were intended
to improve disreputable coinages, as at Amiens,[4] or to achieve parity,
or to facilitate exchange with the relatively strong currencies of wider

[1] When Philip Augustus confirmed the charter of Chambly in 1222, he prescribed
'quod omnes census et redditus nostri predicti [mentioned in charter] solventur nobis de
cetero ad monetam paris. . . . set secundum valorem monete belvacensis, quam de eisdem
censibus et redditibus sepedicti homines commune Chambliaci solebant reddere comiti
Bellimontis . . .', Douët-d'Arcq, 'Comtes de Beaumont', no. 197, art. 48; cf. no. 199, art.
36 (charter for Beaumont by Louis VIII, 1223).
[2] For *monetarii* at Amiens, see 'Cart. Amiens', no. 12 (1121); at Beauvais, text of
c. 1212–14 quoted above, p. 151 n. 4; at Péronne, *PU Frankreich*, iv. *Picardie*, no. 67
(1155); at Ponthieu, *Rec. des actes des comtes de Pontieu*, no. 115 (1186–7); and at Saint-
Quentin, AN, LL 985B, fo. 235 (1216), and *Archives anciennes*, ed. Lemaire, i, no. 26
(1217). At Corbie from the late eleventh century, the *nummularii* had custody of the dies,
and were probably identical with the *monetarii*, Prou, 'Histoire monétaire de Corbie',
MSAF, lv. 86, 88; and at Abbeville in 1186–7, the moneyers held the exchanges as well
as the coinage; so it may be that the changers whose flourishing *tabule* at Saint-Quentin
were mentioned in a charter of Philippe d'Alsace, *Rev. numism. belge*, 4th ser., iv. 282,
had something to do with the mint there. Cf. generally R. S. Lopez, 'An Aristocracy of
Money in the Early Middle Ages', *Speculum*, xxviii (1953), 21–3, who gives earlier examples
of this confusion of interest.
   The moneyer Simon, whose name figures on coins of Amiens and Crépy in the time
of Philippe d'Alsace, came from Flanders; see Poey d'Avant, *Monnaies féodales*, iii.
323–5, 337–8; Richebé, *Monnaies féodales d'Artois*, pp. 47–51. For Artois and Flanders,
see also *Cartulaire de l'abbaye de Saint-Vaast d'Arras . . . par Guimann . . .*, ed. E.-F.
Van Drival (Arras, 1875), pp. 191, 199, 210, 334; Georges Espinas, *La Vie urbaine de
Douai au Moyen Âge*, 4 vols. (Paris, 1913), ii. 133–5; iii, *p.j.*, no. 6; Arthur Giry, *Histoire
de la ville de Saint-Omer et de ses institutions . . .* (Paris, 1877), pp. 385–7; Richebé,
pp. 38, 76; Victor Tourneur, 'Le monnayage dans les villes de Flandre et de Brabant au
XIIᵉ siècle et au XIIIᵉ', *Académie royale de Belgique, Bulletin de la Classe des lettres . . .*,
5th ser., xxvi (1940), 34–6.
[3] Cf. Brussel, *Nouvel Examen des fiefs*, i. 216–17; Adolphe Vuitry, *Les Monnaies et le
régime monétaire de la monarchie féodale de Hugues-Capet à Philippe-le-Bel (987–1285) . . .*
(Paris, 1876), p. 35.
[4] Poey d'Avant, *Monnaies féodales*, iii. 324.

circulation.[1] There is no evidence that the old moneys of Picardy had been very profitable in late years nor, accordingly, that their stabilization was costly either to the rulers or to the people. The bishop of Beauvais was entitled to 4 d. on each pound of minted coin,[2] or less than 2 per cent, which on any reasonable estimate must have netted far less than the 30 l. per annum that the count of Flanders was said in 1127 to have received from his coinage of Saint-Omer.[3] Very comparable sums from *moneta* at four Flemish towns are indicated in the *Gros Brief* of 1187,[4] and Philip Augustus found it worth reserving one-third of the *monetagium* at Tournai (1202),[5] in a charter which has no analogue in Picardy.

Only, perhaps, in the county of Ponthieu did commercial prosperity and political continuity allow for the lucrative exploitation of a coinage. According to their charter of 1186 or 1187, the count and countess were to receive 12 l. per annum in 'rent' (*census*) from moneyers who were to hold the coinage and the exchanges in hereditary homage and fealty. The coinage might be altered, but in that case the count was to receive no less than 200 l. from the first year's receipts. It is difficult to believe that a coinage on this basis was changed very often, and tempting to believe that the parties understood that themselves. Yet on its face this charter was of coldly fiscal design. Witnessed by the count's men, it did nothing to secure the people of the county from the arbitrary manipulations—probably obligatory demonetization, to judge from the discrepancy between the ordinary and the occasional rents—by which minters and lords alike would profit.[6]

The only possible allusion to a tax intended, as in the Île-de-France or in Normandy, to secure the coinage from manipulation occurs in the royal charter for Bruyères, Cherêt, Vorges, and Valbon (1186–7), derived from the charter of Laon. Toward the end we read that these villagers of the Laonnais are exempt from certain obligations imposed on the men of the 'peace of Laon', including the *theloneum*, the *monetagium*, and certain exactions by the bishop on foodstuffs.[7] Now there is nothing in its context

---

[1] See e.g. Douët-d'Arcq, 'Comtes de Beaumont', no. 56; *Rec. des actes de Philippe Auguste*, ii, no. 496; Richebé, *Monnaies féodales d'Artois*, p. 142.

[2] Above, p. 151 n. 4.

[3] 'Le privilège de Saint-Omer de 1127', ed. Georges Espinas, *Revue du Nord*, xxix (1947), 46–7.

[4] *Le Compte général de 1187, connu sous le nom de 'Gros Brief'* ..., ed. Adriaan Verhulst and Maurits Gysseling (Brussels, 1962), pp. 142, 156–7, 163, 190.

[5] *Rec. des actes de Philippe Auguste*, ii, nos. 710, 711.

[6] *Rec. des actes des comtes de Pontieu*, no. 115. For the economic background, see also nos. 4, 5, 8, 17, 27, 41, 54, 65, 70, 73, 77, 101, 109, 112, which suggest a tradition of exchange in larger sums involving various coinages and substitutes for specie. But even Ponthieu came under royal influence, its types being patterned on that of the *parisis*, Dieudonné, *Manuel de numismatique*, iv. 332.

[7] *Rec. des actes de Philippe Auguste*, i, no. 197 (p. 240): '34. Hec autem omnia, ad modum pacis Laudunensis, in hac pace instituta sunt preter hoc quod homines hujus pacis nec theloneum nec monetagium reddant, nec apud eos aliquis dominus capturam panis, vini,

to rule out the conclusion that this 'money-tax' was a levy on persons (or on the community) that had lately been administered or threatened at Laon. If the meaning was *seigneuriage*, in the sense of some share of the profits of minting or exchange, one might expect some limiting reference to money-ers or changers. On the other hand, no imposition associated with confir-mations of coinage figures among the tallages at Laon regulated by the bishop and confirmed by the king in 1185,[1] nor is it mentioned in the royal charter of the peace (1128) confirmed in 1189—a weighty silence in view of the persistent fears for the stability of the deniers of Laon.[2] Moreover, while the term *monetagium* does not otherwise occur in reference to general levies in the Île-de-France or Picardy, we do find it used not only to refer to profits of coining but even—as at Orléans in 1200—to denote a share of the profits of exchange.[3] It seems most unlikely that the *monetagium* renounced in these villages of the countryside had anything to do with the mint, which must have been the preserve of a few men at Laon. Conceivably, however, the king or the bishop had made an effort to rake off some of the mounting proceeds of exchange, a dangerous precedent wherever the tables were being set up. In the last analysis, the interpretation remains doubtful; yet it seems altogether possible that we have here a first, fleeting glimpse of a new effort to tap the swelling incomes of the makers and sellers of money.

E. *Toward a Redefinition of the Public Interest*

Our theme might easily be pursued further along these provincial roads. In Flanders the men of Saint-Omer who momentarily acquired the coinage from the embattled successor to Charles the Good in 1127 surely retained the expectation of its stability when they surrendered it a year later to Thierry d'Alsace (1128–68).[4] A mutation at about that time, or before, resulted in a lighter coin of relatively good alloy; and the new standard was to be maintained during the long, strong reigns that spanned the century in a beautiful series of 'petty deniers'. The institution of this coinage,

carnium vel piscium aut aliarum venalium rerum habeat sicut episcopus in urbe Laudu-nensi habere consuevit.'

[1] *Rec. des actes de Philippe Auguste*, i, no. 145; see generally Stephenson, *Mediaeval Institutions*, pp. 81–4.

[2] See e.g. AD Oise, G 1984, fo. 105; *Rec. des actes de Philippe Auguste*, i, no. 197 (p. 240), art. 33; no. 279. There is little correspondence between the regulation of 1185 and the king's confirmation of the charter of 1189, but neither mentions *monetagium*.

[3] *LTC*, i, nos. 602, 603. Niermeyer, *Lexicon*, p. 703 (*moneta*, *monetagium*), cites sugges-tive precedents for the tenth and eleventh centuries, including *monetagium per cambitum* (*Gallia christiana*, ii, *inst.*, 480; the emendation should be ignored).

[4] 'Le privilège de Saint-Omer', ed. Espinas, 46–7: 'Monetam meam in Sancto Audo-maro, unde per annum xxx lb. habebam [i.e. Guillaume Clito] et quicquid in ea habere debeo, ad restaurationem dampnorum suorum et gilde sue sustentamentum, constituo. Ipsi uero burgenses monetam per totam vitam meam stabilem et bonam, unde villa sua melioretur, stabiliant'; *Recueil de documents relatifs à l'histoire du droit municipal en France...*, *Artois*, ed. Georges Espinas, 3 vols. (Paris, 1934–43), iii, no. 623, art. 18. Cf. Giry, *Hist. Saint-Omer*, p. 61.

extended from town to town with appropriate differentiation of types, engendered a measure of regional confidence comparable to that in the Parisian system.[1]

Such being the case in an urbanized society well endowed with instruments and offices of exchange, the popular or communal interest in coinage was understandably quiescent. The rewards of a reputable coinage, political as well as fiscal, were too precious to risk by resorting to arbitrary mutations. But it was not only the lay princes who arrived at this conception of monetary administration. The bishops of Châlons-sur-Marne, probably from the days of Guillaume de Champeaux (1113–22), had their coinage in parity with the king's;[2] and the very wide currency of the *châlonnais*—from Picardy to Lorraine,[3] to follow it no further—shows again how in some ways and some circumstances a good coinage can drive out a bad. At Verdun toward 1140 a despairing bishop suspended the 'depraved' coinage of which his predecessor had lost control, ordaining that for fifteen years the deniers of Châlons be used instead. Thereafter—presumably *c.* 1147–56—he maintained his coinage unchanged. Motivated by charity, according to the *Deeds of the Bishops of Verdun* (which, unfortunately, leave it at that), these decisions were surely responsive to popular sentiment, the recoinage being described in terms suggestive of a public confirmation.[4]

In Berry the early disappearance of the count had fostered a proliferation of vicecomital or seigneurial mints which were slow to yield to any overriding money.[5] The charters of Saint-Sulpice suggest that the money of

[1] Dieudonné, *Manuel de numismatique*, iv. 184–5, 76–8; Richebé, *Monnaies féodales d'Artois*, pp. 45–52, 124–6, 136–7; Joseph Ghyssens, *Les Petits Deniers de Flandre des XIIᵉ et XIIIᵉ siècles* (Brussels, 1971), pp. 14–16, 49–52, 56–128, and plates i–x.

[2] Le Blanc, *Traité des monnoyes* (1690), p. 162; see also C.-R. Buirette de Verrières, *Annales historiques de la ville et comté-pairie de Châlons-sur-Marne* (Châlons, 1788), pp. 161–71. The *moneta* of Châlons was still very lucrative in 1220, *Catalogue des actes de Philippe-Auguste ...*, ed. Léopold Delisle (Paris, 1856), no. 1949.

[3] Dieudonné, *Manuel de numismatique*, iv. 139; AD Oise, G 1984, fos. 91ᵛ–92ʳ; 'Cart. Saint-Vincent de Laon', no. 37.

[4] *Laurentii gesta episcoporum Virdunensium...*, ed. Georg Waitz, *MGH, Scriptores*, x (1852), 513: '... nec illud de laude episcopi [Albéron] praetereundum est, quod per quindecim annos, quibus praesul sedet, plebiculae suae ita pepercerit, ut percussuram numismatis depravatam mox post primum annum deposuerit, et Cathalaunensem monetam inducens, numquam deinceps nummi percussuram, ne pauperes inde graventur, mutari fecit.'

[5] Paul Chenu, 'De la circulation des monnaies féodales dans les territoires qui ont formé le département du Cher, aux XIᵉ, XIIᵉ et XIIIᵉ siècles', *Mémoires de la Fédération des Sociétés savantes du Centre* (à part, Moulins, 1940), 1–17 (a cautious study based on hoards as well as texts); Guy Devailly, *Le Berry du Xᵉ siècle au milieu du XIIIᵉ ...* (Paris-La Haye, 1973), pp. 227–31, 570–3; Dieudonné, *Manuel de numismatique*, iv. 93–103. For the diversity of currencies in a relatively undeveloped rural economy, see *Catalogue des actes des archevêques de Bourges, antérieures à l'an 1210*, ed. Alfred Gandilhon (Bourges-Paris, 1927), nos. 132, 133, 147, 148, 151, 157, 199, 226, 228, 231, 248, 327, 330, 343, 347–49, 356, 376, 380, 429, 439; *Chartes du Bourbonnais, 918–1522*, ed. Jacques Monicat and Bernard de Fournoux (Moulins, 1952), nos. 6, 10–11, 13, 17, 18, 20, 22–3, 27; *Chartrier de Fontmorigny*, nos. 4, 21, 23, 26, 55, 63, 114.

Bourges, the king's since 1100, was among eight or nine recognized local currencies during much of our period. What might result from such 'monetary anarchy'[1] is illustrated by the customs of La Chapelaude which date from the middle of the twelfth century. It was laid down that 'by the counsel of his monks and retainers, the prior shall impose in the seigneury such a coinage as would be useful to them and the burghers, and which should be accepted around La Chapelle and at Huriel and at Saint-Désiré and other neighbouring regions'.[2] In this hinterland where but little wealth was in specie and where the prior had no coinage of his own, the problem was not the minting nor even, primarily, the stability of money. The villagers had to use what deniers came their way and they were accustomed to dealing in credit. Accordingly, the prior required an administrative council in order to determine what coinage from without should be recognized as current in his lands; and it may be imagined that his choice would depend on the supply of deniers as well as their stability. What was of concern here was the convenience of petty exchange in rural markets rather than the security of seigneurial income.

Over the next half century the situation changed. By 1200 Philip Augustus was active in Berry, minting steady money at Déols (for a time) as well as at Bourges, allowing that of Gien to continue current after assuming that lordship in 1199, while other local coinages lost intrinsic value.[3] In 1213 the king expressed himself with peremptory candour: 'As we have many times ordered you,' he wrote to the bailiffs of Berry, 'you should see to it that our money of Bourges circulates throughout your whole *bailliage* and that other bad money is abolished completely.'[4] This directive, for all

---

[1] The expression is Étienne Cartier's, 'Lettres sur l'histoire monétaire de France, IX. Monnaies baronales', *RN*, vi (1841), 281. See 'Essai de reconstitution du Cartulaire A de Saint-Sulpice de Bourges', ed. Louis de Kersers, *Mémoires de la Société des Antiquaires du Centre*, xxxv (1912), nos. 44, 55, 65, 67, 73, 79, 90, 100, 110, 117–18, 121, suppls. 8, 8 *bis*, 10, 28.

[2] Ed. C. van de Kieft, *Étude sur le chartrier et la seigneurie du prieuré de la Chapelle-Aude (XIe–XIIIe siècle)* (Amsterdam, 1960), p. 242, art. 21: 'Talem monetam in villa prior, consilio tam monachorum quam gliencium, inponet, que sibi et burgensibus utilis sit, et que circa Capellam aut apud Urciacum aut apud Sanctum Desideratum aliisve finitimis regionibus suscipiatur.' Purporting to date from 1073, the text has been shown by Kieft to have been written *c.* 1151–6 (ibid. 89–91, and preceding discussion). There is a translation of some of the articles and commentary by Duby, *L'Économie rurale*, i. 343–56; *Rural Economy*, pp. 412–13. For the lord's imposition of currency at Issoudun, see the regulation of 1190, *LTC*, i, no. 380.

[3] *LTC*, i, nos. 502, 739; *Rec. des actes de Philippe Auguste*, iii, no. 1123; Dieudonné, *Manuel de numismatique*, iv. 93, 98, 321; Poey d'Avant, *Monnaies féodales*, i. 265, 268, 274 (corrected by Dieudonné), 276–86, 288–90, 292–8, 303; Lafaurie, *Monnaies des rois de France*, pp. 18–19, nos. 166–9. Philip later minted at Issoudun, Lafaurie, no. 170. A strong money of Sancerre was cited in 1200 and 1211, *Rec. des actes de Philippe Auguste*, ii, no. 631A; iii, no. 1185. For the persistence of the money or accounting of Gien, see *Actes*, ii, no. 568; iii, no. 1123; *Chartrier de Fontmorigny*, nos. 158, 160, 165; *HF*, xxiii, 660, 661, 669.

[4] *Rec. des actes de Philippe Auguste*, iii, no. 1276, addressed to Gilbert de Chanceaux and Mathieu Dreu: '... et, sicut multociens vobis mandavimus, monetam nostram

its portentous air, cannot have been intended to dismiss all seigneurial moneys (one of which was the king's); rather it was following up on efforts, understandably arduous, to weed out debased or counterfeit pieces that were driving prices up and good deniers out—a late revival of the troubles at Laon and Verdun. It exhibited urgently the same fear for rural revenues paid in diminished coinages that prompted the regulations of Noyon and Beauvais during these very years. This inference is supported by a complaint of the archbishop of Bourges that tenants of Gui de Dampierre, lord of Bourbon (1202–13), wished to pay the 'pentecostal penny' in 'money of less value which was then circulating in the land of the same lord'. In a settlement dated 1214, the lord of Bourbon agreed to direct his *prévôts* and bailiffs to announce 'to his men publicly in all churches of his land' that the payments were to be made in the 'good money' of Souvigny.[1] It is among the more vivid surviving testimonies to the seigneurial perception of the fiscal advantage in promoting the use of strong coinages.

These various incidents serve to remind us of some underlying tendencies in northern experience. By the later decades of the twelfth century coinages were being stabilized in commercially realistic ratios, the weaker ones becoming dependent on some stronger ones of widening currency. This happened with the evident, sometimes express, approval of persons or institutions dependent on agrarian incomes increasingly measured or paid in cash. How far such a fiscal interest motivated townsmen is more difficult to say. The charters of Saint-Omer (1127 and 1128) are equivocal on this point; those of Saint-Quentin (1191–5) and Noyon (1197) suggest that popular convenience was consistent—as it was partly coincident—with the interest of landlords; while only those of Dijon (1187) and Beaune (1203) could possibly be construed otherwise. But the fearful consequences of such uncontrolled debasements as are known to have occurred at Laon must have been a lesson to all. The concern in the Burgundian towns was probably to ensure that no coinage too strong to circulate be imposed; and that concern would not only have been shared by the rulers of the northern principalities, but might have disposed any prudent ruler to administer his coinage openly.

---

bituricensem per totam balliviam vestram currere faciatis et aliam pravam monetam penitus aboleri ....'

[1] AD Cher, G 2, fos. 140–1 (ed. Monicat and Fournoux, *Chartes du Bourbonnais*, no. 42): '...Noverint universi quod cum inter venerabilem patrem dominum G. Bituricensem archiepiscopum et nobilem virum Guidonem dominum Borbonensem contencio esset super moneta minoris valencie que tunc in terra eiusdem domini currebat quam homines de terra sua pro denario pentecostali volebant persolvere, tandem ... idem dominus prepositis et ballivis suis iniunxit quod in omnibus ecclesiis terre sue hominibus suis publice preciperent ut bonam monetam videlicet silviniacensem de anno presenti et de anno proxime preterito [in] quibus predictum denarium non reddiderant solverent ....' On the business of the 'pentecostal denier', see further *Chartes du Bourbonnais*, no. 38.

The instituted consultation on coinage—whether in order to determine currency as at La Chapelaude or to determine standards as at Saint-Quentin—was an original development in the North. It was not parliamentary in nature, although it surely grew out of the kind of experience with petitioning that is exemplified by the charter of 1137–8 for Étampes. It was very different from the ponderous assemblage of Corbigny wherein the great men of the county of Nevers dealt with the coinage as an urgent but passing issue related to their crusade; a coinage confirmed for ever was the last in the world to require statutory consultation. But such a coinage might well require periodic surveillance, as the prelates and barons were realistic enough to grasp, and their provision for this contingency is, ironically, the earliest extant allusion to expert counsel on coinage. In reality, discussions of standards and currency were surely being held in many towns where it was thought unnecessary to prescribe them. Everywhere lords and people alike were finding themselves at the mercy of economic forces that would remould the coinage into a public institution.

In this process the traditional confirmation of coinage persisted tenaciously. The notion that a ruler's good new money should be preserved unchanged during his lifetime figured more or less explicitly in charters for Corbie (*c.* 1080), Saint-Omer (1127), Étampes and Orléans (1137–8), Blois (*c.* 1165), Champagne (1165), Burgundy (1185), and Nevers (1188). Some of these engagements were sworn by or on behalf of the rulers in forms broadly analogous to the meridional charters of confirmation. The solemnity of the concession to Blois and of the ceremonies at Provins (1165) and at Corbigny (1188) show that the stability of coinage continued to be perceived in moral terms of direct interest to the clergy. It remained difficult to distinguish mutations, or at least debasements, from monetary fraud, so that—once again as in the South—we find remedies against counterfeiting or misrepresentation mentioned together with confirmations as well as in separate provisions.[1]

A critical phase was reached in the decade 1185–95. Charters of Burgundy and Picardy continued to salute the conservation of coinage in principle, while that of Nevers carried the principle to its *ne plus ultra*. But already at Châtillon (1185) and Dijon (1187) the possibilities of exchange *secundum valorem* were pointing to a less rigid conception of stability, whereby alterations within designated limits or upon due consultation might be contemplated. At Metz the restraints imposed by the town remained considerable: the bishop had only the right to strengthen his coinage by not more than 8 d. per mark, probably little more than normally acceptable

---

[1] See above, pp. 131, 137, 147; Kieft, *Chartrier de la Chapelle-Aude*, p. 248, art. 8; *Rec. de documents relatifs à l'histoire du droit municipal. Artois*, ed. Espinas, i. 565, art. 7; cf. above, p. 118.

tolerance in the mints.[1] The monetary regulation at Saint-Quentin (1191–5) marks the turning-point; therein the imperative of maintaining the coinage has all but given way to the recognition of due need and occasion for replenishment. Moreover, the final clause—'and we shall cause the old money to circulate with the new'—both evokes and remedies one of the more profound causes for dissatisfaction with mutations. Once exchange had become generally available, and rates of exchange better recognized, arbitrary or clandestine mutations became less profitable, less frequent, and less feared. A new conception of the public interest in coinage began to gain acceptance.

The transformation is well illustrated by the consequences of Bishop Pierre III's failure to give notice (*c.* 1221–4) that his old money of Meaux would become worthless when his new coinage went into circulation. Upon the complaint of people living on royal fiefs 'in places where the old money used to circulate', King Louis VIII remonstrated with the bishop, who agreed in 1225 that whenever in future he or his successors revoked the old coinage upon minting an altered one, he or they would give four months' notice to those people 'so that they might rid themselves of the old money'.[2]

In this settlement almost every vestige of the *confirmatio monetae* has disappeared. Pierre III (1221–55) seems to have been acting on the old understanding that a ruler might change the coinage on accession, but he made no engagement to conserve the coinage for life. On the contrary, he anticipated occasions for mutations whenever Count Thibaut altered his coinage, a detail which—in view of the solidity of the money of Champagne—proves his shrewd grasp of monetary realities. It was no longer practical to forswear mutations, however immoral they might still seem to many. Nor were the demands for such acts so urgent as in the past, for the disadvantage of ageing and depreciating silver in prospering economies dominated by stable currencies had become generally apparent. The new objective was to define the procedures of public recoinage that would be least injurious or inconvenient to the people. Whether an old coinage was to be left in circulation, as was provided at Saint-Quentin, or revoked, as was in prospect at Meaux, such events should be made known.[3]

---

[1] Statement of rights quoted (as from BN, MS. n. a. fr. 4837, fo. 75ʳ; but I have been unable to verify the citation) by Jean Schneider, *La Ville de Metz aux XIIIᵉ et XIVᵉ siècles* (Nancy, 1950), pp. 93–4 (cf. pp. 257–8): 'Mes sires li aveckes . . . fait faire monoie keile k'il welt et en keil flour k'il welt mais il ne lai puet ampairier, ne amandier ke viii d. a mairc. . . .' The uncertain date of this understanding probably falls within the generation ending about 1225. Cf. Blanchet and Dieudonné, *Manuel de numismatique*, ii. 43.

[2] BN, MS. lat. 5528, fo. 45ᵃᵇ, text in the king's name. The better-known text in the bishop's name survives in an original, AN, J 459, no. 1, ed. *LTC*, ii, no. 1704.

[3] Whatever happened at Provins with the famous recoinage of 1224, it seems clear that the event was neither deceptive nor unpopular; see *HF*, xxii. 82; xxiii. 178; cf. Blanchet and Dieudonné, *Manuel de numismatique*, iv. 133.

As a result, the money-tax became harder than ever to justify. If the *monetagium* of Laon in the 1180s was intended to fall on the mass of the people, it left an astonishingly feeble trace in the records. The *cornagium* at Blois, whatever its nature, is known to us only from its repudiation. In the county of Nevers the hearth tax of 1188 'for the perpetuity of the coinage' could not and would not be repeated. These impositions and their circumstances were well known to Philip Augustus and his men, who were at that time regulating the *tallia panis et vini* at Orléans and instituting it at Paris. So it is significant that money-taxes were not introduced in Picardy and Berry as the king's influence and currencies spread. By that time the French and Norman tallages were coming to be regarded popularly as customs rather than utilities; nor did Capetian officials see fit to pretend otherwise.[1] Moreover, the proceeds of these taxes, as must have become apparent in the 1190s, but especially after 1204, were relatively too mediocre to make them worth imposing where mints and exchanges were returning profits and where resistance could be expected.[2]

These shifts in attitude corresponded to changes in social circumstances and administrative policy. Down to the final years of the twelfth century the only men visibly active in monetary policy were the lay magnates who served in princely courts. Raoul de Vermandois, who was on hand as seneschal of France when Louis VII confirmed his coinages and imposed his tallages at Étampes and Orléans (1137–8), was reorganizing his own coinage at Saint-Quentin at about the same time. Anseau de Traînel, who swore security for his lord Henri le Libéral's confirmation of the coinage in 1165, took particular interest in fiscal matters as butler to the count during many years;[3] and he and his brother Garnier had associations in Burgundy and Nevers—Garnier being seneschal to Count Gui of Nevers toward 1170–5—in the period just before the unsteady coinages of those regions were regulated.[4] Most conspicuous among such men was Thibaut V of Blois, one of the principals in the *rapprochement* between France and Champagne that was to be as critical for monetary history as for political. Having confirmed the coinage of his own county almost simultaneously with his

[1] The memorandum *De foagio* is strictly a record of obligations and administrative practice, Appendix, no. 7; see also *LTC*, i, no. 901.

[2] See p. 163 n. 5 below; and for estimates of the fiscal value of these money-taxes, above, pp. 26, 42.

[3] *LTC*, i, no. 118; Bourquelot, *Hist. Provins*, ii. 380–2; Carrière, *Cart. Templiers de Provins*, pp. 103–4; Arbois de Jubainville, 'Catalogue des actes', *Comtes de Champagne*, iii, nos. 8, 11, 15, 19, 24–5, 28, 32–5, 38, 42, 43 *bis*, 44–6, 53–4, 62, 65, 67, 68, 74, 78, 86, 96, 100, 116–17, 119, 124, 136, 136 *bis*, 140, 150, 152, 157, 160, 179, 214 *bis*, 218, 248, 269, 324.

[4] 'Documents pour servir à la généalogie des anciens seigneurs de Traînel', ed. Charles Lalore, *MSAA*, xxxiv (1870), 179–80, 185–7, 194–5; *preuves*, nos. 22, 36, 47, 51, 55, 58, 68, 86, 94, 96, 106, 113, 121, 124–5, 133; 'Cart. Jully-les-Nonnains', 268; AD Cher, 6H 59, nos. 56, 57. Milon de Traînel, brother of Anseau II and Garnier II, was abbot of Saint-Marien d'Auxerre from 1155 to 1202, 'Documents', ed. Lalore, no. 43.

brother's analogous act in Champagne, he was for many years the king's seneschal,[1] and he attended Philip Augustus in almost every enactment relative to monetary confirmations or money-taxes which that sovereign is known to have issued.[2]

These circumstantial contacts prove, if proof were needed, that the monetary practices in the great domains bordering on the Île-de-France were understood among the courtiers as well as among the money-changers. But it is improbable that the seneschals and butlers, for all their experience in administration, had much expertise in coinage. Their approach, like the king's, was seigneurial: through the coinage as through other monopolies or tallages they lived off their tenants, even if their charters showed them willing to reduce or commute this burden. When it came to operations in the mints or the money markets, these men must have been as much in the dark as the magnates of Nevers who, in the charter of 1188, were authorized to consult 'changers and men competent in the knowledge of silver and weight' when the coinage needed testing.

The moneyers and changers were big winners in the increasingly liquid and prosperous economies of France, Champagne, Ponthieu, and Flanders. Godin and Simon evidently enjoyed the power of wealth when they agreed virtually to finance the count of Ponthieu in return for the dies and exchanges in 1186–7.[3] At Orléans the associated changers of Sainte-Croix received the king's privilege in 1200 on condition of paying 15 l. yearly, of which 5 l. was *pro monetagio*.[4] Of moneyers at work under Philip Augustus we know sadly little, but it seems clear that their profits as well as their systematized products were being made to serve the king. By 1225 their 'custom of the fabric of the dies' was lucrative enough so that the king could dispense the masters, minters, and workers of the Parisian money from all other impositions.[5] And in Champagne, as the confirmation of coinage faded away, the moneyers were charged with the kind of tax that subject populations had elsewhere been required to pay.

---

[1] Thibaut replaced Raoul de Vermandois in 1154; see generally Luchaire, *Études sur les actes de Louis VII*, pp. 44–7, and ('Actes inédits'), nos. 3 ff., 279 ff., 298, 330, 333 ff.; see also Pacaut, *Louis VII*, pp. 172–7, and indexed references to Raoul and Thibaut V. The latter served Philip Augustus until his death in 1191, *Rec. des actes de Philippe Auguste*, i, as far as no. 374.

[2] i.e. charters for Orléans, 1183; Dijon, 1187; Nevers, 1188; and that for Bruyères (1189) which mentions the *monetagium* at Laon.

[3] In addition to the cited contract (*Rec. des actes des comtes de Pontieu*, no. 115), see Richebé, *Monnaies féodales d'Artois*, p. 50, with reference to the likewise powerful Simon of Flanders. For the royal domain under Louis VII, see the suggestive evidence cited by Newman, *Domaine royal*, p. 27. A changer, Ébrouin, was probably among the 'six good and legitimate men' appointed consultants to the royal administrators in 1190, Rigord, *Gesta Philippi Augusti*, c. 70, ed. Delaborde, i. 100.

[4] *LTC*, i, nos. 602, 603. I find no evidence of this receipt in the royal accounts of 1202–3.

[5] AN, JJ 26, fo. 89ᵛ, ed. Saulcy, *Rec. de documents*, i. 120–1. Cf. *Rec. des actes de Philippe Auguste*, iii, no. 1220.

Accordingly, the change in supervision of royal finance was symptomatic. The real successor to Thibaut V, upon whose death (1191) the seneschalsy lapsed, was to be Brother Haimard, treasurer at the Temple of Paris from about 1202 to 1227;[1] and Haimard was expert in currency and exchange. Presiding over the king's receipts during the years when the domain was most rapidly expanding, he had to calculate sums in diverse coinages and standards.[2] He was the chief consultant for the ordinance of Caen (1204) relating to currencies and rates of exchange admissible in the Norman Exchequer.[3] Moreover, in 1214 the bishop-elect of Meaux asked Haimard's advice before renewing the pact providing for joint administration of the mints with the countess of Champagne.[4] That Haimard should have been familiar with the original pact of 1208 is hardly surprising, for he was probably a native of Champagne,[5] the administration of the county had been in the king's wardship since 1201 (with the revenues of Bray and Montereau collectible since 1209 at latest), and it was in the treasurer's interest to see that the popular coinages of Meaux, Provins, and Troyes be maintained uniform with one another and sound.[6] If, through the influence of Haimard or otherwise, the contracts with royal moneyers were at all like those surviving in Champagne, then it is easier to understand why Capetian officials made no evident effort to extend the incidence of the money-tax from Orléans and Paris to other *prévôtés*. The secrets of the moneyers and changers were getting out, melting the reverence for the immutable denier. To the likes of Brother Haimard or the town fathers of Burgundy and

[1] Léopold Delisle, 'Mémoire sur les opérations financières des Templiers', *Mémoires de ... l'Académie des inscriptions et belles-lettres*, xxxiii: 2. 61–4. Although there were budding specialists in finance during the 1180s and 1190s—men like Pierre le Maréchal and Adam the clerk—they were significantly less visible than Haimard; see generally Charles Petit-Dutaillis, *The Feudal Monarchy in France and England ...*, tr. E. D. Hunt (London, 1936), p. 182; Lot and Fawtier, *Hist. des institutions*, ii. 52, 54–5.

[2] Allusions to the work of Haimard in the account of 1202–3 are conveniently indexed in Lot and Fawtier, *Compte général de 1202–1203*, p. 255.

[3] *Rec. des actes de Philippe Auguste*, ii, no. 844: 'Ita ordinatum est apud Cadomum coram senescallo Normannie, consilio fratris Haimardi et consilio baronum Normannie, quod ...' Haimard's specialized interest in the matter may safely be distinguished from the general right of the barons to be consulted. Haimard directed sessions of the Exchequer at Easter 1213 and Easter 1214, Delisle, 'Mémoire', 62.

[4] BN, MS. lat. 5993, fo. 30ʳ: '... Notum uobis facimus [Bishop Guillaume I to Countess Blanche] nos cum fratre Aẏmardo loquutus fuisse super societate que facta fuit super monetam inter uos et uenerabilem patrem predecessorem nostrum G. quondam Meldensem episcopum ...'; cf. above, p. 134.

[5] One 'frater Aymardus' was witness to a donation to the Templars of Provins in 1193, *Cart. Templiers de Provins*, no. 7; the associations of 'frater Haymardus' the treasurer with Champagne persisted strongly, until he retired there, Delisle, 'Mémoire', 62–4, and *Cart. Templiers de Provins*, nos. 131, 121, 54, 126; *HF*, xxiii. 676H.

[6] *Rec. des actes de Philippe Auguste*, ii, no. 678; iii, no. 1088. King Philip ordered the countess Blanche to pay Brother Haimard or his messenger 250 l. *pruv.* in February 1203, *Actes*, ii, no. 743. Note further that a 'Hugo monetarius' and his wife submitted to the arbitration of Haimard about 1231 in a dispute with the Templars of Provins in which monetary value was at issue, *Cart. Templiers de Provins*, no. 54.

Picardy, the confirmations and ransoms of coinage no longer made sense. Less restricted than in the past but not less suspiciously overseen,[1] the moneyers were to have the burdens as well as the profits of coinage.

[1] See e.g. *Rec. des actes de Philippe Auguste*, i, no. 237; Arbois de Jubainville, *Comtes de Champagne*, iv: 2. 771–2; Saulcy, *Rec. de documents*, i. 120–1.

VI

THE CORRELATIONS OF THOUGHT

APART from the charters already examined, the conservation of coinage left few traces in the written residues of thought and doctrine. It was a peculiar notion derived from economic and fiscal contingencies of which the moralists and storytellers were oblivious. Even among lawyers and schoolmen the discussions of coinage down to about 1250 had little to do with the question of limiting the monetary prerogative. In this regard, it seems clear, the practical issue preceded the theoretical one. On the other hand, the difficulties resulting from fluctuating coinages and from arbitrary or increasing taxation were too commonly experienced to escape the notice of the literate, whose learned and legal inquiries led to positions quite diversely related to the principle of the stabilized coinage. More generally, of course, the coinage as money was on everyone's mind, with a pertinence to the realities of value and wealth that made it the subject—progressively the tarnished hero—of anecdote, *exemplum*, and song. It would be no less mistaken to disregard these secondary manifestations than to misconceive them. They afford glimpses of the cultural setting in which the conservation of coinage was related to prevailing monetary ideas and to the larger moral and economic issues created by the revival of commercial exchange.

A. Quanto personam tuam (Third Compilation 2.15.4; X 2.24.18)

It was in the realm of moral thought that conservationist practice had its most closely related expression. Of foremost importance were the papal pronouncements on monetary problems in Occitania and Aragon, among which *Quanto personam tuam* (5 April 1199) was to be the monument. What concerned the pope in the latter case was the safety of a king's soul and the welfare of the kingdom of Aragon, and of these Innocent III proclaimed himself the custodian.[1]

---

[1] The argument of this section was anticipated in my article ' "Quanto personam tuam" ' (*X 2. 24. 18*): Its Original Significance', *Proc. Fourth Intern. Congress of Medieval Canon Law* . . . (Vatican City, 1976), pp. 229–49. Professor Stephan Kuttner has kindly permitted me to draw on that article for some of what follows.

For the text and editions of *Quanto*, see below, p. 203. The decretal was destined, after its incorporation in the *Liber Extra*, to become an important *locus* of economic and constitutionalist commentary, which has, in turn, attracted the attention of modern writers: e.g. Émile Bridrey, *Théorie de la monnaie*, pp. 317–34; Ludwig Buisson, *Potestas und Caritas. Die päpstliche Gewalt im Spätmittelalter* (Cologne, 1958), pp. 290–3.

In responding to King Peter's appeal to be absolved from his incautious oath to preserve unaltered his late father's last Aragonese coinage, the pope alluded to the evil counsel on which the king had allegedly acted to confirm the coinage without the consent of the people, and to the scandal aroused by a 'defrauded' coinage of diminished weight. But he pointed out that in this case interpretation rather than absolution was required. For if the king had sworn in the belief that the coinage was good, then the oath should hold firm; but if, unfortunately, he had confirmed a coinage he knew to be 'false', then his oath was null, and he was to do penance by direction of the bishop of Zaragoza. In either case, the king must invalidate the diminished coinage and reissue the best money of his father's reign without revoking the old deniers of full quality still in circulation.[1]

Now it would be difficult to contend that this text was a celebration of the sworn confirmation of coinage. On the contrary, the pope was trying to undo such an act, or its effects, and it could well seem, as it did seem to the early decretalists,[2] that he was more interested in the integrity of the king's oath than in the state of the coinage. Nevertheless, if we hold fast to the words of Innocent III, we shall find his thought consistent with the principle of the justly secured coinage. It was not wrong of Peter to have sworn 'to conserve the money', only imprudent of him to have failed to ascertain in time whether the money in question was good. Moreover, the pope's preferred solution, which depended on the king's innocence *in actu*, was to save the oath while restoring the good old coinage. For a new ruler to retain the good old pieces in circulation while continuing to mint them with the imprint unchanged was fully in keeping with popular conservationist thought. But did Innocent III actively approve of sworn confirmations of coinage?

It is a difficult question. Neither *Quanto personam tuam* nor subsequent writings of the great pope afford a conclusive answer. The most that can be said is that the letter to Peter of Aragon refers to the coinage in terms that had in the past been associated with the pontifical endorsement of the sworn confirmation. For Innocent the coinage must have been either 'false' (or 'defrauded') or 'legitimate'. This distinction did not in itself imply hostility to mutations, not at least to all mutations, for it obviously turned on the issue of deception. A coinage was false if its standards were other than those publicly proclaimed, and most blatantly so if it were diminished —i.e. defrauded—without notice.[3] A coinage thus misrepresented was a kind of counterfeit, a fraud. And the tendency to assimilate deceptive mutations to counterfeits was already apparent in Honorius II's directive

---

[1] Below, p. 203; for the immediate circumstances in Aragon, see above, pp. 83–104.
[2] See below, p. 169.
[3] Would the pope have used other language for a surreptitious *strengthening* of the coinage? Cf. below, pp. 174, 182.

(*c.* 1129) to his vassal Bernard IV of Melgueil that he mint his coinage, adding 'nothing false', on the standards in effect in the time of Calixtus II.[1]

Now in this letter, perhaps the earliest papal pronouncement on a lay ruler's coinage, Honorius II was certainly opposing the mutation of coinage. Indeed, it is conceivable that he was seeking to enforce the confirmation formerly sworn by Bernard IV before judges-delegate,[2] although if so it is puzzling to find no allusion to an oath in the letter of *c.* 1129. But what the pope stressed was the end, not the means, and if we seek the origins of this stress on the soundness of the coinage, we shall find ourselves on another, still older trail leading toward *Quanto personam tuam.*

It will be remembered that the First Lateran Council (1123) had provided for the excommunication of counterfeiters and knowing dealers in false coin. In stigmatizing such persons as 'oppressors of the poor' and 'disturbers of the city', in context with canons relating to the security of roads and the Peace and Truce of God,[3] the council fathers were imposing on Christendom a conception of the sound coinage as an element of public order that was already a century old in the Spanish March. It was there, so far as we know, that men first began to think of debasements as akin to counterfeits; there, too, that acts of either sort came to be regarded as violations of the Peace. And it was there, almost on the eve of the First Lateran Council, that a ruler confirmed the coinage and the peace together under oath.[4] Whether these Catalonian tendencies influenced Popes Calixtus II and Honorius II we do not know; but when the cardinal-legate Jacintus went to Spain a generation later he found there and surely approved a clerical programme, perhaps already traditional, of urging rulers to forswear mutations as a species of fraud and as if in violation of the peace. This programme suffered setbacks, as we have seen, but if Jacintus did not insist upon it during his subsequent legations, he probably continued to favour the sworn confirmation of coinage in principle. For as Pope Celestine III he dispensed Alphonse II of Aragon from such an oath in 1191 on the conditions that a strengthened coinage be minted and, in its turn, be confirmed under oath.[5]

The circumstances of his letter *Cum utilitas publica* significantly anticipated those of *Quanto personam tuam* a few years later; and like Innocent III, whose policy he may have influenced, Celestine evidently regarded a securing of the coinage as in the public interest. But the purpose of both letters was to regulate oaths, not to advocate them. Once the question of the validity of oaths, on which there existed a considerable jurisprudence, had

---

[1] *Bull. Maguelone,* i, no. 24; JL, i, no. 7345. Discussed above, p. 71.

[2] Above, p. 66.

[3] *Conc. oec. decreta,* ed. Alberigo, pp. 192–3 (arts. 13–15). For the legal background, see Peter Herde, 'Römisches und kanonisches Recht bei der Verfolgung des Fälschungs-delikts im Mittelalter', *Traditio,* xxi (1965), 291–302, 319 ff.

[4] Above, pp. 50–64.   [5] Above, pp. 103–4.

become paramount, the substantive principle of conserving the coinage was overshadowed. Was not a pope in duty bound to entertain the plea that a given coinage, even though confirmed, was detrimental? Indeed, the scrutiny of conscience might logically have led the popes to take an interest in determining and regulating coinages, to the confusion of the absolutist tendencies of local opinion. The positions taken by Celestine and Innocent were consistent with the canonist doctrine that licit oaths might be commuted into commitments of improved substance.[1]

Accordingly, it may be said that the papacy, or at any rate the late twelfth-century popes, gave only conditional support to the conservation of coinage.[2] In its extreme form, that principle could hardly have appealed to them; as a temporary or lifetime expedient, it was in the nature of a customary sanction against fraud to which the Roman-canonical test of utility was applicable. Yet the important fact remains that these popes failed to recognize any practical distinction between legitimate and fraudulent mutations. To confirm (or to reconfirm) the Aragonese coinage was to assume that a permanently just standard could be determined and imposed, an assumption left unexamined by Innocent III as it had been by his predecessors. Nor were the early commentators on *Quanto personam tuam* to move far beyond this position.

The text was incorporated in the *Third Compilation* (1210), and later in the *Liber Extra*, under the title *De iureiurando*.[3] What chiefly interested the decretalists were the general implications of its discussion of oaths. The question arising from the word *absolvi* was whether vows and oaths could be dispensed at all, even by the pope: this Huguccio had denied, but most canonists admitted dispensation in case of 'intolerable scandal' or when a misguided vow threatened to become a 'bond to iniquity'.[4] Now there could be no doubt that the monetary issue in Aragon provided a good case in point. Innocent III had spoken of the threats to the king's soul and to the

---

[1] e.g. 1 *Comp.* 2. 17. 10 (*X* 2. 24. 3) Pervenit ad nos; cf. *Decretum* C. 22 q. 4, and Ramon de Penyafort, *Summa . . . de poenitentia et matrimonio . . .* (Rome, 1603), pp. 94–5 (i. 'De iuramento'). See generally Walter Ullmann, *Principles of Government and Politics in the Middle Ages*, 2nd edn. (London, 1966), pp. 67–8; and Zerbi, *Papato, impero e 'respublica christiana'*, pp. 148–50.

[2] Émile Bridrey, *Théorie de la monnaie*, p. 324 n. 1, quotes a letter by which Innocent III is supposed to have supported the bishop of Laon against his canons in the right to manipulate his coinage. But the reference to 'Baluze, *Innocentii epistolae*, l. I, ép. 178' is mistaken, and I have been unable to find any such letter in the Migne edition or in Po.

[3] 3 *Comp.* 2. 15. 4, ed. Aemilius Friedberg, *Quinque compilationes antiquae . . .* (Leipzig, 1882), p. 115; *X* 2. 24. 18. On the *Third Compilation* and its glossators, see Stephan Kuttner, *Repertorium der Kanonistik (1140–1234)*. *Prodromus corporis glossarum*, i (Vatican City: *Studi e Testi*, lxxi, 1937), 355–68; idem, 'Bernardus Compostellanus Antiquus. A Study in the Glossators of the Canon Law', *Traditio*, i (1943), 308, 311–12.

[4] Laurentius to 3 *Comp.* 2. 15. 4, LB Karlsruhe, MS. Aug. XL, fo. 166 (Bisson, '"Quanto personam tuam"', p. 244). Johannes Galensis (Bisson, p. 243) had cited C. 22 q. 4 c. 22 *Inter cetera*, a spurious letter of St. Augustine which (as transmitted by Gratian) was evidently the source of Innocent III's expression *iniquitatis vinculum*.

general welfare, and of the 'grave scandal' resulting from the confirmation of a defrauded coinage. Any attempt to analyse these points in their specific connections would surely have raised the question of the justice of mutations. But the decretalists ignored words such as *detrimentum terre* and *grave . . . scandalum*, preferring to comment on terms pertaining directly to the debased coinage and the king's conscience.

Laurentius Hispanus, followed by Vincentius Hispanus, Johannes Teutonicus, and Tancred, seized upon the word *defraudata* to cite *Digest* and *Code* on penalties for counterfeiters: those who falsify the coinage of the king or emperor (or of the prince, in the version of Teutonicus) are to be burned; as for those who clip or mutilate coins, the free man is tossed to the beasts while the slave suffers the 'ultimate punishment'. No one is dispensed from the obligation to accuse counterfeiters, the one condemned of this crime has no appeal, and the owner of the premises, even if unknowing, is punished as an accomplice to counterfeiting done there.[1] Less academic was the interpretation of *patris* (Peter having been admonished to restore a coinage of legitimate weight *sub nomine patris tui*). Vincentius pointed out that it must be the king's father's coinage because that was the coinage stipulated in the *forma iuramenti*.[2] But as Johannes Galensis asked, followed by other decretalists, would not a coinage thus reformed effectively render 'the king himself a counterfeiter'? For in coinage the 'public form' as well as the weight and the quality is critical. Nevertheless, the pope's injunction is justified. For whereas the terms of the solemn oath are to be observed, the legend on the coin is likened to that upon a funerary monument: it has the nature of an artistic creation in which the painter or poet works with some margin of licence.[3]

In short, the early commentators had no difficulty in accepting Innocent III's conception of the altered coinage of Aragon as a fraud. They thought of it as a counterfeit whose perpetrators were subject to the correction traditionally meted out to individuals who abused a legitimate coinage. Their authorities, among whom we can number the modern civilians as well as the ancient jurists, afforded no examples of rulers debasing public currencies. Not only did most of these decretalists overlook the words *assensu populi*, in which their successors would find justification for some

---

[1] LB Karlsruhe, MS. Aug. XL, fo. 166; SB Bamberg, MS. canon. 20, fo. 132; SB Munich, MS. 3879, fo. 197ᵛ (second layer; Bisson, '"Quanto personam tuam"', pp. 244–7). Bridrey, *Théorie de la monnaie*, p. 324, sees 'quelque chose de nouveau' in the allusion to a 'defrauded' coinage of legitimate mintage, a view which seems to me inconsistent with the precedents and context of *Quanto*: Bridrey does not speak of the early glosses to *defraudata*. For the early history of these penal regulations, see Philip Grierson, 'The Roman Law of Counterfeiting', in *Essays in Roman Coinage presented to Harold Mattingly*, ed. R. A. G. Carson and C. H. Sutherland (Oxford, 1956), pp. 240–61.

[2] SB Bamberg, MS. canon. 20, fo. 132 (Bisson, '"Quanto personam tuam"', p. 245).

[3] SB Munich, MS. 3879, fo. 197ᵛ (both layers); SB Bamberg, MS. canon. 20, fo. 132; Bibl. Apost. Vat., MS. lat. 2509, fo. 196ᵛ (Bisson, pp. 243, 245–7).

kinds of mutations, but they imagined no economic or public necessities through which the scope of ethical monetary policy might reasonably be enlarged. Only Galensis noted the word *populi*, which reminded him of *Code* 5. 59. 5. 2 (*quod omnes tangit*), among other places, but his brief gloss seems to have been forgotten at once; nor was an anonymous Romanist treatment of the liability of counsellors for fraudulent advice to prove influential in the subsequent discussion of the decretal.[1] In considering oaths, the early commentators fixed on their putative solemnity, not (despite the mention of the *forma iuramenti*) on the substantive difficulties that might test the observance of a monetary oath.

Moreover, for all their archaism on some points, these interpretations, like that of Innocent III himself, were true to the conservative temper of contemporary monetary practice. It was in the context of monetary fraud that the clergy had first taken notice of mutations of coinage in southern France and Spain. Not only the conciliar provision of 1155 but also the Catalonian oaths of confirmation dating from 1174 dealt easily with counterfeits and mutations together. And the oaths, whether sworn or projected, were conservative in another respect: it was not that mutations were to be effected only upon consultation with the people, but that they were to be renounced as completely as possible.[2] Accordingly, the reticence of most early decretalists about *assensus populi* may have been more faithful to Innocent III's meaning than the flights of Innocent IV and later commentators, for it is by no means clear from *Quanto* that its author was saying that a ruler should consult his people when he wished to alter the coinage. All he said directly was that Peter II had been induced to *confirm* a weakened coinage without popular approval. The letter avoided giving the impression that the solution of the problem might be a new mutation; it urged the restoration and conservation of Alphonse's legitimate and confirmed coinage.

So, as a monetary text, *Quanto personam tuam* lacked originality. Its author and its early commentators looked to the past in regarding manipulations of coinage as an unnecessary evil. Nor was the tenor of the discussion soon to change. In composing what was to be the ordinary gloss to the *Liber Extra* (*c.* 1241 and after), Bernardus Parmensis virtually reproduced the older commentary on fraud and absolution.[3] Other decretalists preserved the stress on the *casus moralis*.[4] Only toward mid-century, with the work of Innocent IV, Petrus de Sampsona, and Hostiensis, was the decretal

---

[1] SB Munich, MS. 3879, fo. 197ᵛ (first layer); SB Bamberg, MS. canon. 19, fo. 160ᵛᵇ (second layer), s.v. *consiliarii tui* (Bisson, pp. 243, 248).

[2] See Botet y Sisó, *Monedes catalanes*, i. 211–12; iii. 240; ACA, perg. Alfonso I, extrainv. 2602 (Appendix, no. 3); *DI*, viii. 106–9; and the charter cited above, p. 79 n. 1.

[3] *X* (ed. Lyon, 1553) 2. 24. 18 (p. 487).

[4] Citations in my ' "*Quanto personam tuam*" ', p. 249.

reinterpreted in the light of economic and constitutional ideas, marking
a major shift in the climate of opinion.[1]

B. *Pecuniary Obligations*

To say that Innocent III and his early commentators did not deal with the
practical admissibility of mutations is not, of course, to say that they overlooked the legal and moral consequences of fluctuating coinages. Was it just
for lords or creditors to insist on their rents or repayments in strengthened
coinages? Or for debtors and pensioners to take advantage of depreciated
money? These were urgent questions by the later twelfth century, and
although the very forms in which they were put implied adherence to the
principle of a stable coinage, the concrete situations to which they had
reference were so commonplace, the acceptance of imperfect reality so
complete, that their discussion was carried on, so far as we can tell, without
immediate allusion to the conservation of coinage.[2]

Of this conceptual divorce, the decretal *Quanto personam tuam* itself
affords an illustration. Innocent III in one place used the word *reprobata*
to refer to the defrauded coinage unwittingly confirmed by Peter II. This
was a resonant word, quite probably for the learned pope himself, and
certainly for the canonists who glossed the early compilations. It evoked
a familiar passage in the Roman law of actions (*Dig.* 13. 7. 24 *Eleganter*
§*Qui reprobos*) where Ulpian had observed that 'false money [*reproba pecunia*] does not free the payer' from his obligation. Now if this point was
disregarded by most of the early commentators on *Quanto*, it was surely
because they understood it to be peripheral to the main issues posed by that
letter; yet one anonymous decretalist provided a marginal citation to *Qui
reprobos* which shows that the alternative context was perceptible.[3] Moreover, the same writer, alone among the early glossators of *Quanto*, gave a
reference for the word *diminuta* that proves his knowledge of the problem
of monetary obligations and thus serves to link two quite distinct spheres of
discussion. He cited, from the *Second Compilation*, the decretal *Querelam*,
a letter of Urban III dating from 1185–7 which had at first (*c.* 1206) been
incorporated in the collection of decretals by the Englishman Alanus.[4]

---

[1] '"Quanto personam tuam"', 230, 249; Innocentius IV, ... *In v. libros decretalium
commentaria* (Venice, 1570), p. 343; Petrus de Sampsona, *Lectura decretalium*, in SB Vienna,
MS. lat. 2083, fo. 26ᵛ; Hostiensis, *In [quinque] decretalium [libros] commentaria*, 2 vols.
(Venice, 1581), i. 130ʳᵛ.

[2] For related tendencies of thought, see generally John Gilchrist, *The Church and
Economic Activity in the Middle Ages* (London, 1969), ch. 4.

[3] SB Bamberg, MS. canon. 19, fo. 160ᵛ (ed. Bisson, '"Quanto personam tuam"',
p. 247).

[4] Citations in preceding note; JL, ii, no. 15745. Placed under the title *De censibus* ... ,
the decretal is 3. 22. 2 in Alanus, and 3. 25. 3 in 2 *Comp.* (Rudolph von Heckel, 'Die
Dekretalensammlungen des Gilbertus und Alanus nach den Weingartener Handschriften',
ZRG Kan., xxix [1940], 278; *Quinque compilationes antiquae*, ed. Friedberg, p. 89).

In this letter the pope had assigned for judgement the complaint of a priest that the canons from whom he held his church had arbitrarily changed the terms of his rental, demanding full payments in Parisian coin even though it was of better quality than the accustomed money of payment. That such a demand was unjust the pope had no doubt; the only issue was whether the allegation was accurate. If it were found to be so, the canons were to be directed to remain 'content with their old rent'.[1] But what exactly did this last clause mean? Was it Urban's will that only the accustomed coinage should be rendered in payment? Or would he have admitted settlements in Parisian (or other) money according to the value of the old coin? The latter was to be the interpretation of the glossators on the *Second Compilation*, and may already have been that of Urban III himself. For there can be no doubt that the notion of payments by *aestimatio*, as contemporaries spoke of it, was already well understood in the 1180s.

To make this clear is to disclose once again, and even more pertinently than in the case of *Quanto personam tuam*, how thought and deed were linked. The situation of *Querelam* was precisely that of the landlords whose efforts to introduce the strong and steady *parisis* resulted in the dislocations and remedies at Beauvais and Noyon that have been described.[2] Moreover, the appeal to Urban III probably came from a location in Picardy or its near vicinity, for it was just then and there that the deniers of Paris were becoming dominant.[3] Nor is this all. As it happens, the disputes over fixed payments in northern France came to the notice of the theologians at Paris; and the remarkable echo of their discussions which survives in the

---

[1] 2 *Comp.* 3. 25. 3, ed. Friedberg: '. . . cantori et magistro scholarium Re. Querelam P. presbiteri sancti Petri accepimus, quod cum canonicis Dehore certam summam pecuniae pro pensione ecclesiae suae aliquot persolverit annis, idem canonici ab eo summam illam ex integro de Parisiensi moneta exigunt sibi solvi, licet ea melior sit illa, quam pro pensione predicta soluere consuevit. Quia igitur in hoc idem presbiter contra iustitiam grauatur discretioni uestrae per ap. scripta mandamus, quatinus, si verum est quod asseritur, canonicos illos antiqua pensione cogatis appellatione cessante manere contentos.'

[2] Above, pp. 151–3.

[3] The problem is to identify the *canonici Dehore* (in MSS. usually *de hore*, *de horen*; but also *de bore* [Paris, Bibl. Mazarine, MS. 1292, fo. 90va], *de born* [BN, MS. n. a. lat. 2192, fo. 82rb], *deboeye* [BN, MS. n. a. lat. 2127, fo. 78rb]. No place clearly corresponding to *Hore*, *Bore* (or *Dehore*) appears in the ordinary ecclesiastical indices or in those of the Institut de recherche et d'histoire des textes, nor could Dr. Dietrich Lohrmann, who kindly investigated for me, identify such a place in Picardy or the Île-de-France. The house of Boran (-sur-Oise) might seem a possibility, for it was *de bosrenc*, *borrench* in the texts (e.g. AN, L 842, no. 50; S 4195, no. 25), but Boran was a nunnery. If one could suppose an original scribal slip for *de hodenc* (or *hosdenco*), i.e. Hodenc-en-Bray, or for *gerborredi*, i.e. Gerberoy, where there were collegiate churches, the circumstantial link between the legal and theological discussion would be tightened, for Peter the Chanter (see p. 174 n. 1) had ties with both places: see AD Oise, G 7391, reproduced in J. W. Baldwin, *Masters, Princes and Merchants: The Social Views of Peter the Chanter and His Circle*, 2 vols. (Princeton, N.J., 1970), i, facing p. 18. But the location in Picardy or its near vicinity seems confirmed in any case by the assignment to the cantor and master of scholars of Reims as judges-delegate.

Summa of Peter the Chanter, himself a native of the Beauvaisis, is of unique value for our purposes. It is the only one of the early doctrinal and legal texts which deals with monetary obligations in extended theoretical and circumstantial relation to the mutation of coinage.[1]

Like Urban III, the Chanter thought it beyond question that fluctuating coinages effectively altered agreements.[2] 'Concerning debts and rents', he wrote, 'it is certain that if I owe you 100 sous . . . , if the value of the coinage is increased, I am obliged to repay you only so much as the 100 sous were worth when we made the contract. Why should it not be the same with revenue?' Just as a prince cannot justly increase the customary service of fiefs, so is he bound to respect the determined dues of peasants. 'It seems to us that a ruler would sin mortally if he should exact from subjects in new coin unless at the value of the former money.'[3]

In these questions as in others, the Chanter assumed a popular as well as a moral position. He went so far as to postulate a ruler who, with a land full of dues-paying peasants, doubles the value of his coinage, an example that vividly betrays the suspicion aroused by the new movement to strengthen coinages in northern France. Yet the solution for the theologians was not to fix the currencies but to adjust the values. Indeed, the Chanter was singularly explicit about the practical contingencies. Supposing the case of a customary render initiated in a good coinage that was later debased and then restored, he regarded it rightful that the payments remain (if they had remained) unchanged. He regarded it simple-minded to contract for annual payments in Parisian coin without stipulating 'what will be done if the value of the money increases'. But his most interesting observation, from the theoretical point of view, relates to a coinage that is only slightly strengthened: in such a case, he says, the full amount contracted can rightfully be exacted. Where, however, is the line to be drawn? 'When will it be a sin for the prince to collect the 100 sous? We believe that when the value of the coinage has increased so much that the excess of the value and the trouble of the peasants are manifest, the ruler must lessen his demand according to a suitable estimate.'[4]

[1] On the Chanter, see Baldwin, *Masters*; his early years are dealt with in ch. 1.
[2] Could these two clerics have discussed this very question? They were certainly in touch, Baldwin, ii. 236, nos. 12, 15; cf. p. 173 n. 3 above. On the Chanter's canonist expertise, see also Baldwin, i. 7–10.
[3] Pierre le Chantre, *Summa de sacramentis et animae consiliis*, ed. Jean-Albert Dugauquier (Louvain–Lille, 1954–67), part 3, 2a, pp. 415–16: 'De debitis et pensionibus, certum est quod si deberem tibi centum solidos de pensione uel debito, si augeretur pretium monete, non redderem tibi nisi tantum quantum ualebant centum solidi tunc quando interuenit inter nos contractus. Quare non erit simile de censu?
Item. Non posset princeps augere seruitium feodorum. . . . Quare ergo potius sine peccato potest mutare statum et quantitatem census rusticorum? Videtur nobis quod peccaret princeps mortaliter si exigeret a subditis de noua moneta nisi tantum quantum ualet prior moneta.'
[4] Ibid., pp. 415–16: 'Esto quod terra aliqua debeat censum alicui principi, et ille

Only on this last point are we allowed a glimpse of the underlying issue. Committed to the justification of intrinsic values, the Chanter has nothing to say for an opposed view save in the exceptional circumstance where it is expedient. In his day the divergences of monetary weight and alloy had become too pronounced to be overlooked. A century earlier it would have been easier to satisfy Peter's test for settlements by tale. But to argue that pieces nearly identical in intrinsic value were interchangeable for practical purposes was hardly to justify settlements in the stipulated amounts of significantly altered deniers. How was the latter position defended?

By attempting to disregard the matter of intrinsic value, that much seems clear. According to a traditional view preserved by Isidore of Seville, money was something to be counted in pieces rather than weighed.[1] This notion was still perceptible in the twelfth century.[2] But Isidore had weakened the implication of his own assertion when he proceeded to derive the word *moneta* from *monere*: 'because it warns against whatsoever fraud in the metal or in weight'.[3] As early as *c.* 1100 the rabbi Rashi of Troyes had taken a position, based on Jewish law, substantially the same as the Chanter's, although Rashi's discussion possibly bears witness also to the popular view that a change in the imprint affected the value of a coin.[4] In

princeps augeat monetam in duplum pretium. Est ne peccatum si recipiat a rusticis tot solidos quot prius?

Et uidetur, quia centum solidi de noua moneta ualent ducentos de ueteri.

. . . Sed quid si antiquitus fuit moneta ualida et eque pretiosa ut ista noua, medio tempore fuit uilior et semper continue rustici soluebant centum solidos, potest modo dominus eorum petere de noua moneta centum solidos?

Item. Esto quod modo parum augeatur pretium monete, non ideo minus soluent centum solidos in futuro anno.

Item. Parum augeatur; ubi standum? Quando erit peccatum principi exigere centum solidos? Credimus quod quando excreuit pretium monete in tantum quod manifestus est excessus pretii et manifestum grauamen rusticorum, tenetur princeps relaxare de pretio secundum quod condigna fuerit estimatio.

Sed item esto quod ita contrahant inter se aliqui simplices iuramento medio: 'Tu reddes michi singulis annis centum solidos parisiensis monete,' nec determinant quid fiet si excrescat pretium monete, quantum tenetur iste soluere ratione iuramenti in tertio anno cum excreuerit pretium monete?

Credo quod determinandum est pretium et quantitas pretii secundum tempus, sicut secundum locum . . .'

[1] *Etymologiae*, ed. W. M. Lindsay, 2 vols. (Oxford, 1911), ii, xvi. 18. 8: '. . . antiqui enim adpendere pecuniam soliti erant magis quam adnumerare'; cf. Cicero, *Philippics* ii. 38; and, more generally, *Wisdom*, xi: 21: '. . . sed omnia in mensura, et numero, et pondere disposuisti.'

[2] *Lo Codi in der lateinischen Übersetzung des Ricardus Pisanus*, ed. Hermann Fitting, (Halle, 1906), p. 74 (iv. 6): 'Ille res possunt dari in prestancia que possunt numerari uel pessari uel mensurari. numerari: sicut denarii. pessari: sicut aurum et argentum. mensurari: sicuti frumentum, uinum et aleum'; also p. 113 (iv. 51). Cf. Hugolinus, as quoted by Taeuber, *Geld und Kredit*, p. 172 n. 482.

[3] *Etym.*, xvi. 8. 8.

[4] *Responsa of Rashi*, ed. Israel Elfenbein (New York, 1943), no. 222; tr. I. A. Agus, *Urban Civilization in Pre-Crusade Europe* . . . , 2 vols. (New York, 1965), i. 378–9. The following translation is based on versions kindly supplied by Mr. Sheldon Brunswick and

1183 the nuns of Quedlinburg failed to persuade Pope Lucius III that the annual mark of silver they had been paying to the Holy See was equivalent to the pound stipulated in their old privileges,[1] and there is no very strong evidence that the lawyers were impressed with such arguments any more than the theologians. Reason supported the merchants and creditors in extending to coinage the measures appropriate to weights of metal, while the jurists of Bologna, notably Bulgarus, Martinus, and Pillius, put the case for the determining value of the time when the contract was made with reference to variable measures of produce as well as to variable money.[2] The likeness of measures and coins in this respect, also familiar to Peter the Chanter,[3] had become axiomatic by Azo's time: *Eadem mensura vel moneta debetur, quae erat tempore contractus.*[4] The coin was to be regarded as at once a commodity of fluctuating value and a means and measure of exchange.

But the Romanists dealt with the problem differently from the theologians. Influenced not only by legal texts relating to weakened or counterfeit money but also by the practical questions of the validity of settlements subsequently challenged, they were led to examine the vigilance of the creditor as well as the motives of the debtor. Thus Pillius, in one of his 'Saturday questions', arrived at a qualified conclusion based on the distinction 'whether the debtor believed the money good [or] whether he knew it to be bad'. If he believed it to be good, the fault lies with the imprudent creditor or his representative; but even if otherwise, the debtor is freed of his obligation if it can be shown that the creditor knowingly received the bad money.[5] Another *quaestio* of Pillius deals more directly with the alterations that might vitiate a coinage of first payment, and offers

Professor David Jacoby: '. . . (Rashi to R. Solomon of Tours): As to your question concerning [A] who lent [B] money and the coins were invalidated, what should [B] pay [A]. You should know that we rule . . . [that B] give [A] the coin then current unless [value] has been added to it. Our coin was invalidated, no [value] has been added to it except in respect to the alteration of the design. Therefore, [B] must pay [A] what he borrowed from [A; i.e. the same number of coins] before the coin was invalidated. And [B] must repay [A] in the same coins which were invalidated as if they had been exchanged [for the new ones] at the time [A] lent them to him.'

[1] *Cum multam sedes* (14 Apr. 1183), JL, ii, no. 14757; cited by Taeuber, *Geld und Kredit*, pp. 85–6.

[2] See quotation from *Lo Codi* in p. 175 n. 2 above; also (ed. Fitting), p. 308 (viii. 35); *Die Epitome exactis regibus* . . . , ed. Max Conrat (Berlin, 1884), p. 105 (viii); *Quaestiones dominorum Bononiensium. Collectio Gratianopolitana*, ed. G. B. Palmieri, *Scripta anecdota glossatorum*, 3 vols. (Bologna, 1892–1914); i, 2nd edn., *Additiones* (Bologna, 1914), 216, 248 (nos. 29, 60); *Quaestiones* . . . , *Collectio Parisiensis*, ed. Palmieri, *Scripta*, i. 253 (no. 107); and the gloss or brocard of Martinus to *Dig.* 13. 7. 24, cited by Taeuber, pp. 202–3. For Pillius, see below.

[3] *Summa*, part 3, 2a, pp. 148, 415.

[4] *Lo Codi*, ed. Fitting, p. 81 (iv. 15); *Brocardica sive generalia iuris D. Azonis* . . . (Basle, 1567), p. 136 (the collection is traced back to Otto by Taeuber, *Geld und Kredit*, pp. 228–9).

[5] *Pilii Medicinensis quaestiones sabbatinae*, ed. Ugo Nicolini (Modena, 1935), pp. 19–22.

different arguments, in somewhat saucy formulations, in the debtor's favour. As Taeuber has shown, this question *Quidam creditor* drew upon discussions of *Dig.* 12. 1. 3 *Cum quid mutuum* to affirm that form as well as quality determined the lawful identity of goods of payment and repayment; it is not enough that the *genus* of the Luccan deniers be the same, if their *bonitas* were diminished, to discharge the debt.[1] Nor did the arguments attributed to the debtor deny this. They were, first, that 'same kind' in *Cum quid mutuum* referred to the time of repayment, not of payment; second, that in the case of that law, the debtor was responsible for the deterioration, contrary to the present fact; and third, that settlement in the original state and quality was only possible when those remained unchanged. It was unscrupulous to insist on a good old coinage if, in the contrary circumstance, one would refuse a bad old one. These were, for all their panoply of citations, captious arguments, and it is difficult to believe that they can have been effective in practice. In his determination Pillius agreed with Placentinus on the overriding validity of the *lex Eleganter*. If what is loaned cannot be returned in identical form and quality, then the parties must resort to its 'estimation' to settle the debt.[2]

Whether arguments like these were known to the theologians is unclear. The Chanter had some contact with Bolognese jurists,[3] but apart from the comparable conclusions he drew from quite different cases, there is little to connect his discussion with theirs. On the other hand, the Romanist questions certainly influenced the canonists. Huguccio of Pisa examined *aestimatio* in terms which, if they betrayed an unsure grasp of the Roman law of loans, showed his acquaintance with the problem of altered goods of repayment.[4] Decretalists relied on the familiar *Digest* texts to support the papal position taken unequivocally in *Olim causam* (1200) that settlements of pecuniary obligations must take account of alterations or substitutions of coinage.[5] This decretal focused sharply on the intrinsic discrepancy

---

[1] Ed. Taeuber, *Geld und Kredit*, pp. 311–12: '. . . dicit enim pomp. (Pomponius): id agi intelligitur inter dantem et accipientem mutuum, ut eiusdem generis et eadem bonitate solvitur quod datum est. non enim fuit contentus dicere "eius generis", sed adiecit "eiusdem bonitatis". patet igitur, quod hec duo in solvendo sunt necessaria, scilicet genus, ne videatur aliud pro alio reddi, et bonitas. si igitur adfuerit bonitas, sed genus desit, vel eccontra ut hic, solvere non videtur debitor . . .'

[2] Ibid., pp. 312–14. Taeuber discusses this *quaestio* at length, pp. 119 ff.; for the problem of *aestimatio*, see his pp. 178–93, 209–15, 221–32.

[3] See Baldwin, *Masters*, i. 17; ii. 9 n. 3.

[4] Huguccio, *Summa*, to C. 14. 4. 5 *Si quis clericus*, quoted by Taeuber, p. 182, from SB Bamberg, MS. canon. 40, fo. 160ʳ; my transcription is from Stiftsbibliothek Admont, MS. 22, fo. 260ʳ: 'Sic pono casum: aliquis clericus mutuauit alicui pecuniam et prefixus est terminus quando debeat reddi. Dicitur quod si postea uult pro pecunia recipere uinum uel aliam speciem debet extimari quantum species talis uendatur tali tempore quo pecunia debet reddi. Et tantum et non plus accipiat de illa specie quantum ualeat tantam pecuniam. Si autem speciem non uult accipere quia non indiget tantum peccunie et non plus accipiat quantum pecunie dedit.' See also Huguccio to C. 14. 4. 6 *Nullus clericorum*; and generally, Taeuber, pp. 182–4.   [5] 3 *Comp.* 3. 37. 5 (Po., i, no. 1207; X 3. 39. 20).

between two Italian coinages, a *casus* more like the Chanter's than like Pillius's; yet Laurentius surely echoed the glossators in his proposition 'that it [the *synodaticum*] should be paid in the old measure, not the new, and in the old coinage even if the new should be better.'[1] Another decretalist thought that in *Querelam* Urban III had been intentionally general about the substance of the 'old pension' to be restored, since the pope presumably had not known whether the old deniers were still in circulation.[2] But there must have been some agreement that Pope Urban's formulation was insufficiently explicit; for while *Querelam* does not appear in the *Liber Extra*, it provided the form for *Cum canonicis* (1227–34; *X* 3. 39. 26), of which the final clause was revised according to the apparatus of Tancred to 2 *Comp.* 3. 25. 3 *Querelam* so as to overcome the difficulty.[3]

On the other hand, a conservative strain in the canonist treatment of pensions and rents points to a lingering fidelity to the fading world of the standard silver denier. The issue of the creditor's knowledge at the moment of repayment persists in the glosses to *Querelam* by Laurentius (?) and Tancred, although not in such language as to link their thought directly with that of Pillius.[4] More significant are the citations contrary to the propositions based on *Eleganter* in the glosses of Laurentius and others to *Olim causam*, as it appeared in the *Third Compilation*, citations that were

---

[1] LB Karlsruhe, MS. Aug. XL, fo. 208 (3. 37. 5), s.v. *monete declinationem*: 'Ar. quod ad ueteram mensuram non ad nouam soluendum est, et ad ueteram monetam licet noua melior sit, ut S. e. t. Querelam, S. de iure iur. Quanto, dum tamen uetus in usu sit, alioquin soluatur extimatio ut hic scilicet, et contra S. xxxii. q. iiii. Quis ignorat.'

[2] SB Bamberg, MS. canon. 19, fo. 103ᵛ (partly quoted by Taeuber, pp. 212–13), s.v. *antiqua*: 'Non dicit "summa denariorum illorum qui hactenus soluti fuerunt", quia, si denarii de quibus antiquitus soluebantur, abierint in disuetudinem, non illos denarios sed estimationem soluere debebit, ut infra de censibus Olim lege .iii., et ita cum reprobata moneta incipiat teneri ad estimationem poterit soluere inuito creditore, et liberabitur. Et ita fallit hic regula generalis: quod inuito creditori aliud pro alio solui non possit, ut ff. si certum pe. l. ii. § mutui datio. . . .'

[3] *X* 3. 39. 26 (Po., i, no. 9657): '. . . tibi damus nostris literis in mandatis, ut canonicos illos solutione prioris pecuniae, vel, si non sit in usu, aestimatione pensionis antiquae facias manere contentos.' Cf. Tancred to 2 *Comp.* 3. 25. 3, AC Cordoba, MS. 10, fo. 122ʳ, s.v. *pensione*: 'Si illa habetur in usu uel extimatione eius si illa reprobata est, vt infra e. t. Olim causam, lege iii. ff. de rebus creditis. Cum quid. Et est tunc specialis casus quod aliud pro alio soluatur contra illud quod habetur ff. si certum pe. l. Mutuum §i. . . .' (passage continued in next note).

[4] See above, n. 2; also AC Cordoba, MS. 10, fo. 122ʳ, with corrections from SB Bamberg, MS. canon. 19, fo. 103ᵛ, s.v. *pensione*: '. . . [see n. 3] Alium specialem casum habes .x. q. ii. Hoc ius, versu ut [*leg.* inventa?] res estimata detur. Sed quare non solueretur illa que conuenta fuit licet reprobata sit? Respondeo: quia non liberaretur ab obligatione, quia reproba moneta non liberat debitorem, ut ff. de pig. action. Eleganter § Qui reprobos, nisi forte esset alia ab accipiente scienter approbata, vt ff. de con. et demon. Quamuis, ff. mandati Inter causas §iii., et sibi inputet qui talem elegit, ff. pro socio. Socius socio. T.' Cf. Pillius, *Quaest. sabb.*, ed. Nicolini, p. 22.

Pillius's way of putting the issue of the debtor's intention is curiously analogous to the distinction which Innocent III applied to Peter II's oath in 1199; most likely that learned pope was familiar with such legal reasoning. Cf. Baldwin, *Masters*, i. 261–9, for related tendencies of moral discussion.

reproduced in the ordinary gloss to *X*. 3. 39. 20.[1] The rescript *Imperatores* [*Dig*. 18. 1. 71), apparently first noted in this connection by Johannes Teutonicus, adverted once again, although with imperfect relevance, to the matter of intention, for its point was that no one is forced to sell if the price or the measure displeases him.[2] But the decretalists found a very different argument in *Quis ignoret*, a text of Jerome incorporated in the *Decretum* (C. 32. 4. 6):

Who does not know that all past saints under God's other dispensation were of the same merit as those who are now Christians? Just as formerly Abraham was pleasing in marriage, so now virgins please in perpetual chastity. He served the law and his time, let us serve the gospel and our time, in which the ends of the ages have their course.[3]

Coinages, like the times, change, but that does not mean that any differentiation of their 'merit' need be made. In the case at issue, according to this view, the *synodaticum* could justly be collected in the new coinage, even though it was of better quality than the old. Now it had not occurred to Huguccio nor to most other decretists to draw such an analogy between spiritual merit and the values of coinage; but the discussion of *Olim causam* was recalled by Johannes Teutonicus in his gloss to *Quis ignoret*. While reversing the arguments pro and con, he gave precisely the same references as he himself and Tancred had done in their apparatus to 3 *Comp*. 3. 37. 5 *Olim causam*: '*Argumentum*, that if first a stronger coinage was circulating and now a weaker circulates by order of the prince, my obligation is discharged by paying the weaker. . . .'[4] This formulation, although it has the interest of hinting that the ruler's decree might render a diminished coinage lawful for the settlement of old contracts as well as new, falls clearly short of arguing for the external determination of value. The positions diversely taken against the estimation of a former coinage's

---

[1] e.g. SB Munich, MS. 3879, fo. 238; Stiftsbibliothek Admont, MS. 22, fo. 220ʳ (3 *Comp*. 3. 37. 5), s.v. *extimationis*: 'Ar. ad questionem dominicalem quod ad ueterem monetam sit soluendum licet noua sit melior, vt S. de iureiurando Quanto lege e. et S. e. Querelam lege ii. et ff. si certum petatur lege .iii. Ar. contra .xxxii. q. .iiii. Quis ignorat, ff. de contrahenda emptione Inperatores. Io.' Taeuber (who is surely mistaken in attributing this gloss to Galensis) has traced the 'Sunday question' back to an anonymous collection of decretalist *quaestiones* (*c.* 1190?) in SB Bamberg, MS. canon. 45, fo. 48ʳ, *Geld und Kredit*, pp. 238–40 (on this collection, see Kuttner, *Repertorium*, pp. 425–6).

[2] *Dig*. 18. 1. 71 *Imperatores* reads in part: 'quibus mensuris aut pretiis negotiatores uina comparent, in contrahentium potestate esse: neque enim quisquam cogitur uendere, si aut pretium aut mensura displiceat, praesertim si nihil contra consuetudinem regionis fiat.'

[3] Ed. Aemilius Friedberg, *Decretum magistri Gratiani* (Leipzig, 1879), col. 1129. I read *Quis ignorat*, following Jerome (*PL*, xxiii. 288) and some MSS.

[4] *Decretum Gratiani* . . . (Lyon, 1525), ordinary gloss s.v. *tempori nostro*: 'Ar. quod si primo currebat fortior moneta et modo currit vilior de mandato principis liberor solvendo viliorem. ar. ff. de contrahen. em. imperatores. Ar. contra extra de censi. olim in fi. ff. si cer. pe. cum quid. extra de iureiu. quanto.' See generally Walter Taeuber, 'Geld und Kredit im Dekret Gratians und bei den Dekretisten', *Studia Gratiana*, ii (1954), 443–64.

current worth have in common their ignorance of the concept of imposed value—or of what would later sometimes be termed *bonitas extrinseca*.[1] Yet they were all attempts to counter the allegedly deceptive phenomenon of intrinsic mutation, to define value relatively and ethically, as in the analogy of Abraham and the virgins, or nominally and numerically, as in the Chanter's recommendation about coinages of negligible intrinsic difference. Such arguments could only make sense so long as coinages were maintained without abrupt or drastic alteration, so long as they were 'conserved'.

But the realities were otherwise, and nowhere, perhaps, more plainly than in the regions where the known discussions took place. The canonists followed the civilians and (if the Chanter was typical) the theologians in affirming that settlements of pecuniary obligations must take account of substitutions or intrinsic alterations of coinage. Increasingly, the theorists responded to manipulations by rulers, on which the Roman law had been silent, as distinct from abuse or counterfeiting by subjects. That is why, among the texts cited, the word *reproba* (as in *reproba pecunia*, *Dig.* 13. 7. 24. 1) is often replaced by *reprobata*, indicative of coinages debased or declared invalid by the issuing authorities. And while arguments contrary to that based on intrinsic value were preserved in the ordinary glosses to the *Decretum* and the *Liber Extra*, not one decretal clearly espousing such arguments was incorporated in the canonist collections. None of the theorists, so far as we know, saw in the problem of obligations a reason to deplore mutations. The tendency of their thought, consistent with the growth of exchange and credit, can have held little comfort for the provincial élites struggling to stabilize their currencies.

c. *Profit and Taxation*

This doctrinal tendency is the more striking because it extended to a problem of moral inquiry having to do with the exploitation of mints. Could transactions rightly be passed in coinages of tainted origin? According to Master Robert de Courçon, a disciple of Peter the Chanter, it was common practice for rulers to melt down their silver variously acquired from tallage, plunder, and usury for reminting, exchange, and expenditure at the fairs. He postulated the case of citizens petitioning for the restoration of such stolen wealth while the trade went on.[2] Now Peter the Chanter, in his

---

[1] Wilhelm Endemann, *Studien in der romanisch-kanonistischen Wirtschafts- und Rechts-lehre* . . . , 2 vols. (Berlin, 1883), ii. 172 ff., 197–211; Taeuber, *Geld und Kredit*, pp. 186–9, 205–6, 253; cf. Bloch, *Esquisse d'une histoire monétaire*, pp. 40–7.

[2] *Le Traité 'De Usura', de Robert de Courçon*, ed. Georges Lefèvre (Lille, 1902), p. 51: 'Quaestio.—Item difficillima oritur quaestio de hoc quod saepe videmus de facto: ecce aliquis marchatus scilicet princeps aut pseudo qui collegit infimam de foeneratoribus et per tallias et exactiones quam totam redegit in massam quae vulgo dicitur plata; illam transmittit ad nundinas, praecepit ibi fabricari de illa novam monetam quae discurrat per

exposition of the problem, had observed rather practically that the scrupulous rejection of all coins minted from questionable bullion would have the most disruptive consequences for payments and exchange. He concluded that such money could be used if its recipient were free of legal liability to those with a claim on the stolen goods.[1] Master Robert, for his part, accepted the Chanter's realistic premiss, but altered the conclusion, making two moral distinctions. The validity of the transaction depended on the merchant's knowledge of the state of the money in question; somewhat as in the case of the debtor's intention in the legal discussions of repayment, his ignorance, after due investigation, excused his trade in the tainted money. But it also depended on the purpose of such trade. Only when its returns were applied to charity, other needs of the Church, or to 'extreme necessity' was it justified.[2]

It is difficult to believe that Robert's solution had much influence in the market-place. But perhaps we should not lightly dismiss his remark that the 'very difficult question' he discusses arose because 'we often see in fact' that some 'prince or pseudo-prince' effects his recoinage with bullion of doubtful origin.[3] Suspicion of the resources for new coinages was commonplace in the twelfth century, vividly expressed in the complaint of Guibert de Nogent,[4] and by no means allayed when, toward the end of the century, the silver proceeds of taxation increased. Underlying the Parisian debates was the question of the legitimacy of the ruler's profits from coinage, one of the very questions which, from a different angle, occupied the conservationists of coinage. Why, then, did the masters not deal directly with the question of *monetagium*—in connection, say, with profit or just price? If they discussed it at all, they clearly did not think of it as forming a significant *casus*. Was this because excessive or unjustified returns from the mint were too unusual to seem worth mentioning?

Very likely so. Two points require emphasis in this connection. First, we have found little evidence of outlandish profits from coinage, and none at

nundinas, per manus mercatorum et cambiatorum, ut ipse sic lucretur et multiplicet eam. Tu accedens ad has nundinas scis pro certo hanc cursalem monetam totam esse ex rapina et scis quod spoliati in quatuor civitatibus a quibus princeps violenter abstulit eam, petunt illam sibi restitui. Quaeritur ergo in hoc casu utrum liceat tibi vel aliis exercere contractus nundinales mediante hac moneta.' See, on this problem, Baldwin, *Masters*, i. 242–3; cf. J. T. Noonan, Jr., *The Scholastic Analysis of Usury* (Cambridge, Mass., 1957), pp. 31–42.

[1] *Summa*, part 3, 2a, p. 127: '. . . ponatur quod tota moneta alicuius ciuitatis sit fabricata de thesauro regis Sicilie qui totus est collectus de rapina, mercatores pro mercibus quas illic attulerunt retulerunt thesaurum illum in rudi materia que uulgo dicitur plata. Secundum prius iuditium nichil poterit emi pro tali moneta. Cessabunt ergo contractus, solutiones debitorum ut censuum, stipendiorum et huiusmodi. Oportebit ergo nos exire de hoc mundo. Forte in debitis et contractibus, quasi necessitatis humane, dici potest recipi posse de tali summa si non nascatur de tali receptione aliqua actio aduersus recipientem, quod fit cum qui soluit non remanet soluendo erga eos quibus rapuit . . .'
[2] *De Usura*, pp. 53, 55.　　　　　　　　　　　　[3] Above, p. 180 n. 2.
[4] See above, p. 9.

all in later twelfth-century France.[1] The commerce in silver was too delicately balanced, the control of the moneyers too difficult, to admit of sustained profit above moderate levels, while the spread of money-changing and the increasing volume of coined money worked to the manifest advantage of the minters of steady, respectable currencies. That is why, in the second place, some rulers in the Chanter's day, and, indeed, in his homelands, were altering their coinages with a view to securing improved currency for them. It was by no means unknown, and perhaps not uncommon, for coinages to be improved in alloy or weight, a form of mutation that cannot have been expected to return immediate profits. While the Chanter's example of a ruler's doubling the value of his coinage may be hyperbolic, his postulate was not academic.[2]

There is another connection in which one might hope to find some theological opinion on the conservation of coinage. Whether as fees for the renunciation of mutations or as commutations of arbitrary profits of coinage, the money-taxes were analogous to the ransoms and tallages of which the Parisian masters had a good deal to say.[3] It is altogether possible, if not likely, that the Chanter and his colleagues were familiar with the *tallia panis et vini* which was being regulated at Orléans and imposed at Paris in the 1180s[4] in accordance with the very principle of commutation which the scholars discussed in general terms.[5] Would they have regarded such money-taxes licit?

On the one hand, they were inclined to interpret the arbitrary tallage as a species of theft.[6] This position, as John Baldwin has shown, made it difficult for them to justify the commutation of such exactions into regular taxes. On the other hand, since they do not seem to have regarded the exercise of *moneta* as normally dangerous to the soul, they could possibly have thought of the stabilized coinage as one of those public works, like fortifications or houses of charity, for which regulated impositions were appropriate. So far as we know, however, the money-tax did not pose a

---

[1] Was the Catalonian coinage of *c.* 1208–11 exceptional? See above, pp. 96–9.

[2] On this point I differ with Baldwin, *Masters*, i. 244, who concludes that 'Peter's examples . . . may seem academic because . . . the few manipulations which took place were towards devaluation.' The burghers of Dijon would not have wished to restrain reinforcements of coinage if such mutations were unheard of; see also Rashi, in *Teshuvot ḥakhme Tsarefat ve-Loter*, ed. Joel Mueller (Vienna, 1881), *responsum* no. 29 (tr. Agus, *Urban Civilization*, i. 237), a strengthened coinage in the Île-de-France replaces a weaker one; and above, pp. 175–6. The Chanter consistently postulated improved coinages, *Summa*, part 3, 2a, pp. 148, 415–16.

[3] See Baldwin, *Masters*, i. 235–40, and references.

[4] See above, pp. 35–40; and for the remarkable allusion to the triennial minting term in the Île-de-France, the passage from Peter's *Summa* quoted above, p. 174 n. 4.

[5] Pierre le Chantre, *Summa*, part 3, 2a, p. 148; Robert de Courçon, *Summa*, xv. 12, quoted by Baldwin, *Masters*, ii. 173 n. 86.

[6] Robert de Courçon, *De Usura*, pp. 31, 51; *Summa*, xv. 1, quoted by Baldwin, ii. 171 n. 68; Pierre le Chantre, *Summa*, part 3, 2a, pp. 145–8.

moral problem for them. It would surely have been otherwise had they believed, and thought it a matter of common belief, that rulers of their day were accustomed to manipulating their coinages for profit. Only in the special case of minting from stolen silver did they question the practice of *moneta* at all, and the issue there was not mutation. To them mutations were not inherently harmful; their interest lay in the ethics of trade in altered coinages.

The Catalan Ramon de Penyafort, in his moral works composed a generation later, had even less to say about coinage than the theologians of Paris. But he justified tallages and aids imposed for the support of legitimate authority or of public necessities; and his examples of ecclesiastical enterprises and the maintenance of security[1] remind us that in his own homeland the count–kings had attempted to associate the stabilized coinage with the peace and the crusade. Even as he wrote (probably in the new Dominican house at Barcelona, 1222–7), the confirmation of coinage had become a matter of renewed public interest in Aragon, and it is inconceivable that the renowned friar who attended the great *cort* of Monzón in 1236 first heard of the *monetaticum* on that occasion.[2] To the aspiring young canonist fresh home from his studies in Bologna, the exploitation of coinage may have seemed too peculiar, too provincial an issue to examine, but his silence draws our attention once again to the prevailing focus of legal thought on money. Ramon's doctrine in the *Summa* on penitence was profoundly influenced by the compilations of decretals which he himself was to reduce and codify in the *Liber Extra*, and among the well-known pontifical letters down to 1234, only *Quanto personam tuam* dealt with the manipulation of coinage. But while that singular decretal indicated an emphatic contempt for mutations, its *casus* lacked the familiar urgency that rendered the matter of payments in altered currencies a lively and practical issue. Most likely the canonists of this time would have agreed with the theologians that it was more important to confirm the value of money in relation to goods and services than to confirm the weight and alloy of the coin.

D. *Wealth: The Almighty Coin*

When one ventures out from these doctrinal and legal thickets into the open fields of homiletic and literary expression, the problem is dispersed in commonplace descriptions and moral similes. What people most simply and ordinarily thought about coined money, it seems, had less to do with

---

[1] Ramon de Penyafort, *Summa poen.*, pp. 178–84.

[2] *Col. dipl. Zaragoza*, i, nos. 48, 52; Botet y Sisó, *Monedes catalanes*, iii. 252–6; and see below, pp. 194–5. For Ramon's early career, see Fernando Valls Taberner, *San Ramón de Penyafort*, in *Obras selectas*, i: 2, 213–38; Kuttner, *Repertorium*, pp. 438–45; and *San Raimundo de Penyafort. Diplomatario* . . . , ed. José Rius Serra (Barcelona, 1954), nos. 1–17, and pp. 271–5.

the abuses to which it was subject, or their remedies, than with the blunt and overriding truth that it constituted the measure or substance of wealth. Money might be admirable or cherished, the means to *largesse*, as in the *chansons*; or it might be a hazard to the soul, as for the reformers, preachers, and satirists: in both cases the focus was on accumulation instead of exchange. And in both cases one thought naturally of the common coin: 'li deniers', said Pourette to that Courtois d'Arras whose role was the Prodigal Son's, 'est boings compaing.'[1]

It would take us too far afield to trace the origins of these habits of mind in the Scriptures, the Fathers, and old popular literature. Nor would it be useful to try to classify chronologically the allusions to money in the imaginative literature of France and Spain for the periods that concern us. Quite apart from the difficulties of dating much of this material, the fact is that the poets differed extremely in their allusiveness to money: the *Gormont et Isembart* and the *chansons* of Jaufré Rudel, for example, are altogether lacking the references to *or et argent*, *deniers*, and *mailles* that abound in the *Couronnement de Louis* and the *Charroi de Nîmes*.[2] Moreover, there are unmistakably archaic or fantastic touches in the literary allusions to gold and silver—*or et argent* is, indeed, formulaic—making it difficult to say whether a relative preponderance of such allusions in the earlier songs and epics[3] bears any significant relation to the scarcities of coined money shown by some archival records of payments in the eleventh and early twelfth centuries. But it is clear that, from *c.* 1130 at the latest, some poets have an easy familiarity with the denier and the *maille* and their values.[4] Half a century later the diversity of minted deniers has impressed itself on the literary consciousness,[5] although it is only in the thirteenth century that

[1] *Courtois d'Arras* . . . , ed. Edmond Faral, 2nd edn. (Paris, 1967), p. 11 (l. 311).

[2] *Le Couronnement de Louis* . . . , ed. Ernest Langlois, 2nd edn. (Paris, 1966), ll. 84, 140, 154, 179, 225, 252, 442, 488, 595, 600, 914, 1343, 1426, etc.; *Le Charroi de Nîmes* . . . , ed. J.-L. Perrier (Paris, 1968), ll. 254, 334, 536, 564, 645, 653, 704, 843, 1104, etc.

[3] *La Vie de Saint Alexis* . . . , ed. Gaston Paris, 5th edn. (Paris, 1933), l. 526; *Les Chansons de Guillaume IX, duc d'Aquitaine* . . . , ed. Alfred Jeanroy, 2nd edn. (Paris, 1927), p. 2 (l. 18), p. 4 (l. 18); *La Chanson de Roland*, ed. Frederick Whitehead, 2nd edn. (Oxford, 1946), ll. 32, 100, 398, 645; *Couronnement de Louis*, ll. 252, 319, 443, 1343, 1426, 1483, 2261; *Raoul de Cambrai* . . . , ed. Paul Meyer and Auguste Longnon (Paris, 1882), ll. 1398, 1755, 5424, 5529, 6434, 8580; *Les Lais de Marie de France*, ed. Jean Rychner (Paris, 1966), p. 76 ('Lanval', l. 142), pp. 175, 191 ('Eliduc', ll. 645, 1157); Gautier d'Arras, *Ille et Galeran* . . . , ed. F. A. G. Cowper (Paris, 1956), ll. 523, 2202, 4023; *Huon de Bordeaux*, ed. Pierre Ruelle (Brussels–Paris, 1960), ll. 307, 2122, 7534; cf. ll. 696, 1115, 1653, 5073, 7695, 8649. References to *or* and *argent* seem to me distinctly less common in the *fabliaux*, although they persist in a poet–chronicler like Philippe Mousquet.

[4] References above, n. 2.

[5] *Aiol* . . . , ed. Jacques Normand and Gaston Raynaud (Paris, 1877), ll. 3473, 3842, 3914, 5429; *Huon de Bordeaux*, ll. 668, 888, 1497, 9999; *Wistasse le Moine* . . . , ed. Wendelin Foerster and Johann Trost (Halle, 1891), ll. 56–62, cited by U. T. Holmes, Jr., 'Coins of Old French Literature', *Speculum*, xxxi (1956), 316; *Aymeri de Narbonne* . . . , ed. Louis Demaison, 2 vols. (Paris, 1887), ii, ll. 736, 782, 3240; see also Gustav Belz, 'Die

allusions like that of the *Prestre et des .ii. ribaus* to '.v. artisiens, .iii. tornois et .ii. cambrisiens'[1] become at all common; as one might expect of the literature centred in northern courts and towns, the *parisis* was the most famous of the familiar coinages.

The mentions of money in vernacular poetry were characteristically governed by a preoccupation with riches and *largesse*. Such and such, the hyperbolic notion goes, is not worth a denier (or a *maille*). 'Por Deu, Guillelmes, ne te valt un denier', says Gui d'Alemaigne to comfort his lord on the loss of his war-horse.[2] Complains King Louis to Guillelme in the *Charroi de Nîmes*:

> Tant com servi vos ai tenu le chief,
> N'i ai conquis vaillissant un denier
> Dont nus en cort m'apelast chevalier.[3]

And the suggestion that one so rich as a king cannot love well evoked from Alphonse II of Aragon–Catalonia the retort:

> Aissi vos pogratz un denier
> adesmar contr'un marc d'argen.[4]

The denier in this frame of mind was the usual petty constituent of wealth: had not the Oxford poet of Roland spoken of *or et aveir et deners*?[5] It is understandable that allusions to gold and silver, sometimes explicitly to weights of precious metal, remain commonplace in the old vernacular literatures of France and Spain.[6]

There is one genre, however, which treats the coin quite differently. Best represented in Old French by *De dan denier* (*Concerning the Lord Penny*, probably to be identified with the 'flabel du denier' mentioned in the *Bordeors ribeaus*), it portrays the denier as an almighty ruler:

> Denier fet cortois le vilain,
> Denier sorprent le mont à plain
> Sorprent.
> Tout est en son commendement.

Münzbezeichnungen in der altfranzösischen Literatur' (diss., Strasbourg, 1914), pp. 7, 14, 25, 46–8, 52.

[1] *Recueil général et complet des fabliaux des XIIIᵉ et XIVᵉ siècles . . .* , ed. Anatole de Montaiglon and Gaston Raynard, 6 vols. (Paris, 1872–90), iii. 62.
[2] *Couronnement de Louis*, l. 2568.   [3] *Charroi de Nîmes*, ll. 253–5.
[4] Ed. Riquer, 'La littérature provençale', ii. 185.
[5] *Chanson de Roland*, l. 1148.
[6] *Aiol*, ll. 1679, 2199, 3739, 3962, 4483, 5305, 5665, 6298; *Lais de Marie de France*, ed. Rychner, p. 76 ('Lanval', l. 142), pp. 175, 191 ('Eliduc', ll. 645, 1157); *Girart de Roussillon . . .* , ed. W. Mary Hackett, 3 vols. (Paris, 1953–5), i, ll. 1985, 2163, etc.; *Cantar de mio Cid . . .* , ed. Ramón Menéndez Pidal, 3 vols. (Madrid, 1908–11), iii, ll. 135, 161, 184, 473, 513, 521, 845, 1010, 1234, 1285, 1737, 1766, 2426, 2467, 2571, 3204; *Ille et Galeran*, ll. 265, 358, 4194, 5038; *Aymeri de Narbonne*, ii, ll. 1242, 2157, 2226; *Aucassin et Nicolette . . .* , ed. Mario Roques, 2nd edn. (Paris, 1954), xxii, ll. 35–6 (cf. ix, l. 3).

The denier is handled by the rich, is much feared, is the joy of misers, is the guarantee of success in lawsuits at Rome, is the distraction of priests, although 'Dans denier fet les granz sermons'. It empties prisons, makes mills grind, wages war, disinherits orphans, gives 'les granz honors, les granz chastiaus et les granz torz'—in short: 'C'est dans denier qui tout sorprent.'[1]

This fable, which probably dates from the early thirteenth century, was not an altogether new inspiration. Despite a fresh mix of awe with discontent, it manifestly recalls the Latin satirical verses on 'King Coin' or its variants,[2] and some of the French lines correspond closely to the Latin ones:

> Nummus bella gerit, nec si vult, pax sibi deerit.
> Nummus agit lites, quia vult deponere dites.[3]

There is no need to recite the whole litany:

> Ut breviter dicam, dominus facit omnia nummus.[4]

Or, in the clever echo of the *laudes*:

> Nummus vincit, nummus regnat, nummus imperat.[5]

The sovereign coin of this literature is the *nummus* or the *denier* (depending on the language). These words mean, in the present context, the same thing: 'coined money' (in general). The coin of twelfth-century France was the denier, and it was unnecessary in moral discourse to specify which local denier was meant. Unnecessary only because irrelevant? Was not a further reason the lingering disinclination to acknowledge inequalities between deniers of different mints? Down to the last two or three decades of the twelfth century the denier continued in many places to represent a unit of value independent of its intrinsic value in exchange, so that the literary testimony accords with those censiers which persist in referring to

---

[1] *Jongleurs et trouvères* . . . , ed. Achille Jubinal (Paris, 1835), pp. 94–100. See also 'Du denier et de la brebis', ed. Achille Jubinal, *Nouvel recueil de contes* . . . , 2 vols. (Paris, 1839–42), ii. 264–72; and cf. 'De la maaille', ed. Jubinal, *Jongleurs*, pp. 101–6. See generally Charles Muscatine, 'The Social Background of the Old French Fabliaux', *Genre*, ix (1976), 1–19.

[2] *Carmina Burana* . . . , ed. Alfons Hilka and Otto Schumann, 3 parts in 2 vols. (Heidelberg, 1930–41), i: 1, nos. 1, 11, 42; *Lateinische Sprichwörter und Sinnsprüche des Mittelalters* . . . , ed. Jakob Werner (Heidelberg, 1912), pp. 12, 19, 36, 40–2, 63, 72; Paul Lehmann, *Die Parodie im Mittelalter*, 2nd edn. (Munich, 1963), pp. 54–7.

[3] *Carm. Bur.*, i: 1, no. 11 (p. 15).

[4] Ibid., no. 11, l. 48a (p. 27).

[5] Gautier de Châtillon, *Moralisch-satirische Gedichte* . . . , ed. Karl Strecker (Heidelberg, 1929), p. 110, no. 10; see generally E. H. Kantorowicz, *Laudes regiae. A Study in Liturgical Acclamations and Mediaeval Ruler Worship* (Berkeley, Calif., 1946), p. 6, who cites some related texts. Of the wayward archbishop of Narbonne about 1200, Innocent III remarked that his 'Deus nummus est', *PL*, ccxiv. 905.

renders in *nummi* or in deniers unspecified.¹ The literary heroism of the *nummus* is, in this sense, a survival of the age of the standard denier.

Considering that the coin's power in this *topos* was in some respects a tyranny, it is surprising how little was said of its quality. Nevertheless, one finds in the Benedictbeuern manuscript: 'Nummus mentitur, raro verax reperitur',² an allegation apparently consistent with the references to false or counterfeit coinage in other forms of imaginative and religious literature. Humbert de Moyenmoutiers had drawn an elaborate simile between the simoniac bishop and the *nummus falsus*.³ A century later a homilist of uncertain identity, taking up the image of the Christian man as a denier vulnerable in weight, alloy, and inscription, interpreted sin as the debasement of a sound man.⁴ The spectre of the 'bad' or 'falsified' coin haunts the vernacular poetry of France and Spain.⁵ But just as in the legal and doctrinal literature, there is scant evidence for distrust of the coining prince. It is the people or the moneyers who abuse coins; let the honest beware! Only toward 1200 and after do references to *bons deniers* and the like, possibly the belated literary reflection of an irremediable diversity in the values of circulating coinages, become at all common in French literature.⁶ But even then the popular interest, if such it can be called, was only to avoid being cheated. The customer with the wrong coins is a familiar figure;⁷ the ultimate reasons or remedies for his complaint did not interest the poets.

Thus the monetary themes of contemporary moral and literary expression bear only remote relation to the conservation of coinage. It was as the measure of wealth rather than the medium of exchange that the coin typically figured in imaginative situations. One finds in the stress on wealth or in the elaboration of the power of the coin some reflection of those pervasive economic changes which conferred on money 'a new social

---

¹ See e.g. *Cart. Vendôme*, ii, no. 621; *Cart. Longpont*, no. 287; 'Cart. Saint-Jean d'Angély', xxx, nos. 203, 215. Cf. S. D. Goitein, *A Mediterranean Society . . .*, 2 vols. to date (Berkeley–Los Angeles, 1967–72), i. 79: 'These dinars are not good even for beggars and for craftsmen, only peasants would use them.'

² *Carm. Bur.*, i: 1, no. 11 (p. 15).

³ *Humberti cardinalis libri III. adversus simoniacos*, ed. Friedrich Thaner, *Libelli de lite . . .*, 3 vols. (Hanover: *MGH*, 1891–7), i. 109 (i. c. 6).

⁴ Achard de Saint-Victor, *Sermons inédits . . .*, ed. Jean Chatillon (Paris, 1970), p. 225. The editor doubts that the sermon in question is Achard's.

⁵ See e.g. *Huon de Bordeaux*, l. 1793; *Eneas*, ed. J.-J. Salverda de Grave, 2 vols. (Paris, 1925–9), ii, l. 4424; *Cantar de mio Cid*, ed. Menéndez Pidal, iii, ll. 165, 503, 1042; and references in next note.

⁶ *Charroi de Nîmes*, l. 1105; *Aiol*, ll. 3689, 3749, 7245; 'De la maaille', ed. Jubinal, *Jongleurs*, p. 103; Cortebarbe, *Les Trois Aveugles de Compiègne . . .*, ed. Georges Gougenheim (Paris, 1932), l. 150; and *fabliaux* in Montaiglon and Raynard, *Recueil général de fabliaux*, i. 18, 312; ii. 11, 17, 29, 167, 173, 179; v. 215.

⁷ e.g. *Wistasse le Moine*, ll. 56–62; Jean Bodel, . . . *Le Jeu de Saint-Nicolas*, ed. Alfred Jeanroy (Paris, 1925), ll. 274 ff.

value' in the twelfth century.[1] As the chasms deepened between the fortunes of merchant and artisan, debtor and creditor, people felt a new abhorrence of avarice which promoted, in turn, the virtue of poverty. Could any coin, from this point of view, be really sound? To Julien de Vézelay money epitomized the transient goods of this world: the coin is advisedly made round 'so that like a ring it rolls from you to another. . . . O how similar to this are the propertied brethren who love their little coins more than Christ. . . .'[2]

[1] Michel Mollat, 'Le problème de la pauvreté au XIIe siècle', in *Vaudois languedociens et Pauvres Catholiques* (Toulouse, 1967), esp. pp. 29–30; L. K. Little, 'Pride Goes before Avarice: Social Change and the Vices . . .', *Amer. Hist. Rev.*, lxxvi (1971), 20–31, 37–47.

[2] Julien de Vézelay, *Sermons*, ed. Damien Vorreux, 2 vols. (Paris, 1972), ii. 546: 'Mobilia bona sunt bona mundi huius, et in statione non permanent, sed semper ab uno mouentur et rotantur ad alterum. Huius rei consideratione numismata rotunda fiunt ut, uelut rotula, a te uoluatur ad alium; haec est ut uulgo ioco dicitur rotula Martineti, quam non rebus maximis commutaret. O quam similes huic sunt proprietarii fratres qui nummulos suos plus Christo diligunt, et malunt perire quam perdere rotulas suas!'

VII

CONCLUSION

THE conservation of coinage was the response of provincial societies to the exploitative *moneta* of the eleventh and twelfth centuries. People began to tire of obligatory exchanges, often at unfavourable rates, and of surreptitious debasements; as their use and need of coined silver quickened, they began to notice discrepancies in the intrinsic value of deniers from different mints; the inherited notion that any denier represented a denier's worth weakened. The authorities themselves must have been among the first to notice these changes, for it was in charters devised to protect shares of revenues from coinage that some of the early prescriptions for monetary stability appear. Thus in Aquitaine, that spacious corridor through which two worlds were coming again into touch, the coinages of Saintes and Poitou were regulated in the mid-eleventh century so as to discourage fraud in the mints. The Poitevin charter—obtained by the reformed monks with the widest connections in France and Spain—bears a startling verbal resemblance to the great confirmation-charters of the twelfth century; yet its substantive affinity is rather with the persistent efforts, evident in the charter of Cardona (986) and the Pyrenean peace movement, to provide for the uniformity and security of the old regalian coinage. The idea of protecting circulating pieces from public abuse, basically Carolingian (and ultimately Roman), was to subsist in the conservation of coinage. But the emphasis of the sanctions shifted as the moneyers and even the lords themselves came to be identified as violators. In many regions,[1] the exploitation of the mints had become too crudely fiscal by the close of the eleventh century to be easily reformed. Whether in the *pretium* renounced in Poitou or in the redemptions of coinage elsewhere, one cannot fail to discern the characteristic seigneurial disposition to charge, to demand, for every concession to right or convenience.

The coinages of this harsh age having become customs, all too often bad customs, the remedies of the charters tended henceforth to assume the native forms of customary restraint. Just as the ruler swore to uphold other good customs, so he swore to maintain the coinage unaltered. The inherited coinage, preferably: such was the literal meaning of *conservare* as Innocent III employed the term, and the principle is manifest in Catalonia and the Île-de-France as well as in Aragon. For life, typically: the

---

[1] Even, by 1103, in Poitou, where the persistence of the good old money into the high tide of the ecclesiastical reform must have made its collapse seem the more shocking.

engagement *in vita mea* is first clearly attested in Cerdanya in 1118,[1] it was sworn at Étampes and Orléans in 1137–8, and was common thereafter. The more extreme form of confirmation, best exemplified by the count of Nevers's oath in 1188 'to conserve' the coinage 'perpetually henceforth', may have been more faithful to the underlying if increasingly irrelevant principle of a standard regalian currency; it had precedents dating back to the tenth and eleventh centuries in the Spanish March and to 1120 in Capetian France. Down to the middle of the twelfth century the manifestations remained isolated as well as local. While some of them attracted the interest of the clergy—and those at Melgueil the support of the pope— there was still no sign that the leaders of Christian society would support the maintenance of coinage as a common cause. In this sense the confirmed coinage lagged behind the territorial order with which it had already become associated: it remained an adjunct of the diocesan peace for a generation after Pope Urban II preached the militant peace of Christendom.

These currents of restraint persisted and widened in the second half of the twelfth century. The solemn confirmation of coinage occurred in one form or another (to cite only ascertained instances) in Champagne (1165) and at Blois about the same time; at Vich (1174); in Burgundy (1185, 1187); in Nevers (1188) and soon after in Picardy; in Aragon and probably Catalonia (1196); and in the following half-century it was celebrated at Toulouse (1205, 1222), in Urgell (1210), at Cahors (1212), repeatedly in Aragon (1218–36), and in Agenais (1232, 1234). The legate Jacintus, from his experience of Spain dating back to the 1150s, brought some of these initiatives to the notice of Rome, where he himself, as Pope Celestine III, followed by Innocent III, acted in accordance with the pontifical surveillance of oaths and the canonical sanctions against fraud.

Nevertheless, the conservation of coinage remained a provincial phenomenon. It never attained the rank of a Lateran conciliar canon. Its geographic incidence remained limited; for while it seems likely that the principle became familiar throughout the successor-principalities of West Frankland, it cannot be altogether accidental that we have no written confirmations of coinage from the north-western and south-eastern zones of that territory. Even where it was instituted, moreover, there were signs of weakening in the later twelfth century: the charter for Étampes became a dead letter, while those of Provins, Dijon, and Saint-Quentin represented the principle in increasingly qualified forms.

To explain this *échec* we have to observe that the conjuncture of economic, legal, and moral imperatives was changing. The discrepancy of monetary standards, which had already resulted in the abandonment of the Roman system of weights, seems to have reached its extreme toward

---

[1] But cf. above, p. 147.

the middle of the twelfth century. Thereafter, while less is heard of abusive manipulations, a movement to adjust and stabilize coinages in practical ratios becomes perceptible: in Occitania and the Spanish realms toward 1173-4 and in France, Burgundy, and Picardy beginning about the same time.[1] Increasing supplies of coin together with the spread of monetary exchange into remote countrysides were breaking down the monetary autonomy of *pays* and towns. For a Gascon landlady dealing with travellers returning from Spain to refuse to accept their *tornois* and *paresis* save at an enormous discount was either wicked or benighted, and it is no wonder that unpleasant things happened to her in the Old French tale of the early thirteenth century.[2] The predominance of certain territorial moneys—the Melgorian and the Barcelonan as well as the Parisian, for instance—had become so extended and assured as to overcome their seigneurial attributes. How could one recall such a coinage?—and what point in manipulating it? As the alloys of the leading deniers were fixed, typically in the vicinity of 4 or 5 d. fine, and as their weights in terms of the regional marks became better known, the local black moneys had to be adjusted in determined relation to the strong ones if they were to remain current: the process is clearly visible in Picardy. The masters of the favoured moneys put their faith in the open administration of stabilized coinages.

Moreover, the revival of the Roman law of pecuniary obligations together with the growth of exchange tended to divert efforts from the prohibition of mutations to the remedy of their consequences. The old insistence on renders in deniers that need not be exchanged (tolerably equivalent, that is, to the preferred coinage) disappears after 1150 or so.[3] That settlements *per aestimationem* became easier and more frequent was itself a reason why arbitrary debasements became less profitable and less frequent. The French moralists, like the Romanist lawyers, worried more about exchange than about mutations, and so, too, did the canonists and popes from the 1180s on. It was in commentaries on directives relating to repayments in altered coinages, not on *Quanto personam tuam*, that the early decretalists dealt with the subject of mutations of coinage. Nor had the monks and poets any very urgent concern with mutations: one's soul, burdened by commerce and gain, could be quite indifferently endangered by coined money of any quality.

[1] Paul Guilhiermoz dated the establishment of the regional marks to about 1125, but his evidence suggests that it was only in the second half of the twelfth century that the new system—symmetrical with the new zones of strong money—became generally recognized: see his 'De la taille du denier dans le haut moyen âge', *BEC*, lxxxiv (1923), 281-2, also 268 ff.; 'Note sur les poids du moyen âge', *BEC*, lxvii (1906), 197-8, 424, 439; 'Remarques diverses sur les poids et mesures du moyen âge', *BEC*, lxxx (1919), 21, 52-3, 57, 78.

[2] *Wistasse le Moine*, ll. 56-62 and *passim*. In 1178 landlords at Saint-Gilles swore not to engage in money-changing with pilgrims on the way of Rome, that work being reserved to the changers under oath, *LTC*, i, no. 288.

[3] Cf. above, pp. 121, 130.

In these circumstances, it may seem puzzling that the conservation of coinage persisted at all. But the principle was flexible in practice. It was not, after all, inconsistent with the new interest in stabilizing the regulated currencies. Where it had sanction in local custom it might well survive together with other old customs, or be adjusted to fit the changed economic reality. Philip Augustus could in good conscience reserve his tallage 'for the stability of the coinage' at Orléans in 1183 while jettisoning his oath of confirmation. One could limit the renunciation to debasements, as did Thibaut V of Blois, or to reinforcements, as did Hugues III of Burgundy. When Henri le Libéral confirmed the coinage of Meaux, and then promised to hold it in parity with his coinages of Provins and Troyes, he was effectively creating a regional monetary standard, somewhat as Guilhem VIII had done in Aquitaine a century before; but it is worth noting that while the latter had simply sought to co-ordinate the issues of his several mints, the count of Champagne laid stress on the conservation of the co-ordinated issues.

But the main reason for the survival of efforts to confirm the coinage was that anxieties about monetary stability were slow to disappear. When the old custom of Jaca was adapted by the compilers of the *fueros* of Aragon in the thirteenth century, the word 'to change' (*mudar*) in the phrase 'the king can change his coinage' was replaced by the word 'to make' (*fabricare*).[1] What were people afraid of? Nowhere are we told in so many words. Surely the paramount concerns were to prevent trouble in the exchange of coins and, more specifically, to secure the value of incomes. Of these concerns the latter presumably increased in importance, while the former decreased, over time. In any case, the grounds for such fears were persistent enough. The stabilizing of coinages was not everywhere and promptly effective in the later twelfth century, the countervailing effects of commerce were still imperfect, and a long generation was to pass before the cautious specifying of deniers of payment—and not everywhere even then—ceased once again to seem urgent.

In major respects, however, the phenomena that have occupied us defy such general summation. The rhythms of regional change were diverse, the patterns of incidence and diffusion problematical. If only we could know what engagements accompanied the institution of the Norman *monnéage*, more than one secret might be unlocked. Only then could it be confirmed that the Capetian money-tax owed something to the influence of the Norman one, or that the northern charters were altogether independent of the southern ones. What is beyond doubt is that the southern confirmations of coinage were more homogeneous than those of the North, more

---

[1] *Fueros, observancias y actos de corte del reino de Aragón*, ed. Pascual Savall y Dronda and Santiago Penén y Debesa, 2 vols. (Zaragoza, 1866), ii. 109A; see also *Los Fueros de Aragón según el manuscrito 458*, ed. Tilander, p. 153 (art. 265).

traditional in character and more persistent. In their association with the peace and their attendance by the great men of the region (or of the county town), these enactments long continued to evoke the structural character-istics of the late Carolingian county. Right into the thirteenth century the diplomatic forms in which the confirmations were cast went on stressing the solemnity of the event in terms first apparent in the earliest extant charters. Nor is this conservatism difficult to explain, for it was chiefly in the South that the widely attested efforts to stabilize and regulate currencies were disrupted in the turbulent years that ended in the Albigensian wars.

In the North, where the ceremonial assembly only exceptionally exhi-bited a regional composition—perhaps only, indeed, in the case of the charter of Corbigny (1188)—the solemn confirmation of coinage had its heyday in the generation *c.* 1120–65, that is, in the last years of the un-regulated coinages. Its spectacular recurrence in Nevers, where monetary disorder had continued in the absence of a strong, competitive coinage, was out of phase with more pragmatic tendencies in the Capetian lands, Burgundy, Champagne, and Picardy. The charters of Dijon and Saint-Quentin, although they surely owed something to conservationist senti-ment, were intended rather to define the limits of permissible mutation than to confirm the coinage. In Champagne the objective shifted from confirmation to the open management of profitable coinages. In the Île-de-France a progressive royal administration, itself in close touch with the government of Champagne, likewise found the confirmation of coinage irrelevant to its reorganization of fiscal affairs. At the same time some northern charters begin to prescribe consultations on the currency or on standards of coinage, and even, in the otherwise traditional charter for Nevers, to recognize that the regulation of monetary standards was a technical matter to be referred to experts.

It is from the fiscal point of view that the changes of the later twelfth and early thirteenth centuries are most significantly clarified. Owing partly to the moral sentiment against arbitrary mutations or ransoms of stable coinage and partly to the inadequacy of the revenues they yielded, there could be no question of persisting in the proprietary exploitation of mints. The instituted money-taxes of Normandy, Orléans, and Paris could be maintained in the new circumstances, could even be justified; but the newly stabilized coinages of Paris and Tours were not made the excuse for extending the levy to populations hitherto immune. Royal administrators, of whom the Templar Haimard was the first whose expertise in coinage is demonstrable, shifted the burden to the prospering moneyers (if the scanty evidence is not misleading) in order to secure a better share of the profits of coinage. With the exception of the newly consolidated tallage at Orléans and of the *ad hoc* crusading *fouage* in Nevers, no effort was made in the North to amplify the occasions, or to extend the incidence, of the money-tax in order to meet the new financial demands on the larger feudal states.

In the South it was very different. From its early days the Catalonian ransom of the coinage had been allied with the purchase of peace, and as early as 1196 the former had been justified by the requirements of war against the Saracens. But Peter II had no such expanding resources as Philip Augustus to tap, nor were his increasing needs of money matched by his fiscal skill. His imposition of the *monedaje* (1205), which violated custom in both of his realms, could only have been excused by necessities larger than fluctuating coinages, and it seems clear that Peter's later money-taxes, like the equally traditional peace taxes with which some of them were confused, were levied systematically by paid collectors. The proceeds of these taxes represented a substantial portion of the royal income in their day. In short, the monarchs of the fledgling Crown of Aragon, at a critical juncture in their history, felt obliged to fall back on their only customary subsidies in order to create a modern tax adequate to their extraordinary need. So transformed, the *monedatges* and *bovatges* were the southern analogues of the new property taxes of the northern kingdoms. How is this adaptability of the old Catalonian imposition to be explained?

In its original form, the subsidy for the money and the peace was much more nearly public and territorial than the Capetian tallage on bread and wine. Only the Norman *fouage* was comparable in this respect, so that it can be said that the two oldest money-taxes shared a utilitarian justification within older structures of princely authority. But unlike the *fouage*, which assumed the form of a fixed and modest custom, the Catalonian payment remained occasional. Had its recurrence been envisaged at the outset, and its recurrent form defined, its destiny might not have been much different from that of the *fouage*. As it happened, the magnates of Catalonia could pretend that the charter *Cunctis pateat* did not commit them or their tenants to the payment of an accession tax, but to press such a claim was only to encourage the count–kings to redefine the occasions on which such a payment was needed and justified, and to increase the incidence or burden of the levy. In the absence of customary impositions on vassals, this redefinition of a basically territorial subsidy was to be a powerful influence in the rise of public taxation in the Crown of Aragon.

Moreover, it can hardly be doubted that the fiscal importance of Peter II's money-taxes was a major cause for the persistence of the confirmation of coinage in Occitania and the Pyrenees. Of nine confirmations directly attested in those regions between 1212 and 1253, at least six were attended by grants, *fouages*, or *monedatges*.[1] Except for the events in Quercy and

---

[1] At Cahors (1212), in Aragon (1218, 1221, 1223, 1236), and Agenais (1232); the confirmation of 1234 in Agenais is a probable case; no evidence of grants at Toulouse (1222) or at Barcelona (1253). For the evidence, see above, pp. 104–19.

Catalonia, there is little evidence to connect these ceremonies with unstable or wilfully manipulated coinages. The popular insistence on the confirmed coinage, having been ingrained in custom, could now be exploited for fiscal motives; yet for just that reason it became impossible for the ruler to dispense with the witness or consent of his expanding community of notables. The composition of this community varied with the socio-political structures of the several regions: what was done before enlarged councils or the 'general parliament' at Toulouse and Narbonne required the convocation of men from the two or three orders of the land in Agenais and Aragon. In diplomatic forms remarkably continuous with the tradi-tional Pyrenean expressions, the immutability of coinage figured among the most basic customary imperatives upon which an enlarged consultative representation was founded.

So in several ways—in their fidelity to the conservation of coinage, in their cultivation of the money-tax, and in their recognition that the stability of coinage formed a constitutional interest of society—the peoples and rulers of the Midi arrived at an altogether distinct experience, a broader and slower current than flowed in the North. While older provincial anxieties were largely dispelled through administrative reform in the North, they persisted long enough in the South to assume customary or in some places parliamentary forms. But even in the South efforts had been made, notably in Aragon and at Melgueil and Vich, to administer the coinages openly, and the renewal of these efforts in the second and third decades of the thirteenth century there, too, serves to mark an epoch. There, too, a closer surveillance of the moneyers must have worked to the fiscal advantage of the ruler. Just as in Capetian France, the Templars were occupied in the monetary work of Aragon and Catalonia, and their written receipts for profits of the money of Barcelona (1208–11, 1222), together with other evidence of improved publicity for the coinage, suggest that there, too, the work of the minters was becoming a public institution of the Crown. Moreover, it is in the South that we first hear of a new kind of mutation: the imposition of an altered value on an otherwise unchanged coin. This practice must have developed out of attempts to regulate the concurrency of pieces of different intrinsic value; and so long as the decrees, like those for Noyon (1197) and Beauvais (1215), merely sanctioned current rates of exchange, there could be no difficulty. But when James I tried, in effect, to favour, to overvalue, one coinage of Barcelona against another, there was protest of a kind also perceptible in the renunciations sworn by the same king in the Aragonese courts of his early years. An abuse of the new age thus helped to perpetuate the old-fashioned vigilance of the South.

Everywhere, the second quarter of the thirteenth century formed a watershed in monetary history. The solitary reign of the denier (and its fractions), whether in the more famous and stabilized issues or in the less reliable and less plentiful ones from petty mints, was at its end. Already *gros* coins of Italy were finding their way to the West, the more eagerly welcomed as the purchasing power of the denier and the obol declined; gold coins would soon be common even in the North. In these conditions some main tendencies of the preceding generations were to be consolidated. Stabilized royal moneys would increasingly prevail over seigneurial ones. As multiples of the denier became current, the statutory ascription of exchange values would become more common and more troublesome. The public interest in coinage, soon to be more cogently argued than had been possible before the social teachings of Aristotle were known, would increasingly be seen to lie in its regulation instead of its conservation, although the *confirmatio monetae* would survive or recur here and there. The more money that was handled and the more rapidly it circulated, the less likely were people to be concerned with the weight and fineness of individual pieces and the more likely to be interested in amounts or sums. The expanding markets would tend to attract popular interest away from money to prices, and so, perhaps, to encourage some measure of tokenism.[1] The technicalities of coinage would increasingly determine the forms of consultation on monetary policy. To be sure, the mid-thirteenth century was a time of economic stability, and when the old order collapsed in the reign of a new (and sophisticated) manipulator of coinage, popular cries for the good old money were heard again; yet the remedies of the fourteenth century were usually less absolute and more realistic than those of the past.[2] The profound changes had occurred much earlier. As the 'age of the silver denier' ended, the coinages of France and the Spanish March had largely recovered their public and utilitarian character.

The conservation of coinage was easily among the more reactionary economic notions known to history. A confused child of rural anxieties, it betrayed an astonishing innocence of the natural behaviour of minted money. Some ways in which this innocence was dispelled by inexorable new economic forces have been examined at some length. But it would be mistaken to conclude that the problem was simply one of economic ideas in conflict. For the conservation of coinage as revealed to us by the charters was not so much an economic as a psychological and legal idea. It resounded

---

[1] See generally Cipolla, *Money, Prices and Civilization*, esp. ch. 6. The work of W. J. Courtenay on token coinage and imposed value likewise points to the transitional importance of the middle decades of the thirteenth century: 'Token Coinage and the Administration of Poor Relief during the Later Middle Ages', *Journal of Interdisciplinary History*, iii (1972–3), 278–82; 'The King and the Leaden Coin . . .', *Traditio*, xxviii (1972), 185–209.

[2] Especially in France: see e.g. AN, J 459, no. 22, ed. J. R. Strayer in (Strayer) and C. H. Taylor, *Studies in Early French Taxation* (Cambridge, Mass., 1939), pp. 98–103; AN, JJ 41, fo. 121, ed. André Artonne, *Le Mouvement de 1314 et les chartes provinciales de 1315* (Paris, 1912), p. 174 (art. 11).

deeply with that instinctive and associative suspicion of arbitrariness inherited from the 'law societies' of the early medieval West. That coins should be anything other than what they purported to be was likely to arouse indignation regardless of economic tests. This is why mutations of coinage were so easily assimilated to fraud, why the concept of legitimate mutation was slow to regain acceptance. The coinage, in its natural and peculiar way, 'touched all', so that lordly efforts to establish monetary prerogatives in custom sooner or later collapsed before the popular insistence on the good old coinage. Few lords anywhere—and none, perhaps, in France and Spain—managed to secure the written guarantee of an unlimited power of *moneta* such as appears in the early charter of Dinant; the charters of confirmation were consistent with virtually all documentary expressions of the right and custom of coinage in their tendency to limit its exploitation.

Accordingly, the problem of explaining how the conservation of coinage found its way around the west European hinterlands is less basic than might otherwise have appeared. An effort has necessarily been made to discover the provincial circumstances that determined the forms and contents of the charters of confirmation. But those charters, to change the metaphor, were only the outcroppings of a bedrock of popular sentiment perhaps no less widespread than the Carolingian silver coinage itself. The capricious administration of coinage had upset a balance inherent in the social nature of minted money. That is why the ceremonial occasions of confirmation— rites of coinage, they might almost be called—were among the most profoundly representative assemblies of their day. They might have been more frequent and more memorable had not economic influences coincided with popular constraints to recommend the public regulation of coinage. But the provincial vigilance in monetary affairs, once aroused, would long survive the conditions of its origins in the age of the conservation of coinage.

APPENDIX

SELECT DOCUMENTS

REPRODUCED below are eight of the texts most fundamental to the present study. Two of them (nos. 3 and 6) are printed from originals not heretofore published as such, one (no. 8) is printed from a manuscript copy independent of its only and incomplete edition in an exceedingly rare book, while the other five (nos. 1, 2, 4, 5, and 7) seemed too long to reproduce fully in the notes. For all but no. 2 (here printed from a reliable edition) the best extant manuscripts have been used, but no attempt has been made to identify the manuscripts, editions, and indications systematically.

I

[4 April 1118]

Ramon Berenguer III and Bishop Pere I of Elne institute a peace in the county of Cerdanya–Conflent for the protection of oxen, other domestic animals, their possessors, and the coinage. The count has confirmed the coinage for his lifetime under oath, and he is to be compensated for this one time.

ACA, Canc., Reg. 4, fo. 42[rab] (copy of early thirteenth century; Plate V; ed. Miquel Rosell, *LFM*, ii, no. 691). Discussed above, pp. 50 ff.

[C]vnctis pateat hanc uidentibus uel audientibus scripturam quoniam ego Raimundus, Dei gratia Barchinonensis comes et marchio Prouincie, atque domnus Petrus Helenensis episcopus, consilio et iussione magnatum et militum tocius comitatus Cerritanensis atque Confluentis, mittimus pacem in predicto comitatu de bubibus atque ceteris animalibus arantibus et omnibus hominibus tangentibus illos uel arantibus, ita ut nullus homo uel femina cuiuscumque sit ordinis audeat tollere uel capere illos qualicumque modo uel ingenio, quod qui fecerit boues restituat cui tulerit et insuper .lx. solidos monete comitis componat prenominato comiti et tantum interim ab episcopo interdictus mane(r)at quoadusque hoc restitutum pleniter habeat. Quapropter predictus comes consilio omnium supradictorum mittit suam monetam quam habet propria manu firmatam in predicto comitatu sicut et in ceteris suis comitatibus habet missam, ut omni tempore quandiu ipse superstes extiterit prephatam monetam non mutet uel minuet lege uel penso, tali uero ratione ut omnes homines uel feminas tocius predicti comitatus donet per paria boum .xii. denarios et per unum hominem .vi. denarios et exaders .iii. denarios. Prephatus uero comes promittit Deo et hominibus omnibus iamdicti comitatus quod postquam iam dictos denarios fuerint donati pretitulato comiti numquam amplius predictos denarios requirat iam dictis hominibus, sed predicta pax illibata atque firma semper maneat et a nullo homine uiuente uel femina disrumpatur neque per guerram quam comes uel prephati principes seu milites inter se habeant. De predicta uero iusticia sexaginta solidorum habeat prephatus episcopus terciam partem. Actum est hoc secundo nonas Aprilis., anno decimo Leouico rege. S†Raimundi comes. †Petrus Helenensis episcopus. Bernardus huius scriptor die et [*sign*] anno quo supra.

2

[*c.* 1151]

Provisions of the Establissement *of Saint-Quentin: customary payments are to be made in the stipulated coinages and lords are enjoined against deceit in the handling of coin.*

From AM Eu, 'Livre Rouge', fos. 2–61, translation-copy of *c.* 1340, ed. Arthur Giry in Lemaire, *Archives de Saint-Quentin*, i. lxxx (later ed. Albert Legris, *Livre Rouge d'Eu [1151–1454]* [*Rouen–Paris*, 1911], pp. 12–13). Discussed above, pp. 147–8.

Giry

41. Et se aucun devera chens a son seigneur, de terre, ou de meson, ou de pré, ou de bois, ou de quelconques heritage, il rendra sans forfait a son seigneur a son terme[a] le chens premierement establi et nommé u convenant;[b] et se le seigneur devant nommé[c] voloit avoir par forche meilleur monnoie de ychely par aucune maniere, il ne le porra faire par droit en nulle maniere; mais telle monnoie li paiera et combien il li a enconvenanchié.

42. Et se le seigneur felon, mené par convoitise, ara faussé les deniers de son homme, pour greigneur cange, il convendroit par le tesmoing d'un homme estre prouvé que eux soient faux et refusés; et donquez le seigneur ne[d] les porroit refuser; et[e] l'onme nient plus en pledier n'en porroit, et de chen en la volenté de l'onme seroit pour la monnoie recangier.

43.[f] Et se le seigneur de le quemune, ou autre seigneur dessous li, wellent requerre de leurs hommes autre monnoie que u pays establie et forgie et anchianement acoustumée, il ne le porront faire, mais rendront denier pour denier sans nul cange. Et ensement cheste chose doit estre tenue des acoustumanches des estaux.

    [a] (Giry's apparatus.) Les mots *sans forfait a son seigneur a son terme* ajoutés en interligne.

    [b] Les mots *et nommé u convenant* ajoutés en interligne, ont remplacé *en le convenanche* biffés.

    [c] Il y avait d'abord: *Et se le chens devant nommé a son terme a son seigneur sans forfait paie; et se le seigneur voloit avoir par forche meilleur monnoie . . .* qui a été corrigé.

    [d] *ne* ajouté en interligne.

    [e] *et* ajouté en interligne.

    [f] Tout cet article a été ajouté par le correcteur à la marge inférieure de la page.

3

[*c.* 1174]

Alphonse II, king of Aragon, count of Barcelona, and marquis of Provence, institutes a new coinage of Barcelona at 4 d. fine and 18 s. of deniers to the mark (and obols at 3 d. and 26 s.), swears to preserve it unchanged for life, and establishes sanctions against violators.

ACA, Canc, perg. Alfonso I, extrainv. 2602, contemporary parchment minute or copy, without authentication. 175 × 230 mm. (Ed. Botet y Sisó, *Monedes catalanes*, iii. 240, from copy in Reg. 2, fo. 47ʳ.)[1] Discussed above, p. 76.

In Christi nomine. Sit notum cunctis quod ego Ildefonsus, Dei gratia rex Aragonensis, comes Barchinonensis et marchio Prouincie, facio et stabilio monetam nouam barchinonensem bonam et legalem que omnibus diebus uite mee per terram curret. Quam monetam facio et statuo fieri ad quatuor denarios[a] argenti fini siue puri et quod exeat marcha denariorum[b] ad .xviii. solidos. Predictam ergo monetam uolo et facio firmam et stabilem in predicto penso et lege cunctis diebus uite mee sine omni fraude et absque malo ingenio et sine omni engan, ita quod mutabitur nec cambiabitur neque peiorabitur. Quicumque autem iamdictam monetam ausu temerario falsauerit uel minuerit seu in aliquo defraudauerit, promitto siquidem in mea bona fide et legalitate quod faciam tam de eo quam de illo qui hoc inquam consenserit uel cognouerit et mihi statim non reuelauerit iusticiam secundum quod ius dictauerit. Similiter statuo et fieri facio ipsas medalias iamdicte monete ad .iii. denarios argenti fini et quod exeant ad .xx. solidos ipsa marca.[c] Supradictum autem stabilimentum facio et firmiter obseruari precipio uolens et cupiens prouidere communi utilitati tocius populi mei et terre.

4

1188 Corbigny

Pierre de Courtenay, count of Nevers, and his wife Agnès, with the counsel and consent of bishops, abbots, and barons of the county of Nevers, have minted at 4 d. fine and 16 s. 8 d. to the mark of Troyes, and have sworn to conserve this coinage perpetually. So long as they do, their coinage is to be lawful tender, and provision is made for testing in the mint. The count and countess are granted a hearth-tax of 12 d. for this one time.

[a]   or
.iiii. denarios *added (or possibly written over erasure).*
[b] denariorum *written over erasure.*
[c] Similiter statuo . . . ipsa marca *added.*

[1] Dorse: *Carta qua Ildefonsus rex ordinauit certam cudi monetam in Barchinona in uita sua* (thirteenth or fourteenth century), and later marks of classification.

Prou, 'Recueil de documents monétaires', *RN*, 3rd ser., xiv. 287–8, reproducing AD Nièvre, G 64 (today 2G 11, no. 1, presently missing); described by Prou as 'Original sur parchemin autrefois scellé de deux sceaux suspendus par des lanières de cuir'. Discussed above, pp. 135 ff.

In nomine sancte et individue Trinitatis. Noverint universi quod ego Petrus, comes Nivernensis, et ego Agnes, comitissa, uxor ejusdem comitis, ad consilium et consensum episcoporum, abbatum et baronum comitatus Nivernensis, monetam fecimus ad IIII^{or} denarios de fino argento et XVI solidos et VIII denarios de pondere in marca Trecensi. Quam ego comes et ego comitissa juravimus perpetuo de cetero in jam dicto pondere et legalitate fideliter conservandam. Quam etiam jurabit filius noster vel filia et filii filiorum vel filiarum successive in posterum ut duret in perpetuum. Si vero ego Petrus comes, et ego Agnes, comitissa, / uxor ejusdem comitis vel filius noster vel filia aut filius filii vel filie monetam ipsam de supradicto pondere et valore in aliquo defraudaremus vel fraudari sustineremus, ecclesiastice persone vel barones terre nostre monetam nostram deinceps non tenerentur recipere, set monetam quam vellent in terra nostra sine occasione mitterent et episcopi Altissiodorensis et Nivernensis de nobis et terra nostra heredibus nostris justitiam facerent. Si autem fabricatores monete predictum pondus et valorem minuere presumerent, de ipsis justitia districta fieret nec eis favore aliquo aut gratia parceretur. Et ut nulla possit in moneta ipsa fieri diminutio vel falsitas, frequentius probabitur a cambitoribus et discretis viris in cognitione argenti et ponderis, et ecclesiastice persone vel barones eam quandocumque voluerint probari facient. Pro perpetuitate vero istius monete et pro via Jherosolimitana placuit personis ecclesiasticis et baronibus terre nostre ut de singulis domibus que proprium habent mansionarium et ignem XII denarios, hoc tantum anno, acciperemus per civitates et castella et burgos et villas in quibus moneta nostra debitum cursum habet. Ne vero beneficium XII denariorum, quod nobis sponte hoc tantum anno impenditur, ecclesiis vel baronibus in consequentiam trahatur, quod nunquam fuerat nec amodo erit, litteras nostras eis patentes tradidimus tam de monete perpetuitate quam de indempnitate pro beneficio nobis semel gratis impenso. Quod ut in posterum ratum illibatumque permaneat, presentem paginam sigillorum nostrorum auctotate precepimus confirmari. Actum Corbiniaci, anno ab incarnatione Domini M^{o}C^{o}LXXX°VIII°, comitatus vero nostri anno V^o.

5

November 1197   [Noyon]

In response to complaints about uncertain rates of local exchange, Bishop Étienne I of Noyon gives currency to parisis *at 12 d.* par. *to 18 d. of black coin, adding other regulations as to* cens, tolls, *and other customary payments.*

AD Oise, G 1984, fos. 116^v–17 (copy of fourteenth century, ed. Lefranc, *Noyon*, pp. 204–5). Discussed above, pp. 152–3.

Stephanus, Dei gratia Nouiomensis episcopus, uniuersis paginam presentem inspecturis in Domino salutem. Quoniam propter incerte cursum monete ecclesie nostre totique capitulo Nouiomensi damna non minima proueniebant et maiora in posterum imminebant, eorum indempnitati prouidere uolentes, concessimus eis ut moneta parisiensis Nouiomi cursum habeat quamdiu nostre fuerit uoluntatis, ita quod census qui infra metas communie debebantur de parisiensi moneta, computatis duodecim parisiensibus pro decem et octo nigris, reddantur de cetero, hoc addito quod census qui obolum non excedit, de obolo parisiensi, et qui non excedit denarium, de denario parisiensi soluatur. Et si denarium excesserit, ea ratione qua pro decem et octo nigris duodecim parisienses soluuntur reddatur. Ceterum si a nobis siue a successoribus nostris aliquo in tempore monetam ad legem trium denariorum et oboli fieri contigerit, predicti census ex eadem moneta, computatis .x. et octo nigris pro duodecim parisiensibus, exsoluantur. Item si cariorem monetam quam de tribus denariis et obolo nos seu nostri fecerimus successores, omnes census, sicut prescriptum est et ordinatum, de moneta parisiensi reddantur. Ad hec quecumque moneta Nouiomi cucurrerit, teloneum et alie consuetudines preter wionagium nostrum quod ad nostram dabimus uoluntatem ex ea persoluentur. Quod ut firmiter obseruetur in posterum presentis pagina cyrographi et nostri munimine sigilli confirmamus. Actum anno Domini .m°.c°.xc°.vii°., mense Nouembri.

6

5 April 1199   Lateran

Pope Innocent III responds to King Peter II's appeal to be released from his oath to conserve his father's debased coinage by posing the issue whether that oath was sworn in knowledge of the fraud or not. In the former case the oath is null and penitence is ordered, in either case the best coinage of Alphonse II is to be restored.

ACA, Canc., Bulas, Inocencio III, legajo 3, no. 4 (Plate XI). Original parchment letter, formerly sealed and closed. 234 × 302 mm. Indicated by F. J. Miquel Rosell, *Regesta de letras pontificias del Archivo de la Corona de Aragón* . . . (Madrid, 1948), no. 46. For editions and indications of the Vatican copies, see Mansilla, *Documentación pontificia*, no. 183.[1] Discussed above, pp. 86 ff., 166–73.

Innocentius episcopus, seruus seruorum Dei, karissimo in Christo filio [Petro][a] illustri regi Aragonensi salutem et apostolicam benedictionem. Quanto personam tuam inter alios principes christianos sinceriori caritate diligimus tanto serenitati regie diligentiori sollicitudine uolumus precauere nequid ei quod absit immineat quod uel in periculum anime aut detrimentum terre ualeat redundare. Ex tenore siquidem litterarum tuarum et plurium prelatorum necnon et aliorum multorum in tuo regno consistentium nobis innotuit quod cum aduersus inimicos christianitatis qui pre magnitudine sue potentie terram Hispanie tunc temporis occupabant in auxilium karissimi in Christo filii nostri [Alphonsi][a] Castelle

---

[a] *Space for king's name left blank.*

---

[1] Dorse: *illustri regi Aragonensi*, and later marks of classification.

regis illustris cum armatorum multitudine festinares, quidam consiliarii tui quin immo potius deceptores tuum animum induxerunt ut iurares irrequisito assensu populi usque ad certum tempus patris tui conseruare monetam que tamen circa mortem ipsius fuerat legitimo pondere defraudata. Quoniam autem eadem moneta est adeo diminuta et minoris ualoris effecta quod graue propter hoc in populo scandalum generatur, tu quod egeras indiscrete discrete cupiens reuocare ac necessitati populi satisfacere ab obseruatione iuramenti predicti ex quo tibi et regno tuo metuis graue periculum imminere postulasti suppliciter a nobis absolui. Super quo diligens indagator ueritate comperta potuisset facile intueri quod non tam erat absolutio necessaria quam interpretatio requirenda, quoniam cum iuramentum fecisti, monetam aut falsam aut legitimam esse credebas. Si falsam, quod de regia serenitate non credimus, iuramentum fuisset illicitum et nullatenus obseruandum, et pro eo tibi esset penitentia iniungenda, cum iuramentum ut esset iniquitatis uinculum non fuerit institutum. Si uero ipsam legitimam esse credebas, iuramentum licitum fuit et usquequaque seruandum, et ut irreprehensibiliter obseruetur, consulimus et mandamus ut, reprobata moneta que a legitimo pondere fuerat diminuta, alia sub nomine patris tui moneta cudatur quam ad legitimum pondus reducas secundum eum statum quem tempore patris tui habuit meliorem, ita quod et antiqua moneta que ab illo statu falsata non fuerat cum ea minime[a] expendatur per quod et dispendium uitari poterit et iuramentum seruari. Verumptamen si forte monetam ipsam in prestatione iuramenti credebas a legitimo pondere diminutam et tua super hoc conscientia te remordet, venerabili fratri nostro [Raimundo][b] episcopo Cesaraugustano, cui super hoc scribimus, tuum humiliter confitere reatum, et satisfactionem quam indixerit tibi pro illicito iuramento deuote suscipias et studeas adimplere. Datum Laterani, nonas Aprilis, pontificatus nostri anno secundo.

7

[*c.* 1205–1210]

Memorandum concerning the levy of fouage *in Normandy.*

Bibl. Apost. Vat., MS. Ottoboni 2796, fo. 46rb (copy [?] of 1205–12; Plate IV); other early copies in AN, JJ 8, fo. 71[rv]; JJ 26, fo. 292[rv]; etc. Facsimile edn. by Delisle, *Premier Registre de Philippe Auguste*; other editions cited by Bridrey, 'Le chapitre *De monnéage*', 82 nn. Discussed above, pp. 14 ff.

Ottoboni

Scriptum de foagio.

Foagium capiendum est in Normannia in tercio anno, ita videlicet quod duo anni pretermittuntur sine foagio et in tercio anno capitur. Tali autem modo accipitur: de una quaque villa secundum hoc quod villa est summonentur quatuor homines uel sex uel plures, si opus est. Et illi summoniti iurant quod fideliter colligent foagium, videlicet de quolibet foco xii. denarios et si in eadem domo manserint quatuor homines uel plures siue pauciores de quibus unusquisque uiuat de suo

---

[a] minime *written over erasure, apparently replacing* pariter.
[b] *Space for bishop's name left blank.*

proprio et habeat de catallo xx. solidos aut amplius, quislibet illorum reddit foagium. Vidua etiam si habeat de mobili xl. solidos aut amplius dat foagium; si non habeat xl. s. non reddit. De foagio autem quiti sunt omnes presbiteri et diaconi et milites et omnes persone qui habent ecclesias. Molendinarii etiam et furnarii episcoporum et abbatum et baronum et omnium militum qui deseruiunt dominis suis per membrum lorice exinde quiti sunt. Et preterea quilibet episcopus et abbas et baro habet .vii. seruientes quoscumque uoluerint quitos de foagio. Sciendum est autem quod duo ex iuratoribus de singulis villis afferent ad balliuos regis foagium et habebunt in scriptum nomina illorum de quibus receperint foagium, que tradent balliuis cum foagio, et illi duo habebunt .xii. denarios de quitancia de foagio suo pro illis afferendis. Illi autem ipsi colligent foagium de hominibus templariorum et hospitalariorum, et similiter afferent ad balliuos regis et per manum balliuorum reddetur ad scacarium templariis et hospitalariis. Sciendum uero quod hee terre quite sunt de foagio, videlicet totum feodum Britolii quicumque illud teneat, et Vallis Moritolii usque ad Petras Albas et usque ad Doet Herberti, et tota terra de Passeis et Alenconii et Alenconesium usque ad Pissotum Heraudi, et Molins et Boens Molins et terra ad ea pertinens, et castrum de Aumenesche in ballia de Argenton. In ciuitate Lexouiensi capietur foagium per manum episcopi Lexouiensis et extra ciuitatem ut alibi capietur.

8

July 1212

Bishop Guillem IV of Cahors, responding to the petition of barons of Quercy and burghers of Cahors, who have paid 10,000 s., has instituted a coinage at 3 d. fine and 20 s. 6 d. to the mark, has provided for its exclusive currency, and has promised to preserve it unchanged for his lifetime, admitting that subsequent bishops will have the right to one mutation.

BN, Coll. Doat, cxviii, fos. 7–8ᵛ (copy of 1669 'de loriginal en parchemin trouvé aux archives de lhotel de ville de Caôrse'); ed. incompletely by Lacroix, *Acta episcoporum Cadurcensium* (1617), p. 88, from an unidentified manuscript (possibly the original later copied by order of Doat). Discussed above, pp. 108–12.

Doat (with significant variants from L[acroix])

Notum sit omnibus has litteras cernentibus quia nos Vuillelmus, Dei gratia Caturcensis Episcopus, uolumus facere monetam in Caturcinio ad quatuor denarios et Barones Caturcenses et Burgenses Caturci rogauerunt nos quia[a] faceremus eam ad tres denarios, et per preces eorum et per decem milia solidorum[b] quos dederunt nobis Burgenses, nos fecimus fieri. Et haec moneta debet esse ad tres denarios de argento ad undecim denarios et[c] obolum, et uiginti solidi et sex denarii quando exeunt de moneta debent ponderare marcham unam, et sex

---

[a] quòd *L*.　　　[b] pro decem mille solidis *L*.　　　[c] et *om. L*.

denarii debent esse de obolis eiusdem legis et ponderis quorum denarii.[a] Et Burgenses Caturci mandauerunt et conuenerunt nobis quia[b] de caetero non acciperent denarios Ruthenenses nec obolos ueteres Caturcenses nisi ad cambium, et si aliquis acciperet uel expenderet Burgenses concesserunt[c] nobis septem solidos de justitia et ut amitteret Ruthenenses et obolos quos acceptos habuerit.[d] Sed si forte aliquis fuerit qui reciperet Ruthenenses uel obolos nescienter dum modo praestaret iuramentum[e] non debet dare septem solidos sed admittere[f] Ruthenenses et obolos quos acceperat.[g] Et nos assecurauimus praedictam monetam, ne quamdiu uixerimus in Episcopatu eam mutemus nec deterioremus suo pondere et lege. Et Barones et Burgenses cognouerunt quia[h] unusquisque Episcoporum Caturci post nos potest mutare semel monetam per dominium suamque iuridictionem. Et si Burgenses Caturci fecerant[i] nobis iniuriam de moneta usque modo nos remisimus eis. Et hoc totum factum est bona fide partis utriusque. Et ut conuentiones supradictae sint[j] firmius obseruatae,[k] nos imposuimus praesenti cartae sigillum nostrum et Consules Caturcenses de comuni ciuitatis[l] Consilio similiter posuerunt suum. Et hoc factum est Anno ab incarnati uerbi millesimo ducentesimo duodecimo, mense Julii.

[a] quorum denarii *doubtful reading. L:* cuius unus denarius; *Doat:* quo et d.
[b] quòd *L.*   [c] Burgensium concederet *L.*   [d] habuerint *L.*
[e] nesciens Dominium, iuramentum praestando *L.*   [f] amittere *L.*
[g] acceperit *L.*   [h] quòd *L.*   [i] fecerunt *L.*
[j] conuentum suprà dictum sit *L.*   [k] obseruatae *om. L.*   [l] ciuium *L.*

BIBLIOGRAPHY

WORKS fully cited in the List of Abbreviations (pp. xxi–iii) are omitted here, with one exception there noted. Place-names are given in native forms, except in cases of familiar English equivalents (such as Rome, Munich, Brussels). The lists of primary and secondary publications are limited to the more pertinent works. To avoid confusion, numismatic publications are represented as secondary even though they often include editions of coins; many other secondary works have been used for the documents printed in them.

I. MANUSCRIPTS CITED

ADMONT. Stiftsbibliothek, MS. 22.

AGEN. AD Lot-et-Garonne, new G 2, no. 1.

AMIENS. AD Somme, H 16, no. 1.

AUXERRE. AD Yonne, G 510, H 488.
   BM, MS. 161 (cartulary of Saint-Germain d'Auxerre).

BAMBERG. Staatsbibliothek, MSS. canon. 19, canon. 20, canon. 40, canon. 45.

BARCELONA. ACA, Sección Cancillería Real, pergaminos Ramón Berenguer I, 182, 228, 361; Ramón Berenguer IV, 233; apéndice 6, 8, 9; extrainventario 2502; Alfonso I, 13, 46–8, 55, 56, 59, 60, 62, 65, 67, 94, 108, 126, 146, 160, 194, 408, 417, 442, 478, 567; Pedro I, 13, 26, 64, 76, 84, 155, 164, 200, 201, 226, 265–8, 271, 274, 315, 316, 320, 325, 355, 361, 377, 381, 382, 384, 385, 416, 434–6, 441, 445, 455, 568, apéndice 3; Jaime I, 35, 207; extra-inventario 3131, 3235; bulas pontificias, Inocencio III, legajo 3, nos. 1, 3, 4; registros 2, 4, 22, 309, 310, 340.
   Sección Monacales, St. Benet de Bages, 501, 504, 506.
   Sección Gran Priorato de Cataluña de la Orden de San Juan de Jerusalén, sección 1, armario 17, no. 321.
   AC, 'Libri antiquitatum', 4 vols. (cartulary of cathedral chapter); pergamins Diversorum A 1115 (26 XII 1211); C capsa 9, 315 (17 III 1212); capsa 14, 1264 (6 XII 1212); capsa 20, 2350 (1211).
   Biblioteca Central, MSS. 193, 729, 1619 (cartulary of Gerri); pergamins Miret y Sans, 3170, 4000.

BEAUVAIS. AD Oise, G 1984 (cartulary of cathedral chapter of Noyon), G 7391.

BLOIS. AD Loir-et-Cher, 3H 66, no. 1; 3H 110; 46H 3, no. 30.

CAHORS. AD Lot, F 349–53.
   AM, DD 1.

CASBAS. Archivo del monasterio, cajón 10, no. 16; legajo no. 1.

CERVERA. AM, pergamins.

CHÂLONS-SUR-MARNE. AD, H 585, H 714, 18H 33, no. 2.

CORDOBA. AC, MS. 10.

DIJON. AD Côte-d'Or, 1H 14, no. 1; 15H 13 (cartulary of Fontenay [diocese of Autun]).
   AM, B 1.

GIRONA. AC, MS. 7 ('Llibre verd,' cartulary of cathedral chapter); privilegis reials, 7.
   Arxiu diocesà, 'Carles Many' (cartulary of cathedral chapter).

KARLSRUHE. Landesbibliothek, MS. Aug. XL.
LAON. AD Aisne, G 39, G 1850 (cartulary of cathedral chapter).
LÉRIDA. AM, privilegis, no. 5.
LILLE. AD Nord, 28H 46 (*pièce* 1196).
MADRID. AHN, Sección Clero, Poblet, carpetas 2019, 2040, 2109; códice 597B (cartulary of Templars).
MONTAUBAN. AD Tarn-et-Garonne, G 998.
MONTPELLIER. Société archéologique de Montpellier, MS. 10 (cartulary of the Trencavel).
MONTSERRAT. Arxiu del monestir, pergamins de Sant Cugat.
MUNICH. Staatsbibliothek, MS. 3879.
NARBONNE. AM, AA 109.
NEVERS. AD Nièvre, 2G 11.
ORLÉANS. AM, AA 1.
PARIS. AN, J 318, no. 15; J 321, no. 28; J 459, nos. 1, 22; J 896, no. 33; K 24A, no. 3 (1); K 192, nos. 202, 260, 312; L 842, no. 50; S 4195, nos. 21, 25; JJ 26; JJ 41; LL 985B ('Livre Rouge' of chapter of Saint-Quentin).
Bibliothèque Mazarine, MS. 1292.
BN, MSS. lat. 5471 (cartulary of Froidmont), 5528 (cartulary of cathedral church of Meaux), 5650 (cartulary of La Trinité, Caen), 5993 (cartulary of counts of Champagne), 9930 (cartulary of chapter of Arras), 9994 (cartulary of Grandselve), 11070 (cartulary of chapter of Saint-Quentin), 17098 (cartulary of cathedral church of Troyes), 17758 (cartulary of Corbie); n. a. lat. 2127, 2192; fr. 11988; n. a. fr. 4837 (? see p. 161, n. 1), 6278; collections: Champagne lviii; Doat cxviii; Dupuy ccxxvi; Moreau lvi, lxxi, lxxx; Picardie clxii, ccii, ccxxxv.
PERPIGNAN. AD Pyrénées-Orientales, B 8, B 58, J 20D 1 (cartulary of Arles-sur-Tech).
AM, AA 9.
POITIERS. AD Vienne, Jacques de Font-Réaulx, MS. 'Catalogue des actes des ducs d'Aquitaine'.
PROVINS. BM, MSS. 85, 92 (cartularies of Provins).
REIMS. AD Marne, H 318, H 1384.
SANT JOAN DE LES ABADESSES. Arxiu del monestir, pergamins.
LA SEU D'URGELL. 'Liber dotaliorum', 2 vols. (cartulary of cathedral church), pergamins.
TARRAGONA. AM, pergamins, cartoral-rotlle.
TORTOSA. AC, pergamins, privilegis reials, 41.
AM, calaix Bisbe i Capitol 78, no. 8.
TOULOUSE. AD Haute-Garonne, E 501; E 508, no. 1; H Malte, Caignac, no. 31; Toulouse 1, no. 100.
AM, AA 1.
TROYES. AD Aube, G 2857, 20H 9, MS. n. a. 524.
VATICAN CITY. Biblioteca Apostolica Vaticana, MS. lat. 2509, MS. Ottoboni 2796 ('First Register' of Philip Augustus).
VICH. AC, calaix 6, nos. 25, 28–31, 368, 373, 384, 394, 402, 1659, 1926, 2404; calaix 9 (April 1196); calaix 37, nos. 38, 57*bis*, 68; Mensa episcopal, registre 'Variarum rerum'.
AM, Privilegis, IX, no. 172.
VIENNA. Staatsbibliothek, MS. lat. 2083.

2. PRINTED SOURCES

A. *Cartularies*

AGDE. *Cartulaire du chapitre d'Agde*, ed. Odile Terrin. Nîmes: Publ. Société d'histoire du droit et des institutions des anciens pays de droit écrit, i, 1969.

AMIENS. 'Cartulaire du chapitre de la cathédrale d'Amiens', ed. Edmond Soyez and Joseph Roux, *MSAP, Documents inédits concernant la province*, xiv (1897–1905), xviii (1912).

ANGOULÊME. *Cartulaire de l'église d'Angoulême*, ed. J. Nanglard. Angoulême, 1900.

ARRAS. *Cartulaire de l'abbaye de Saint-Vaast d'Arras rédigé au XIIe siècle par Guimann* . . . , ed. E.-F. Van Drival. Arras, 1875.

—— 'Un cartulaire de l'abbaye de Saint-Vaast d'Arras, codex du XIIe siècle', ed. A. Guesman, *Bulletin historique et philologique du Comité des travaux historiques et scientifiques* (1896), pp. 240–305.

AUTUN. *Cartulaire de l'église d'Autun. Première et deuxième parties*, ed. Anatole de Charmasse. Paris–Autun, 1865.

BAYEUX. *Antiquus cartularius ecclesiae Baiocensis (Livre noir)*, ed. l'abbé V. Bourrienne, 2 vols. Rouen–Paris, 1902–3.

BEAUVAIS. *Cartulaire de la Maladrerie de Saint-Lazare de Beauvais comprenant 406 chartes*, ed. Victor Leblond. Paris, 1922.

—— *Cartulaire de l'Hôtel-Dieu de Beauvais comprenant 529 chartes* . . . , ed. Victor Leblond. Paris, 1919.

BÉZIERS. *Cartulaire de Béziers. Livre noir de Béziers*, ed. J.-B. Rouquette. Paris–Montpellier, 1918.

BLOIS. 'Cartulaire de la ville de Blois (1196–1493). Recueil manuscrit conservé à la Bibliothèque nationale . . .', ed. Jacques Soyer and Guy Trouillard, *Mémoires de la Société des sciences et lettres de Loir-et-Cher*, xvii (1903–7).

BOURGES. 'Essai de reconstitution du Cartulaire A de Saint-Sulpice de Bourges', ed. Louis de Kersers, *Mémoires de la Société des antiquaires du Centre*, xxxv (1912), 1–350.

CASBAS. *Documentos de Casbas*, ed. Agustin Ubieto. Valencia: *Textos medievales*, xxi, 1966.

CLUNY. *Recueil des chartes de l'abbaye de Cluny* . . . , ed. Auguste Bernard, revised by Alexandre Bruel, 6 vols. Paris, 1876–1903.

COMPIÈGNE. *Cartulaire de l'abbaye Saint-Corneille de Compiègne*, ed. Émile Morel, 2 vols. Compiègne, 1904–9.

CORBIGNY. 'Chartes de l'abbaye de Corbigny', ed. Anatole de Charmasse, *Mémoires de la Société éduenne*, new ser., xvii (1889), 1–40.

DIJON. *Chartes et documents de Saint-Bénigne de Dijon, prieurés et dépendances des origines à 1300*, ii (*990–1124*), ed. Georges Chevrier and Maurice Chaume. Dijon, 1943.

—— *Les Chartes de Saint-Étienne de Dijon des origines au XVe siècle*, i:2 (*1098 à 1140*), ed. Adrien Bièvre-Poulalier. Dijon, 1912; i:3 (*1140 à 1155*), ed. P. Bourrier. Paris–Dijon, 1912; i:4 (*1155 à 1200*), ed. Georges Valat. Dijon–Paris, 1907.

ÉCHARLIS. 'Chartes inédites relatives à la famille de Courtenay et à l'abbaye des Écharlis (XIIe–XIIIe siècles)', ed. Henri Stein, *Annales de la Société historique & archéologique du Gâtinais*, xxxvi (1922), 141–65.

FONTMORIGNY. *Le Chartrier ancien de Fontmorigny, abbaye de l'ordre de Cîteaux. Étude générale et catalogue des actes antérieures au XIVe siècle (1135–1300)*, ed. Albert Huchet. Bourges, 1936.

GELLONE. *Cartulaire de Gellone*, ed. Paul Alaus, Léon Cassan, and Edmond Meynial. Montpellier, 1898.

GIRONA. 'Cartoral de Carles Many: index cronòlgich . . .', ed. Joaquím Botet y Sisó, *BRABLB*, iii (1905–6), iv (1907–8).

GUILLEMS (see MONTPELLIER).

HÉRONVAL. *Cartulaire de Héronval publié par le Comité archéologique de Noyon.* Noyon, 1883.

HOSPITALLERS. *Cartulaire général de l'ordre des Hospitaliers de S. Jean de Jérusalem (1100–1310)*, ed. Joseph Delaville le Roulx, 4 vols. Paris, 1894–1901.

HUESCA. *Colección diplomática de la catedral de Huesca*, ed. Antonio Durán Gudiol, 2 vols. Zaragoza: CSIC, 1965–9.

—— 'Cartulario de San Pedro el Viejo', numerous pieces ed. Ricardo del Arco, *Huesca* . . . (cited below).

ÎLES NORMANDES. *Cartulaire des Îles Normandes. Recueil de documents concernant l'histoire de ces îles* . . . Jersey: Société jersiaise, 1918–24.

IRACHE. *Colección diplomática de Irache*, ed. J. M. Lacarra, 1 vol. to date. Zaragoza: CSIC, 1965.

JACA. *Jaca: Documentos municipales, 971–1269*, ed. Antonio Ubieto Arteta. Valencia: *Textos medievales*, xli, 1975.

JULLY-LES-NONNAINS. 'Cartulaire du prieuré de Jully-les-Nonnains', ed. Ernest Petit, *Bulletin de la Société des sciences historiques et naturelles de l'Yonne*, xxxiv (1880), 249–302.

JUMIÈGES. *Chartes de l'abbaye de Jumièges (v. 825 à 1204) conservées aux Archives de la Seine-Inférieure*, ed. J.-J. Vernier, 2 vols. Rouen–Paris: Société de l'histoire de Normandie, 1916.

LA CHAPELLE-AUX-PLANCHES. *Cartulaire de l'abbaye de La Chapelle-aux-Planches. Chartes de Montierender, de Saint-Étienne et de Toussaints de Châlons d'Andecy, de Beaulieu et de Rethel*, ed. Charles Lalore. Paris: *CCDT*, iv, 1878.

LA CHARITÉ-SUR-LOIRE. *Cartulaire du prieuré de La Charité-sur-Loire (Nièvre), ordre de Cluni*, ed. René de Lespinasse. Nevers, 1887.

LAON. 'Cartulaire de Saint-Vincent de Laon, analyse et pièces inédites', ed. René Poupardin, *MSHPIF*, xix (1902), 173–267.

LA RÉOLE. 'Cartulaire du prieuré de Saint-Pierre de La Réole', ed. Charles Grellet-Balguerie, *Archives historiques de la Gironde*, v (1863).

LIMOGES. 'Sancti Stephani cartularium', ed. Jacques de Font-Réaulx, *Bulletin de la Société archéologique et historique du Limousin*, lxix (1922), 5–258.

LIMOUSIN. 'Chartes du Limousin antérieures au XIIIe siècle', ed. Alfred Leroux, *Bulletin de la Société des lettres, sciences et arts de la Corrèze*, xxii (1900), 204–46.

LONGPONT. *Le Cartulaire du prieuré de Notre-Dame de Longpont de l'ordre de Cluny, au diocèse de Paris*, ed. (anonymously) Jules Marion. Lyon, 1880.

LONGUEVILLE. *Chartes du prieuré de Longueville de l'ordre de Cluny au diocèse de Rouen antérieures à 1204*, ed. Paul Le Cacheux. Rouen–Paris: Société de l'histoire de Normandie, 1934.

MÂCON. *Cartulaire de Saint-Vincent de Mâcon connu sous le nom de Livre Enchaîné*, ed. Camille Ragut. Mâcon, 1864.

MAGUELONE. *Cartulaire de Maguelone*, ed. J.-B. Rouquette and Augustin Villemagne, 7 vols. Montpellier, 1912–24.

MARMOUTIER. *Cartulaire de Marmoutier pour le Dunois*, ed. Émile Mabille. Châteaudun, 1874.

—— *Marmoutier. Cartulaire blésois*, ed. Charles Métais. Blois, 1889–91.

MÊVES-SUR-LOIRE. 'Titres du prieuré de Mêves-sur-Loire (XIIe, XVIIIe siècles)', ed. René de Lespinasse, *BSN*, 3rd ser., vii (1899), 171–232.

MONTPELLIER. *Liber instrumentorum memorialium. Cartulaire des Guillems de Montpellier*, ed. Alexandre Germain. Montpellier, 1884–6.

MORES. 'Chartes de l'abbaye de Mores (Aube)', ed. Charles Lalore, *MSAA*, xxxvii (1873), 5–107.

MORIGNY. *Cartularium abbatiae Morigniacensis prope Stampas*, ed. Ernest Menault, ... *Morigny: son abbaye, sa chronique et son cartulaire suivis de l'histoire du doyenné d'Étampes*. Paris, 1867.

MORLAAS. *Cartulaire de Sainte Foi de Morlaas*, ed. Léon Cadier. Pau, 1884.

NEVERS. *Cartulaire de Saint-Cyr de Nevers*, ed. René de Lespinasse. Nevers–Paris, 1916.

—— 'Les chartes de Saint-Étienne de Nevers', ed. René de Lespinasse, *BSN*, 3rd ser., xii (1908), 51–130.

NÎMES. *Cartulaire du chapitre de l'église cathédrale Notre-Dame de Nîmes*, ed. Eugène Germer-Durand. Nîmes, 1874.

NOUAILLÉ. 'Chartes de l'abbaye de Nouaillé de 678 à 1200', ed. P. G. de Monsabert, *AHP*, xlix (1936).

ORLÉANS. *Cartulaire de l'église cathédrale Sainte-Croix d'Orléans (814–1300) contenant le* Chartularium ecclesiae Aurelianensis vetus ... , ed. Joseph Thillier and Eugène Jarry. Paris: *MSAHO*, xxx, 1906.

—— *Cartulaire du chapitre de Saint-Avit d'Orléans (1112–1418)*, ed. Gaston Vignat. Orléans: *Collection des cartulaires du Loiret*, ii. 1886.

OURSCAMP. 'Cartulaire de l'abbaye de N.-D. d'Ourscamp, de l'ordre de Cîteaux, fondé en 1129 au diocèse de Noyon', ed. Achille Peigné-Delacourt, *MSAP*, *Documents inédits* ... , vi (1865).

PARACLET. *Cartulaire de l'abbaye du Paraclet*, ed. Charles Lalore. Paris: *CCDT*, ii, 1878.

PARIS. *Cartulaire de l'église Notre-Dame de Paris*, ed. Benjamin Guérard, 4 vols. Paris, 1850.

—— *Recueil des chartes de l'abbaye de Saint-Germain-des-Prés des origines au début du XIIIe siècle*, ed. René Poupardin, 2 vols. Paris, 1909–32.

—— 'Recueil de chartes et documents de Saint-Martin-des-Champs, monastère parisien', ed. Joseph Depoin, *Archives de la France monastique*, xiii (1912), xvi (1913).

POBLET. *Cartulari de Poblet. Edició del manuscrit de Tarragona*, ed. Joan Pons i Marquès. Barcelona: IEC, 1938.

POITIERS. 'Cartulaire de l'abbaye de Saint-Cyprien de Poitiers', ed. Louis Rédet, *AHP*, iii (1874).

—— 'Cartulaire du prieuré de Saint-Nicolas de Poitiers', ed. Louis Rédet, *AHP*, i (1872).

POITOU. 'Chartes poitevines de l'abbaye de Saint-Florent près Saumur (de 833 à 1160 environ)', ed. Paul Marchegay, *AHP*, ii (1873).

PONTOISE. *Cartulaire de l'abbaye de Saint-Martin de Pontoise*, ed. Joseph Depoin. Pontoise: Société historique du Vexin, 1895–1901.

PROVINS. Carrière, Victor, *Histoire et cartulaire des Templiers de Provins avec une introduction sur les débuts du Temple en France*. Paris, 1919.

ROUEN. *Cartulaire de l'abbaye de la Sainte-Trinité du Mont de Rouen* ... , ed. Achille Deville, in *Cartulaire de l'abbaye de Saint-Bertin*, ed. Benjamin Guérard. Paris, 1840.

ROUSSILLON. *Cartulaire roussillonnais*, ed. Bernard Alart. Perpignan, 1880.

SAINT-GABRIEL. 'Actes inédits du XIe siècle. I.—Les plus anciennes chartes du prieuré de Saint-Gabriel (Calvados)', ed. Lucien Musset, *BSAN*, lii (1952–3), 117–53.

SAINT-JEAN-D'ANGÉLY. 'Le cartulaire de l'abbaye royale de Saint-Jean-d'Angély', ed. Georges Musset, *Archives historiques de la Saintonge et de l'Aunis*, xxx (1901), xxxiii (1903).

SAINT-MAIXENT. 'Chartes et documents pour servir à l'histoire de l'abbaye de Saint-Maixent', ed. Alfred Richard, *AHP*, xvi (1886), xviii (1886).

SAINT-QUENTIN. *Le Livre Rouge de l'Hôtel de Ville de Saint-Quentin*, ed. Henri Bouchot and Emmanuel Lemaire. Saint-Quentin, 1881.

SAINT-WANDRILLE. Lot, Ferdinand, *Études critiques sur l'abbaye de Saint-Wandrille*. Paris: *BEHE*, cciv, 1913.

SAINTES. *Cartulaire de l'abbaye royale de Notre-Dame de Saintes*, ed. P.-Th. Grasilier. Niort: *Cartulaires inédits de la Saintonge*, ii, 1871.

SANT CUGAT DEL VALLÈS. *Cartulario de 'Sant Cugat' del Vallés*, ed. José Rius Serra, 3 vols. Barcelona: CSIC, 1945–7.

SANTES CREUS. *El 'Llibre Blanch' de Santas Creus (cartulario del siglo XII)*, ed. Federico Udina Martorell. Barcelona: CSIC, 1947.

SÉLINCOURT. 'Le cartulaire de l'abbaye de Sélincourt (1131–1513)', ed. Georges Beaurain, *MSAP*, xl (1925).

SOISSONS. 'Cartulaire de l'abbaye de Saint-Léger de Soissons (1076–1666)', ed. L.-V. Pêcheur, *BSS*, 2nd ser., ii (1870), 183–396.

TALMOND. 'Cartulaire de l'abbaye de Talmond', ed. Louis de la Boutetière, *Mémoires de la Société des antiquaires de l'Ouest*, xxxvi (1872), 41–498.

TAVERNOLES. *El cartulario de Tavernoles*, ed. Josefina Soler Garcia. Castellón de la Plana, 1964.

TEMPLARS. 'Los Templarios de la Corona de Aragón. Índice de su cartulario del siglo XIII', *BRAH*, xxxii (1898), 451–63; xxxiii (1898), 90–105.

THENAILLES. Piette, Amadée, 'Histoire de l'abbaye de Thenailles (ordre de Prémontré)', *BSS*, 2nd ser., vii (*recte* viii, 1878), 17–241.

TINSELVE. 'Cartulaire de Tinselve', ed. L.-V. Pêcheur, *BSS*. 2nd ser., v (1875), 212–46.

TOULOUSE. 'Le cartulaire du consulat: édition critique', ed. Roger Limouzin-Lamothe, *La Commune de Toulouse et les sources de son histoire (1120–1249)* ... Toulouse–Paris, 1932.

TROYES. *Cartulaire de l'abbaye de Saint-Loup de Troyes*, ed. Charles Lalore. Paris: *CCDT*, i, 1875.

VENDÔME. *Cartulaire de l'abbaye cardinale de la Trinité de Vendôme* ..., ed. Charles Métais, 5 vols. Paris, 1893–1904.

YONNE. *Cartulaire général de l'Yonne* ..., ed. Maximilien Quantin, 2 vols. Auxerre, 1854–60.

ZARAGOZA. *Colección diplomática del concejo de Zaragoza*, ed. Angel Canellas Lopez, 2 vols. Zaragoza, 1972.

B. *Other Collections, Narratives, and Literary Sources*

Achard de Saint-Victor, *Sermons inédits. Texte latin* ..., ed. Jean Chatillon. Paris: *Textes philosophiques du Moyen Âge*, xvii, 1970.

Actes des comtes de Namur de la première race, 946–1196, ed. Félix Rousseau. Brussels, 1937.

Aiol. Chanson de geste, ed. Jacques Normand and Gaston Raynaud. Paris: *SATF*, iii, 1877.

(Alanus) 'Die Dekretalensammlungen des Gilbertus und Alanus nach den Wein-
gartener Handschriften', *ZRG Kan.*, xxix (1940), 116–357.
Anonymum S. Martialis chronicon . . . , ed. Henri Duplès-Agier, *Chroniques de
Saint-Martial de Limoges.* Paris: SHF, 1874, pp. 172–83.
Archives anciennes de la ville de Saint-Quentin . . ., ed. Emmanuel Lemaire, 2 vols.
Saint-Quentin, 1888–1910.
El Archivo condal de Barcelona en los siglos IX–X. Estudio crítico de sus fondos, ed.
Federico Udina Martorell. Barcelona: CSIC, 1951.
Aucassin et Nicolette. Chantefable du XIIIe siècle, ed. Mario Roques, 2nd edn.
Paris: *CFMA,* xli, 1954.
'Avis sur la question monétaire donnés aux rois Philippe le Hardi, Philippe le Bel,
Louis X et Charles le Bel', ed. Paul Guilhiermoz, *RN,* 4th ser., xxv (1922), 73–
80, 173–210 (series continued in later vols. of *RN*).
Aymeri de Narbonne. Chanson de geste, ed. Louis Demaison, 2 vols. Paris: *SATF,* i,
1887.
(Azo) *Brocardica sive generalia iuris D. Azonis* . . . Basel, 1567.
Breve chronicon Autissiodorense, in *HF,* x. 270; xi. 292; xii. 299–300.
Bullaire de l'église de Maguelone, ed. J.-B. Rouquette and Augustin Villemagne,
2 vols. Montpellier, 1911–14.
*Cahors: inventaire raisonné & analytique des archives municipales. Première partie,
XIIIe siècle (1200–1300),* ed. Edmond Albe. Cahors, n.d.
Capitularia regum Francorum, ed. Alfred Boretius and Victor Krause, 2 vols.
Hanover: *MGH, Legum Sectio II,* 1883–97.
Carmina Burana . . . , ed. Alfons Hilka and Otto Schumann, 3 parts in 2 vols.
Heidelberg, 1930–41.
Cartas de población y franquicia de Cataluña, ed. J. M. Font Rius, 1 vol. in 2 parts.
Madrid–Barcelona: CSIC, 1969.
Cassiodorus, *Variae,* ed. Theodor Mommsen. Berlin: *MGH, Auctores Anti-
quissimi,* xii, 1894.
Catalogue des actes de Philippe-Auguste . . . , ed. Léopold Delisle. Paris, 1856.
Catalogue des actes des archevêques de Bourges, antérieures à l'an 1210, ed. Alfred
Gandilhon. Bourges–Paris, 1927.
La Chanson de Roland, ed. Frederick Whitehead, 2nd edn. Oxford, 1946.
Le Charroi de Nîmes. Chanson de geste du XIIe siècle, ed. J.-L. Perrier. Paris: *CFMA,*
lxvi, 1968.
Chartes de commune et d'affranchissement en Bourgogne, ed. J. F. Garnier, 4 vols.
Dijon, 1867–1918.
Chartes des libertés anglaises (1100–1305), ed. Charles Bémont. Paris, 1892.
Chartes du Bourbonnais, 918–1522, ed. Jacques Monicat and Bernard de Fournoux.
Moulins, 1952.
Chronicon anonymi Laudunensis canonici, HF, xiii. 677–83; xviii. 702–20.
Chronicon Barcinonense, ed. Henrique Florez, *España sagrada* . . . , xxviii (1794),
331–6.
Chronicon (Barcinonense) de rebus alibi notis, VL, viii. 230–3.
Chronicon Briocense, ed. Hyacinthe Morice, *Mémoires pour servir de preuves à
l'histoire ecclésiastique et civile de Bretagne* . . . , 3 vols. Paris, 1742–6, i. 7–102.
Chronicon Rivipullense, VL, v. 241–9.
Chronicon Rotomagense, HF, xxiii. 331–43.
Chronicon sancti Maxentii Pictavensis, ed. Paul Marchegay and Émile Mabille,
Chroniques des églises d'Anjou. Paris: SHF, 1869, pp. 349–433.

(Cid) *Cantar de mio Cid. Texto, gramática y vocabulario*, ed. Ramón Menéndez Pidal, 3 vols. Madrid, 1908–11.

Clarius, *Chronicon sancti Petri Vivi Senonensis* . . . , ed. Luc d'Achery *et al.*, *Spicilegium* . . . (q.v.), ii. 463–86.

Lo Codi in der lateinischen Übersetzung des Ricardus Pisanus, ed. Hermann Fitting. Halle, 1906.

Colección diplomática de Pedro I de Aragón y Navarra, ed. Antonio Ubieto Arteta. Zaragoza: CSIC, 1951.

'Commentarios a los privilegios dados por Alfonso II el Casto a la ciudad de Lérida', texts ed. Concepción Pérez Pérez, *VII Congreso de Historia de la Corona de Aragón*, 3 vols. Barcelona, 1962, ii. 247–54.

Le Compte général de 1187, connu sous le nom de 'Gros Brief', et les institutions financières du comté de Flandre au XIIe siècle, ed. Adrien Verhulst and Maurits Gysseling. Brussels, 1962.

'Compte général des revenus tant ordinaires qu'extraordinaires du Roi pendant l'an 1202', ed. Nicholas Brussel, *Nouvel Examen* . . . *des fiefs* (q.v.), ii. cxxxix–ccx.

Conciliorum oecumenicorum decreta, ed. Josephus Alberigo *et al.*, 3rd edn. Bologna, 1973.

Cortebarbe, *Les Trois Aveugles de Compiègne. Fabliau du XIIIe siècle*, ed. Georges Gougenheim. Paris: *CFMA*, lxxii, 1932.

Córtes de los antiguos reinos de Aragón y de Valencia y principado de Cataluña, 26 vols. Madrid, 1896–1920.

Córtes de los antiguos reinos de León y Castilla, 5 vols. Madrid: Real Academia de Historia, 1861–1903.

'Cortes y Usajes de Barcelona en 1064.—Textos inéditos', ed. Fidel Fita, *BRAH*, xvii (1890), 385–428.

Le Couronnement de Louis. Chanson de geste du XIIe siècle, ed. Ernest Langlois, 2nd edn. Paris: *CFMA*, xxii, 1966.

Courtois d'Arras. Jeu du XIIIe siècle, ed. Edmond Faral, 2nd edn. Paris: *CFMA*, iii, 1967.

Decretum magistri Gratiani, ed. Aemilius Friedberg. Leipzig, 1879. Also in glossed edn., Lyon, 1525.

La Documentación pontificia hasta Inocencio III (965–1216), ed. Demetrio Mansilla. Rome: Instituto Español de Estudios Ecclesiasticos, 1955.

Documentos de Jaime I de Aragón, ed. Ambrosio Huici Miranda and María Desamparados Cabanes Pecourt, 2 vols. to date. Valencia, *Textos medievales*, xlix-l, 1976.

'Documentos para el estudio de la numismática navarro-aragonesa medieval (1.a serie)', ed. Antonio Ubieto Arteta, *PSANA*, i (1951), 113–35; '. . . (2.a serie)', *PSANA*, ii (1953), 85–102; '. . . (3.a serie)', *Caesaraugusta*, v (1954), 147–59.

'Documentos para el estudio de la reconquista y repoblación del Valle del Ebro (primera serie)', ed. J. M. Lacarra, *EEMCA*, ii (1946), 469–576.

'Documents pour servir à la généalogie des anciens seigneurs de Traînel', ed. Charles Lalore, *MSAA*, xxxiv (1870), 177–273.

Domesday Book, 2 vols. London: Record Commission, 1783.

Droits et privilèges de la commune de Nevers, ed. Henri Crouzet. Nevers, 1858.

Eneas, ed. J.-J. Salverda de Grave, 2 vols. Paris: *CFMA*, xliv, lxii, 1925–9.

Epistolae pontificum Romanorum ineditae, ed. Samuel Loewenfeld. Leipzig, 1885.

Die Epitome exactis regibus mit Anhängen und einer Einleitung. Studien zur Geschichte des römischen Rechts im Mittelalter, ed. Max Conrat (Cohn). Berlin, 1884.

España sagrada . . . , ed. Henrique Florez *et al.*, 58 vols. Madrid, 1747–1918.

(Folquet de Marseille) *Le Troubadour Folquet de Marseille. Édition critique* . . . , ed. Stanisław Stroński. Cracow, 1910.
Fragmentum de Petragoricensibus episcopis . . . , ed. Philippe Labbé (q.v.), *Novae bibliothecae* . . . *tomus secundus*, 737–40.
El Fuero de Jaca, ed. Mauricio Molho. Zaragoza: CSIC, 1964.
Los Fueros de Aragón según el manuscrito 458 de la Biblioteca nacional de Madrid, ed. Gunnar Tilander. Lund, 1937.
Fueros, observancias y actos de corte del reino de Aragón, ed. Pascual Savall y Dronda and Santiago Penén y Debesa, 2 vols. Zaragoza, 1866.
Gallia christiana . . . , 16 vols. Paris, 1715–1865.
(Gautier d'Arras) *Ille et Galeran par Gautier d'Arras*, ed. F. A. G. Cowper. Paris: *SATF*, lxxxviii, 1956.
(Gautier de Châtillon) *Moralisch-satirische Gedichte Walters von Châtillon* . . . , ed. Karl Strecker. Heidelberg, 1929.
Die Gesetze der Angelsachsen, ed. Felix Liebermann, 3 vols. Halle, 1903–16.
Gesta abbatum S. Germani Autissiodorensis, *HF*, x. 296; xi. 377; xii. 306–7.
Gesta comitum Barcinonensium, textos llatí i català, ed. Louis Barrau Dihigo and J. J. Massó Torrents. Barcelona: IEC, 1925.
Gesta pontificum Autissiodorensium, ed. L.-M. Duru, *Bibliothèque historique de l'Yonne* . . . , 2 vols. Auxerre, 1850–63, i. 309–509.
Girart de Roussillon. Chanson de geste, ed. W. Mary Hackett, 3 vols. Paris: *SATF*, lxxxvii, 1953–5.
La Grande Charte de Saint-Gaudens (Haute-Garonne). Texte gascon du XIIe siècle . . . , ed. S. Mondon. Paris, 1910.
Guibert de Nogent, *Histoire de sa vie (1053–1124)*, ed. Georges Bourgin. Paris, 1907; tr. C. C. Swinton Bland, revised by J. F. Benton, *Self and Society in Medieval France. The Memoirs of Abbot Guibert of Nogent (1064?–c. 1125)*. New York, 1970.
(Guilhem IX) *Les Chansons de Guillaume IX, duc d'Aquitaine (1071–1127)*, ed. Alfred Jeanroy, 2nd edn. Paris: *CFMA*, ix, 1927.
Guillaume de Puylaurens, *Chronique*, ed. Jean Duvernoy. Paris: *Sources d'histoire médiéval*, 1976.
(Guillem de Tudela) *La Chanson de la croisade albigeoise*, ed. Eugène Martin-Chabot, 3 vols. Paris, 1931–61, i (2nd edn., 1960).
(Hostiensis) *Henrici de Segusio cardinalis Hostiensis* . . . *in [quinque] decretalium [libros] commentaria*, 2 vols. Venice, 1581.
Hugues de Poitiers, *Historia Vizeliacensis monasterii*, ed. Luc d'Achery, *Spicilegium*, 2nd edn., ii. 498–560.
Humberti cardinalis libri III. adversus simoniacos, ed. Friedrich Thaner, *Libelli de lite* . . . , 3 vols. Hanover: *MGH*, 1891–7.
Huon de Bordeaux, ed. Pierre Ruelle. Brussels–Paris, 1960.
Innocentii III Romani pontificis opera omnia, ed. J.-P. Migne, *PL*, ccxiv–ccxvii, 1891.
(Innocent IV) . . . *In v. libros decretalium commentaria*. Venice, 1570.
Inventaire des titres de Nevers de l'Abbé de Marolles . . . , ed. Georges de Soultrait. Nevers, 1873.
Isidori Hispalensis episcopi etymologiarum sive originum libri XX, ed. W. M. Lindsay. Oxford, 1911.
Jean Bodel, trouvère artésien du XIIIe siècle. Le jeu de Saint Nicolas, ed. Alfred Jeanroy. Paris: *CFMA*, xlviii, 1925.
Jongleurs et trouvères, ou choix de saluts, épitres, rêveries et autres pièces légères des XIIIe et XIVe siècles . . . , ed. Achille Jubinal. Paris, 1835.

Julien de Vézelay, *Sermons*, ed. Damien Vorreux, 2 vols. Paris: *Sources chrétiennes*, cxcii, cxciii, 1972.

Jurisdiccions i privilegis de la ciutat de Vich, ed. Eduard Junyent. Vich, 1969.

(Labbé) *Novae bibliothecae manuscript[orum] librorum, tomus primus [secundus]* ..., ed. Philippe Labbé, 2 vols. Paris, 1657.

Lambert de Waterlos, *Annales Cameracenses*, ed. G. H. Pertz, *MGH, Scriptores*, xvi (Hanover, 1859), 509–54.

Lateinische Sprichwörter und Sinnsprüche des Mittelalters aus Handschriften gesammelt, ed. Jacob Werner. Heidelberg, 1912.

Laurentii gesta episcoporum Virdunensium et abbatum S. Vitoni, ed. Georg Waitz, *MGH, Scriptores*, x (1852), 486–525.

Leges Visigothorum, ed. Karl Zeumer, Hanover–Leipzig: *MGH, Legum Sectio I*, 1902.

Libre dels feyts, ed. Ferran Soldevila, *Jaume I, Bernat Desclot, Ramon Muntaner, Pere III. Les quatre grans cròniques*. Barcelona, 1971.

Magni rotuli scaccarii Normanniae sub regibus Angliae, ed. Thomas Stapleton, 2 vols. London, 1840–4.

(Marie de France) *Les Lais de Marie de France*, ed. Jean Rychner. Paris: *CFMA*, xciii, 1966.

Miracula S. Marculfi, Acta sanctorum ..., 70 vols. Antwerp–Brussels–Paris, 1643–1940. Mai, vii. 531–9.

Miscellaneous Records of the Norman Exchequer, 1199–1204, ed. S. R. Packard. Northampton, Mass.: *Smith College Studies in History*, xii, 1927.

Monuments historiques: cartons des rois ..., ed. Jules Tardif. Paris, 1866.

Orderici Vitalis Angligenae, coenobii Uticensis monachi, historiae ecclesiasticae libri tredecim ..., ed. Auguste Le Prevost, 5 vols. Paris, 1838–55.

Ordonnances des roys de France de la troisième race, 22 vols. Paris, 1723–1849.

PU Frankreich. v. Berry, Bourbonnais, Nivernais und Auxerrois, ed. Wilhelm Wiederhold. Berlin: *Nachrichten von der königlichen Gesellschaft der Wissenschaften zu Göttingen, philologisch-historische Klasse*, 1910.

PU Frankreich. Neue Folge. ii. *Normandie*, ed. Johannes Ramackers. Göttingen: *Abh.*, 3rd ser., xxi, 1937.

PU Frankreich. iv. *Picardie*, ed. Johannes Ramackers. Göttingen: *Abh.*, 3rd ser., xxvii, 1942.

PU Spanien. Vorarbeiten zur Hispania pontificia. i. *Katalanien*, ed. Paul Kehr. Göttingen: *Abh.*, neue Folge, xviii, 1926. ii. *Navarra und Aragon*, ed. Paul Kehr. Göttingen: *Abh.*, neue Folge, xx, 1928.

(Peter of Blois) *Petri Blesensis Bathoniensis in Anglia archidiaconi opera omnia, PL*, xxvii, Paris, 1855.

Pierre le Chantre, *Summa de sacramentis et animae consiliis*, ed. Jean-Albert Dugauquier. Louvain–Lille: *Analecta medievalia Namurcensia*, iv, vii, xi, xvi, xxi, 1954–67.

Pierre des Vaux-de-Cernay, *Hystoria albigensis*, ed. Pascal Guébin and Ernest Lyon, 3 vols. Paris, 1926–30.

Pilii Medicinensis quaestiones sabbatinae, ed. Ugo Nicolini. Modena, 1935.

Les Plus Anciennes Chartes en langue provençale. Recueil des pièces originales antérieures au XIIe siècle, ed. Clovis Brunel. Paris, 1926.

Le Premier Registre de Philippe-Auguste: reproduction héliotypique du manuscrit du Vatican, ed. Léopold Delisle. Paris, 1883.

'Le privilège de Saint-Omer de 1127', ed. Georges Espinas, *Revue du Nord*, xxix (1947), 43–8.

Privilèges et titres relatifs aux franchises, institutions et propriétés communales de Roussillon et de Cerdagne depuis le XIe siècle jusqu'à l'an 1660. Ière partie, ed. Bernard Alart. Perpignan, 1874.

Privilegis i ordinacions de les valls pirenenques, ed. Ferran Valls Taberner, 3 vols. Barcelona, 1915–20.

(Ptolemy of Lucca) *Divi Thomae Aquinatis doctoris angelici opuscula philosophica*, ed. R. M. Spiazzi. Rome, 1954.

Quaestiones dominorum Bononiensium. Collectio Gratianopolitana, ed. G. B. Palmieri, *Scripta anecdota glossatorum*, 2nd edn., 3 vols. and *Additiones*. Bologna, 1892–1914, i. 209–42.

Quaestiones dominorum Bononiensium. Collectio Parisiensis, ed. G. B. Palmieri, *Scripta anecdota* . . . , i, 2nd edn., 235–66.

Quinque compilationes antiquae nec non Collectio canonum Lipsiensis . . . , ed. Aemilius Friedberg. Leipzig, 1882.

(Ramon de Penyafort) *Summa Sti. Raymundi de Peniafort Barcinonensis ord. praedicator. de poenitentia et matrimonio cum glossis Ioannis de Friburgo* . . . Rome, 1603.

Raoul de Cambrai. Chanson de geste, ed. Paul Meyer and Auguste Longnon. Paris: *SATF*, xliv, 1882.

(Rashi) *Responsa of Rashi*, ed. Israel Elfenbein. New York, 1943.

(——) *Teshuvot ḥakhme Tsarefat ve-Loter*, ed. Joel Mueller. Vienna, 1881.

Recueil de documents inédits concernant la Picardie publiés d'après les titres originaux conservés dans son cabinet, ed. Victor Beauvillé, 4 vols. and supplement. Paris, 1860–82.

Recueil de documents relatifs à l'histoire des monnaies frappées par les rois de France depuis Philippe II jusqu'à Francois Ier, ed. Félibien de Saulcy, 4 vols. Paris, 1879–92.

Recueil de documents relatifs à l'histoire du droit municipal en France des origines à la Révolution. Artois, ed. Georges Espinas, 3 vols. Paris, 1934–43.

'Recueil de documents relatifs à l'histoire monétaire', ed. Maurice Prou, *RN*, 3rd ser., xiv (1896), 283–305; 4th ser., i (1897), 174–91.

Recueil des actes de Henri II, roi d'Angleterre et duc de Normandie, concernant les provinces françaises et les affaires de France, ed. Léopold Delisle and Élie Berger, introduction and 3 vols. Paris, 1909–27.

Recueil des actes de Philippe Ier, roi de France (1059–1108), ed. Maurice Prou. Paris, 1908.

Recueil des actes de Philippe Auguste, roi de France, ed. H.-F. Delaborde, Charles Petit-Dutaillis, Jacques Monicat, and Jacques Boussard, 3 vols. to date. Paris, 1916–66.

Recueil des actes des comtes de Pontieu (1026–1279), ed. Clovis Brunel. Paris, 1930.

Recueil des actes des ducs de Normandie de 911 à 1066, ed. Marie Fauroux. Caen: *MSAN*, xxxvi, 1961.

Recueil général et complet des fabliaux des XIIIe et XIVe siècles . . . , ed. Anatole de Montaiglon and Gaston Raynard, 6 vols. Paris, 1872–90.

(Rigord) *Œuvres de Rigord et de Guillaume le Breton*, ed. H.-Fr. Delaborde, 2 vols. Paris: SHF, 1882–5.

(Robert de Courçon) *Le Traité 'De Usura', de Robert de Courçon*, ed. Georges Lefèvre. Lille: *Travaux & Mémoires de l'Université de Lille*, x, no. 30, 1902.

(Robert de Torigni) *Chronique de Robert de Torigni . . . suivie de divers opuscules historiques de cet auteur* . . . , ed. Léopold Delisle, 2 vols. Rouen: Société de l'Histoire de Normandie, 1872–3.

Spicilegium, sive collectio veterum aliquot scriptorum . . . , ed. Luc d'Achery, 2nd edn. by Étienne Baluze and Edmond Martène, 3 vols. Paris, 1723.

(Suger) *Vie de Louis le Gros par Suger, suivie de l'Histoire du roi Louis VII*, ed. Auguste Molinier. Paris, 1887.

Summa de legibus Normannie in curia laicali, ed. E.-J. Tardif, *Coutumiers de Normandie, textes critiques*, 3 parts in 2 vols. Rouen–Paris, 1881–1903, ii.

Le 'Te Igitur', ed. Paul Lacombe and Louis Combarieu. Cahors, 1874.

'Un texte inédit du XIIe siècle sur l'atelier monétaire de Toulouse', ed. Georges Boyer, *Annales de la Faculté de Droit d'Aix*, new ser., no. 43 (1950), 37–45.

Thesaurus novus anecdotorum, ed. Edmond Martène and Ursin Durand, 5 vols. Paris, 1717.

Travaux pratiques d'une conférence de paléographie à l'Institut catholique de Toulouse, ed. Célestin Douais. Toulouse–Paris, 1892.

Le Très Ancien Coutumier de Normandie, ed. E.-J. Tardif, *Coutumiers de Normandie* (see *Summa de legibus*), i:1.

Usatges de Barcelona, ed. Ramon d'Abadal i Vinyals and Ferràn Valls Taberner. Barcelona: *Textes de Dret català*, i, 1913.

Veterum scriptorum et monumentorum historicorum, dogmaticorum, moralium amplissima collectio, ed. Edmond Martène and Ursin Durand, 9 vols. Paris, 1724–33.

La Vie de Saint Alexis. Poème du XIe siècle, ed. Gaston Paris, 5th edn. Paris: *CFMA*, iv, 1933.

Wistasse le Moine. Altfranzösischer Abenteurroman des XIII. Jahrhunderts . . . , ed. Wendelin Foerster and Johann Trost. Halle: *Romanische Bibliothek*, iv, 1891.

3. SECONDARY WORKS

Abadal i de Vinyals, Ramon d', *L'Abat Oliba, bisbe de Vic, i la seva època*, 3rd edn. Barcelona, 1962.

Altisent, Agustí, 'Notícies socials i econòmiques de Montblanc, la Guàrdia dels Prats i la Riba, pels voltants del 1200, en els documents de Poblet', *VIII Assemblea intercomarcal d'estudiosos: Montblanc, 1966*. Montblanc, 1967, pp. 49–65.

—— 'Un poble de la Catalunya nova en els segles XI i XII. L'Espluga de Francolí de 1079 a 1200', *AEM*, iii (1966), 131–213.

Anselme de Sainte Marie, Pierre de Guibours, *Histoire généalogique et chronologique de la maison royale de France, des pairs, grands officiers de la Couronne* . . . , 3rd edn., 9 vols. Paris, 1726–33.

Arbois de Jubainville, Henri d', *Histoire des ducs et des comtes de Champagne*, 6 vols. in 7. Paris, 1859–67.

Arco, Ricardo del, 'Archivos históricos del Alto Aragón', reprint from *Universidad: Revista de Cultura y Vida universitaria* (Zaragoza, 1929).

—— *Huesca en el siglo XII (Notas documentales)*. Huesca, 1921.

Asso y del Rio, Ignacio, *Historia de la economía política de Aragón*. Zaragoza, 1798; new edn. José Manuel Casas Torres, Zaragoza: CSIC, 1947.

Babelon, Ernest, 'La théorie féodale de la monnaie', *Mémoires de l'Institut national de France: Académie des inscriptions et belles-lettres*, xxxviii:1 (1909), 279–347.

Balari y Jovany, José, *Orígenes históricos de Cataluña*. Barcelona, 1899; 2nd edn., 3 vols. Barcelona, 1964.

Baldwin, J. W., *Masters, Princes and Merchants: The Social Views of Peter the Chanter and his Circle*, 2 vols. Princeton, N.J., 1970.

Barthélemy, Anatole de, 'Essai sur la monnaie parisis', *MSHPIF*, ii (1876), 142–71.

Barthélemy, Anatole de, 'Explication de quelques monnaies baronales inédites. Troisième article', *RN*, xi (1846), 285–94.

—— 'Monnaie', in Arbois de Jubainville, *Histoire des ducs et des comtes de Champagne*, iv:2 (1865), 759–88.

—— 'Notice sur les monnaies ducales de Bourgogne (Première race, 1031–1361)', in Petit, *Histoire des ducs de Bourgogne* (q.v.), v (1894), 339–60.

Bautier, Robert, 'Les foires de Champagne. Recherches sur une évolution historique', *La Foire (Recueils de la Société Jean Bodin*, v, Brussels, 1953), 97–145.

Beltrán Villagrasa, Pío, 'Los dineros jaqueses, su evolución y su desaparición', *PSANA*, i (1951), 51–112.

Belz, Gustav, 'Die Münzbezeichnungen in der altfranzösischen Literatur', diss., Strasbourg, 1914.

Benton, J. F., 'The Revenue of Louis VII', *Speculum*, xlii (1967), 84–91.

Bernier, Jean, *Histoire de Blois contenant les antiquitez & singularitez du Comté de Blois* . . . Paris, 1682.

Bimbenet, Eugène, 'Examen critique de la charte octroyée par le roi Loius VII aux habitants d'Orléans, en l'année 1137', *Mémoires de la Société d'agriculture, des sciences, et des belles-lettres et arts d'Orléans*, 2nd ser., xvi (1874), 67–98.

Bisson, T. N., *Assemblies and Representation in Languedoc in the Thirteenth Century*. Princeton, N.J., 1964.

—— '*Confirmatio monete* à Narbonne au XIIIe siècle', *Narbonne. Archéologie et histoire*, 3 vols. Montpellier, 1973, ii. 55–9.

—— 'An Early Provincial Assembly: The General Court of Agenais in the Thirteenth Century', *Speculum*, xxxvi (1961), 254–81.

—— ' "Quanto personam tuam" (*X* 2. 24. 18): Its Original Significance', *Proceedings of the Fourth International Congress of Medieval Canon Law, Toronto, 21–25 August 1972* (Vatican City, 1976), pp. 229–49.

—— 'Sur les origines du *monedatge*: quelques textes inédits', *Annales du Midi*, lxxxv (1973), 91–104.

—— 'An "Unknown Charter" for Catalonia (A.D. 1205)', *Album Elemér Mályusz; Székesfehérvár-Budapest, 1972* (Brussels: *Études présentées à la Commission internationale pour l'histoire des assemblées d'États*, lvi, 1976), 61–76.

Blanchet, J.-Adrien, *Histoire monétaire du Béarn*. Paris, 1893.

—— and Dieudonné, Adolphe, *Manuel de numismatique française*, 4 vols. Paris, 1912–36.

Bloch, Marc, *Les Caractères originaux de l'histoire rurale française*, new edn. with supplementary volume compiled by Robert Dauvergne. Paris, 1955–6.

—— *Esquisse d'une histoire monétaire de l'Europe*. Paris: *Cahiers des Annales*, ix, 1954.

Bonnassie, Pierre, *La Catalogne du milieu du Xe à la fin du XIe siècle. Croissance et mutations d'une société*, 2 vols. Toulouse, 1975–6.

—— 'Une famille de la campagne barcelonaise et ses activités économiques aux alentours de l'An Mil', *Annales du Midi*, lxxvi (1964), 261–303.

Bonnaud-Delamare, Roger, 'Fondements des institutions de paix au XIe siècle', *Mélanges d'histoire du moyen âge dédiés à la mémoire de Louis Halphen*. Paris, 1951, pp. 19–26.

Bonnet, Émile, 'Des variations de valeur de la monnaie melgorienne', *Bulletin archéologique du Comité des travaux historiques et scientifiques* (1903), 490–514.

Borrelli de Serres, L. L., *Recherches sur divers services publics du XIIIe au XVIIe siècle*, 3 vols. Paris, 1895–1909.

Borrelli de Serres, L. L., *La Réunion des provinces septentrionales à la couronne par Philippe Auguste: Amiénois, Artois, Vermandois, Valois*. Paris, 1899.

Botet y Sisó, Joaquím, *Les Monedes catalanes. Estudi y descripció de les monedes carolingies, comtals, senyorials, reyals y locals propries de Catalunya*, 3 vols. Barcelona: IEC, 1908–11.

Bourgin, Georges, *La Commune de Soissons et le groupe communal soissonais*. Paris: BEHE, clxvii, 1908.

Bourquelot, Félix, 'Études sur les foires de Champagne, sur la nature, l'étendue et les règles du commerce qui s'y faisait aux XIIe, XIIIe et XIVe siècles', *Mémoires présentés par divers savants à l'Académie des inscriptions et belles-lettres* . . . , v (1865–6).

Boussard, Jacques, 'Le comté de Mortain au XIe siècle', *Le Moyen Âge*, lviii (1952), 253–79.

—— *Le Gouvernement d'Henri II Plantagenêt*. Paris, 1956.

—— 'La seigneurie de Bellême aux Xe et XIe siècles', *Mélanges d'histoire du moyen âge dédiés à la mémoire de Louis Halphen*. Paris, 1951, pp. 43–54.

Bridrey, Émile, 'Une page oubliée des Coutumiers normands. Le chapitre *De monnéage*', *BSAN*, xlviii (1940–1), 76–519.

—— *La Théorie de la monnaie au XIVe siècle. Nicole Oresme (Étude d'histoire des doctrines et des faits économiques)*. Paris, 1906.

Brooke, G. C., *English Coins*, 3rd edn., rev. C. A. Whitton. London, 1950.

—— ' "Quando moneta vertebatur": The Change of Coin-Types in the Eleventh Century, its Bearing on Mules and Overstrikes', *British Numismatic Journal*, xx (1929–30), 105–16.

Brussel, Nicolas, *Nouvel Examen de l'usage général des fiefs en France pendant les XIe, XIIe, XIIIe et XIVe siècles*, 2 vols. Paris, 1750.

Brutails, J.-A., *Étude sur la condition des populations rurales du Roussillon au moyen âge*. Paris, 1891.

Buisson, Ludwig, *Potestas und Caritas. Die päpstliche Gewalt im Spätmittelalter*. Cologne, 1958.

Bur, Michel, 'Remarques sur les plus anciens documents concernant les foires de Champagne', *Les Villes. Contribution à l'étude de leur développement en fonction de l'évolution économique*. Reims: *Publications de l'Université de Reims, Faculté des Lettres* . . . , iii (1972), pp. 45–60.

Carlet, Auguste, 'Archéologie et histoire monétaire. Monnaies dijonnaises de la fin du XIIe siècle', *Annales de Bourgogne*, xi (1939), 24–30.

Caron, Émile, 'Essai de classification des monnaies de Louis VI et Louis VII', *Annuaire de la Société française de numismatique*, xviii (1894), 249–75.

—— *Monnaies féodales françaises*. Paris, 1882.

Cartellieri, Alexander, *Philipp II. August, König von Frankreich*, 5 vols. Leipzig, 1899–1922.

Cartier, Étienne, 'Lettres sur l'histoire monétaire de France. IX. Monnaies baronales', *RN*, vi (1841), 256–84.

—— 'Recherches sur les monnaies au type chartrain . . . Septième article', *RN*, xi (1846), 28–55.

Caruana, Jaime, 'Itinerario de Alfonso II de Aragón', *EEMCA*, vii (1962), 73–298.

Castaing-Sicard, Mireille, *Monnaies féodales et circulation monétaire en Languedoc (Xe–XIIIe siècles)*. Toulouse, 1961.

Cazel, F. A., Jr., 'The Tax of 1185 in Aid of the Holy Land', *Speculum*, xxx (1955), 385–92.

Chalande, J.-F., 'Monnaies baronales & épiscopales de la province de Languedoc', *HL*, vii (1879), 388–418.

Chapin, Elizabeth, *Les Villes de foires de Champagne des origines au début du XIVe siècle.* Paris: *BEHE*, cclxviii, 1937.

Chédeville, André, *Chartres et ses campagnes (XIe–XIIIe siècles).* Paris, 1973.

Chenu, Paul, 'De la circulation des monnaies féodales dans les territoires qui ont formé le Département du Cher, aux XIe, XIIe et XIIIe siècles', *Mémoires de la Fédération des Sociétés savantes du Centre* (1940).

Cipolla, Carlo, 'Currency Depreciation in Medieval Europe', *EcHR*, 2nd ser., xv (1963), 414–22.

—— *Money, Prices and Civilization in the Mediterranean World, Fifth to Seventeenth Century.* Princeton, N.J., 1956.

Colson, Achille, 'Recherches sur les monnaies qui ont eu cours en Roussillon', *Société agricole, scientifique et littéraire des Pyrénées-Orientales*, ix (1854), 29–260.

Costa y Bafarull, Domingo, *Memorias de la ciudad de Solsona y su iglesia*, 2 vols. Barcelona, 1959.

Delisle, Léopold, *Études sur la condition de la classe agricole et l'état de l'agriculture en Normandie au moyen âge*, Paris, 1903.

—— 'Mémoire sur les opérations financières des Templiers', *Mémoires de l'Institut national de France: Académie des inscriptions et belles-lettres*, xxxiii (1889), 1–248.

—— 'Des revenus publics en Normandie au douzième siècle', *BEC*, x (1848-9), 173–210, 257–89; xi (1949), 400–51; xiii (1851-2), 97–135.

Deloye, Augustin, 'Des chartes lapidaires en France', *BEC*, viii (1840), 31–42.

Dessalles, Léon, *Histoire du Périgord*, ed. G. A. J. Escande, 3 vols. Périgueux, 1883-5.

Devailly, Guy, *Le Berry du Xe siècle au milieu du XIIIe. Étude politique, religieuse, sociale et économique.* Paris–La Haye, 1973.

Dieudonné, Adolphe (see also Blanchet), *Catalogue des monnaies françaises de la Bibliothèque nationale. Les monnaies capétiennes ou royales françaises. 1ère section (De Hugues Capet à la réforme de Saint Louis).* Paris, 1923.

—— 'Les conditions du denier parisis et du denier tournois sous les premiers capétiens', *BEC*, lxxxi (1920), 45–60.

—— 'Histoire monétaire du denier parisis jusqu'à Saint Louis', *MSAF*, lxxi (1911), 111–47.

—— 'Les lois générales de la numismatique féodale', *RN*, 4th ser., xxxvi (1933), 155–70.

—— 'Le melgorien. Exemple de variations de monnaie médiévale', *RN*, 4th ser., xxxv (1932), 31–5.

—— 'La numismatique normande. Les monnaies féodales', *BSAN*, xxxvi (1927), 301–8.

Doehaerd, Renée, 'Un paradoxe géographique: Laon, capitale du vin au XII siècle', *Annales: Économies-Sociétés-Civilisations*, v (1950), 145–65.

Dolley, R. H. M., *Anglo-Saxon Pennies.* London, 1964.

—— *The Norman Conquest and the English Coinage.* London, 1966.

Douët-d'Arcq, L.-C., 'Recherches historiques et critiques sur les anciens comtes de Beaumont-sur-Oise, du XIe au XIIIe siècle avec une carte du comté', *MSAP Documents inédits . . .* , iv, 1855.

Douglas, D. C., *William the Conqueror: The Norman Impact upon England.* London–Berkeley, Calif., 1964.

Du Bouchet, Jean, *Histoire généalogique de la maison royale de Courtenay* . . . Paris, 1661.

Duby, Georges, 'Économie domaniale et économie monétaire : le budget de l'abbaye de Cluny entre 1080 et 1155', *Annales* . . . , vii (1952), 155–71.

—— *L'Économie rurale et la vie des campagnes dans l'Occident médiéval*, 2 vols. Paris, 1962; tr. Cynthia Postan, *Rural Economy and Country Life in the Medieval West*. London, 1968.

—— *Guerriers et paysans, VIIe–XIIe siècle. Premier essor de l'économie européenne*. Paris, 1973; tr. H. B. Clarke, *The Early Growth of the European Economy* . . . , London, 1974.

—— *La société aux XIe et XIIe siècles dans la région mâconnaise*. Paris, 1953; 2nd edn., Paris, 1971.

Du Cange, Charles Dufresne, *Glossarium ad scriptores mediae et infimae latinitatis*, 3 vols. Paris, 1678; re-ed. C. A. L. Henschel, 7 vols. Paris, 1840–50.

Dumas-Dubourg, Françoise, 'Le début de l'époque féodale en France d'après les monnaies', *Cercle d'études numismatiques, Bulletin*, x (1973), 65–77.

—— *Le Trésor de Fécamp et le monnayage en France occidentale pendant la seconde moitié du Xe siècle*. Paris, 1971.

Dupré, Alexandre, 'Étude sur les institutions municipales de Blois', *MSAHO*, xiv (1875), 441–550.

Endemann, Wilhelm, *Studien in der romanisch-kanonistischen Wirtschafts- und Rechtslehre bis gegen Ende des 17. Jahrhunderts*, 2 vols. Berlin, 1883.

Engel, Arthur, and Serrure, Raymond, *Traité de numismatique du moyen âge*, 3 vols. Paris, 1891–1905.

Engels, Odilo, 'Die weltliche Herrschaft des Bischofs von Ausona-Vich (889–1315)', *Gesammelte Aufsätze zur Kulturgeschichte Spaniens*, xxiv (Münster, 1968), 1–40.

Erdmann, Carl, *Das Papsttum und Portugal im ersten Jahrhundert der portugiesischen Geschichte*. Berlin: *Abhandlungen der preussischen Akademie der Wissenschaften*, 1928.

Espinas, Georges, *La Vie urbaine de Douai au Moyen Âge*, 4 vols. Paris, 1913.

Fabrège, Frédéric, *Histoire de Maguelone*, 2 vols. Paris–Montpellier, 1894–1900.

Fleureau, Basile, *Les Antiquitez de la ville, et du duché d'Estampes* . . . Paris, 1683.

Font Rius, J. M., *Orígenes del régimen municipal de Cataluña*. Madrid, 1946.

Fontette, François de, *Recherches sur la pratique de la vente immobilière dans la région parisienne au moyen âge (fin Xe–début XIVe siècle)*. Paris, 1957.

Fossier, Robert, *La Terre et les hommes en Picardie jusqu'à la fin du XIIIe siècle*, 2 vols. Paris, 1968.

Fournial, Étienne, *Les Villes et l'économie d'échange en Forez aux XIIIe et XIVe siècles*. Paris, 1967.

Friedensburg, Ferdinand, *Die Münze in der Kulturgeschichte*, 2nd edn. Berlin, 1926.

Garcia, Arcadi, 'Orígens del mercat de Vich', *Ausa*, v (1964–7), 129–34.

García de Valdeavellano, Luis, *Historia de España. i. De los orígenes a la baja Edad Media*, 5th edn. in 2 parts. Madrid, 1973.

Gasparri, Françoise, 'Études sur l'écriture de la chancellerie royale française de Louis VI à Philippe Auguste d'après vingt-cinq actes originaux jusqu'ici inconnus', *BEC*, cxxvi (1968), 297–331.

Gautier-Dalché, Jean, 'L'histoire monétaire de l'Espagne septentrionale et centrale du XIe et XIIe siècles: quelques réflexions sur divers problèmes', *AEM*, vi (1969), 43–95.

Germain, Alexandre, 'Étude historique sur les comtes de Maguelone, de Sub-stantion et de Melgueil', *MSAM*, iii (1850–4), 523–640.

—— 'Mémoire sur les anciennes monnaies seigneuriales de Melgueil et de Mont-pellier', *MSAM*, iii (1850–4), 123–255.

Ghyssens, Joseph, *Les Petits Deniers de Flandre des XIIe et XIIIe siècles*. Brussels, 1971.

Gil Farrés, Octavio, 'The Billon Dineros of Barcelona. Their Origin, Evolution and End', *Seaby's Coin and Medal Bulletin* (1957), pp. 192–8, 290–4, 338–42, 389–92, 426–9, 468–71.

—— 'Consideraciones acerca de las primitivas cecas navarras y aragonesas', *Numa-rio hispánico*, iv (1955), 5–37.

—— *Historia de la moneda española*. Madrid, 1959.

Gilchrist, John, *The Church and Economic Activity in the Middle Ages*. London–New York, 1969.

Giry, Arthur, *Étude sur les origines de la commune de Saint-Quentin*, in *Archives anciennes . . . de St-Quentin*, ed. Lemaire (q.v.).

—— *Histoire de la ville de Saint-Omer et de ses institutions jusqu'au XIVe siècle*. Paris: *BEHE*, xxxi, 1877.

—— *Manuel de diplomatique . . .* Paris, 1894.

Grierson, Philip, 'Mint Output in the Tenth Century', *EcHR*, 2nd ser., ix (1957), 462–6.

—— 'Money and Coinage under Charlemagne', *Karl der Grosse: Lebenswerk und Nachleben*, ed. Wolfgang Braunfels, 4 vols. Düsseldorf, 1965–7, i. 501–36.

—— 'Numismatics and the Historian', *NC*, 7th ser., ii (1962), i–xiv.

—— 'The Roman Law of Counterfeiting', *Essays in Roman Coinage presented to Harold Mattingly*, ed. R. A. G. Carson and C. H. Sutherland. Oxford, 1956, pp. 240–61.

Gudiol i Cunill, Joseph, *Les Monedes episcopals vigatanes*. Vich, 1896.

Guilhiermoz, Paul, 'De la taille du denier dans le haut moyen âge', *BEC*, lxxxiv (1923), 265–83.

—— 'Note sur les poids du moyen âge', *BEC*, lxvii (1906), 160–233, 402–50.

—— 'Remarques diverses sur les poids et mesures du moyen âge', *BEC*, lxxx (1919), 5–100.

—— and Dieudonné, Adolphe, 'Chronologie des documents monétaires de la numismatique royale des origines à 1330 et 1337', *RN*, 4th ser., xxxiii (1930), 85–118, 233–54.

Guillot, Olivier, *Le Comte d'Anjou et son entourage au XIe siècle*, 2 vols. Paris, 1972.

Halphen, Louis, *Paris sous les premiers capétiens (987–1223): Étude de topographie historique*. Paris, 1909.

Harmand, Auguste, 'Notice historique sur la léproserie de la ville de Troyes . . .', *MSAA*, xiv (1848), 429–680.

Haskins, C. H., *Norman Institutions*. Cambridge, Mass., 1918.

Heiss, Aloïss, *Descripción general de las monedas hispano-cristianas desde la invasión de los Árabes*, 3 vols. Madrid, 1865–9.

Herde, Peter, 'Römisches und kanonisches Recht bei der Verfolgung des Fäl-schungsdelikts im Mittelalter', *Traditio*, xxi (1965), 291–362.

Higounet, Charles, 'Mouvements de population dans le Midi de la France du XIe au XVe siècle d'après les noms de personne et de lieu', *Annales . . .*, viii (1953), 1–24.

Hinojosa, Eduardo de, *El régimen señorial y la cuestión agraria en Cataluña durante la edad media*. Madrid, 1905.

Hoffmann, Hartmut, *Gottesfriede und Treuga Dei*. Stuttgart: *MGH, Schriften*, xx, 1964.

Holmes, Urban T., Jr., 'Coins of Old French Literature', *Speculum*, xxxi (1956), 316–20.

Huesca, Ramón de, *Teatro histórico de las iglesias del reyno de Aragón*, with Lamberto de Zaragoza, 9 vols. Pamplona, 1780–1807.

Johanneau, Éloi, *Mémoire sur deux inscriptions latines de la ville de Blois, du XIe et du XIIe siècle*. Blois, 1840.

Kehr, Paul, *Das Papsttum und die Königreiche Navarra und Aragon bis zur Mitte des XII. Jahrhunderts*. Berlin: *Abhandlungen der preussischen Akademie der Wissenschaften*, 1928; tr. into Castilian by Ma. Luisa Vázquez de Parga, *EEMCA*, ii (1946), 74–186.

Kieft, C. van de, *Étude sur le chartrier et la seigneurie du prieuré de la Chapelle-Aude (XIe–XIIIe siècle)*. Amsterdam, 1960.

Kuttner, Stephan, 'Bernardus Compostellanus Antiquus. A Study in the Glossators of the Canon Law', *Traditio*, i (1943), 277–340.

—— *Repertorium der Kanonistik (1140–1234). Prodromus corporis glossarum*, i. Vatican City: *Studi e Testi*, lxxi, 1937.

Labande, L.-H., *Histoire de Beauvais et de ses institutions communales jusqu'au commencement du XVe siècle*. Paris, 1892.

Lacarra, J. M., ' "Honores" et "tenencias" en Aragon (XIe siècle)', *Structures*, pp. 143–74.

Lacoste, Guillaume, *Histoire générale de la province de Quercy*, 2nd edn. by Louis Combarieu and François Cangardel, 4 vols. Paris, 1968.

Lacroix, Guillaume de, *Series & acta episcoporum cadurcensium* . . . Cahors, 1617.

Lafaurie, Jean, *Les Monnaies des rois de France*. i. *Hugues Capet à Louis XII*. Paris, 1951.

(La Lande, Jacques de) *Coutume d'Orléans commentée par Monsieur de La Lande, ancien conseiller au Présidial, et Professeur en Droit à Orléans* . . . , 2nd edn., 2 vols. Orléans, 1704.

Lavoix, Henri, *Catalogue des monnaies musulmanes de la Bibliothèque nationale*. ii. *Espagne et Afrique*. Paris, 1891.

Lebeuf, Jean, *Mémoires concernant l'histoire civile et ecclésiastique d'Auxerre et son ancien diocèse* . . . , original edn., 1743; ed. Ambroise Challe and Maximilien Quantin, 4 vols. Auxerre, 1848–55.

Le Blanc, François, *Traité historique des monnoyes de France*. Paris, 1690.

Lecaron, Frédéric, 'Les origines de la municipalité parisienne', *MSHPIF*, vii (1880), 79–174.

Lecointre-Dupont, Gabriel, *Lettres sur l'histoire monétaire de la Normandie et du Perche*. Paris, 1846.

Ledesma Rubio, María Luisa, *La Encomienda de Zaragoza de la Orden de San Juan de Jerusalen en los siglos XII y XIII*. Zaragoza, 1967.

Lefranc, Abel, *Histoire de la ville de Noyon et de ses institutions jusqu'à la fin du XIIIe siècle*. Paris: *BEHE*, lxxv, 1887.

Legrand, Maxime, 'Essai sur les monnaies d'Étampes', *RN*, 4th ser., xvi (1912), 236–67, 390–409.

Leineweber, Johannes, 'Studien zur Geschichte Papst Cölestins III.', diss. Jena, 1905.

Lemarignier, J.-F., *Le Gouvernement royal aux premiers temps capétiens (987–1108)*. Paris, 1965.

Lemarignier, J.-F., *Recherches sur l'hommage en marche et les frontières féodales.* Lille: *Travaux et mémoires de l'Université de Lille,* new ser., *Droit et lettres,* xxiv, 1945.

Le Patourel, John, *The Norman Empire.* Oxford, 1976.

Lépinois, Eugène de Buchère de, 'Recherches historiques et critiques sur l'ancien comté et les comtes de Clermont-en-Beauvoisis, du XIe au XIIIe siècle', *MSO,* x:1, 1877.

Lespinasse, René de, *Le Nivernais et les comtes de Nevers,* 2 vols. Paris, 1909–11.

Limouzin-Lamothe, Roger (see *Cartularies . . .* TOULOUSE).

Little, L. K., 'Pride Goes before Avarice: Social Change and the Vices in Latin Christendom', *American Historical Review,* lxxvi (1971), 16–49.

Lladonosa i Pujol, Josep, *Història de Lleida,* i. Tàrrega, 1972.

—— 'Marchands toulousains à Lérida aux XIIe et XIIIe siècles', *Annales du Midi,* lxx (1958), 223–30.

Lluis y Navas Brusi, Jaime, 'Le droit monétaire dans la région de Vich pendant la reconquête espagnole: essai sur les traditions carolingiennes en relation avec les tendances géopolitiques de l'Espagne pendant le moyen âge', *RN,* 5th ser., xviii (1956), 209–32.

—— (with collaboration of Salvador Clotet Madico), 'La moneda "nova" barcelonesa de Alfonso I', *Numario hispánico,* x (1961), 123–6.

Longpérier, Adrien de, 'Recherches sur les monnoies de Meaux', *RN,* v (1840), 128–53.

Lopez, R. S., 'Continuità e addattamento nel medio evo: un millenio di storia delle associazioni di monetieri nell'Europa meridionale', *Studi in onore di Gino Luzzato,* 4 vols. Milan, 1949–50, ii. 74–117.

—— 'An Aristocracy of Money in the Early Middle Ages', *Speculum,* xxviii (1953), 1–43.

Lot, Ferdinand, 'L'état des paroisses et des feux en 1328', *BEC,* xc (1929), 51–107, 256–315.

—— and Fawtier, Robert, *Histoire des institutions françaises au moyen âge,* 3 vols. to date. Paris, 1957–62.

—— —— *Le Premier Budget de la monarchie française: le Compte général de 1202–1203.* Paris: *BEHE,* cclix, 1932.

Luchaire, Achille, *Études sur les actes de Louis VII.* Paris, 1885.

—— *Histoire des institutions monarchiques de la France sous les premiers capétiens (987–1180),* 2nd edn., 2 vols. Paris, 1891.

—— *Louis VI le Gros. Annales de sa vie et de son règne (1081–1137).* Paris, 1890.

Luneau, Victor, 'Deniers normands inédits du XIe siècle', *RN,* 4th ser., x (1906), 306–16.

—— 'Quelques deniers normands inédits du XIe siècle: nouvelle trouvaille', *RN,* 4th ser., xv (1911), 86–96.

Mabillon, Jean, *De re diplomatica . . .* Paris, 1681.

Magnou-Nortier, Élisabeth, 'Fidélité et féodalité méridionales d'après les serments de fidélité (Xe–début XIIe siècle)', *Structures,* pp. 116–35.

Manneville, Ch.-A.-A. de, 'De l'état des terres et des personnes dans la paroisse d'Amblainville (Vexin français) du XIIe au XVe siècle', *MSO,* xiii:2 (1887), 451–570; xiii:3 (1888), 761–810; xiv:1 (1889), 119–218; xiv:2 (1890), 478–549.

Marca, Petrus de, *Marca hispanica sive limes hispanicus, hoc est, geographica & historica descriptio Cataloniae, Ruscinonis, & circumjacentium populorum . . . ,* ed. Étienne Baluze. Paris, 1688.

—— *Histoire de Béarn.* Paris, 1640.

Mas, Joseph, *Notes històriques del bisbat de Barcelona*, 12 vols. Barcelona, 1906–15.

Mateu y Llopis, Felipe, *La moneda española (breve historia monetaria de España)*. Barcelona, 1946.

—— '"Super monetatico o morabetino" (Breve noticia documental sobre el impuesto del monedaje en Aragón, Cataluña, Valencia, Mallorca y Murcia) (1205–1327)', *Mélanges offerts à René Crozet* . . . , ed. Pierre Gallais and Y.-J. Riou, 2 vols. Poitiers, 1966, ii. 1115–20.

Menéndez Pidal, Ramón, *El Imperio hispánico y los cinco reinos. Dos épocas en la estructura política de España*. Madrid, 1950.

Miret y Sans, Joaquím, *Les Cases de Templers y Hospitalers en Catalunya aplech de noves y documents històrichs*. Barcelona, 1910.

—— 'Los ciutadans de Barcelona en 1148', *BRABLB*, ix (1921), 137–40.

—— 'Itinerario del rey Pedro I de Cataluña, II en Aragón (1196–1213)', *BRABLB*, iii (1905–6), 79–87, 151–60, 238–49, 265–84, 365–87, 435–50, 497–519; iv (1907–8), 15–36, 91–114.

—— 'Pro sermone plebeico', *BRABLB*, vii (1913), 30–41, 101–15, 163–85, 229–51, 275–80.

—— 'Los vescomtes de Cerdanya, Conflent y Bergadà', *MRABLB*, viii (1901), 115–75.

Molinier, Auguste, 'Étude sur l'administration féodale dans le Languedoc (900–1250)', *HL*, vii (1879), 132–213.

Mollat, Michel, 'Le problème de la pauvreté au XIIe siècle', *Vaudois languedociens et Pauvres Catholiques*. Toulouse: *Cahiers de Fanjeaux*, ii (1967), 23–47.

(Moncada, Juan Luís de) *Episcopologio de Vich escrito a mediados del siglo XVII por el Deán D. Juan Luís de Moncada*, ed. Jaime Collell, 3 vols. Vich, 1891–1904.

Monsalvatje y Fossas, Francisco, *Noticias históricas*, 26 vols. Olot, 1889–1919.

Mor, C. G., 'En torno a la formación del texto de los "Usatici Barchinonae"', *AHDE*, xxvii–xxviii (1957–8), 413–59.

Mundy, J. H., *Liberty and Political Power in Toulouse, 1050–1230*. New York, 1954.

Musset, Lucien, 'A-t-il existé en Normandie au XIe siècle une aristocratie d'argent? Une enquête sommaire sur l'argent comme moyen d'ascension sociale', *Annales de Normandie*, ix (1959), 285–99.

—— 'Recherches sur quelques survivances de la fiscalité ducale', *BSAN*, lv (1959–60), 1–29.

—— 'Sur les mutations de la monnaie ducale normande au XIe siècle: deux documents inédits', *RN*, 6th ser., xi (1969), 291–3.

—— 'La vie économique de l'abbaye de Fécamp sous l'abbatiat de Jean de Ravenne, 1028–1078', *L'Abbaye bénédictine de Fécamp. Ouvrage scientifique du XIIIe centenaire, 658–1958*, 3 vols. and tables. Fécamp, 1959–63, i. 67–79, 345–9.

Newman, W. M., *Le Domaine royal sous les premiers capétiens (987–1180)*. Paris, 1937.

—— *Les Seigneurs de Nesle en Picardie (XIIe–XIIIe siècle). Leurs chartes et leur histoire*, 2 vols. Philadelphia–Paris, 1971.

Niermeyer, J. F., *Mediae latinitatis lexicon minus*, 11 fascicules (of 12) to date. Leiden, 1954–64.

Noonan, J. T., Jr., *The Scholastic Analysis of Usury*. Cambridge, Mass., 1957.

Oman, Charles, *The Coinage of England*. Oxford, 1931.

Pacaut, Marcel, *Louis VII et son royaume*. Paris, 1964.

Petit, Ernest, *Histoire des ducs de Bourgogne de la race capétienne avec des documents inédits et des pièces justificatives*, 9 vols. Dijon, 1885–1905.

Petit-Dutaillis, Charles. *Les Communes françaises. Caractères et évolution des origines au XVIIIe siècle*. Paris, 1947.

Pierfitte, Georges, 'Monnaies des comtes de Toulouse', *RN*, 4th ser., xxxviii (1935), 47–65.

Plancher, Urbain, *Histoire générale et particulière de Bourgogne, avec des notes, des dissertations et les preuves justificatives . . .*, 4 vols. Dijon, 1739–81.

Poey d'Avant, Faustin, *Monnaies féodales de France*, 3 vols. Paris, 1858–62.

Powicke, F. M., *The Loss of Normandy, 1189–1204. Studies in the History of the Angevin Empire*, 2nd edn. Manchester, 1961.

Procter, E. S., 'The Development of the Catalan *Corts* in the Thirteenth Century', *Homenatge a Antoni Rubió i Lluch . . .*, 3 vols. Barcelona, 1936, iii. 525–46.

Prou, Maurice, *Catalogue des monnaies françaises de la Bibliothèque nationale: les monnaies carolingiennes*. Paris, 1896.

——— 'Esquisse de la politique monétaire des rois de France du Xe au XIIIe siècle', *Entre Camarades*. Paris: Société des Anciens Élèves de la Faculté des lettres de l'Université de Paris (1901), 77–86.

——— 'Essai sur l'histoire monétaire de l'abbaye de Corbie', *MSAF*, lv (1895), 55–92.

——— 'Essai sur l'histoire monétaire de Beauvais à propos d'un denier de l'évêque Philippe de Dreux', *MSAF*, lvi (1897), 61–82.

Quantin, Maximilien, 'Note sur une trouvaille de monnaies du moyen-âge faite à Accolay', *Bulletin de la Société des sciences historiques et naturelles de l'Yonne*, xxxix (1885), 226–33.

Richard, Alfred, *Histoire des comtes de Poitou, 778–1204*, 2 vols. Paris, 1903.

Richard, Jean, *Les Ducs de Bourgogne et la formation du duché du XIe au XIVe siècle*. Paris, 1954.

Richebé, Claude, *Les Monnaies féodales d'Artois du Xe au début du XIVe siècle*. Paris, 1963.

Riquer, Martín de, 'La littérature provençale à la cour d'Alphonse II d'Aragon', *Cahiers de civilisation médiévale*, ii (1959), 177–201.

Rolland, Henri, *Monnaies des comtes de Provence, XIIe–XVe siècles. Histoire monétaire, économique et corporative, description raisonnée*. Paris, 1956.

Rovira i Virgili, Antonio, *Història nacional de Catalunya*, 7 vols. Barcelona, 1922–34.

Russell, J. C., 'The Medieval Monedatge of Aragon and Valencia', *Proceedings of the American Philosophical Society*, cvi (1962), 483–504.

Säbekow, Gerhard, 'Die päpstlichen Legationen nach Spanien und Portugal bis zum Ausgang des XII. Jahrhunderts', diss. Berlin, 1931.

Salat, Josef, *Tratado de las monedas labradas en el principado de Cataluña, con instrumentos justificativos . . .*, 2 vols. Barcelona. 1818.

Sánchez-Albornoz, Claudio, *La curia regia portuguesa. Siglos XII y XIII*. Madrid, 1920.

——— 'Devaluación monetaria en León y Castilla al filo del 1200?' *Homenaje a Jaime Vicens Vives*, 2 vols. Barcelona, 1965, i. 607–17.

——— 'La primitiva organización monetaria de León y Castilla', *AHDE*, v (1928), 301–45.

Sarriau, Henri, 'Numismatique nivernaise', *BSN*, 3rd ser., vi (1896), 1–152.

Schlumberger, Gustave, *Description des monnaies, jetons & médailles du Béarn*. Paris, 1893.

Schneider, Jean, *La Ville de Metz aux XIIIe et XIVe siècles*. Nancy, 1950.

Serrure, Raymond, 'L'atelier monétaire de Châlons-sur-Marne', *Bulletin de numismatique*, viii (1900), 22–8.

Setton, K. M., ed., *A History of the Crusades*, 2nd edn., 4 vols. to date. Madison, Wis., 1969–77.
Sobrequés Vidal, Santiago, *Els grans comtes de Barcelona*. Barcelona, 1961.
Soldevila, Ferràn, *Història de Catalunya*, 2nd edn. Barcelona, 1963.
—— *Els Primers Temps de Jaume I*. Barcelona: IEC, 1968.
—— 'A propòsit del servei del bovatge', *AEM*, i (1964), 573–87.
Soultrait, Georges de, *Dictionnaire topographique du département de la Nièvre*. Paris, 1865.
—— *Essai sur la numismatique nivernaise*. Paris, 1854.
Spufford, Peter, 'Assemblies of Estates, Taxation and Control of Coinage in Medieval Europe', *XIIe Congrès international des sciences historiques*. Louvain–Paris: *Études présentées à la Commission internationale pour l'histoire des assemblées d'États*, xxxi (1966), 113–30.
Stephenson, Carl, *Borough and Town: A Study of Urban Origins in England*. Cambridge, Mass., 1933.
—— *Mediaeval Institutions: Selected Essays*, ed. B. D. Lyon. Ithaca, N.Y., 1954.
Strayer, J. R., *The Royal Domain in the Bailliage of Rouen*. Princeton, N.J., 1936.
—— and Taylor, C. H., *Studies in Early French Taxation*. Cambridge, Mass., 1939.
Suchodolski, Stanisław, '*Renovatio monetae* in Poland in the 12th Century', *Polish Numismatic News* (1961), 57–75.
Taeuber, Walter, 'Geld und Kredit im Dekret Gratians und bei den Dekretisten', *Studia Gratiana*, ii (1954), 443–64.
—— *Geld und Kredit im Mittelalter*. Berlin, 1933.
Tessier, Georges, *Diplomatique royale française*. Paris, 1962.
Tourneur, Victor, 'Le monnayage dans les villes de Flandre et de Brabant au XIIe siècle et au XIIIe', *Académie royale de Belgique, Bulletin de la Classe des lettres* . . . , 5th ser., xxvi (1940), 34–49.
Tropamer, Henry, *La Coutume d'Agen* . . . Bordeaux, 1911.
Udina Martorell, Federico, 'Una moneda inédita de Cervera', *Numisma*, iii (1953), 31–40.
Usher, A. P., *The Early History of Deposit Banking in Mediterranean Europe*, i. Cambridge, Mass., 1943.
Valin, Lucien, *Le Duc de Normandie et sa cour (912–1204): étude d'histoire juridique*. Paris, 1910.
Valls Taberner, Ferràn, 'Carta constitucional de Ramon Berenguer I (vers 1060)', *Obras selectas de Fernando Valls-Taberner*, 4 vols. in 6 tomes. Madrid–Barcelona, 1952–61, ii. 55–62.
—— 'La cour comtale barcelonaise', *RHDFE*, xiv (1935), 662–82, reprinted in *Obras selectas*, ii. 258–75.
—— 'Ein Konzil zu Lerida im Jahre 1155', *Papsttum und Kaisertum: Forschungen zur politischen Geschichte . . . Paul Kehr zum 65. Geburtstag dargebracht*, ed. Albert Brackmann. Munich, 1926, pp. 364–8.
—— 'La primera dinastia vescomtal de Cardona', *Obras selectas* . . . , iv. 207–15.
—— *San Ramón de Penyafort*, in *Obras selectas* . . . , i:2.
Veissière, Michel, *Une communauté canoniale au Moyen Âge. Saint-Quiriace de Provins (XIe–XIIIe siècles)*. Provins, 1961.
Vincke, Johannes, *Staat und Kirche in Katalonien und Aragon während des Mittelalters*. 1. Teil. Münster: *Spanische Forschungen der Görresgesellschaft*, 2nd ser., i, 1931.

Vuitry, Adolphe, *Les Monnaies et le régime monétaire de la monarchie féodale de Hugues-Capet à Philippe-le-Bel (987–1285)* . . . Paris, 1876.

Werner, Joachim, 'Fernhandel und Naturalwirtschaft im östlichen Merowingerreich nach archäologischen und numismatischen Zeugnissen', *Moneta e scambi nell'alto medioevo.* Spoleto: *Settimane di Studio del Centro italiano di Studi sull'alto Medioevo,* viii (1961), 557–618.

Werner, K. F., 'Königtum und Fürstentum im französischen 12. Jahrhundert', *Probleme des 12. Jahrhunderts* . . . Stuttgart: *Vorträge und Forschungen,* xii (1968), pp. 177–225.

Wohlhaupter, Eugen, *Studien zur Rechtsgeschichte der Gottes- und Landfrieden in Spanien.* Heidelberg, 1933.

Wolff, Philippe, 'Le problème des cahorsins', *Annales du Midi,* lxii (1950), 229–38.

Zerbi, Piero, *Papato, impero e 'respublica christiana', dal 1187 al 1198.* Milan: *Pubblicazione dell'Università cattolica del S. Cuore,* new ser., lv, n.d. (1955).

Zurita y Castro, Gerónimo, *Anales de la Corona de Aragón,* 6 vols. Zaragoza, 1578–85; also 4 vols., 1668–70; new edn. by Antonio Ubieto Arteta *et al.,* 4 vols. to date, Valencia, 1967–72.

INDEX OF CHARTERS, DECRETALS, AND REGULATIONS PERTAINING TO COINAGE

864. Edict of Pîtres, 2, 5 n. 3.
986. Cardona, 57–8, 66, 189.
1020–3. England, 52.
1033. Vich, 52–3.
1047. Saintes, 5, 49–50.
1047–64. Dinant, 5–6, 197.
1056–66. Barcelona, 6.
c. 1070. Aquitaine, 45, 48–50, 112, 189, 192.
c. 1080. Corbie, 147, 150, 160.
1091. Normandy (*Consuetudines et iusticie*), 17–18, 33 n. 3.
1100. England, 15–16.
1101. Burgundy (confirmed 1177), 120–1.
1118. Cerdanya (*Cunctis pateat*, q.v., General Index).
c. 1120. Compiègne, 32–4, 44, 120.
1121. Melgueil, 65–6.
1125. Melgueil, 6 n. 6, 66–7, 69–74.
1127. Saint-Omer, 156, 159–60.
1128. Melgueil, 6 n. 6, 12, 69–71, 113.
1125–9. Melgueil, 71–3, 113.
1130. Melgueil, 6 n. 6, 69–73, 113.
1132. Melgueil, 73.
1137–8. Étampes, 29–31, 120, 129, 132–3, 160, 162, 190.
1138. Orléans, 29–31, 44, 89, 120, 129, 160, 162, 163 n. 2, 190.
c. 1140. Verdun, 157.
1146. Melgueil, 73.
c. 1060–1150. Catalonia (*Moneta autem*), 53–4, 58, 64, 66, 81 n. 1, 101, 117.
1151. Saint-Quentin (*Establissement* of), 147–9, 153, 200.
1155. Aragon–Catalonia, 81–2, 102–3.
1151–6. La Chapelaude, 158–60.
1165. Champagne, 131–3, 160, 162, 190, 192.
c. 1165. Blois, 126–30, 132, 160, 190, 192.
1173. Provence, 75 n. 1, 113, 191.
1174. Melgueil, 74, 91.
1174. Aragon, 75–7, 103, 113, 191.
1174. Vich, 77–81, 102–3, 106, 109, 113–14, 171, 190–1.
c. 1174. Barcelona, 76–8, 81, 87, 102, 113, 171, 191, 201.
1176. Vich, 80, 102.
1183. Orléans, 35, 36 n. 6, 37 n. 3, 141, 191.
1185. Burgundy, 121, 124, 160, 190–1.
1186–7. Bruyères (etc.), 155–6.
1186–7. Laonnais, 156–7.
1186–7. Ponthieu, 6 n. 6, 155.
1187. Burgundy (Dijon), 125–6, 141–2, 159–60, 190–3.
1188. Nevers (Corbigny), 120, 136–43, 160, 163, 190–1, 193, 201–2.
1190. Issoudun, 158.
1190. Melgueil, 106–7.
1191. *Cum utilitas publica*, 85, 104, 168, 190.
1191. Saint-Quentin (confirmed 1195), 149–51, 154, 159–61, 190, 193.
1197. Noyon, 152–4, 159, 190, 195, 202–3.
1197. Vich, 90, 114, 194.

1197. Jaca, 86–7, 101.
1199. *Quanto personam tuam*, 86–7, 104, 166–73, 190, 203–4.
1203. Beaune, 125–6, 159.
1204. Caen, 164,
1205. Catalonia (Girona), 88–91, 98, 102, 117.
1205. Aragon–Catalonia (Huesca), 84, 87–8, 90, 92–4, 96–8, 115, 194.
1205. Toulouse, 104–7, 112, 114, 190, 194.
1208. Champagne (renewed 1214), 134–5, 164, 193.
1210. Urgell (Agramunt), 102, 106, 113, 190.
c. 1205–10. Normandy (*De foagio*), 14–15, 18–19, 21 n. 2, 26–7, 162 n. 1, 204–5.
1211–12. Cahors, 108–14, 190, 194, 205–6.
1213. Barcelona, 101–2, 118.
1213. Berry, 158–9.
1214. Bourbon, 159.
1215. Beauvais, 151–2, 154, 159, 173, 190, 195.
1215. Melgueil, 118.
1218. Lérida, 114–15, 117, 190, 194–5.
1221. Barcelona, 118–19.
1221. Huesca, 114–15, 119, 190, 194–5.
1222. Toulouse, 112, 114, 190, 194 n. 1.
1223. Daroca, 114–15, 190, 194–5.
1224. Meaux, 134–5, 193.
1225. Champagne, 161, 193.
1225. Paris, 163.
?*c.* 1190–1225. Metz, 160–1.
1231. Auxerre, 143.
1232. Agenais, 112–13, 117, 190, 194–5.
1234. Agenais, 112, 117, 190, 194–5.
1236. Monzón, 114–16, 183, 190, 194–5.
c. 1250. Normandy (*De monetagio*), 14–15, 18–19, 25.
1253. Barcelona, 116, 194 n. 1.
1258. Barcelona, 116–17, 119.
1265. Narbonne, 113, 194.

GENERAL INDEX

The main abbreviations are: abp. = archbishop; abt. = abbot; ar. = *arrondissement*; Aug. = Augustinian canons regular; Ben. = Benedictine (abbey, if not further specified); bp. = bishop; c. = coin(s), coinage(s), or, in place-names, *canton*; ch.-l. = *chef-lieu*; Cist. = Cistercian (abbey, if not further specified); Cl. = Cluniac; ct. = count; ctess. = countess; cty. = county; dép. = *département*; p.j. = *partido* (or *partit*) *judicial*; Prem. = Premonstratensian; vct. = viscount; vcty. = viscounty. In locations, the *département* or *provincia* is indicated before the *arrondissement*, *canton*, or *partit judicial* (see, e.g., Argentan). With few exceptions, cross-references to proper names are given in regional listings (e.g. Vermandois) only for persons mentioned simply by title in the text (e.g. bishops of Meaux; *see* Meaux). Modern scholars are indexed only for opinions or assistance.

Abadal i de Vinyals, Ramon d', 54 n. 1.
Abbeville (Somme, ch.-l. ar.), c. of, 152 n. 3, 154 n. 2; moneyers of, 154 n. 2.
abuse of coins, coinage, 113, 118, 168, 180. *See also* fraud, mutation of c.
Accolay (Yonne, ar. Auxerre, c. Vermenton), hoard of, 138 n. 6.
accounts, accounting, 83, 94–5, 100, 143, 155; of c. of Barcelona, 100, 118, 195; of Flanders, 155; of France (royal, 1202–3), 35 n. 1, 36, 39–40, 42–3, 163 n. 4, 164 n. 2; of Lérida, 85 n.
Adam the clerk, 164 n. 1.
administration, *see* coinage.
aestimatio, *see* 'estimation'.
Agen (Lot-et-Garonne, ch.-l. dép.), bps. (Géraud, Raoul), c., citizens, customs, diocese of, 117. *See also* confirmation(s) of c. (in Agenais).
Agenais, *see* confirmation(s) of c., general courts, money-taxes.
Agnès, ctess. of Nevers and Auxerre: her confirmation-charter (1188), 136–44, 201–2.
Agonac (*Castrum Agoniacum*: Dordogne, ar. Périgueux, c. Brantôme), 48 n. 5.
Agramunt (Lérida, p.j. Balaguer), 106; c. of, 102.
aids, 26, 140, 183; of crusade, 141–2. *See also* tallage, taxation.
Aisne valley, 141.
Alanus, 172.
Albéron, bp. of Verdun: his monetary decree (c. 1140), 157.
Albi-Bonafos (Albi: Tarn, ch.-l. dép.), c. of, 55 n. 2.
Aldebert II, ct. of Périgord: his monetary policy, 48.
Alençon (Orne, ch.-l. dép.), 19–20, 205.
Alençonnais, 19 n. 2, 205.
Alexander III, pope, 103 n. 3.

Alfons-Jordan, ct. of Toulouse: confirms c. of Melgueil (c. 1132), 73.
Aliénor, ctess. of Vermandois: her charter for Saint-Quentin (1191–2), 149–50; c. of, xix.
Alix, ctess. of Blois: her charter (c. 1165), 126–30.
alloy, viii, 33, 75, 80–1, 126, 138, 143, 153, 156, 187, 196; diversity of, 6, 24, 100 n. 5, 175; mutation of, 7, 32 n. 2, 38, 67, 85, 152–3, 182; of mark, 87. *See also* confirmation(s) of c., value(s) (of c.).
Al-Mansur, 57, 63.
Almenêches (*castrum de Aumenesche*: Orne, ar. Argentan, c. Mortrée), 19 n. 2, 205.
Almorávides, 68.
Alphonse I, k. of Aragon: c. of, xviii.
Alphonse II (I in Catalonia), k. of Aragon, ct. of Barcelona (etc.), 80 n. 5, 89, 91, 92 n. 2, 97–104, 106–7, 110, 113; his c.: in Aragon, xvii, 8, 75–6, 81–2, 84–7, 167–8, 170–1, 203–4; in Catalonia, xviii, 76–8, 81–2, 87, 98–9; his draft confirmation in Catalonia, 76–8, 81, 102, 113, 171, 191, 201; his finance and politics, 77–8, 97–100; his recoinage in Aragon (1174), 75–7, 103, 113, 191.
Alphonse VII, k. of Castile and Leon, emperor, 81–2, 103.
Alphonse VIII, k. of Castile, 82–3, 86 n. 1, 203–4.
Alphonse IX, k. of Leon: sells c. (1202), 93.
amends, 5, 9, 109, 126, 141 n. 2.
Amiens (Somme, ch.-l. dép.), c. of, 10, 145–6, 147 n. 1, 154; cty. of, 145; moneyers at, 154 n. 2; mutations of c. at, 8, 146, 154.
Andeli (Les Andelys: Eure, ch.-l. ar.), manor of, 26.
angevins, *see* Anjou, c. of.
Anglo-Saxon minting, *see* England.
Angoulême (Charente, ch.-l. dép.), c. of, xvi, 49.

Anjou, 4; c. of (*angevins*), 20, 24–5, 49, 145; cts. of, 25, 50 n. 1.

Anseau, bp. of Meaux, 134.

Anseau de Traînel, butler, 131, 132 n., 162.

anxiety, fears: about coinage, *see* stability of coinage; about value of rents, 151.

appeals, *see* petitions.

Aquitaine, c. and regulations of c. in, 45, 48–50, 112, 189; d. or duchy of, 45, 48–50, 52, 55–6, 192; economic conditions in, 48–50. *See also* confirmation(s) of c., Guilhem VII, mutation of c.

Aragon, barons, churches, *infançones* of, 86, 101, 114; c. of, vii, xvii, xviii, 8, 75–8, 81–7, 93, 98, 101–4, 106–7, 167, 169–71; *fueros* of, 75, 116, 192; k. or kingdom of, vii, 8, 81, 83, 85, 99, 101–2, 104–7, 110, 112, 201; mines in, 99; mints in, 93; moneyers in, 48, 195; taxation, consent in, 92, 114. *See also* confirmations of c., general courts, Jaca (c. of), money-taxes, mutation of c.

archives, 64, 76, 127; lack of secular, 143 n. 8.

Argentan (Orne, ch.-l. ar.), 19 n. 2, 205.

Aristotle, 196.

Armagnac, great men of, 55.

Arnal, abp. of Narbonne: papal deputy, 70.

Arnal de Lérida, 110.

Arras (Pas-de-Calais, ch.-l. dép.), 145; c. of (*artisiens*), 145, 149 n. 2, 151 n. 2, 185; k.'s c. at, 145 n. 4. See also *Courtois*.

Artois, 144, 154. *See also* Arras, c. of.

assemblies, 21, 114–15, 129, 193–5; of confirmation of c., 31, 35, 51–2, 79, 102, 106, 109, 114–18, 121, 136–7; parliamentary or representative, 22, 197; of the peace, 53, 59, 111. *See also* consultation, general courts, representation.

Auberoche (*Alba Rocha*: Dordogne, ar. Sarlat, c. Montignac), 48 n. 5.

Ausona, 78. *See also* Vich.

Autun (Saône-et-Loire, ch.-l., ar.), 126 n. 3; canons of Saint-Nazaire of, 140 n. 1; c. of (*hyilenses*), 126 n. 3.

Auxerre (Yonne, ch.-l. dép.), bps. of, 135–7, 138 n. 5, 139–40, 143, 202; clergy, men of, 136–7, 140, 143–4; c., mint of, 137 n. 1, 138, 142–4; c. of Provins at, 143 n. 1; ct., cty. of, 143; disputes over c. at, 137 n. 1, 143; tithing at, 142 n. 5; wine-trade at, 144. *See also* Hugues IV, bp., Milon de Traînel, Saint-Germain, Saint-Marien.

avarice, 188.

Azo, 176.

Babelon, Ernest, 30 n. 1.

Bagneux (dép. Seine, ar. and c. Sceaux), 40 n. 3.

baillis, 15, 39; in Berry, 158; at Gisors, 25.

Baldwin, J. W., 182.

Bar (Bar-sur-Aube: Aube, ch.-l. ar.), fair of, 134.

Barcelona (provincial capital), bps. of, 98–9; citizens, merchants, vicar of, 64, 118–19; c. of, xvi–xviii, 6–8, 53–4, 59–60, 63; quaternal, ternal, *doblench* c. of, 75, 81–3, 87–8, 100–2, 118, 191, 195, 201; ct., ctess., or cty. of, 6, 50–1, 53–4, 56–8, 68 n. 8, 74, 80, 82, 90, 99, 119, 201; economy of, 63, 77, 99; mint of, 76, 96–100, 118; moneyers of, 6, 58, 121, 147; peace legislation of, 53–4, 64, 81; recoinage of, 76–8, 96. *See also* Bernat de Berga, Catalonia, confirmation(s) of c., Pere de Cirach, *Usatges*.

Barthélemy, Anatole de, 126 n. 3, 131 n. 3.

Barthélemy, bp. of Cahors, 110.

Baudouin VIII, ct. of Flanders, 149.

Baudri, k.'s sergeant, 27 n. 2.

Baumel, Jean, 72 n. 1.

Béarn, clergy, magnates, peace and truce of, 55–6; vcty., diocese of, 54–6. *See also* Morlaas, c. of.

Béatrice, ctess. of Ponthieu, 155.

Béatrix, ctess. of Melgueil, 73–4.

Beaumont (Beaumont-sur-Oise: Seine-et-Oise, ar. Pontoise, c. L'Isle-Adam), cts., charter of, 149, 154 n. 1.

Beaune (Côte-d'Or, ch.-l. ar.), charter of (1203), 125–6, 159.

Beauvais (Oise, ch.-l. dép.), bp. or canons of, 151–2; c. of, 142 n. 1, 145, 151–3; c. of Paris at, 151; commune of, 152; mint of, 152; moneyers of, 154 n. 2; ordinance of (1215), 151–2, 154, 173, 190, 195.

Beauvaisis, 144 n. 5, 146 n., 174.

Bellême, castle of (Orne, ar. Alençon, ch.-l. c.), 20.

Beltrán, Pío, 87 n.

Benavente (Leon), full court at, 93.

beneficium, money-tax of Nevers, 138, 142 n. 5, 202.

Benton, J. F., 43 nn. 1, 2, 130 n. 2.

Berenguer, abp. of Narbonne, 186 n. 5.

Berenguer (? cf. *HL*, iv. 795), prior of Corneilla-de-Conflent, 96 n. 2.

Berenguer Ramon, ct. of Provence, 73.

Berenguer Seniofred I de Lluçà, bp. of Vich, 61.

Berguedà, 61; *marcha de Bergitano*, 61 n. 5; population of, 62 n. 1.

bernagium, 26.

Bernard, Saint, 56 n. 5.

Bernard IV, ct. of Melgueil, 12; his confirmations of c. (1125–30), 65–73, 168; vassal of pope, 68, 71–3.

Bernard Amel, 71 n. 1.

Bernard At, vct. of Béziers, 71 n. 1.

Bernard-Pelet, 73–4.

Bernardus Parmensis, his gloss on *Quanto personam tuam*, 171.

Bernat, scribe, 51, 200.

Bernat II, ct. of Besalú, 91 n. 1.

Bernat III, ct. of Besalú, 60 n.

Bernat de Berga, bp. of Barcelona, 98.

Bernat Guillem, ct. of Cerdanya, 50.

Bernier, Jean, 126 n. 5, 127.

Berry, 4, 157–8; c. in, 157–9, 162; economy, hoards of, 157 n. 5; mints in, 157–8; regulation of c. in, 158–9. *See also* Bourges, Gilbert de Chanceaux, Mathieu Dreu, mutation of c.

Bertrand, ct. of Toulouse, 107.

Besalú (Girona, p.j. Olot), c. of, 60 n., 62, 79, 82; ct. or cty. of, 59, 60 n., 91 n. 1; Santa Maria of, 91 n. 1.

Béziers (Hérault, ch.-l. ar.), c. of, 67, 82; vct. of (Bernard At), 71 n. 1.

billon, 100 n. 5.

'black money', *see* money.

Blanche, ctess. of Champagne and Brie: her monetary pact with bp. of Meaux (1208), 134, 164.

Blois (Loir-et-Cher, ch.-l. dép.), barons, lords, peasants, proprietors at, 127–30; c. of (*blesensis*), xviii, 126–30, 142; ct. or cty. of, 126–30, 136, 142, 162; economy, monetary conditions at, 128–9; exactions, *cornagium* at, 126–30, 162; *patria* of, 127, 129; portal of Saint-Fiacre at, 126, 130. *See also* Bourgmoyen, *communitas terre*, confirmation(s) of c., mutation of c., Peter of Blois, Saint-Lomer, Saint-Sauveur.

'boconaylla', *see* billon.

Bologna, 183; jurists of, 176–7.

bona moneta, see money, 'good'.

Bonfill Fredal, moneyer at Barcelona, 6.

bonitas, 177; *bonitas extrinseca*, 180. *See also* imposed value.

Bonnassie, Pierre, 54 n. 1.

Bonsmoulins (*Boens Molins*, castle near Moulins, q.v.), 19 n. 2, 205.

Boran-sur-Oise (Ben. priory of nuns: Oise, ar. Senlis, c. Neuilly-en-Thelle), 173 n. 3.

Bordeors ribeaus, 185.

Borrell II, ct. of Barcelona and marquis: his charter to Cardona, 57–8.

Botet y Sisó, Joaquím, 76, 78 n. 2, 90 n. 1.

Boulogne (Pas-de-Calais, ch.-l. ar.), cty., c. of, 145.

Bourbon (Bourbon-l'Archambault: Allier, ar. Moulins, ch.-l. c.), lord, *prévôts*, bailiffs of, 159.

Bourg Saint-Germain, *see* Paris.

Bourges (Cher, ch.-l. dép.), 32; abp. of (Girard de Cros), 159; *bailliage* of, 158; c. of, 157–8; ct. or vct. of, 157. *See also* Berry, Saint-Sulpice.

Bourgin, Georges, 33 n. 4.

Bourgmoyen (Aug.: Blois), 129.

bovatge, see *bovaticum*.

bovaticum (or *bovatge*), Catalan 'peace of beasts' or redemption thereof, 61, 88–91, 100–1, 111, 117, 128, 194; its association or identity with *monetaticum*, 92, 94–8, 100; proceeds of, 95–7.

Bray (Bray-sur-Seine: Seine-et-Marne, ar. Provins, ch.-l. c.), revenues of, 133 n. 3, 164.

bread, grain, 6, 30–1, 35, 40, 43, 133 n. 3, 153. See also *tallia panis et vini*.

Breteuil (Eure, ar. Évreux, ch.-l. c.), 19, 205.

Bridrey, Émile, 14, 15 n. 1, 17–18, 21–2, 25 nn. 4, 6, 36 n. 3, 166 n. 1, 169 n. 2, 170 n. 1.

Brittany, duchy of, 4, 19–20; hearths in, population of, 26 n.

bronze, c. in, 7, 9–10.

Brooke, Christopher, 128 n. 2.

Brunswick, Sheldon, 175 n. 4.

Brussel, Nicolas, 14 n. 1, 29 n. 1, 36 n. 3.

Bruyères (Bruyères-en-Laonnais: Aisne, ar. and c. Laon), charters of, 146, 155, 163 n. 2.

Buisson, Ludwig, 166 n. 1.

Bulgarus, 176.

bullion, 180 n. 2, 181.

bullion clauses, 63, 67–8, 73, 79 n. 3, 113.

Bur, Michel, 131 n. 3.

Burchard, bp. of Meaux, 134 n. 1.

Burgundy, d. or duchy of, vii, 4, 120–1, 124–6, 130, 141–2, 151, 162, 193; economy of, 124, 126; numismatic history of, 121 n. 1; townsmen of, 164. *See also* confirmation(s) of c., Dijon (c. of), Hugues (son of Eudes I), mutation of c.

Caen (Calvados, ch.-l. dép.), 26; ordinance of, 164. *See also* Sainte-Trinité.

Cahors (Lot, ch.-l. dép.), bps., cty., diocese, men of, 104, 108–12, 118, 204–5; c. of (*caorcencs*), xviii, 108–12; recoinage of, 108. *See also* Barthélemy, confirmation(s) of c., money-taxes, mutation of c., Quercy.

'Cahorsins', 109.

Calixtus II, pope, 71, 72 n. 2, 168.

Cambrai (Nord, ch.-l. ar.), c. of, 185.

Cambrésis, 144 n. 5.

capitularies, 3, 5, 58.

Carcassonne (Aude, ch.-l. dép.), mutation of c. of, 8.

Cardona (Barcelona, p.j. Berga), charter of (986), 57–8, 66, 189; economic conditions around, 57; magnates of, 58; town, vct., vcty. of, 57–8, 80. *See also* Ermemir.

Carmina Burana, 186–7.

carnotensis, see Chartres, c. of.

Carolingian (or Frankish) institutions, influence, survivals, 2–3, 5, 10 n. 2, 48, 51, 56, 58, 71 n. 3, 189, 197.

carta sacramentalis, carta del sacramental, 70–1.
cartularies, viii, 88, 105, 137 n. 1.
Casbas (Cist. nuns: Huesca, p.j. Huesca), charter for, 91.
Castaing-Sicard, Mireille, 106 n.
Castile, c. of, 74, 75 n. 1, 81–3, 115; k., kingdom of, 81–3, 86 n. 1, 103, 203–4. *See also* Alphonse VIII.
Catalonia, vii–ix, 50–66, 80, 90, 106, 110, 116–17, 124; c. in, 51–4, 56–64, 74–5, 78, 83, 93, 96, 99, 106, 182 n. 1, 194–5; economic conditions in, 57–8, 63–4, 99; fiscal administration, revenues, taxation in, 62–3, 85 n., 88–100, 113; legislation on peace and c. in, 53–5, 89 n. 2, 101, 112; mines in, 99; mints in, 93. *See also* Barcelona, Cerdanya, confirmation(s) of c., *Cunctis pateat, Moneta autem*, money-taxes, mutation of c., Vich.
cattle-tax, see *bovaticum*.
Celestine III, pope, 85, 114, 168–9, 190; his letter *Cum utilitas publica*, 85, 104. *See also* Jacintus.
cens, census, see rents.
censiers, 186.
Cerdanya, c. of or in, 63 n. 1, 65 n. 1; clergy, knights, magnates, merchants of, 50–1, 59–61, 63, 114; ct. or cty. of, vii, 51–2, 59–63, 81, 89, 95–7, 168, 190, 199–200; *pagi* of, 59, 61; peace of, 50–2, 60–1; peasants, agrarian property of, 50–1; population of, 62 n. 1, 94–6; redemption of c. and peace in, 45, 60–2, 112. *See also* Bernat Guillem, *bovaticum*, confirmation(s) of c., *Cunctis pateat*, money-tax.
ceremonies, *see* assemblies, confirmation(s) of coinage, courts.
Cervera (Lérida, p.j.), charter for (1202), peace legislation of (1203), 55 n. 3.
Chalon-sur-Saône (Saône-et-Loire, ch.-l. ar.), c. of, 124 n. 3, 139 n.
Châlons-sur-Marne (Marne, ch.-l. dép.), bps. of, 157; c. of (*châlonnais*), 130–1, 145, 157.
Chambly (Oise, ar. Senlis, c. Neuilly-en-Thelle), charter of, 154 n. 1.
Champagne, changers of, 133 n. 4; c. of, 127 n. 1, 130–6; cts., ctess., counties of (*see also* Provins, Troyes), 129–36, 147, 162–3; economy, fairs, revenues, trade in, 130–1, 133–4, 164; mints of, 133 n. 4, 140; moneyers of, 163; regulation of c. in, 134–5. *See also* confirmation(s) of c., Haimard, Larrivour, money-taxes, Montiéramey, mutation of c.
changers, 37, 133 n. 4, 137, 154 n. 2, 156, 163–4, 181 n., 182, 191 n. 1, 202.
Chanson de Roland, 184 n. 3, 185.
chansons de geste, 184–5, 187.
Charlemagne, k. of Franks and emperor: his monetary reform, 3.
Charles the Bald, k. of West Franks, 5 n. 2.

Charles the Good, ct. of Flanders, 156.
Charroi de Nîmes, 184–5.
Charte aux Normands, 22.
charter(s), forged, 91–2; of 'land', 130; of liberties in England (1100), 15–16; royal: in Aragon, 10, 91, 105; in Catalonia, 55 n. 3, 91, 98, 100–2; in France, 35, 36 n. 6, 37, 40, 141, 154, 163. *See also* Index of charters (etc.) pertaining to c., *carta sacramentalis*, confirmation(s) of c., *Cunctis pateat*.
Chartres (Eure-et-Loir, ch.-l. dép.), c. of, (*carnotensis*) 128, 132.
Châteaurenard (Loiret, ar. Montargis, ch.-l. c.), toll at, 142 n. 6.
Châtillon-sur-Seine (Côte-d'Or, ar. Montbard, ch.-l. c.), co-lordship of, 121–4; regulation of c. of, 160.
Chauny (Aisne, ar. Laon, ch.-l. c.), charter of, 154; *Scripta de feodis* of, 146 n.
Cherêt (Aisne, ar. and c. Laon), charter of, 155.
Chronicle of Saint-Maixent, 7, 32.
Church, interest, influence of, 45, 82, 102, 168; Fathers of, 184. *See also* law, canon.
Cipolla, Carlo, 196 n. 1.
Clermont (Puy-de-Dôme, ch.-l. dép.), council of (1095), 56 n. 5.
clipping of c., 51–2, 66, 118.
clippings, of mint of Troyes, 133.
Cluny (Saône-et-Loire, ar. Mâcon, ch.-l. c.), 124, 189; charters for abbey (Ben.) of, 45, 48–50, 121, 124. *See also* Morlaas, Pons.
Cnut, k. of England, 52.
Code 5. 59. 5. 2, see *quod omnes tangit*.
coinage, administration of, 42, 57–8, 151, 153, 157–9, 162–5, 171, 189, 191, 195–7; expertise in, 18, 100, 115, 137, 160, 163–4, 193, 196, 202; popular or constitutional interest in, vii, 20–2, 29–32, 48–9, 69–70, 88–9, 101–6, 121, 129, 150–1, 157, 189–97; public interest in, 28, 50, 58, 66, 102, 125, 156–65, 168, 199; policy (especially fiscal) of, 13, 39 n. 6, 40 n., 49, 74, 80, 96–101, 118–19, 134–5, 193–5; limitation of prerogative of, 1–2, 13, 51 ff., 111–19, 142–3; becomes proprietary, 5–13, 189; reform of, 3, 18, 21, 28, 78–80, 162–3, 195; shortage of, 23, 57, 62, 83, 138 n. 6, 139, 150; supply of, 49, 63, 113, 118, 133, 144, 146, 158, 191; as public utility, 1–5, 154, 156–65, 196. See also *moneta*, mutation of c., right of c., stability of c.
coins (deniers, obols, etc., referred to as such), 1, 8, 12, 23–4, 31, 37, 41, 45, 74–6, 108–9, 153, 189, 196, 200–1, 203, 205–6; classified, illustrated, Frontispiece, Plates I–III, and xv–xix; described, 9–10, 54–6, 61, 78, 146 n. 1, 148; extant, 8, 17, 33 n. 5, 34, 58, 138, 154 n. 2; *gros* c. of Italy, 196; literary allusions to, 184–8. *See also* coinage, *nummus*.

collectors, 15, 26, 35, 40 ,96, 100 ,194, 204.
comitatus, 4.
commerce, 41, 79, 83, 107, 130, 144, 153, 183, 191–2; in money or silver, 153, 182.
Comminges, bps. of, peace in, 56 n. 3, 110.
communes, 35 n. 1, 142, 145, 152, 200, 203.
communitas terre Blesis, 129 n. 4.
commutation, of profits of c., 45, 182; of tallage, 35–6 n. 6, 39. *See also* money-taxes.
Compiègne (Oise, ch.-l. ar.), 33; c. of, 32–4; charter for (1120), 32–4, 44, 120; mint at, 33 n. 5; *fumagium* of, 34 n. 1.
compilations of decretals, 172; 1 *Comp.*, 169 n. 1; 2 *Comp.*, 172–3; 3 *Comp.*, 166, 169, 172, 178–9; *X.*, 166, 169, 171, 178–80; Alanus, 172. *See also* decretals.
Compostela (Santiago de Compostela: La Coruña, p.j.), 98.
comune, peace tax in Quercy, 111–12.
confirmation(s) of c., vii, 45, 83, 161, 163, 165, 183, 189–90, 192–206; diverse forms of, 192–3; economic inconvenience of, 119, 161–5, 196; for life (usually sworn; *see also* oaths), 29–30, 59, 76, 81, 85, 88–90, 93, 102–4, 106, 108–9, 113–14, 119, 124–5, 160, 189–90, 199–201, 205–6; associated with customary restraints, 189; tradition of, 84, 113–14; in or at: North and South, 113–19, 192–5; Agenais, 112–13, 117, 190, 194–5; Aquitaine, 45, 48–50; Aragon, 75–7, 85–7, 102–3, 115–17, 167, 183, 190, 194–5, 203–4; Aragon-Catalonia (1155), 81–2, 102–3, 171; Barcelona, 76–8, 81, 100, 102–3, 113, 116–17, 119, 171, 191, 194 n. 1, 201 (see also *Moneta autem*); Blois, 126–30, 132, 142, 160, 190, 192; Burgundy, 120–1, 124–6, 141–2, 151, 159–60, 163 n. 2, 190–3; Cahors, 108–14, 190, 194, 205–6; Cardona, 57–8, 66, 189; Catalonia, 81–2, 88–91, 102, 117, 190, 194 (*see also* Barcelona, *above*; Vich, *below*); Cerdanya, see *Cunctis pateat*; Champagne, 127 n. 1, 129, 131–4, 160, 162, 190, 192; Corbie, 147, 160; Étampes, 29–31, 120, 129, 132–3, 160, 162, 190; Melgueil, 64, 66–7, 69–74, 106–7, 113, 118, 168; Narbonne, 113, 195; Nevers, 120, 136–43, 160, 163, 190–1, 193, 201–2; Orléans, 29–31, 35, 44, 89, 120, 129, 141, 160, 162–3, 190; Picardy, 190 (*cf.* 147, 150, 156); Saint-Omer, 160; Toulouse, 104–7, 112, 114, 190, 194–5; Urgell, 113, 190; Verdun, 157; Vich, 78–81, 102–3, 106, 109, 113–14, 190–1. *See also* Index of charters (etc.) pertaining to c.
Conflent, cty. of, 59, 61, 91, 95, 97, 114, 199; population of, 62 n. 1. *See also* Cerdanya.
consent, 70, 86–7, 96 n. 2, 103–4, 109, 124, 149–50, 167, 195, 204; to money taxes, 21–2, 45, 112, 114–15, 117, 137–8; *assensus populi*,

115, 203; *assensu et consilio*, 153 n. 1. *See also* counsel.
conservation of coinage, 1, 13, 53, 166, 171–2, 180–2, 187, 189–90, 195, 204; as economic or psychological and legal idea, 196–7; incidence, diffusion, different forms of, 45, 57, 71, 74, 86, 102–3, 118, 120, 130, 137, 143, 150, 160–1, 192–3; as provincial phenomenon, 190.
Constança, daughter of Alphonse II, 94 n. 3.
Constance, abbess of Notre-Dame (Saintes), 50.
consuetudines, 4, 18 n. 1, 30 n. 1, 36 n., 152, 201–2. *See also* renders, rents, revenues.
Consuetudines et iusticie, 17–18, 33 n. 3.
consultation, 13, 86–7, 101, 111–12, 129, 163, 171, 193, 196; on c., an original development in North, 160; plenary, 116. *See also* assemblies, consent, counsel, general court(s).
contracts, 6, 11 n. 5, 32, 53 n. 3, 164, 181 n. 1. *See also* Index of charters (etc.) pertaining to c.
conventions, 6, 71 n. 1; consular accords, 111.
copper, 53.
Corbie (Ben.: Somme, ar. Amiens, ch.-l. c.), abts. of, 145 n. 5, 147; c. of, 145, 147 n. 1; moneyers, *nummularii* of, 154 n. 2; regulation of c. at, 147, 150, 160. *See also* Evrard, Josse.
Corbigny (Nièvre, ar. Clamecy, ch.-l. c.), Ben. abbey-town, 136; assembly of, 136, 160; charter of (1188), 120, 136–43, 160, 163, 190–1, 193, 201–2.
cornagium, of Berry, 162; of Blois, 126, 127 n., 128, 130, 162.
Corneilla (Aug.: Corneilla-de-Conflent: Pyr.-Or., ar. and c. Prades), levy on prior's (? Berenguer's) tenants, 96 n. 2.
cort, see general court(s).
Cortes, 115.
coruagium, 128 n. 2. See *cornagium*.
councils: Clermont (1095), 56 n. 5; First Lateran (1123), 72, 168, 190; Second Lateran (1139), 82; of Lérida (1155), 81–2, 103, (1173), 103; of Toulouges, 55; of Valladolid (1155), 82 n. 2; of peace, 195; in towns, 195. *See also* peace, Vich (synod of).
counsel, 30 n., 31, 53 n. 2, 69 n. 7, 76, 81 n. 1, 171; on c., 51, 64, 78, 103–4, 158, 160, 164 n. 3, 167, 199; and approval, 53 n. 2, 54; 'and command', 50, 59, 199; and consent, 69–70, 136, 201–2. *See also* consent.
counsellors, 86, 171, 203.
counterfeiting, 2, 9, 51–3, 57, 113, 137, 167, 170, 176, 180, 187; akin: to mutations, 167, 171; to simony, 187; penalties, remedies for, 76, 81, 118, 131, 160, 168. *See also* fraud, mutation of c.
Courtenay, W. J., 196 n. 1.
Courtois d'Arras, 184.
courts, *see* general courts.

Couserans, bps. of, 56 n. 3.
credit, 152, 180.
creditors, 49, 51, 70, 73, 172, 176, 178, 188.
Crépy (Crépy-en-Valois: Oise, ar. Senlis, ch.-l. c.), charter of, 154; c. of, 154 n. 2; *Scripta de feodis* for, 146 n.
Crown of Aragon, 83–4, 100, 107; persistence of confirmation of c. in, 194–5; rise of public taxation in, 194. *See also* Aragon, Catalonia.
crusade(s), 51, 56, 104, 160, 183, 203; First, 49, 56 n. 5, 68 n. 5; Third, 136, 142; Albigensian, 83, 104, 111, 193; aid and finance of, 137–8, 140–2, 193–4, 202; crusaders, 49, 65, 68–9, 72, 125, 138.
Cum canonicis (X 3. 39. 26), 178.
Cum multam sedes (JL ii, no. 14757), 176.
Cum utilitas publica (4 September 1191), 104, 168.
Cunctis pateat, charter of peace for Cerdanya (1118), 66, 79, 81, 101, 107, 113, 116–17, 142; its concession and background, 50–64, 168; its influence, 89–90, 94, 104, 194; text of, 199–200.
currency, 41, 125, 138 n. 6, 145, 151–3; concurrency, 109; guarantees of, 1, 3, 158, 160; legal, 10, 52, 75, 121, 137, 142, 202–3, 205–6.
custom, 35, 38, 44, 105, 139, 173–4, 189, 195, 197; of dies or c., 101, 163; of Agen, 117; of Aragon and Catalonia, 194; of Catalonia (see also *Usatges*), 54, 88–90, 116; c. as, 115, 162; of Jaca (see also *fueros*), 192; of La Chapel-aude, 158; of Normandy, 15, 28, 43. *See also* renders.
Cuxa, *see* Saint-Michel-de-Cuxa.

Dalmau de Creixell, 95 n. 2.
Daroca, general court of (1223), 117 n. 3, 119 n. 1, 194 n. 1.
Daube, David, 3 n. 4.
debasements, *see* mutation of c.
debtors, 51, 172, 176–7, 181, 188.
debts, *see* loans.
decimatio, see tithing.
Decretales Gregorii IX (*Liber Extra*, or *X*), *see* compilations of decretals.
decretals and papal letters: see *Cum canonicis, Cum multam sedes, Cum utilitas publica, Olim causam, Pervenit ad nos, Quanto personam tuam, Querelam, Quod irreprehensibile est.*
Decretum, C. 10. 2. 2 *Hoc ius*, 178 n. 4; C. 14. 4. 5 *Si quis clericus*; C. 14. 4. 6 *Nullus clericorum*, 177 n. 4; C. 22. 4, 169 n. 1; C. 32. 4. 6 *Quis ignorat*, 178 n. 1, 179.
De dan denier, 185–6.
De foagio Normannie, 14–15, 18–19, 21 n. 2, 26–7, 162 n. 1, 204–5.
'Dehore' (?), canons of, 173 nn. 1, 3.
Delisle, Léopold, 14 n. 1, 17, 30 n. 1, 36 n. 3.

De monetagio, 14–15, 18–19, 25.
demonetization, 5, 7, 10, 13, 21, 37, 139, 150, 155, 189. *See also* recoinage, mutation of c.
denariata, 41 n. 6.
deniers, *see* coins.
Déols (Indre, ar. and c. Châteauroux), 158.
depreciation of c., 7, 16, 63.
Dessales, Léon, 48 n. 5.
devices, *see* types.
dies, 5, 6 n. 6, 8, 48, 58, 132, 154 n. 2, 163.
Dieudonné, Adolphe, 14 n. 1, 29 n. 1, 32 nn. 2, 3, 36 n. 3, 37 n. 3, 107 n. 3.
Digest, 12. 1. 2. 1 *Mutuum*, 178 nn. 3, 4; 12. 1. 3 *Cum quid mutuum*, 177; 13. 7. 24 *Eleganter*, 172, 176 n. 2, 177, 178 n. 4, 180; 18. 1. 71 *Imperatores*, 179.
Dijon (Côte-d'Or, ch.-l. dép.), c. of (*digenois*), xviii, 9; lords, townsmen of, 120–1, 125, 141, 182 n. 2; moneyer of, 120. *See also* confirmation(s) of c. (in Burgundy), Saint-Bénigne.
Dinant (province and ch.-l. Namur), right of c. at, 5–6, 197.
dinars (Muslim c.), xvi, 187 n. 1.
dispensation, *see* law, canon.
divellere, 149–50.
Doet Herberti (Normandy), 19 n. 2, 205.
Domesday Book, 6, 15–16, 18.
Domfront (Orne, ar. Alençon, ch.-l. c.), 20.
donations, 41 n. 3, 75 n. 2, 105; donation-sale, 77 n.
Duby, Georges, 3, 158 n. 2.
Du Cange, Charles Dufresne, 14 n. 1, 36, 37 n. 2, 134.
Duero river, 93 n. 2.

Ebro valley, 68, 112.
Ébrouin, changer, 163 n. 3.
economy, economies, economic circumstances, 3, 13, 83, 160–1, 171, 192, 196. *See also* confirmation(s) of c., exchange, mutation of c., *and entries for regions* (Aquitaine, *etc.*).
Edict of Pîtres, 2, 5 n. 3.
Edgar 'the Peaceful', k. of England, 52.
Edward the Confessor, k. of England, 15.
Eleganter (*Dig.* 13. 7. 24. 1), 176 n. 2, 177, 178 n. 4, 180
Élisabeth, ctess. of Vermandois, 149.
Elne (Pyr.-Or., ar. and c. Perpignan), bp. of, 50, 66, 199–200; church of, 62; diocese of, 56.
Elvira de Subirats, ctess. of Urgell, 102.
emptio monete, 93. *See also* purchase (of c.).
Empúries, c. of, 62.
England, 6, 11, 18–21, 24, 66; charter of (1100), 15–16; c. of, 16, 52, 56 n. 1; legislation in, 52; Anglo-Saxon minting in, 16, 18; sterling, 25. *See also* money-taxes.
Ermemir, vct. of Cardona, 58.
Ermessinde, 65 n. 3, 68 n. 3.

Ermessinde, daughter of Béatrix and Bernard-Pelet, 74.

Escaro (Pyr.-Or., ar. Prades, c. Olette), 91.

Espanolus, vicar at Toulouse, 107 n. 6. See also *Ispanoli*.

Establissement of Saint-Quentin, 147–9, 153, 200.

'estimation', payments or settlements by, 173–4, 177, 178 n. 3, 179, 191.

Étampes (Seine-et-Oise, ar. Rambouillet, ch.-l. c.), c. and mint of, xv, 24, 29–31, 34, 38, 162; commune, knights, men of, 30–3, 35; redemption of c. at, 29–35; tallages of, 35 n. 1, 42. *See also* confirmation(s) of c., money-taxes.

Étienne, ct. of Sancerre, 132.

Étienne I, de Nemours, bp. of Noyon: regulates c., 152–3, 202–3.

Étienne de La Chapelle, bp. of Meaux: c. of, xviii, 130–2.

Eudes, constable, 131, 132 n.

Eudes I, d. of Burgundy: confirms c. of Dijon, 120–1.

Eudes III, d. of Burgundy: c. of, xviii, 125; confirms c., 126.

Eudes of Burgundy, ct. of Nevers, 143.

Eugene III, pope, 80 n. 1.

Evrard, abt. of Corbie: his regulation of c. (*c.* 1080), 147, 150, 160.

Exactis regibus, 176 n. 2.

exchange, 6–7, 42, 129 n., 148, 151–4, 158, 166, 180–1; in c., 12, 22, 77 n., 79, 84, 85 n., 118, 132 n., 139, 147, 155 n. 6, 156–7, 160–4, 174–5, 186, 191–2, 200, 206; money as means of, 2; obligatory, 5; public, 5 n. 2; tables of monetary, 10–11, 153, 154 n. 2, 156. *See also* demonetization, rates of monetary exchange.

Exchequer, 15, 164.

Extremadura, 93 n. 2.

fabliaux, 184 n. 3.

fairs, 133, 180; of Lendit, 41 n. 1; of Saint Ayoul (Troyes) and Bar, 134.

'falsity', 71–2. *See also* fraud.

farms of revenue, 24, 26, 40, 42, 135.

Fawtier, Robert, 25 n. 3, 32, 36 n. 3, 37 n. 3.

fealty, 51, 56, 66, 71, 73 n. 2, 111, 116.

Fécamp (Seine-Maritime, ar. Le Havre, ch.-l. c.), *see* hoard(s).

fees, *see* money-taxes.

Ferdinand II, k. of Leon, 82.

fief(s), 4, 6, 66, 69–70, 73–4, 80, 136, 155, 161; feudal aids, 140; 'feudal c.', 6–7; feudal rights, 4; feudalistic engagements, 6 n. 6, 65–71; on revenue of c. of Melgueil, 69. *See also* fealty, homage, vassals.

Figeac (Lot, ch.-l. ar.), 111.

'flabel du denier', 185.

Flanders, c. of, 145, 156–7; cts. cty. of, 140, 144, 149, 154–6; economy of, 163; communal

interest in c., 156; moneyers of, 163; towns of, 155–6. *See also* Baudouin VIII, Guillaume Clito, Philippe d'Alsace.

focagium, see *fouage*, *De foagio Normannie*.

fogatge, 96, 112 n. 2. See also *fouage*.

Foix, vassal (Bernard Amel) of ct. of (Roger II), 71 n. 1.

Folquet de Marseille, bp. of Toulouse, 107.

Fontenay (Cist.: Côte-d'Or, ar. Semur, c. Montbard), 124.

Fontette, François de, 41 n. 3.

Fontevrault (Ben. nuns: Maine-et-Loire, ar. and c. Saumur), 25 n. 3.

Forum iudicum, 53, 58, 81 n. 1.

Fossier, Robert, 146, 148.

fouage (money-tax), in: Agenais, 117; Nevers, 137, 142, 193; Normandy, viii, 14–15, 18 n. 4, 19, 21, 25–7, 29, 44, 120, 194, 204–5. See also *fogatge*, taxation.

fraud, 2–3, 50, 57, 64, 81 n. 2, 148, 167–71, 175, 190, 199–203; by moneyers, 58, 120 n. 1, 121, 147, 187, 189; mutation of c. likened to, 72, 160, 167–8, 197; by users of c., 5, 52, 58, 76, 187.

Freeman, E. A., 17.

fuero(s), of Aragon, 75, 116, 192; of Jaca, 84 n .3; *antich fuero* of Jaca, 10, 11 n. 1.

fumagium, 34.

Galensis, *see* Johannes Galensis.

Garnier de Traînel, seneschal of Nevers, 162.

Gascony, vii, 112, 191.

Gaudri II, bp. of Laon: his manipulations of c., 7, 9–10, 12.

Gaufred, bp. of Tortosa, 91.

Gaufred de Rocabertí, 88.

Gautier, abp. of Sens, 143.

Gautier de Coutances, abp. of Rouen, 26.

Gelasius II, pope, 68.

general court(s), 115; of: Agenais (1232, 1234), 117–18, 195; Aragon, 114–17, 119, 183, 195; Catalonia, *see* Lérida, *below*; Daroca (1223), 117 n. 3, 119 n. 1; Huesca (1221), 119, 194 n. 1; Leon, Castile, 93, 115; Lérida (1214), 116–17; (1218), 117; Monzón (1217), 117; (1236), 114, 116, 183.

Geoffroy Martel, ct. of Anjou and Saintes: his directive to moneyers of Saintonge, 50 n. 1.

Géraud, bp. of Agen: confirms c. of Agen (1232), 112, 117.

Géraud de Gourdon, bp. of Périgueux: his monetary policy, 48.

Gerberoy (Oise, ar. Beauvais, c. Songeons), 173 n. 3.

Germain, Alexandre, 65 n. 3, 72 n. 1.

Gévaudan, 98.

Gien (Loiret, ar. Montargis, ch.-l. c.), c. of, 138, 139 n.

Gil Farrés, Octavio, 87 n. 3.
Gilbert de Chanceaux, *bailli* in Berry, 158.
Girard de Cros, abp. of Bourges, 159.
Girbertus, 48 n.
Girona (provincial capital), c. of, 63, 82; charter of (1205), 88–91, 98, 102, 117; *moneta* of, 62; *monetaticum* and other proceeds from, 94 n. 3; *questia* of, 94 n. 3, 95.
Giry, Arthur, 127 n. 3.
Gisors (Eure, ar. Les Andelys, ch.-l. c.), *bailli* at, 25.
glossa ordinaria, to *Decretum*, 179–80; to *X*, 171, 179–80.
Godefroi de Tressy, bp. of Meaux: his monetary pact (1208), 134–5, 164 n. 4.
Godin, moneyer of Ponthieu, 155, 163.
Goitein, S. D., 187 n. 1.
gold, gold c., 3, 91 n. 1, 113, 184–5, 196. See also mancus, mazmudins, morabetins.
'good money (or coin)', see money.
Gormont et Isembart, 184.
grain, see bread.
grains, in c., 7.
Grandselve (Ben. then Cist.: Tarn-et-Garonne, ar. Castel-Sarrasin, c. Verdun), 69.
graveria, 26.
Grierson, Philip, 3, 23 n. 4.
Gros Brief, account of Flanders, 155.
Gualter, bp. of Maguelone: recipient of confirmation of c. at Melgueil, 66, 68.
Guerau II, ct. of Roussillon: c. of, xvii, 55.
Gui, brother of ct. of Nevers, 139.
Gui, ct. of Nevers, 162.
Gui de Dampierre, lord of Bourbon, 159.
Gui de Forez, ct. of Auxerre: his new c., 143.
Guibert de Nogent, 9–10, 12, 146 n. 1, 181.
Guilhem VII, d. of Aquitaine, 50 n. 1.
Guilhem VIII, d. of Aquitaine, 45, 48–50; his statute, 45, 48–50, 192.
Guilhem IX, d. of Aquitaine: as ct. of Toulouse, 55; his debasement of c. in Poitou, 10, 12, 49.
Guilhiermoz, Paul, 37 n. 2, 191 n. 1.
Guillaume II, ct. of Nevers, 136.
Guillaume IV, ct. of Nevers, 138–40.
Guillaume de Champeaux, bp. of Châlons, 157.
Guillaume Clito, ct. of Flanders: his charter to Saint-Omer, 155–6.
Guillaume de Nemours, bp.-elect of Meaux: renews monetary pact (1214), 134, 164.
Guillaume de Toucy, bp. of Auxerre, 135, 138 n. 5.
Guillem IV, de Cardaillac, bp. of Cahors: his c. and confirmations of c. (1211–12), xviii, 108–12, 118, 205–6.
Guillem V, lord of Montpellier, 65, 68 nn. 4, 5; his daughter, 69 n. 7.
Guillem VI, lord of Montpellier: his interest in c. of Melgueil, 66, 68–73.

Guillem VII, lord of Montpellier: his fief on c. of Melgueil, 74.
Guillem VIII, lord of Montpellier: his monetary engagement (1190), 106.
Guillem de Creixell, 95 n. 2.
Guillem Durfort, fiscal administrator in Catalonia, 100.
Guillem de Montpellier, 66 n.
Guillem Ramon de Montcada, V Seneschal, co-lord of Vich, 80.
Guillem de Tavertet, bp. of Vich, 80 n. 5; his gift to k., 98.
Guillem de Tudela, 110 n. 3.
Guillemette (or Guillelma), 65, 70.

Haimard, Templar and monetary expert, 164, 193.
Haskins, C. H., 17 n. 3, 23.
hearths, see *fogatge, fouage*, taxation.
helianensis, see Périgueux (c. of).
Hélie, ct. of Périgord, 48.
Henri I le Libéral, ct. of Troyes, 136; confirms c. (1165), 129–33, 162–3, 192.
Henri II, ct. of Troyes, 140.
Henry I, k. of England, d. of Normandy, 15–16, 18, 20, 22; his coronation charter (1100), 15.
Henry II, k. of England, d. of Normandy, 15, 19, 21.
Henry of Huntingdon, 17.
Hervé de Donzy, ct. of Nevers, 138, 140, 144; c. of, xix; alters c., 143.
Higounet, Charles, 107 n. 4.
Hiver, [? Alfred], 134.
hoard(s), 23; of Accolay, 138 n. 6; in Berry, 157 n. 5; of Fécamp, 17 n. 2, 23 n. 2.
Hoc ius (C. 10. 2. 2), 178 n. 4.
Hodenc-en-Bray (Oise, ar. Beauvais, c. Le Coudray-Saint-Germer), 173 n. 3.
homage, 111.
Honorius II, pope: his admonition concerning c. of Melgueil, 71–2, 167–8, 190.
Hospitallers, 94 n. 1.
Hostiensis, 171.
Hoveden, see Roger of.
Huesca (provincial capital), cathedral chapter's share of c. at, 84; general court of (1221), 119, 194 n. 1; institution of *monedaje* at (1205), 84, 90, 92–4, 96–8, 115, 194; mint at, 84; scribes of, 85.
Hugo de Lisigniano, 48 n.
Hugo monetarius, 164 n. 6.
Hugolinus, 175 n. 2.
Huguccio of Pisa, on dispensation, 169; on *aestimatio*, 177, 179.
Hugues, son of d. Eudes I of Burgundy, 120.
Hugues I, d. of Burgundy, 120.
Hugues III, d. of Burgundy, 142; his c., charters and confirmations of c. (1177, 1185,

1187), xviii, 121, 124–6, 141–2, 192.
Hugues IV, de Noyers, bp. of Auxerre, 137
n. 1, 139–40.
Hugues d'Amboise, 128.
Hugues de Plancy, 131, 132 n.
Humbert de Moyenmoutiers, likens simoniac
bp. to *nummus falsus*, 187.
Huriel (Allier, ar. Montluçon, ch.-l. c.), 158.
hyilenses, see Autun, c. of.

iaccensis, see Jaca, c. of.
Île-de-France, vii–viii, 4, 11, 21, 29–44, 120,
124, 144 n. 5, 173, 189–90; c. of, 4, 9, 24, 109,
182 n. 4; economy of, 40–4, 163; mints of,
29, 42; Capetian monetary policy in, 37–44,
163, 193, 195; moneyers in, 37, 43, 163–5,
193; *prévôtés* of, 39, 42, 164; revenues of,
42–3, 99; townsmen of, 29–32, 35, 44. *See
also* confirmation(s) of c., money-taxes (of
Étampes, Orléans, Paris), mutation of c.
Imperatores (*Dig.* 18. 1. 71), 179.
imposed value, 33, 118–19, 179–80, 195.
imprint, *see* types.
inflation, *see* price(s).
Innocent III, pope, 86, 104, 114, 166–72, 178
n. 4, 186 n. 5, 189–90, 203–4; his attitude
toward confirmation and conservation of c.,
167, 169; his conception of debased c. of
Aragon, 170. See also *Quanto personam tuam.*
Innocent IV, pope, 171.
intrinsic value, *see* value(s).
Ispanoli, brothers, 107.
Issoudun (Indre, ar. Châteauroux, ch.-l. c.),
158 nn. 2, 3; mint of, 158 n. 3.
Italy, 23; c. of, 178, 196.

Jaca (Huesca, p.j.), charter of (1197), 86, 101;
c. of (*iaccensis*), 8, 75–8, 81–7, 93, 98, 101
n. 2, 102–4, 106–7, 115, 195; new c. of, 84–5,
103; moneyers of, 101; right of Templars on
c. of, 101. *See also* confirmation(s) of c.,
fuero(s), money-taxes, mutation of c.
Jacintus, cardinal-deacon and legate: promotes
confirmation of c. in Spain, 81 n. 3, 82,
103–4, 114, 168, 190. *See also* Celestine III.
Jacoby, David, 176 n.
James I, k. of Aragon (etc.), ct. of Barcelona,
98 n. 5, 114, 195; his confirmations and
regulation of c., 114–16, 117 n. 1, 118–19.
Jaufré Rudel, 184.
Jean, abt. of Saint-Bénigne (Dijon), 120–1.
Jean, ct. of Vendôme, 128 n. 2.
Jean, moneyer at Dijon, 120.
Jean, ct. of Ponthieu: his regulation of c., 155.
Jerome, Saint, 179.
Jersey, 24.
Jerusalem, 56, 121; fall of (1187), 142. *See also*
crusade(s).

Jews, 39 n. 6, 175.
Johannes Galensis, 179 n. 1; his glosses on
Quanto personam tuam, 170–1.
Johannes Teutonicus, his glosses to *Quanto
personam tuam*, 170; and to *Quis ignorat*, 179.
John of Salisbury, 41.
Josse, abt. of Corbie, 145 n. 5.
judges-delegate, *see* papacy.
Julien de Vézelay, 188.
jurea, 19.
jurisdiction, 66; of c., 5, 14, 18–20, 43, 131–2,
137, 206.
jus monetae, see moneta, right of c.
justice, 136; of peace, 199; revenues of, 94
n. 3, 95, 99.

'King Coin', Latin satire of, 186.
Kuttner, Stephan, 166 n. 1.

La Chapelle, *see* La Chapelaude.
La Chapelaude (Ben.: Allier, ar. Montluçon, c.
Huriel), prior and monks of, c. and consulta-
tion on currency, customs of, 158.
Lacroix, Guillaume de, 108.
La Ferté-Milon (Aisne, ar. Soissons, c. Neuilly-
Saint-Front), *Scripta de feodis* for, 146 n.
La Grande Chartreuse (Carthusian: Isère, ar.
Grenoble, c. Saint-Laurent-du-Pont), 136.
La Lande, Jacques de, 31 n. 3.
La Marche, ct. of: debases c., 11.
Lambert de Waterlos, 148 n. 7.
Landfriede, 53. *See also* peace.
landlords, 68, 125, 130, 139, 147, 150, 152, 159,
172ff., 191 n. 2.
Langres (Haute-Marne, ch.-l. ar.), bp. and c.
of, 121, 124 n. 1, 125 n. 2.
Languedoc, vii, 64, 67, 77, 103, 112, and chs. 4,
7 *passim. See also* Occitania.
Laon (Aisne, ch.-l. dép.), bp(s). of, 7, 9–10, 12,
155–6, 169 n. 2; charter of (1128), 155; c. of
(*laudunensis*), xv, 7, 9–10, 12, 145–6, 156; mint
of, 9, 156; *monetagium* at, 156, 162, 163 n. 2;
moneyers at, 9, 156; tallages of, 36 n. 6, 156.
See also mutation of c., Roger de Rozoy.
largesse, 184–5.
Larrivour (Cist.: Aube, ar. Troyes, c. Lusigny-
sur-Barse), 133 n. 3.
Las Navas de Tolosa, campaign of, 100.
laudunensis, see Laon, c. of.
Laurentii gesta episcoporum Virdunensium, 157.
Laurentius Hispanus, his glosses: on *Olim
causam* and (?) *Querelam*, 178; on *Quanto
personam tuam*, 170.
law, canon: 166–74, 176–80, 183; of oaths and
dispensation, 166–72; on repayments, pensions, rents, 178–80, 191; sanctions against
fraud, 72, 190; its test of utility, 169. *See also*
compilations of decretals, decretalists, papacy.

law, Roman: of c., 2–3, 58, 170–2, 177, 180, 189; of loans, payments, obligations, 172, 177–8, 191. See also *Code*, *Digest*, lawyers.

lawyers: Romanist, 170–1, 176, 180, 191.

Le Blanc, François, 36 n. 3, 38 n.

Lecointre-Dupont, Gabriel, 25 n. 3.

Le Crès (Hérault, ar. and c. Montpellier), *see* Saint-Martin du Crès.

legend, *see* types.

legislation, 45, 52, 64, 78, 82, 105, 112, 116; of Normandy, 17, 22. See also councils, peace.

Lemaire, Emmanuel, 148 n. 4.

Le Mans (Sarthe, ch.-l. dép), c. of (*mançois*), 20.

Lemarignier, J.-F., 56.

Lendit, *see* fairs.

Leon, k. or kingdom of, 74, 75 n. 1, 82, 93; c. of, 74, 83, 93, 115; sale of c. of, 84, 93. See also Ferdinand II.

Lérida (provincial capital), 77 n. 1, 103 n. 3; account of, 85 n., 89 n. 2, 99; councils of: (1155), 81–2, 103; (1173) 103; general courts at, 115 n. 4, 116–17; men of Cahors at, 110; Toulousans at, 107.

Lescar (Basses-Pyr., ar. Pau, ch.-l. c.), bp. (Sanche) of, 55.

Lespinasse, René de, 137 n. 1.

Lillebonne (Seine-Maritime, ar. Le Havre, ch.-l. c.), statutes of, 17.

Limoges (Haute-Vienne, ch.-l. dép.), c. of (*barbarinus*), xvi, 49.

Limousin, 11.

Lisieux (Calvados, ch.-l. ar.), bp.'s right to collect *fouage* in, 19 n. 2, 27 n. 2, 205.

Lleida, *see* Lérida.

Lluis y Navas Brusi, Jaime, 78 n. 2, 87 n. 3, 90 n. 1.

loans, 39 n. 1, 73–4, 97–9, 101, 107, 174, 177, 181 n. 1; Roman and canon law of, theologians on, 172–80. See also pledges.

Lo Codi, 175 n. 2, 176 nn. 2, 4.

Lohrmann, Dietrich, 173 n. 3.

Longpont (Cl. priory: Seine-et-Oise, ar. Corbeil, c. Longjumeau), 39 n. 1.

Lorraine, 157.

Lot, Ferdinand, 25 n. 3, 32, 36 n. 3, 37 n. 3.

Louis V, k. of the Franks, 58.

Louis VI, k. of France, 30–4, 44, 50, 146; his c., xv, 30–4; confirms c. of Compiègne, 32–4; redeems and confirms c. of Orléans, 31–4.

Louis VII, k. of France, 29–31, 32 n. 1, 35–9, 42–3, 163 n. 3; his c., xv, 29–31, 32 n. 1, 35–9, 83, 149; redeems and confirms c. of Étampes and Orléans, 29–35, 129, 133, 148, 162.

Louis VIII, k. of France, 154 n. 1, 161.

Luc de Male, knight of Étampes, 30, 133.

Lucca (Tuscany), c. of, 177.

Luchaire, Achille, 33 and nn. 1, 4, 36 n. 3.

Lucius III, pope: his letter *Cum multam sedes*, 176.

Lyon (Rhône, ch.-l. dép.), c. of, 8–9, 124 n. 3. *See also* mutation of c.

Mabillon, Jean, 32 n. 5, 33.

Mâcon (Saône-et-Loire, ch.-l. dép.), c. of, 124 n. 3.

Mâconnais, 121 n. 1, 124.

Maguelone, 65; bp. and see of, 64 n. 2, 66, 68–9. See also Gualter.

mailles (*medalie*), 45, 76, 184–5, 201. *See also* coins.

Maine, cty. of, 19–20, 24.

Mallorca, crusade against, 68; planned invasion of, 97.

Manasses, bp. of Langres: his regulation of and interest in c., 121, 124, 125 n. 2.

mancus, gold c. of or at Barcelona, 7, 53, 63–4. *See also* gold.

manipulation of c., *see* mutation of c.

Marcus, moneyer at Barcelona, 6

Maria de Montpellier, 97.

Marie, ctess. of Troyes, 132 n., 133 n. 3.

Marie de France, 129 n. 4.

Marigny (Marigny-sur-Yonne: Nièvre, ar. Clamecy, c. Corbigny), lordship of, 139.

mark (monetary weight or value), 74 n., 75–6, 78, 87, 99 n. 1, 108, 118, 136, 138 n. 5, 143, 152 n. 1, 160, 201–2, 205–6; establishment of regional marks, 191; payments by, 80 n. 2, 126, 140–1, 176, 185.

markets, 40–1, 51–2, 67, 77f., 139, 144–5, 181, 196; rights over, 3, 57–8, 64, 158; in money and silver, 99, 143, 163.

marque and reprisal, 111.

Martinus, 176; his gloss on *Eleganter*, 176 n. 2.

Mateu y Llopis, Felipe, 92 n. 2.

Mathieu, ct. of Beaumont, chamberlain of France, 149.

Mathieu Dreu, *bailli* in Berry, 158.

Mathilde of Burgundy, 141.

mazmudins (Muslim–Spanish gold coins), 97.

measures, 30, 35, 36 n., 40, 42–3, 133 n. 3, 175, 178 n. 1, 179.

Meaux (Seine-et-Marne, ch.-l. ar.), bps., clergy of, 130–4, 161, 164; c. of, xviii, 130–5, 145, 148, 161, 164, 192; mint of, 131, 133 n. 4, 134–5; moneyers of, 134; regulation of c. of, 131–3, 161, 192. *See also* Anseau, Burchard, Étienne de La Chapelle, Godefroi de Tressy, Pierre III de Cuisy.

Melgueil (now Mauguio: Hérault, ar. Montpellier, ch.-l. c.), 7, 68, 71, 73–4; c. of xvii, 6 n. 6, 8, 62, 64–75, 77–8, 97, 107, 109 n. 2, 118, 191; cts.; cty. of, 12, 64 n. 2, 65–6, 68, 70–4, 106–7, 168; economic conditions at, 67–8; mint of, 65, 118; people, knights, vassals of, 69 n. 7, 70–1, 74. *See also* confirmation(s) of c., mutation of c.

Merced, Nuestra Señora (Barcelona), 92 n. 2.

Metz (Moselle, ch.-l. dép.), bp., c. of, 160, 161 n. 1.

Millau (Aveyron: ch.-l. ar.), 98.

Milon de Traînel, abt. of Saint-Marien d' Auxerre, 162 n. 4.

mines, of silver in Aragon and Catalonia, 99.

mints, minting: contracts of, 6, 11 n. 5, 53, n. 3; houses of, 6; periods of (*see also* renewals of c.), 19, 21, 37, 44, 75, 135, 175 n., 182 n. 4, 204–5; revenues of (*see also* revenues, of c.), 20, 26, 50, 73, 80, 96, 99–100, 133, 162, 181; right and practice of, 2–7, 12, 33, 106, 193; (minting) from stolen silver, 183. *Local and regional mints are indexed by place-names.*

Miret y Sans, Joaquím, 90 n. 1, 92 n. 1.

Modus colligendi bovaticum . . . , 94.

Moià (Barcelona, p.j. Manresa), tallage at, 80 n. 2.

Moissac (Tarn-et-Garonne, ar. Castelsarrasin, ch.-l. c.), 110.

Moncada, Juan Luís de, 90 n. 1.

monedagium, mentioned in Domesday Book, 18.

monedaje, money-tax proclaimed in Aragon and Catalonia (1205), 13, 84, 88, 91, 97, 113; its original character, 93; contrary to custom, 194. See also *monetaticum*.

monedatge, Catalonian redemption of c., 13, 100, 117, 194. See also *monetaticum*, money-taxes (in Catalonia).

monedatgue (?), seigneuriage at Melgueil, 69, 73.

monedaticum, 91, 94, 100. See *monetaticum*.

moneta, *reproba*, 178 n. 4, 180; *reprobata*, 178 n. 2, 180; meaning: house of c. (mint), 6; revenue of c., 62, 99, 112, 157 n. 2; right of c., vii, 2–5, 21, 48, 50, 118, 121, 155, 182–3, 189, 197. *See also* mints, revenues (of c.), right of c.

Moneta autem, monetary regulation for Catalonia (*c.* 1060–1150), 53–4, 58, 64, 66, 81 n. 1, 101, 117.

monetage, see *montagium*.

monetagium, 181; of exchanges, 156 n. 3, 163; cf. 155–6, 162; as money-tax, 135, 138; in: England, 15–18, 20–1, 28, 97; Laonnais, 155–6, 162, 163 n. 2; Normandy, viii, 13, 18–21, 27 n. 2, 97, 135. *See also* money-taxes (in Normandy).

monetaticum, as *seigneuriage*, 5, 13, 91; as money-tax in Aragon and Catalonia, 13, 91–3, 96–7, 98 n. 5, 114, 117 n. 3, 183; associated or identified with *bovaticum* in Catalonia, 92, 94–8, 100. *See also* money-taxes (in Aragon, Catalonia).

money, as wealth, 183–8; 'black money' (*nigri*), 37, 146, 147 n. 2, 151 n. 2, 191, 202–3; 'good money' (*bona moneta*), 24, 64, 79, 131, 146,

147 n. 2, 158 n. 3, 187. *See also* coinage, mints, *moneta*.

money-changers, *see* changers.

money of account, 33 n. 5, 78, 106 n. 1, 130, 153, 191.

money-taxes, vii, 11 n. 4, 12, 128; in: Agenais, 112 n. 2, 194 n. 1; Aragon, 13, 45, 84, 88, 90–5, 100, 112, 114, 183, 194–5; Blois, *cf.* 128; Burgundy, 165; Cahors, cf. 109, 112, 194 n. 1, 205–6; Catalonia, 13, 84, 89–90, 92–8, 100–2, 112–14, 117, 194–5; cf. 81; Cerdanya, 45, 94–7, 112–13; cf. 51, 56, 60, 89–90, 198–9; Champagne, *cf.* 134–5, 163; Conflent, 94–7; England, 17–18, 20–1, 45; Étampes, 35, 42, 162; Île-de-France, 13, 29–45, 62, 84, 89–90, 97, 113, 135, 155, 162–3; Leon, 93; Melgueil, cf. 73, 118; Navarre, 45, 112; Nevers, 45, 137–44, 193–5; Normandy, viii, 13–28, 34, 43–5, 62, 84, 91, 97, 113, 135, 155, 192–4, 204–5; Orléans, 29 n. 1, 30–1, 34–40, 42–3, 89, 141, 162, 164, 182, 192–4; Paris, 29 n. 1, 35 n. 1, 36–40, 42–3, 162, 164, 182, 192–4; Picardy, cf. 115–16, 164–5; Quercy, 194; Roussillon, 92, 94–7; Vich, 45, 90, 92, 98; assessment of, in: Agenais, 117; Aragon and Catalonia, 51, 60–2, 94–5, 199–200; Cahors, 108, 205–6; Île-de-France, 29–30, 35, 40, 43; Nevers, 137, 139–40, 201–2; Normandy, 14–15, 21 n. 2, 27, 204–5; exemptions or immunities from, 14–15, 19, 21, 25, 27, 35, 44, 91–2, 95; as fees for confirmation of c., 34, 109, 182 (and see *Cunctis pateat*); analogous to ransoms and tallages, 182. See also *beneficium*, *cornagium*, *focagium* (*fouage*), *monetagium* (*monnéage*), *monetaticum* (*monedatge*, *monedaje*), *servitium*, *tallia panis et vini*.

'moneyage', 5, 13. See also *seigneuriage*.

moneyers, 2, 5–7, 182, 187, 189. *See also* listings by region and town.

monnéage, money-tax in Normandy (q.v.), 13, 192.

montagium, 91.

Montargis (Loiret: ch.-l. ar.), fief of, 136.

Montauban (Tarn-et-Garonne, ch.-l. dép.), 110.

Montereau (Montereau-faut-Yonne: Seine-et-Marne, ar. Provins, ch.-l. c.), revenues of, 164.

Montiéramey (Ben.: Aube, ar. Troyes, Lusigny-sur-Barse), 133 n. 3.

Montlhéry (Seine-et-Oise, ar. Corbeil, c. Arpajon), 39 n. 1.

Montpellier (Hérault, ch.-l. dép.), 107; lords, lordship of, 64–6, 68–74, 98, 100, 106; people, vassals (or knights), consuls of or near, 66, 69–70, 74, 118; regional economy of, 65, 67.

Monzón (Huesca, p.j. Barbastro), Templars of, 104 n. 1; general courts of, 117 (1217), 114, 116, 183 (1236). *See also* San Juan de Monzón.

Moors, *see* Saracens.

morabetins, Muslim–Spanish gold pieces, 79, 80 n. 2, 93; as money of account, 76, 78, 83, 86 n. 1, 87, 118.

moravetinus, 91 n. 2. *See also* morabetins.

Morlaas (Basses-Pyr., ar. Pau, ch.-l.c.), c. of ('morlans'), xvii, 54–6; mint of, 7; Cl. priory's tithe of c. of, 55.

Mortain (Manche, ar. Avranches, ch.-l. c.), collegial of, 20 n. 1; valley of, 19, 205.

Moulins (*Molins*: Orne, ar. Alençon), 19 n. 2, 205.

Muret (Haute-Garonne, ar. Toulouse, ch.-l. c.), campaign of, 100.

Musset, Lucien, 23, 24 n. 7, 26 n. 4.

mutation (debasement, manipulation) of c., 1, 113, 150, 160–1, 189, 191–3, 197; different forms of, 5–11; economic impact of, 12–13, 24, 62–3, 68, 121, 125, 128, 146–7; remedy of consequences of, 172–83, 191; in form of imposed value, 118–19, 195; in or at: Aquitaine (*see also* Poitou *below*), 45, 48–50, 55; Aragon, 8, 10–11, 74–7, 83–7, 98, 104, 167–71; Berry, 158; Blois, 128; Burgundy, 8, 125–6; Cahors, 108–9, 112; Carcassonne, 8; Catalonia, 7–8, 53, 57, 74–80, 83, 87, 89–90, 93, 100, 102, 117; Champagne, 135; England, 16, 21; Île-de-France, 9, 33–4, 37–9, 182 n. 2; La Marche, 9; Laon, 7, 9–10, 12, 146, 159; Lyon, 9; Melgueil, 7–8, 12, 67–70, 72–4; Morlaas, 7, 55; Nevers, 9, 135, 139, 143; Normandy, 8, 11, 16–18, 20, 25; Picardy, 8–9, 146, 149–50, 154; Poitou (*see also* Aquitaine *above*), 7, 8 n. 5, 10, 12, 32; Provence, 74; Roussillon, 55; Saint-Omer, 156; Toulouse, 8, 74, 75 n. 1, 104; Verdun, 7 n. 4, 157, 159. *See also* bullion clauses, confirmation(s) of c., demonetization, value(s) (of c., intrinsic).

Mutuum (*Dig.* 12. 1. 2. 1), 178 nn. 3, 4.

Narbonne (Aude, ch.-l. ar.), abps. of, 70, 186 n. 5; c. of, 65, 67, 82; confirmation of c., parliament of (1265), 113, 195. *See also* Berenguer.

Navarre, kingdom of, 82, 98, 110 n. 3; c. of, 83. *See also* money-taxes, San Salvador de Leire.

necessity, 98–100, 140 n. 1, 181, 194, 204; fiscal, 90–1, 97, 101, 114, 141–2; public, 171, 183.

Nevers (Nièvre, ch.-l. dép.), 136, 140–1; barons, bps., clergy, landlords, towns of, 136–7, 139–40, 143, 163; c. of, xix, 9, 109, 136–9, 141–4, 160; expert consultation on c. in, 137, 160, 202; cts., ctess., cty. of, 120, 135–44, 160, 162, 201–2; economy and exchange in, 139, 143–4; mints of cty. of, 140; moneyers in, 137, 143, 201; taxation in, 137–42. *See also*

confirmation(s) of c., Eudes of Burgundy, money-taxes, mutation of c., Thibaut bp.

nigri, *see* money, 'black'.

Niort (Deux-Sèvres, ch.-l. dép.), c. of, 45, 48; mint of, 48.

Nivernais, 140, 142. *See also* Nevers.

Normandy, c. of, xv, 14, 17–25, 43, 113; custom of, 15, 28, 43; d. or duchy of, vii–viii, 4, 11, 14, 16–17, 19–20, 29, 43–4; economy of, 22–3, 27–8, 40–1; Exchequer of, 15, 164; farms, revenues of, 26, 97, 99; *graveria* and *bernagium* of, 26; mints of, 18, 25; moneyers of, 23; population of, 26–7; regulation of c. in, 17, 22, 66; townsmen of, 44; villagers of, 15, 26–7. *See also* *De foagio Normannie, De monetagio*, money-taxes, mutation of c.

notariate, 102, 118; of monetary charters, 70, 76–9, 88, 105–6, 131, 189, 193, 195; of Occitanian charters compared with Catalonian, 109, 113.

Notre-Dame (Ben. nuns: Saintes), abbess (Constance), 50.

Novempopulania, vii.

Noyon (Oise, ar. Compiègne, ch.-l. c.), bp. and clergy of, 152–3, 202–3; black c. of, 145–6, 152–3; commune of, 152, 153 n. 1; economy of, monetary disorder at, 152–3, 173; ordinance on c. of (1197), 152–4, 159, 195, 202–3.

Noyonnais, 144 n. 4.

Nullus clericorum (C. 14. 4. 6), 177 n. 4.

nummus, 9 n. 5, 186–7; *falsus*, 187. *See also* coins, money.

oaths, 60, 69–71, 116, 121, 139, 189–92; of confirmation of c., 103, 113, 166–72, 189–90, 192; of confirmation in: Aragon, 85–6, 104, 166–7; Blois, 129, 160; Cahors (?), 109; Catalonia (*see* Cerdanya, Girona, Vich); Cerdanya, 51, 56–60, 64, 113, 116, 190, 199; Champagne, 129–32, 160; Girona, 88; Melgueil, 66–7, 70, 72, 73 nn. 2, 3, 113, 168; Nevers, 136, 160; Toulouse, 104–6; Urgell, 102, 113; Vich, 78–9; of peace, 56, 60, 67, 116; canon law of dispensation from, 166–72, 203–4.

obligations, monetary, 151, 172–81; canon law on, 172–3, 176–80; Jewish law on, 175; Roman law of, 172, 191; Romanist discussion of, 176–7, 180; theological discussion of, 173–5, 177, 180. *See also* renders.

obols, *see* coins.

Occitania, vii n. 1, viii, 74, 104, 110, 124, 166, 191, 194–5. *See also* Languedoc.

Oise valley, 144.

Old Catalonia, 96, 99. *See also* Catalonia.

Oliba, abt. of Ripoll, Cuxa, bp. of Vich: his legislation on peace and c., 52, 54.

Olim causam (3 *Comp.* 3. 37. 5; *X* 3. 39. 20), 177–9.

Olleguer, abp. of Tarragona, 69 n. 1.

or et argent, 184. *See also* gold.

Orderic Vital, 17.

ordinance of Caen (1204), 164. *For other ordinances see* Index of charters (etc.) relating to c.

Oresme, Nicolas, vii, 2.

Orléans (Loiret, ch.-l. dép.), 29–32, 34–5; changers of, 163; c. of, xv, 24, 29–31, 34, 162; hospice of, 142 n. 1; mint of, 34; *monetagium* of, 156; redemption of c. at, *see* money-taxes; tallage of, 35, 36 n. 6, 40, 193. *See also* Saint-Euverte, Sainte-Croix, *tallia panis et vini*.

Otto, 176 n. 4.

P., priest of Saint Pierre (?), 173 n. 1.

Pallars, cty. of, 60 n. 2; Pallars Jussà, 100.

papacy, 64, 68, 85, 107, 141, 166–77, 189–91; judges-delegate of, 66, 69 n. 1, 71, 168, 173 nn. 1, 3; legates, legations of, 70, 81 n. 3, 82, 103–4, 114, 168, 190; its suzerainty over Melgueil, 71–3. *See also* Calixtus II, Celestine III, Eugene III, Gelasius II, Honorius II, Innocent III, Innocent IV, Lucius III, Urban II, Urban III, Jacintus.

Paris (Seine, ch.-l. dép.), 31, 111, 137; Bourg Saint-Germain, 40, 43; c. of (*parisis, paresis*), xv–xvi, 24, 34, 37–44, 83, 139 n., 141 n. 2, 142, 145, 148–9, 151–3, 155–7, 173–4, 185, 193, 203; drapers, furriers, Jews, rents at, 39 n. 6; mint of, 34, 163; tallage of, 42; Templars at, 164; theologians at, 37, 182–3. *See also* money-taxes, Saint-Magloire, *tallia panis et vini*.

parliament, of Toulouse, 104–5, 195; of Narbonne, 195. *See also* general court(s).

parliamentarism, parliamentery interest in c., *see* coinage (interest in, limitation of prerogative of), consultation, general court(s).

pasnagium, 27 n. 2.

Passeis, Le (*Passeis*, march district: Orne, ar. Domfront), 19 n. 2, 205.

patz, in Comminges, 56 n. 3; in Quercy, 111. *See also* peace.

pax, bestiarum, 61 n. 3, 89 n. 2, 95; as device on c., 54–6, 107. *See also* peace.

payments, 131, 143, 177, 181, 184; by *aestimatio*, 173, 183; in altered c., 183; in kind, 62; by tale, 175; by weight of deniers, 23, 41. *See also* obligations (monetary), renders.

peace, peace and truce, 49–58, 66, 114, 130, 183, 189–90, 193–4; c. protected by, 50–2, 55–6, 58, 81–3, 113; constitutions or legislation of, 49–54, 56 nn. 3, 5, 81–3, 88–9, 91, 101, 112–13, 116–17, 190, 199–200; taxes or redemptions of, 60, 88–98, 194 (and see *bovaticum*); in or

of: Agenais, 118; Aquitaine, 49; Barcelona, 54; Béarn, 55; Cerdanya–Conflent, 50f.; Cervera, 55 n. 3; Comminges, 56 n. 3, 110; Quercy, 111; Vich, 52–4, 61. *See also Landfriede*.

Peace of God (or Peace and Truce of God), *see* peace.

'pentecostal penny', 159.

Pepin (?III), 38 n.

Pere, abt. of Sant Joan de les Abadesses: his loan, tenants, 95.

Pere, ct. of Melgueil, 65 n. 3.

Pere Bernat I, bp. of Elne: institutes peace in Cerdanya (1118), 50–1, 59, 66, 199–200.

Pere de Caors, 110.

Pere de Cirach, bp. of Barcelona, 99.

Pere de Lluçà, 78, 80.

Pere de Redorta, bp. of Vich, 77, 103; confirms c. (1174), 78–81, 104, 109, 114, 118.

Pere Sanz, notary of Toulouse, 105 n. 1, 107.

Pere de Tavertet, canon and sacristan of Vich, 78, 80.

Pere Vidal, troubadour, 107.

Périgord, ct. of. *See* Aldebert II, Hélie.

Périgueux (Dordogne, ch.-l. dép.), bp. of, 48; c. of (*helianensis*), 48 n. 5, 49.

Péronne (Somme, ch.-l. ar.), c. of, 145–6, 151 n. 2; k.'s c. at, 145 n. 4; cty. of, 145; moneyers of, 154 n. 2.

perpetuitas monete, 137, 202. *See also* conservation of c.

Perpignan (Pyr.-Or., ch.-l. dép.), 91–2, 96.

Perroy, Édouard, 27 n. 1.

Pervenit ad nos (1 *Comp.* 2. 17. 10; *X* 2. 24. 3), 169, n. 1.

Peter I, k. of Aragon, 8.

Peter II (I in Catalonia), k. of Aragon, ct. of Barcelona (etc.), 80 n. 5, 84–104, 106–7, 110, 113–16, 118–19; c. of, xviii, 78 n. 2, 86–102; confirms his father's debased c. in Aragon, 86–7, 166–7, 171–2, 178 n. 4, 203–4; his draft-charter of Girona (1205), 88–90; proclaims *monedaje* in Aragon-Catalonia, 84, 90–5, 194; his monetary policy, 86–90, 93, 116.

Peter of Blois, 142 nn. 4, 5.

Peter the Chanter, 37, 173–8, 180–3; on settlements in altered c., 174–5.

Petit-Dutaillis, Charles, 148 n. 7, 149 n. 5.

petitions, appeals, 30–3, 108, 152, 160, 205–6.

Petrus de Sampsona, 171.

Philip I, k. of France, 31 n. 3, 32.

Philip II Augustus, k. of France, 14, 26, 32, 40, 100, 111, 154–6, 192, 194; c. of, xvi, 4, 37, 39, 44, 83, 145, 149–52, 158; his charter for Orléans (1183), 35–6, 141; his policy in Burgundy and Nevers, 136–7, 141–2; his monetary policy, 4, 39, 44, 83, 145, 149–52, 158, 162–4.

Philip IV the Fair, k. of France, 196.
Philippe d'Alsace, ct. of Flanders, 9, 149, 154 n. 2.
Philippe de Dreux, bp. of Beauvais: his c., 151–2.
Philippe Mousquet, 184.
Picardy, 144–57; bps. and cts. of, 144; c. in, 144–56; k.'s c. in, 145, 149, 151–5, 162, 193; economic conditions in, 145–6, 148, 151; lords, peasants in, 145, 173; moneyers in, 154, 156; regulations of c. in, 147–56, 160, 190–1; towns, townsmen in, 144–56, 164–5.
pictavensis, see Poitiers.
Pierfitte, Georges, 107 n. 3.
Pierre I, de Courtenay, 142 n. 1.
Pierre II, de Courtenay, ct. of Nevers and Auxerre: his confirmation of c. (1188), 120, 136–43, 160, 163, 190–1, 193, 201–2.
Pierre III, de Cuisy, bp. of Meaux: his monetary regulations (1224–5), 134, 161.
Pierre le Maréchal, 164 n. 1.
Pierres Aubes ('*ad Petras Albas*': Manche, ar. Avranches, c. Chalandrey), 19 n. 2, 205.
Pillius, 176–8; on problem of debtor's knowledge, his question *Quidam creditor*, 176–7.
Pissotum Heraudi (rivulet in vicinity of Alençon), 19 n. 2, 205.
Placentinus, 177.
pledges, 80 n. 2, 98 n. 5, 99, 131, 141 n. 2; c. as pledge, 65, 69; stipulations of c. in, 75, 79 n. 3, 85, 86 n. 1, 138 n. 5. *See also* loans.
Poblet (Cist.: Lérida, p.j. Montblanc), 77 n., 83.
Poey d'Avant, Faustin, 25 n. 3, 34 n. 4.
Poitiers (Vienne, ch.-l. dép.), c. of (*pictavensis*), 7, 8 n. 5, 12, 32 n. 3, 45, 48–50. *See also* Saint-Nicolas.
Poitou, 7, 8 n. 5, 9 n. 5, 10, 50; for c. of, *see* Poitiers.
Pomponius, 177 n. 1.
Pons, abt. of Cluny, 68.
Ponthieu, c. of, 145, 152 n. 3; ct., ctess., cty. of, 144 n. 5, 155, 163; economy of, 155, 163; moneyers of, 6 n. 6, 154 n. 2, 155, 163; regulation of c. of, 6 n. 6, 155, 163. *See also* Jean, ct.; Béatrice, ctess.
Pontlevoy (Ben.: Loir-et-Cher, ar. Blois, c. Montrichard), 129.
Portugal, 83.
poverty, 188.
Powicke, F. M., 16 n. 4.
Prestre et des .ii. ribaus, 185.
price(s), 148, 179, 196; of c., 113; of confirmation or concession, 81, 83, 90, 126, 135, 189 (*see also* money-taxes); 'of the money', 37, 175 n.; inflation of, 10, 26, 43, 100, 148, 159; just price, 181.
proceeds, *see* revenues.
profit, 181, 183. *For* profits of c. *see* revenues.

Prou, Maurice, 33, 137 n. 1.
Provence, c., recoinage of, 74, 75 n. 1, 76, 77 n. 1; ct., cty., marquis of, 73–4, 75 n. 1, 83, 199, 201.
Provins, c. of (*provinois*), 39 n. 1, 124–5, 129–31, 133 n. 4, 134–5, 138, 139 n., 143, 164; ct., cty. of, 129–33, 136, 140, 162–3, 192; mint of, 133 n. 4, 134; moneyers of, 134–5. *See also* confirmation(s) of c. (Champagne).
provisions of Huesca (1205), *see* Huesca, institution of *monedaje*.
Ptolemy of Lucca, 1.
purchase, of c., 90, 92–3, 144; of c. and peace, 194. *See also* redemption of c.

quaestiones, collection of decretalist, 179 n. 1.
Quaestiones dominorum, 176 n. 2.
Quanto personam tuam (3 *Comp*. 2. 15. 4; *X* 2. 24. 18), 1, 86–7, 104, 166–73, 190, 203–4; its purpose, 167, 204; commentators on its words: *absolvi*, 169; *assensu populi*, 170–1; *defraudata*, 170; *diminuta*, 172; *patris*, 170; *populi*, 171; *reprobata*, 172.
Quedlinburg (Ben. nuns: Saxony), 176.
Quercy, barons, knights, townsmen of, 108–9, 111, 205–6; c. in, 108–11, 205–6; c. and peace a diocesan interest in, 111–12. *See also* Cahors.
Querelam (2 *Comp*. 3. 25. 3), 172–3, 178, 179 n. 1.
questa, questia, 80 n. 2, 94 n. 3, 140. *See also* tallage.
Quidam creditor, question of Pillius, 176–7.
Quis ignorat (C. 32. 4. 6), 178 n. 1, 179.
Quod irreprehensibile est (JL, i, no. 7345), 71–2.
quod omnes tangit (*Code* 5. 59. 5. 2), 171, 197; cf. 204.

Raimond (?), 65 n. 3.
Raimond II, ct. of Melgueil, 65, 68 nn. 4, 5; his daughter, 65.
Raimond IV, ct. of Melgueil, *see* Raimond V, ct. of Toulouse.
Raimond V, ct. of Toulouse, 74, 77, 104; as ct. of Melgueil, secures c. of Melgueil, 107.
Raimond VI, ct. of Toulouse, 98, 107, 110–11; confirms *septena* c. (1205), 104–7, 112, 114, 190, 194.
Raimond VII, ct. of Toulouse, confirms c. (1222), 112, 114, 190, 194 n. 1.
Raimond de Rabastens, bp. of Toulouse, 105.
Ramiro II, k. of Aragon, 8.
Ramón, bp. of Zaragoza, 167, 204.
Ramon Berenguer I, ct. of Barcelona, 53, 60.
Ramon Berenguer III, ct. of Barcelona and marquis of Provence, 68; his c., 62–3; confirms c. and peace of Cerdanya (1118), 50–1, 53, 54 n. 1, 59–63, 81 n. 2, 89, 168, 199–200. See also *Cunctis pateat*.
Ramon Berenguer IV, ct. of Barcelona and

prince of Aragon, 54 n. 1, 68 n. 8, 81–2, 91, 99; his c., 77, 81–2.
Ramon de Cervera, 55 n. 3.
Ramon Galcerà de Pinós, 88.
Ramon de Malla, 78, 80.
Ramon de Manresa, collector in Catalonia, 94–5, 100.
Ramon de Miralpeix, brother of, 77 n.
Ramon de Montcada, 78.
Ramon (Saint) de Penyafort, on public obligations, 183.
Ramon de Pou, moneyer at Vich, 80.
ransom, 182. *See also* redemption of c.
Raoul, bp. of Agen: confirms c. (1234), 112, 117.
Raoul I, ct. of Vermandois, seneschal of France, 162, 163 n. 1; his monetary policy, 9, 148–9.
Raoul Taisson, 27 n. 2.
Rashi, rabbi of Troyes, 182 n. 2; on obligations in altered c., 175–6.
Ratbod, 144 n. 4.
rates, ratios of monetary exchange, 24, 28, 62, 82, 86 n. 1, 124, 130–1, 138, 143, 146 n. 1, 147–8, 151–4, 159–61, 164, 195, 203; c. in ratios with mark, 74 n., 76, 78, 87, 102, 108, 133 n. 4, 143, 160, 205. *See also* bullion clauses, exchange, value(s).
recall of c., 75, 86–7. *See also* demonetization.
recoinage, 6, 11–13, 157, 161, 181; in: Île-de-France, 37; Normandy, 23, 25; Picardy, 149, 153; South, 74–80, 83–4, 96, 108.
redemptio, 93, 138; *monete redemptio*, 30 n.; *redimere*, 89. *See also* redemption of c.
redemption of c., 134, 148, 165, 189, 199; of c. and peace, 60, 88–9, 92, 101, 113, 116; in: Catalonia, 89–92, 98, 113, 194; Île-de-France, 29–31, 38, 44, 142; Quercy, 112. *See also* money-taxes, purchase, relief.
Reims (Marne, ch.-l. ar.), cantor and master of, as judges-delegate, 173 nn. 1, 3.
relief, 60, 140, 147 n. 1; of c., 29 n. 1, 36, 38, 44. *See also* redemption of c.
renders, 6, 74, 83 n. 4, 125, 133, 146, 148, 153, 187, 191; customary or fixed, 41, 63, 68, 108, 125, 128, 139, 143 n. 1, 146–8, 153, 173–4. *See also* rents, revenues.
renewals of c., 5, 11, 16.
rents, 60 n. 3, 124, 138 n. 6, 146–7, 151–2, 154 n. 1, 172–8, 181 n. 1, 200, 202–3; *census* of moneyers, 155. *See also* renders.
representation, 58–9, 67, 106, 114–15, 119 n. 3, 150, 195, 197. *See also* consultation, general court(s).
revenues, 24, 63, 70, 133 n. 2, 142 n. 6, 154 n. 1, 158–9, 173–4, 178; comital or royal, in Catalonia, 62, 95, 97–8, 194; ducal, in Normandy, 23; royal, in France, 41–2, 164; of c., 4, 11–12, 165, 181–2, 193, 195; of c. in:

Aquitaine, 48–50; Aragon, 84–5; Cahors, 112; Catalonia, 80, 90 n. 1, 91–2, 95–8, 101, 118, 195; Champagne, 134–5, 165; Île-de-France, 43, 165; Laon, 156; Melgueil, 65, 67, 73, 118; Normandy, 25; Toulouse, 106; of exchange, 156; of money-taxes, in: Catalonia, 97–8, 194; France, 42–3; Normandy, 25–6; inadequacy of revenues of money-taxes, 193. *For fixed revenues see* renders; *see also* taxation.
Rhône river, 67.
Richard I, ct. of Poitou, 8 n. 5.
Richard, Alfred, 32 n. 3.
right (prerogative) of coinage, 3–6, 13, 112, 166, 193; in: Aragon, 83, 93, 101–4, 112; Burgundy, 126; Catalonia, 54–5, 80, 83, 89–90, 93, 96, 101–3, 112, 116; Champagne, 130–1, 135, 163; Île-de-France, 31, 33–4, 163; Melgueil, 65, 69–70, 72, 107, 112; Nevers, 137, 144; Normandy, 22; Picardy, 153, 163. See also *moneta*.
Rigord, 141 n. 2.
Ripoll (Ben.: Girona, p.j. Puigcerdà), abt., monks of, 52–3.
Robert, d. of Normandy, 22.
Robert de Bellême, 20.
Robert de Courçon, on payments in tainted c., 180–1.
Rocamadour (Ben. priory: Lot, ar. Gourdon, c. Gramat), shrine of, 110.
Rodez (Aveyron, ch.-l. dép.), c. of, 55 n. 2, 108–9, 206.
Roger II, ct. of Foix, 71 n. 1.
Roger of Hoveden, 26.
Roger de Rozoy, bp. of Laon, 156.
Rome, pilgrim route of, 191 n. 1.
Rouen (Seine-Maritime, ch.-l. dép.), 25; abp. of (Gautier de Coutances), 26; c. of, 25. *See also* Normandy (c. of).
Rouergue, 98. *See also* Rodez.
Rougemont (Côte-d'Or, ar. and c. Montbard), 124–5.
Roussillon, clergy, magnates of, 56; c. of, xvii, 54–6, 62, 67, 82–3; ct., cty., or diocese of, vii, 54–6, 92, 100; Truce of God in, 55; wealth of, 96.
Roye (Somme, ar. Montdidier, ch.-l. c.), charter of, 150, 154.

Saint-Bénigne (Ben.: Dijon), charters for abt. and monks of, 120, 126. *See also* Jean, abt.
Saint-Chaffre (Ben., then Cl.: Saint-Chaffre-du-Monastier: Haute-Loire, ar. Le Puy, ch.-l. c.), 69.
Saint-Denis (Ben.: Seine, ch.-l. ar.), charter for men of abbey, 36 n. 6.
Saint-Désiré (Allier, ar. Montluçon, c. Huriel), 158.

Saint-Étienne (Cl. priory: Nevers), privilege for, 139; *bourg* of, 140.
Saint-Étienne (Aug.: Toulouse), 105.
Saint-Euverte (Ben., then Victorine: Orléans), 38 n. 1.
Saint-Fiacre, portal at Blois, 130.
Saint-Germain-(d'Auxerre: Ben.), 138 n. 6, 140.
Saint-Gilles (Gard, ar. Nîmes, ch.-l. c.), money-changing at, 191 n. 1.
Saint-James (Saint-James-de-Beuvron: Manche, ar. Avranches, ch.-l. c.), castellany of, 19.
Saint-Jean-d'Angély (Charente-Maritime, ar. Saintes, ch.-l. c.), c., mint of, 45, 48.
Saint-Lomer (Ben.: Blois), 129; tenants of, 128 n. 2.
Saint-Magloire (Ben.: Paris), charter for, 37–8; house at Orléans, 38.
Saint-Marien (Prem.: Auxerre), abt. of, 162 n. 4.
Saint-Martin (Prem.: Laon), 146.
Saint-Martin du Crès: (Le Crès: Hérault, ar. and c. Montpellier), 66.
Saint-Martin (canons regular: Tours), c. of, 32 n. 3.
Saint-Michel-de-Cuxa (Ben., congregation of Saint-Victor, Marseille: Pyr.-Or., ar. Prades, c. Codalet), 65 n. 1; abt. of, 52–3.
Saint-Nazaire (Autun), canons of, 140 n. 1.
Saint-Nicolas (Ben. priory: Poitiers), its tithe on c. of Poitiers, 48.
Saint-Omer (Pas-de-Calais, ch.-l. ar.), c. of, 155–6; k.'s c. at, 145 n. 4; men of, 156; charter of (1127), 156, 159–60.
Saint-Quentin (Aisne, ch.-l. ar.), 145; c. of, xix, 9, 145, 147–9, 162; *Establissement* (*c.* 1151) of, 147–9, 153, 200; charters to (1191, 1195), 149–51, 154, 159–61, 190, 193; commune, mayor, men of, 147–50, 153–4; moneyers, changers of, 154 n. 2; mutation of c. at, 9, 149–50, 154.
Saint-Sauveur (Blois), charter for, 129 n. 2.
Saint-Sernin (Aug.: Toulouse), 105.
Saint-Sulpice (Bourges), charters of, 157.
Sainte-Croix (Orléans), changers of, 163.
Sainte-Marie de la Daurade (Ben.: Toulouse), 105.
Sainte-Trinité (Ben.: Caen), revenues of in Jersey, 24.
Sainte-Trinité (Ben.: Vendôme), 129.
Saintes (Charente-Maritime, ch.-l. ar.), 5, 49; abbess, ct., cty. of, 50; c., mint, moneyers of, 5, 49–50, 189. *See also* Notre-Dame.
Saintonge, *see* Saintes.
'Saladin tithes', 26, 39, 142.
sales, 41 n. 3, 75, 85.
Salimbene, 144.
Salomon de Regina, 77 n.

Salses (Pyr.-Or., ar. Perpignan, c. Rivesaltes), 89 n. 2.
salvamentum, 133 n. 3, 139.
San Juan de Monzón, Templars of, 104.
San Salvador de Leire (Ben.: Navarre), 103 n. 3.
Sança, daughter of Alphonse II, 94 n. 3.
Sancerre (Cher, ar. Bourges, ch.-l. c.), c. of, 139 n., 158 n. 3; ct. of, 132.
Sanche, bp. of Lescar, 55.
Sánchez Albornoz, Claudio, 115.
Sancia, queen of Aragon, ctess. of Barcelona, 55 n. 3.
Sangorrín, Dámaso, 86 n. 5.
Sant Cugat del Vallès (Ben. Barcelona, p.j. Terrassa), domains of, 57.
Sant Joan de les Abadesses (Ben.: Girona, p.j. Puigcerdà), abt. of (Pere), 95; valley of, 79.
Sant Pere (Vich), cathedral chapter of, 78, 80.
Santa Cilia (Huesca, p.j. Jaca), forged privilege for, 91 n. 2.
Santa Christina de Somport (Huesca, p.j. Jaca), 75 n. 2.
Santa Maria (Besalú), receives tithe of c., 91 n. 1.
Saracens, 63, 86, 90, 98–9, 194; tribute of, 78.
Sarriau, Henri, 137 n. 1, 138 n. 3.
Schneider, Jean, 161 n. 1.
Segarra (Lérida, comarca), 83.
seigneuriage, 5, 13, 25, 67, 134–5, 137, 155–6. *See also* revenues (of c.).
Seine valley, 41.
Sens (Yonne, ch.-l. ar.), abp. of (Gautier), 143; *decimationes* at, 142 n. 5; revenues at, 142 n. 6.
septena c. of Toulouse, 75 n. 1, 104–8, 111.
Septimania, vii.
servitium, tax on c. in Champagne, 134–5.
Seu (La) d'Urgell, *see* Urgell.
Si quis clericus (C. 14. 4. 5), 177 n. 4.
Sicily, k. of, 181 n. 1.
silver, 9, 78, 91 n. 1, 113, 143, 180, 182–3, 185; content of in c., 53, 137, 146, 163; weights of, 67, 73, 185. *See also* alloy, bullion clauses, mark, value(s).
Simon, moneyer of Flanders, 154 n. 2, 163 n. 3.
Simon, moneyer of Ponthieu, 163.
Simon de Montfort, 111.
Soissons (Aisne, ch.-l. ar.), 145; charter of, 125; c. of, 145–6, 151 n. 2.
Soissonnais, 144 n. 5.
Solsona (Lérida, p.j.), 57 n. 2.
Somme valley, 144.
Soultrait, Georges, de, 137 n. 1.
Southern, R. W., 128 n. 2.
Souvigny (Allier, ar. Moulins, ch.-l. c.), c. of, 138, 139 n., 159.
Spain, 58, 68–9, 81–2, 84, 168, 171, 184, 191. *See also* Castile, Leon.

Spanish March, vii, 13, 52, 54, 57, 59–60, 62, 91, 168, 190, 196. *See also* Aragon, Catalonia.
specifying of c., *see* stipulation.
stability of c., anxiety or fears concerning, 49, 83, 124, 131, 138, 141, 146, 156, 192, 195; as a constitutional interest, 195.
standards of c., 8, 190, 192; in Aquitaine, 49, 192; Aragon, 8, 74–6, 83, 86–7, 119; Blois, 128; Cahors, 108; Catalonia, 53, 58, 62, 74, 76–8, 83, 87; Champagne, 164, 192; Flanders, 156; Île-de-France, 33–4, 37, 164; Melgueil, 8, 66–74; Nevers, 137–8, 143; Normandy, 17–18, 164; Picardy, 147, 151 n. 2, 160; Provence, 74; Toulouse, 8, 74, 104. *See also* alloy, weight(s).
Stapleton, Thomas, 16 n. 4, 25 n. 6.
Stephenson, Carl, 18 n. 1, 36 n. 6, 44.
sterling, *see* England, c. of.
stipulation (or specifying) of c., 192; in: Aquitaine, 49; Aragon, 83; Berry, 159; Blois, 128; Burgundy, 121, 124–5; Catalonia, 77 n. 3, 79, 83, 102; Champagne, 130; Île-de-France, 39 n. 1, 174; Melgueil, 67, 68 n. 2; Nevers, 143; Normandy, 23; Picardy, 146–7.
Substantion, cty. of, 70. *See also* Melgueil.
Summa de legibus Normannie, 14.
synod, *see* Vich.
synodaticum, 178–9.

Taeuber, Walter, 177, 179 n. 1.
taille du pain et du vin, 31 n. 3, 37. See also *tallia panis et vini*.
tallage, 13, 88, 92, 95, 97, 100, 155, 163, 180, 182–3, 193; of bread and wine, see *tallia panis et vini*; in Île-de-France, 35, 36 n. 6, 40, 42, 44; in Nevers, 139–40, 142. *See also* taxation.
tallia panis et vini, money-tax in Capetian France: viii, 29 n. 1, 31 n. 3, 36f., 97, 162, 182, 192, 194.
talliata panis et vini, 36.
Tancred, his glosses, on *Quanto personam tuam*, 170; and on *Querelam*, 178–9.
Tardif, E.-J., 15 n. 1.
Tarragona (provincial capital), 63, 92 n. 1, 99; abp. of, 69 n. 1.
taxation, 18, 35, 61, 101, 114, 141, 166, 181, 194; on hearths (see also *fogatge*, *fouage*): in Agenais, 117; in Catalonia, 95–6, 100; in Nevers, 137, 139, 142, 162, 201–2; in Normandy, 14–15, 25, 27, 42. *See also* aids, money-taxes, tallage.
Templars, 85, 94 n. 1, 97 n. 1, 100, 101 n. 2, 104, 118, 164, 193; as administrators of c., 100, 118, 195.
tensamentum, 40 n. 3.
Teutonicus, *see* Johannes Teutonicus.
Thibaut, bp. of Nevers, 139–40.
Thibaut II, ct. of Troyes (etc.), 131 n. 3.

Thibaut III, ct. of Champagne and Brie, 133–4.
Thibaut IV, ct. of Champagne and Brie, 161; his monetary regulation (1224), 134.
Thibaut V, ct. of Blois, seneschal of France, 136; his charter for Blois (c. 1165), 126–30, 132, 142; as k.'s fiscal administrator, 162–4, 192.
Thibaut the Great, ct. of Blois and Troyes, 136.
Thierry d'Alsace, ct. of Flanders, 156.
Thuir (Pyr.-Or., ar. Perpignan, ch.-l. c.), profits of justice at, 94 n. 3, 95.
tithe(s), 40 n. 3. 60 n. 3, 100, 133; of confiscated c., 81; on revenues of c., 55, 85, 91 n. 1, 97 n. 1, 98–9; *decima panis et vini*, 40 n. 3; *tallia vel decima*, 142.
tithing (*decimatio*), 140, 142.
Toledo (provincial capital), 101 n. 2.
tolls, 3, 23, 67–8, 88, 131, 133 n. 2, 142 n. 6, 152–3, 155, 202–3.
Tonnerre (Yonne, ar. Avallon, ch.-l. c.), 141; c., mint of, 138, 139 n.; cty. of, 143.
Tortosa (Tarragona, p.j.), 68, 89 n. 2, 115 n. 4; bp. of (Gaufred), 91.
Toulouges (Pyr.-Or., ar. and c. Perpignan), councils of, 55.
Toulouse (Haute-Garonne, ch.-l. dép.), Aragonese, Catalans at, 107; bps. of, 55, 105, 107; clergy, patricians, consuls of, 105–7, 110–12; c. of, xvii, 8, 54–5, 74, 104–8; *septena* c. of, 75 n. 1, 104–8, 111; cts., cty. of, 54–5, 73–4, 77, 98, 104, 106–7, 116; mint of, 106–7; notariate of, 106. *See also* Bertrand.
Toulousain, 111.
Tournai (Hainaut, ch.-l. Mons), 9; *monetagium* of, 155.
Tours (Indre-et-Loire, ch.-l. dép), c. of (*tornois*, *tournois*), xvi, 32 n. 3, 109 n. 2, 111, 142, 185, 191, 193; quaternal c. of, 111; c. of Saint-Martin of, 32 n. 3.
Très Ancien Coutumier, 15 n. 1.
tribute, 83, 99.
Troyes (Aube, ch.-l. dép.), c. of, 130, 133–5, 164; cts., cty. of, 129–33, 136, 140, 162–3, 192; fair of Saint-Ayoul of, 134; mark of, 136; mint of, 133–4; moneyers of, 134–5; Rashi, rabbi of, 175.
Truce of God, 52–3, 55–6, 60, 81. *See also* peace.
Turenne (Corrèze, ar. Brive, c. Meyssac), c. of, 49.
types (imprint, devices, legends), viii, 3, 5, 7–8, 170; change of, 31, 33–4, 85; change of affects value of c., 175; in: Aragon, 75, 87, 107, 167; Burgundy, 126; Catalonia, 58, 78; Champagne, 132; England, 21; Flanders, 157; Île-de-France, 31, 33–4, 38, 155 n. 6; Laon, 10; Nevers, 144; Occitania, 54–6, 65, 105, 107; Picardy, 149; Poitou, 48; Ponthieu, 155 n. 6.

Ulpian, on obligations paid in bad c., 172.

Urban II, pope, 56 n. 5, 190.

Urban III, pope, 141; on payments in altered c., 172-4, 178.

Urgell, c. of, 62, 82, 102; ctess. of (Elvira de Subirats), 102; cty., diocese of, 56 n. 3, 57, 100, 102; peace in, 56 n. 3. *See also* confirmation(s) of c.

Urse, bp. of Verdun, 157.

Usatges of Barcelona, 51 n. 1, 53, 54 n. 1, 57, 101, 116. See also *Moneta autem.*

usury, 180.

utility (common, public, social), 1-2, 11, 76, 85 n. 2, 154, 162, 169-70; *communis utilitas populi,* 201.

Vaissete, J.-J., 65 n. 3.

Valbon (Vauxbuin: Aisne, ar. and c. Soissons), charter of, 155.

Valencia, campaign of, 100.

Valladolid (provincial capital), council of (1155), 82 n. 2.

Vallès (Barcelona, comarca), 57.

Vallis Moritolii, see Mortain.

Valls Taberner, Ferràn, 54 n. 1.

value(s), of account, 153 n. 3; of c. in exchange, 12, 42, 63, 88, 102, 118, 126, 133 n. 3, 166, 174; of c., intrinsic, viii, 1, 16, 23-4, 58, 62-3, 76, 83, 106, 118, 121, 124, 130, 133 n. 4, 170, 186; of c., intrinsic value altered, 8, 11, 67, 158, 175, 177-8, 180, 189; of incomes, 192. *See also* alloy, bullion clauses, mutation of c., rates of monetary exchange.

Vanderkindere, Léon, 149 n. 5.

vassals, vassalage, 6, 59-60, 65-6, 68 n. 8, 69-71, 74, 113, 168.

Vendôme, abbey Sainte-Trinité of, 129.

Verdun (Meuse, ch.-l. ar.), bps. of (Albéron, Urse), 157; c. of, 7 n. 4, 157, 159. *See also* mutation of c.

Vergy (Côte-d'Or, ar. Dijon, c. Gevrey-Chambertin), war of, 141.

Vermandois, c. of, xix, 149; cts., ctesses. of, 148-9. *See also* Élisabeth.

Veruela (Cist.: Zaragoza, p.j. Tarazona), 92 n. 2.

Vézelay (Ben.: Yonne, ar. Avallon, ch.-l. c.), 136.

Vich (Barcelona, p.j.), 57, 78-80; bps., diocese, lords of, 45, 52-3, 61, 63, 90, 98, 103, 118; c.

of, xv (and Frontispiece), 52, 61-2, 75, 78-80, 90 n. 1, 109; markets, enterprise of, 77, 99; men (clergy, three classes) of, 78-80, 90, 97; mint of, 52, 80; moneyers of, 58, 80; recoinage of, 78-80, 102; redemption of c. at, 45, 90, 92, 98; regulation of c. at, 52-3, 64, 66, 81, 195; synod of (c. 1033), 52-3, 64, 66, 81. *See also* confirmation(s) of c., Guillem de Tavertet.

Villefranche-de-Conflent (Pyr.-Or., ar. and c. Prades), 96; proceeds of justice and *monetaticum* from, 94 n. 3, 95.

Villeneuve-sur-Yonne (Yonne, ar. Sens, ch.-l. c.), pension at, 142 n. 6.

Vincentius Hispanus, his glosses on *Quanto personam tuam,* 170.

Vincke, Johannes, 92 n. 2.

violations, violators of c., 52-4, 60, 76, 79, 81, 131-2, 189, 201. *See also* fraud.

Vorges (Aisne, ar. and c. Laon), charter of, 155.

wages, 27, 181 n. 1.

Walter Map, 42 n. 2.

wealth, 95-6, 166, 180; ideas concerning, 183-8.

weight(s), viii, 64, 125, 137-8, 163, 176, 187, 191, 196; diversity of, 6, 100 n. 5, 175; mutation of, 7, 74, 87, 143, 160, 167, 182; payments by, 23-4, 41, 63, 185; Roman system of, 190, 191 n. 1; test of, 2-3, 170. *See also* confirmation(s) of c., mark.

Willelmus Arnaldus de Montetotino, 105 n. 1.

William I the Conqueror, d. of Normandy, k. of England, 14, 27; c. and mints of, 16-21, 56 n. 1; reforms c. of Normandy, 22, 24, 28; his money-tax, 15-21.

William II Rufus, k. of England, 17-18, 22.

wine, viticulture, 10, 30-1, 35, 40, 42 n. 2, 43, 144, 153.

wionagium, 202.

Wistasse le moine, 191.

works, public, 182.

Yaḥyā al-Muʿtalī, c. of, xv.

Zaragoza (provincial capital), assembly at (1174), 75, 103; bp. of (Ramón), 167, 204; reconquest of, 68.

Zurita, Gerónimo, 84, 91-4, 96-7, 101.

I. Selected coins

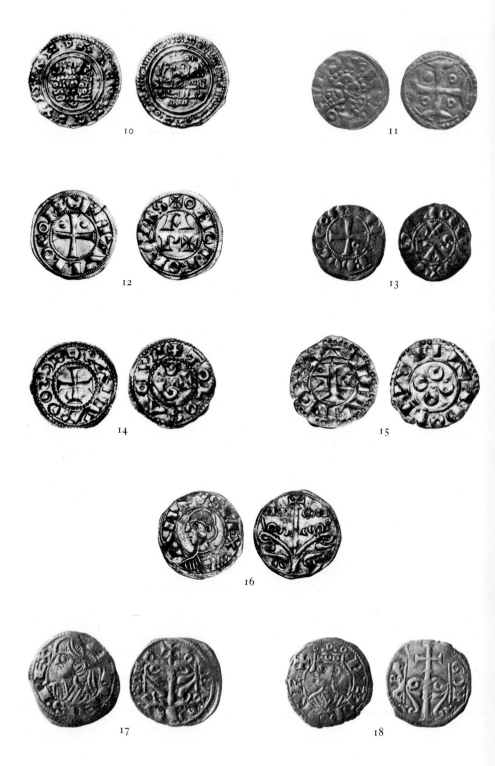

II. Selected coins

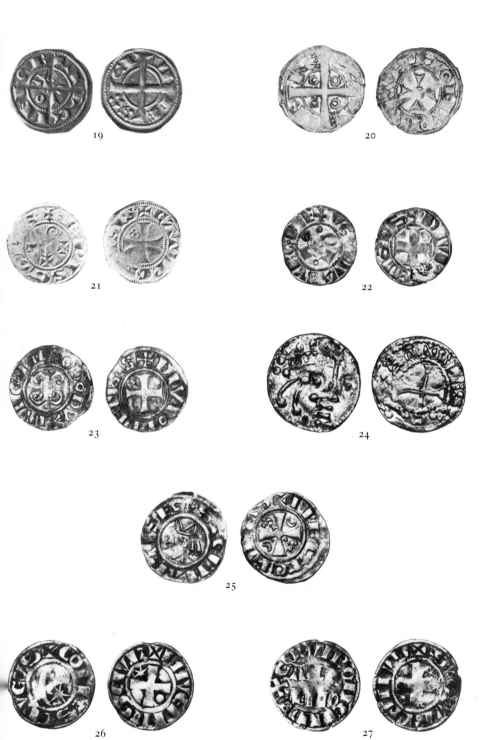

III. Selected coins

IV. 'Memorandum concerning *fouage*' (*Scriptum de foagio*), from 'First Register of Philip Augustus' (Appendix, no. 7)

159

160

IN NOMINE SANCTE ET INDIVIDUE TRINITATIS AMEN. PHILIPPUS DEI GRATIA FRANCORUM REX.

Ad regiam anime clementiam pertinent subiectis miseracioribus parcere, et mole grauaminis laboraturos leuarabiles ab subuenire. Nouerint igitur uniuersi presentes pariter et futuri quia nos de nutritu et ob remedium anime nostre et anime patris sui Ludouici bone memorie, et predecessorum nostrorum homines tam manentes qui manituros duraturos, et in talliis sui quaram, et in talliis sui iobis apud Toldriam, et apud Gremmiuillam, de cetero ab omni talia et tallia liberos et immunes esse uolumus et precipimus, concedentes etiam quod eos placitare non faciam in remotiori loco quam apud Stampas, ut apud curiam, ut apud Lorriacum. De eos nec res nec greges nec fetus, nec filios eorum capiam, nec eis uim aliam faciam quam sui iudicium capere uiese iustare uoluerint et portauerint. Quod nisi causa pro aliquo iure facto plurium seraginta soldzos nobis emendabitur. nisi pro furto rapina. homicidio. murtro. et potuame. ut nisi aliam pedem ut manum ut nasum ut oculum ut aurem ut aliquo alius membrum abstulerit. Et siquis submonitus fuerit ad submonitionem nram non ante octo dies, respondere teneatur. Teneatur omnia eis concedim sub hac condicione. quod quilibet illorum quibus hec indulgemus quos uidelicet talliare poteram ut possem de cetero singulis annis eo singulis modnis unum et bladi quod habuerit. tam de hibernagio qui de maresdina quartam; illa foi nob duos denarios dabit. Sed scedendum quod duos annos colleco suo iada de blaco et uino, que quid colleco uulgo nuncupatur talia panis et uini. anno pro gentacione colece et talia. et pro superficis conuicuentibus eis concedus. Ceutsilabet ut anni cuturi colleco anno pro stabilitate monaca. Illo quid anno uetuo, alii homines qui illi quis iuradas immunitates concedus. quo uidelicet talliam nob non debebant nisi panis et uini talliam pro monaca. allam panis et uini talliam pro monaca. allam panis et uini talliam pro stabilitate monaca nob etiolatio esse modo.

VI. Royal charter for Orléans, Fontainebleau 1183. Original parchment, 543 × 417 mm. Refers to 'tax . . . [which] is commonly called tallage of bread and wine . . . for the stability of coinage' (*collectio . . . uulgo nuncupatur tallia panis et uini . . . pro stabilitate monete*)

VII. Bishop Pere de Redorta restores and confirms the coinage of Vich, 13 December 1174. Original parchment, 140×240 mm

VIII. Peter II promises nonprejudice to the liberties of the people of Vich in return for their grant of the current 'redemption of the coinage' (*redemptionem hanc monete*), March 1197 (N.S.). Original parchment, formerly sealed, 445 × 243 mm

Moyses J.B. Fouard fecit.

IX. View of Blois from the south showing the Old Bridge and the Porte Saint-Fiacre, from the engraving in
Jean Bernier, *Histoire de Blois* (Paris, 1682), p. 1. The gate, together with its inscription (see Plate X), was
demolished in 1780.

X. Comital charter for Blois, c. 1164–5(?), including a confirmation of the coinage, formerly inscribed on the Porte Saint-Fiacre of Blois (Bernier's facsimile)

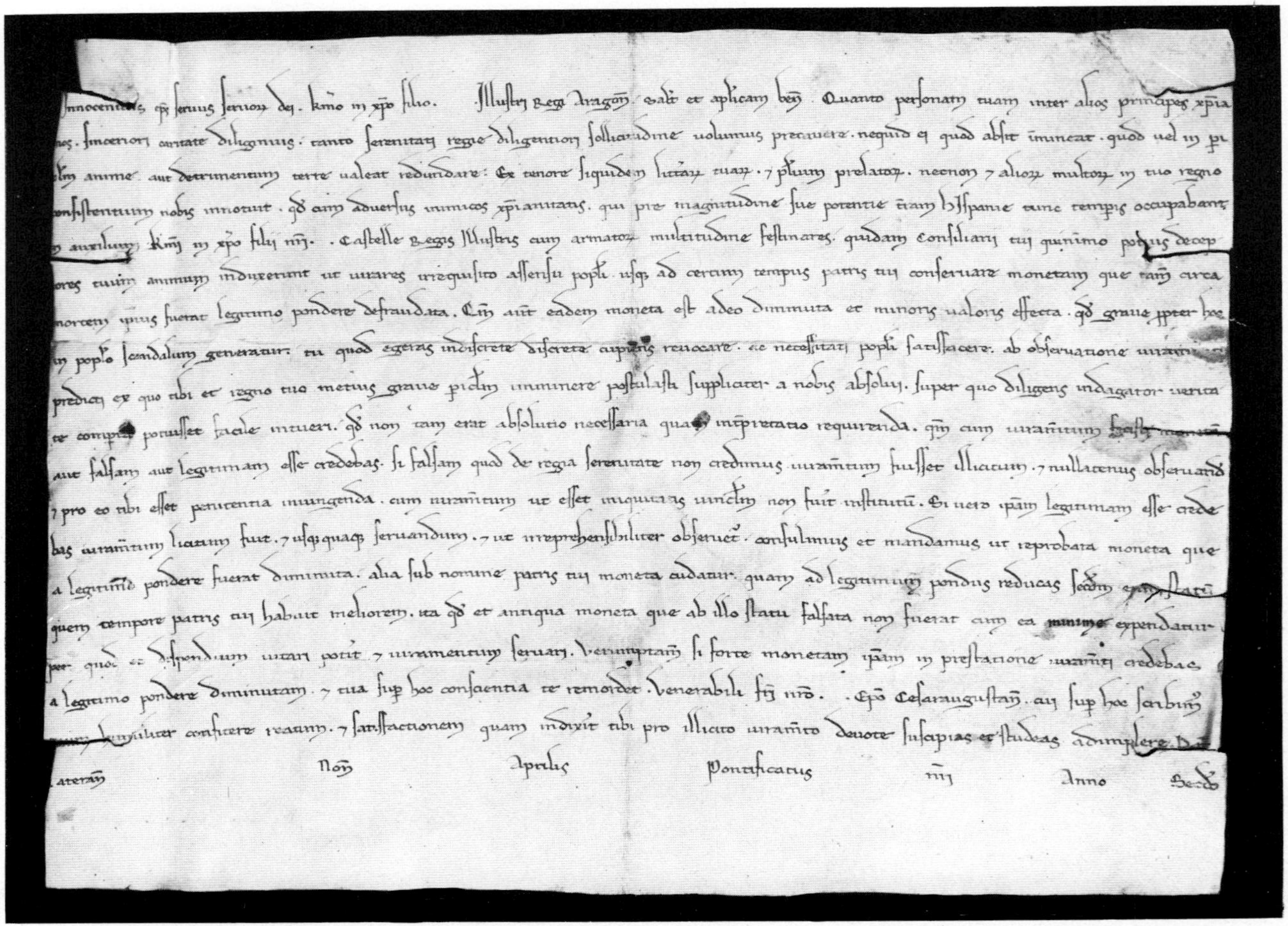

XI. Pope Innocent III's letter *Quanto personam tuam*, Lateran 5 April 1199, concerning the coinage of